Options Explained²

Finance and Capital Markets series

Options Explained²

Robert Tompkins

© Macmillan Press Ltd, 1994

First published in the United Kingdom by
MACMILLAN PRESS LTD, 1994
Companies and representatives throughout the world.

Distributed by Macmillan Direct
Brunel Road, Houndmills,
Basingstoke, Hants RG21 2XS, England.

ISBN 0-333-62807-1

A catalogue record for this book is available
from the British Library.

10   9   8   7   6   5   4
03   02   01   00   99   98   97   96

Printed and bound in Great Britain by
Antony Rowe Ltd, Chippenham, Wiltshire

Dedication

This book is dedicated to Stuart David Katz, who not only taught me everything I needed to know about options but also taught me the true meaning of friendship and to my wife, Barbara who taught me the meaning of true love.

Contents

Preface

In almost every human generation, a revolution occurs. Some generations are blessed by beneficial innovations that forever change the world in which they live. Some of us are fortunate enough to witness these events and assume the task to explain their significance. This is the quest I have undertaken with this book. In my generation, the financial world experienced such a revolution. Many brilliant minds were able for the first time to discern the basic building blocks which form our financial markets and then turn these insights into products which touch the lives of us all. My career has been intertwined with the development of one of the most basic building blocks of financial markets: that of options.

The Mecca of option markets was Chicago in the 1970s where in April 1973, the Chicago Board Options Exchange opened. For the first time, standardised option contracts were listed on a regulated market open to all. In addition, two professors at the University of Chicago, Fischer Black and Myron Scholes were able to uncover the puzzle of options pricing with a brilliant insight. Fate led me to the University of Chicago in 1976 where I was quickly caught up in the electricity of that time. After earning three degrees from the University, I started my career in the Research Department of the Chicago Mercantile Exchange, where Fred Arditti was leading a team of economists investigating the introduction of options contracts on a wide variety of financial products and commodities. The opportunity to work with three brilliant financial economists, Michael Asay, Rick Kilcollin and Galen Burghardt, allowed me to immerse myself in the options area and help develop products (on currency options, Stock index products and interest rate securities) which would forever change world financial markets.

I was also fortunate to have the opportunity to apply these concepts in the marketplace at Harris Trust and Savings Bank and at Continental Illinois National Bank. At Harris, I helped set up one of the first currency option desks in Chicago and later at Continental Illinois, I traded and managing options on interest rate products. At both institutions, I was again fortunate to come into contact with extremely clever colleagues who helped me understand the limitations of options theory.

While my education was comprehensive, I found that the concepts underlying options contracts eluded me. The seminal papers were buried in exotic mathematics which were removed from my daily experiences. Slowly, the common sense of these concepts became uncovered as I read and re-read the seminal papers and combined these concepts with daily trading activity. Then, with extraordinary luck, I was asked to prepare seminars on these markets for banks in America and

Europe. My first seminar in Finland for Postipankki in January 1985 literally changed my life as I could no longer veil options concepts in mathematical terms but had to find a common sense explanation for these products. With the assistance of the educational departments from many of the major futures and options exchanges, a series of seminars were developed that distilled the consistencies among the markets. As this occurred, certain patterns became obvious and the mystery of options was solved for me. Since that first course, I have delivered over 300 courses on options in 28 countries worldwide. As these courses were refined and extended to a wide variety of different underlying instruments, it became even more apparent to me that options contracts were fundamental securities that applied equally well to all markets.

Currently, 22 countries worldwide possess markets for exchange traded options on a range of contracts from energy, metals, commodities, stocks, indices, fixed income securities, interest rates, and currencies. As will be demonstrated in this book, the concepts which spurred the development of options imply that any risky instrument can have an options market associated with it. Given, the growth of exchange traded options markets and other related markets, there is little doubt that many more countries will include options in their capital markets in the near future. Yet as I devoured each new option book that came to press, I found that most books were either too technical, hid behind mathematics, were too basic or specialised. Many books would only concentrate on one kind of underlying instrument (like stocks, commodities or financial products) and seemed to suggest that the conceptual framework of options depends on the asset that underlies the option. These books failed to recognise that all options are based upon the same fundamental concepts. I felt that a book needed to be written that showed the similarities among options instead of the dissimilarities. In addition, I could find no book that could explain the logic behind these products without hiding behind the mathematics. It became apparent that others shared my viewpoint. Many well informed people found the literature on options markets unsatisfying. Books could not answer basic questions such as: Why do options exist, what gives these contracts value and how can these products be used for trading and hedging needs? Furthermore, since these products are so fundamental to an economy, why has their introduction been delayed until this generation only then to grow faster than any other financial product in history? In this book, I will examine all these questions and hopefully will provide the reader with satisfactory answers.

To examine these critical issues, I have broken the book into five broad areas of coverage. In the first three chapters, I will examine options basics and pricing. Each chapter (and throughout this book) will feature a different underlying market with the goal of both explaining the concepts and leading the reader to recognise the overlap that exists among all options markets. Chapter 1 presents basic definitions but differs from other texts by showing how options are created from any underlying market by separating that market into "good" and "bad" parts. In Chapter 2, the basics of options pricing are presented, it also features a different explanation of the Black and Scholes pricing formula; by examining how they solved the problem. For the first time, the tie between the Black and Scholes model and the world of physics is explained without the need to resort to solving partial differential equations. In Chapter 3, the reader is shown how options prices are used by options traders and also a variety of alternative pricing formulas are presented. However, rather than emphasising the trivial differences between these formulae and the Black and Scholes model, this text explains the similarities shared by these options formulae. Finally, I will describe the fundamental relationship between options and their underlying markets (Put-Call Parity) that reaffirms my presentation in Chapter 1, that options are nothing more than an underlying asset split into two parts. To show this, both formulae and "magic graphing" rules are presented to help both the mathematically inclined and visually inclined understand this critical concept.

The next major area of coverage will concentrate on volatility estimation. Chapter 4 will introduce the concept of volatility with a review of stochastic processes, normal and lognormal distributions, and estimation techniques for volatility including historical volatility, implied volatility and cyclical volatility. Chapter 5 will examine more esoteric issues in volatility estimation including the term structure of volatility, the dispersion of volatility across strike prices (known as the smile), forward volatilities and introduce a new kind of pricing model which may revolutionise the entire world of options. This will lay a foundation for later chapters in the book that will discuss the pricing of interest rate and exotic options and will figure prominently in the subsequent chapter on volatility trading.

The third major area this book will cover includes trading strategies with options. Unfortunately, too many texts overemphasise this area and lead the reader to conclude that options are simply a more sophisticated way to gamble. In Chapter 6, I will present how to use options to benefit from a viewpoint on the movement of the underlying market. However, I will present not only the possible returns from various strategies but will also discuss how options allow the investor to limit his risk exposure. In Chapter 7, I will examine the most fundamental use for options, the trading of volatility. I will present the range of possible strategies and also indicate when these are most appropriate. Finally, in Chapter 8, I will review the trading strategies that assure that an equilibrium occurs in these markets. These arbitrage trades are probably outside the realm of experience of most users of options but must be understood to appreciate the mechanisms within which options pricing works. A new chapter has been added for this edition which examines the trading of options in different markets. This is Chapter 9 that examines the theory and practice of trading options between markets. In this chapter, I will examine the trading opportunities that exist in related interest rate and currency markets and explore the relationships between individual stock options and stock index options. These type of strategies have become more prevalent in derivative markets especially with futures and will for the first time be presented here for options.

The fourth area, I will cover is how the investor can use options to manage the risk of his or her investments. Chapter 10 examines how to protect fixed income securities using options and explains how options and futures contracts compare for managing risk. In Chapter 11, I will examine applications of options to the portfolio manager by discussing how options can be used to revise a portfolio manager's risk/return objectives. There I will examine stock index products and show how to achieve guaranteed investment funds, discuss how portfolio insurance works, why to avoid delta "neutral" hedging techniques and how to create options hedging strategies with no cost.

The fifth area to be covered in this book will examine the more esoteric options that have evolved in parallel with the booming success of the exchange traded products. Interest Rate options including OTC options on Bonds, Interest Rate Cap Agreements, Interest Rate Guarantees and Swaptions have all become staple products offered by most investment banks. Chapter 12 examines these products with special emphasis on the pricing difficulties of these products and their applications to the end users. Chapter 13 covers the expanding area of exotic options. No area of derivative products has experienced greater growth or mutation as has the realm of exotic options. This chapter will examine both the range of path dependent contingent claims as well as how these products are engineered. A general methodology will be presented for pricing all these products which will allow the user to fit new and more complex structures into a framework as these products are developed. Finally, in Chapter 14, I present how to measure and hedge the risk of an option portfolio. With the use of a popular options risk management computer program, the reader will see how all the theoretical concepts presented in Chapter 3 apply in the daily world of the risk manager. In this chapter, I will also show the reader how to choose the best trading strategy using the computer program.

The final area I will examine can roughly be categorised as the structure of options markets and the regulatory environment for these products. Chapter 15 reviews how exchange traded options markets work. Specifically I will describe the role of the Clearing House in options markets, how margin works and outline the differences in the structures of four popular options markets around the world. The last chapter, Chapter 16, provides a current review of the regulatory, accounting and tax environments for those countries where options contracts are currently trading.

The goal of this book is to show that the concepts which underlie options are consistent across all markets. I hope that for most readers Options Explained² will be the only book they will need in order to understand these products and then to apply them to their investment needs.

Since I first put pen to paper in November 1989 for the first edition, many of my staff at Minerva Consulting Limited have been involved in the evolution of the final book. For this edition of the book, Piero Costantini, Alberto Parise, and Beth Ragheb have made a superhuman effort to complete the entire update in record time. Many thanks are in order to Miles Davis of Kleinwort Benson Investment Management, who proof-read drafts of this book and provided invaluable suggestions. Finally, my wife Barbara was crucial in keeping everything from becoming derailed. Without their help, this book would never have made the deadline we promised to our patient editor, Andrea Hartill. There were also a number of individuals who were kind enough to provide me with data for inclusions in the chapters on volatility analysis. They will be acknowledged at that point in the text where their contribution resides. For the chapter on exotic options, Les Clewlow provided tremendous assistance on the theoretical side. Without his input, there would not have been the complete coverage the chapter required. I also would like to thank Arthur Andersen and Company for their contributions to the final chapter of this book which examines the accounting issues world-wide, especially Victor Levy and Philip Broadley in the London office. Any mistakes or errors remaining are solely my own responsibility.

Robert G. Tompkins
August 1994

1: The Basics of Options

INTRODUCTION

Obviously, the best way to become familiar with trading options is to trade. As happens in many fields, a book can serve as a useful guide to new concepts and later provide a perspective once experience has been gained - but there can be no substitute for the experience itself. I have written this book therefore as a guide and not as a text book, to assist and accompany the reader as he or she learns, applies and trades the financial products described hereafter. Additionally, the book is meant to help develop an understanding of the mechanics of how option trading works and thereby also help potential market traders anticipate and benefit from the experiences encountered in the actual market.

The material for this book has been derived from over 300 workshops on options that I have delivered since 1985. These courses have allowed me at one time or another to explain options on stocks, stock indices, fixed income securities, interest rates, currencies, commodities and a whole range of exotic options such as options on interest rate swaps, Cap agreements and options on options. Fortunately, the concepts that underlie almost all options markets are the same. Once one understands the theoretical underpinnings for one of these securities, one can apply the same rationale to almost any other option or option-like security. To illustrate the degree of overlap that option securities have, each chapter of this book will feature a different kind of options contract in the examples. The reader can be confident that when he understands the basics of stock or currency options pricing, the same principles will apply to other options. In addition, the trading and hedging examples covered can apply equally well to all markets. As in my courses, I have arranged the text here in a progression of topics. My ultimate objective is to give the reader a sufficient understanding of these products and their markets to be able to trade competently in them and understand the foundations of all options markets.

I begin the book by describing what options are and what they can do, and defining the terminology commonly used in the industry. Then, theoretical topics such as options pricing and arbitrage are examined. I will thereafter address the problem of volatility estimation in sufficient detail to allow readers to begin their own systematic approach for estimating this most important parameter in options pricing. This is followed by a practical explanation of how to use options, including trading approaches, hedging strategies and portfolio applications. After this, I will examine the development of Over The Counter (OTC) option products. Then, I

1

will discuss how to manage the risk of an options portfolio. The book ends with a review of exchange traded options markets in four representative exchanges and finally surveys the regulatory environment for option trading throughout the world.

WHY OPTIONS EXIST

Options serve several purposes. On a purely speculative level they offer investors a sort of limited risk wager. Buying options is analogous in some ways to playing the casino game of roulette. In roulette, what one risks on each spin of the wheel is simply the cost of the chips placed on the table. But at the same time, depending on where the chips happen to be placed and where the ball comes to rest in the wheel, there is an opportunity for significant gain. Similar to roulette, someone who purchases an option is buying the right to wager for profit, but in this case by buying or selling an asset of some kind. The option to buy or sell, like the face value of a roulette chip costs a fixed and known amount. In option trading, the face value of this "roulette chip" is called the "option premium". Once an option is purchased, it is immediately placed on the table, so to speak, and the market begins to spin.

Again, viewing option trading as a speculative product, an investor can wager for amounts significantly greater than the value of his option premium, because the cost of the premium is nearly always a very small percentage of the potential value of the asset it represents. This is called leverage or gearing and in simple terms is defined as the opportunity to gain an equivalent profit at the risk of a capital sum considerably smaller than the actual purchase and sale of the asset itself would involve. Again, the likeness of the roulette chip to the option premium may be applied - very large potential gain in relation to the size of the risk.

We will leave the roulette table here though, because options have an important feature not shared by simple games of chance. In addition to loss or gain, options are defined in terms of time. An option contract to buy or sell an asset has a specific buy-by or sell-by date and in most markets exercising that option may occur at any time within that period. This allows the myriad forces of the market to act upon the option and thereby permits those traders skilled in the market to create effective trading strategies both in the long and short term. Market volatility, interest rates, and time to expiration, indeed all the things which effect our economic markets generally come to bear in option trading, and if properly allowed for, may be beneficially used. With so many possible variables the permutations of creating option trading strategies are endless but I have endeavoured to provide a number of examples later in the book by way of illustration of how such strategies work.

If we put the purely speculative uses to one side, the primary purpose of options trading, and in fact the main reason options came to exist in the first place, is one especially suited to industry. Options function as insurance and in this area the needs of the world of commerce and the services provided by the world of finance dovetail perfectly. As insurance, traded options are bought or sold against actual requirements. A typical example is the need of an export manufacturer to protect the exchange rate on a particular contract. Having taken an order on a price calculated at a given exchange rate in a foreign currency, the manufacturer wishes to protect the price against adverse changes in the exchange market for the period between accepting the order and being paid for it. To do so, he purchases an option for the foreign currency covering the period of manufacture, delivery and payment. Another typical case would be a processing company wishing to protect the cost of imported raw materials on long deliveries. This would be done by purchasing an option in local currency against anticipated future delivery requirements of the material. In both cases, however, the option offers a significant flexibility over either simple insurance or plain speculation, because it offers the benefit of both at no additional cost. The insurance is obtained by buying the option at a known exchange or commodity rate and at a known option premium. But should the exchange or commodity rate have changed to the advantage of the option holder by the time the option is to be exercised then the speculative choice becomes available as well. If it is more profitable for the option holder to purchase the required asset on the open market than to exercise the option, the option is simply allowed to lapse. Option trading is one of the rare financial instruments which really does let traders have it both ways.

THE TWO KINDS OF OPTIONS

A call option gives the holder the right to buy the underlying asset at a fixed price. This is also known as the strike price. A put option provides the holder with the right to sell the underlying position at the strike price (see Table 1.1). When buying either type of option, whether a call or a put, the buyer must pay the option seller a premium (either immediately or, at some later point as is the case at some marketplaces where the premium payment is deferred until the expiration date).

A call option is the right to acquire an asset, hold an asset, or own the underlying asset at a fixed price. A put option is the right to sell an asset at a fixed price. A call option gives the holder the ability to assume a buying (also known as a long) position in the underlying market. A put option gives the holder the right to a selling (also known as short) position in the underlying market.

I must explain here a point which confuses many people. The principal difference between options and futures contracts relates to rights and obligations. Futures contracts are *obligations* to perform. Option contracts, conversely, provide the *choice* to perform.

To understand the beneficial aspects of the rights provided by options, think about everyday rights that you have. One right is to cross the street as you please, excluding jay walking. Now picture yourself deciding whether to use that right. You approach the curb at the street corner, and what do you do? If you follow your mother's advice, you will look both ways to see if the street is clear and free from traffic. If it is, and you want to cross the street, you will choose to exercise your right. What happens if the street is not clear but instead heavily congested with speeding traffic? You will choose not to use your right at that moment, but instead will wait until it is safe.

When you purchase an option, you have the right, but not the obligation, to buy or sell the underlying market. Your criterion for crossing the street is the traffic. For options, the criterion is called the strike price, or exercise price. The terms are interchangeable. Given you have the right to buy or not to buy, you will decide what to do depending on whether exercising your right would be profitable to you.

Suppose the market is trading below the strike price of your option contract. If you had the right to buy (a call option) and you did so, you would have a cash outflow, so you will choose not to buy. If, however, the prevailing market price exceeds the strike price, you may choose to buy since that would result in a cash inflow. Therefore, with options, the strike price is the benchmark by which a decision to buy or sell will be made, just as the curb is the "threshold" to evaluate the traffic.

For example, assume a situation where a Gold future contract is trading at $387 per ounce, and a call and put option on the Gold futures both have strike prices of $380. Someone holding a $380 call option will have a cash inflow if he exercises his right. He can buy at $380 and immediately sell the underlying futures at $387 for an inflow of $7 per ounce. Someone holding a put option under similar circumstances would not choose to exercise his right. He would have an outflow of $7 if he exercised into a selling position at $380 and then had to buy the position back at $387. However, he could also wait and hope that the market price will fall below his strike price of $380 at some point prior to the expiration of his option.

In contrast to an option, a Gold futures contract is an obligation which one must accept regardless of the outcome. It is as if one were forced to cross the street regardless of the traffic conditions. Options obviously provide a tremendous benefit because of the rights they confer. Maybe all the best things in life are free, but, understandably, the benefits provided by options have a cost, which is the premium.

DEFINITIONS

While we are here, what does the term "underlying" mean? This is the asset you will deal in if you exercise the option, and the range of financial instruments that can be used with options is quite diverse. Options theoretically can be offered on any kind of asset. Option contracts exist on stocks, currencies, interest rates, gold, commodities and many other markets. The appendix at the end of this book lists the worldwide exchanges where options contracts are traded. Fortunately, all the basic principles of options hold regardless of the characteristics of the underlying asset. Thus, the reader can be assured that all the concepts in this book can be applied to any option he might trade. To prove it, I will examine a different underlying asset in almost every chapter:

Now consider the option on Gold futures traded at the Commodity Exchange (COMEX) in New York which I will use in this chapter. The prices will be in Dollars per ounce. Table 1.1 outlines the contract specification[2] for this underlying asset. The asset underlying the option is a COMEX Gold futures contract which is the obligation to either buy or sell gold in the month following the expiration of the option.

Trading Hours	8:20 a.m. to 2:30 p.m. New York time.
Trading Symbol	OG
Underlying Asset	One COMEX gold futures contract.
Contract Months	The nearest four of the following contract months: February, April, June, August, October and December. Additional contract months - January, March, May, July, September and November - will be listed for trading for a period of two months.
Minimum Price Fluctuation	Price changes are registered in multiples of ten cents ($.10) per troy ounce.
Strike Price Increments	$10/oz. apart for strike below $500. $20/oz. apart for strike prices between $500 and $1,000. $50/oz. apart for strike prices above $1,000. On the first day of trading for any option contract month, there will be 13 strike prices each for puts and calls.
Expiration	Second Friday of the month *prior* to the delivery month of the underlying futures contract.
Exercise	Until 3:00 p.m., New York time, on any business day for which the option is listed for trading. On New York time to exercise an option. Upon exercise, option holders receive the appropriate short or long COMEX gold futures contract by a way of a book entry. Writers of options who receive a notice of exercise are assigned the opposite futures position.

Table 1.1 Contract Specification for Options on Gold Futures (COMEX).

[1] See Appendix 1 for the complete names of the exchanges.
[2] Most exchanges provide free documentation detailing the options that are traded there with complete contract specifications and other materials.

EXPLANATION OF CONTRACT TERMS

The contract terms for any option contract are essentially the rules of the game all participants must adhere to when trading these products. Let us carefully consider these contract terms as we will see similar tables throughout this book for different options.

For any instrument which is traded in an organised marketplace, fixed times for trading exist which are the only times at which dealing in that product can occur. For the options on Gold Futures at the Comex this is between 8:20 a.m. to 2:30 p.m. New York time. A symbol is assigned to the contract to facilitate consistency of the transmission of prices for the instruments across the newswires and data vendor services. For the Gold options, all contracts will begin with the two letter code, OG. Letters and numbers which follow this prefix will indicate the month the options expire, the strike price code and whether the option is a call or a put. For example OGZ380P would indicate an option on COMEX Gold futures (OG) expiring in December (Z) with a strike price of 380 and the option type is a put (P).

As with all option contracts, upon the exercise of the option something is either bought (in the case of a call) or sold (in the case of a put) and in the contract terms, the user must know exactly which asset he or she must transact. In this case, they do not receive or deliver physical gold but a futures contract which settles in the delivery of the actual gold in the month following the expiration of the options contract.

At least four expiration months will be offered at any one time with the available months being listed in the contract terms of the option. As many as six expiration months may be traded as the nearest term months may be added for trading if they fall within two months of the current date. The options contract price change is limited to a minimum fluctuation of ten US cents per troy ounce of Gold for each contract. Given that the underlying Gold futures contract is for 100 ounces of Gold, this means that the option contract can experience a minimum change in value of $10 for each contract (100 ounces times 10 cents).

The number of strike prices that may be traded at any one time is limited and only available in increments of $10, $20 or $50 per ounce depending on the current price of the underlying Gold futures. This means that the maximum trading activity (also known as liquidity) is assured for the limited number of options that are available. If the current price of the Gold Futures is $387 per ounce, then option contracts will be offered with $10 increments stuck at the levels which are divisible by ten. For example, strike prices would be offered at 370, 380, 390, 400 and 410. Indeed, in the contract terms at the initiation of every new option contract 13 such strike prices will be offered spread above and below the current level of the underlying futures price as symmetrically as possible. As the price of the Gold futures rises or falls, new options strike prices are offered and once traded these options cannot be withdrawn but continue to exist until the end of their life. Therefore, it is possible to have dozens of strike prices available for any expiration period if the underlying asset price rises or falls sufficiently to allow new strike prices to be added.

As one might imagine, the date that the option expires is critical to all those trading these products and this is clearly defined in the contract specification. It is interesting to note that this occurs in the month preceding the actual settlement of the underlying Gold futures into the actual physical Gold market. This is common in those options contracts which may eventually become involved in some sort of physical delivery of real assets. The reason is that having both the options and their underlying futures expire at the same date may introduce a "logjam" delivery problem: too many traders may have positions at the same moment. This would require the actual acquisition of the physical Gold and could lead to disruptions in the market. To avoid this problem, the options and futures expire at different times to smooth out the potential demand for settling of the actual Gold. For other types of options contracts we will discuss later in this book (stock index and Eurodollar options), the underlying instruments do not require any physical delivery but instead provide for a cash settlement on the expiration date and thus do not possess the potential for disruptive effects on the cash market. For these types of options, the expiration of the options and futures markets will often occur on the same date.

A recent development in options markets has been the addition of serial expiration periods for the same underlying futures market. For example, in the Gold futures at the COMEX there is an October Futures contract available. Options are offered on this October futures that expire on the second Friday prior in September. This would be called the October option on Gold futures (even though it expires in September). A serial option would involve having another expiration on the Gold futures which would expire on the second Friday in August and this would be referred to as an August option on the October Gold futures. In some markets, such as foreign exchange, Bond futures and EuroDeposit futures serial options are actively traded. In the Gold futures market at the COMEX, there exists a futures expiration for every month, so there is no need for serial options. Every option settles into whichever futures contract expires in the next calendar month.

The final key element in the option contract specifications is that of how and when exercise can occur. As the reader can see, this can occur by notifying the COMEX (clearing house) up to 3:00 p.m., New York time, on any business day for which the option is listed for trading. This feature indicates that these kinds of options can be turned into the appropriate Gold futures contract on any trading day. There is a special term for these kinds of options with this "everyday" ability to exercise and this will be introduced later in this chapter. Finally, upon the exercise, those who have bought the options (holders) and those who have sold the options (writers) will be assigned positions in the underlying futures market the options are based upon.

Clearly, whenever one is playing a new game, the first step is to understand the rules. Likewise, when trading an option on any market for the first time, the trader is strongly advised to obtain a copy of the contract specifications and the rule book for the market they are trading and to study the contract terms and regulations carefully. For without knowing the rules, how can anyone be expected to win at the game?

For the rest of this book, I will dispense with explaining in detail all the contract specifications for each market. Only when the rules are sufficiently different from the option on the Gold future to warrant a closer look will the salient points be examined.

Before proceeding, let us define some more terms. There are holders and writers in the options market. A holder is a buyer of an option in an opening transaction. Writers are sellers of an option in an opening transaction.

All options which trade on the same financial instrument belong to a particular option class. Options of a particular class which have the same strike price (exercise price) and the same expiration date are classified as an option series. With options, the underlying instrument is defined in the contract specifications (see Table 1.1). However, there is a difference between August Gold futures and December Gold futures because they represent different points of time in the future; therefore, options on these different underlying instruments belong in different option classes.

DISPOSITION OF OPTIONS CONTRACTS

Assume you have acquired an option position. What can you do with it? You have four alternatives to dispose of that option. You can offset the option in the market, let the option expire worthless, exercise the option, or allow the exchange to exercise the option automatically for you. Let us look at each of these in turn.

Offsetting an option means cashing it in by doing an opposite trade. Exchanges provide a marketplace where people can find an opportunity to offset positions acquired earlier. In the best markets, one can offset a position at any time until the position matures. Therefore, if the rationale for the transaction has changed, you can cash in the option, get some money back and, who knows, you might even make a profit! The principal role of any market is to facilitate trading on the products offered there and to disseminate price information to the world as a matter of public record. Such release of price information is transmitted almost immediately to trading desks around the world. At the end of each day, a summary of trading during the day is released to the financial press for publication the following day.

Table 1.2 displays such a summary for options on the Gold futures as published by the Wall Street Journal, Europe as of 20 August 1994. In this table, there is an indication of the prices at which traders could have bought or sold options with a variety of strike prices and maturities. As the reader can see, both calls and puts are available for October, November and December expirations. The strike price ranges are between 360 and 410 US $ per ounce. This does not mean that other strikes or expirations are not available for the investor but that these options were the ones most actively traded on that day. At the bottom of the Table, some terms are presented which require explanation. "Est Vol 6,800" indicates the estimated volume of both call and put options that were traded on the previous day, 19

August 1994. To the right of this is the phrase: "Thur 8,479 calls 1,446 puts". This indicates the actual trading volume in both calls and puts that occurred on the day before yesterday, Thursday, 18 August 1994. At the very bottom of the Table, one finds the phrase: "Op int Thur 102,848 calls 36,206 puts". This indicates the number of open positions (which are known as Open Interest) that were held by traders as of the close of trading on Thursday. These numbers, which are broken down by calls or puts, indicate the cumulative trading activity in the markets. They are also used to indicate whether the market as a whole has more of a bullish bias with a higher call open interest relative to the put open interest and the potential trading activity than might be expected as option holders offset their positions prior to the final trading date.

The second alternative to getting rid of an option is to let the option expire worthless. If a potential loss would occur if you exercised the option, you have the ability to walk away from the option and let it expire worthless. Your only loss for not using the option is the premium you paid to acquire it.

The third alternative is to transform the option into a position in the underlying market by exercising it. Once the option is transformed, it cannot be changed back into an option. A transformed option is analogous to a caterpillar which has metamorphosed into a butterfly. It cannot decide after it has emerged from the cocoon as a butterfly that it preferred being a caterpillar, munching leaves all day long.

Once an option is exercised into the underlying asset it is likewise transformed. The trader now holding the new position in the underlying asset cannot return to the features of the option. When the holder transforms an option it remains a full position in the underlying asset as either long (if a call) or short (if a put). As with all options, it is the right of the holder to exercise. An important question is: Who actually provides the position to the holder who exercises?

The individual who must assume the opposite side to the holder is the one who has written that option. If only one holder and one writer exist, then it is obvious who exercises and who honours the options contract. In reality, many option writ-

GOLD (CMX)					
100 troy ounces; $ per troy ounce					
Strike	Calls—Settle			Puts—Settle	
Price	Oct	Nov	Dec	Oct	Nov	Dec
360	24.00	27.40	27.30	.10	.50	.90
370	14.30	18.00	18.70	.40	1.10	2.10
380	6.00	10.00	11.40	2.00	3.00	4.50
390	1.90	5.30	6.50	7.90	8.40	9.60
400	.80	2.60	3.90	16.70	15.70	17.00
410	.20	1.40	2.50	26.10	24.50	25.40
Est vol 6,800	Thur 8,479 calls 1,446 puts					
Op int Thur	102,848 calls 36,206 puts					

Table 1.2 Options on COMEX Gold Futures: 20 August 1994.

ers exist, and the one assigned to honour a contract when a holder exercises his or her options is determined by the clearing house associated with an exchange market. This is done by random assignment on the COMEX, whose structure will be discussed extensively later in Chapter 15. In practice, because options can be offset easily, very few people choose to exercise their options, and most people generally offset the option contracts before their expiration.[3]

The fourth alternative for options at a number of option markets (and at the COMEX) is an automatic exercise. Sometimes the situation occurs in which a profitable option has been forgotten, and the profit can be lost when the option expires. To avoid this oversight, the market provides procedures for automatically exercising the option. At the COMEX, if the underlying Gold futures price is $1 or more above the strike price of a call option (or $1 or less the strike price of a put), then the option will be automatically exercised.

For example, suppose you had a call option on Gold with a $380 strike price, and the futures market ends up at $385 on the expiration day of your option. Let us say you were on holiday on this day and were unable to be reached regarding whether or not to exercise the option. The COMEX would assume that you would want to exercise the option at $380 and receive the inflow of $5. That is an instance where automatic exercise would come in handy.

One might think that automatic exercise makes automatic sense. This is not always true. Risks may be introduced by automatic exercise which the holder may not want. Imagine that the price of an underlying physical security was barely above the strike price of a call option. If automatic exercise occurred, the option holder would have to deal in the underlying market to realise the profit. It could be that significant transactions costs in doing this would wipe out any small positive cash flow for the option. If instead the option was cash settled at the moment of exercise, the holder simply has cash deposited into his account and no position in the underlying asset. So, for cash settled options (especially on Stock indices) automatic exercise makes sense. However, given that many options are exercised into an underlying asset that may require physical delivery, an irrevocable automatic exercise feature might be detrimental.

Imagine that on a particular date that the underlying Gold market settles at $380.50 and a $380 call option expires on that same date. Since you have the right to buy at $380, you might want to exercise the call and have a 50 cents inflow. However, if the 50 cents profit is not immediately paid in cash but instead one is assigned a futures position to immediately realise the cash inflow one would have to place an offsetting trade in the futures market. Now suppose that the last traded price on the Gold futures is $380.50, but the market makers on the floor of the COMEX will only buy the futures at a price of $379.50 (that is known as the bid price). If you exercised the option, you would receive a buying position in the Gold futures at $380 but you could only sell it at $379.50 for a loss of 50 cents. In this

---

[3]The reason why people generally prefer to offset an option by selling it rather than by exercising it will be discussed in Chapter 2.

case, since the bid price for the futures is lower than its strike price, you will lose if an automatic exercise forced you to buy the underlying futures. If you decided not to close the futures position immediately, you could hold the futures position uncovered and wait until the final settlement occurs for the futures (in the next calendar month), but by then the futures market could have dropped below $380 and you would have a loss on the exercised option. So, in this example, the automatic exercise would not be beneficial to the option holder.

An even more stark example is for options on stocks or other actual securities, where one might have to come up with substantial capital to perform on the contract only to be stuck with the proverbial truckload of Soyabeans dumped on the front lawn. To add to your misery, you might be unable to unload the position you have just been automatically exercised into at a profit. So for most options on physical securities, exercise of these contracts is left up to the discretion of the trader.

EXERCISE AND ASSIGNMENT OF OPTIONS

Now that your brain is brimming with new terms, let us squeeze in a few more. Two styles of exercise features exist for most options: American and European.[4]

An American style option allows you to exercise the option into the underlying asset at any time until expiration. For example, if one buys a December 1994 expiration option on Gold futures, it can be converted to a Gold future at any time from the date of purchase until November 8, which is the final trading day for the December options (while the expiration date is November 11).

The European style options can only be exercised on a single day, usually the expiration day of the option. In our example, if the option on COMEX Gold were European style, then only on November 11 could it be transformed into the underlying Gold futures market. The COMEX options instead have an American style exercise feature which gives confidence to holders that at any time they can "force" the options to follow movements in the underlying asset through the mechanism of exercise and liquidation of the futures thus obtained. If at any time American option prices become unreasonable, holders can exercise them to receive the appropriate cash inflow rather than have to accept unfair offsetting option prices which would be below the "fair" amount (in the next chapter I will discuss what this amount is).

As mentioned earlier, when an option is exercised there has to be someone on the other side who is assigned to honour that particular contract. Note that assignment means the obligation of the writer to fulfill the contract terms. As discussed, the Clearing House must assign these positions to writers in a fair and equitable way. The random solution process used at the COMEX is similar to a box full of bingo balls. If a holder decides he wants his position immediately and he exercises

---

[4]Sometimes, compound options, or options that allow one to exercise at the average price for a period, are referred to as having an "Asian" exercise feature and these will be discussed in Chapter 13.

his option before expiration, the Clearing House pulls a numbered ball at random from the box. Each number is associated with a particular selling option position held by a particular option writer and this random process determines who takes the opposite position to the holder. In reality, no bingo balls exist, but a random number generator on the Clearing House computer performs a similar task.

The number of exercises that has occurred is entered into the clearing system. The computer matches exercised options with writers each night and assigns futures positions to holders and writers of options which appear on their statements the next morning. When the holder of a call option exercises, the option writer who is selected by the (Clearing House of) COMEX will be assigned a selling position in Gold futures at the strike price of the option. Furthermore, the short option position the writer previously had then disappears. Suppose someone sold ten call options and that night the (Clearing House of) COMEX assigned three contracts to this writer. The next morning, on the writer's books he would have seven short call options and three short futures.

However, people generally do not exercise options prior to expiration unless there is illiquidity, silly prices, or if they have made a mistake. If they made a mistake, they essentially have given the writer "free" money.[5] Most options are only exercised if they are deep "in-the-money" (which I will define in the second chapter) and at that point the writers already expect them to be exercised. However, the existence of the exercise feature is generally sufficient to assure that option prices behave efficiently. If it were the case that option positions did not mirror a position in the underlying market, the mechanism of early exercise would allow the holder to cash in the option immediately if fair prices were not available in the market.

WHY OPTIONS ARE TIED TO THE UNDERLYING MARKET

Because of the threat of exercise, option positions must behave like positions in the underlying market. Call option premiums have to increase as the underlying market prices increase because if they do not, people who hold call options can exercise them into the underlying market and realise this gain. If your put option price does not increase as the market price falls, you can exercise it to realise the gain associated with the downward movement in the underlying market. The call option becomes an underlying long position when you transform it by exercise, and exercising the put option yields a short position in the underlying market. Thus, holding a call option must act like a long underlying position, and holding a put option must act like a short underlying position (see Figure 1.1). What about those who sell the options to the holders? Option writers must have positions which have payoffs exactly opposite to the payoffs of options holders. Let us return to our insurance analogy. People who sell options act like insurance agents. If I sold someone "buying" insurance, or a call option, then he/she has the right to buy the underlying

---

[5]This will be discussed in some detail in Chapter 2 when we examine the relationship between the prices of American and European options.

asset in consideration for the payment of a premium. When the holder exercises the "buying" insurance he assumes a long position in the underlying asset. The call option writer must assume the opposite side to this transaction; therefore, he has the obligation to sell the underlying asset to the holder. When the holder transforms his option, the writer's position is also transformed into a selling position in the underlying market. Thus, writers of call options have positions that behave like short positions in the underlying market (see Figure 1.1). That is, they will make money when the market goes down and lose money when the market goes up, exactly the opposite payoff structure to the call option holder.

Let us now consider the writer of the put option. If the put holder decides to exercise his right to sell, the writer of the put must assume a buying position. Therefore, the writer must assume a long position when the put holder decides to exercise. Holding a put provides the buyer with the right to have a short position. Those who write puts, however, have an obligation to provide a long position to the holder whenever exercise occurs (see Figure 1.1).

Now wait a minute! Can you think of any other market where when you buy something you become a seller, or when you sell something you become a buyer? Options are unique: buying or selling options may not act in the same way as buying or selling the underlying market.

Buying or selling calls behave in a similar way to buying or selling the underlying market. If you buy calls when (underlying asset) prices go up, you expect to make money, and when market prices fall you expect to lose. Writers of call options have similar profit and loss biases to selling the underlying market. When prices fall they expect to profit and when prices rise they expect to lose.

Puts act conversely. Buyers of puts expect to lose money when prices rise and expect to make money when prices fall. Writers of puts expect to profit when prices rise and lose money when prices fall. The key point to remember is that holders of options, either calls or puts, have a limited loss potential equal to their premium expenditure with potentially unlimited profits. The maximum amount writers of options can make is the premium that has been paid to them. For this assured initial cash inflow, they accept an unlimited risk potential.

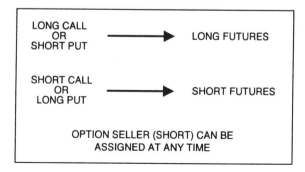

Figure 1.1 Exercise & Assignment Results of Options.

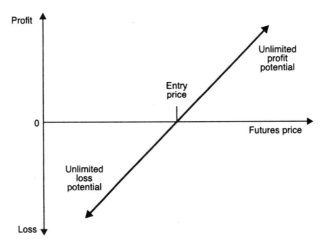

Figure 1.2 Long Futures Profit/Loss Profile.

Options are currently traded on underlying assets as diverse as currencies, interest rates, raw materials, stocks, and a wide variety of other markets. Theoretically, any asset you can buy or sell can be the basis for an options market. Before I can demonstrate this, I must clearly define what a profit/loss profile is. A profit/loss profile is the profit and the loss associated with a range of underlying market prices for a particular transaction.

PROFIT/LOSS PROFILES

Assume that you buy a Gold futures contract at a price of $380.[6] As the futures price increases to $383, your profit will be $3. If you buy the futures contract at $380 and the market remains constant, then the profit or loss is zero. Had you bought it at $380 and it dropped to $378 you would have a loss of $2. So now, we put a point at the intersection of these profit/loss numbers and the associated prices and connect the points with a line. This has been done for you in Figure 1.2.

This illustrates the relationship between profit/loss and prices for buying the underlying asset (in our case, futures) described above. The line going to the northeast on the table continues in that direction infinitely and the line towards the southwest until the Gold futures price is zero. For didactic purposes, I consider this to be an infinite loss. The logic is that if Gold futures prices are at zero that probably means the end of the world. What I really mean is not an infinite loss but a linear loss which has a constant slope equal to the profit slope until the Gold futures is worthless. So, I do grant the point that the individual who purchases a Gold futures knows his maximum loss potential. However, given these contracts are

---

[6]This is the obligation to buy at $380 a certain date in the future.

margined, the actual dollar loss potential could be much greater than the initial investment the holder of the futures initially placed as margin.[7]

OPTIONS AS THE "GOOD" AND "BAD" FEATURES OF THE UNDERLYING ASSET

Where do options come in? Option contracts simply take this position which is long on the underlying asset and split it into a good part and a bad part. The good part is the profit line which rises to the northeast and the bad part is the loss potential portion of the diagram which falls to the southwest.

First, consider the good part. If we cleanly divided the good and bad parts as in Figure 1.3, then the good part is terrific: no losses and only gains. This would be akin to going to the casino and the croupier gives you an unlimited supply of free chips. If this were the case, what would you do? Play roulette all the time, of course. However, the casino does not do this. To prevent you from playing the roulette wheel infinitely the casino charges you for the chip. Likewise, to keep you from playing the option market perpetually with no risk, you are charged a premium, and that premium is what you stand to lose.

People only vaguely familiar with options cannot fathom why it is necessary to pay for options. By paying the premium, you pay for an unlimited upside potential and you have the ability to walk away from it with a fixed loss (the premium). Would those same people expect to play roulette at no expense or receive their fire insurance policies for free? Of course not. Nor should they expect option contracts to be free.

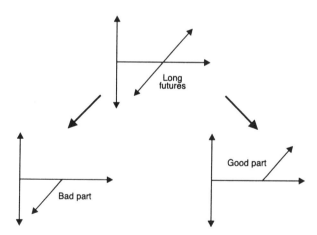

Figure 1.3 Long Futures Split into the Good and Bad Parts.

---

[7]Margin is a deposit placed with futures or options exchanges which is sufficient to guarantee that the holder of the position will be able to perform at the levels agreed to when the position was established. This is generally a small percentage of the value of the contract.

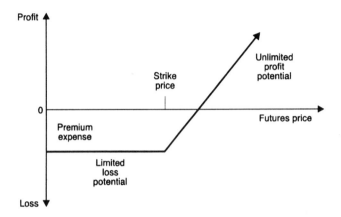

Profit

Strike
price

0

Unlimited
profit
potential

Futures price

Premium
expense

Limited
loss
potential

Loss

Figure 1.4 Holding a Call Profit/Loss Profile.

Therefore, when you purchase a call option, you have to pay a premium to gain the right to buy the underlying asset and get the good parts of buying the market. The most you can lose is your premium when the market is at or below your strike price and you have an unlimited profit potential when the market rises. The profit/loss diagram for buying the call can be seen in Figure 1.4.

What about the "bad" part of going long in the market? This is the unlimited loss potential which in Figure 1.3 goes towards the bottom left hand corner (or southwest). If you made this kind of transaction where you only got the "bad" things and never any gains, you would be most unhappy. This trade is not the way to get ahead in any business. Therefore, if you decided to accept this terrible trade, you would only be induced to do so if someone made it worth your while.

Again, this situation can be compared to insurance. Insurance companies assume the potentially unlimited losses of their policy holders. What do they get from the insurance buyer in exchange for taking this risk? They receive a premium. An insurance company assumes all the risks in return for the receipt of a premium. Furthermore, the maximum gain it can hope for is the amount received for assuming that risk. Therefore, writers of options, like insurance writers, face an unlimited loss potential in exchange for a limited gain. Thus, the trade which is the unlimited loss potential in Figure 1.3 is the obligation to buy, which is writing a put option. The most you can make is the premium received when the market is stable or rises and you have an unlimited loss potential when the market price falls. The profit/loss diagram for writing a put can be seen in Figure 1.5.

Hence, we take the original long underlying position and simply split it into the right to buy (holding a call option) and the obligation to buy (writing a put option) (see Table 1.3). Consider a put writer. He sold a Gold option to someone who is now holding the right to sell at a strike price of $380. The put writer sold the option and received $5 in premium. If the market goes up to $390, the put holder who has the right to sell at $380 will choose instead to sell at the market price which is

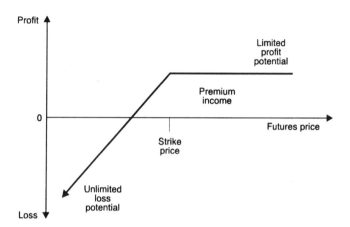

Figure 1.5 Writing a Put Profit/Loss Profile.

higher than this strike price (if he decides to sell at all). At any price equal to or above the strike, the put writer walks away with the entire premium of $5. At $380, the put holder is indifferent to exercising the put option or selling the underlying asset directly because he will achieve the same selling price of $380. When the market price is at $380, the put writer is still happy because he retains the entire premium paid to him.

If the market collapses to $370, the put holder has the right to sell at $380. He could conceivably cover it by buying the underlying market at $370, and the put holder would have a tidy sum less the premium he paid. The put writer must take the loss by buying the underlying asset at $380 from the put holder, and the best price he can sell at is the prevailing price of $370. Hence, by writing put options, the writer loses money when the market goes down, and makes money when the market goes up. This is comparable to the loss potential from holding the underlying asset.

SPLITTING A SHORT UNDERLYING POSITION
INTO "GOOD" AND "BAD" PARTS

Now I will examine the selling side of the underlying market. Short selling is selling something without owning it, with an implicit agreement to buy it back later. Futures contracts are ideal for this kind of transaction because they can be established with only a margin payment.

In futures markets, buying and selling positions are equally as easy to do and are no different in terms of transaction costs. If you sell a Gold futures contract at $380 and the market decreases to $378, then there is a profit of $2. If you sell at $380 and it remains at $380, you have no profit or loss. If you sell at $380 and the

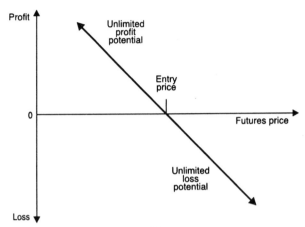

Figure 1.6 Short Futures Profit/Loss Profile.

market increases to $383, there is a loss of $3. Therefore, you have an unlimited profit potential as market prices fall and an unlimited loss potential as market prices rise (see Figure 1.6). Again, the options market simply splits this position into two parts: a good part and a bad part.

Figure 1.7 shows the short position split into its good and bad parts. The put option, the right to sell, has an unlimited profit potential heading towards the northwest (or top left hand corner). Once you have paid the premium for the put, you acquire an unlimited profit potential and a limited loss potential (see Figure

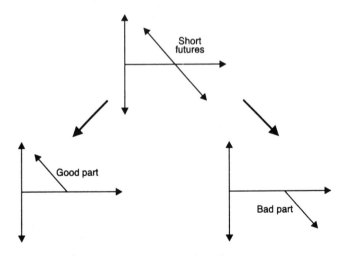

Figure 1.7 Short Futures Split into Good and Bad Parts.

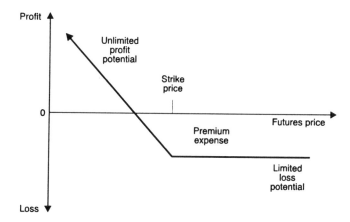

Figure 1.8 Holding a Put Profit/Loss Profile.

1.8). The bad part, the unlimited loss, goes to the writer of the call option. He has a limited gain as prices fall but can lose a bundle as prices rise (see Figure 1.9).

The writer of the call option has the obligation to sell the market at the strike price no matter how high the price goes. The writer receives a premium and assumes for that premium an unlimited loss potential as the market rises. People who purchase options pay for the right to unlimited gain potentials. Those who sell options, the writers, accept the unlimited loss potential in exchange for the premium paid to them by the option holders.

SUMMARY

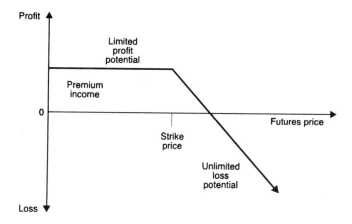

Figure 1.9 Writing a Call Profit/Loss Profile.

Summing up, option markets split buying or selling positions in the underlying market into purely "good" and "bad" parts. If we wanted to establish a buying position, meaning trades which benefit as prices rise, we now have three alternatives (if we use both the option and underlying markets). First of all, we could purchase a futures contract with unlimited profit and loss potential. Second, we could purchase a call option with unlimited profit potential and a limited loss. Finally, if we write a put option we achieve a limited gain potential with an unlimited loss.

If we wish to establish selling positions, meaning trades which profit as prices fall, we also have three possible transactions. First, the most straightforward way to benefit from drops in market prices is to sell a futures contract. Second, we can purchase put options (the right to sell) without a potentially unlimited loss by paying a premium. Finally, we can sell a call option which yields a limited premium if the market moves down and an unlimited loss if the market moves up. These position for both the buying and selling sides of the market are presented in Table 1.3. Holding options confers rights while written options impose an obligation.

The final figure in this chapter (Figure 1.10) displays the profit and loss profiles of the four basic options strategies plotted against each other. In this figure, the held and written call options profiles are displayed on the left hand side and the puts on the right hand side. In the middle, these four profiles have been grouped together.

If one examines the resultant pattern, it resembles the shape of a diamond. For many of those new to the world of options, this pattern is extremely helpful in visualising the differences between the four basic option strategies. At this point, our "diamond" is somewhat rough. However, throughout the remainder of this book

Underlying Market

	Buying	Selling
Holding	Holding a Call Right to Buy	Holding a Put Right to Sell
Writing	Writing a Put Obligation to Buy	Writing a Call Obligation to Sell

Table 1.3 Alternative Strategies.

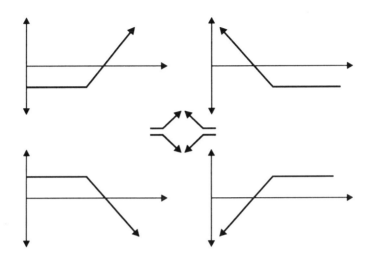

Figure 1.10 The Option Diamond.

my goal is to polish the basic principles outlined here to yield a multi-faceted understanding of these interesting securities. The first facet we will polish is that of option pricing.

   As can be discerned from all the profit and loss profiles in this chapter, a key difference between trading options and trading their underlying assets is the option premium paid or received. Therefore, it is crucial to understand how this is determined and what the critical factors are in that determination. This will be discussed in the next chapter.

2: Basic Concepts In Options Pricing

In this chapter, I will examine option concepts by using options on IBM stock as our sample underlying asset. Table 2.1 displays the contract specifications for this option contract traded at the Chicago Board Options Exchange (CBOE). This allows one to either buy or sell 100 shares of IBM stock at or before a variety of expiration dates.

Symbol	For listed stock, the option symbols are the same as for the underlying stock. Symbols for options on qualified over-the-counter (OTC) securities vary according to the vendor. Please consult your vendor's symbol guide for its specific methodology.
Underlying	Generally, 100 shares of common stock or American Depository Receipts ("ADRs") of companies that are listed on securities exchanges or trade over-the-counter. Call 1-800/OPTIONS for a list of stocks.
Premium Quotation	Stated in points and fractions. One point equals $100. Minimum tick for options trading below 3 is 1/16 ($6.25) and for all other series, 1/8 ($12.50).
Strike (Exercise) Prices	In-, at- and out-of-the-money strike prices are initially listed. New series are added when the underlying stock trades through the highest or lowest strike price available.
Strike Price Intervals	2 1/2-points when the strike price is between $5 and $25, 5-points when the strikeprice is between $ 25 and $ 200, and 10-points when the strike price is over $200. Strikes are adjusted for splits, recapitalisations, etc.
Position and Exercise Limits	Limits vary according to the number of outstanding shares and past six-month trading volume of the underlying stock. The largest in capitalisation and most frequently traded stocks have an option position limit of 10,500 contracts (with adjustments for splits, recapitalisations, etc.) on the same side of the market; smaller capitalisation stocks have position limits of 7,500 or 4,500 contracts (with adjustments for splits recapitalisations, etc.) on the same side of the market. The number of contracts on the same side of the market that may be exercised within any five consecutive business days is equal to the position limit. Equity option positions must be aggregated with equity LEAPS positions on the same underlying position and exercise limit purposes. Exemptions may be available for certain qualified hedging strategies.

Margin	Uncovered writers must deposit 100% of the option proceeds plus 20% of the aggregate contract value (current index level multiplied by $100) minus the amount by which the options is out-of-the-money, if any. Minimum margin is 100% of the option proceeds plus 10% of the aggregate contract value. Long puts or calls must be paid in full.
Expiration Date	Saturday immediately following the third Friday of the expiration month.
Expiration Months	Two near term months plus two additional months from the January, February or March quarterly cycles.
Exercise Style	*American* - Equity options generally may be exercised on any business day before the expiration date. Exercise notices are not accepted whenever trading is halted in the option or the underlying security.
Settlement of Option Exercise	Exercise notices properly tendered on any business day will result in delivery of the underlying stock on the fifth business day following exercise.
Last Trading Day	Trading in equity options will ordinarily cease on the business day (usually a Friday) preceding the expiration date.
Trading Hours	8:30 a.m. - 3:10 p.m. Central Time (Chicago time)

Table 2.1 Options on IBM Shares (CBOE).

Before option pricing can be properly examined, a few important terms must be introduced. Three key concepts to understand are: in-the-money, at-the-money and out-of-the-money.

IN-THE-MONEY

If, as a holder of an option, you transact at the strike price of the option and relative to the underlying market, you have a cash inflow, that option is called in-the-

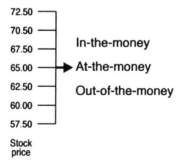

Figure 2.1 65.00 IBM Stock Call Option.

24

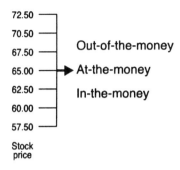

Figure 2.2 65.00 IBM Stock Put Option.

money. For example, if the current price of IBM stock is $70.50 and you could buy it at $65 using a call option, you would have money coming in. Thus, a $65 option would be known as an in-the-money call (see Figure 2.1). In this table, the price of the underlying stock is displayed on the vertical axis with the strike price fixed at 65. When the underlying price is 70.50 for example, the call option is defined as in-the-money. In fact, for any stock price above 65, the call will be defined as in-the-money.

AT-THE-MONEY

An option is at-the-money when the market price is trading at the same level as the strike price. If you have a $65 call option on IBM and the current market price of IBM is $65, the option is an at-the-money call option.

OUT-OF-THE-MONEY

If you transact at the strike price of the option and relative to the underlying asset you have a cash outflow, that option is called out-of-the-money. Consider a put option on IBM with a strike price of $65. If you exercised the put option, selling the stock at $65 and then bought the stock at $70.50, you would have an outflow of $5 per share. The $65 put option would then be called out-of-the-money (see Figure 2.2).

THE FUNDAMENTAL COMPONENTS OF AN OPTIONS PRICE

In this section, I will examine the basis of option pricing. The fundamental idea in option pricing is that an option price can be split into two components, intrinsic value and time value (see Figure 2.3).

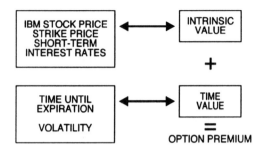

Figure 2.3 Principal Components of an Options Price.

Intrinsic Value

The intrinsic value is simply the in-the-money amount. In-the-money is a cash in-flow from exercising the option. What happens if you hold a call option on IBM with the right to buy at $65, and the IBM stock price is currently at $65.5? If the option were exercised, the inflow of $0.5 per share would result, making it an in-the-money option. Since the intrinsic value is the in-the-money amount, it is also $0.5. If the price of IBM decreased to $65, the in-the-money amount and the intrinsic value dwindle to zero (see Table 2.2).

What occurs if the price of IBM shares decreased further to $64? You would not exercise this call option at $65 because it is out-of-the-money. Because the option is out-of-the-money, the in-the-money amount is zero. The intrinsic value must then also be zero. It follows that the intrinsic value of an option will always be either greater than or equal to zero. It can never be negative.

The put option is the mirror image of the call option. A positive inflow will not result if you could sell at $65 when everyone else can also sell at that price (i.e., the put is at-the-money).

If the underlying market price falls to $62, you could exercise the put and establish a short position at $65. Then, one could buy the underlying market back at

IBM STOCK PRICE	INTRINSIC VALUE 65.00 CALL	INTRINSIC VALUE 65.00 PUT
62.00	0.00	3.00
. . . . .	. . . . .	. . . . .
64.50	0.00	0.50
65.00	0.00	0.00
65.50	0.50	0.00
. . . . .	. . . . .	. . . . .
68.00	3.00	0.00

Table 2.2 Intrinsic Value Calculation.

$62, resulting in a $3 inflow per share. The put option is in-the-money by an amount of $3 when the price of IBM is $62.

Determining the Time Value

Calculating the intrinsic value is very straight forward; but how do we determine the time value? It is easy. Just take the actual option's price and subtract the intrinsic value. That gives you the time value.

For example, suppose that IBM is trading at $65 and you can buy a $60 call and a $60 put. The price of the $60 call is $5.75, and the price of the $60 put is $0.75 (see Table 2.3). The in-the-money amount for the call option is $5, thus the intrinsic value is also $5. As the call option is trading at $5.75, the remaining $0.75 is the time value for the call. What about the $60 put? Since the market price is higher than the put strike price, the put is out-of-the-money and its intrinsic value is zero. Since the put has a price of 0.75 of a dollar, the entire value of the option is composed of time value.

IBM STOCK PRICE		60.00 CALL	60.00 PUT
65.00		5 3/4	3/4
CALL:	INTRINSIC VALUE	= 65.00 - 60.00	= 5.00
	TIME VALUE	= 5 3/4 - 5.00	= 3/4
	OPTION PREMIUM	= 5.00 + 3/4	= 5 3/4
PUT:	INTRINSIC VALUE	= 60.00 - 65.00	OR 0
	TIME VALUE	= 3/4 -0	= 3/4
	OPTION PREMIUM	= 0 + 3/4	= 3/4

Table 2.3 Intrinsic Value versus Time Value.

THE BLACK AND SCHOLES MODEL

As anyone can see, the intrinsic value component of an option price is trivial to estimate. The problem with option pricing, by process of elimination, must lie with the time value. Fischer Black and Myron Scholes, two professors then at the University of Chicago, made a breakthrough in options pricing in 1972-73 when they "cracked the nut" of time value.[1] To understand the steps they took to solve the problem, I need to introduce the stochastic dominance arguments which they used to define the boundary limits for option prices.

---

[1]This is the "big one": Black, F. and Scholes M., "The Pricing of Options and Corporate Liabilities". Journal of Political Economy, May-June 1973, pp.637-59. While Black and Scholes got all the glory, Robert C. Merton of MIT was hot on the trail of solving the problem and barely missed out. See Merton, R. "Theory of Rational Option Pricing". Bell Journal of Economics and Management Science, Spring 1973, pp.141-83 for what may be the best of the early articles on options pricing.

Stochastic Dominance Arguments

A stochastic dominance condition is a statement about the relative benefit of different alternative investments. Stochastic is a word that means probabilistic or random and comes from the Greek root, "Stochastikos" which means skilful in aiming. Dominance, as it sounds, means that one of the instruments dominates the other in terms of the return that will be provided to the investor. For instance, suppose we are comparing two alternative investments in a market that can go up, down, or remain the same. If investment 1 provides the same payoff as investment 2 when the market goes up or down, but provides a superior payoff when the market is stable, then we say that investment 1 is stochastically dominant over investment 2. Furthermore, we can say that the value of investment 1 must be greater than or equal to the value of investment 2.

The first stochastic dominance condition compares the option's price to its intrinsic value. Consider that an option is American style, meaning it can be exercised at any time. The option's price must be greater than or equal to its intrinsic value (see Figure 2.4).

If the option price were less than the intrinsic value, the option buyer could earn immediate and risk-free profits by purchasing the option, exercising it and covering the exercised position in the underlying market. For example, suppose a $60 call option on IBM was trading at $2 when the underlying IBM stock was trading at $65. Then the option buyer could buy the call for $2, immediately exercise it and simultaneously sell the IBM stock at $65. The result of these series of transaction is an inflow of $5 from the stock trades (long IBM stock through the call exercise at $60 and selling the stock obtained at $65) and an outflow of $2 on the options purchase. The net effect is a risk-free inflow of $3.

1) FOR AMERICAN OPTIONS, OPTION PRICE ≥ INTRINSIC VALUE

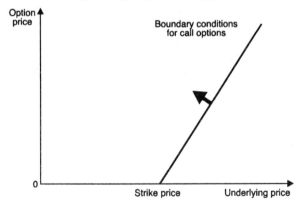

Figure 2.4 Boundary Condition Number 1: Relative to the In-the-Money Amount.

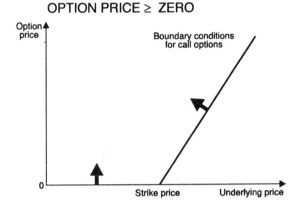

Figure 2.5 Boundary Condition Number 2: Relative to Zero.

The second stochastic dominance condition is that an option must be worth at least zero (see Figure 2.5). As discussed before, options can be compared to insurance policies. Imagine an insurance broker providing you with insurance and not only giving you the insurance for free, but throwing in a cash rebate as well. That is a negative insurance price and, of course, impossible. While an insurance agent gives you a free calendar, he will not give you free insurance and then pay you money to take on your risk. Likewise with an option, the option price conceivably could be zero if there is no risk, but it can never be negative. An option price must be greater than or equal to zero.

The third stochastic dominance condition is that an option price must be less than or equal to the value of the underlying asset price (see Figure 2.6).

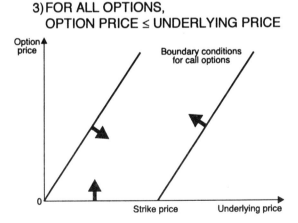

Figure 2.6 Boundary Condition Number 3: Relative to the Underlying Asset Price.

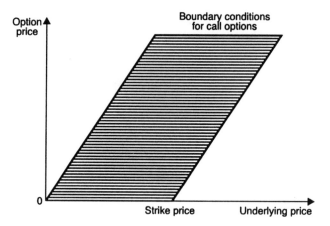

Figure 2.7 *Boundary Conditions: Potential Range for Call Option Price.*

For example, consider the relationship between the value of a six month option on gold with the actual price of gold. The option will only last six months while the gold may well last forever. So, how can the option on gold be worth more than the gold itself? It cannot. The value of the option will be less than or equal to the value of the underlying asset.

The option price must be some positive non-zero value between the intrinsic value and the value of the underlying asset. This is shown in Figure 2.7.

ASSUMPTIONS OF THE BLACK AND SCHOLES MODEL

With these stochastic dominance arguments defining the boundaries for call option prices, Black and Scholes set about determining where in that range the call option price would be. To make things simpler, they assumed that the call option has a European style exercise feature, the underlying market price is distributed lognormally, interest rates and volatility of the underlying asset are constant, and that the asset pays no dividends or coupons before the expiration of the option. These assumptions are critical not only to their solution but also to the "holes" in the Black and Scholes model that will be discussed thoroughly throughout this book.

What does a lognormal process for returns imply? Assume that yields are at present 7% and the market can fluctuate up or down. Over the short term, there is a higher probability that yields will be at 6.90% or 7.10% rather than at 12%. If I had to guess what tomorrow's yields will be, my best guess would be that they will remain at 7%. This is the fundamental assumption of the normal curve, also called the Gaussian curve, displayed in Figure 2.8.

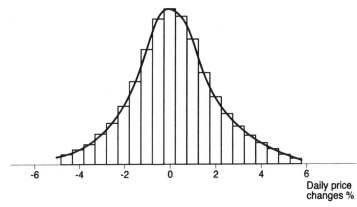

-BELL SHAPED CURVE
-PILED AROUND THE BEST GUESS

Figure 2.8 Normal Distribution.

However, since interest rates cannot fall below zero, but can go up to infinity, we must adjust the normal distribution to take this into account. To do this, we simply multiply the normal distribution by a natural logarithm to enable the rates to be non-zero but retain the ability to reach positive infinity. Black and Scholes assume that the price for assets also follow this pattern of distribution; that is, prices also cannot fall below zero.

With these few assumptions regarding how underlying markets behave (which turns out to be the same as geometric Brownian motion in physics), Professors Black and Scholes were able to identify and solve a partial differential equation for the option's value. Curiously, their assumptions about how markets tend to behave is similar to the random movement of particles in physics. Therefore, it is not sur-

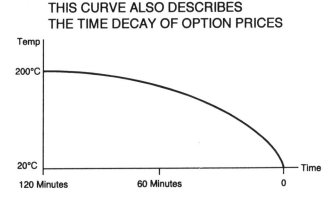

THIS CURVE ALSO DESCRIBES
THE TIME DECAY OF OPTION PRICES

Figure 2.9 Black and Scholes Model "Heat Transfer Equation".

31

prising that an important breakthrough in solving the Black and Scholes formula for option pricing was the adaptation of an equation for heat transfer from physics.

To illustrate the comparative logic between the heat transfer equation and option pricing, assume you have a block of metal in a room which is at 20 degrees Celsius. If the block was heated until its temperature reached 200 c° and then allowed to cool, the centre of the block would remain hot for quite some time, but at some point will begin cooling down rapidly. If you plotted the decay of heat over time, you would see a curve similar to that in Figure 2.9.

This pattern of decay is identical to the time decay predicted for options by the Black and Scholes option pricing model. This breakthrough allowed, for the first time, a closed form solution for the pricing of European call options. The theory behind adapting the heat transfer equation to options was that if one could simply determine the market volatility (the "heat") that exists and the time left until expiration, the time value of an option could be estimated. Once this is added to the intrinsic value, you have determined the "fair" option price.

Black and Scholes Option Pricing Model

$$CALL = S \cdot N(d_1) - E \cdot N(d_2) \cdot e^{-rt}$$

where:

$$d_1 = \frac{\ln(S/E) + (R + \sigma^2/2) \cdot t}{\sigma \cdot \sqrt{t}}$$

$$d_2 = d_1 - \sigma \cdot \sqrt{t}$$

t   = time to expiration % of a year
E   = exercise price of option
R   = risk free interest rate of period t
ln   = natural logarithm function
N   = cumulative normal density function
σ^2 = variance of the rate of return
S   = share price
e   = exponential function
σ = square root of variance, i.e. volatility

The formula is really quite easy to understand when one remembers that the price of an option is simply made up of its intrinsic value and time value. For a call option, the intrinsic value is determined by the difference in the underlying stock price and the exercise price. In the equation, the reader can see that S is the price of a stock and $E \cdot e^{-rt}$ is the present value of the exercise price of the option. If the price of an option were only made up of the intrinsic value (as is the case at the expiration of the options) then the Black and Scholes formula simply subtracts the difference between the stock price and today's equivalent exercise price $S - E \cdot e^{-rt}$ to yield the intrinsic value of the call. The intrinsic value for this can be seen later in this chapter in Figure 2.11b. The reader will notice that the exercise price has been discounted to present value.[2] Obviously at expiration, the "future is now" and the intrinsic value is simply $S - E$.

EUROPEAN VERSUS AMERICAN CALL OPTION PRICES

This factor is critical in understanding the relationship between American and European call option prices. In Figure 2.10, the stochastic dominance argument is provided for the minimum price of the call option relative to its intrinsic value for both American and European calls.

In this figure, since the strike price for the European call is discounted back by the interest rate ($E \cdot e^{-rT}$), the line going to the top right corner is higher than the line for the American option whose strike price E is not discounted to present value. This means that the price of the European call option must be greater than or equal to the price of an American call option and can never be less than the value of the American call. The reader may consider this counter-intuitive since an American option allows the trader something (an early exercise feature) that the European option does not. Thus, the American option should be worth more. This appears not to be the case from Figure 2.10. What is the common sense rationale for this apparently unreasonable assumption?

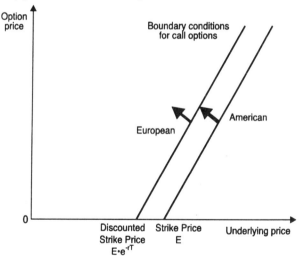

Figure 2.10 Boundary Condition Number 1: American versus European.

---

[2]The exercise price is discounted because the Black and Scholes formula works only for European Style options. For the American Style option, the fact that immediate exercise could occur means that the intrinsic value must be equal to the difference between the current underlying price and the strike. For the European option, the only time exercise could occur to realise the intrinsic value is at the expiration in the future. To determine today's equivalent exercise price, we must discount the future exercise price back to present value and e^{-rt} is the continuous interest rate factor that achieves this.

To solve their partial differential equation, Black and Scholes had to make some pretty onerous assumptions. Since most options have an American exercise feature (including the stock options on IBM) and the Black and Scholes model is only for European style options, is this a not a serious problem? The answer is "not necessarily" and I can illustrate this best through an analogy. How many people do you know who will reach in their pocket, take out a $100 note, drop it on the floor and then walk away? I would endeavour to guess not very many. Consider the theoretical difference between an American option and a European option. The American should be more valuable because you can do something with it that you cannot do with the European option - you have the choice to exercise early. However, consider what one actually receives when one exercises the option. One would assume a position in the underlying market at the strike price of the option. Thus only when the option is in-the-money will the holder decide to exercise it. When he exercises the option, it "disappears" and a position in the underlying market replaces it. The amount of the money he will receive is equal to the difference between the strike price and the prevailing underlying price.The reader will recognise that this is simply equal to the intrinsic value of the option. However, prior to expiration, an option's price will also contain time value. Upon exercise before the final expiration date, this time value is lost. It is comparable to taking the $100 note out of your pocket and throwing it away. If one wanted to offset the option rather than exercising it, one could sell it back and will always receive at least as much and in almost all cases considerably more. So, for almost all assets, the American exercise feature does not add value to the value of call option because there is no value in being able to exercise early if you could instead sell the option back.[3] This also explains why most people choose to offset options rather than exercise them (with this I fulfill my promise to explain the statement made in Chapter 1).

How Time Value is Estimated from the Black and Scholes Model

By process of elimination, the time value for the Black and Scholes model must be determined by the other factors in the formula which are N(d1) and N(d2). The N factors are the cumulative normal distribution of the stock price centered at the current price S and at the discounted exercise price $E \cdot e^{-rT}$. The factors d1 and d2 simply apply the logarithmic function outlined above and determine how big these distributions are. Let us return to the logic of the process. The two sources of value to the buyer of a call option are:

(1) An unlimited profit potential when the stock price S is above E, and
(2) A limited loss potential when the stock price S is below E.

---

[3]This may not be the case for a call option on an asset which pays coupons or dividends. However, for options on futures this is not a problem. Furthermore, there exist circumstances where the early exercise of a put option may make sense and an elegant argument is presented in the Robert C. Merton article previously referenced.

Clearly when one is "betting" on the market using an option, the trader is interested in the probability that the option will be profitable at the end of its life. As with any asset, what the investor is willing to pay for the option is the present value of the potential future profits. To assess the probabilities, some function must be applied to the possible movements of the underlying stock price. Black and Scholes assume that this process is that of a normal distribution for the returns of the stock (and a lognormal distribution for the prices). Why a normal distribution has been selected is discussed extensively in Chapter 4 of this book.[4] If this is written more formally as an equation the result would be:

$$C = p \cdot e^{-rT} \cdot \left(EV\left(S_T | S_t > E\right) - E \right)$$

where:
  C is the price of the European call
  p is the probability that the Stock price $S_T > E$
  e^{-rT} is the continuous discount factor to time T
  EV is the expected value
  S_T is the price of the Stock at expiration T
  S_t is the current price of the Stock at today t
  $|$ is the statement meaning "given that"
  E is the exercise price of the option

This equation says that we are interested in the probability that the terminal stock price S_T is greater than the strike price E. The expected value of this depends on the "odds" that the terminal stock price rises above the strike given the current stock price S_t. Then, this value is discounted back to present value.

Most discussions of the Black and Scholes model only examine the probability function for the stock S rising above the strike price E. The value of the option is solely based upon the present value of this expected payoff. While there is no doubt that this approach is correct, I was puzzled by the Black and Scholes formula. If we are only concerned with the probability that the stock price rises N(d1), then why is another normal distribution N(d2) found in the formula which is then multiplied by the exercise price E? Is not the exercise price E fixed? The answer is yes. So why does the model have another normal distribution N(d2) associated with it? There are two explanations: one mathematical and one intuitive.

First, the mathematical answer: It can be shown that to solve the Black and Scholes formula, one must estimate the relative probability of the stock price moving above the exercise price E. That is, one asks oneself what the ratio is of the probability that the stock price will rise above the strike price divided by the prob-

---

[4]For those readers unfamiliar with this concept, it may make sense to read the first few sections of Chapter 4 now and then return to this section to continue the explanation.

ability that the stock price will remain below the strike price.[5] Finding the formula for the call option price requires integrating the normal distribution curve over the range from the exercise price E to positive infinity (∞). Why infinity? Because the profit potential is unlimited. What we are trying to solve is:

$$EV\left(S_T \middle| S_t > E\right)$$

where:
- EV is the expected value
- S_T is the price of the Stock at expiration T
- S_t is the current price of the Stock at today t
- $\mid$ is the statement meaning "given that"
- E is the exercise price of the option

When this is solved, the result is:

$$EV\left(S_T \middle| S_t > E\right) = S_t \cdot e^{rT} \cdot N(d1) / N(d2)$$

Taking this result and plugging it into the equation from the last page and assuming that $p = N(d2)$ we obtain:

$$C = N(d2) \cdot e^{-rT} \cdot \left[S_t \cdot e^{rT} \cdot N(d1) / N(d2) - E \right]$$

where:
- C is the price of the call
- $N(d2)$ is the probability that the Stock price $S_T > E$
- $N(d1)$ is the probability that the Stock Price $S_t > E$
- S_t is the current price of the Stock at today t
- E is the exercise price of the option
- e^{-rT} is the continuous discount factor to time T
- e^{rT} is the continuous future value factor to time T

When this is multiplied through the result is the Black and Scholes Formula:

$$C = S_t \cdot N(d1) - E \cdot N(d2) \cdot e^{-rT}$$

and this completes the mathematical rationale for the use of both distributions.

---

[5]See Lawrence Galitz, Financial Engineering, Financial Times/Pitman Publishing, 1994 pp 210 -216 for a very clear exposition or see the notes of this Chapter.

Regarding the commonsense approach, we must recall that the two fundamental sources of value for the call option include the unlimited profit potential above the strike price E and the limited loss potential below the strike price. While this approach is somewhat unconventional, my approach makes the trader quantify the value of *both* elements of the option.

Again let us return to the formula. It tells us that we must take the difference between these distributions centred at the current stock price S_t and the exercise price E. Figure 2.11a displays these two bell shaped distributions plotted against one another. The probability that the stock will rise above the strike price E is the area of the N(d1) curve which lies above the strike price. This is seen in the right portion of the distribution and has been shaded to help the reader see it. In addition, the area of the probability distribution N(d2) that lies below the current stock price is also shaded. The time value of the option can be thought of as the summation of both probabilities. The first is the probability that the stock price will rise above the strike price and the second probability is that relative to the strike price E, the stock price will fall further. The first probability is the value of the unlimited gain potential of the option and the second probability is the value of the limited loss the option provides relative to holding a position in the stock. The summation of the probabilities associated with these two bell shaped distributions is a "pointy" peaked area and is equal to the time value of the option.

What will happen to time value as the stock price increases or decreases? Since the exercise price is fixed, only the distribution of the stock price can move around. If S rises, then the peak of the two distributions rises as well. In the mind's eye, the reader can see that as the stock price goes to the right, the summation of the probabilities from the two distributions will increase. When the stock price is equal to the discounted exercise price, the distributions are exactly on top of each other and the summation of the joint probabilities is at the highest level. If the stock price continues to rise above the discounted exercise price, then summation of the joint probabilities can be thought of as the area where both distributions crossover. The reader can see that this total area will begin to decrease (Figure 2.11a). Since the time value of the option can be thought of as the total joint probability of the unlimited profit and the limited loss potentials, the time value is proportional to the total area under both curves. The maximum total area for the joint probabilities is when the option is at-the-money, thus these options have the most time value. The further away from the strike price the underlying asset price is, the lower the time value of the option.

There is one factor in this simplified analysis which seems inconsistent: When the option is out-of-the-money or at-the-money I look at what appears to be a different probability than when the option is in-the-money. Why do I now take the crossover area as opposed to the entire region under both distributions? This is because the option is now in-the-money. Using the previous definition, when the option is in-the-money would lead to the total area under both probability curves to be much larger. But if this is consistent, the options price will be higher but it will also include the intrinsic value. That means that the probability of finishing above

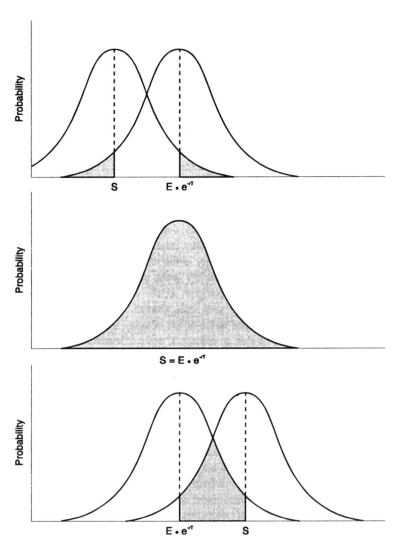

Figure 2.11a The intersection of the distributions at various stock price levels.

the strike price is above 50%. When this occurs, to strip out only the time value from the total option price, we must determine the amount of the distribution which lies between the current probabilities and 100%. Thus, we turn the analysis around.

Since the option is in the money with a 70% probability, any remaining time value of the option is based upon the remaining 30% probability that the underlying market could rise further (or fall below the strike price of the option). Therefore, the crossover area is the joint probability area we are interested in when the option is in-the-money.

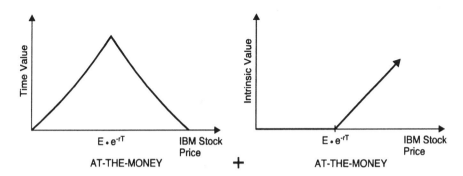

Figure 2.11b The Time Value and Intrinsic Value of an IBM Call Option.

In conclusion, the Black and Scholes formula implies that the intrinsic value is equal to the difference in the prices of the stock and strike and that the time value is equal to the difference in the probability distributions of the stock price at current levels and at the level of the exercise price.

To show the relative contributions of the time value and intrinsic value to the total value of a call option, Figure 2.11b had been drawn which is an extension of Figure 2.11a. This shows both the intrinsic and time values of a call option over a continuous range of possible stock prices.

The reader can clearly see the "pointy" shape described previously with the maximum time value when the option is at-the-money ($S = E \cdot e^{-rt}$). When the price of the stock is lower or higher than the strike price, the time value will fall for the reasons indicated previously. Ultimately at some level of the underlying stock the time value will approach zero and the option will either be deeply in or out of the money.

Again, the intrinsic value of an option is determined by using the market price and the discounted strike price and this is presented in the righthand portion of Figure 2.11b. Volatility, time to expiration, and our normal distribution function allow us to determine the time value component. Figure 2.12 displays prices generated by the Black and Scholes model for call options. In this table, the intrinsic value and the time value are combined. So, if the reader combines the two graphs in Figure 2.11b, he will achieve the same result as Figure 2.12.

After the addition of the time value, the relationship between the option's premium and the underlying price is represented by a smooth curve. Prior to expiration, a call option's relationship to the underlying market is defined by this curve instead of the angular "hockey stick" shape of the (intrinsic value) profit/loss profiles I have presented until this point. What the reader will notice is that the longer the period until expiration, the greater the price for an option and the straighter the shape of the curve. Only at expiration, when there is no time remaining, does the call option's profit/loss profile resemble a "hockey stick" shape and the price of the option is only determined by the prices of the underlying asset and the strike.

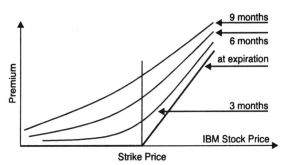

TIME AND INTRINSIC VALUE
AT VARIOUS POINTS IN TIME

Figure 2.12 3-6-9 Month Call Options.

In a similar vein, the put option's price is also made up of two components, the intrinsic value and the time value.[6] The intrinsic value for a put option is its in-the-money amount. That is, the strike price minus the current underlying price (if that amount is positive), or else zero. Again, the time value is equal to the summations of the probabilities drawn from the distributions centered at the strike price and at the discounted exercise price of the option.

Since the assumption of the Normal distribution process for the returns of asset prices may not seem obvious, Chapter 4 will explain in some detail why this assumption may still be reasonable. Perhaps the other assumptions of the Black and Scholes model seem more severe: that volatility and interest rates are constant over time and no cash flows (like dividends) are associated with the underlying asset over the life of the option. What would be the point of having options if the underlying asset and the risk of that market were fixed? There would be no point. Furthermore, almost all stocks pay dividends (and bonds pay coupons) and when these dividends are paid the stock price will fall. These are indeed serious drawbacks to the formula. However, I will examine these problems later in the book and show the reader how adjustments can be made to address them. Nevertheless, the Black and Scholes model is remarkably good as an estimation tool for the "fair" price of an option. Essentially, Black and Scholes required these assumptions to take a "snap shot" of what the options price would be at a single point in time. At the moment of estimation, the Black and Scholes formula is as accurate as a Nikon camera. It will give you a "fair" picture of the situation. If, however, the scene changes, the photograph you have taken is no longer an accurate representation of current reality. As with the Black and Scholes model, one must retake the picture when the scene changes and do so every time a change occurs. Does that imply that a Nikon camera is not good simply because the scenes it records change? Of

---

[6]Black and Scholes did not actually come up with a model for pricing put options. However, through some very simple arbitrage techniques that will be explained in the next chapter, one can determine put prices from the Black and Scholes call option prices.

course not and equally so that does not mean that the Black and Scholes model is invalid because it assumes the underlying market conditions will remain unchanged. Remember, the Black and Scholes formula is referred to as a "model" and not as the Black and Scholes "reality".

Rather than dwell upon the assumptions of the model now, I will examine in detail the variables required to determine the Black and Scholes option prices. In subsequent chapters, I will discuss the practical application of theoretical options pricing models and how these assumptions are factored in. In review, the two components that determine intrinsic value are the strike price and the underlying price (discounted by the interest rate for the life of the option). The elements used to assess the time value include the time until expiration and the expected volatility.

The Key Element in the Estimation of Time Value from the Black and Scholes Formula

If one carefully examines the Black and Scholes formula it is apparent that the elegance comes from the estimation of the time value. The key components are the estimation of the d1 and d2 factors which are input into the normal distribution function. The output of this operation is a probability number which is both multiplied by the current stock price and the discounted exercise price. The difference between these numbers is the options price. If the two factors d1 and d2 were identical, then the output from the normal distribution function would be the same number. This constant number would mean that the price of the option would simply be $S = E \cdot e^{-rT} \cdot$ a constant. In a situation where the output of the normal distribution function is 1.0, the value of the option would simply be the discounted intrinsic value. If the output was 0.0, the value of the option would be zero. This is the result one would find at expiration. The option would be worth its positive intrinsic value or zero. However, these two factors, d1 and d2 are not identical. They are slightly different:

$$d2 = d1 - \sigma\sqrt{T}$$

The only difference between these factors and the key element which determines the time value of an option is therefore:

$$\sigma\sqrt{T}$$

where:

σ is the volatility of the underlying stock

$\sqrt{T}$ is the time to expiration of the option in the percentage of a year

This element defines both the impact of volatility and time on the price of an option. The first variable I will examine is that of time.

Effects of Time on the Price of an Option

How does time affect the time value of an option? Once again, we can apply an in-surance example to infer an answer. If we compare a one year insurance policy to a two year insurance policy, both beginning tomorrow, we would expect them to have different prices. The longer the term of the policy is, the more expensive the insurance will be. Since we now know that options are similar to insurance, the greater the time to expiration, the higher the time value of the option. However, time value is not a linear function of time as one can see from the above formula. The impact of time is a function of the square root of the time to expiration. Because of this fact, one might conclude that there are optimal times to consider purchasing options, and times when it is optimal to sell them, purely from the as-pect of time decay.

For example, assume you have two choices for purchasing 125 days of option protection. Figures 2.13a and 2.13b describe the time decay of two potential strategy.

The first choice would be to buy an at-the-money IBM call option with 125 days left until expiration for $6 and hold it until it expires. Upon expiration there is no time left, and the time value is zero. Since the 125 days of protection cost $6, the total cost is $6 per share and since each IBM option contract is for 100 shares that represents a loss of $600. This can be seen at the top of Figure 2.13a. The sec-ond alternative would be to buy an at the money option with 250 days until expirat-ion. The cost is $8.5. After 125 days, when it is no longer needed, you offset the

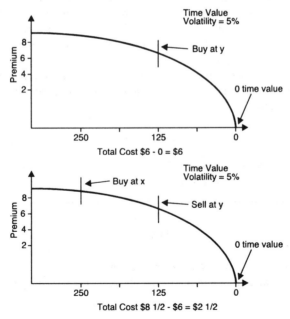

Figures 2.13a & 2.13b The impacts of Time Decay on Options Prices.

option by selling it back. If you sold it back for $6, then your total cost is only $2.5. This can be seen in the bottom Figure 2.13b.

A significant problem for commercial users of options is that they consider them too expensive for their needs. They are only too expensive if you buy them at $6 and hold them until expiration when they become worthless. However, if you buy the option at $8.5 and sell it back at $6, then the expected cost is only $2.5.[7] The time to consider buying options from a time decay standpoint is when the option has a long term until expiration. The time to consider selling options is when the option has a short term until expiration. If one recognises this fact, then why would anyone buy options close to the expiration date? This is especially puzzling when one considers that the most concentrated trading activity in exchange traded options seems to occour in those options closest to expiration. Obviously that means a lot of people are buying options at a time where the heaviest rate of time decay occurs. To understand why people choose to buy options close to expiration, one must consider another factor I previously introduced: that of leverage. By examining when during the life of an option the heaviest trading activity occurs, we can draw some interesting conclusions about who is buying these option contracts and why. Suppose there are three kinds of players in the market: hedgers, market makers, and speculators. A hedger is interested in reducing his risks and -when buying options- reducing his expected net cost of hedging. Therefore, hedgers are more likely to buy long dated options and sell them back prior to expiration to reduce the expected cost. Most economists would categorise hedgers as "risk adverse". Market makers should be indifferent about when they buy or sell options because they generally hold the positions only long enough to find someone else to pass the contracts on to. Therefore, market makers might be called "risk neutral" regarding the time decay of options. On the other hand, the speculator wants to make a quick profit; therefore, he is interested in leverage (percentage returns) and would be a "risk seeker". Since these individuals have an appetite for risk, they will want to maximise the amount of leverage. As Figure 2.14 shows leverage is maximised as options approach expiration. Leverage in this figure is defined as the percentage profit for an at-the-money option for a certain fixed movement in the underlying market. In Figure 2.14, I assumed an at-the-money call option on IBM and determined the percentage profit for a movement in the stock price of $5 at various points prior to expiration. To contrast the leverage with the time value of the option, I plotted the percentage returns on a logarithmic scale on the right hand side of Figure 2.14 and the time value of the option on the left hand side of the graph. As the reader can see, the further back in time one goes, the greater the option's cost and the lower the leverage. However, if one does purchase a long dated option, the time decay impact is significantly less. Hedgers, who often have more capital to

---

[7]This only works if the other variables which determine an options price are constant. This argument is known as *Ceteris Paribus*. However, given you cannot predict the future, you must base your decisions upon expected outcomes. One expects that buying longer dated options and selling them back prior to expiration will be a cheaper alternative than buying shorter dated options and letting them expire.

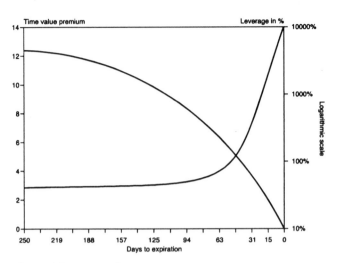

Figure 2.14 Time Value versus Leverage.

work with, want to minimise the net cost of their option premium. They can achieve this by paying more for the options initially and then offsetting them before the heavy time decay begins to occur (as was demonstrated in Figure 2.13b).

Why would a speculator prefer inexpensive options near the expiration date? Suppose the speculator considers buying an option with 200 days until expiration costing $8, or an option with approximately a week of life left (that costs only $0.25). If the underlying stock price increases by $5, then the long dated option's value would increase to $10.5 from $8 for the $5 increase in the price of the underlying share. This is only a 31% return on the investment of premium. Now, consider the short dated option, bought at $0.25. When the market moves by $5, then the option's value would increase to $5. The percentage return is then 2,000%. As a result, the leverage is inversely related to the time remaining and the shape of the leverage curve is the mirror image of the time decay curve.

Of course, this kind of leverage could lead the unscrupulous to contemplate manipulation. For this reason, many exchanges have very strict regulations on trading near expiration. Unscrupulous speculators can make a huge percentage return by buying options with strike prices which are close to the prevailing market price. If the market happens to move dramatically, the returns can often exceed 100%. For example, with one day to expiration, someone buys an IBM $65 call for $0.25 when the underlying share is trading at $64.75. If IBM's price just happened to move to $65.5 the next day, the holder would exercise the option, sell the stock and make a profit of $0.25. This would be a return of 100% in one day on the capital invested. Therefore, there exists an incentive to manipulate the underlying market near expiration to drive the market price through an option strike price. Because of the highly levered, limited loss gamble that exists during the last week before expiration, many option professionals have coined this period "lottery time".

The Implications of the Lognormal Distribution

The reader will recall that the Black and Scholes model assumes that markets are distributed in a lognormal distribution. To understand the implications of this, the game of roulette is a good way to explain the probabilistic features of time value.

There are 38 numbers on (an American) roulette wheel. These numbers run from 1 to 36, which pay off the gambler who has placed a bet on one of these numbers, and 0 and 00 which pay off nothing. The object is to win by betting on a particular number and having the ball land in the slot represented by that number. If the ball lands on the number, you win. By placing a one Dollar bet on a single number, the probability of winning is 1 in 38, with a payoff of $35. The payoff is very high, but the probability is very low that your number will be a winner.

To guarantee you get some payoff in roulette, you could place a bet on each of the 36 available numbers. In this strategy, the amount of cash winnings is high and the probability of winning is also high (94.74%). However, the net payoff is negative because the cost of this betting tactic ($36) exceeds the potential payoff of $35, and you will always lose. However, if over time a particular bias can be discerned on the wheel, then the player can devise a strategy to earn superior profits. Basically, the highest expected return strategy would be to place selected bets on those numbers observed to occur most often.

Since Black and Scholes assume that markets are distributed lognormally (instead of a uniform distribution on a fair roulette wheel), the highest probability event is at the current market price and this is the best guess for the outcome of the next market price. Thus, at-the-money "bets" have the highest probability and, as a result, the highest time value. When the option's strike price is deeply out-of-the-money, the option is a long shot and not very expensive. If the option is deeply in-the-money, it will be very expensive. This is similar to the strategy of putting a chip on every number in roulette. One reduces the leverage and potential profits of the option because of the high premium expenditure. So, from a net profit standpoint, the lowest expected profits are for deeply out-of-the-money and deeply in-the-money options. The greatest profit potential is for the at-the-money options. Thus again the expected payoffs (probability times payoff minus the cost of the bet) will resemble the bell shaped curve in Figure 2.8.

The Impact of Volatility on the Price of an Option

The other major component in determining time value is volatility. Volatility is by far the most important variable in the determination of the time value of an option premium. Assume you want to buy health insurance. If you are in perfect health, the policy will be less expensive than if you had a terminal disease. The policy is more expensive if you become gravely ill because the perceived risk (the probability of pay out) is much higher.

However, if you had purchased the insurance when healthy and then were told that you had a terminal disease, you could probably sell the policy back to the insurance agent. You could receive more than you had paid for it initially if the insurance agent is anxious enough to get out of his obligation. If you did this, you would be able to recognise a monetary gain due to the fact that the perception of risk had changed.[8] If you did sell back the insurance and then learned your terminal disease was simply a misdiagnosis, you could go to another agent and buy insurance again at a lower premium. Hence, you were able to buy low risk, sell high risk, buy low risk again, and make money in the process. Your underlying health did not change, but the perception of the risk of your health did change.

The key to understanding volatility is that the greater the risk, the higher the option premium. Hence in options markets, risk is measured by a concept known as volatility. The more volatile the underlying market, the riskier it is. The riskier the market, the greater the time value of the option. As one can see from the above key element, $\sigma\sqrt{T}$, the impact on the option from a change in the volatility parameter is directly proportional. The higher the volatility σ, the bigger the difference between the factors d1 and d2 and the higher the time value of the option.

HOW VOLATILITY IS MEASURED

Volatility is such an important concept in options that I have devoted two entire chapters in this book to its estimation (Chapters 4 and 5). However, I will introduce here the basic types of volatility and how it is estimated for input into the Black and Scholes pricing model. Volatility is measured in three primary ways: historical, implied, and forecasted.

Historical Volatility

Historical volatility is measured by the actual deviations in the underlying market over some recent past period. As an example, assume that IBM shares are currently trading at \$65.75. Suppose the price of the market yesterday was \$66 and the day before yesterday the price of the market was \$65.5. The difference between these numbers shows a profit of \$0.5 on the underlying markets yesterday and a loss of \$0.25 today. To standardise things, I will convert this number into a percentage change since it is easier to compare. Some days it will increase by 0.10% and other days it will decrease by 0.10%. However, in a world with random fluctuations over time, percentage returns average to around zero and are distributed in a bell shaped normal curve similar to that seen in Figure 2.8.

---

[8]The comparable situation in the options market is to sell the option previously purchased back into the market. If the volatility has risen, the option will be worth more and result in a profit to the option holder.

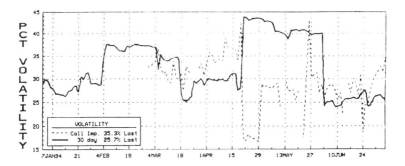

Figure 2.15 Historical Volatility (Source: Bloomberg).

Suppose we took the distribution of the movements up and down which have occurred in the market over the last 30 days. In most markets, we would get a normal curve as I discussed previously. The nice thing about normal curves is that they can be completely described and understood by two numbers: the average (or mean) and the volatility (standard deviation). If we assume that the average change is zero, the only thing we must concentrate on is the standard deviation. A useful feature with the standard deviation is that it gives you defined probabilities about what could occur between certain prices.

The time value of options is simply a method to securitise risk or volatility. When the volatility in any market changes, option prices on that market also can change. Options prices not only reflect market moves but also reflect on fluctuations in volatility. Figure 2.15 displays the historical volatility of IBM shares from January to July 1994. This series is represented by the solid line in the figure. Because significant changes in risk have occurred over this period, substantial opportunities existed for volatility traders. For example, if the option prices are a function of the actual volatility in the market, then as volatility increases so will the option prices. During the periods of February/March and late April/May, the actual movement in IBM shares increased substantially to an annualised rate approaching 40%. However, in June, the volatility dropped to around 25% which would be associated with a drop in the prices of options. Trading option volatility is really no different in principle than trading any price series: these opportunities can be realised into profits simply by buying low volatility and selling high volatility. Just like our health insurance example, if one can predict changes in the perceptions of risk, one can make money trading risk.

Implied Volatility

The implied volatility is the risk perceived by the market today and built into the time value of the premium. It can change as quickly as any market generated factor. To determine implied volatility, all one requires is an actual option price and a theoretical option pricing model. You simply input the strike price of the option, the underlying asset price, the expiration date, a short term interest rate, the expected dividends that will be paid and finally the actual option price into a theoretical option pricing model. The price of the underlying market, the option premium, the term, the short term interest rates, the dividends and the time to maturity are all known factors. The only unknown variable is the volatility. One determines the implied volatility by running the option pricing formula backwards with the actual price as an input. The model will inform the trader what volatility input had to be entered into that model to yield the actual option's market price. The trader can then assume that the market's price for volatility should be consistent for other option strike prices on the same underlying asset and maturity. If a 25% volatility is implied by the price of a $65 call option, you would expect the volatility of a $70 option to be equal given both options share the same underlying asset. Therefore, one could use the implied volatility of the $65 call to predict the price of the $70 option. Essentially, implied volatility is determined by supply and demand for risk in the market just like any price series. Figure 2.15 also displays the plot of the implied volatility for IBM options versus the 30 day actual historical volatility. As one can see the series diverge, with at best a tenuous relationship. Then, the key question that must be asked is which volatility is of interest to the trader of options. For the prices of options today, the relevant volatility measure is the implied volatility. However, for the eventual profits one earns on the options, the key volatility is the actual future volatility that occurs.

Forecasted Volatility

Another way to determine volatility is to forecast it using statistical techniques. Heteroscedasticity is a statistical term for nonconstant variance. Since volatility perceptions in the market are based on people's perceptions, there must be a link between volatility and real events which affect risk. In both Chapters 4 and 5, I will examine how to forecast the future volatility one expects to occur over the life of an option. But for the time being, it is sufficient to say that the most important element in the option price is the volatility you predict; since it is the only unknown element, it is the only factor you can trade.

IMPACT OF CHANGING VOLATILITY
ON THE PRICE OF A CALL OPTION

Consider the situation where you buy a $65 call option when the market is trading at a 20% volatility and the price paid for the option is $2.75. If the price of IBM falls to $60, the value of the call should decrease. However, if implied volatility

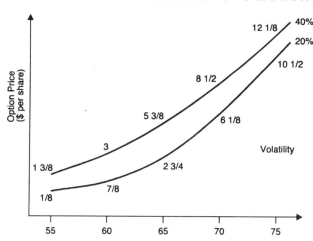

Figure 2.16 The impact of a change in the Implied Volatility on the Price of a 65 IBM Call options with 90 days to expiration.

increased to 40% concurrently when the market fell, the value of the option would increase to $3. Thus, the increase in time value caused by a rise in volatility can sometimes overwhelm the impact from underlying market moves (see Figure 2.16). In addition, if the market price for IBM rose as the volatility increased to 40%, the holder of the call option would experience double profits. In fact, if the IBM share price remains static but the volatility increases, the holders of the call will double their money (from a price of 2.75 to 5.5). Clearly, volatility is too important to the change in options prices to be ignored.

What is interesting about this graph is that an at-the-money option will experience the greatest absolute change in its price for a change in the implied volatility. However, if we compare the percentage changes in the option's prices for the same change in the implied volatility, when an option is out-of-the-money it will experience the greatest percentage change in price.

Underlying Price	55	60	65	70	75
Old Option Price	1/8	7/8	2 3/4	6 1/8	10 1/2
New Option Price	1 3/8	3	5 3/8	8 1/2	12 1/8
Absolute Change	1 1/4	2 1/8	2 5/8	2 3/8	1 5/8
% Change	1000.0%	242.9%	95.45%	38.8%	15.5%

Table 2.4 Percentage and Absolute Price Changes for an IBM 65 Call option for an increase in the Implied Volatility and as a Function of the Price of IBM shares.

In Table 2.4, the results of Figure 2.16 are tabulated for the change in the price of the 65 IBM call option at the various levels of the underlying IBM share price. When the IBM share price is at $55, the 65 call option is deep out-of-the-money and at a volatility of 20% is worth only 1/8th When the implied volatility rises to 40%, if the price of IBM has remained at $55, the 65 call option price rises to 1 and 3/8. The absolute change is the lowest amount at only 1 1/4. However, in percentage terms of the initial value of the option, the percentage rise is the greatest at 1000%. When the IBM price was at $60, the 65 call is still out-of-the-money and will once again have a lower absolute change in value compared with the situation that the option is at-the-money. However, once again the percentage change in the price is greater. When the option is at-the-money, as we can see, the option practically doubles in value. The reason why it has not exactly doubled (100% increase) is because the options on IBM are expressed in minimum 1/8th increments and the theoretical values of the call have been rounded to the nearest 1/8th. When the options are in-the-money, the absolute gains in the time value of the option drop. The drop is roughly symmetrical with the out-of-the-money options. What is important is that the percentage change in the options price starts to fall. In fact, the further the option is in-the-money the lower this percentage change becomes.

This effect puzzled me when I traded treasury bond options in the United States in the mid 1980s. I had bought put options while the market was rising. Theoretically, the puts should have lost their value. However, exactly the opposite occurred because the level of the implied volatility increased. I made a greater percentage return than I would have made by buying calls because the increase in the perception of risk overwhelmed the loss potential from the move in the market. In addition, because the put options were out-of-the-money, they had a higher percentage change in their prices for the same change in the implied volatility when compared to the call options (which for the same strike price were in-the-money). Remember, volatility is easily the most critical element in the time value of an option.

In conclusion, while the absolute sensitivity in the price of an option is greatest when the option is at-the-money, the greatest percentage sensitivity in the price of an option to a change in the implied volatility is for the out-of-the-money options.

IMPACTS OF INTEREST RATES AND DIVIDENDS ON OPTIONS

The final variable in the Black and Scholes options pricing formula is the interest rate factor. When they developed their model, they wanted to cover all the angles and to do so they needed to consider what alternative investments an option investor might consider. What made sense to Black and Scholes was an investment in risk-free deposits for the term of the options life, especially if the investor could combine the option purchased (or sold) with a position in the underlying asset to create a risk-free position. Then the combined position should have a return equal to the interest rate offered on the comparable deposit. This final variable made sure that the option holder (or writer) would not be able to make money for nothing (this condition is also known as a "no arbitrage" constraint). For many option markets, this interest rate factor is trivial. For options on futures contracts which I will discuss later, the impact can be completely eliminated. However, to show this to be the case, I need to cover a little more theoretical ground and this will be done in the next chapter.

The effects of dividends and other cash inflows like coupons are fairly straightforward. One can treat these payments as "negative" borrowing and a reduction in the net borrowing cost required to purchase equity or bonds. Later, I will discuss both continuous dividend payments and what happens when dividends are paid in a lump sum.

NOTES[9]

The Black-Scholes Equation

The value of any option written on S depends just on S and t.
We write it as C(S,t)
At a later time $t + \Delta t$, S has changed to $S + \Delta S$.

By Taylor series expansion,

$$C(S+\Delta S, t+\Delta t) = C(S,t) + \frac{\partial C}{\partial t}\Delta t + \frac{\partial C}{\partial S}\Delta S + \frac{1}{2}\cdot\frac{\partial^2 C}{\partial S^2} + \Delta S^2 + \ldots\ldots$$

Return on a portfolio of 1 option, C, minus $\partial C/\partial S$ units of S is riskless and

$$= \frac{\partial C}{\partial t}\Delta t + \frac{1}{2}\cdot\frac{\partial^2 C}{\partial S^2}\cdot\sigma^2 S^2 \Delta t \quad \text{(from above)}$$

$$= \left(C - S\cdot\frac{\partial C}{\partial S}\right)\cdot r\cdot\Delta t \quad \text{(to earn the rate r)}$$

This gives

$$\frac{\partial C}{\partial t} = rC - S\frac{\partial C}{\partial S} - \frac{\sigma^2 S^2}{2}\cdot\frac{\partial^2 C}{\partial S^2}$$

[9]Acknowledgement to the Financial Options Research Centre, Warwick University.

This equation characterises the value of all options.
It does not involve the expected rate of return on S.
This tells us we can use neutral valuation approach.

Derivation Of Black-Scholes In A Risk Neutral World

Lemma - The Lognormal Distribution

The kth moment of a lognormal distribution truncated at a is given by

$$\int_a^\infty e^{ky} dN(y) = e^{k\mu + \frac{1}{2}k^2\sigma^2} N\left(\frac{\mu - a + k\sigma^2}{\sigma}\right)$$

where $y \equiv N(\mu, \sigma)$

Proof: See Aitchison J and J A C Brown, the Lognormal Distribution, Cambridge University Press, 1957.

The Black-Scholes Formula

Current share price = S, standard deviation of annual log wealth relatives = σ.
In a risk neutral world expected future share after time T is Se^{rT},

which $= e^{\mu + \frac{1}{2}\sigma^2 T}$ (by the lemma)

Rearranging gives $\mu = \log S + rT - \frac{1}{2}\sigma^2 T$

Expected future value of call with exercise price E

$$= \int_{\log X}^\infty \left(e^y - E\right) dN(y) \quad, \text{so using the lemma}$$

$$= Se^{rT} N\left(\frac{\mu - \log X + \sigma^2 T}{\sigma\sqrt{T}}\right) - EN\left(\frac{\mu - \log X}{\sigma\sqrt{T}}\right)$$

$$= Se^{rT}N(d_1) - EN(d_2)$$

where, $d_1 = \left(\dfrac{\mu - \log E + \sigma^2 T}{\sigma \sqrt{t}} \right) = \dfrac{\log S - \log E + rT + \dfrac{1}{2}\sigma^2 T}{\sigma \sqrt{T}}$

$$d_2 = d_1 - \frac{1}{2}\sigma^2 T$$

Finally, discounting at the risk free rate: r,

$$\boxed{C = SN(d_1) - Ee^{-rT}N(d_2)}$$

3: Advanced Concepts in Options Pricing

Now that I have identified the key factors in options pricing (the underlying instrument market price, the strike price, the underlying instrument volatility, the time to expiration, and the risk-free rate) and examined how these factors are synthesised into an option pricing model, I will now discuss how such models are used by most traders in the options markets.

In this chapter, the underlying asset which will serve for our examples will be the US Dollar/£ exchange rate. Options on foreign exchange are traded in the interbank market on an over the counter basis (OTC) and are also traded at a number of exchanges worldwide. Of these exchange traded currency options, the Philadelphia Stock Exchange (PHLX) and the International Monetary Market (IMM) in Chicago are the most popular. I will examine both the OTC currency options market and the US Dollar/£ options traded at both the PHLX and IMM markets. The contract specifications for both the PHLX US Dollar/£ option on physical currency and the IMM US Dollar/£ option on currency futures are presented in Tables 3.1 and 3.2.

Trading Unit	One £ Futures contract (£62,500).
Expiration Months	All contract months deliverable into January, March, April, June, July, September, October and December.
Expiration Date	19:00 on the last trading day.
Premium Quotation	US Dollar per £.
Minimum Price Movement (Tick size)	0,0002 (2 pt) ($6.25 pt) ($12.50).
Trading Hours	7:20 - 14:00 (Chicago Time).
Last Trading Day	Two Fridays before the third Wednesday of the contract month.

Table 3.1 Options on £ (IMM).

Contract Size	31,250
Base Currency Quotation	US Dollar
Exercise Price Intervals the nearest months 5,9 and 12 months over 12 months	2.5 cents per unit 2.5 cents per unit cents per unit
Premium Quotations	Cents per unit

55

Minimum Premium Change	$ 0.0001 per unit = $3.125
Margin	US Dollar
Expiration Months	**Regular Options:** March, June, September and December - Nearest term months -. **Months End Options:** Three nearest months Long. **Term Options:** 18, 24, 30, 36 months (June and December).
Expiration Date	**Regular Options:** Friday before the third Wednesday of expiring month. **Month End Options:** Wednesday following the last Friday of the month. **Long Term Options:** Friday before the third Wednesday of expiring month.
Expiration Settlement Date	**Regular Option:** Third Wednesday of expiring month. **Month End Options:** Wednesday following the last Friday of the month. **Long Term Options:** Third Wednesday of expiring month.
Last Trading Day	**Regular Options:** Friday before the third Wednesday of expiring day. **Month End Options:** Last Friday of the month. **Long Term Option:** Friday before the third Wednesday of expiring month, *provided it is a business day otherwise the day immediately prior.*

Table 3.2 Options on US Dollar/£ (PHLX).

THE ROLE OPTION PRICING MODELS PLAY IN OPTION EVALUATION

A common misconception about option pricing models is that their typical use by options traders is to indicate the "right" price for an option. Options pricing models do not necessarily give the "right" price of an option. The "right" price of an option is what someone is willing to pay for a particular option. The best pricing method found up to now is the market; an efficient market will give the best and truest prices for options. The true benefits of an options pricing model are that they provide an accurate "snap shot" of current market conditions (remember the Nikon camera example in Chapter 2) and more importantly the options pricing models break the option's market price into each of the factors that comprise it. Thus, you can examine each factor separately and assess its individual contribution to the determination of the option's price. Furthermore, by forecasting each of the individual factors, one can forecast an option's price over a wide variety of different scenarios.

For example, once you have an actual market price for an option, you can determine the implied volatility associated with that market price by setting the theoretical price generated by your model of choice equal to the actual price. Furthermore, an options pricing model can predict how the market price of the option should change given that the volatility changes, or given that any of the other factors that determine the value of an option change. Therefore, options pricing models should be used to inform you how options prices can change in the market and not necessarily what the correct option price is. This might seem to undermine the usefulness of options pricing models. However, this is far from being the case.

OPTION DERIVATIVES COMPARED TO AEROPLANE GAUGES

For an analogy of the options pricing model, let us look at another model that has the sole purpose of measuring the present state of the world and indicating the impact on that state from changes in several factors. Consider the instruments in an aeroplane. When you fly an aeroplane you will probably rely mostly on the visual feedback you receive from looking out of the window. However, you also have gauges to confirm and quantify your visual feedback, and also to guide you when your view out of the window is unreliable, such as when you are flying through a storm.

Suppose you were designing an aeroplane instrument board. If you could select only one instrument, which one would you choose? Would you measure the altitude, acceleration, speed, fuel or the outside temperature? As you contemplate which gauge is most important, you will begin to realise that since many factors are necessary to keep the aeroplane airborne, you will require gauges on all these factors. If you had altitude but not speed, you might stall the plane and crash. If you had altitude and speed but not fuel, you could also plummet to earth as your aeroplane runs out of fuel and the engine stops. However, regardless of the gauges you choose, only a very foolish pilot would rely only on his instruments and never look out of the window. With options markets, relying on the market price is like looking out of the window when flying an aeroplane. The option pricing model acts as a surrogate for reality by providing gauges to inform you how the options price could change as the factors determining options prices change. But no matter how good your options pricing model, you cannot neglect to "look out of the window" as you trade options. Remember that at some point, however, your gauges can be the difference between success and "crashing" when the actual market conditions may become too foggy to fathom.

The factors we need to measure and, therefore, create "gauges" for include: the underlying instrument market price, the underlying instrument volatility, the time to expiration, and the interest rates.

THE DELTA CONCEPT

The first and perhaps most important gauge we will use in options markets is commonly called the delta. The delta tells us how sensitive the option's price is to changes in the value of the underlying asset. There are at least four ways to think about delta.

Delta as the Measure of Relative Change to the Underlying Asset

The first way to define delta is as the relative change that an option price will experience for a given change in the underlying market. Suppose that the futures exchange rate for Dollars and the £ is $1.525, and the price of a call option on the
exchange rate is trading at 2.25 cents. Suppose the underlying market moves from
$1.525 to $1.535, a change of 1 cent, and at the same time, the option on £ futures
changes from 2.25 cents to 2.75 cents. The option has experienced a change of 0.5
cents simultaneously with the underlying market changing by 1 cent (see Table 3.3).

Delta: the amount the option price changes
for a small change in the underlying price

Example:			
	T	T + 1	Δ
$/£ Price	1.525	1.535	0.010
Option Price	0.0225	0.0275	0.005

Table 3.3 Definition and Example of the Delta Derivative.

The delta is the actual change in the option's price divided by the actual change
in the underlying price. Therefore, the relative change (or delta) for the option
would be one half of a cent divided by the underlying market change of 1 cent, or
0.5 (see Table 3.3). This suggests that for every point of the underlying asset
movement, the option price will move by 50%. For this reason, the delta is also
known as a hedge ratio. This allows one to determine the proper hedged position
for an options contract using a position in the underlying £. If the size of the underlying foreign exchange transaction were £1,000,000, then in this example, two options would be required to offset 100% of the movement in £1,000,000.
Conversely, you could also create a risk-free position with one option and
£500,000 (1/2) of the underlying amount of the £.

Delta as the Sloped Relationship between the Option Price
and the Price of the Underlying Asset

The second way to understand delta is to define it as the ratio between the change
in the option's price for a change in the underlying price. This ratio is equal to the
slope of the curved relationship between the option's price and the price of the underlying market. This relationship is shown in Figure 3.1. At expiration, the value
of the option is zero or it is the in-the-money amount (intrinsic value). If the option
is out-of-the-money, it has a value of zero everywhere from $1.525 to the left.
Since a slope of zero implies a horizontal line, the option's price is flat from $1.525

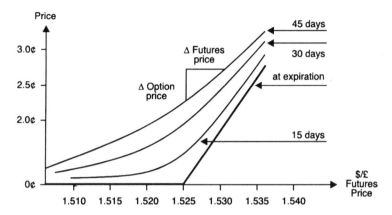

Figure 3.1 Fair Value Call Option Premiums.

to the left. If the option is in-the-money it will be exercised into a long underlying position. This will occur everywhere to the right of $1.525. So, the value of the option at that point will be solely determined by the level of the underlying asset. The value of the option will then increase one point for every one point increase in the underlying asset. Therefore, the slope for the option in this region is 1.0 or at a 45 degree angle. Hence, at expiration the option will have either a slope of zero (if out-of-the-money) or one (if in-the-money).

Only at the expiration of the option will we know for certain whether the option is exercised or not. Prior to this date, it is unknown whether the underlying market price will finish above or below the option's strike price. Therefore, before the expiration, the slope of the relationship of the option's price to the underlying market lies somewhere between zero and one. The higher the probability the option will finish at a value of 0, the closer the slope will be to 0. The higher the probability the option will be exercised into a full underlying position, the closer the slope will be to 1. Intuition should tell us that at some point the slope should be halfway between 0 and 1 and that value would be 0.5. Suppose a slope of zero is associated with an out-of-the-money option and a slope of one with an in-the-money option. We could surmise that the at-the-money option (which lies in the middle between these extremes) might have a slope of 0.5. Hence, anytime before expiration, an out-of-the-money option will have a delta between 0 and 0.5, and an in-the-money option will have a delta between 0.5 and 1.0. This can be seen for a 1.525 call option with 45 days until expiration in Figure 3.2. The delta of the option will approach zero if the option is sufficiently out-of-the-money and will curve upwards again approaching 1.0 when the option is deep in-the-money. This "s" shaped curve indicates how the exposure of the call option relative to the underlying asset has a limited loss when the price of the underlying asset falls and assumes full exposure when the underlying price rises.

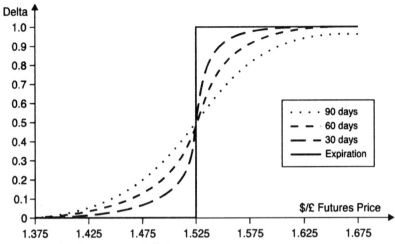

Figure 3.2 Delta for a 1.525 Call Option.

Delta as the Measure of Relative Risk of the Option to a Buying Position in the Underlying Market

The third way one might evaluate the delta is to examine the relative risk of the option to an underlying position as the underlying price changes. For example, if one held £1,000,000 in nominal value of £ at a price of $1.525 that means the contract value is $1,525,000. If the price changes from $1.525 to $1.515 the new contract value is $1,515,000 or a loss of $10,000. To eliminate completely the risk of holding this position, we must sell an equivalent amount of £ which in this example would be £1,000,000.

An option's risk relative to the exchange rate of the $/£ is thus dependent on two factors: the amount held in the underlying asset, suppose £1,000,000 and the delta factor which might be 0.50 if the option's strike price is $1.525 (at-the-money). Suppose a call option with a strike price of $1.525 has a premium of 5 cents at a market price of $1.525. If the market price fell to $1.515, then the new option premium would be 4.5 cents. Thus, the contract value was originally worth $50,000 (0.05 x 1,000,000) and the new value is $45,000 (0.045 x 1,000,000) for a loss of $5000. What would be the equivalent position in £ which would generate the same loss for the same price change from $1.525 to $1.515? Recalling that £1,000,000 in £ lost $10,000, then it is clear that £500,000 in £ would generate a loss of $5000 for the same price change. Therefore, the call option with a strike price of $1.525 would have the same equivalent risk as holding 50% of a £1,000,000 position. Again, to eliminate the price risk of holding the option, one would be required to establish an equivalent short position in £ with the same relative exposure and this would be £500,000.

Since the delta indicates the relative risk of an option to a full long position in the underlying market, deltas allow easy consolidation of complicated options and underlying positions. This is because the netting of all "positive" and "negative" deltas provides the trader with his total risk relative to holding a long position in the underlying market. Remember that a long position in the market corresponds to a delta of +1, and a short position corresponds to a delta of -1.

Delta as the Probability that the Option will Finish In-the-Money at Expiration

The fourth way to define delta is as the probability that the option will finish in-the-money. Suppose the current spot exchange rate for $/£ is $1.55 and the forward price of £ at expiration date of the option is $1.525. Since we are interested in the expected future rate of the currency exchange, the forward price is the appropriate rate to compare. What is the probability that the next price of the forward $/£ could be either $1.524 or $1.526 when the current forward rate is $1.525? In a random market the probability is 50/50. Therefore, if I have an option with the right to buy (or sell) at $1.525, the probability is 50/50 that it will be in-the-money after the next trade. What would be your guess that an option would be in-the-money in 5 minutes given the prevailing market price and the strike price are both at $1.525? Again the probability is 50/50. What about in an hour, a day, a week or a month? It is always the same, 50/50. Therefore, the delta of an option which is at-the-money is always approximately 0.5.

Now, consider options which are out-of-the-money (i.e. call 1.550). These options have less than a 50% chance of finishing in-the-money (i.e. the delta is below 0.5). This is because if the prevailing price remains where it is, when the options expire they will finish out-of-the-money. Therefore, the probability that the market will be 2.5 cents lower in 45 days is less than 50/50; it might be only 33%. On the other hand, there is an approximately 67% probability that the market will be higher than that level in 45 days. Hence, the delta states the probability that the option will be above or below the strike price at the maturity depending on whether it is a call or a put option.[1] For calls, the delta is the probability that the market price will be above that level and for puts it is the probability that the market will be below that level.

Uses of Delta

Deltas are very valuable because they show both the probabilities of exercise and the risk relative to the underlying market. Also, deltas show you how many options

---

[1] This is actually a rule of thumb. In Table 3.5, the reader will see that the delta is the N(d1) factor. The actual probability that the option will be exercised is N(d2) but in almost all cases this is very close to N(d1).

or underlying asset positions are required to hedge the underlying market price risk. Finally, the delta indicates what the profit or loss will be for a particular option contract when the underlying price changes. When the option is at-the-money, the delta is always approximately 0.5. When an option is deeply in-the-money, the delta approaches 1.0 for a call and -1.0 for a put. If the option is out-of-the-money, then you will not exercise the contract, and the delta of these options approaches 0.

As you approach expiration, people who hold in-the-money call options have a position which mimics a full long position in the underlying asset. As a result, their exposure relative to the underlying asset (definition 3) is 100% of a position, or a delta of one. The person who holds an in-the-money put has a position that acts like a full short position in the underlying asset which compared with an underlying long position would be -1. Similarly, if you have agreed to buy £1,000,000 for dollars in the future and you want to be flat or risk-free, you can close out the position by selling £1,000,000 for that same date. If you are long the equivalent of one delta and want the position to be flat or zero, you must simply combine with it some strategy that yields a -1 delta position. Since one minus one equals zero, you would then have a flat position relative to the underlying exchange rate.

Therefore, deltas allow you to evaluate the risk of any options position (or combination of options) as if it (they) were a position in the underlying foreign exchange market. Then, it is a simple step to establish offsetting delta exposures (with either spot or forward currency contracts, or with other options) until the net delta exposure is zero; achieving a position with no exposure to the underlying market. Alternatively, one can become delta positive or negative to benefit from a bullish or bearish sentiment. Since a positive delta offsets a negative delta and we have identified those option positions that are long (positive delta) or short (negative delta) relative to the underlying market, the relative risk can easily be determined. They cancel out if they are balanced correctly, yielding a hedged position. Determining the overall delta position is crucial to assessing the overall risk of a combination of options. The ability to determine the net delta is an important feature in risk management.

Delta Exposures of the Basic Strategies

Generally, if you buy any underlying market, your exposure will always be one or 100% of that market. If you buy a put option (the right to sell), the relative exposure to a long underlying position is negative. That is, if the price of the underlying asset rises and the other factors do not change, the value of the put option will fall and the holder of the put will lose money. Therefore, relative to the underlying asset, holding put options is a negative position and provides negative deltas. When the market rises, put options should lose money; conversely, if the market falls, put options should make money. Therefore, put prices have an inverse relationship to movement in the price of the market. If an option is out-of-the-money, it will have a relatively small exposure relative to the underlying market; that is, if the market price changes the price of the option will remain almost unchanged. If it is deeply in-the-money, it acts exactly like a full long or short position in the underlying market. When it is eventually transformed into the underlying market by exercise, it assumes the risk of the underlying market and then has a delta of either +1 or -1.

In the currency markets, if you have a position with a delta of positive 0.95, then you have a position which is as risky (in nominal term) as 95% of one million £ (or £950,000). The buyer of a put option finds that his risk will range from no exposure to a full short position (minus one delta) depending on whether the market price lies above or below the strike price. Similarly, this inverse exposure also exists for those who sell call options. As I discussed in the previous chapter, both writing calls and holding put positions are equivalent short positions relative to the underlying market and, thereby, have delta exposures which are negative. All deltas are relative to one standard, which is a position buying £1,000,000 for dollars in our examples.

The Concept of Delta Neutral

Because of the wide variety of strike prices for calls and puts that are available for $/£ both on exchange markets and on over-the-counter (OTC) basis, the ways to achieve a flat position are almost infinite. When the net delta for a combination of options (and spot or forward contracts) is equal to zero that is commonly referred to as a "Delta Neutral" position. Consider hedging a single $/£ option series with an offsetting position in the $/£ forward market. To determine a "risk-free" hedge ratio, one simply takes the inverse of the option's delta to determine the number of options required for each $/£ forward contract. Alternatively, one would simply multiply the delta by one $/£ forward position to determine the quantity of the currency that must be sold forward to hedge each option position. Unfortunately, because option deltas are by definition less than or equal to 1.0, the amount of currency required to hedge a single option may easily be less than the £1,000,000 which is the amount representing the minimum dealing size for most forward contracts. In the exchange traded £ futures market (and in almost all exchange markets) it is not possible to buy or sell less than one futures contract. So, if we adjust the quantity of the forward currency position to hedge the option, we will have to either deal in a size smaller than is generally traded and have to pay a wider spread or use standardised futures contracts in "round lots" (i.e. integer amounts). Let us consider instead using the inverse of the delta to determine the number of options for a one million $/£ forward contract. For example, assume the $/£ forward price is at $1.525, the volatility is 10.5%, there are 45 days to expiration and the differential in interest rates between the United States and Britain is 2%. The call option with a strike price of $1.55 is out-of-the-money and therefore has a delta of 0.33 (which is less than 50%). If one purchased this call option it would be equivalent to being long 33% of a single million £ forward contract. If you bought a $/£ forward contract to create an equivalent position, how many would you have to buy? To create an equivalent position you would have to buy 33% of one million £ in the forward market which would be equal to £330,000 for each call option you bought. What happens if we decide that we want to only deal forward contracts at a minimum size of £1,000,000? We must find out how many options are required to establish a position exactly equal to buying a £1,000,000 forward contract. In delta terms, this strategy would have to be equal to a positive one delta. Let us consider an example. Suppose you are short one million $/£ in the forward market and you wish to offset the risk of this transaction using these call options expiring on that forward date. Since the options are equivalent to one third of a long position in a $/£ forward contract, you would need to purchase three call options to offset the risk exposure and become delta neutral. So, the proper hedge ratio would be the inverse of 0.33 which is three option contracts.

The real beauty of deltas is that they not only allow comparisons between options and the underlying forward market but also between call and put options with a wide variety of strike prices. Now, we will apply this technique to hedge a $/£ option's exposure with another $/£ option. When we purchase a call, we have an equivalent long position. If we sell a call, by symmetry, we have an equivalent short position. If these calls were on the same underlying asset, the same maturity and the same strike price, buying and selling these options would provide an exact offset. Suppose the options have different strike prices; then the options are also quite different. Suppose you purchased a Mercedes Benz automobile and then sold it. What would your risk position be, relative to the price of Mercedes Benzes? One might intuitively think the position is offsetting or flat. But what if the Mercedes purchased was a 600 SL model and the Mercedes sold was a C 180 model? The position may or may not be "flat" relative to the overall price of Mercedes Benzes because you are holding two positions which do not exactly offset. Since the 600 SL costs more than the C 180, we must adjust the number of cars held to be equivalent in value. What is important is that the relative exposure of each offsets the other. Since the 600 SL is more valuable than the C 180, more C 180's must be sold to provide a truly "hedged" position.

Let us now return to the options on foreign exchange market. Suppose you have an $1.55 strike price call option and an $1.575 strike price call option. As indicated above the $1.55 call has an equivalent risk of one third worth of one million $/£ forward contract because its delta is 0.33. Suppose the $1.575 call option has a delta of 0.20 (i.e., it is further out-of-the-money). If you sold the $1.575 call option it would create a position equivalent to selling one fifth of a million $/£ forward contract (0.20 is approximately 1/5). This occurs because when you sell a call, the delta position is negative (if you instead bought the call, the delta would be a positive 0.20). If your goal is to achieve an offsetting and risk-less position with these two options, then you must adjust the number of calls bought or sold to reflect their different relative risks. So, if buying the $1.55 call is equivalent to buying one third of a million £ forward and selling the $1.575 call is equivalent to selling one fifth of a million £ forward, to have a position with no exposure to the forward $/£ exchange rate (that is a delta neutral position) you would have to sell five $1.575 calls for every three $1.55 call you bought. The reader may be curious as to the reason why we did not sell one $1.575 call and then sell half of the $1.55 call. We could have. However, this would require the underlying $/£ amount for the $1.55 call option to only be equal to £500,000. Again, most options trade on a minimum underlying amount and it could be that the price for a "micro" option might be less advantageous. In addition, the hedge ratio would not be exact due to the fact that 0.20/0.33 is not equal to half.

In exchange traded foreign exchange markets it would not be possible to sell half of the $1.55 call option because these trades are restricted to whole numbers. Nevertheless, even if we are restricted to a minimum purchase or sell of one option, the true risk of the option may not be equivalent to one lot in the underlying market. The risk for an option is defined by both the number of lots bought or sold multiplied by the delta for that option.

The Problem with the Delta

The problem with deltas is that they only provide instantaneous information; they change as market conditions change. As with the aeroplane analogy, the speedometer will provide a valid measure of the speed at that moment; however, as other factors such as acceleration, altitude or fuel change, so will the speed. As the pilot must monitor how his speed may change as the other factors which keep his aeroplane airborne change, so the options trader must also monitor how his deltas can change as the other variables that determine options prices change. To remain perfectly risk-free, a hedged position in options may have to be revised continuously.

For example, the £ forward market is at $1.525 and you buy three $1.55 calls with a delta of 0.33 (out-of-the- money call options). The relative risk of these options is therefore 1.0 delta (0.33 x 3) and this strategy is equivalent to buying a million £ on the expiration date of the option. Suppose that to hedge this risk, you sell a million £ forward for that date. Since shorting the underlying forward contract provides a -1 delta, when you combine this trade with the three calls you have purchased, the net position is zero (a delta neutral position). If the market then increased to $1.55, the $1.55 call would now be at-the-money and the delta has increased to 0.50. This implies that the three call options each have an equivalency to 50% of one million £. In total, the equivalent delta position for all three together is a positive 1.50 or £1,500,000. The short position has remained at a -1.0 delta or short £1,000,000 because it is still a single short position in £. As the reader can see, the "hedged" position is no longer neutral but has become an equivalent long position with the same risk as holding 50% of one million £ or a risk of £500,000.

As the market moves, the delta does not remain constant. Therefore, the option trader must measure the sensitivity of the deltas to changes in other factors, in this case to the movement in the underlying market. Again, the true value of option pricing models is that they allow you to determine this sensitivity. By using calculus and taking the derivatives of the option pricing formula relative to those factors of interest to us, we can easily generate additional gauges.

I can just imagine the words "derivative" and "calculus" hitting the reader right between the eyes and the attention starting to wane. Do not fear, as I will leave these concepts to other books where they are more appropriate. My objective here is not to show you how to produce your own "option gauges" but rather to show you how to read them and understand what they mean.

When I studied calculus, most examples seemed very abstract and sometimes even trivial to me. One of the most popular examples to explain derivatives used a graph with a vertical axis representing distance such as kilometres or miles and a horizontal axis representing time. A sloped line (very much looking like our call option in Figure 3.1) was drawn representing the change in distance for a given change in time. The intuition was quite straightforward, the relationship between the changes in distance and time is simply speed. Likewise, the relationship between an option's price and the underlying price is called the delta. So, the delta is like the speed of the option. However, speed is not the only thing that sells cars. Another important performance feature (besides the Dolby sound system) is the acceleration. This is the change in speed for a given change in time. While the speed (delta) is the first derivative of the distance per time at a particular point (simply the slope), the acceleration is the second derivative at that same point (the change in the slope). This derivative is determined by taking another derivative of the speed with respect to time. Since in options we are interested in determining how the delta changes when the underlying market changes, we simply take the derivative of the delta with respect to the underlying market and we get a new "gauge" which is commonly referred to as the gamma. The gamma is analogous to the acceleration of the option as the underlying price changes.

THE CONCEPT OF GAMMA

Of all the concepts in options there are fewer more critical than that of the gamma. Options are different than positions in the underlying asset in that they change their exposure depending on what the price of the underlying asset is. Over a certain range, options behave just like the underlying asset (in-the-money) and over a different range they have no exposure (out-of-the-money). Their price relationship is curved in a beneficial (or positive) way for the holder. The amount of this curved relationship is the gamma and gamma is essentially what makes options unique.

By definition, the higher the gamma value is, the more the delta will change when the underlying market price changes. Intuitively, gamma jointly measures how close the current market is to the strike price of your option and how close the option is to expiration. The closer the market price is to the strike price and the closer the maturity of the option is to the expiration date, the higher the gamma will be. For example, an at-the-money option with one minute remaining until expiration will have the highest possible gamma value of 1.0. This is because if the underlying asset price moves the tiniest increment up, the option will become in-the-money with a delta of 1.0. If on the other hand, the underlying asset price falls by an infinitesimally small amount, the option will be out-of-the-money with a delta of zero.

Consider a $1.55 call option with the underlying market trading at $1.5495 and one minute remaining until expiration. The delta is close to zero because it is out-of-the-money. If the market moves up 0.0010 (to $1.5505), the option is now in-the-money and the delta has become close to 1.0 due to the very small change in the underlying market. If the market oscillated above and below the strike price of $1.55, the delta would also swing between a 100% exposure and a zero exposure. For those who purchase options, this impact represents an incredible leverage and many professional speculators purchase options at or near expiration with the goal of maximising this gamma impact. This effect was demonstrated in the last chapter in Figure 2.14 with the effect of gearing versus the time decay of the option. As the reader may remember, the two effects offset each other. The reason why traders buy options near the expiration is that the gearing effect of the gamma directly offsets the expected loss in time decay that occurs over the period.

The more one moves away from this extreme situation of being at-the-money at expiration, the lower the gearing effect of the option and the lower the gamma. An option with more time remaining will have a lower gamma. The further the option's strike price is away from the current underlying asset price the less time value in the option and the lower the gamma. Figure 3.3 indicates gamma values for a particular $/£ call option with a variety of different maturities.

The increments of the gamma are often referred to as the number of deltas that will change for a change of one tick in the underlying asset price. Suppose that the futures market is currently at 1.525, there are 45 days to expiration, the volatility is

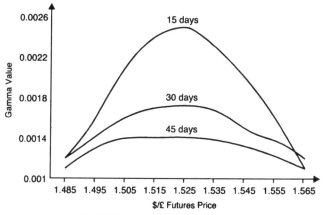

Figure 3.3 Gamma for a 1.525 Call Option.

at 10.5% and the at-the-money call option has a delta of 0.505 with a gamma of 0.0014. If the market moves up by one tick to 1.5252 (for the IMM contract each tick is 2 hundredths of a US cent), the new delta would be 0.5064. If instead the change in the underlying exchange rate was 50 ticks to a new level of 1.535 (50 ticks: 0.01/0.0002) the new delta would be 0.505 + 0.0014 · 50 or 0.575. Thus, when the market price increases, the call option gains exposure making even greater profits.

As with deltas, gamma positions can either be positive or negative. A positive relationship is just as it sounds, for those positive gamma positions, they benefit from actual movement in the price of the underlying market. Consider a holder of a call option. If the option is at-the-money, the delta is close to 50%. If the underlying market price rises such that the call option is deeply in-the-money, then the delta of the option will approach 100%. Thus, for an increase in the price of the underlying asset, the delta has also increased, which is a positive relationship. Likewise, if the underlying asset price falls, the delta of the call option falls to zero. Because a decrease in the underlying asset has been associated with a decrease in the delta once again the relationship is positive. What about put option holders?

Let us say someone is holding an at-the-money put option. The delta is -50%. When the price of the underlying asset rises, the option delta also rises to 0% as the option is now out-of-the-money. When the asset price falls, the put exposure becomes more negative and at some point will approach -100%. Thus, as the gamma relationship is again positive the change in the amount of the delta is in the same direction as the movement of the underlying market. All buyers of options gain from movements in the price of the underlying assets. For this reason, holders of options are often referred to as being "long gamma". The concept of gamma can be seen as:

Gamma is a measure of the exposure the position has to a change in the actual volatility of the underlying market

For sellers of options, the gamma exposure is exactly opposite to that of buyers of options. The gamma has probably turned more hair white, caused more ulcers and broken more marriages than any other feature in options markets. Those who sell options can be hurt when the gamma is high and the underlying market price moves. Therefore, they are often referred to as "short gamma".

One easy method to assess if a position is gamma positive overall is to look at the profit/loss profile of the strategy prior to expiration. If the curved relationship to the price of the underlying asset is curved in a convex manner and this can be assessed if the curve turns upwards like a smile, then one is gamma positive. If the curve turns downwards like a frown, then the position is gamma negative. This will be demonstrated later in this book in the chapters on trading strategies (Chapters 6 and 7) and when I discuss risk management of options books (Chapter 14). The reader may wish to flip through the figures in these chapters to see the "smiling" or "frowning" effects of gamma.

Of course, if we are going to build gauges that measure the option's sensitivity to movement in the underlying market, we are also interested in all the other factors which determine an option's value. I have so far examined the speed (delta) and acceleration (gamma) features of options over the underlying market price. Now, I will look at the other factors, the most important of which is the volatility.

THE MEASURE OF VOLATILITY EXPOSURE - THE VEGA

The change in the option's price for a given change in the implied volatility is called, among other things, vega. I prefer to call this measure the vega, but this is by no means a convention. In some markets, this derivative is called kappa, zeta, sigma, omega[2], epsilon and a variety of other Greek letters. Vega, as anyone who has pledged to a sorority or fraternity knows, is not a Greek letter but a now extinct sub-compact American car made by Chevrolet or a star. I like vega because it has a "V" for volatility and sounds rather Greek. Anyway, the vega measures the amount of money you make or lose from a given change in volatility. If the options market is trading at an implied volatility of 15% and your option position has a vega of +1.4, this indicates the amount to some fixed level you will make (lose) $1,400 for every 1% increase (decrease) in volatility. If that fixed level was $ 1000 per 1% change in implied volatility, your profit or loss from such a change would be $1400. Thus, if you had this vega positive position and volatility increased to 16%, then if everything else remains constant you will expect to make this amount of money. Of course, if volatility drops to 14% you would also expect to lose this amount (see Figure 3.4). The concept of the vega can be summarised thus:

Vega is a measure of the exposure the position has to
a change in the implied volatility of the options market

Let us go through an example. Suppose that the futures price for the expiration of an option we are holding is at 1.555, the volatility is currently at 10% and there are 30 days to the option expiration. The price of a call option 1.525 is 0.0364 with a vega of 1.403. If the implied volatility of the options market moves up to 11%, the new price of the call option will rise to 0.0378. The price changed by 0.0014, which is equal to $1400 (7 ticks · $200), roughly the same amount indicated by vega. Whenever we purchase options we are purchasing the time value component as well as the intrinsic value component of the premium. Thus, when the implied volatility rises, the time value and the total option premium also rise. It can be fair to say that when one buys options, the exposure to changes in the implied volatility is positive and the vega is positive. By symmetry, when one sells options, they benefit from a decrease in the implied volatility and therefore have a vega negative exposure.

---

[2]In the foreign exchange market, omega is sometimes referred to as the risk that appears when dealing in options where neither currency in the pair is the accounting currency for the bank.

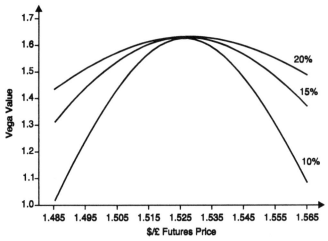

Figure 3.4 Vega for a 1.525 Call Option.

As was alluded to earlier, options are the most straightforward method to turn risk into a security.[3] As risk changes, so does an options contract. Therefore, options dealing is nothing more than risk (or volatility) dealing. It is easy to understand why one must measure the vega to know what the volatility exposure of an option is. A key feature of most computer programmes based upon the Black and Scholes model is that they can quickly and accurately determine the exposure of the option to each factor that determines its value including this vega measure. Using our aeroplane analogy, one could consider the vega as the measure of an option's "altitude". Obviously the altitude is one of the most critical elements in flying an aeroplane and the volatility is one of the most critical elements in determining an option's time value.

What are the other variables which determine a currency option's value? These include the strike price of the option, the time until maturity and the interest rates for each country. Of these, there is no derivative relative to the strike price because the strike price is fixed. Since the strike price cannot change, it makes no sense to examine how the option's price will change for a change in the strike price. While this is true for most options, some option-like securities such as convertible bonds can have a variable "strike" price and then such a derivative may be appropriate.

THE EXPOSURE OF THE OPTION TO TIME DECAY - THE THETA

Of these three remaining variables (time, interest and the strike price), the most important one to measure is the option price's time decay as the option approaches maturity. While time passing is not a probabilistic (sometimes known as stochastic)

---

[3]The reader is referred to the health insurance example in Chapter 2 where the policy holder is "trading" risk.

factor (since everyone knows that time is passing), the options price impact from the passage of time is not as easy to determine as one might think. If you recall from earlier chapters, options prices do not decay over time in a straight line but rather in the shape defined by the heat transfer equation. So, to determine the amount of time decay that would occur from today until tomorrow, one could simply plug in today's underlying price, volatility, interest rates and time to maturity (making sure that the theoretical price from the model equals the market price of an option). Then, one would reduce the amount of time to maturity by one day, keeping the other variables constant, and revalue the option. The difference between today's market price and tomorrow's theoretical price is the time decay. As one can imagine, this is tedious and time consuming. To speed up the process, one can simply use calculus to determine the derivative of the option price with respect to time, which is commonly known as the theta. This derivative is simply the slope of the time decay curve at a particular point and it gives the change in option's market price from one day to another. The theta decay (which is exactly the same as the time decay curve in Figures 2.13a and 2.13b) can be seen in Figure 3.5. We can summarise the theta effect as:

> *Theta is a measure of the exposure*
> *the position has to the passage of time*

Using our aeroplane gauge analogy, the theta derivative can be thought of as the fuel gauge. It measures how long the option will live and when it starts running out of "fuel".

In this figure, the theta values have been included for at-the-money, in-the-money and out-of-the-money call options. Theta informs us how the value of the

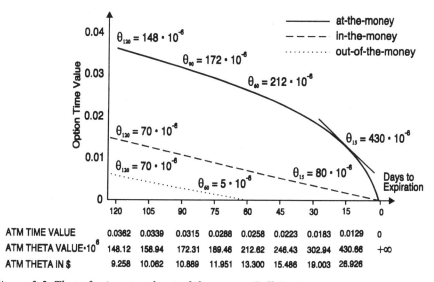

	120	105	90	75	60	45	30	15	0
ATM TIME VALUE	0.0362	0.0339	0.0315	0.0288	0.0258	0.0223	0.0183	0.0129	0
ATM THETA VALUE·10^6	148.12	158.94	172.31	189.46	212.62	246.43	302.94	430.66	$+\infty$
ATM THETA IN $	9.258	10.062	10.889	11.951	13.300	15.486	19.003	26.926	

Figure 3.5 Theta for in, at and out-of-the-money Call Options.

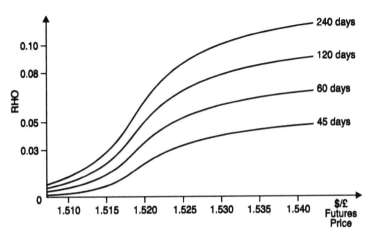

Figure 3.6 Rho for a 1.525 Call Option at Various Points Prior to Expiration.

option will lose day by day. For instance with the at-the-money option, the 60 days' theta, 0.0002126 means that in one day the option value loses 0.0002126/0.0002 = 1.063 ticks, or 1.063 · $12.50 = $13.28. One will notice that the options which are not at-the-money have an almost linear rate of time decay. One reason for this is the fact that the options time value is relatively smaller. This impact is important when comparing option trading strategies for the time decay impact. Later in Chapter 7, this will become evident when we compare the volatility strategies.

THE SENSITIVITY OF OPTIONS TO INTEREST RATES - THE RHO

Next, we will measure is the sensitivity of the option's price to changes in short term interest rates. The derivative of an option's prices relative to interest rates is commonly called rho. For currency options, two interest rates are important: the domestic currency interest rate and the foreign currency interest rate. Thus, currency options will have two rho derivatives. Again, using our aeroplane gauge analogy, the rho can be thought of as a thermometer measuring the outside temperature. For most flights in a small aeroplane, the outside temperature is fairly unimportant to the safe operation of the aeroplane. However, if the altitude is very high, the temperature gauge can be quite important because at those altitudes ice can form. If ice forms on the wings, the aeroplane might become too heavy and plummet to earth. Figure 3.6 displays the domestic interest rate ($) rho for a call option on $/£. Rho can be summarised as:

> *Rho is a measure of the exposure the position has to a change in interest rates from today until expiration*

To properly examine interest rate impact on options prices, we must wait until after I have covered put-call parity at the end of this chapter . Until then, it is sufficient to say that the interest impact is generally of minor significance relative to the volatility, underlying market price movements and the passage of time. For options on forward foreign exchange, the interest rate impact is trivial and for certain kinds of options there is no effect from interest rates at all. However, for certain kinds of options (especially long dated OTC options) the interest rate impact can be important and will be closely monitored by dealers in these products.

THE GEARING OF AN OPTION TO THE UNDERLYING - THE LAMBDA

Another "Greek letter" that is sometimes referred to is the lambda. This is similar in principal to the delta but instead of measuring the absolute change in the options price for a change in the price of the underlying asset, lambda measures the percentage change in the options price for a percentage change in the price of the underlying asset. This is simply calculated by multiplying the delta of the option by the ratio of the underlying price divided by the price of the option. The formula for the lambda is:

Delta · Underlying Price/Option Price.

Let us return to the example in Table 3.3 of this chapter for some numbers. In that table the underlying US$/£ exchange rate was 1.525 and an option (in this case a call) had a price of 2.25 US cents per £. The delta of the option was 0.505. Applying the formula, the lambda is equal to 34.22 (0.505 · [1.525/0.0225]). Figure 3.7 displays a similar figure as was produced for the delta (Figure 3.1) but this

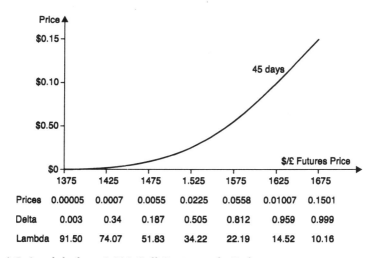

	1375	1425	1475	1.525	1575	1625	1675
Prices	0.00005	0.0007	0.0055	0.0225	0.0558	0.01007	0.1501
Delta	0.003	0.34	0.187	0.505	0.812	0.959	0.999
Lambda	91.50	74.07	51.83	34.22	22.19	14.52	10.16

Figure 3.7 Lambda for a 1.525 Call Option with 45 days to expiry.

time, the delta and the lambda are presented and the scale for the movement of the underlying asset has been expanded to see the full impact.

As the reader can see, some of these numbers have become astronomical indicating that the options provide much greater kick from a movement in the price of the underlying asset than the asset itself. It is therefore no surprise that options have now replaced spot dealing for many speculative foreign exchange institutions given the incredible gearing that can be achieved. Nevertheless, this "Greek letter" is not often referred to by option traders. However, this derivative can be of interest and will re-emerge in Chapter 11. If one were to summarise the lambda, it would be:

Lambda is a measure of the gearing the position has relative to a position in the underlying asset

THE APPROPRIATE PRICING MODELS FOR OPTIONS ON FOREIGN EXCHANGE

I feel that this is the point to present to the reader the appropriate pricing models for options on foreign exchange. I will also demonstrate how these same models are adapted for other kinds of underlying assets. The choice of the appropriate pricing model (for any kind of underlying asset) depends on whether the option is based upon the spot currency or upon the forward currency rate and whether the option can be exercised early.

European Options on Spot Currency

The formula for an option based upon the current (or spot) foreign exchange rate that can only be exercised at expiration can be seen below. This formula was developed by Mark Garman and Steven Kohlhagen[4] and is remarkably similar to the Black and Scholes formula discussed in the last chapter. In fact, the only difference between the two is that an additional interest rate factor is added to the Garman/Kohlhagen model for the "foreign" country. It is one of the most comforting facets of option pricing theory that essentially all option pricing models are a refinement of the basic Black and Scholes methodology I have discussed so far.

One can view the evolution of option pricing theory as an adaptive progression from the initial innovative breakthrough. Consider as an analogy, the evolution of internal combustion petrol engines. In the 1880's, Mr. Daimler developed the first internal combustion petrol engine. This was a fundamental breakthrough that changed our world for ever. Since that time, many refinements have been made to

---

[4]Garman, Mark B. and Steven W. Kohlhagen, "Foreign Currency Option Values", Journal of International Money and Finance (1983), 2, pp. 231-237.

the initial model. However, every engine produced is still based upon the conceptual framework invented by Mr. Daimler.

Garman/Kohlhagen FX Option Model:

$$CALL = S \cdot N(d_1) \cdot e^{-Rf \cdot t} - E \cdot N(d_2) \cdot e^{-Rd \cdot t}$$

where:

$$d_1 = \frac{\ln(S/E) + (Rd - Rf + \sigma^2/2) \cdot t}{\sigma \cdot \sqrt{t}}$$

$$d_2 = d_1 - \sigma \cdot \sqrt{t}$$

t   = time to expiration % of a year
E   = exercise price of option
Rd = risk free domestic interest rate
Rf = risk free foreign interest rate
ln   = natural logarithm function
N   = cumulative normal density function
σ^2 = variance of the rate of return
S   = spot currency rate
e   = exponential function

One can think of the Black and Scholes model as being as great a breakthrough in the financial world as the first petrol motor was in the transportation world. As was the case with petrol motors, option pricing models since the initial invention have become more refined and sophisticated. Nevertheless, like the evolution of petrol engine, all option models are based upon the basic premises of Black and Scholes. From the extensive number of models that have been published in the financial literature, one might think that each new option pricing model is another breakthrough (for example the Binomial model which will be examined in the next few pages). However, this is not the case. The plethora of option pricing models do not reflect the invention of new "engines" but rather present refinements to the original. It is as if when the first turbo-charger or fuel injection device was invented, the developer claimed that a new engine had been created. This is obviously not the case. The innovation would not be of any use had Mr. Daimler not invented the basic engine for the refinements to fit onto.

So it is not surprising that the Garman/Kohlhagen "model" is really the Black and Scholes model with a "currency interest rate" "carburettor". Furthermore, the most popular model for European options on dividend paying stock, the Merton 1973 model, is identical to the Garman/Kohlhagen model except that a continuous dividend payment is substituted for the foreign interest rate. So, the Merton model is really the Black and Scholes model with a Garman/Kohlhagen "carburettor" painted a different colour.[5] Later in this book, I will present other models which have achieved fame in the pricing for a variety of underlying assets. But the reader can rest assured that most of these models are simply a refinement of the original Black and Scholes model presented in Chapter 2 and for the most part are only cosmetic changes.

European Options on Currency Forwards

The most appropriate model for European options on currency forwards is the Black (1976) model for options on forward contracts.[6] Once again this "model" is almost identical to the Black and Scholes model. The only differences are that a forward price F has replaced the stock price S and both the forward price and the strike price are discounted to present value. So, once again a simple refinement to the original "engine" has been introduced. However, this model has much broader applications than just for currency options. The Black (1976) model applies equally well to all futures contracts (for options with a European exercise feature) and many interest rate products I will discuss in Chapter 12.

The Black (1976) Option Pricing Model:

$$CALL = e^{-rt} \cdot \left[F \cdot N(d_1) - E \cdot N(d_2) \right]$$
$$PUT = CALL + e^{-rt} \cdot (E - F)$$

where:

$$d_1 = \frac{\ln(F/E) + (\sigma^2/2) \cdot t}{\sigma \cdot \sqrt{t}}$$

$$d_2 = d_1 - \sigma \cdot \sqrt{t}$$

t   = time to expiration % of a year
E   = exercise price of option
r   = risk free interest rate of period t
ln = natural logarithm function
N   = cumulative normal density function
σ^2 = variance of the rate of return
F   = future price
e   = exponential function
σ = square root of variance, i.e. volatility

---

[5]Actually, since the Merton dividend adjustment came first in 1973, it is the original "carburettor" and the Garman/Kohlhagen model is really the Merton "carburettor" painted a different colour.
[6]Black, Fischer, "The Pricing of Commodity Contracts", Journal of Financial Economics, January 1976, 3: pp. 167-179.

The reason why the Black (1976) model has such a broad appeal is because it assumes the underlying asset price that should be analysed is not the current price but what the asset price should be in the future (using basic arbitrage relationships). It has been convincingly argued by Mark Garman that the expected future price of the underlying asset on the expiration date of the option is more important than the current price of the asset.[7] In fact, all option pricing models estimate first what the expected forward price of the underlying asset will be at the expiration date of the option and then from this knowledge, estimate the option price. If instead the trader estimated the forward price himself, then for European options, the Black (1976) model would provide the correct price for any kind of option contracts.

American Options on Foreign Exchange

Some have argued that the early exercise feature is so important that the Black and Scholes model cannot be correct. However, this argument is somewhat exaggerated in my viewpoint. If one remembers our discussion of the difference between European and American options in Chapter 2, one will recall that for securities that do not have discrete cash flows, the early exercise of options is like throwing a $100 bill on the ground and walking away. The supposed problem is for those securities like stocks and bonds that do have cash flows periodically and would induce the option holder to exercise early to claim these cash flows. The most popular of the corrections to the Black and Scholes model for the possibility of American early exercise is the Binomial approach suggested by Bill Sharpe and Cox, Ross and Rubinstein.[8]

Basically, the development of the Binomial model was spurred by an attempt by Professors Cox, Ross and Rubinstein to find an easier way to teach their students how the Black and Scholes formula works. They used simple tree diagrams which can be seen in Figure 3.8a to explain how the price of the underlying security could change. These diagrams indicate that given you start out at a particular price for the underlying asset ($100 in Figure 3.8a), the market price could either rise or fall by a discrete amount, say $1. After the initial up or down movement, the price could again move up or down by $1 and could be anywhere in the range $98 to $102. Then after this point, the process continues until the expiration date of the option.

The reader may recall that in the movement of markets, two factors are required to fully understand what is going on. One factor is the amount of the movement and the other is the probability of the movement. This was the same case when I discussed the expected return from playing roulette. How the Binomial approach incorporates probabilities is that it assigns to each branch of the tree the probability

---

[7]Garman, Mark B., "Forward Prices, Option Prices and "Dividend Corrections"", Working Paper, Department of Business Administration, University of California, Berkeley, April 1983.

[8]Cox, John S., Steven Ross and Mark Rubinstein, "Options Pricing: A Simplified Approach", Journal of Financial Economics, September 1979, 7: pp. 637-654.

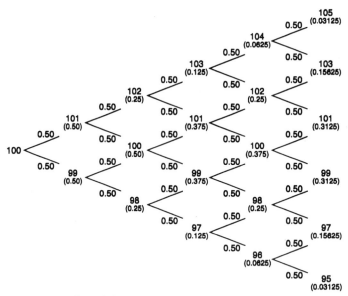

Figure 3.8a Binomial Model.

of an upward movement or a downward movement. Now consider that we are at $100 and the probability is 50/50 that the market could rise or fall.[9]So, this means a 50% chance that in one unit of time, the price of the underlying market will be at $101 and a 50% chance that the underlying market will be at $99. What about the probabilities for the next "round"? Again, they will be 50/50. So if we are at either $101 or at $99, we face the same chances of upward or downward movement.

However, if we are pricing the option at the beginning of the period when the market price was at $100, we do not know whether the price will be at $101 or $99 after the first "round". To determine the probability that a given price would occur in "round" two given that we are starting at $100, we can simply multiply the probabilities along the branches to provide our estimate. These probabilities are also displayed on the tree diagram in Figure 3.8a. For example, what is the probability now that in the second "round" the price of the underlying asset will be $102 (or $98)? Well, it is a 50% chance that the price will rise to $101 (or fall to $99) in the first round and another 50% chance that if it is at $101 (or $99) the next price will be $102 (or $98). So, we multiply 50% by 50% and that gives us 25% chance that in round two the price will be $102 (or $98). Furthermore, by the second round the market price could either rise to $101 and then fall back to $100 or fall to $99 and

[9]This assumes a pure random walk process, or a simple Martingale process but is not critical to the Binomial methodology. For example, Cox, Ross and Rubinstein used a 60% probability for upward movements and a 40% probability for downward movements. However, we will assume a 50/50 probability and the reader is referred to the Cox, Ross and Rubinstein article to verify the result for a non-pure random walk environment.

then rise back to $100 each with a probability of 25%. The combined probability that the market price will be at $100 in the second round is 50% (25% + 25%). This carries on overtime and the reader can see that the further the market price branches up or down, the lower is the probability of occurrence and that the highest probability remains at the current market price of $100. Does this sound familiar? The reader will recall that the lognormal distribution has a similar probability spread. The only difference between these distributions is that the Binomial distribution is plotted with discrete movements (like 100, 101 or 99) rather than continuous ones (like 100, 100.000001 or 99.999999).

The Cox, Ross, Rubinstein Options Pricing Model

$$CALL = S \cdot \theta \cdot [a; n, p'] - E \cdot e^{-rt} \cdot \theta \cdot [a; n, p]$$

where:

    t = amount of time until expiration
    S = price of the underlying exchange rate
    E = exercise price of option
    r = short term interest rate until expiration
    n = number of discrete periods until expiration
    r = interest rate for a single period
    u = possible upward movement in prices
    d = possible downward movement in prices
    p = (r - d) / (u - d)
    p' = (u/r) p
    a = smallest non-negative integer greater than $\ln(E/Bd^n)/\ln(u/d)$
    ln = natural logarithm function
    θ = binomial function (which can be thought of as a distribution in discrete time)
    e = exponential function

Instead of assuming a smooth lognormal distribution like Black and Scholes, Cox, Ross and Rubinstein assume this jagged Binomial distribution in their model. Their equation, that can be seen in the above table, is often used for pricing American options on foreign exchange. While it initially looks different from the Black and Scholes formula presented in Chapter 2, it really is based upon similar assumptions. Once again, the model has the underlying price S minus the strike price E which determines the intrinsic value just like the Black and Scholes model. The difference between the Binomial and Black and Scholes models is the θ function in the Binomial formula. This is just like the lognormal distribution in the Black and Scholes model but here the Binomial distribution with discrete time (assuming that the change in market prices is not continuous but can only vary by a minimum amount) is used. Essentially, one takes the binomial tree diagram in

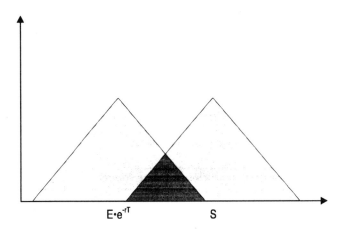

Figure 3.8b The intersection of the binomial distributions when the stock price is above the exercise price.

Figure 3.8a turns it sideways, and puts it on the graph in Figure 3.8b centred at the spot underlying price and at the discounted exercise price.

Once again, the difference between the two distributions is taken to determine the time value of the options price. If the reader compares the result with the earlier Figure 2.14a for the Black and Scholes model, he will see a remarkable resemblance. In fact as the Binomial approach is extended to continuous time, the curve becomes identical to the lognormal distribution and the Binomial result is equal to the Black and Scholes result.

This line of argument seems to suggest that the Binomial model is really not different to the Black and Scholes model. If this is so, what is the point of the Binomial approach? When dividends or other cash flows occur at a single point in time, the Binomial model can take this into account and the Black and Scholes model cannot. For example, in Figure 3.9 we have again a tree diagram with the underlying asset paying a dividend in the third period of 50 cents. When this occurs, the price in the branch at that point will drop by this amount. Then the branching process continues as before from these new prices which have been reduced by the dividend payment.

Also, the Binomial model is often used for American style options where an early exercise feature exists. The Binomial model estimates the value of early exercise by assuming that at a particular price for the underlying asset, the option will be exercised. Thus, all subsequent branches in the tree diagram have been "pruned". Because the option after that point no longer exists, it is no longer necessary to continue the branching process. When the option price is calculated (assuming the possibility of early exercise), once again all the possible prices for the underlying asset are multiplied by their probability of occurrence to give us the option price adjusted for the exercised event.

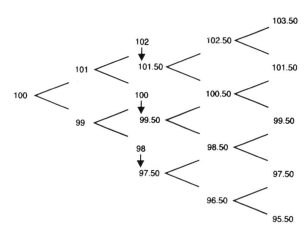

Figure 3.9 Binomial Model (Dividends Paid).

Therefore, it appears that all options pricing models are based upon the same basic premises. But as was indicated in the beginning of this chapter, the purpose of an option pricing model is not necessarily to provide the correct price for an option but rather to indicate how an option price will change when the variables that determine that option price change. So I will return to the popular pricing models for currency options and examine the formulae for the derivatives of the important variables.

Formulae for the Derivatives of the Currency Option Pricing Models

The next list of equations gives all the derivatives I have spoken of and their respective formulae for calculation. As the reader can see, Table 3.4 lists the derivatives for the Garman/Kohlhagen Model and is choc-a-bloc with exotic formulae. He should take comfort that unless he is a real "quant" enthusiast (expert in quantitative methods) the formulae may look like a lot of graffiti. Not to worry! Almost all the popular computer programmes have these equations automatically coded in their routines. Therefore, the reader can leave the high level mathematics to the "rocket scientists" who solve these kind of equations as a matter of course. The reader should instead try to understand the intuition I have presented in this text. Remember, you are not supposed to create the "gauges" only be able to read them. In addition, I have also included the Black and Scholes model and its derivatives for comparison's sake in Table 3.5. Finally, in Table 3.6, the derivatives of the Black (1976) model are also presented. These derivatives are the most important outputs for the option pricing models as they provide the critical "gauges" necessary for hedging the risk of these securities.

$$CALL\ DELTA = e^{-rf \cdot t} N(d_1)$$

$$PUT\ DELTA = -e^{-rf \cdot t} N(-d_1)$$

$$CALL\ GAMMA = PUT\ GAMMA = \frac{e^{-rf \cdot t} N'(d_1)}{S \cdot \sigma \sqrt{t}}$$

$$CALL\ THETA = r_f \cdot S \cdot e^{-rf \cdot t} N(d_1) - r_d \cdot E \cdot e^{-rd \cdot t} N(d_2) - S \cdot e^{-rf \cdot t} \cdot \sigma \cdot N'(d_1) / (2\sqrt{t})$$

$$PUT\ THETA = -r_f \cdot S \cdot e^{-rf \cdot t} N(-d_1) + r_d \cdot E \cdot e^{-rd \cdot t} N(-d_2) - S \cdot e^{-rf \cdot t} \cdot \sigma \cdot N'(d_1) / (2\sqrt{t})$$

$$CALL\ VEGA = PUT\ VEGA = e^{-rf \cdot t} \cdot S\sqrt{t} \cdot N'(d_1)$$

$$CALL\ DOMESTIC\ RHO = t \cdot e^{-rd \cdot t} \cdot E \cdot N(d_2)$$

$$PUT\ DOMESTIC\ RHO = -t \cdot e^{-rd \cdot t} \cdot E \cdot N(-d_2)$$

$$CALL\ FOREIGN\ RHO = -t \cdot e^{-rf \cdot t} \cdot E \cdot N(d_1)$$

$$PUT\ FOREIGN\ RHO = t \cdot e^{-rf \cdot t} \cdot E \cdot N(-d_1)$$

Table 3.4 The Garman/Kohlhagen Model (Derivatives).

$$CALL\ DELTA = N(d_1)$$

$$PUT\ DELTA = -N(-d_1)$$

$$CALL\ GAMMA = PUT\ GAMMA = \frac{N'(d_1)}{S \cdot \sigma \sqrt{t}}$$

$$CALL\ THETA = \frac{S \cdot \sigma \cdot N'(d_1)}{2\sqrt{t}} + r \cdot E \cdot e^{-rt} \cdot N(d_2)$$

$$PUT\ THETA = \frac{S \cdot \sigma \cdot N'(d_1)}{2\sqrt{t}} - r \cdot E \cdot e^{-rt} \cdot N(-d_2)$$

$$CALL\ RHO = t \cdot e^{-rt} \cdot E \cdot N(d_2)$$

$$PUT\ RHO = -t \cdot e^{-rt} \cdot E \cdot N(-d_2)$$

Table 3.5 The Black and Scholes Pricing Model (Derivatives).

$$CALL\ DELTA = e^{-r \cdot t} N(d_1)$$

$$PUT\ DELTA = -e^{-r \cdot t} N(-d_1)$$

$$CALL\ GAMMA\ = PUT\ GAMMA\ = \frac{e^{-r \cdot t} N'(d_1)}{F \cdot \sigma \sqrt{t}}$$

$$CALL\ THETA = -r \cdot F \cdot e^{-r \cdot t} N(d_1) + r \cdot E \cdot e^{-r \cdot t} N(d_2) + F \cdot e^{-r \cdot t} \cdot \sigma \cdot N'(d_1)/(2\sqrt{t})$$

$$PUT\ THETA = r \cdot F \cdot e^{-r \cdot t} N(-d_1) - r \cdot E \cdot e^{-r \cdot t} N(-d_2) + F \cdot e^{-r \cdot t} \cdot \sigma \cdot N'(d_1)/(2\sqrt{t})$$

$$CALL\ VEGA = PUT\ VEGA = e^{-r \cdot t} \cdot F\sqrt{t} \cdot N'(d_1)$$

$$CALL\ RHO = -t \cdot CALL$$

$$PUT\ RHO = -t \cdot PUT$$

Table 3.6 The Black (1976) Pricing Model (Derivatives).

PUT - CALL PARITY:
THE FUNDAMENTAL ARBITRAGE RELATIONSHIP

The final major theoretical topic which I will introduce in this chapter is Put-Call-Parity. When theoretical option pricing was in its nascent stage, many people began to discern that a relationship between the prices of call and put options seemed to exist. The only conundrum was that the payoff diagrams for these securities and their premiums seemed to be inversely related. As was discussed in the first chapter, all options can be created by simply splitting the underlying market positions into "good" and "bad" parts. Therefore, if we can break the underlying market into two parts, we can just as easily recombine them to recreate the underlying asset or try other combinations to see what we get. This can be done using a simple formula known as the Put-Call Parity.

The formula for Put-Call Parity is:

$$C - P = F - E$$

C is the value of a call, P the value of the put, F the value of the underlying forward foreign exchange market, and E the strike price for both the call and the put.[10]

---

[10]In the original Black/Scholes formula, the strike price (E) in the Put-Call Parity formula should be discounted at the risk free interest rate for the appropriate time to maturity and F is replaced by S which is the current spot rate.

The put-call parity is the fundamental arbitrage relationship which forces call and put prices to be tied to their underlying market and to each other. For example, let us examine the value of a call and the value of a put on the options contract's expiration day. Suppose the strike price for a $/£ put and call is $1.60. At expiration, relative to $1.60, the underlying price can be in one of three possible states of the world: the price could finish higher, lower, or exactly equal to $1.60. In the first case, when the market finishes higher than $1.60, consider the call option which is the right to buy at $1.60. With the market at $1.625, the value of the option would be equal to its intrinsic value of 2.5 cents. The $1.60 put option (the right to sell) would expire worthless. Hence, 2.5 cents (the value of a call) minus zero (the value of a put) must be equal to F minus E (1.625 - 1.60) which it does.

The second case is when the £ exchange rate finishes below $1.60 at $1.585. If someone has the right to buy at $1.60 and the market is at $1.585, you will abandon the call because it is out-of-the-money. Thus, the value of the call is zero. Since the put option confers the right to sell at $1.60, with the market at $1.585, the put option will be worth its intrinsic value of 1.5 cents. So, on the left side of the equation, we find zero (C) minus 1.5 cents (P) must be equal to $1.585 minus $1.60 on the right side. Once again the arbitrage formula holds. Finally, if the market finishes at $1.60, equal to the strike price, both the call and the put are at-the-money with no intrinsic value and worthless. The left side of the equation reads zero minus zero equal $1.60 minus $1.60. Hence, regardless of what happens to the market price at expiration, the put-call parity arbitrage formula will hold.

The reader can rest assured that put-call parity works not only at expiration but at all points prior to the expiration as well. For example, if the reader turns back to Chapter 2 and reviews Table 2.2, he will see that put-call parity works for stock options in exactly the same way as it does for currency options. In that example, the price of IBM stock is $65 and the price for the $60 call is $5.75 and the $60 put is $0.75. The put-call parity formula holds if $5.75 minus $0.75 is equal to $65 minus $60. In this case, because $5 on the left side of the equation is equal to the $5 on the right hand side, the formula is not violated. This example not only demonstrates the arbitrage relationship between call and put prices but also indicates the fact that the time value is identical ($0.75) for calls and puts with the same strike price and time to maturity.[11]

Using Put-Call Parity to Create Synthetic Securities

Apart from defining the most fundamental arbitrage relationship in the options markets, put-call parity also allows the trader a simple method to break strategies

---

[11]Later in this chapter we will discuss the impacts of interest rates and dividends for the Put-Call Parity equation for stock options. With dividends and interest rates, both the stock price must be reduced by the dividend paid and the exercise price discounted by the interest rate. In this example, the interest rate impact was exactly offset by the payment of dividends so the put-call parity relationship was easily determined to be equal to the difference between the strike price and current stock price.

into their component parts and to recombine them. In essence, it helps the trader combine the basic building blocks of futures and options to create new "synthetic" securities. To use put-call parity for this purpose, we first need to learn a few "tricks". The first trick in using put-call parity to develop synthetics is to put parentheses around the F - E and treat this new variable as a buying position in the underlying market initiated at E.

Now the equation reads:

$$C - P = (F - E)$$

and we have three components: a call option, a put option, and the underlying market. The second trick is that if any of these three components has a positive or plus sign associated with it, it will be defined as a buying, holding or long position (this is also true for the case that there is nothing in front of it). If any of the variables has a minus sign in front of it, then it will be defined as a short, selling or writing position. Now, you can read the above equation aloud: if you buy a call (C) and sell a put (-P), that is equal to buying the underlying market at the price of E. Simple enough? I hope that the reader realises that we have just created our first synthetic security. When you buy a call and sell a put at the same strike price, that is the same payoff as buying a futures contract. Put-call parity allows us to determine many other synthetic positions as well.

In the first chapter, I defined three positions which are equivalent long positions relative to the underlying market: Buying that market (or a forward contract on that market), buying a call option and selling a put option. I also defined three positions which are equivalent short positions: Selling that market short (or a short forward contract), buying a put option and selling a call option. Since I have demonstrated how easy it is to create a synthetic long forward or futures position, I will give the reader in Table 3.7 the whole packet of actual and synthetic positions.

For example, what would you have if you had purchased £1,000,000 with dollars and expected to convert the £ back into dollars in the future? To protect against

	Actual **Position**	**Synthetic** **Position**
Buying the Underlying	+ (F - E)	C - P
Buying a Call Option	+ C	(F - E) + P
Selling a Put Option	- P	(F - E) - C
Selling the Underlying	- (F - E)	- C + P
Buying a Put Option	+ P	- (F - E) + C
Selling a Call Option	- C	- (F - E) - P

Table 3.7 Actual versus Synthetic Positions.

an adverse move in the exchange rate one would purchase a put option on £. That series of trades would fit into our put-call parity equation as + (F - E) and + P. To determine what the position would look like, all we need to do is to review our equation: C - P = (F - E) and see if we can get (F - E) + P on one side of the equation. If we can, we will find the other side of the equal sign what this combination is equivalent to. Those who excelled at algebra will see immediately that to get a + P over to the other side of the equation, along with the (F - E), they simply have to add a + P to both sides. On the left side you will get C - P + P and on the right side you get (F - E) + P. On the left side, the - P and the + P cancel, leaving only C. So, the equation reduces to C = (F - E) + P.

This means that buying a call is an equivalent position to buying a futures contract and buying a put option. The left side of the equation is an "actual" call and the right side is the synthetic call.

The "Magic" Graphing Rules and Put-Call Parity

For those of you who like algebra, this process can make a lot of sense. But the rest of you are probably visually oriented. Therefore I will provide a picture worth a thousand words. Indeed, we can tackle put-call parity with pictures. To do this I must first explain what we call the "magic" graphing rules.

- firstly, *unlimited opportunities dominate limited opportunities*;
- secondly, *unlimited opportunities offset unlimited opportunities*; and finally,
- *limited opportunities offset limited opportunities*.

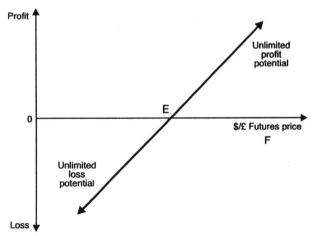

Figure 3.10 Put Call Parity: Applying Graphing Rules.

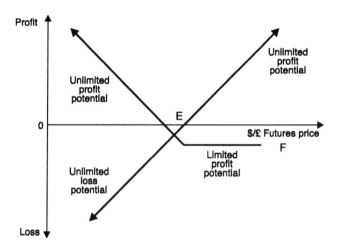

Figure 3.11 Put-Call Parity: Applying Graphing Rules.

Let us use these rules to prove the example I have just discussed: the composition of the synthetic call option.

Figure 3.10 is a graphic example of a long underlying position (F - E). If you buy a $/£ forward contract at E and the market price F rises, the profit of that position will be equal to F - E. This implies the current price minus the price where you purchased it. Imagine you buy it at a price of $1.60 (E) and the market price (F) falls below $1.60 (E). The loss for the position E is equal once again to whatever the current price is minus $1.60 (F - E). There is an unlimited profit potential to the north-east (top right) and an unlimited loss potential to the south-west (bottom left). Figure 3.11 displays a long put option which has an unlimited profit potential on the downside (to the north-west or top left). The most you can lose when you buy the put option is the premium paid, which is a limited loss potential. This can be seen in the lower right quadrant. Now, let us consider the left of E in Figure 3.11. One line goes to the north-west (the profit potential for the put) and one line goes to the south-west (the loss potential for the futures). It is important to consider that these potential exposures are equivalent and unlimited in an opposite way. The rule says unlimited and unlimited offset; so these two potentials cancel out each other.[12] Now, let us look at the right side of the graph. The underlying long position extends indefinitely to the north-east with a profit opportunity that is unlimited. What about the put option? It has a limited loss component to the right of E. Since the unlimited gain dominates the limited loss, the net effect is that the net position has an unlimited gain potential. To the left, the underlying market losses

---

[12]The intuition is: If F = 1.55, the loss on the forward contract = -5 cents, the profit on the put = (+5 cents - premium), therefore, the profit/loss of the net position = - premium. This will occur whenever the $/£ forward price is less than $1.6000.

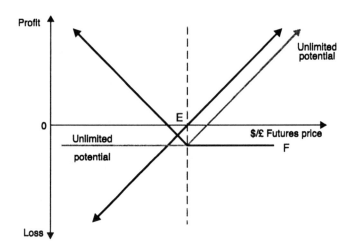

Figure 3.12 Put-Call Parity: Applying Graphing Rules.

cancel the put's gains and to the right, the unlimited gains overwhelm the limited loss on the put. What does the net position end up looking like? This can be seen in Figure 3.12. It has a limited loss to the left (which looks like an option premium) and an unlimited gain as the market prices rise. Upon reflection, the reader will see that a synthetic call has been produced. This is hardly surprising. You will remember that when we combined buying the underlying asset with buying a put this produced a synthetic buying call: $C = (F - E) + P$. Hence, the put-call parity is a very easy way to separate each of the components in the forward (or futures) and options market and later recombine them.

It is probably not surprising that this simple technique is critical to ensure that fair and efficient pricing of each of the individual components occurs. For example, consider the value of a call option. As you will remember, it is made up of two components: time value and intrinsic value. Intrinsic value is simply $F - E$.

So, a quick review of call and put prices in put-call parity would imply that the only difference between calls and put prices must be due to the intrinsic value. The time value for these must be exactly the same. If this turns out not to be the case, then an extremely low risk transaction can take place which will reap this profit through arbitrage. If the actual call option is "over-valued" then it is a simple matter to sell this option and buy a fair valued synthetic call. Then the put-call formula would read:

$$0 = (F - E) + P - C$$

If this is valued at greater than zero, "bingo!" an arbitrage profit exists. Later in this book I will carefully examine these and other kinds of arbitrage strategies and will at that time use put-call parity extensively.

The Effects of Interest Rates on Options Prices

Now that I have introduced you to put-call parity, I can use this formula to gain further insight into the interest rate impacts on options. The interest rate impact for an option depends on the characteristics of the underlying asset. I will break these available underlying assets into three broad categories: costly assets, costless assets and neutral assets.

Costly assets require an immediate substantial cash outflow. For example, if you buy a 100 oz bar of gold when gold is trading at $380 per ounce, you will have to pay $38,000 to be "long" Gold. A call option on gold might only cost $1200 and would still allow you the right to hold that asset if you bought the option instead of the gold. The remaining $36,800 could be placed on deposit to earn interest. Thus, the call option increases the leverage and frees up cash to place on deposit. As short term interest rates rise, this leverage factor becomes more and more attractive. Therefore, buying gold call options and placing the balance in deposits will become increasingly more attractive compared to buying the actual gold. To remain at equilibrium (also known as a "no arbitrage" state), the call option's price must increase when the short term interest rate rises to make the investor indifferent to either investing in the option/deposit trade or the outright gold purchase. Therefore, the higher the deposit rate, the higher the value for a call option. Conversely, the higher the short term interest rate the lower the value of the put option. The actual formula for this put-call parity relationship can be seen in Table 3.8.

The formula in Table 3.8: $C - P = S - E \cdot e^{-rt}$ does require a little further explanation. First, let us define the terms. I bet you can guess what C and P are. The S is the value of a spot security which is a costly asset, like gold or non-dividend paying shares. As before, E is the strike price for both the call and put, but now we have another factor e^{-rt}. This is the interest rate factor. First, what is e? This is a continuous compounding factor. The letter "e" is the mathematical exponential function also known as an anti-logarithm. This determines the present value of a pure continuously discounted instrument like a zero coupon bond or treasury bill.

$$C - P = S - (E \cdot e^{-rt})$$

where:
  C: value of a call option
  P: value of a put option
  S: cash security price
  E: exercise price for call & put
  e: exponential function
  r: interest rate for option's life
  t: time (in % of a year) until expiry

Table 3.8 Interest Rate Impacts for "Costly" Assets.

The letter "r" is the deposit interest rate at which you could invest the money that buying options would free up (instead of buying the entire asset). Finally, "t" is the time period in the percentage of a 365 day year until the option expires and the deposit matures.

Say we want to find out what the continuous discount factor could be at 4.5% for 182 days. It would be $e^{-(0.045)\,(0.50)}$ or 0.9777. Suppose we return to our put-call parity formula with an S equal to $100 and E equal to $90. Then C - P = $100 - ($90 x 0.9777) = $12. If the r rises to 5.5% what happens? The new discount factor has become 0.9728. So back to the put-call parity formula: C - P = $100 - ($90 x 0.9728) = $12.44. This increase from $12 to $12.44 reflects the increase in the value of the call relative to the put.

To further prove this effect, I determined theoretical option prices with a maturity of 182 days and the strike and underlying prices consistent with the above example. Further, I assumed the underlying asset was a non-dividend paying stock with a volatility of 25%. At an interest rate of 4.5%, the $90 call option is worth $14.26. When the interest rises to 5.5% the call is now worth $14.59. So, the call gained in value by 0.33. The $90 put conversely was worth $2.26 at a 4.5% interest rate and at the higher interest rate has dropped to $2.15 for a loss of $0.11. The put-call relationship at 4.5% interest was $14.26 minus $2.26 for a difference of $12. At the 5.5% interest rate the new put-call relationship is $14.59 minus $2.15 and a difference of $12.44. The reader can see that this result is the same as that shown above.

In the currency option market, the formula is slightly different and reflects that both the currencies of the two countries involved in the contract pay an interest rate. This formula is seen in Table 3.9 and is almost identical to the formula I have just presented. The only difference is that the S is also discounted back to present value by e^{-rf}, where rf is the foreign interest rate and rd is the domestic interest rate.

If the reader simply substitutes a dividend yield for rf in the formula, he will have defined the put-call parity relationship for stocks (or bonds) with continuous dividend (coupon) payments.

$$C - P = S \cdot e^{-rf \cdot t} - E \cdot e^{-rd \cdot t}$$

where:
C : value of a call option
P : value of a put option
S : cash security price
E : exercise price for call & put
E : exponential function
Rd : domestic interest rate
Rf : foreign interest rate
T : time (in % of a year) until expiry

Table 3.9 Interest Rate Impacts for "Costly" Assets (for Currency Options).

It must be noted that there is a problem applying the put-call parity formula, when American options are concerned. The reader may remember that in the last chapter, it was demonstrated that American calls must not be worth more than European calls assuming no cash payments like dividends occur. This is generally true for currency options. The only time one would wish to exercise an American currency option early would be if the time value of the option were less than the interest that could be earned by exercising the option for the other currency.[13]

The second type of underlying assets I will consider are assets termed "costless". Examples of these kind of assets include options on forward foreign exchange and most options available on futures contracts.

If you decide to buy a forward contract in foreign exchange, you decide upon a price at which you will deal in the future. You pay nothing today because the agreement is to be settled at the forward date. If I buy an option instead of the forward contract, I have to pay a premium today. So, when comparing the value of an option to a forward contract, I must take into account that if I buy the option I give up a premium, and if I had deposited the premium, I could have earned interest. Thus, you give up interest by buying an option on a forward contract instead of simply dealing on the forward market and in this case, options actually reduce the leverage. In many world exchanges (particularly in the United States), the premium for options on futures must be paid upon purchase while the underlying futures contract is margined. In these cases, non-margined options on futures have the same interest rate impact as options on forward foreign exchange. The reader can imagine that these kinds of options will have a completely different interest rate impact when compared to options on costly assets. What is interesting about cost-less asset options is that the interest rate impact for them is almost opposite to the impact of options on costly assets. That is, as interest rates rise, both the value of call options and put options fall. However, the impact tends to be small because the interest involved is on the option premium and not on the value of the underlying asset. In fact, for those futures options most likely to be traded (that is, options with maturities of three months or less), the effect on the option price from interest rate moves is generally minuscule. The put-call parity formula for these kinds of options can be seen in Table 3.10. In that formula, the variables are identical to those in Table 3.8. The only differences are that F is the futures or costless asset price and both the costless asset price and the strike price are discounted using the continuous discount factor.

The final interest rate impact is for options on assets which we will call "neutral". Neutral assets are in some ways similar to costless assets, except that both the underlying asset and the options are "costless". For example, options at London International Financial Futures Exchange, the LIFFE, options on futures do not require payment when they are purchased but are margined (like the underlying

---

[13]For put options, this is not the case and the reader is referred to the Merton (1973) article which was previously referenced for proof of why one might be willing to exercise a put early for options on shares.

$$C - P = (F - E) \cdot e^{-rt}$$

where:
C : value of a call option
P : value of a put option
F : futures price
E : exercise price for call & put
E : exponential function
R : interest rate for option's life
T : time (in % of a year) until expiry

Table 3.10 Interest Rate Impacts for "Costless" Assets.

futures) and are "paid for" at some point in the future. Consider the interest rate implications of such an arrangement. Suppose you do not have to pay for an option up front, but are permitted to margin it just like a futures contract. Since you can margin both futures and options, they can be considered "costless" especially if you are able to use interest bearing securities as the basis for your margin. There is no opportunity cost lost from either the purchase of the underlying futures or the option on the futures. Therefore, there is no impact on the options prices from changes in the short term interest rate because the investor comparing the two securities does not have to consider foregone interest. The value of the call minus the put will simply equal the difference between the strike price and the underlying futures contract (see Table 3.11 for this final put-call parity formula). This is the purest form of the put-call parity formulae.

With this final formula, we have "broken the back" of the theoretical bases for options pricing. In the next two chapters, we will apply the theories learned to this point for the all important estimation of volatility. Later we will build upon these concepts when we discuss the concepts of interest rate options and exotics. Apart

$$C - P = F - E$$

where:
C : value of a call option
P : value of a put option
F : futures price
E : exercise price for call & put

Table 3.11 Interest Rate Impacts for "Neutral" Assets.

from these sections, Options Explained[2] will now turn from the realm of the theoretical to the real world and the practical issues users must face when trading these securities.

4: Volatility Estimation

Of all the noble aims of mankind, surely the incessant search for identifying patterns which govern our world must rank near the top. With the wide range of disciplines which could find the rules we seek, clearly mathematics has been one discipline which has solved more questions than it posed. One could argue that the truest goal of mathematics is to define rules which can lead to predictable behaviour in the future. In this spirit, this chapter will examine the long and colourful history of volatility estimation and show the reader how these principles can be practically applied to the fundamental problem when pricing options, that of an accurate measure of volatility.

This chapter is organised as follows:

- an introduction to volatility analysis
- how volatility is actually estimated for the pricing of options using
- historical analysis,
- implied estimation and
- future forecasting techniques.

The following chapter will address more complicated issues in volatility estimation. This will include non-constant volatility, and the means to adjust for this fact, volatility patterns across the strike prices (known as the smile) and how volatility changes through time (the term structure of volatility).

INTRODUCTION TO VOLATILITY ANALYSIS

The estimation of uncertainty in the outcomes of events has a long and interesting history. The first mathematicians were interested in a clockwork world where all events would follow defined rules and the only problem was finding the rules that applied. As the outcomes became more complex, the clockwork simply needed to be made more detailed. This worked quite well for simple closed systems. Also, a real and pressing practical problem had to be solved, and more importantly, those who needed the solution had money to spend to find the answer. These patrons of the sciences were appropriately for the options markets, professional gamblers.

Let us return to the 1600s, where bored but wealthy aristocrats spent an inordinate amount of time gambling. It is not surprising that many of these gamblers lost their shirts. Those gamblers who were successful had to develop a feeling for the odds through trial and error. But a few looked elsewhere to develop systematic rules

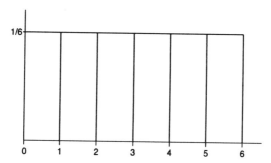

Figure 4.1 Distribution of Single Die Outcomes versus their Probabilities.

to gamble by. Girolamo Cardano was the first to write about probability (based on his long personal experience at the card tables) and to benefit from his insights. Obviously, other less learned (but more wealthy) card sharks became concerned when the travelling scholar began to beat their pants off. One of these less learned gamblers, the Chevalier de Mere, set up the first "quantitative" research department in 1654 when he asked Blaise Pascal, the famous mathematician, to come up with some rules for the odds in card games. Pascal formed his "research team" with Pierre de Fermat and Christian Huygens and three years later published the first quantitative research report titled appropriately enough, *On Reasoning in Games of Chance*. Given the lack of facsimile machines or even reliable post at the time, the ideas of how to beat the odds spread slowly.

However, mathematics had taken a fundamentally new turn in its development. A new discipline was born: the mathematics of chance. Probability became a discipline in its own right when Laplace published the *Analytic Theory of Probabilities* in 1812. The fundamental idea that events could be weighted by their probabilities was a key concept for the estimation of expected and fair values of gambles and options.

For example, let us throw a dice (you know, the cube with little dots on all six sides that is indispensable to such fundamental human activities such as the games of craps and Monopoly™). Laplace stated that the possible outcomes were from 1 to 6 and each had a probability of occurrence of 1/6th. In order to calculate the expected payoff from the throw of the die one would multiply each of the possible outcomes by their probability and this results in the expected value of 3.5. As any one who has ever thrown a die knows it would be extremely inconvenient if this outcome would actually be realised especially in the game of Monopoly™ when it is not possible to move 3 and one half spaces.

In 1846, Adolphe Quetelet continued the work of Laplace by plotting distributions of probabilities (P) relative to the events they were associated with. If we toss

A:	1	2	3	4	5	6
P:	1/6	1/6	1/6	1/6	1/6	1/6

Table 4.1 The outcome from the Toss of One Die.

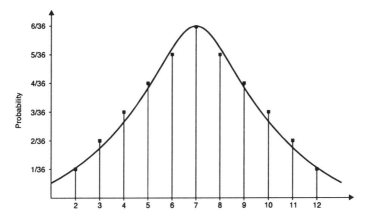

Figure 4.2 Distribution of Two Dice Outcomes versus their Probabilities.

one die (A), the possible events are from 1 to 6 landing each with a probability of 1/6th. This is summarised in Table 4.1. When the distribution of the events are drawn relative to their probability of occurring a graph can be produced which is portrayed in Figure 4.1. This distribution is totally flat and is known as a uniform distribution.

But something most curious happened when you threw two dice (A & B). Using the Laplace methodology of listing all the possible events and then summing them to find the probability of each event occurring, a totally new distribution was born.

In Table 4.2 are presented all the possible outcomes that could occur from throwing two dice. One could get 1 on the first die and 1 on the second die or any number on the second die up to 6. Likewise, die 1 could also have any value from 1 to 6. When all the combinations are analysed there are 36 possible outcomes that could arise. The number of occurrences is estimated when the same value appears on both dice and the expected outcome is determined as in the example, with one die.

When Quetelet plotted the possible outcomes against their probabilities he had come up with something that looked remarkably like a normal distribution (see Figure 4.2). When he tried other data series, the same pattern was found: from the

B＼A	1	2	3	4	5	6
1	2	3	4	5	6	7
2	3	4	5	6	7	8
3	4	5	6	7	8	9
4	5	6	7	8	9	10
5	6	7	8	9	10	11
6	7	8	9	10	11	12

Table 4.2 Outcomes from the Toss of Two Dice.

average height of men in a village to the number of apples on individual trees in any given orchard. Whenever two events occur simultaneously and independently, no matter what the distributions of each event is, in combination their distribution will be a normal one. This principle, which is known as the "Central Limit Theorem", is crucial to the discipline of probability and applies equally well to natural and financial series.

Since Adolphe was more concerned with philosophy than with gambling, his findings were used to justify the moral justification of the "average man" instead of the average profits and therefore did not generate as much interest as they deserved.

Just to prove that money is not only the source of all evil but also of most research, we continue the story in 1860 with Francis Galton, who, while initially training as a physician, fell into an inheritance and immediately dropped out of medical school deciding first to go out and see the world and later to study probability (no doubt to replenish his spent fortune). Galton, in his study of probabilities, was the first to develop a curious instrument called a quincunx which was a board with nails pounded into it at regular intervals. Galton used to amuse his friends by pouring lead balls into the top to see what would happen. As the balls fell and hit a nail, they could either turn right or left with an equal probability. When enough balls had been dropped into the quincunx a pattern began to emerge that looked exactly like a normal distribution. This is shown in Figure 4.3.

You may ask what this has to do with options prices. From Chapter 2, we indicated that in the Black and Scholes model the cumulative normal probability distri-

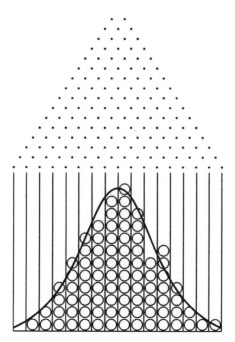

Figure 4.3 The Result from Dropping Balls into a Quincunx.

bution functions N(d1) and N(d2) are the key to the estimation of the time value of the option. However, it was not indicated why a normal distribution was chosen. One of the principal assumptions of the aforementioned pricing model is that returns for the markets are normally distributed and therefore, building on this assumption it is possible to extend the analysis to pricing options.

Of course, Professors Black and Scholes could use almost 150 years of solid research theory from various fields that suggested this to be appropriate. In 1828, the botanist Robert Brown observed in his microscope that small particles of pollen seemed to move erratically. The term for this irregular movement became known as Brownian motion. In 1900, the brilliant (and totally ignored) Louis Bachelier found that Brownian motion could be used to model the movement of stock prices. In Chapter 14, we will once again look at his contribution to this field. Then, in 1905, Albert Einstein began studying the probability density functions resulting from Brownian motion processes which linked heat transfer equations with Brownian motion. This process was treated more rigorously by Norbert Wiener in 1923 which lent his name to the Brownian motion process for this link. In the late 1940s the entire field of stochastic theory was applied to a wide variety of applications including nuclear energy, telecommunications and computers. With all this backing, how could Black and Scholes go wrong?

The good news about normal distributions is that all one needs to accurately draw them is to know the expected value (from Laplace) and a measure of how disperse the events are above and below the expected value. Other useful features of normal distributions are that they are symmetrical, and describe the likely outcomes of random events. This is perfect for the pricing of the uncertain outcomes for an underlying asset and therefore an options price which only pays off if the outcomes are above a certain level known as the strike price.

The estimation of the expected value of the events is fairly simple: multiply the probability of the event by the quantity of the event and add up all the possibilities. However, the measure of the dispersion is more of a problem. This measure of dispersion which is known as the variance or more commonly in its square root form, the standard deviation is essentially the volatility estimate we require when pricing options.

ESTIMATION OF THE NORMAL DISTRIBUTION

Normally, one might think that normal distributions have nothing to do with real money. For those who saw the film "The Graduate", one key line of dialogue addressed to Dustin Hoffman, was "There's money in Plastics!" By symmetry, is there money in normal distributions? Maybe not but there are normal distributions in money. When one looks at a 10 Deutsche Mark note (see Figure 4.4a) one finds a portrait of another mathematician Carl Friedrich Gauss[1]. Immediately next to the portrait is the normal distribution and the formula for drawing it which Gauss dis-

---

[1]To avoid problems with the Bundesbank, the Deutsche Mark note has been modified slightly to render it unable to be used in any inappropriate manner. The picture of Herr Gauss has been substituted by that of an interloper. That interloper is myself.

Figure 4.4a A Slightly modified 10 Deutsche Mark Note.

covered in 1801. From the 10 Deutsche Mark note, the formula has been magnified (in Figure 4.4b) to allow the reader to see it more clearly. In this formula, all that is needed to draw the normal (or Gaussian) distribution is two variables: the expected value and the standard deviation.

What exactly is this standard deviation? It measures the deviations from what you expect to receive (the mean) expressed in a standardised way. The first step is to take a data series and determine what it is you expect. For example with the two dice we discussed previously, you might expect to get a combination of dots which is equal to 7. However, you might receive something besides 7 (in fact 5/6s of the time you will). How do we determine the dispersion from what we expect. Well, we throw the dice 50 times and record the results. This has been done for you and can be seen in Table 4.3.

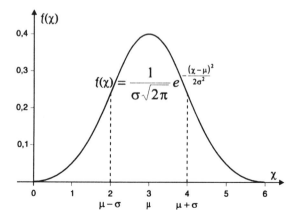

$$f(\chi) = \frac{1}{\sigma\sqrt{2\pi}} e^{-\frac{(\chi-\mu)^2}{2\sigma^2}}$$

Figure 4.4b The Formula for the Normal Distribution from the Note.

OBSERV.	FIRST DIE	SECOND DIE	SUM Xi	Xi - Xm	(Xi - Xm)^2
1	2	5	7	-0.060000	0.003600
2	5	3	8	0.940000	0.883600
3	1	4	5	-2.060000	4.243600
4	4	4	8	0.940000	0.883600
5	4	4	8	0.940000	0.883600
6	6	2	8	0.940000	0.883600
7	3	6	9	1.940000	3.763600
8	2	5	7	-0.060000	0.003600
9	2	6	8	0.940000	0.883600
10	5	5	10	2.940000	8.643600
11	4	2	6	-1.060000	1.123600
12	1	2	3	-4.060000	16.483600
13	4	3	7	-0.060000	0.003600
14	6	4	10	2.940000	8.643600
15	6	1	7	-0.060000	0.003600
16	3	2	5	-2.060000	4.243600
17	1	5	6	-1.060000	1.123600
18	4	4	8	0.940000	0.883600
19	2	1	3	-4.060000	16.483600
20	4	6	10	2.940000	8.643600
21	4	3	7	-0.060000	0.003600
22	3	6	9	1.940000	3.763600
23	3	5	8	0.940000	0.883600
24	3	3	6	-1.060000	1.123600
25	6	2	8	0.940000	0.883600
26	1	4	5	-2.060000	4.243600
27	2	3	5	-2.060000	4.243600
28	3	1	4	-3.060000	9.363600
29	4	6	10	2.940000	8.643600
30	5	4	9	1.940000	3.763600
31	1	5	6	-1.060000	1.123600
32	3	1	4	-3.060000	9.363600
33	5	2	7	-0.060000	0.003600
34	5	3	8	0.940000	0.883600
35	4	3	7	-0.060000	0.003600
36	2	5	7	-0.060000	0.003600
37	2	6	8	0.940000	0.883600
38	3	4	7	-0.060000	0.003600
39	3	1	4	-3.060000	9.363600
40	1	2	3	-4.060000	16.483600
41	1	3	4	-3.060000	9.363600
42	5	3	8	0.940000	0.883600
43	4	3	7	-0.060000	0.003600
44	3	6	9	1.940000	3.763600
45	5	5	10	2.940000	8.643600
46	5	5	10	2.940000	8.643600
47	3	5	8	0.940000	0.883600
48	2	5	7	-0.060000	0.003600
49	5	4	9	1.940000	3.763600
50	3	3	6	-1.060000	1.123600
			Mean Xm 7.06	Sum (Xi - Xm) 0.000000	Sum (Xi -Xm)^2 190.820000
			Std. Deviation 1.973394465		

Table 4.3 Outcomes from Tossing 2 Dice 50 times.

The average value is 7.06 and dispersed between 2 to 12 as expected. When the result is 2 that is less than you expected by 5.06 (which is 2 - 7.06) if you get 12 that is more than you expected by 4.94 (which is 12 - 7.06). If we are looking for the ordinary (or standard) deviation, we must take all the results subtracted from what we expected, add them all up and what do we get? The answer is zero. This has been done for you in the column second to the right of Table 4.3. If we divide this result by the number of observations (50) this will still result in zero which would mean no risk? Absolutely not! The problem is that we are subtracting all the observations by the average for all the observations, and by the definition of the average one half will be below the average and one half above the average so the result is zero.

What we are more interested in is the absolute positive deviation away from what we expect. One way to assure that all the deviations are positive is to multiply all of them by themselves (negative times negative and positive times positive will always be positive). This result is added up and then divided by the number of occurrences to produce the average squared deviation from what you expected. This is formally called the variance. This can be seen in the furthest right column of Table 4.3. Unfortunately, this result is in squared units. The reader may ask what squared dots on the die are or look at Figure 4.4a and contemplate what a squared Deutsche Mark looks like. Clearly, you would be immediately thrown out of your neighbourhood beer garden if you tried to pass a "squared Deutsche Mark" in payment for your genuine German brew. The solution? Take the square root of this result and you are back to normal Deutsche Marks and this can be compared directly to your expected value. This number can also be seen at the bottom centre of Table 4.3 as the Standard Deviation. This number is 1.973394465. The formula for the Standard Deviation is simply:

$$\sqrt{\sum (X_i - \chi)^2 / N - 1}$$

where:
N is the Number of Observations
x_i is each Observation
χ is the Average Observation
Σ is the Summation Sign which means
that we add up over all Observations

With the expected value of the two dice outcomes and the standard deviation from the 50 tosses, we can apply Herr Gauss' equation to draw a normal distribution which is superimposed upon the actual outcomes for the 50 tosses in Figure 4.5. As the reader can see, the fit between what actually occurred and the normal distribution curve is fairly close. The reader may be asking himself at this point: So

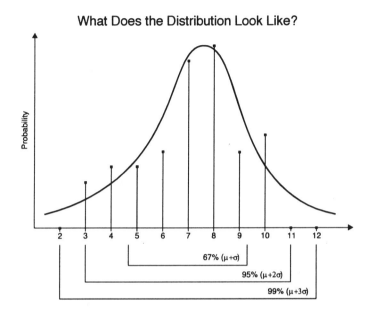

Figure 4.5 The Two Dice Normal Distribution with Probability Ranges.

what? If that is the case, let me remind the reader that our goal is to discern the rules underlying variability away from what we expect and in options markets such variability is the volatility. This normal distribution formula not only tells you the expected number of occurrences that could happen at any level but also provides a function which identifies the probabilities that would be associated at a single point or over a range of possible outcomes.

For example, in the dice distribution of outcomes, just knowing the expected value and the standard deviation will give you a normal distribution which can tell you exactly the probabilities of certain events or a range of events occurring. It is fairly obvious that when you throw two dice you will expect to get 7, but what are the chances that the dice will be between 5 and 9? While you could add up all the instances where these results occurred, you could simply use the normal distribution function with the fact that you know the expected value of 7 and the standard deviation of 1.973 to estimate the total probabilities. This is achievable due to the fact that Herr Gauss took his function and realised that the entire normal distribution has to encompass 100% of all possible outcomes. Furthermore, because the expected value is the average of the series, 50% of the possible events must lie below this number and 50% above this number. Then, he started looking at other sections of the distribution and he discovered (using the quincunx no doubt) that if he moved up and down from the average expected value by one standard deviation, that would hold approximately 67% of all the events and if he moved up and down by two standard deviations that would hold approximately 95% of all the events. In fact, he produced tables for all movements away from the average value expressed in units of standard deviations. This can be seen for the dice distribution and its normalised distribution counterpart in Figure 4.5.

What does all this mean? Just by knowing the expected value and the standard deviation, you can find any probability of an occurrence either at one level or over a range of values. From Chapter 2, the reader will remember that the essence of the time value in call options prices is assessing the joint probabilities that the underlying price (which is the expected value) will be greater than the strike price at expiration and the probability that the underlying price will drop further relative to the strike price of the option. Once again, the option buyer is paying for the probability of the unlimited profit potential and the probability of the limited loss potential which are inherent in the option.

Problems in Financial Markets with Normal Distributions

It is evident that normal distributions permeate throughout the world whenever we have uncertain outcomes. Do normal distributions also apply in the financial markets? Because normal distributions are symmetrical and continuous, it is assumed that the possible data points can range from positive to negative infinity. This would imply that prices for underlying assets or interest rates could potentially be below zero. Clearly, this could not occur.

The solution is to convert the actual price levels or rates into their logarithmic equivalent by simply multiplying the levels by the logarithmic function. This was introduced in Chapter 2. The resultant modified series has the useful feature of being bounded by zero and the ability to rise to positive infinity. Figure 4.6 displays the difference between the lognormal distribution and the normal distribution.

Therefore, it makes sense that the price series for assets or interest rates must be distributed lognormally (so as to not be below zero) while the returns for these series must follow a normal distribution since they can be both negative and positive. Having said this, it must be remembered that the return series is also limited to a maximum loss potential of minus 100% while the profit potential (in percentages) remains infinite.

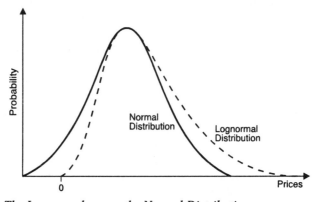

Figure 4.6 The Lognormal versus the Normal Distribution.

Practically, this may be irrelevant because if the market prices go to zero (or the loss is minus 100%) those who deal in those markets most certainly will face the career equivalent of an unlimited loss potential: they will lose their jobs. While this may seem far fetched, in the next chapter when we discuss volatility smiles, I will present one hypothesis that the market ignores the potential of the underlying price going to zero (thus representing a limited loss potential) due to the fact that put option volatilities for lower strike prices are consistently higher than the higher strike price call option volatilities. Thus, according to the Black and Scholes methodology assuming a limited loss potential, the markets may treat the potential as truly unlimited.

The Random Walk Hypothesis

Now with that introduction over, we can return to the application of this methodology into the pricing of options. When Black and Scholes examined the problem of pricing options, they drew from the world of physics. It was indicated both in Chapter 2 and in the notes to Chapter 2 how this was done with a heat transfer equation. We must return to this once again to fully appreciate how volatility impacts the price of an option.

As the reader will realise by this point, I normally shy away from formulae due to the fact that they often hide the common-sense behind variables and symbols which often leads more to confusion than to understanding. However, the following formula is so important that we must not only display it but truly understand it to appreciate how volatility really impacts option prices.

$$\Delta S / S = \mu \Delta t + \sigma^2 \Delta z, \text{ where } \Delta z = N(0,t)$$

Firstly, let us define a few terms: N is the normal distribution function as discovered by Herr Gauss, z is a standardised normal distribution function where the average value is set to zero and the variance is defined by σ^2 multiplied by time (or t). As the reader will remember it is not possible to spend a squared Deutsche Mark at the Beer Garden, so to return the value to a meaningful number, we must take the square root of the whole thing. If this is done the formula changes slightly to become:

$$\Delta S / S = \mu \Delta t + \sigma \sqrt{\Delta t},$$

Since the mean of the z distribution is 0, all we care about is the variance multiplied by the time. Since variance multiplied by time is measured in squared units, we must take the square root of the whole thing to return to a meaningful unit of measure. When this is done, all we need concern ourselves with is the standard deviation times the square root of time. For those of you that read Chapter 2 quite carefully, this standard deviation multiplied by the square root of time figures critically in the estimation of the time value of the option. For those of you who did not read as carefully, the entire rationale for the existence of the time value is that the d1 and d2 inputs into the cumulative normal density function N differ by $\sigma \sqrt{t}$. When one considers that the t in that equation is exactly the same as Δt in the above equation, then there is something quite important about this latest formula.

So, what does our final formula really say in English? The first factor in the equation which is $\Delta S/S$ is simply the absolute change in the price of an asset such as a share price divided by the price of the share. This is simply the percentage change in the price of the asset. For example, if the change in the price of the S&P 500 index was 1.5 points from the last quoted price (one micro second ago) and the current price is 430, then $\Delta S/S$ would be 1.5/430 or 0.00348837 which is equal to 0.348837%.

This represents the actual instantaneous percentage changes in the stock index level. The purpose of the equation is to predict this change (thus the "=" sign) with the two factors on the right hand side providing an estimate of how the underlying asset will change through time. The first element in the equation, $\mu \Delta t$, is relatively straightforward. This takes the average or mean change in the asset price and simply multiplies this by the amount of time that has elapsed. For example, if the S&P 500 index on average goes up by 10% per year then 10% or 0.10 is the expected change in a year. In two years, the change would be expected to be 20% and in three years 30% and so forth.

Thus, one could say that the predicted level of the S&P 500 index would be a function of the level today times the average change multiplied by the number of periods that have elapsed relative to one year. Another way to define the prediction would be to divide the current level of the index by the number of periods the Δt represents relative to a single year. Which ever way, the results will be the same. But just to prove it to the "doubting Thomases" in the audience here are the results:

Expected Level Forecast using $\mu = 10\%$ and
Multiplying by Number of years relative to period

Level Today	in 3 mths	in 6 mths	in 1 year	in 2 years	in 3 years
430	*.10*.25	*.10*.50	*.10*1	*.10*2	*.10*3
430	+10.75	+21.50	+43.00	+86.00	+129.00
430	440.75	451.50	473.00	516.00	559.00

Expected Level Forecast using $\mu = 10\%$ and
Dividing by Number of periods relative to 1 year

Level Today	in 3 mths	in 6 mths	in 1 year	in 2 years	in 3 years
430	*.10/4	*.10/2	*.10/1	*.10/.5	*.10/.333
430	+10.75	+21.50	+43.00	+86.00	+129.00
430	440.75	451.50	473.00	516.00	559.00

The reader will note that a three month period represents 25% of one year which is the same thing as saying that there are 4 three month periods in one year. While, the results will be the same in either case, I have chosen only to apply the second formula the reason of which will become clear when we discuss the second factor, $\sigma \sqrt{t}$.

Obviously, if we are predicting the future value of the S&P 500 index there will be deviations away from what we expect. I hope this sounds familiar and that the number we need to measure how dispersed the actual results will be away from where we expect is measured by the standard deviation. In the second portion of the random walk formula the σ is the standard deviation of the returns for the S&P 500.

It also makes sense that the further out in time you forecast, the more error you will have. Said another way, the actual results will experience greater dispersion the further out in time we go from today's level. I am more confident about tomorrow's price forecast than for my price forecast for three years.

Assuming that the standard deviation of returns for the S&P 500 index is 20% per year. The formula indicates that the error effect on our forecasted returns will not be directly related to the time period of our forecast but is instead a function of the standard deviation times the square root of the time period. To be 95% confident of the possible outcomes that could occur, we would have to take 2 standard deviations as was discussed earlier. Then we must add and subtract this amount from our forecasted level at that point in the future. If we do this to determine our 95% confidence interval, we will obtain the levels in this table.

Expected Errors of Forecast using $\sigma = 20\%$ and Taking
the Squared Root of the Number of periods relative to 1 year

Time Period	in 3 mths	in 6 mths	in 1 year	in 2 years	in 3 years
Formula	$2*.20/\sqrt{4}$	$2*.20/\sqrt{2}$	$2*.20/\sqrt{1}$	$2*.20/\sqrt{.5}$	$2*.20/\sqrt{.333}$
% Range	±20%	±28.28%	±40%	±56.56%	±69.28%
Lower Level	352.60	323.82	283.80	224.2	171.72
Expected Level	440.75	451.50	473.00	516.00	559.00
Upper Level	528.90	579.18	662.20	807.85	946.30

If we draw the expected levels of the S&P 500 as a function of time, the reader will see that the forecasted values are a straight line rising at a slope of 10% per year. In addition, there is the 95% confidence interval of S&P 500 levels at these same points in time and the reader can see the range is widening out the farther out we go. This is seen in Figure 4.7a.

What does this tell us? One thing is that we expect the S&P 500 to rise over time and the amount it will rise depends on the average rise that we expect multiplied by the time elapsed. Secondly, the further out in time our forecast occurs, the more error we expect to have above or below the forecasted value.

Let us once again think of a similar simple process which acts in the same way. Suppose we are trying to predict how dispersed pellets from a shotgun will be scattered against the side of a barn door somewhere in the heartland of America. Vis-

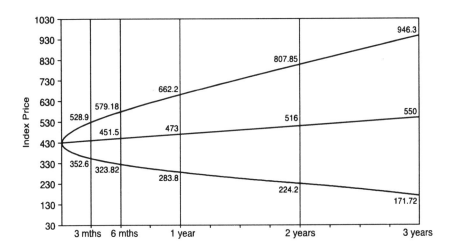

Figure 4.7a The Dispersion Process for the S&P 500 (Supra Martingale).

ualise yourself pointing the shotgun, pulling the trigger and the pellets explode out of the barrel hitting the barn door. How dispersed will the pattern of pellets be? Or, said another way, what would my prediction be of where any individual pellet would hit. If there was a target on the door, I would expect that the pellet would hit the centre of the target. Why? Because I would have aimed at the target. If I pointed the shotgun up, the expected spot would be above the vertical, if I held the shotgun parallel to the ground, the spot would be straight ahead of me and if I pointed the shotgun downwards, the shot would hit the door below where I was holding the shotgun. This is the expected spot where the pellets would hit and this corresponds to the μ of my formula.

Of course, the pellets will be dispersed not hitting all at the same spot. What will determine how disperse the pattern of pellets will be against the door? Intuitively, the dispersion will depend on two factors, the length of the shotgun barrel, and the distance away from the door I was when the shotgun was fired.

If the shotgun barrel was very long, the dispersion of pellets would be fairly tight and not very dispersed away from the target where I pointed the shotgun. On the other hand, if the barrel was a "Chicago" special with a sawn off barrel (very short and intended to hit everything in front of the shotgun and the weapon of choice of Gangsters in the 1930s), the dispersion would be very wide. Supposing that we have a box standard shotgun with no lethal modifications, then the key factor in determining the amount of the dispersion would be how far away from the door I was when the gun was discharged.

If I was standing one meter away from the door when the gun was fired, the dispersion would be very tight. If, instead, I was standing ten meters away from the door when pulling the trigger, the dispersion would be wider. Suppose, I stood twenty meters away from the door and fired the shotgun, the dispersion would be wider still. Finally, if I stood 1 kilometre away and fired, the dispersion would be even wider. Of course, at one kilometre, the pellets wouldn't travel far enough to hit the barn door at all but in theory, if they made it that far, they would be spread all over the barn yard and it would also be very likely that we would be having chicken for dinner (if any of the unfortunates happened to be out and about at the time of the conflagration).

What does this example have to do with the random walk formula for markets? Everything! The aim of the gun is the expected value or the μ. The standard deviation, σ, is the length of the gun and where the pellets hit depends on how far away I am from the door upon firing the shotgun. This is the time until the realisation of the event which in the case of the random walk formula is the time until the expiration of the option. The closer I am to that realisation point (tomorrow for example), the less the dispersion. The further out in time my forecast is, the more possible dispersion of actual results that may occur.

The reader may also visualise that the dispersion of the shotgun blast will not be spread out linearly but focused or aimed at the target which we point the shotgun at. Thus, the dispersion of the pellets will be reverting back to the expected point where we aimed. The spread of pellets as a function of the distance to the door will be curved just like the curve we saw in Figure 4.7a.

Depending on the "aim" of the series (that is the μ), the random walk process will be classified further. If the aim is tilted upwards (or a positive μ) then the process is called a supra Martingale process. If the aim is parallel to the ground (a μ of zero), the process is called a normal Martingale process and if the aim is tilted downwards (a negative μ) this is called a sub Martingale process. The second two processes are portrayed in Figures 4.7b and 4.7c.

It may interest the reader to know where the term Martingale comes from. A Martingale is a rather chaotic bird that when it flies, it seems to flutter around ran-

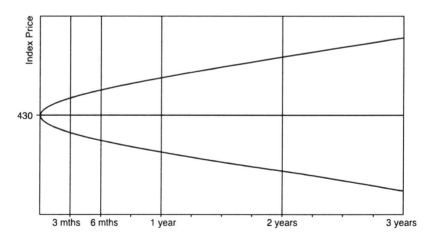

Figure 4.7b Normal Martingale Process.

domly. Thus, some statistician must have been at a loss to describe the process of random movements and looked to heaven for an answer. Lo and behold, a humble bird provided the answer to his prayers.

Anyway, Black and Scholes also assumed this type of dispersion for their under-lying asset, a share in a company, and they assumed a Random Walk normal Martingale process (see Figure 4.7b). This is why they assumed the stock price in the future to be equal to its price today. This has led many analysts to reject the Black and Scholes model at first sight because everyone knows that a stock price should rise over time. If this were not the case, then no one would buy it. This fun-damental principle was summarised by my fellow American (and Oklahoman) Will Rogers when he made the brilliant stock market investing guideline: "Investing in shares is easy, find a good share buy it and when it goes up sell it. If it fails to go up don't buy it in the first place."

However, this need not nullify the value of the Black and Scholes methodology. If the share markets tend to rise over time, then all we need to do is apply the supra Martingale process (in Figure 4.7a) which assumes an upward drift in share values. Indeed, Black himself realised the importance of this effect and that is why his later pricing model, Black (1976), uses the future price of the asset rather than the cur-rent asset price. In this approach, the future price is assumed to be equal to the cur-rent price plus some μ rate of growth wich is equal to the risk free rate.

Why have I spent so much time on this dispersion process? As was stated ear-lier, this is because all options pricing is based upon this fundamental assumption and only in this light can volatility truly be understood. In addition, the reader will see that many of the problems with volatility estimation which will be discussed in the next chapter are a direct consequence of the assumptions in this dispersion process. For example, while we all know that if you fire a shotgun one kilometre away from the barn door the pellets will not reach the door, the simple random walk

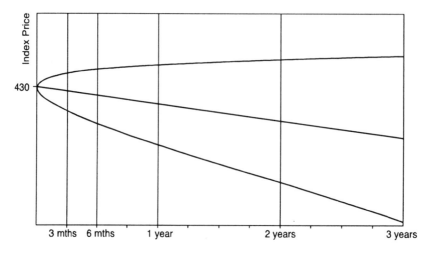

Figure 4.7c Sub Martingale Process.

Martingale processes would assume that it would hit the door. Furthermore, if you fired the shotgun 100 kilometres away from the barn door, the model will still assume that the pellets hit the door. Hold this thought in mind for the next chapter when I discuss the problems with the term structure of volatility.

Volatility as the Standard Deviation

As the reader can see, the random walk model provides just what is needed for both estimating future values of the underlying asset and the range of plus or minus values that could occur given the random nature of markets. In the example of the S&P 500 all that was needed was the mean of 10% and the standard deviation of 20%.

As the previous examples show, both numbers are expressed in annualised terms, that is the percentage growth and dispersion in one year. The volatility number most often associated with options is the one standard deviation price change (expressed in percentage terms) in one year's time. However, since most options are traded for time periods of less than one year, the volatility must be adjusted from an annualised basis to the basis of the time period of the option's life.

Adjusting the volatility for the time period of interest simply involves using the fact that the dispersion is assumed to be related to the square root of time. This has already been done for you in the previous table wich presented the dispersion process of the S&P 500. With the assumed annualised volatility of 20%, if we are interested in the volatility for three months, we simply divide 20% by the square root of the number of trading periods in the year. In the previous example, we were interested in the two standard deviation ranges for the 95% confidence interval. In this case, we are interested in only the one standard deviation ranges so in this example the three month standard deviation is 10%. This is simply $20\%/\sqrt{4}$ (3 month periods in a year).

What if we were interested in the daily volatility of the S&P 500 index? If the annualised volatility is 20% then the daily volatility can be estimated using the same formula. This is simply $20\%/\sqrt{252}$ (business days in a year). This is equal to 1.26% and it implies that you would be 95% confident that in a single business day the S&P 500 index would not move by more that 2.52% of its current level. In real numbers, if the index were 430, then this would reflect a range of 10.84 index points plus or minus. In a week, if the annualised volatility were 20%, the weekly volatility would be 2.77% which is $20\%/\sqrt{52}$ (weeks in a year). Not only can we use the formula to convert annualised volatility to that of daily or weekly volatility, we can invert the formula to estimate annualised volatility from daily or weekly volatility. This will become important later in this chapter when we will analyse the actual volatility of markets over time.

To convert the volatility from a daily or weekly measure to an annual measure, we simply take the measure of the volatility measured over the single time period and multiply this result by the square root of the number of periods the analysis period represents in a single year. For example, let us assume a pure random walk process for the S&P 500 index with no drift (ordinary Martingale process). If the S&P 500 index closed today at 430 and closed yesterday at 425, we could say that the index experienced a change of 1.176% from yesterday to today ((430-425)/425). If we look at the formula for the standard deviation displayed earlier in this chapter, we would have an expected mean of zero and an actual change of 1.176%. This would be squared and divided by N-1. But in this instance, we ignore the "-1" and divide by N (which is in this case 1 day). When we take the square root, we get back to 1.176% and this would be our estimate of the volatility. To find the annualised volatility estimate, we simply multiply this daily estimate by $\sqrt{252}$ and obtain 18.67% annualised volatility.

Of course, when estimating the volatility for the lives of options, they rarely have only one day or one week or one month to expiry. More often they have something like 45 calendar days until expiration. How would we then adjust the volatility from an annualised basis to that of 45 calendar days? Well, how many 45 day periods exist in 365 days? The answer is 365/45. So the formula above would yield $20\%/\sqrt{(365/45)}$ or 7.02%. Clearly, this is inconsistent since first the number of trading days in a year were used to estimate the volatility and then we use calendar days when converting the annual volatility for pricing the option. Indeed, there is an inconsistency. In the period of 45 calendar days only 32 trading days exist. If we express this volatility as the percentage of time in business days then our result becomes: $20\%/\sqrt{(252/32)}$ or 7.13%.[2] As the reader can see, the difference is not very great and only becomes important when the options have a few days left until the expiration where the proportional difference between calendar time and business days can become more extreme. For example, if there were a three day weekend for an option which has only 4 calendar days to expiry then there would be a big difference between 4/365 and 1/252. Otherwise, the difference is generally not worth bothering about.

I hope the reader is not starting to worry that he or she will have to convert all the annualised volatility numbers he is given into period specific volatility (or vice versa) for the estimation of an options price. When anyone prices options using a formula based upon the random walk hypothesis above, one needs not worry. As was mentioned in Chapter 2, the impact of the volatility on the price of the option is automatically adjusted for the time period of the options life. How do we know that? The whole ball game for the time value of an option is simply the difference between d1 and d2. This difference is simply $d2 = d1 - \sigma \sqrt{t}$ and furthermore since the σ is the annualised volatility input and $\sqrt{t}$ is the square root of the time period as a percentage in one year, this is all done for you. The volatility input for the pricing of options is almost always quoted on an annualised basis. The pricing models recognise that the impacts of the volatility on the price of an option are not directly proportional to the time period of the option life but proportional

---

[2]This begs the question: Which data series should be used for the basis for volatility estimation or conversion; Calendar days or Business days. All will be revealed later in this chapter when we discuss the estimation of historical volatility.

to the square root of the % of a year the time period represents and this occurs within the calculations imbedded in the formulae.

We have spent an enormous amount of time and space discussing the principles underlying volatility estimation without discussing how to estimate the volatility input into the option pricing model. The final conceptual bridge we must pass before we can do that is to define what the types of volatility are.

The Types of Volatility

There are five principal types of volatility that we need concern ourselves with. They are: Historical Volatility, Seasonal Volatility, Implied Volatility, Forecasted Volatility and Actual or Spot Volatility.

The problem of the estimation of volatility can be thought of in a similar light to the problem one faces when going to work in the morning and has to solve this fundamental forecasting problem: Do I take my umbrella? How does one make the decision whether or not to take the umbrella?[3]

One approach would be to look at the calendar and try to remember if it rained on this day in the past. This would be a historical estimation of the probability of rain. It could also be the "rainy" season and that would lead one to use a seasonal estimation of the probability of rain. Another approach would be to look out of the window and see if other commuters are carrying umbrellas. If I then took my umbrella, then the rationale for the rain forecast would be an estimation based upon the implied behaviour of my supposedly better informed colleagues. Of course, I could turn on the radio or television and listen to the weather service. If my decision to carry an umbrella were based upon this information, then I would be using a forecasted estimation of the weather. Only after the day is over would I know for certain if the umbrella was needed or not. This would be the actual (or spot) weather.

Volatility estimation can be done in a similar fashion. Volatility can be estimated from historical data with the assumption that the future will be like the past. Seasonal volatility estimation is based upon the premise that patterns of volatility are repeated at fixed points in a year or on some regular basis. This occurs most often with the volatility of commodities although there are some patterns that occur for financial markets as well. Volatility can be implied by the prices of options traded in the marketplace and volatility can be forecasted using varieties of statistical techniques. Finally, actual or spot volatility is the actual movement associated with the movement of an underlying market and can only be ascertained after the fact.

The rest of this chapter will examine in detail all of these concepts and show the reader how to use these techniques for the estimation of volatility for the correct pricing of options contracts.

---

[3]This example was inspired by a similar analogy presented by Shelly Natenberg in his courses on Options.

Estimation of Volatility Historically

As was previously stated, historical volatility is based upon statistical analysis of data in the past with the assumption that the past will bear some relevance to the future. The key issue that I will discuss in this section is what data series to use in the estimation. Two approaches exist: that of using percentage changes in the prices of assets through time, or logarithmic price changes. I will also examine what is the most appropriate data frequency for estimation: should weekly, daily, business days or economic days be considered. Another key question is what sample period should be used for the estimation of the historical volatility and finally what prices should be used: market closing prices, high/low or opening/closing prices when determining the historical asset return dispersion.

The volatility estimation using the historical approach is similar in principle to that of estimating the standard deviation of the return series of the underlying asset. This was done previously in this chapter with the dice outcomes. When determining the standard deviation of asset market returns, we simply determine the returns for a given number of observations, determine the average or mean return, subtract each observed return from this average return, square all these results and add them up. Then we divide this result by the number of observations (minus one) and take the square root. The first step is to determine the returns.

Methods of Determining Asset Returns

The two methods for determining asset returns are with percentage price changes and the second is by using logarithmic price changes. Percentage price changes are fairly easy to estimate from the following formula:

Formula for Estimating Percentage Returns for an Asset:

$$X_i = \left(P_{i+1} - P_i \right) / P_i$$

where:
X_i is the Percentage Return in the Asset
P_i is the Price of the Asset Yesterday
P_{i+1} is the Price of the Asset Today

For the examples in this chapter and the next, I will use actual market data from the Futures and Options contracts on the Italian Government Bond contract (BTP) traded at the London International Financial Futures and Options Exchange

(LIFFE). The contract specifications for the futures and options contracts can be seen in Tables 4.4a and 4.4b.

Unit of trading	ITL 200,000,000 nominal value notional Italian Government Bond with 12% coupon
Delivery Month	March, June, September, December
Delivery Day	Tenth calendar day of delivery month. If such day is not a working day for the Stanza di Compensazione Titoli in Italy, then the Delivery day will be the next following working day for the Stanza di Compensazione Titoli in Italy.
Last Trading Day	12.30 Italian time Four Stanza di Compensazione Titoli working days prior to the Delivery Day
Quotation	Per ITL 100 nominal value
Minimum Price Movement (tick Size & Value)	ITL 0.01 (ITL 20,000)
Trading Hours	08.00 - 16.10 London Time
APT Trading Hours	16.21 - 17.58 London Time

Table 4.4a Italian Government Bond (BTP) Future.

Unit of trading	1 BTP futures contract
Delivery/Expiry Months	March, June, September, December
Delivery Day/ Exercise Day/ Expiry Day	Exercise by 17.00 on any business day, extended to 18.30 on Last Trading Day. Delivery on the first business day after the exercise day. Expiry at 18.30 on the last Trading Day.
Last Trading Day	16.10 Seven business days prior to first day of the delivery month
Quotation	Multiples of ITL 0.01
Minimum Price Movement (tick Size & Value)	ITL 0.01 (ITL 20,000)
Trading Hours	08.02 - 16.10 London Time

Table 4.4b Option on Italian Government Bond (BTP) Future.

Using this contract, we will now estimate the percentage return achieved on this contract from 20 April to 21 April 1994 for the June 1994 BTP futures. On 20 April, the BTP June futures settled at 110.64 and on the following day settled at 111.51. Applying the above formula, we obtain:

$$0.007863 = (111.51 - 110.64) / 110.64$$

$$0.007863 \cdot 100 = 0.7863\%$$

There are two approaches to employing logarithmic price changes. One formula uses the logarithm of the price ratio and the other subtracts the logarithm of the prices. Here are the formulae for both:

Formula for Estimating Logarithmic Returns Approach #1

$$X_i = \ln\left(P_{i+1} / P_i\right)$$

where:

    X_i is the Logarithmic Return for the Asset
    P_i is the Price of the Asset Yesterday
    P_{i+1} is the Price of the Asset Today
    ln   is the Natural Logarithmic Function

Formula for Estimating Logarithmic Returns Approach # 2

$$X_i = \ln\left(P_{i+1}\right) - \ln\left(P_i\right)$$

where:

    X_i is the Logarithmic Return for the Asset
    P_i is the Price of the Asset Yesterday
    P_{i+1} is the Price of the Asset Today
    ln   is the Natural Logarithmic Function

Now let us go through an example with both formulae using the BTP data on the 20 and 21 of April. Our results are:

Using Formula # 1

0.007833 = ln (111.51 / 110.64)
0.007833 · 100 = 0.7833%

Using Formula # 2

0.007833 = ln (111.51) - ln (110.64)
0.007833 = 4.714114 - 4.70682
0.007833 · 100 = 0.7833%

As the reader can see, the results are identical with both logarithmic formulae. In addition, the results are similar to that achieved with the percentage change formula. The difference between the formulae results is fairly small from 0.7863% for the percentage returns and 0.7833% for the logarithmic returns.

Why are the results different? It is due to the assumptions one makes when using percentage versus logarithmic returns. Percentage returns assume that prices change at fixed discrete intervals while logarithmic returns assume that prices are continuously changing. This is similar in principle to the difference between compound interest at regular intervals (percentage returns) and interest which is continuously compounded (logarithmic returns). In the Black and Scholes model the assumption is continuous price movement and this may be inferred from the fact that the strike price is discounted back to present value by a continuous interest rate factor e^{-rt}. Therefore, for this model, the appropriate method for determining the volatility would be the logarithmic returns.

Indeed, for most underlying markets, we can assume more or less continuous potential changes in prices and would therefore conclude that for the historical volatility estimation logarithmic returns are more appropriate.

Example of Historical Volatility Estimation using Logarithmic Returns

By using a sample of 20 days from the 20 April 1994 until 18 May 1994, we can determine the historical volatility for the BTP futures over this period. Table 4.5 displays this. The first column on the left is the date for each observation. The next column is the actual closing price of the June 1994 BTP futures contract. The next column is the natural logarithm of the price and to the immediate right of this is the difference in these logged prices. At the bottom of this column is the sum of all the changes in logged prices and below that the mean or average change. In this example, this number is 0.001264. Using this number, we can calculate the difference for each observation away from the mean and this appears for each day in the next column. Second furthest from the right these differences have been squared. At the bottom of this column is the sum of these squared deviations and this number is 0.000752.

Below that the Daily Variance is displayed. This is estimated by taking the sum of the squared deviations and dividing it by 18 (which is the number of observations 19 minus 1). This number is 0.00004176. This can then be multiplied by the number of business days in a year (252) which will produce an annualised variance number (0.01052322). Once again we have the same problem as was experienced with the squared Deutsche Mark; a squared Lira makes no sense. After we take the square root of the annualised variance number, we have produced the standard deviation, which is the historical volatility for this period. This number can be seen in the lower right hand corner of the table and is 0.102582748. This would be expressed as a volatility of 10.26%. It should be noted that this volatility is the actual volatility that occurred over the period and could only be estimated on 18 May.

One thing that can be said about this estimate is that it leaves no doubt to how dispersed the BTP futures was over the 20 day period. However, that may not be our goal in volatility estimation. What we are trying to achieve is an estimation that can be used outside of the sample period from 20 April to 18 May. We may want to estimate the volatility that would actually occur from 18 May until 10 June when the futures contract expires. What is needed is some measure of the potential error that could occur from our estimation of the volatility. To consider this problem, we must examine where the potential sources of error could come from.

DATE	BTP FUT.	LOG PRICE	DIFF. IN LOG Xi	Xi - Xm	(Xi - Xm)^2	
20-Apr-94	110.64	4.7063	-	-		
21-Apr-94	111.51	4.7141	0.00783	0.00657	0.000043142	
22-Apr-94	111.85	4.7172	0.00304	0.00178	0.000003169	
25-Apr-94	110.44	4.7045	-0.01269	-0.01395	0.000194620	
26-Apr-94	112.10	4.7194	0.01492	0.01365	0.000186449	
27-Apr-94	112.40	4.7221	0.00267	0.00141	0.000001983	
28-Apr-94	111.89	4.7175	-0.00455	-0.00581	0.000033780	
29-Apr-94	112.31	4.7213	0.00375	0.00248	0.000006162	
03-May-94	111.90	4.7176	-0.00366	-0.00492	0.000024222	
04-May-94	111.31	4.7123	-0.00529	-0.00655	0.000042914	
05-May-94	110.68	4.7066	-0.00568	-0.00694	0.000048167	
06-May-94	111.39	4.7130	0.00639	0.00513	0.000026318	
09-May-94	111.12	4.7106	-0.00243	-0.00369	0.000013625	
10-May-94	112.05	4.7189	0.00833	0.00707	0.000049987	
11-May-94	111.89	4.7175	-0.00143	-0.00269	0.000007254	
12-May-94	112.44	4.7224	0.00490	0.00364	0.000013244	
13-May-94	112.12	4.7196	-0.00285	-0.00411	0.000016928	
16-May-94	112.43	4.7223	0.00276	0.00150	0.000002240	
17-May-94	112.50	4.7230	0.00062	-0.00064	0.000000412	
18-May-94	113.33	4.7303	0.00735	0.00609	0.000037044	
			SUM		SUM	ANNUALISED
			0.024022		0.000752	VARIANCE
						0.01052322
			MEAN Xm			STD. DEV.
			0.001264		VARIANCE	
					0.00004176	0.102582748

Table 4.5 Example of Historical Volatility Estimation for BTP Futures.

Sources of Error in the Volatility Estimate

The first major source of error could be that the 20 day period we selected for the estimation of the historical volatility was not a typically volatile period for the BTP. It could have been more volatile or less volatile than normal. Another problem is that the period we are trying to forecast the volatility for is also untypical. This is a fundamental problem in the statistical analysis of data series where the series are uncooperative and change over time. This problem is known as heteroscedasticity and unfortunately it sounds sexier than it really is. It simply means that variance (or what we are after, the volatility) is not constant over time. This problem will be dealt with in some detail in the next few pages when we introduce the concept of economic days and use this information to forecast actual volatilities.

The second source of error would be that we have a well behaved price series (i.e., it is homoscedastic) but we simply have not taken enough data to get a reasonable estimation. Think of this problem as one with the proverbial urn filled with blue and red balls. If the balls are relatively well mixed together and one were trying to find out the proportions of both red and blue balls in the container, one would not have to empty out the whole urn and start counting but could instead take a smaller sample and imply what the proportions were. If this is the problem we are facing, then it is a trivial statistical test that will tell us how many observations we need to sample to have a reasonable estimate. This statistical test is based upon another statistic called the standard error.

The standard error is simple to estimate and the formula makes a certain amount of logical sense. The formula for the error of the standard deviation (or volatility) is simply:

$$\sigma / \sqrt{2N}$$

where:
  σ is the Volatility Estimate
  N is the number of Observations
  used in making the estimate.

In the example for the BTP futures, the σ estimate was 10.258% and the number of observations used to get the estimate was 19. Well, multiply 19 by 2 and we get 38. Then, take the square root of this and this yields 6.164414. Our volatility estimate of 10.258% is divided by this to get our standard error of 1.664%. This number is like a standard deviation itself. It states that when we take a sample to make a guess about the true value of an entire population, we will have errors. Our estimated volatility could be higher or lower than the real true nebulous volatility which is lurking just outside our statistical tools. You can treat the standard error just like the standard deviation and start producing probabilities. That is, if we go up and down by one standard error away from our estimate, we will have about 66% of all sample observations (if we repeated this sampling process over and over). And that is right: If we take two standard errors, we will have about 95% of all sampled estimates. So, the standard error can be thought of as the standard deviation of the standard deviation.

Back to the BTP problem: The true volatility could be between 8.594% and 11.922% if we wanted to be sure two out of three times. If the margin for error is too high and we must have 95% certainty, then the true volatility would be between 6.930% and 13.586%. Of course, even in the BTP market this is a wide enough spread to drive a fleet of trucks through. With that degree of potential error, the analyst may as well throw dice, multiply the result by 23.5 and then take the cubed root! So what's the solution? Well, if the series is well behaved, it is a simple matter to reduce the statistical sampling error by adding more observations. Suppose we chose instead of 19 observations 1000 observations for the BTP series. Assuming the same volatility estimate, our new standard error would only be ± 0.229% ($10.258\%/\sqrt{2 \cdot 1000}$). Of course, the statisticians would now be happy, but the BTP analyst would have big problems given there have not been 1000 observations for the June 1994 futures. In addition, even if there had been, a serious conceptual problem is raised: Are the price changes for BTPs from four years ago as important to the forecasted volatility as yesterday's price changes? Probably not!

Data Frequency for Estimation of Historical Volatility

This raises a very good point which will now be addressed. What data frequencies should be used for the estimation of historical volatility? Should business days, calendar days, weekly, monthly or quarterly data be used? In theory, the results should all be equal for our estimation, if the data series are well behaved. If the results are dramatically different, then alarm bells should start going off! We have identified a badly behaved data series and we must be extremely careful with these "Peccatori" (Italian for misbehaved) of the time series world.

To see if the BTPs are "Santi" (Saints) or "Peccatori" (Sinners), we look again at the time series data for the June 1994 futures. Only, this time we look at it from the beginning of its life: 4 of January 1994 until the final expiration of the futures on 10 June 1994. In Figures 4.8a, 4.8b and 4.8c , I have presented the annualised volatility estimates using all the trading days, Mondays to Mondays, Tuesdays to Tuesdays, Wednesdays to Wednesdays, Thursdays to Thursdays, Fridays to Fridays and finally the differences between BTP prices every two weeks (on a Wednesday). As the reader can see the results are not the same. Even when one controls for the few sampling periods of the weekly and biweekly estimates (compared with the daily estimates) the volatility estimates are not the same. Alarm bells should be going off at this point.

So what should one do? To minimise statistical errors and also to gain a clearer picture of what is going on, most analysts (and myself) use as frequent a sampling period as possible and this means at least daily data. Clearly, the problem of volatility estimation is not as simple as determining the percentage of coloured balls in an urn. Or is it? To answer this question (which will no doubt surprise and delight the reader), we have a little more ground to cover.

Now that we have determined that at a bare minimum of daily data should be taken, the next question is which days to choose. Should we take calendar days,

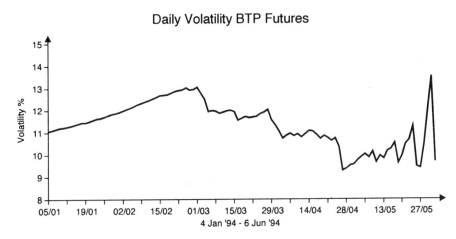

Figure 4.8a Historical Volatility for BTP Futures Estimated Daily.

only those days when the markets are open (i.e. trading days) and should special days such as those when important economic events took place be given special consideration? To answer all these burning questions and many more, let us define what we mean by days.

Calendar days are the actual number of days that elapsed for the period of the estimation of the volatility. Trading days are the number of days on which the underlying instrument (which we are estimating the volatility for) can be traded. Simply said, this is the calendar days minus the weekends and holidays. Finally, we will define a new kind of day which is called an Economic Day. These are the days when some significant economic event takes place which causes the price movement of the underlying market to be greater than it normally would be.

First things first. Should we use calendar days or trading days for the estimation of the volatility of the underlying asset? I believe that trading days should be observed. I have always converted the daily volatility to annual volatility and vice versa using the number of trading days in a year. Still, the reader may wonder why.

If you believe that markets are well behaved, then volatility would more or less be at the same level throughout time. If any changes in the volatility were to occur they would be caused solely by the random effects of new information that would change how the market evaluates the risk of the asset. Many market participants find that when the markets close, obviously the prices cease to move. Furthermore, on most occasions, the prices will only start moving again when the market is re-opened. This is not dissimilar to what happens when you are watching a video at home and you feel the urge to load up on refreshments. What you do is hit the pause key on your video player and take five. As long as you do not take an inordinate amount of time filling your plate and cup, when you return the film will be frozen at the point where you paused the tape. However, many academics who believe in "efficient" markets would say that events that would increase volatility should occur

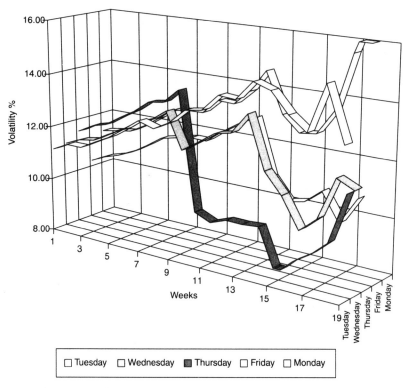

Figure 4.8b Historical Volatility for BTP Futures Estimated Weekly.

continuously through time including weekends. It is as if markets never close: a Saturday or Sunday is no different than a Monday as far as price movements are concerned.

This important question of whether volatility for assets is identical when the markets are open and closed was tested by two professors of mine at the University of Chicago, Eugene Fama and Ken French.[4] They concentrated their analysis on American share prices and used the closing prices to determine the variances of two share price return series. The first was the variance between trading days where there was no break in between the days (like holidays or weekends). The second variance was only between the close of trading on Fridays and the close of trading on Mondays. If the academics are correct about the events which cause volatility being spread evenly throughout time, then the variance of the second series should be three times as great as the variance on the day to day series. This is because there are three days between Friday's and Monday's closes while only one day between

[4]Fama, E.E., "The Behavior of Stock Market Prices", Journal of Business, 38 (January 1965), pp. 34-105; French, K.R., "Stock Returns and the Weekend Effect", Journal of Financial Economics, 8 (March 1980), pp. 55-69.

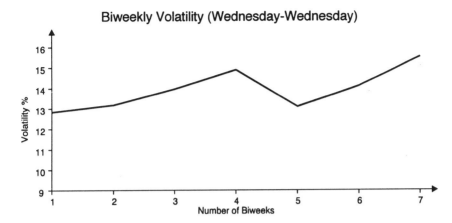

Figure 4.8c Historical Volatility for BTP Futures Estimated Biweekly.

Monday's and Tuesday's closes. Fama found that instead of a 300% increased variance, the variance was only 22% higher. French found that the variance was only 19% higher. Thus, the results of both studies blow enormous holes in the constant volatility hypotheses.

The conclusion is that the variability of underlying asset prices is much larger when the markets are open than when they are closed. The academics may still argue that the relevant information which impacts the price of a stock is only released during trading days. While this may be true, we can test this impact on another set of underlying assets, that are impacted by relevant information which is not only released on days markets are open but truly year round. Which assets are these? Commodities. These assets are impacted by a variety of factors, the most important of these is the weather. If the weather only occurred on days when commodity futures were traded, we would have the same problem as the stocks. However, this is obviously not the case, as weather occurs all year.[5]

Taking the same approach to commodity price series as was taken by Fama and French for shares, has shown that they act pretty much the same as shares. Their volatility is greater when the markets are open. Even though news about the weather is equally likely to be released on all days throughout the year and any releases of news on the weekends would have a knockon effect on Mondays price changes.

The only reasonable conclusion is that prices change because the markets and trading cause volatility. This makes a certain amount of sense, for if no one were buying and selling, prices would never change. In conclusion, volatility is a function of trading and open markets. When we are estimating the historical volatility, we should use as many daily observations as possible and only those days when the markets are open.

---

[5]In fact it seems that there is a negative relationship between non-trading days and the quality of the weather, but this is purely anecdotal. That implies that on working days the weather is good and on days off the weather is miserable!

The Impacts of Economic Days on the Historical Volatility

While both the empirical results and common sense would lead us to use only business day observations for the estimation of the historical volatility, can we assume that on these business days volatility is the same day in and day out? In more formal terms, is volatility homogeneous over time? Again, common sense would say not. On some days markets move more than on other days when markets may not move at all. One might conclude that volatility will be at some level over time but there will be periods of extremely high volatility. We will call these days "Economic Days" when something happens that fundamentally impacts the price of an asset. Clearly, most of the time the market volatility will be "lower" since substantial "Economic Days" do not occur that often. Then the summation of all these individual observations would yield the actual volatility one would expect over time. This problem of actual movement and potential movement is the key to understanding and possibly predicting volatility. In fact, the same problem exists in physics and relates to energy.

One of the cornerstones of physics is the law of the conservation of energy. Every object has a given amount of energy which is in one or the other state. An object has either potential energy or kinetic (or actual) energy but both add up to the total energy of the object. For example, consider a boulder sitting on the top of a hill. While it sits there it is expending no kinetic energy but has 100% of its energy due to the potential that it may roll down the hill. As the boulder begins rolling down the hill the potential energy is transformed to kinetic energy such that when the boulder reaches the bottom of the hill the energy is now 100% kinetic and no potential is left. The same principle applies to volatility and I will call this the Theory of the Conservation of Volatility.

In my theory, there exists an actual level of volatility that can only be determined at the end of the time period. Prior to the end of the period, all volatility day by day will either be an actual expenditure of risk (resulting in a highly volatile day) or will remain a potential expenditure of risk (due to the passage of a low volatility day). Regardless, the absolute level of true volatility will not change, it will only be a composition of the transition between actual and potential volatility (just like energy). In our task of estimating historical volatility, we must therefore take into account the number of transitions from potential to actual realised volatility. Then, our volatility forecasts for future movements of the underlying asset would take into account how much further potential should exist for highly volatile observations. Essentially, this would require the analyst to count through time the instances of "normal" days and of "highly volatile" days and adjust his estimates following the conservation of volatility principle. This process of counting observations to obtain a better forecast is really nothing new, especially when considering other situations with uncertain outcomes. The most direct example of this is the rule for winning at the card game of Blackjack.

Blackjack (also known as 21) is a popular card game at many of the world's casinos. It is a very simple game where the dealer deals two cards to himself and to the player. One card is played down and one up. The objective of the game is to have a hand of cards with the total value of all the cards as close to 21 as possible without going over.

The player knows what he has but only knows half of what the dealer has. He then bets based upon the probability that his hand will beat the dealer. If his hand is well below 21, he may request more cards dealt to him but as soon as his hand exceeds 21 he loses. What the player needs to assess is the probability of the unseen card the dealer holds being a particular card and also the probabilities of what card he will receive if he asks for another one from the dealer.

To assess the probabilities, he lays out all the cards and groups them together depending on their values. Since all the face cards (Jacks, Queens and Kings) and the "tens" have a value of 10, he combines these across all suits to have a pile of 16 "ten" cards. He has 4 Aces which can either be 11 or 1 depending on what the player wishes and the rest of the cards which go from 2 to 9. Then, he starts calculating probabilities. The chance of receiving a "ten" card is simply 16/52 which is 30.77% and the chance of receiving any other card from a 2 to an Ace is 4/52 which is 7.69%. The basic logic in winning at Blackjack is to receive "ten" cards or Aces as many times as possible and not the lower cards which in combination will more probably bust your bet. Assuming that 20 cards are dealt from a deck of 52 and they are all "low" cards, then, the odds have changed for the probability of receiving "ten" cards and Aces from this point forward. In fact, the probability of receiving a "ten" has improved to 16/32 which is 50% and the probability of getting an Ace is now 4/32 which is 12.5%. Thus, the gambler now has a better probability estimate of what the down card is for the dealer and what cards he is most likely to receive if he asks for another card. While, the outcome is not certain, the odds are improving for the player as he is more certain than at the beginning of the game of receiving "high" cards which are better. The only certainty is that when all 52 cards are dealt there will have been 16 "ten"s played and 4 Aces. This is the conservation rule of Blackjack. The same principle applies to the "Conservation of Volatility".

Suppose that over the next 260 business days (roughly one year) the expected volatility should be 20%. Furthermore, three quarters of the time or 195 days, the market movements will be normal and one quarter of the time or 65 days the markets will be highly volatile. Then like with the card game of Blackjack, we would expect 65 highly volatile days to occur and 195 low volatility days to occur but we cannot be sure when. One thing we can be sure of is that the combination of normal and highly volatile days must be equal to the total volatility over the period. Suppose that normal volatility days are 10% and highly volatile days are 50%. If we further suppose that the overall volatility of BTPs should be equal to 20%, we can then very simply estimate the proportion of both types of days that should occur over our period of analysis. Does this hold to the principle of the conservation of volatility?

Composite Volatility	= %Normal Days in Period X Normal Volatility	+ %High Volatile Days in Period X High Volatility
20%	= 195/260 · 10%	+ 65/260 · 50%

In this example, yes. But this could be cheating because we knew all the variables for the composite volatility, normal and high volatility. However, this may not be totally unreasonable when one considers that it may be possible to use the historical volatility to ascertain what these values may be.

The logic is that when estimating historical volatility from past data, the data will be mixed between normal days and more highly volatile days. When the analyst is forecasting future volatility, he cannot do so blindly. He must adjust his future projections based upon the number of "Economic Days" that have already occurred over his sample period. When he counts the "Economic Days" that have already occurred, he will then have a better feel for the remaining number of "Economic Days" that are expected to occur in the future. Obviously, the more the "Economic Days" that are expected to occur, the higher the volatility estimate for the future and the fewer the "Economic Days" the lower the forecasted volatility.

This insight first came to light in a series of articles by Kenneth Leong published in Risk Magazine book in 1992.[6] His premise is that as economic data are released, the price of the underlying asset can be expected to change. One would suppose that the expected volatility will depend upon both the release of economic data and the number of such events in the forecasted period.

Mr. Leong presented an extremely simple example: a three day period where two days were normal days with a 15% volatility and one economic day with a volatility of 30% sandwiched in the middle. He produced a chart of the daily volatilities which peaked in day 2 and can be seen in Figure 4.9.

Then the problem of volatility estimation occurs. The average volatility for the period of three days would be 20% which is $2/3 \cdot 15\% + 1/3 \cdot 30\%$. Even though this is mathematically correct, it is clear that after day one passes for the remaining two days the volatility would no longer be 20% but would rise to 22.5% which is $1/2 \cdot 30\% + 1/2 \cdot 15\%$, and on the final day the expected volatility would only be 15% because the highly volatile day was now past. Clearly, this approach would be

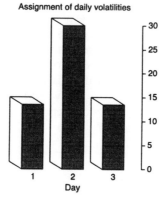

Assignment of daily volatilities

Figure 4.9 Volatilities on Normal and Economic Days.

[6]Leong, Kenneth, 1992, "Exorcising the Demon", pp. 57-62; in *From Black-Scholes to Black Holes*, edited by Robert G. Tompkins, London, England, Risk Magazine Publishing, 1992.

superior to that of a constant 20% volatility just as counting cards in the game of Blackjack is a superior technique compared with assuming constant probabilities. While Mr. Leong's articles were compelling, it remained to determine what an economic day was and how one could project economic days in the future.

The only thing to be sure of was that volatility is neither constant nor homogeneous over time. When major economic developments occur volatility should be higher. When they do not occur, volatility should be lower. But how does one measure economic events? A first approach was to look at a time series of data and find those days where extremely high volatility occurred. The daily observations were calculated using the differences in the logged prices and multiplied by $\sqrt{252}$. This was done for the BTP futures from 25 May 1993 to 4 May 1994. The reader can see this in Figure 4.10. Each day that had a high spike, was defined as an economic day and I went back to find out what happened on that date. My logic was simple: if the release of economic numbers or Bundesbank meetings or BTP auctions caused the increased volatility, then all I needed to do was determine what effect they had in the past and then project forward our volatility estimates using the calendar of economic data releases, Bundesbank meetings and BTP auctions that would occur over the forecasted volatility period and then weight the volatility by:

the number of normal days · the normal volatility

+

the number of economic days · the "economic" volatility.

While this made a lot of sense, a priori, the review of the economic events that caused high volatility seemed to have no general pattern or consistency. It just appeared to be random. A little distraught, another tack had to be tried and that was applying the principle of the conservation of volatility.

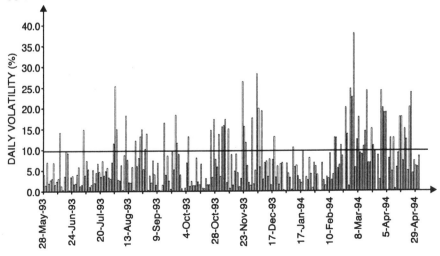

Figure 4.10 Daily Volatility of BTP Futures Nearby Contract.

Looking at Figure 4.10 again, I decided that it did not matter what caused the highly volatile days only that they occurred throughout time with some expected probability. So, I imposed a probability of 25%. The daily volatility data was ranked from the lowest result to the highest result and all results from the 180th observation and below were classified as "normal". Since the total number of observations in the historical analysis period was 240 days, 180 represents 75% of all the observations (or the third quartile). All observations above the 180th ranked observation (and there were 60 of these) were classified as highly volatile days. In Figure 4.10, the reader will see a line at little below 10% (9.6138% actually) which represents this dividing level between normal and high volatile observations.[7] The graph thus allows the analyst to distinguish the two groups of data more easily. Now comes the interesting part: we will use this information to forecast the future actual volatility from 5 May until 20 May which represents the expiration of the options on the BTP futures. This will be done by both using historical estimates of BTP normal and economic volatilities and "counting the cards" as they are dealt day to day.

The problem remains the same. As of 5 May we need to forecast the actual levels of BTP volatility from today until the expiration of the options on 20 May. Our assumption is that in the next 12 trading days until expiration, 25% of those days will be economic (or high volatility) and 75% will be normal (or low volatility). Next, we need to determine both the average volatility that occurred for the economic days (which is the simple arithmetic average of the top 60 days described above) and for the 180 normal volatility days. This turned out to be 16.326% for the highly volatile economic days and 4.077% for the lower volatile normal days. The final step was to then weight these volatilities by the expected number of normal and economic days that would occur in the sample period. This done, we have our forecast of the actual volatility that should be expected to occur over the period.

DATA: 4/5/94
Volatility Forecast Until 20 May 1994

$$\frac{9 \text{ days} \cdot 4.077\% + 3 \text{ days} \cdot 16.326\%}{12 \text{ days}} = 7.1393\%$$

Of course, when tomorrow comes we will know if today was an economic day or not if the actual volatility fell below our 3rd Quartile cut-off point of 9.6138. In fact, as time goes by, the volatility forecast is recalculated daily to take into account both the passage of economic and normal days that have passed. Let us go to 12 May and 6 days have passed from our original period of 12 days. When we look at the daily volatility two days (the 6th and 10th) had volatilities above the 9.6138 threshold and would be considered economic days. These must be dropped from

---

[7]By the way, the volatility series was not normally distributed but extremely skewed to the right and also displayed a certain degree of leptokurtosis.

our future estimates. The other four days were below the threshold and would therefore be considered normal. The day by day evaluations of whether the days were normal or economic plus the forecasted volatilities can be seen in Table 4.6. If the day were assessed to be normal (or economic), then it gets a "1" otherwise it gets a "0". Now our forecast for 12 May would assume that for the remaining 6 days, 5 would be normal and 1 would be an economic day. This being the case, here was our forecast:

DATA: 12/5/94
Volatility Forecast Until 20 May 1994

$$\frac{5 \text{ days} \cdot 4.077\% + 1 \text{ day} \cdot 16.326\%}{6 \text{ days}} = 6.1185\%$$

As the reader can see from Table 4.6, this has been done day by day and can be seen under the column **Volatility Forecast**. The column directly to the right of this, titled **Effective Volatility**, is the actual volatility that occurred for the BTP futures over the period from that day to 20 May. Of course, this can only be calculated after 20 May as the series represents what the actual "true" volatility was.

The furthest right column is the **Implied Volatility** which was the market's guess of the actual volatility imbedded in options prices. This concept will be discussed extensively in the next section of this chapter. But it will suffice to say that these are the market's "odds" regarding the expected volatility. One thing that is striking is how accurate the volatility forecast is with the effective volatility and equally how bad the implied volatility is as a forecast of the actual volatility. This can be seen to its greater effect in Figure 4.11 where the volatility series are plotted across time.

Date	Normal Day	Economic Day	Expected Volatility	Effective Volatility	Implied Volatility
04/05/94	1	0	7.1393	1.920	10.800
05/05/94	1	0	7.4176	7.754	11.100
06/05/94	1	0	7.7517	7.347	10.890
09/05/94	0	1	6.7990	7.269	10.140
10/05/94	1	0	7.1393	7.423	9.100
11/05/94	0	1	5.8269	6.633	9.200
12/05/94	1	0	6.1185	7.020	8.800
13/05/94	1	0	6.5268	7.061	8.380
16/05/94	1	0	7.1393	7.414	8.920
17/05/94	1	0	8.1600	8.344	12.780
18/05/94	1	0	10.2015	10.216	12.830
19/05/94	0	1	4.0770	4.874	13.900
	9	3			

Table 4.6 Example of BTP Futures Volatility Forecasting.

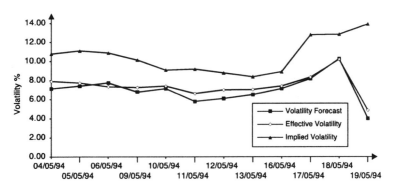

Figure 4.11 Implied Volatility, Forecasted Volatility and Effective Volatility.

While all the three series move in the same general directions, the implied volatility is consistently higher than the actual volatility in the markets. This finding is consistent with other empirical research that will be presented in Chapter 10 which also shows that the implied volatilities consistently seem to overshoot the actual volatility that occurs. The forecasted series is almost too good to be true; fitting the actual volatility like a glove. Having been trained as a statistician, I am extremely worried about "overfitting" a series so tests were performed to confirm that the results were possible. All the statistical tests we ran indicated that the forecast results were not a fluke but were statistically significant. Then the ultimate test was to extend the prediction to another time period which is displayed in Figure 4.12.

While the perfect fit is lost, the reader can see the predictions are close. Furthermore, the results of the formal statistical analysis still indicate that the forecasts are statistically significant in predicting the actual volatility achieved.

One problem is that market volatility may not be like a deck of 52 cards which always have 16 "ten" cards. There may be more economic days or fewer in the actual market than you would predict. In essence, the market volatility could funda-

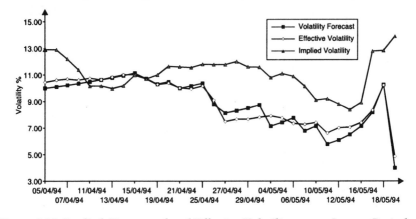

Figure 4.12 Implied, Forecasted and Effective Volatility over a Longer Period.

mentally change. This simply implies that the nature of the game and the probabilities have changed. How would you know that the rules had changed until the game was over? Going back to Blackjack, if we expected 4 Aces to be dealt in the game and Ace number 5 is dealt, we know something is amiss. If in our sample period, we start receiving economic days one after another, the analyst can apply simple statistical rules to see if the probabilities are beyond the realm of reasonable chance. But remember: all volatility estimation does is to provide the analyst with a better guess to the probabilities than simply naively throwing darts at a board. The card counters do not win every hand at the casino, but they have the edge in their favour such that as soon as the casino discerns a card counter being present, he is promptly escorted to the door. The last person a casino wants is someone who has a reasonable chance of winning. In the estimation of volatility, the trader must play the odds as effectively as the card counter in Blackjack. The good news is that traders will not be thrown out of the options market for forecasting volatility better than their rivals.

(1) when estimating the Historical Volatility the goal
   is to forecast future levels of volatility,
(2) As many observations should be used to assure that
   the results will be statistically significant,
(3) Trading Days should be used as opposed to
   Calendar Days and
(4) Volatility forecasts must take into account the difference
   between normal trading days and Economic trading days.

Next, we will examine other crucial questions in the estimation of Historical Volatility including the sample period of the estimation and which prices during the trading days should be used for the calculation of volatility.

Sample Period for the Estimation of the Historical Volatility

If the "true" volatility for an underlying asset is assumed to be constant, then the sample period and frequency for the estimation should be irrelevant. But this is clearly not the case. As was demonstrated earlier in this chapter there is a difference between daily, weekly and bi-weekly estimates of volatility. In addition, the fact that volatility is not homogeneous due to normal days and economic days means the analyst must choose his time period for estimation with care.

What the analyst needs is a sufficiently accurate measure of the historical volatility to serve as input into the volatility forecasting technique just outlined. Clearly, there is a trade-off between the reduction of the standard error of the forecast, by increasing the sample size of the estimation period, and drawing upon data which is too old to have any current relevance.

The analyst can have three choices for the sample period when estimating the historical volatility. The first choice would be the longer term volatility using trad-

ing days for the past one year. The second choice would be a shorter sampling period, e.g. the last 30 or 90 trading days. The third choice would be a variable period
in the past equal to the time horizon the analyst wishes to forecast in the future. For
example, if the analyst wishes to forecast volatility for the next 45 days, he would
look at the historical volatility for the last 45 days, carefully adjusting for the
economic and normal trading days that occurred in this period. If the analyst assesses all three sample periods and finds the composite volatility (as well as the
normal and economic volatilities) are almost the same, he may assume that volatility is probably stable for this asset over time and should choose the longer term estimate due to the smaller standard error of the estimate.

If, however, the results of the three sample periods are grossly different, most
analysts prefer to use the estimate based upon the more recent data or for the period
which matches the forecasted period. Again, all these estimates should be adjusted
for the economic days projected to occur or that can be forecasted (like elections,
releases of company results or other predictable economic events).

Another approach to determining the sample period is drawn from the conservation of volatility principle that the volatility levels will eventually revert to some
long term or average value. In this way, the analyst will adjust the most recent
volatility estimate to be closer to the longer term volatility depending on how far it
is away from the long term mean. This is achieved by weighting volatility estimates
of various periods to arrive at a composite volatility.

For example, assume that the long term volatility for the BTP futures is 7.140%
as measured for the past year. In the last 10 days, the BTP futures volatility was
9.256% and for the last 65 days it was 10.276%. It is the problem of the analyst to
arrive at forecasted volatility levels for future periods of 30 days, 65 days and 100
days. Assuming this is the composite volatility including both normal and economic
days, we have a problem since the numbers for the sampling periods are all very
different. We will blend these three forecasted numbers in different ways, by
including in our forecast each of the past volatilities but with different amounts of
emphasis. This is called weighting.

POSSIBLE WEIGHTING TECHNIQUES

EQUAL WEIGHTING
$1/3 \cdot 7.140\% + 1/3 \cdot 10.276\% + 1/3 \cdot 9.256\% = 8.891\%$

LONGER TERM WEIGHTING
$1/2 \cdot 7.140\% + 1/4 \cdot 10.276\% + 1/4 \cdot 9.256\% = 8.453\%$

MEDIUM TERM WEIGHTING
$1/4 \cdot 7.140\% + 1/2 \cdot 10.276\% + 1/4 \cdot 9.256\% = 9.237\%$

SHORT TERM WEIGHTING
$1/4 \cdot 7.140\% + 1/4 \cdot 10.276\% + 1/2 \cdot 9.256\% = 8.982\%$

Unfortunately, this is all rather silly in the BTP market given the volatility bid/offer spreads are sometimes 2%, but for more efficient markets, this technique is used with some success. The reader must be aware that the weightings for the longer term, medium term and shorter term volatilities are not always 1/2 or 1/3 or 1/4 but will be determined by statistical analysis of what weightings produce the least error in the actual volatility realised in the future.

In the analysis for the BTP futures volatility forecasting, we simply used the long term historical volatility and split it into the economic and normal days. However, the divergence between the volatility results from different time periods will be the clue the analyst needs that the game has changed. Different volatilities especially for the short term will be the dealing of the fifth Ace in the Blackjack of volatility forecasting.

The final topic that will be discussed for Historical Volatility estimation is that of which prices should be used from the trading days for the estimation of volatility.

Which Prices Should be Used for the Estimation of Volatility

In most instances, the prices used for the estimation of the historical volatility are the closing prices of the market each day. But these are certainly not the only prices that could be used and for many markets like foreign exchange the markets do not close. So how do we get closing prices for US Dollar vs. Yen for example?

An alternative method for estimating the historical volatility does not use the closing prices of the data series but the highest and lowest prices that occurred during the trading day. This was first described by Parkinson in 1980.[8] It is not surprising that Professor Parkinson was not a financial economist but rather a physics professor using a technique well known in the estimation of particle dispersions. His formula for the estimation of the historical volatility using high and low prices is simply:

$$\sigma = \sqrt{(0.361 / N) \cdot \sum \left[\ln(H_i) - \ln(L_i) \right]^2}$$

where:

σ is the estimated volatility
N is the number of observations
ln is the natural logarithmic function
H_i is the highest price occurring in the day
L_i is the lowest price occurring in the day

---

[8]Parkinson, Michael. "The Random Walk Problem: The Extreme Value Method for Estimating the Variance of the Displacement." Journal of Business, Vol. 53 (January 1980), pp. 61-65. (ch. 7).

The advantage of the Parkinson approach is that it is five to six times as accurate (from a statistical standpoint) an estimate of the historical volatility as compared to using closing prices. This means that the periods of analysis can be reduced by as much as 80% without loss of accuracy. The disadvantage of the approach is that the analyst must have access to real high and low prices and not simply bid or offer rates.

In many markets such as foreign exchange, this is the only reasonable approach for the estimation of historical volatility as closing prices simply do not exist.

A question the reader may ask is: If using high/low data improves the accuracy of the estimate so much, why not use other measures as well? Indeed, this approach has been expanded to include combined high/low and closing prices by Stan Beckers[9] and by Garman and Klass who used both high/low and opening/closing prices[10]. As if these approaches were not complicated enough, Ball and Torous applied a multiple regression approach[11]. All of these approaches warrant review by the serious volatility forecaster and are recommended reading. However, regardless of the approach one takes in estimation of the historical volatility, one must see the estimate only as good as what the actual volatility turns out to be. In addition, this forecast can only make the trader money if the forecasted volatility is different from the market consensus of volatility. What this consensus volatility is and how it is measured will be discussed later in this chapter, when I cover the implied volatility.

Estimation of Seasonal Volatility

In many markets, especially agricultural commodity markets, volatility is extremely sensitive to factors arising from seasonal weather patterns. Immediately prior to the harvest, the volatility increases and after the harvest volatility drops. For example look at frozen orange juice futures: Frosts in Florida during January and February will have a devastating effect of the supply and price of orange juice. Later in this book when we discuss Volatility Trading, we will examine coffee futures. In 1994, weather disasters in Brazil turned a normally docile coffee market into a wildly volatile beast as a substantial portion of the coffee crops were ruined by frosts in that country.

Clearly, an analyst must consider these factors when estimating the future volatility for these kinds of assets. Figure 4.13 displays the range of historical volatilties for frozen orange juice futures as a function of the months in a year.

For this figure, I have gone back five years and estimated the actual volatility in every month. Then I grouped the months together across the five year period. That is, all the January volatilities together and so forth. With the series broken into cal-

---

[9]Beckers, Stan. "Variance of Security Returns Based on High, Low and Closing Prices." Journal of Business, Vol. 56, (January 1983), pp. 97-112. (ch. 7).

[10]Garman, Mark B., and Michael J. Klass. "On the Estimation of Security Price Volatilities from Historical Data." Journal of Business, Vol. 53 (January 1980) pp. 67-78. (ch. 7).

[11]Ball, Clifford A., and Walter N.Torous. "Futures Options and the Volatility of Futures Prices." Journal the Finance, Vol. 41, No. 4 (September 1986), pp. 857-870. (ch. 5).

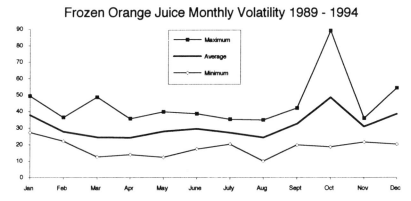

Figure 4.13 Frozen Orange Juice Volatility on a Monthly Basis during the Year.

endar months, I determined the highest volatility that had occurred in that calendar month, the lowest volatility and the average volatility over the five year period. Finally, this was plotted as a function of the calendar month over a year. As the reader can see, the volatility average and spread is not constant but changes throughout the year. Certainly, there is a cyclical pattern that must be considered when estimating the volatility for this asset. The spread between the maximum and minimum monthly volatilities is smallest in February and July. In September the spread starts to widen and by October it is at its maximum. In addition the average actual monthly volatility for this period also peaks in October every year and is at its lowest in August. Why October? That is the critical time in a year when the orange crop is just developing and most subject to weather damage.

Another interesting pattern of seasonal volatility occurs for the proverbial butt of all jokes in the financial markets, the pork belly. Figure 4.14 displays the same type of seasonal volatility chart for the "bellies".

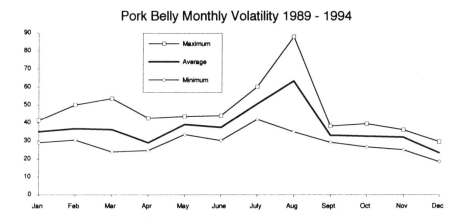

Figure 4.14 Pork Belly Volatility on a Monthly Basis during the Year.

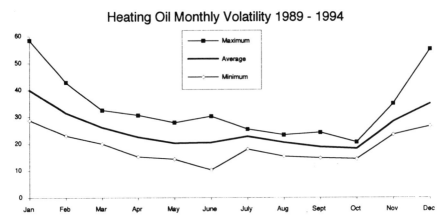

Figure 4.15 Heating Oil Volatility on a Monthly Basis during the Year.

It is interesting that there appear to be two periods of volatility each year from June until August and from February to April. The rest of the year the spreads between the five year historically maximum, minimum and average volatilities are not that different. But it is clear that the highest volatility will occur in August and volatility will be at its lowest in December. I once wanted to know the answer to the question: Why do the bellies always go crazy in August? Fortunately, I was still working at the Chicago Mercantile Exchange where the bellies trade and so it was convenient to simply walk over to the Agricultural Economist who specialised in the meat complex and get it from "the horse's mouth". The reason why pork bellies become so volatile in summer is because the demand is at its peak in August for what is made from the bellies, smoked bacon. Officially, the CME will tell you that it is the demand for lighter foods in the summer that spurs the demand for bacon. When you talk to them privately you get the real answer: more bacon, lettuce and tomato sandwiches are consumed in August than at any other time by folks having picnics.

When you think about seasons, the one thing you are certain about is that it tends to be cold in the winter and warm in the summer. What commodity would you expect to be tied to this classic and never ending cycle: of course, those commodities necessary for keeping us warm in the winter, and in major parts of the world the heating fuel of choice is heating oil. Figure 4.15 displays the monthly volatility dispersion across the year for the heating oil Futures contract traded at the New York Mercantile Exchange.[12]

It is hardly surprising that during the summer until October the volatility of heating oil is at the lowest level during the year. Thereafter, winter begins to set in and the volatility of heating oil depends on how good or bad the winter weather turns out to be. After March, when winter is practically over, the volatility starts to fall again to its low point in October.

---

[12]This data was estimated for the years 1989 to 1994 but due to the Gulf Crisis and later War, the data for these months was removed and replaced by monthly data from an earlier year. For each month in the year, at least five observations were available for evaluation.

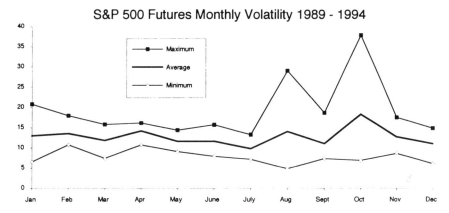

Figure 4.16 S & P 500 Volatility on a Monthly Basis during the Year.

What does all this mean? When the analyst is trying to predict the future volatility of commodities, he can be assured that the volatility will not be homogeneous over time. The existence of seasonality must be considered when he makes his forecasts. For example, while heating oil volatility might average around 25% in a year, for options in December or January, the volatility will certainly be much higher than the yearly average. Also if the volatility estimation period is from July to October, the estimate should be considerably below the yearly average of 25%. Analysis of the seasonal behaviour of asset volatility is a critical element in successful forecasting volatility. While it is clear that seasonal factors must be considered when estimating the volatility of commodities, a burning question remains: Do seasonal factors affect financial assets as well? The answer is maybe yes and maybe no. Figure 4.16 displays the actual monthly volatility for the S&P 500 futures displayed month by month through the year.

Again the analysis period was from August 1989 to July 1994 where at the end of each month, I estimated the actual volatility that had occurred for that month and did this for each month in the five years. Again, the months were all grouped together. Thereafter, the maximum, average and minimum volatilities for each month were determined. They appear in this figure. There does not seem to be the same sort of seasonal behaviour that is clearly observable in the commodity markets. While it does appear that the volatility is higher in August and October this was simply due to the Russian coup that happened in August 1991 and the mini crash of October 1989. The average levels of volatility do differ but not significantly (at least statistically) over the year. So it would appear that S&P 500 futures volatility is not tied to the annual cycle dictated by the seasons. But that does not mean that S&P 500 could not be impacted by some other kind of cycle.

For example, if we recall the example in an earlier chapter of the impact of the health of an individual on the price of his health insurance, we recalled that the sicker the individual the higher the insurance premium and the healthier the policy applicant the lower the insurance premium. Could not the same be said about financial markets? But how to measure the health of an economy? The answer is: Gross National Product (GNP) growth. That is how the economic cycle is defined; when the economy is expanding the GNP grows, and when GNP growth is negative the economy is defined as being in recession.

Back in 1983, I wrote my first paper on volatility analysis by looking at the relationship between the actual volatility of the US stock market as a function of the business cycle. That is, my periods of analysis for the estimation of volatility were broken into periods of expansion prior to a recession, for the duration of the recession and for an equal time period of expansion after the recession was over. I completed the study for all the business cycles from 1970 to 1981 and found a most curious result. When the economy was expanding the volatility was low. When the economy was in recession, the volatility rose often by a factor of 50%. Then after the recession was over and the economy expanded again, the volatility fell back to the previous low levels. This occurred for every business cycle over the period.

From 1983 until the first edition of this book in 1991, there had been no further complete business cycles and so it was not possible to test the findings on a new business cycle. Fortunately for this study (but unfortunately for those who suffered), another US recession came about in 1990 and the prediction of the earlier study was confirmed. For the one year expansionary period from June 1989 to June 1990, the actual S&P 500 volatility was 14.19%. During the recession from June 1990 to June 1991, the volatility rose to 17.11%. Thereafter, during the recovery from the recession from June 1991 to June 1992, the S&P 500 volatility fell back to 12.14%. These results are reproduced in Figure 4.17.

This implies that other seasonal or cyclical factors will affect financial assets as certainly as weather cycles will affect commodities. But with all volatility forecasting, it is important to use common sense when making forecasts. All volatility rep-

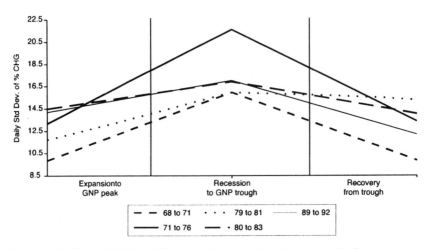

Figure 4.17 S & P 500 Volatility as a function of the Business Cycle.

resents is the uncertainty of future price levels. The more the uncertainty the greater the risk and the greater the actual volatility that will be realised.

I will finish this chapter by examining the market's consensus for future volatility which is the volatility implied in the price of options today.

Estimation of the Implied Volatility

Of all the estimation techniques for future volatility, the most accessible and intuitive is that of the implied volatility. As was noted in Chapter 2, the implied volatility is the risk perceived by the market today for the period up until the expiration of a particular option series. To determine implied volatility, all that one requires is:

(1) a real traded option price and a theoretical option pricing model
(2) strike price of the option, the underlying asset price, the
    expiration date, a short term interest rate, the expected dividends
    that will be paid and
(3) these are entered into a theoretical option pricing model and
    the model is run backwards to yield the implied volatility.

The price of the underlying market, the option premium, the term, the short term interest rates, the dividends and the time to maturity are all known factors. The only unknown variable is the volatility. One determines the implied volatility by "tricking" the option pricing formula. Since we already know the actual price, we use the model to tell us what the other traders must have entered as their volatility input to arrive at that price.

What should be the relationship between the implied volatility coming from the market and the actual volatility that should occur in the future? In the absence of arbitrage opportunities, they should be the same. The assumption here is that if the implied volatility is different from the actual realised volatility over time, then arbitrageurs will simply initiate trading strategies which will benefit from that fact. From Chapter 3, the reader may remember that there are two kinds of volatility impacts on an options price: that of the implied volatility and of the actual volatility. The Greek letter vega measures the sensitivity to changes in the options price for a change in the implied volatility as the gamma measures the changes in the options price for a change in the actual volatility of the market. Essentially, if the implied volatility is consistently below the actual realised market movements (the actual volatility), then the trader should maximise his vega exposure by buying cheap options and then if possible minimise his gamma exposures (or even go short gamma). On the other hand, if the implied volatility is consistently higher than the realised true asset price volatility, then the trader should sell the implied volatility and buy the actual volatility by having a negative vega exposure (that is selling options) and having a positive gamma position.

While it is a little premature at this point to discuss arbitrage strategies, the reader can rest assured that these will be discussed at length in Chapter 8 when we discuss arbitrage trades. At this point, it will have to suffice that the only reasonable objective in using the implied volatility to project future volatility is that the market consensus implied in the options price is better than any other technique. While the evidence is that the implied volatility tends to be higher than the realised true volatility, it may be the case that the mechanisms for a complete arbitrage are indeed not complete (and therefore risk free) thus allowing the discrepancy to continue to exist over time. At the very least, the implied volatility gives the trader or analyst a current level of the market consensus for future risks and provides a measure which can be compared over time to indicate how the prices of options change. As was discussed previously, the implied volatility is a parallel concept to yield to maturity for fixed income interest rates. Everyone knows in their hearts of hearts that the yield to maturity is not perfect but it does provide a momentary snap shot of the internal rate of return implied by the current price of the bond and can be useful for "standardising" different fixed income instruments to a yield to maturity benchmark for comparisons. In addition, bond analysts will look at changes in the yield to maturity to explain changes in bond prices but this is a spurious argument as changes in the bond price cause changes in the yield to maturity and not the other way around. Of course, the same ideas apply to the implied volatility measure for options. A change in the option price will cause a change in the implied volatility and not necessarily the other way around. Still with all these limitations, implied volatility is almost always the volatility concept people mean when that topic is mentioned among those trading options.

In this section, we will examine a variety of issues in the estimation of the implied volatility. First of all, since the implied volatility comes from turning around an options pricing model, we had better look more closely at the assumptions of the popular pricing models we are using to determine our number. Then we will examine the techniques for obtaining the implied volatility given that the pricing model can not simply be inverted to provide our answer. Finally, we will examine what needs to be done when a number of options is inverted to determine a sample of implied volatilities and the implied volatility numbers are different. This final topic which starts out rather innocently turns into a festering can of worms that will require most of the next chapter to resolve. The good news is that the differences in the implied volatilities provide tremendous insights into how those in the markets perceive future asset price distributions and how risk changes over time. But before we can get to these very exciting topics, we must cover the ground work in this chapter.

Assumptions of the Options Pricing Models

First we assume that the analyst is attempting to gauge the market consensus on volatility by reversing the options valuation model to back out what the volatility input had to be to arrive at the observed market price. Obviously, if the model is wrong, the estimate will be wrong as well. Given that the mathematics for the Black and Scholes type models are irrefutable, the only other potential sources of errors in the models could be back at square one with one of the assumptions which underlie the mathematics.

Almost all of the Black and Scholes type models we would use to estimate the implied volatilities share the following assumptions:

(1) Past prices are irrelevant for predicting the future,

(2) Volatility remains constant over time, and

(3) Relative price changes are normally distributed with a variance directly proportional to the length of the time interval over which the relative price change can take place.

What are the implications of these assumptions? If past prices are irrelevant, then technical and seasonal analyses have no value. While I will not debate the merits or demerits of technical analysis, it is clear that a large number of extremely successful market participants do use this technique quite successfully. From the evidence that seasonal factors do seem to influence commodity volatilities, I am more prepared to argue that seasonal analysis dues have merit.

The second assumption that volatility is constant over time is more onerous. If this is the case, then no-one could trade volatility and all the evidence in this book (see Figure 4.10 on the BTPs for example) which clearly demonstrates that volatility is non-stationary would be faulty. In the next chapter we will discuss the problems that this assumption presents and how adjustments can be made. Furthermore, in Chapter 13 on exotic options, we will discuss the evolution of pricing models which allow for variable (or stochastic) volatility.

The third assumption concerning the relative price changes comes directly from the random walk process I discussed earlier in this chapter. If the relative price changes are directly proportional to time, then this suggests that the dispersion of prices will increase infinitely as time goes to infinity (or goes to zero). This is the same problem as the dispersion of the shotgun hitting the barn door if we fire the gun 1 kilometre or 100 kilometres away. The dispersion process only works over a short range. In price series, it is not gravity that is pulling the prices to zero but rather extensive empirical evidence that prices or trends tend to return to a long term average over time.

But what is the point of estimating the implied volatility? The answer is to then use this number to price another option than the one we are inverting and to obtain a "fair" price assuming the implied volatility is an unbiased estimate of the true volatility. It makes no sense to use the implied volatility for pricing the same option that we are inverting because we already have that price in the first place. So essentially, the implied volatility is used to price an option similar to an existing traded option. However, it is not clear how similar the two options have to be to ensure that it is appropriate to use the same volatility for both. If the options have to be extremely similar, then the usefulness of such an approach is quite limited. In those instances where no other similar options are traded with observable prices, then there will be no reference available to determine the implied volatility. Finally, if every market participant relies on others to make the decision regarding the volatility input, then no consensus can be formed as to the implied volatility. It is like a nervous cocktail party where everyone is waiting for the other person to get the conversation going and there is a dead silence until the first bold partygoer introduces the first topic of conversation.

Still, the implied volatility is an anchor that allows the participants some basis for comparison and is necessary to kickstart the trading in individual option series. But how is the implied volatility actually calculated?

Techniques for the Determination of Implied Volatility

When I was first involved with options at the Chicago Mercantile Exchange research department, one of my first tasks was to determine the implied volatilities for the contracts traded at the exchange. I took the Black (1976) pricing model and tried to solve the equation for the volatility input. After one week of trying various algebraic tricks, nothing worked and I learned that it is impossible to invert the formula to solve it for the implied volatility. The only way to find the implied volatility was to introduce a sample volatility number and if the resulting theoretical option price was lower than the real traded option price, to put in a higher volatility. When the theoretical option price was too high then I needed to put in a lower volatility. Thus, the implied volatility was estimated by trial and error until it simply happened that the actual option price was equal to the theoretical price. In later research, I discovered that there are three basic techniques for determining the implied volatility in a more systematic manner. These include: using a volatility/price graph, applying a Newton-Raphson algorithm or employing a Method of Bisection.

The reader will remember the importance of the term $\sigma\sqrt{t}$ in the determination of the time value of an option. If the volatility term, σ, increases then the difference between d1 and d2 goes up as does the time value of the option. Thus, an option's price is almost linearly related to an increase in the volatility. The relationship can be seen best by plotting the relationship between the option price and the level of volatility as has been done in Figure 4.18.

All the analyst needs to do to estimate the implied volatility is to find the intersection point on the curve which represents the current option price and then read down to find the volatility associated with this price. Consider a BTP call option at-the-money that has a price of 1.41. As you draw the dotted line to the curve and then draw another dotted line straight down, you will obtain an implied volatility of 12.75%. However intuitive this approach is, it presents major problems for the analyst. First of all, it assumes that the pricing model one uses is correct, that the price of the underlying asset does not change and that the analyst has a steady hand. Clearly, if any of the other variables which influence the price of an option changes,

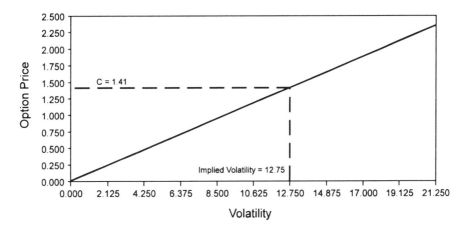

Figure 4.18 Relationship between the Option Price and the Volatility.

one would need another price versus volatility plot to determine the implied volatility. Having said that, the plot does provide an insight into the price volatility input and can provide a good starting point for iteratively finding the implied volatility.

Probably the most used technique for the estimation of the implied volatility relies on the Newton-Raphson iterative process.[13] This process involves making an initial guess as to the implied volatility of the option and then uses the Greek derivative of the options price relative to changes in volatility (the vega) to make new guesses if the first guess is off the mark. This technique will converge very quickly upon the correct answer if the option price relationship to time is continuous and relatively linear (as it is for normal European options for example). The actual formula is:

$$X_{i+1} = X_i' - (Y_i - P)/V_i$$
$$\text{until} \quad |Y_i - P| \leq E$$

where:

P   is the traded options price
X_i is the volatility estimate
Y_i is the option theoretical value with X_i volatility
V_i is the options vega at theoretical price Y_i
E   is the desired degree of accuracy

---

[13] Again the world of the pure sciences interacts with the options market. The "Newton" is Sir Isaac Newton and the "Raphson" is Joseph Raphson another English mathematician who published a method similar to Newton's in the 17th century.

143

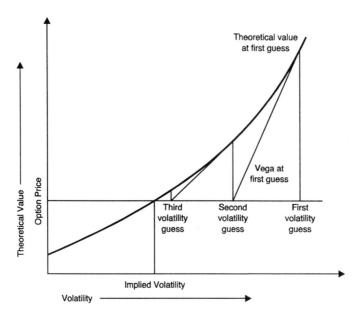

Figure 4.19 Example of Newton-Raphson Estimation of Implied Volatility.

The way the Newton-Raphson iterative process works is best shown with a graphical example. In Figure 4.19 such an iterative process is portrayed. On the left hand side of the graph one can see the vertical dimension which represents option prices (both the actual and theoretical prices). On the horizontal dimension the volatility is plotted increasing as we move to the right. The curve represents the theoretical value of an option and at the first volatility guess, the theoretical option price is too low relative to the actual option price. Using the vega slope at that point, a new volatility estimate is introduced which gives us a lower price but it is still too high. With the new vega slope, another volatility estimate is introduced and we then have converged on the theoretical price which is equal to the market traded price. At this point, we have determined the implied volatility for this particular option.

While the Newton-Raphson iterative process is extremely efficient and will converge to the answer within only two or three iterations, the approach may not be appropriate for all kinds of options. For example, with simple European options, the method is quick and accurate. This is because the price/volatility relationship is a smooth, relatively linear curve. For other kinds of options including American options where a significant probability of early exercise exists or for complex options which have a kinked rather than a smooth price/volatility relationship, the technique may not work. For these types of options, another method is preferred which is the method of bisection.

The method of bisection does not require any estimation of vega and is in some ways simpler in that it is not sensitive to the choice of the starting level of the volatility. The method works by first choosing a "high" estimate of volatility which would correspond to an option value well below the current market price of the options. This input could be the lowest historical volatility that has been recorded for this asset. The "low" option value will be christened C_l and the actual option price is referred to as C_0. Next the analyst chooses a "high" estimate of volatility which would produce a theoretical option price which is well above the current option price C_0. Again, this input could be the highest historical volatility for the asset on record. This "high" option value is known as C_h.

The final step is to estimate the implied volatility as the linear interpolation between those two points. At this point, a new theoretical option price is calculated using the volatility at that point and if this is equal to the market traded price, then the process stops and the implied volatility has been found. Otherwise, the new estimate price is used as a new high or low guess and the process is repeated. Generally, this process is as quick as the Newton-Raphson iterative process and just as accurate. The formula for the iterations is:

$$\sigma_o = \sigma_1 + \left(C_o - C_1\right) \cdot \left(\sigma_h - \sigma_1\right) / \left(C_h - C_1\right)$$

where:

σ_0 is the estimated volatility for the next iteration
σ_l is the lowest volatility estimate
σ_h is the highest volatility estimate
C_0 is the actual market price of the option
C_l is the theoretical option price with σ_l
C_h is the theoretical option price with σ_h

Again, a picture is worth a thousand words and Figure 4.20 displays how the method of bisection would work for an exotic option which is known as a compound option that does not have a smooth price/volatility relationship but is kinked.

The method of bisection is at least as accurate as the Newton-Raphson technique and is indeed much faster because it is not necessary to estimate the vega of the option at each iteration. The method is also more general applying to all kinds of options contracts only requiring the user to specify the appropriate options valuation model. In summary, most computer systems used by traders of options will automatically produce the implied volatilities for the user. While, the reader may never need to program these formulae for the estimation of the implied volatilities into his computer, he should know what the program is doing. A major problem for a number of systems is that they were originally developed for simple European options or American options where there was no concern about early exercise. Thus, these models used the Newton-Raphson process. Then, these same systems were modified to evaluate more exotic options but without changing the method for determining the implied volatilities and upon occasion the resulting numbers were meaningless. Therefore, it is recommended that for all kinds of options the method

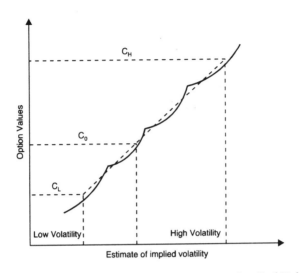

Figure 4.20 Example of Bisection Method for Estimating Implied Volatility.

of bisection be used so that the user can be fairly confident the resulting implied volatility will be of use.

But another fundamental problem that has arisen in the estimation of the implied volatility springs from the question: Which market traded options should I use to estimate the implied volatilities? If the assumptions which underlie most options pricing models are met, then the implied volatilities for all options given the same expiration date should be the same. That is only accurate if one assumes that the implied volatilities are an unbiased estimation of the true underlying volatility expected to occur from now until the expiration. In practice, these implied volatilities differ across strike prices for the same maturity and the analyst must choose which implied volatility to use. In Table 4.7 you will find a selection of the options that were available on 1 November 1993 for the options on the December BTP futures. The strike prices that were available on this day ran from 113.00 to 121.00. On this date the December futures closed at 115.47 and all of the prices presented in the table also reflect their closing prices. To the right of the prices for both the calls and puts is another column which has the heading **Implied Volatility** and this is the implied volatility for that particular option series. To the right of this column the amount of trades is indicated that occurred in that option series on that day. As the reader can see, each strike price has a different implied volatility and the resultant differences can be substantial. For example, the lowest implied volatility is 8.11% and the highest is 11.75%. Which one is right?

Given that the implied volatility is supposed to be the market wide guess of the future price dispersion, market practice attempts to arrive at a consensus of the consensus by applying weighting schemes to all the available implied volatilities that can be estimated so as to determine a composite volatility. The goal is to try to grasp the true opinion of the market as a whole.

	Call			Put		
Strike	**Price**	**Implied Volatility**	**Volume**	**Price**	**Implied Volatility**	**Volume**
110.00	5.53	0	11.75	0.06	0	11.75
110.50	5.04	0	11.20	0.07	0	11.20
111.00	4.56	0	10.86	0.09	3	10.86
111.50	4.07	0	10.15	0.10	0	10.15
112.00	3.59	0	9.59	0.12	0	9.59
112.50	3.13	0	9.28	0.16	0	9.28
113.00	2.70	0	9.22	0.23	4	9.22
113.50	2.29	0	9.11	0.32	0	9.11
114.00	1.90	0	8.93	0.43	56	8.93
114.50	1.54	0	8.75	0.57	51	8.75
115.00	1.23	184	8.71	0.76	214	8.71
115.50	0.94	1248	8.50	0.97	0	8.50
116.00	0.71	445	8.45	1.24	5	8.45
116.50	0.51	220	8.29	1.54	0	8.29
117.00	0.37	2411	8.35	1.90	0	8.35
117.50	0.25	115	8.24	2.28	0	8.24
118.00	0.16	0	8.11	2.69	0	8.11
118.50	0.11	625	8.24	3.14	0	8.24
119.00	0.08	60	8.51	3.61	0	8.51
119.50	0.05	205	8.51	4.08	0	8.51
120.00	0.04	0	8.94	4.57	0	8.94
120.50	0.03	0	9.24	5.06	0	9.24
121.00	0.02	0	9.35	5.55	0	9.35

Table 4.7 BTP Call & Put Prices, Trading Volume and Implied Volatilities.

Weighting of Implied Volatilities to Determine a Composite Estimate

There are many different kind of weighting schemes that are used to arrive at a composite volatility estimate. These methods can be roughly broken into three generic types:

(1) weighting by the percentage of the total trading volume that
     occurred in that option series relative to all options of that class,
(2) weighting the option series by how close it is to being
     at the money and,
(3) weighting the implied volatility of an options series
     depending on its vega.

Let us return to the BTP implied volatilities and see how we might arrive at a composite implied volatility. If we return to Table 4.7, it is important to consider that a number of the options with implied volatility estimates had no trading volume. For example, the 120 calls and puts did not have a single trade all day. So, where does the implied volatility number come from? From indicative bids or offers by market makers. Most of the trading volume occurred from the 115 to the 119.50 strike prices for the calls and from the 114 to 115 strike prices for the puts. If the implied volatilities are a good measure of what the expected volatility is supposed to be that is because the people who are trading options are betting on that volatility by putting real money on the table. As they say in my business, there is no better way to focus one's attention on a problem than to have serious money riding on the outcome.

Given this makes a certain amount of sense, then the only volatilities we should concern ourselves with are those where traders have taken a stake. The implied volatilities of the options which have the most trading volume should have the most weighting in the composite volatility because more traders put their money on those options. Those options with lesser volumes are counted less and options with no trading volume are ignored. Let see how this approach would be applied to the BTP options in Table 4.7. The results of the volume weighting scheme can be seen in Table 4.8.

Option Series	Option Price	Volume	W_i % of Total Volume	V_i Implied Volatility
115.00 call	1.23	184	3.15%	8.71%
115.50 call	0.94	1248	21.38%	8.50%
116.00 call	0.71	445	7.62%	8.45%
116.50 call	0.51	220	3.77%	8.29%
117.00 call	0.37	2411	41.30%	8.35%
117.50 call	0.25	115	1.97%	8.24%
118.50 call	0.11	625	10.71%	8.24%
119.00 call	0.08	60	1.03%	8.51%
119.50 call	0.05	205	3.51%	8.51%
113.00 put	0.23	4	0.07%	9.22%
114.00 put	0.43	56	0.96%	8.93%
114.50 put	0.57	51	0.87%	8.75%
115.00 put	0.76	214	3.67%	8.71%

Composite Volatility
$$= \Sigma \, W_i \cdot V_i = (0.0315 \cdot 8.71\%) + (0.2138 \cdot 8.50\%) +$$
$$(0.0762 \cdot 8.45\%) + (0.0377 \cdot 8.29\%) + (0.4130 \cdot 8.35\%) +$$
$$(0.0197 \cdot 8.24\%) + (0.1071 \cdot 8.24\%) + (0.0103 \cdot 8.51\%) +$$
$$(0.0351 \cdot 8.51\%) + (0.0007 \cdot 9.22\%) + (0.0096 \cdot 8.93\%) +$$
$$(0.0087 \cdot 8.75\%) + (0.0367 \cdot 8.71\%)$$
$$= \mathbf{8.415788\%}$$

Table 4.8 Weighting of Implied Volatility using Volume Weights.

This approach assumes that the options which trade the most will have the highest interest among traders and will thus possess the "fairest" prices. In this example, the composite volatility is being determined mostly by the 117.00, 115.50 and the 118.50 calls. The other options, especially the puts, would have almost no contribution to the estimation of the composite volatility.

This approach makes a lot of sense when volume information is available, but often this is not the case. For example, during a trading day, the volume for the individual option series may not be available (or at best it is estimated). It is only at the end of the day when all the trades are cleared that the volume figures will be released. Another problem is with OTC (over the counter) options where indicative option prices and volatilities may be provided but the amount of trading volume occurring between counterparties in the interbank market is impossible to determine in aggregate. How is it possible to weight volatilities without being able to discern if the interest for that option (and hence its volatility) in the market is real or just an indication? This can be done by employing a weighting scheme which magnifies the impact of the near to the money options and reduces the importance of out-of-the-money options. This technique is often call Distance Weighting.

If you believe that out of the money options should be ignored because their prices are distorted by the lack of liquidity and minimum price quotes, then this may be the technique for you. Here is a typical weighting factor formula you could apply:

If $|(F - E)/F| < 5\%$
then apply the weight $W_i = X_i / \Sigma X_i$
where:
$X_i = (|(F - E)/F| - 5\%)^2 / (5\%)^2$

If $|(F - E)/F| > 5\%$
then apply a weight of ZERO (0)

The results of the distance factor weighting for the determination of the composite implied volatility can be seen in Table 4.9. In this case, the analyst wishes to ignore all BTP options prices which are more than 5% away from the current market price of 115.47. Furthermore, as the strike moves further away from the current market price, its importance to the composite volatility estimate lessens. Here is an example of how this weighting scheme would work with our BTP implied volatility data of 1 November.

In this example, the composite volatility using the Distance Weighting Technique is 8.665% which is substantially different from the one arrived at using the volume weighting technique. The reader will notice that this technique will automatically weight most heavily the 115.50 calls and puts even though only a small percentage of trading volume occurred for these options on that day. Also, the 117.00 calls which represent 41.3% of the trading volume only have a weighting of 7% (0.070002) in the distance weighting technique. Thus, if you are using the distance weighting technique as a substitute for volume weighting this will only work if the most traded options are at the money and the volume trails off the further the strike price away from the current market price. If, as is the case in the BTPs, the volume is actually greater in the out-of-the-money options, the differences in the weighting techniques will be more extreme.

Option Series	Option Price	Out of the money	Wi Weighting Factor	Vi Implied Vol.
110.00 call	5.53	-4.737	0.000358	11.75
110.50 call	5.04	-4.304	0.002510	11.2
111.00 call	4.56	-3.871	0.006605	10.86
111.50 call	4.07	-3.438	0.012644	10.15
112.00 call	3.59	-3.005	0.020627	9.59
112.50 call	3.13	-2.572	0.030554	9.28
113.00 call	2.70	-2.139	0.042424	9.22
113.50 call	2.29	-1.706	0.056238	9.11
114.00 call	1.90	-1.273	0.071996	8.93
114.50 call	1.54	-0.840	0.089697	8.75
115.00 call	1.23	-0.407	0.109343	8.71
115.50 call	0.94	0.025	0.128238	8.50
116.00 call	0.71	0.458	0.106883	8.45
116.50 call	0.51	0.892	0.087471	8.29
117.00 call	0.37	1.325	0.070002	8.35
117.50 call	0.25	1.758	0.054478	8.24
118.00 call	0.16	2.191	0.040897	8.11
118.50 call	0.11	2.624	0.029260	8.24
119.00 call	0.08	3.057	0.019567	8.51
119.50 call	0.05	3.490	0.018170	8.51
120.00 call	0.04	3.923	0.006011	8.94
120.50 call	0.03	4.356	0.002149	9.24
121.00 call	0.02	4.789	0.000230	9.35

Composite Volatility

$= \Sigma\, W_i \cdot V_i = (0.000358 \cdot 11.75) + (0.00251 \cdot 11.2) +$
$(0.006605 \cdot 10.86) + (0.012644 \cdot 10.15) + (0.020627 \cdot 9.59)$
$+ (0.030554 \cdot 9.28) + (0.042424 \cdot 9.22) + (0.056238 \cdot 9.11)$
$+ (0.071996 \cdot 8.93\,) + (0.089697 \cdot 8.75) + (0.109343 \cdot 8.71)$
$+ (0.128238 \cdot 8.5) + (0.106883 \cdot 8.45) + (0.087471 \cdot 8.29) +$
$(0.070002 \cdot 8.35) + (0.054478 \cdot 8.24) + (0.040897 \cdot 8.11) +$
$(0.02926 \cdot 8.24) + (0.019567 \cdot 8.51) + (0.011817 \cdot 8.51) +$
$(0.006011 \cdot 8.94) + (0.002149 \cdot 9.24) + (0.00023 \cdot 9.35)$

$= \mathbf{8.665\%}$

Table 4.9 Weighting of Implied Volatility using Distance Factors.

Option Series	Option Price	Option Vega	Wi Weighting Factor	Vi Implied Vol.
110.00 call	5.53	0.0536	0.018542	11.75
110.50 call	5.04	0.0615	0.021275	11.2
111.00 call	4.56	0.0741	0.025634	10.86
111.50 call	4.07	0.0829	0.028678	10.15
112.00 call	3.59	0.0962	0.033279	9.59
112.50 call	3.13	0.1161	0.040163	9.28
113.00 call	2.70	0.1418	0.049054	9.22
113.50 call	2.29	0.1668	0.057702	9.11
114.00 call	1.90	0.1895	0.065555	8.93
114.50 call	1.54	0.2085	0.072128	8.75
115.00 call	1.23	0.2165	0.074895	8.71
115.50 call	0.94	0.2262˙	0.078251	8.50
116.00 call	0.71	0.2212	0.076521	8.45
116.50 call	0.51	0.2066	0.071471	8.29
117.00 call	0.37	0.1853	0.064102	8.35
117.50 call	0.25	0.1574	0.05445	8.24
118.00 call	0.16	0.1264	0.043726	8.11
118.50 call	0.11	0.1009	0.034905	8.24
119.00 call	0.08	0.0831	0.028125	8.51
119.50 call	0.05	0.0598	0.020687	8.51
120.00 call	0.04	0.0496	0.017158	8.94
120.50 call	0.03	0.0395	0.013665	9.24
121.00 call	0.02	0.029	0.010032	9.35

Composite Volatility

$= \sum W_i \cdot V_i = (0.018542 \cdot 11.75) + (0.021275 \cdot 11.2) +$
$(0.025634 \cdot 10.86) + (0.028678 \cdot 10.15) + (0.033279 \cdot 9.59)$
$+ (0.040163 \cdot 9.28) + (0.049054 \cdot 9.22) + (0.057702 \cdot 9.11)$
$+ (0.065555 \cdot 8.93) + (0.072128 \cdot 8.75) + (0.074895 \cdot 8.71)$
$+ (0.078251 \cdot 8.5) + (0.076521 \cdot 8.45) + (0.071471 \cdot 8.29) +$
$(0.064102 \cdot 8.35) + (0.05445 \cdot 8.24) + (0.043726 \cdot 8.11) +$
$(0.034905 \cdot 8.24) + (0.028125 \cdot 8.51) + (0.020687 \cdot 8.51) +$
$(0.017158 \cdot 8.94) + (0.013665 \cdot 9.24) + (0.010032 \cdot 9.35)$

$= \mathbf{8.883\%}$

Table 4.10 Weighting of Implied Volatility using Vega Weights.

The final weighting scheme that is applied for determining a composite volatility is to use the vega of the options as the weighting for the importance of their contribution to the whole. The logic is that since the values of certain options are more sensitive to the correct measure of volatility than others, it can be argued that these options should be weighted more heavily than the implied volatilities of those options that are less sensitive to volatility. Since the vega is the measure of this sensitivity it will determine the weighting scheme for the composite estimation. As an example, we will once again use the BTP options from 1 November. In this case we will take the total vega of holding all options in the available quoted series (traded or otherwise) and divide each option's vega to arrive at the weighting scheme. This can be seen in Table 4.10.

As the reader can see, the new composite volatility estimate of 8.883% is also totally different from the earlier estimation. However, since a vega for an option is maximised when the option is at the money (for the same maturity options) then this weighting scheme acts in a similar manner to the distance weighting scheme discussed earlier.

After all this weighting business, one may stop and ask why we would we want to weight all these implied volatilities to get one number. One possible reason is that for revaluation purposes only one volatility input would be required for determination of the theoretical profit and loss of the positions held open. Another reason could be that perhaps the composite volatility is a better predictor of the future actual volatility. But the very existence of different volatilities at different strike prices for the same underlying asset and maturity should be a serious cause for concern.

The analysis of how the implied volatilities differ both across the strike prices and maturities has spawned a whole new area of volatility research. Thus, the next chapter will devote most of the coverage to this problem of non-constant implied volatilities with the introduction of volatility smiles and the term structure of volatilities.

5: Advanced Issues
in Volatility Estimation

While the last chapter examined the standard approaches to volatility estimation, this chapter will cover more advanced issues and cutting edge developments in this area.

The general viewpoint regarding volatility estimation assumes that the Black and Scholes model accurately describes conditions in actual options markets. The major assumptions are that the prices of underlying assets evolve through time lognormally with a constant volatility σ at any time and market level. If this is the case, then the volatilities implied from the actual option prices in the market would be the same regardless of the strike price of the option or its maturity. The fact that the implied volatilities differ across strike prices for the same maturity and across diverse expiration periods has led many to question the efficacy of the traditional Black and Scholes methodology and all those pricing models based upon similar assumptions.

In the implied volatility section of the last chapter, I demonstrated that the implied volatilities are different across strike prices. However, one could adjust for these differences by applying a variety of weighting schemes to arrive at one composite volatility number. Unfortunately, it has become apparent that this technique may do more harm than help by the elimination of valuable information that could be understood by examining more closely the patterns of implied volatilities across strike prices and maturities instead of ignoring them. The current wisdom is (instead of simply estimating one implied volatility) to estimate the patterns of volatilities and then evaluate options prices versus these patterns.

This area is so important that it will not only require this entire chapter but will probably consume the minds of options theorists and market participants for years to come.

- Initially, we will examine how the implied volatilities form patterns both across strike prices and time. To do this we will introduce Volatility Matrices and examine them for a variety of markets.
- Then, we will concentrate on the patterns of implied volatilities for the same maturity which has been called the "Smile". In this section, we will show the reader not only how to estimate this pattern but to standardise it to allow the user to spot mispricing opportunities.
- I will continue the analysis by looking at the patterns of implied volatilities for different maturities for a variety of assets and examine why these patterns may exist.

- All this will lead us to a potential breakthrough in options pricing methodology. This is the development of a Supermodel for pricing options which incorporates the patterns of implied volatility both across strike prices and time.
- Finally, I will examine how the implications of volatility relationships through time are being exploited for the forecasting of volatility. In this section, I will introduce the concept of forward volatilities which may become an entirely new market as large as the markets for other kinds of forward contracts such as those on interest rates and foreign exchange.

THE VOLATILITY MATRIX

The easiest way to see how implied volatilities vary across strike prices and maturities is to gather all the data and then tabulate the volatilities across both dimensions. This is done using a volatility matrix which has become one of the most important tools in the repertoire of option traders and analysts. Such a volatility matrix is presented in Table 5.1 for options on the Financial Times 100 Stock Index Futures (FTSE) and for Over the Counter (OTC) options on the FTSE with expirations out to five years in duration.

	-30%	-20%	-10%	-5%	ATM	5%	10%	20%	30%
1 Month	25.75	22.00	19.00	17.75	16.50	16.00	15.50	14.75	14.00
3 Months	24.75	21.25	18.75	17.75	16.75	16.25	15.75	15.00	14.25
1 Year	22.50	20.25	18.50	17.75	17.25	16.75	16.25	15.50	14.75
2 Years	21.75	19.75	18.25	17.75	17.25	17.00	16.75	16.25	15.75
3 Years	21.5	20	19	18.5	17.75	17.5	17.25	17	16.75
4 Years	21	20.25	19.5	19	18.5	18	17.75	17.5	17
5 Years	21	20.75	20	19.25	18.75	18.25	18	17.75	17.25

Table 5.1 Volatility Matrix for Options on the FTSE Index.

The data for this matrix was compiled on 9 August 1994 and was kindly supplied by BZW, London[1]. In this table, the different implied volatilities are produced across a range of standardised strike price range and maturities. The implied volatility for the option series that has a strike price closest to the current market level is deemed the at-the-money or ATM option. This can be seen in the middle of the top line of the matrix. Thereafter, option strike prices in 10% increments are analysed up to 30% above and below the current level of the underlying FTSE market price. To aid the analysis, the results of the volatility matrix are often graphed to show the patterns that exist both across strikes and time. This has been produced in Figure 5.1. As the reader can see, almost all the implied volatilities are

---

[1]Many thanks to Niran de Silva and Leigh Baxendale of BZW, London for kindly providing this information.

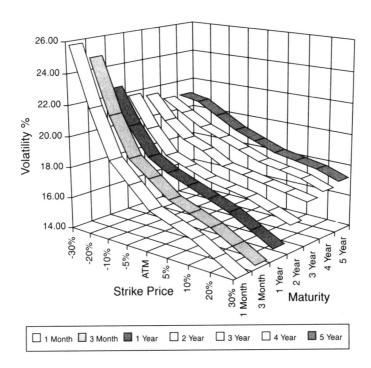

Figure 5.1 Volatility Smiles of Options on the FTSE Index.

different. For the same maturity, the further away from the ATM level one goes the more divergent the implied volatilities become.

In the graph, you can see that the shape of the pattern is curved upwards the lower one goes from the ATM. When the strike price is higher then the ATM level the implied volatility fall; Reaching the lowest level when the strike price is 30% above the current market price. For many markets (as we will soon see) this curved relationship is symmetrical. That is, the further away from the current underlying price one goes, the higher the implied volatility will be. When this is graphed it looks like a smile. Thus, the name for this pattern for the same maturity options is known as the "Volatility Smile" (☺).

Traditional options volatility analysis would imply: If significant differences in the implied volatilities between options on the same underlying asset exist, options would be mispriced and, therefore, would indicate a trading opportunity. In the old days, traders would scan their computers for these anomalies, buying all "cheap" options with low implied volatilities and selling "dear" options with high implied volatilities. However, no matter how long they did this, the anomalous patterns of different implied volatilities would persist. Why was it that these patterns continued to exist? These are patterns, where out of the money options (especially those with lower strike prices that the current underlying market price) have volatilities considerably higher than the ATM implied volatilities. Generally, there are three explanations given for this effect.

(1) The first explanation is that the inflated implied volatilities for deep out-of-the-money options are due to the existence of a disproportionally large bid and offer spread for these options relative to the ATM options. For example, if a deep out of the money option has a theoretical value of 0.02 and the bid price is 0.01 offered at 0.03, the evaluation of the implied volatility at a price of 0.03 will lead to a much higher implied volatility for that option than at its fair price. Because the theoretical options pricing models cannot incorporate transaction costs or the bid/offer spread then this will exaggerate the impact of the implied volatility result from inverting the options pricing model.

(2) The second explanation is that options prices are only partly determined by the theoretical assumptions which underlie options pricing methodology. Another factor could be the supply and demand for leverage that these out-of-the-money options offer to speculators. On the other hand, the sellers of options will be devastated when the out-of-the-money options become in-the-money and will only sell them if they receive a minimum amount for their trouble. There is an old adage in the options market that one should never sell an option for less than 2 ticks. If this is the case, then it could be that the actual options prices and their associated implied volatilities could be much higher than the fair price and "fair" volatility of the option.

(3) The third explanation and the one that is gaining more credence is that the market does not believe that the dispersion of the underlying asset follows a lognormal distribution. There are a wide variety of possible distributions that could be followed depending on:
   • if the market expects a skewed distribution
   (such as can be seen in the volatility matrix for the FTSE) or,
   • that the markets will either not move at all or will experience explosive price changes (like crashes).

This situation which often occurs in real markets is called leptokurtosis, where there are higher probabilities of the markets either staying put or moving well beyond 2 standard deviations. This is portrayed in Figure 5.2 relative to the lognormal distribution.

It is clear that all these factors could combine to cause the implied volatility patterns to deviate from what would be expected from the assumptions of the traditional option pricing models. As was stated before, these models would assume that the volatilities would all be at the same level across the strike prices and over time. It is interesting that these effects are different in different markets yielding implied volatility patterns that are unique to each.

In today's more sophisticated markets, rather than simply buying options with the lowest implied volatilities and selling options with the highest implied volatili-

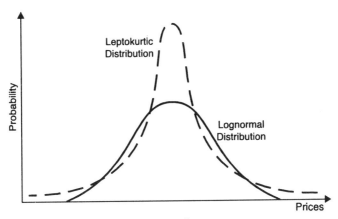

Figure 5.2 Lognormal and Leptokurtic Distribution.

ties, traders are comparing the option implied volatilities to their historical smile relationships to then assess if they are "cheap" or "expensive". With this thought in mind, I will show the reader a methodology allowing assessment of mispriced options not relative to a single implied volatility but rather to the smile pattern of implied volatilities for that particular underlying asset.

VOLATILITY SMILES FOR VARIOUS MARKETS

Analysis of the Smile Pattern for the FTSE

When we carefully consider the patterns of implied volatility in Figure 5.1, they clearly indicate that the options on the FTSE imply greater than "lognormal" chances of extreme movements, especially downwards. This can be deduced because lower strike prices' implied volatilities are so much higher than both those of ATM and higher strike price options. This indicates a bias in the marketplace for a higher probability of a significant collapse compared to a significant explosion to the upside. It is interesting that this kind of shape only appeared recently. In the old days, the volatility patterns were fairly flat or at least symmetrical. However, everything changed in October 1987 with the great stock market meltdown. The fact that extreme downward moves in the index have been proven to be more severe than extreme upward moves is supported by the historical data. Almost all index options world-wide have this downward skew in their smiles which reflect the fear by sellers (and greed of speculators) that they will more likely be hurt (profit) from out-of-the-money puts than they will from out-of-the-money calls. However, this does not imply that this offers a low risk trading strategy by selling out-of-the-money puts (which are over valued) and using the proceeds to buy out-of-the-

157

money calls (which are supposedly undervalued) as anyone who has watched the dramatic FTSE collapse in the first half of 1994 could observe.

Many market participants compare the differences between the lognormal probabilities and the implied probabilities coming from the options prices. To estimate the lognormal probabilities, one must input the implied volatility of the ATM option and let a computer package such as EXCEL™ generate all the probabilities. According to Bill Margrabe, now at Solomon Brothers, "If the lognormal curve says there's a 1% chance that stock will go above 110 at expiration, and the smile [probabilities] shows the chance is 10%, it is a strong statement of market expectation[2]". Indeed, smile patterns are now being included in the Technical Analysis of underlying asset prices to provide more objective probability estimates of certain prices being reached at defined points in the future.

The FTSE smile tells us that a different kind of probability distribution exists in the minds of those that trade these options than the lognormal probability distribution. Also, the further out in time one goes, the implied volatility of the option markets becomes higher. If it is true that the smile is skewed because of the fear an eventual crash will occur, then the longer the time to go (and the more potential for the ultimate economic day) the higher the probability that a crash will indeed happen. This could explain the increasing implied volatilities out in time. However, as we move further out in time, the smile seems to be flattening. Only as we start approaching the final maturity of the option do the curves of the smile turn from a gentle pout to a maniacal grin. This same pattern will appear for other assets that I will examine now.

Analysis of the Smile Pattern for US Dollar/Deutsche Mark

In Table 5.2 and Figure 5.3, the reader will find a volatility matrix and accompanying graph for US Dollar/Deutsche Mark options. The information for this matrix is based upon implied volatilities from 9 August 1994.[3] The data for this matrix only goes out for one year but after that the pattern does not change all that much. In this case, the smile pattern across the strike prices is more symmetrical for both higher and lower strike prices. Furthermore, if we go further out in time, the implied volatilities also rise (as occurred for the FTSE). What do these patterns mean?

It has been shown in many empirical studies that the movements in the foreign exchange markets are neither normally nor lognormally distributed. The chance for big moves is relatively high as is the probability of no movement at all. This may be due in part to the existence of Central Banks that intervene periodically to "stabilise" markets. However, whenever the Central Banks beat the market, it was

---

[2]Quotation from an Article in the May 1994 Futures Magazine, "Mining for value in option pits" by Miriam Bensman, page 30.
[3]The data for the US Dollar/Deutsche Mark volatility matrix was kindly supplied by Paul Akeroyd of a London currency options brokerage house. Many thanks.

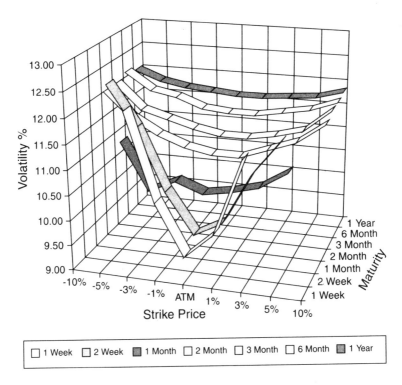

Figure 5.3 Volatility Smiles of the Options on US Dollar/Deutsche Mark.

because the level of the exchange rate was not to their liking and they suddenly and aggressively knocked it back to a level they felt to be more appropriate. If this does not work, the market sits at the current level until the Central Banks give up. When the Battle of the Titans (Central Banks vs. "The Market") is over, the exchange rate tumbles anyway as the markets lose confidence in the ability of the Central Banks to maintain order. This happened to the Bank of England in September 1992 when the Pound departed the ERM in a rather ignominious manner.

	-10%	-5%	-3%	-1%	ATM	1%	3%	5%	10%
1 Week			12.20	10.50	9.50	10.00	11.50		
2 Weeks		12.50	11.70	10.50	9.70	10.00	11.00	11.70	
1 Month		11.20	10.25	10.50	10.30	10.40	10.55	10.90	
2 Months	12.00	11.50	11.20	11.00	10.90	10.90	11.10	11.30	11.70
3 Months	12.00	11.50	11.35	11.20	11.10	11.10	11.20	11.35	11.80
6 Months	12.10	11.75	11.65	11.45	11.40	11.40	11.50	11.60	11.80
1 Year	12.00	11.80	11.70	11.65	11.60	11.60	11.65	11.70	11.85

Table 5.2 Dollar-Deutsche Mark Volatility Matrix.

But the possibility of extreme movements can be equally on the upside and downside because the collapse of the Pound in September 1992 was also an equivalent rallying of the Deutsche Mark. In this case, when the intervention works, the currency will shoot back to a better level (from the Central Bank's viewpoint) and if it fails, the currency will shoot the other way. This may be one reason for the smile at one maturity as traders simply adjust the prices of out-of-the-money options to reflect this factor. But why do implied volatilities rise the further out in time we go?

It may very well be that the longer term volatility for the US Dollar vs. Deutsche Mark is normally higher than that which is currently implied by option contracts maturing in the next few months. The rising pattern for the long dated implied volatilities could simply suggest that the volatilities are returning to their longer term average. Another possible explanation is that the markets expect that sooner or later some extreme economic event will once again occur and the markets will be disrupted. If this is the explanation, then the "Boogie Man will eventually get me" viewpoint could be leading to a higher volatility further out in time.

Analysis of the Smile Pattern for US Interest Rates

In Table 5.3 and Figure 5.4, the reader will find a volatility matrix and accompanying graph for options on US Interest Rates. Again, this data is taken from the implied volatilities of the underlying instruments as of 9 August 1994. These implied volatilities are those associated with Interest Rate Cap Agreements which are simply a string of options on interest rates. While these financial products will be discussed in some detail in Chapter 12 of this book, it will suffice to say that caps are OTC options on interest rates and financial institutions offer them to clients essentially as interest rate insurance policies.[4]

	-20%	-15%	-10%	-5%	ATM	5%	10%	15%	20%
1 Month			21	19.06	18.2	20.6	23		
4 Months		18.88	17.42	18.07	17.97	17.14	17.14	16.98	
7 Months		21	20.4	19.2	18.87	18.69	18.11	17.81	
1 Year	21.72	21.62	21.61	21.58	21.5	21.37	21.34	21.26	
2 Years	22.72	22.62	22.59	22.54	22.5	22.48	22.46	22.44	22.41
3 Years	21.75	21.75	21.75	21.75	21.75	21.75	21.75	21.75	21.75
4 Years	21.5	21.5	21.5	21.5	21.5	21.5	21.5	21.5	21.5
5 Years	20.75	20.75	20.75	20.75	20.75	20.75	20.75	20.75	20.75
7 Years	19.75	19.75	19.75	19.75	19.75	19.75	19.75	19.75	19.75
10 Years	18	18	18	18	18	18	18	18	18

Table 5.3 Volatility Matrix for Options on the US Interest Rates.

---

[4]This data was supplied by Intercapital Brokers, USA and was facilitated by Richard Mannell.

Cap Agreements are generally limited to a minimum of a one year term and extend out to as long as 10 years in duration. So in this case it is not possible to draw a volatility smile for any short time period using the implied volatilities of Interest Rate Caps. However, one can get the implied volatilities from the equivalent products which trade on exchanges. These products are options on Eurodollar futures which I will cover later in Chapter 8. It sufficient at this point, if the reader understands that both Cap Agreements and Options on Eurodollar futures both allow traders to benefit from changes in London Interbank Offer (Interest) Rates for US Dollars. The only difference between the two products is the maturities of the options and that Eurodollar options are exchange traded instruments whereas and the Cap Agreements are OTC products. Therefore, I have included these options with maturities of 1 month, 4 months and 7 months in addition to the Cap Agreement volatilities for comparisons sake.[5]

Now the reader will see a totally different pattern for the smiles as well as for the term structure when compared either to the FTSE options or the US

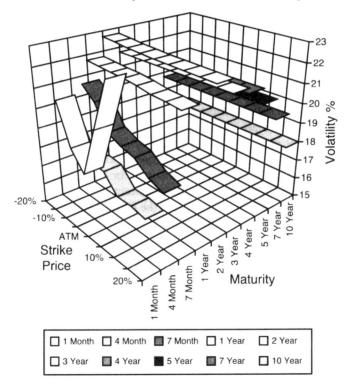

Figure 5.4 Volatility Smiles of the Options on US Interest Rates.

---

[5]It was not possible to include more Eurodollar option maturities in the analysis because in August 1994, when this chapter was composed, the available implied volatilities for the Eurodollar Options were only for September 1994, December 1994 and March 1995 expirations.

Dollar/Deutsche Mark options shown previously. While it is clear that the shorter dated interest rate options do display a curved smile relationship the pattern is completely different to either of the markets so far examined. If we go out further in time, the volatility will rise until one year and thereafter fall. Finally, from one year out to ten years, the curvature of the smile is almost non-existent. For these longer maturity options, a flat volatility pattern would suggest that the assumption of a lognormal dispersion process for interest rates is reasonable.

Why the smile curves are more pronounced for short dated options will be discussed later in this chapter. However, it is curious that in these markets, the implied volatility is decreasing the longer the maturity of the option. Does this imply that the risk is dropping out in time? Maybe so, but most probably not. A more likely explanation of this effect will be offered later and it has to do with both interest rates and volatility tending back to a long term average value.

THE CONSTRUCTION OF THE VOLATILITY MATRIX FOR BTP OPTIONS

In all of these examples, the volatility matrices have been constructed at a particular point in time to allow a comparison of the relative levels of the implied volatilities and the smile structures. The problem is that this matrix can only be used on that one day, for tomorrow the entire structure may change. As an example, the reader is referred to the chart in Figure 5.5 which is a different kind of three dimensional graph. This graph which is produced by the Research Department at the LIFFE displays the smile structure for the options on the December 1993 BTP futures. This also shows the smile pattern that existed for every day from 20 October until 18 November 1993. One thing that can be discerned from the graph is that the smile structure changes through time. As with the FTSE example portrayed earlier, the smile is skewed to the downside but seems to become more symmetrical and more "smiley" near 18 November which is the expiration of the option.

Apart from this, I find these kinds of charts very difficult to interpret. This is because the scale at the front lists a fixed range of strike prices and I never know where the underlying BTP was on that day to determine which options were at-the-money. Secondly, the overall level of the implied volatilities could be rising or falling which would make the curvature of the smile appear greater or lesser than the picture demonstrates. Finally, and this is my major concern, the graph tells me nothing about the future smile shapes that should occur for the BTP.

The FTSE Volatility Matrix portrayed in Table 5.1 is constructed with a standardising methodology that uses smile information from the past to determine what the smile patterns should be in the future. Thus, the goal of estimating the smile structure must be to construct a consistent and predictable method for both pricing the options and identifying mispricing opportunities. In this section, I will take the reader step by step through my own methodology for the construction of a volatil-

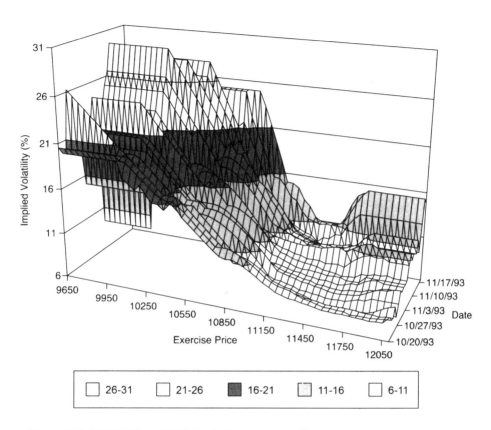

Figure 5.5 LIFFE Plot of BTP Smile Patterns over Time.

ity smile estimation procedure for options on BTP futures. I have chosen this market because the only meaningful volumes that currently trade are for the nearby options and thus, the analysis will only require following 96 calendar days (which corresponds to roughly 72 trading days) of changing smile relationships. However, this methodology can be extended to any markets the reader may be interested in.

The story begins with a real consultancy problem faced by one of my company's Italian clients that wanted to begin market making on BTP options. A major problem was that they did not have a clue as to how to estimate the volatility. Having looked at the three dimensional graphs that came from LIFFE (Figure 5.5), I felt that this was interesting but still would not allow the trader to use the information to properly assess future implied volatility smile structures for the pricing of options. As with all such problems, I went back to the data and started playing around. The first thing I did was to draw the smiles myself and the first one was drawn from the data in Table 4.7 of the last chapter. Since a smile is simply constructed by plotting the implied volatilities for all the individual options relative to the strike prices, the reader can see that the curvature of a smile is apparent. The

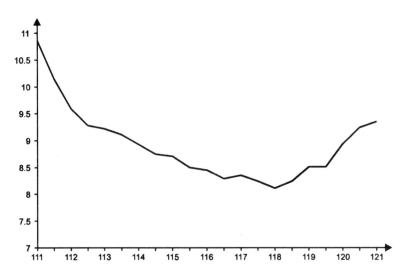

Figure 5.6 BTP Option Volatility Smile 1 November 1993.

smile graph for 1 November 1993 appears in Figure 5.6. While this is an interesting artefact of what happened on that day, my objective was to see if this information could be used to predict what the smile structure should be on any other day. To see if this pattern could be used for prediction, it was necessary to look at smile patterns on other days to see if they were similar. Having first seen the LIFFE graph in Figure 5.5, I already guessed they would be different.

Figure 5.7 shows the three dimensional patterns of smile structures not day by day but every two weeks approximately from the beginning to end of the lives of the options for the December 1993, March 1994 and June 1994 BTP futures.

Problems immediately became apparent: Firstly, the smile structures change over time becoming more extreme the closer one comes to expiration. Secondly, because the levels of volatility are varying constantly, it is not possible to directly compare the relative levels of implied volatilities to the level of the ATM volatility. Finally, because the underlying BTP futures price was moving around throughout the period, drawing each smile relative to the same fixed strike prices is misleading because the strike associated with the ATM option (and the bottom of the smile supposedly) will be moving around with the price of the underlying BTP. In short, I was no closer to my goal of being able to discern systematic patterns in the evo-lution of the smile patterns for BTPs (than is already provided by the LIFFE graphs). What I needed was some standardisation.

To allow the use of historical smiles patterns for the estimation of the implied volatility levels for pricing options in the future, historical smiles must be standard-ised relative to both the current level of the underlying asset and to the absolute level of the volatilities across the strike prices. This can be achieved through the creation of what I have called: a Volatility Smile Index (VSI).

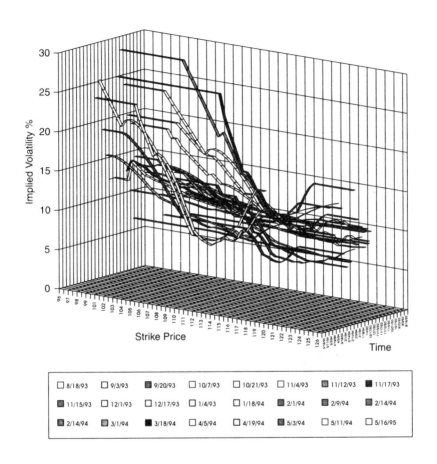

Figure 5.7 Plot of BTP Smile Patterns at Two Week Intervals.

The steps in the construction of this index are as follows. For every day that the smile structure is estimated, the actual strike prices are replaced by a relative strike price index constructed by dividing that strike price by the current price of the underlying asset. The strike price/current underlying price ration which is closest to 1.0 is defined as being at-the-money (ATM). This technique standardises all strike prices in the smiles so that they can be compared to the same relative distance from the current market price.

The second problem is that the implied volatilities are at different levels through time and must also be standardised to allow comparison of smile structures through time. This was done simply by dividing the volatilities at each relative strike price by the volatility of the ATM option and then multiplying by 100. Once

165

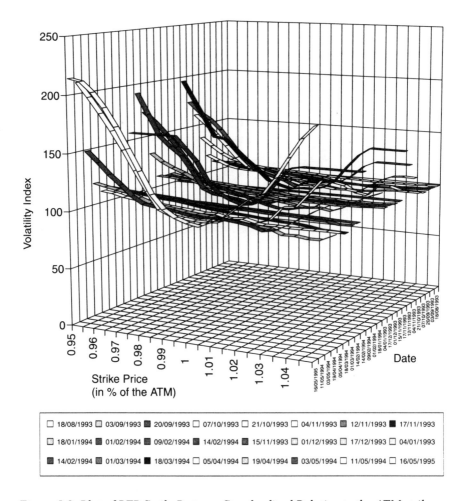

Figure 5.8 Plot of BTP Smile Patterns Standardised Relative to the ATM strike.

these steps are done, the major difficulties in comparing smiles over time have been overcome. The results of this can be seen in Figure 5.8 again for the three BTP futures expirations. Even when these have been standardised, the reader can see they change through time. So once again, it seemed the analysis was stuck. But then I saw it: the volatilities for the same underlying were different through time because each smile structure was for options with different days to expiration.

If I compared not the smile structures for the same underlying BTP futures contract through time but instead compared smile structures across different underlying BTP futures contracts all with the same time to expiration, a consistent pattern emerged. Figure 5.9 displays this and the reader can begin to see that there is some consistency if

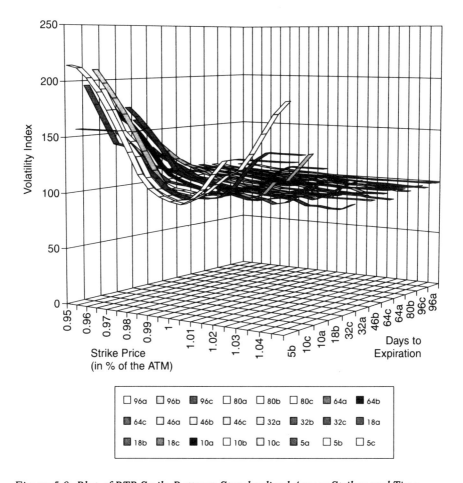

Figure 5.9 Plot of BTP Smile Patterns Standardised Across Strikes and Time.

the time to expiration is held constant across the three underlying contracts.

Given the relative stability of the volatility smile graph when compared at the same point in time, an index of the volatility smile patterns can now be constructed. This is done by averaging the standardised smile patterns for the same period to expiration. I then use this general pattern to estimate the appropriate volatility input that should be used for pricing options at any relative strike price, and at any time between 96 days to expiration, until the final expiry date for the options is reached. Figure 5.10 shows the VSI plotted over time.

All the analyst needs to do is to input the ATM implied volatility and the number of calendar days to expiration. The expected smile structure is automatically reproduced based upon the average of the historical smile relationships at compa-

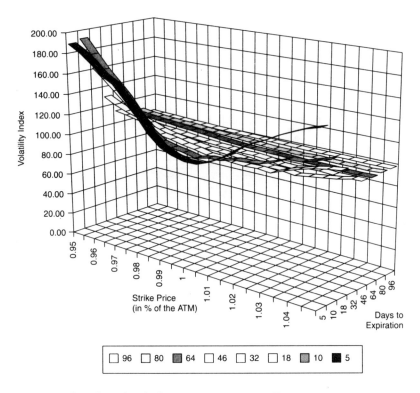

Figure 5.10 Plot of VSI levels for BTP Options over Time.

rable periods in the past. Let us say that the analyst needs to determine the volatility for an out-of-the-money option to either determine the fair price of the option or to evaluate if a traded option is mispriced. He simply applies the following simple formula:

$$V_{est} = VSI \ / \ 100 \cdot V_{ATM}$$

where:
  V_{est} is the Volatility of the Strike Price Option
       the Trader wishes to Estimate for Pricing
  VSI is the Historical Volatility Smile Index level
       for that Maturity of the Option & Relative Strike Level
  V_{ATM} is the Current Implied Volatility of the ATM option
       with the same maturity as the Option to be Analysed

To illustrate better how this would work, I will present an example. Suppose on 22 July 1994, a trader wishes to determine the fair price of a 115.50 call option when the current underlying price of the BTP September futures is 113.00. To determine the fair price, he must estimate the volatility of this out-of-the-money option.

(1) The first step is to estimate the implied volatility of the ATM 113.00 call option using the techniques outlined in the last chapter.

(2) Then this result is multiplied by the VSI/100.

To find the VSI number, we must consider that the calendar days to maturity for the BTP option are 32 and the strike price ratio to the underlying market price is 115.50/113.00 or 1.02212. The actual ATM implied volatility for both the 113.00 call and put options is 10.03%.[6] All we need to find now is the VSI value for a relative strike factor of 1.02212 with 32 days until expiration. In Table 5.4 you will find a table of VSI factors with the relative strike price ratios from 0.95 to 1.05 and various maturities from 96 days to 5 days until expiration.

	Calendar Days to Expiration							
	96	80	64	46	32	18	10	5
0.950	103.65471	108.07722	110.12044	112.47089	129.44986	160.90153	191.85215	188.82789
0.955	103.37042	106.61180	109.18219	110.53562	123.84854	152.17089	178.46722	182.37051
0.960	103.04133	105.61850	108.11665	108.01899	119.37399	142.35229	165.67436	173.71642
0.965	102.48635	104.91647	107.05204	106.72563	115.91949	132.38735	154.69432	163.81373
0.970	101.91531	104.07150	106.24402	105.27059	112.35224	121.55067	143.00215	158.12317
0.975	101.66494	103.80624	104.95145	104.69692	108.47448	112.33353	128.53076	145.51046
0.980	101.01518	102.74655	104.17328	103.47757	105.48091	108.76237	114.87283	132.79597
0.985	100.83251	102.03658	103.12307	102.19110	103.71003	107.00511	107.27183	118.08844
0.990	100.65137	101.32229	101.91299	101.21845	101.83819	104.30409	104.50305	107.98163
0.995	100.30873	100.67838	100.83664	100.49523	100.30219	102.53821	102.74025	103.01352
1.000	100.00000	100.00000	100.00000	100.00000	100.00000	100.00000	100.00000	100.00000
1.005	99.64831	99.03872	99.35470	98.51144	99.18363	99.56841	102.77990	100.33814
1.010	99.45639	98.30035	98.94128	98.63234	98.07143	98.48138	103.18979	104.91272
1.015	99.13330	98.22372	98.58074	97.46020	96.74873	97.82924	106.50671	112.17457
1.020	98.84820	97.89412	98.01636	95.22635	**96.12154**	98.39116	107.30834	121.40771
1.025	98.76303	98.50931	97.23315	94.80851	**96.12358**	97.24205	108.69275	129.31247
1.030	98.81352	97.92894	97.32414	97.71109	94.52361	102.15715	112.87250	134.76649
1.035	98.75440	97.72511	97.17207	98.15440	96.36174	106.06436	118.38262	141.76397
1.040	98.58212	97.90174	96.75652	97.26481	98.25709	109.67157	118.64987	147.31585
1.045	98.65629	97.53401	96.83494	97.58214	100.07376	112.12381	122.62518	152.68767
1.050	98.59062	98.45206	97.31839	97.71888	103.04208	113.73148	126.62228	156.42442

Table 5.4 The VSI matrix for Options on BTP Futures.

Since the days to expiration are exactly 32 days, we simply read down the 32 day column until we find the VSI factor associated with the relative strike price ratio of 1.022123. Unfortunately, there is not a relative strike price ratio which exactly corresponds to this value. However, the relative strike price ratio is between 1.02 and 1.025. To aid the reader find these VSI factors, the two VSI factors for

---

[6]This is due to put-call parity.

these relative strike price ratios of 1.02 and 1.025 have been bolded. Since our ratio is between these factors, a simple linear extrapolation is performed to find exactly our VSI factor. This is done in the following way:

$$VSI_{1.022123} = VSI_{1.02} + (VSI_{1.025} - VSI_{1.02}) \cdot \frac{(1.022123 - 1.02)}{(1.025 - 1.02)}$$

$$VSI_{1.022123} = 96.1215 + 0.00204 \cdot \frac{0.02123}{0.05}$$

$$VSI_{1.022123} = 96.12162$$

Having now determined the appropriate VSI for the 115.50 strike for 32 days to expiration, we simply put this into the formula to estimate the correct volatility for the estimation of the option's price.

$$V_{est} = VSI / 100 \cdot V_{ATM}$$

$$V115.50 = 96.12162 / 100 \cdot 10.03\%$$

$$V115.50 = 9.641\%$$

With the volatility estimate of 9.641% we can then apply an ordinary Black and Scholes type pricing model [actually in this case, the Black (1976)] and determine the "fair" price of the option to be 0.42 or 42 ticks.

Of course, this technique is somewhat cumbersome, requiring a lot of calculations to estimate the volatility for a single strike price (to say nothing of a wide range of strike prices). But this problem is easily solved by putting the above formulae and the VSI table into a computer program that will automatically extrapolate between calendar days and the relative strike price ratios. This is what we did ultimately for our Italian client, which as far as I know is the only participant in that market with this invaluable tool. As we understand, the bank has made good use of it in both market making and arbitrage.

IMPLICATIONS FOR THE EXISTENCE OF SMILES

As was stated earlier, the existence of smile patterns for the implied volatilities across strike prices indicates that something is fundamentally wrong with the assumption of a lognormal dispersion process for the price of the underlying asset. Having said that, the degree to which the lognormal distribution for asset prices produces incorrect results is not constant over time. For example, at 96 days to expiration, the smile pattern for BTP options is almost flat indicating that the lognormal distribution does coincide with the markets perception of price dispersion at that point in time. However, as we approach the expiration of the options, the smile first turns up to the left and the closer to expiration we come, the more both sides of the smile are curled upwards. This indicates that the shorter the time period to expiration, the less the lognormal distribution describes the market's perception of BTP price dispersion.

It is as if the market participants had a different distribution in their minds than that of the lognormal distribution. This can be deduced using the smile structures. Figure 5.11 shows the distributions implied by the smile structures for a variety of maturities relative to the lognormal distribution. One will immediately notice that at 96 days to expiration, the implied distribution is almost identical to the lognormal distribution. However, as we move closer to the expiration of the options, the more the implied distribution changes from the lognormal standard. In fact at expiration, the discrepancy is greatest with what clearly looks similar to a leptokurtic distribution.

If this pattern of implied distribution discrepancies is indeed consistent over time for the same number of days until expiration, then one should be able to build this information into a better pricing model. This is exactly what is being done and will be described in detail later in this chapter when I describe the recent development of the "Super" option pricing model.

Whether or not the reader has realised it, so far we have only been concentrating on analysing the distortions of the implied volatility structures at single points in time. While it is true that he may have examined how the "smiles" change over time, we have not examined in any great detail how the implied volatilities change

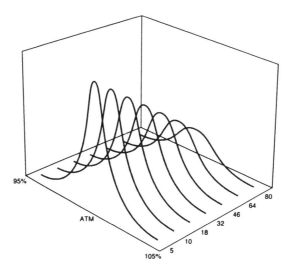

Figure 5.11 Implied Distributions for BTP Options over Time.

as the expiration of the options extends out in time. This is the topic of the next section of this chapter where I will examine how the implied volatility is distributed over time. This is known as the Term Structure of Volatility.

THE TERM STRUCTURE OF VOLATILITY

First, I will define what is meant by the term structure of volatility. When one uses a Black and Scholes model (or something similar) to determine implied volatilities of at-the-money options over a variety of expirations, one will then plot the resulting implied volatilities versus each respective expiration period. With these points, a curve can be fitted which will define the structure of volatilities over the term of the analysis and thus, the term structure of volatility. Let us look at a few examples.

From the volatility matrices presented earlier in this chapter, for the FTSE, US Dollar/Deutsche Mark and US interest rates, we can find the implied volatilities for the ATM options for all the available maturities. When these are plotted relative to the maturity of the options, the term structures can be evaluated. Figures 5.12a, 5.12b and 5.12c display the volatility term structures for options on these assets.

The reader will notice that both the FTSE and the US Dollar/Deutsche Mark term structures are upward sloping out in time, while the term structure for US interest rate volatilities initially rose and then sloped downwards. How could these types of patterns occur and why do they differ across different assets? To answer these questions, let us return to the typical volatility assumptions that underlie the pricing models which generate the implied volatilities. The first assumption is that volatility is a known constant and stationary, i.e., it does not change over time.

Clearly the evidence I have presented in these last two chapters refutes this. Secondly, volatility is homogeneous over time. Again this assumption is belied by the evidence in the last chapter regarding economic days which can be seen in Figure 4.10.

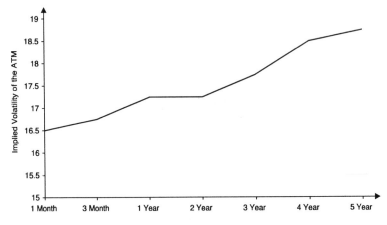

Figure 5.12a Term Structure of Volatility for FTSE Options.

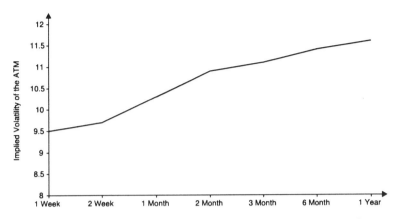

Figure 5.12b   Term Structure of Volatility for US Dollar/Deutsche Mark Options.

The final assumption is that uncertainty regarding the price of the underlying asset at expiration is directly proportional to the square root of the time to expiration. That means that the dispersion of the pellets from a shot gun will carry on infinitely until they hit the barn door, even if that barn door is hundreds of kilometres away.

These assumptions imply that the option pricing model is mis-specified (or in plain terms wrong) if the volatility is not at the same level over time. The evidence in Figures 5.12a, 5.12b and 5.12c clearly shows this not to be the case. This means we have major problems with the assumptions of the pricing models. What are the possible reasons why the term structure is not flat over time? There are three alternative explanations:

- Non-Stationarity in the Price Series
- Non-Uniformity of Volatility
- Mean Reversion of Volatility back to some Average.

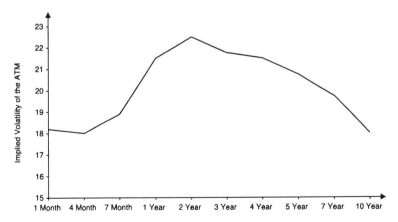

Figure 5.12c   Term Structure of Volatility for Options on US Interest Rates.

173

Non-Stationarity in the Price Series

What does non-stationarity mean? Basically, this says that the underlying economic fundamentals can change over time causing a permanent revision in the expected dispersion of the prices of the underlying assets. If analysts anticipate that some fundamental change will occur for some underlying asset in the future, then the implied volatilities of options will differ for expiration periods prior to and after the economic event occurs.

Economic events that would increase volatility could be such where some economic event changes a previously stable price relationship. For example, the Italian Lira volatility versus the other European currencies used to be extremely low. After the Lira fell out of the ERM mechanism, the volatility of the currency exploded versus the other currencies. If the Bank of Italy (Italian Central Bank) had intended to withdraw the currency from the ERM a few months before it actually occurred and informed the market of this intention, then the volatility of the Lira versus the other European currencies would have been low prior to this date and higher afterwards. This scenario would lead to an upward sloping term structure of volatility perhaps looking like the pattern in Figure 5.13.

Of course, the opposite situation could occur for a reduction in the volatility across maturities. Consider the Russian Rouble which is a highly volatile currency. The volatilities could drop dramatically if an announcement was made by the Russian government that the Rouble would be tied to the US Dollar in three months' time. Then the volatility of the Rouble versus, let us say, the Deutsche Mark would drop to the levels of US Dollar volatilities but would remain at the currently high level prior to the fixing point. This would lead to a downward sloping term structure of volatility that would drop precipitously after the fixing point in three months and remain at this level for options with expirations after that point. This might look like the pattern in Figure 5.14.

Both these figures indicate that an anticipated jump or drop in the implied volatilities would occur following the economic event. Before and after that date,

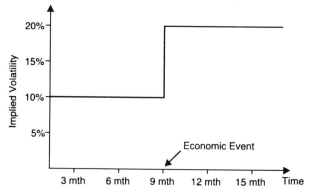

Figure 5.13 Effects of Non-Stationarity on the Term Structure of Volatility #1.

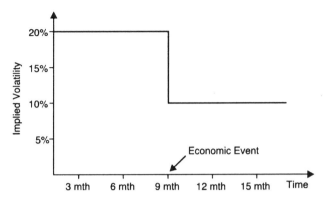

Figure 5.14 Effects of Non-Stationarity on the Term Structure of Volatility #2.

the volatility is assumed to be constant. In my years of experience, there has never appeared such a bizarrely shaped term structure of volatility. Therefore, I doubt that this kind of "one-off" non-stationarity explains the non-flat term structure of volatility. A major reason for this is that it is fairly rare that governments or corporations are as forthcoming with planned policy changes with specified time tables. Furthermore, it is even rarer that they can make these policy changes stick. What may happen is that the markets may expect some drastic economic event to occur but when this will happen is unknown. Thus, market participants may have either an upward sloping or downward sloping term structure of volatility if they are convinced a fundamental change will happen to the underlying market at some unknown point in the future.

Non-Uniformity of Volatility

Non-uniformity of volatility means that the actual volatility is expected to be different on different days depending on the economic events that occur (or the lack thereof) on certain days. We defined these higher than normal volatile days as Economic Days in the last chapter. In a similar vein to non-stationarity, volatility could be a function of the number and importance of economic events that are supposed to occur during the term of the option's life. The more economic events that are expected, the higher the volatility throughout time. What is the evidence for non-uniformity?

It is clear from the empirical results presented in the last chapter that volatility should be expected to be different on days when major economic events occur. The actual volatility is indeed higher on these days, while the volatility on days that are not trading days will be low or even zero. Such non-uniformity would lead to a term structure of volatility. The existence of non-uniformity would suggest that a difference does exist between economic time and calendar time. Economic time (or days) includes those days when significant economic events can take place and influence the price of the underlying asset. Calendar time is simply the number of days until the expiration of a particular option. The evidence for non-uniformity is extremely strong. Apart from the impact of economic days that was presented in the last chapter, two well known instances of market phenomena both support this hypothesis. The first is the Weekend Effect and the second is the Economic Statistics Effect.

The Weekend Effect is the curious result in many markets that the implied volatilities of the ATM call options tend to rise, on average, from before to after the weekend. Why would the implied volatilities be higher on Mondays compared to Fridays? It can not simply be that everyone world-wide hates Mondays. The most probable reason for this effect is that most users of the options pricing models that are determining the implied volatilities use calendar days as the time input into the model. The passage of the weekend represents a loss of calendar time instead of economic time. Therefore, the economic value of an option has not changed over the weekend. On the other hand the options pricing model does not distinguish between calendar days and economic days and the options pricing model would have expected the options price to have fallen due to the loss of the two calendar days. If the options price remains unchanged from Friday to Monday because nothing has happened, the implied volatility produced by the options pricing model has to increase to counterbalance the negative impact of the passage of calendar time. Therefore, it would appear that this effect supports the findings presented in the previous Chapter: While the marketplace does consider economic time, the popular Black and Scholes type pricing models do not. Economic time is the critical element in the volatility of markets, not calendar time.

The Economic Statistics Effect is the curious result that the implied volatilities of traded options tend to fall rather than rise after the release of important economic statistics. Sometimes on that day the actual volatility reflected by the price movements in the underlying asset will rise dramatically as the implied volatilities fall. How can this be? Again, the most probable answer is that the announcement of economic statistics represents the passage of economic time in addition to calendar time. However, the economic day that had passed results in a significant loss in the uncertainty the market had prior to the release. Said in another way, the loss of the economic day is more important in terms of time decay than of a non-economic day. However, the most utilised options pricing models do not recognise that a particularly important economic day has passed. As far as they are concerned, it was just another calendar day. The effective time decay caused by the passage of the economic day is so great that the pricing model can only counter-effect this more than expected loss in the option price by a reduction of the implied volatility associated with that option's price.

If markets are efficient and properly anticipate the impacts of economic time, then the implied volatility will incorporate this. As economic time passes, the drop in the implied volatility will be larger than that predicted by the simple passage of calendar time. This leads to the interesting and perhaps counter-intuitive result that the actual spot volatility may increase as the implied volatility decreases for those days when significant economic statistics are released.

It is most probable that the rising term structure effects seen for Stock Indices and in the Foreign Exchange markets are due to this effect of non stationarity in the underlying asset price series.

Mean Reversion of Volatility Back to some Average

This explanation is as it sounds: Volatility does not remain at extreme levels but will instead settle back to the long term average volatility for a given market. When the level of volatility is excessive relative to the long term average, the volatility is more likely to return to the "normal" level than to continue or extend the discrepancy relative to the average. Many examples of other economic time series also revert back to a long term mean value. These include government management of interest rate levels and Central Bank interventions in the currency markets. Therefore, it is unreasonable to assume that the statistical dispersion of asset prices will widen indefinitely as we move into the future. What effect would this have on the term structure of volatility? It could cause the term structure of volatility to be downward sloping the further out in time we go. When the reader refers back to the volatility matrices presented at the outset of this chapter, he will notice that only the US interest rate ATM option implied volatilities are lower the further out in time one goes. To find one possible cause for this effect, we must return to the shotgun and the barn door analogy.

As I suggested, if we go too far away from the barn door when we discharge our shotgun, the pellets will simply not travel far enough to hit the door. In the same way, the effective variance ($\sigma\sqrt{t}$) of an asset price cannot increase indefinitely as the option expiration lengthens. However the standard options pricing model does not know this. Therefore when the actual option prices are below what would be expected for the calendar time input into the model, the model can only deduce that the implied volatility must have gone down. Thus, the implied volatility has to decrease to counteract the effects of the increase in the time to expiration. The decline in the implied volatility is just a convenient way to artificially induce the mean reversion effect which is not built into any of the pricing models like Black and Scholes.

To correct for the fact that the pricing models are mis-specified, the analyst has two choices:

(1) The first is to continue using the standard options pricing model but to trick it by putting in different volatilities depending on the maturity of the options (or across different strikes).

(2) The other choice is to choose another kind of pricing model which incorporates the mean reversion process in its workings. If this is done, then a constant volatility can be made entered regardless of the maturity of the option.

Four popular option pricing models are used to solve for this kind of mean reversion assumption. These models have been developed for the interest rate markets since as our term structure for US interest rates shows, the volatilities are most probably reverting back to some long term average. The four models are the Ho and Lee Model[7], the Black, Derman and Toy Model[8], the Hull and White Model[9], and the Heath, Jarrow and Morton Model[10]. In Chapter 12 when I discuss Interest Rate Options, these models will all be discussed in some detail.

For all of these models, an adjustment is made that will "aim" at the same result. When Mean Reversion is perceived to occur, the assumed stochastic process driving that market must be adjusted. Just for reminders sake, the basic Wiener Process model for the movement of asset prices is:

$$\Delta S / S = \mu \Delta t + \sigma \sqrt{\Delta t}$$

An adjustment is made either to the mean (or drift) term, μ or to the volatility term, σ. The first three models adjust the mean term and the last model adjusts the volatility term. These adjustments allow the statistical dispersion of the terminal asset price (in these cases interest rates) to be dampened and rendered no longer simply proportional to the time to expiration.

It is as if one fires the shotgun and the pellets fail to hit the target on the barn door due to the effects of gravity pulling the heavy shot downwards. What is the solution? Either point the shotgun high enough to offset the effects of gravity (adjust the mean of the dispersion process) or get a shotgun with a longer barrel such that the dispersion of the pellets is reduced and more focused on the target (by adjusting the volatility). But as the reader might surmise these models have been specifically developed only to handle the mean reversion problem and mean reversion may not be the only reason why the term structure of volatility is not flat. Therefore, the models may be limited in correcting for all the factors causing the term structure to be sloping instead of flat.

CORRECTIONS FOR THE SMILE
AND TERM STRUCTURE OF VOLATILITY

Now for the first punch line of this section: What can the analyst do to correct for the fact that the assumption of constant volatilities in most pricing models is not valid? The answers depend on the kinds of options the analyst is trying to evaluate.

---

[7]Ho, Thomas, S. Y. and S.B. Lee, "Term Structure Movements and Pricing Interest Rate Contingent Claims," Journal of Finance, Vol. 41 (December 1986), pp: 1011-29.

[8]Black, Fischer, Emanuel Derman and William Toy, 1990, "A One-Factor Model of Interest Rates and its Application to Treasury Bond Options", Financial Analyst Journal (January-February 1990), pp. 33-39.

[9]Hull, John, and Alan White. "Pricing Interest-Rate-Derivative Securities. "The Review of Financial Studies, Vol. 3, No. 4 (1990), pp. 573-592.

[10]Heath, David, Robert Jarrow and Andrew Morton, 1990, "Bond Pricing and the Term Structure of Interest Rates: a New Methodology for Contingents Claims Valuation", Journal of Financial and Quantitative Analysis 25 (December 1990), pp. 419-440.

For simple standard options with relatively short time periods to expiration, the Volatility Smile Index approach with the input of the current ATM implied volatility will ameliorate the biases of the pricing models. Then, the modified volatility can be used to price the standard option with a regular options pricing model.

For longer dated options, it may not be possible to obtain a VSI number of the option: e.g. for an OTC (over-the-counter customized product) where it is difficult to get implied volatilities as a benchmark for comparison. The solution is to return to our old friend, historical volatility, and apply the techniques discussed in the last chapter in a rather clever way.

I was fortunate in my career to work with a gifted financial economist, Galen Burghardt, now at Dean Witter in Chicago, who came up with a solution to obtain volatilities for long dated, non-standardised options. His approach is universally known as the "Volatility Cone" technique.

THE VOLATILITY CONE

The basis for this approach is the assumption that the implied volatilities for options must reflect certain forecasts of what the actual market volatility will be over the remaining life of the option. If that is the case, then when evaluating the volatility input into an options pricing model, it would be fairly safe to say that this input would probably not exceed the highest actual volatility that had occurred over a comparable time period in the past or be below the lowest actual volatility that had ever occurred. All the analyst needs to do is find out what the range of actual volatility occurred in the past. This is how it is done:

(1) The analyst will select a variety of sample time horizons (for example one month, three months, one year and so forth) and then estimate the historical volatilities for these constant periods over time. In this way, a running series of one month historical volatilities will be estimated as each new month passes. If this is done for three years, then one will have a sample of historical volatilities to compare.

(2) Then the maximum, minimum and average volatilities will be estimated for the total sample of all historical volatilities which were estimated over the entire period of the analysis. In this way, the analyst can easily determine what the long term average volatility is for that sample time horizon and also the highest or lowest volatilities that have ever occurred.

The theory would say that the volatility estimate one would use to price an option would have to fall between the lowest and highest actual volatility levels that have occurred and would tend to the average level.

Table 5.5 shows an example of how such a volatility cone is constructed for the BTP futures market. I took the futures from the introduction of BTP futures in October 1991 until May 1994 as my estimation period. The sample time horizons are one month, two month, three month, six month and one year periods, respectively.

	1 Month %	2 Months %	3 Months %	6 Months %	1 Year %
01-Oct-91	-	-	-	-	-
01-Nov-91	3.15117	-	-	-	-
01-Dec-91	2.63920	2.94384	-	-	-
01-Jan-92	3.52857	3.18141	3.15138	-	-
01-Feb-92	2.58822	3.03348	2.99109	-	-
01-Mar-92	2.34212	2.44773	2.81301	-	-
01-Apr-92	2.84004	2.68614	2.67800	2.91079	-
01-May-92	2.99980	2.96344	2.78471	2.88260	-
01-Jun-92	2.97195	2.96098	2.94200	2.90603	-
01-Jul-92	7.50903	5.86799	5.13302	4.06499	-
01-Aug-92	7.56603	7.47427	6.54037	5.11570	-
01-Sep-92	9.98979	8.88945	8.39434	6.37551	-
01-Oct-92	12.73065	11.45035	10.25279	8.16485	6.13659
01-Nov-92	17.15345	15.04225	13.59036	10.67199	7.85538
01-Dec-92	4.97700	12.63467	12.64004	10.71431	7.94424
01-Jan-93	8.18725	6.69216	11.30593	10.80234	8.19406
01-Feb-93	7.09458	7.60023	6.79012	10.75246	8.42875
01-Mar-93	7.36583	7.17518	7.47334	10.42478	8.64205
01-Apr-93	7.35408	7.28020	7.21497	9.46638	8.85578
01-May-93	10.25996	8.79638	8.31123	7.56637	9.26914
01-Jun-93	5.31020	8.13738	7.91500	7.67161	9.37182
01-Jul-93	4.59609	4.87832	7.03303	7.18160	9.22436
01-Aug-93	5.70397	5.13042	5.14223	6.97798	9.05865
01-Sep-93	9.12970	7.72428	6.81224	7.45549	9.09880
01-Oct-93	7.36206	8.62008	7.73670	7.38084	8.53702
01-Nov-93	6.99803	7.10691	8.17042	6.82426	7.25325
01-Dec-93	11.19539	9.45599	8.77011	8.13383	7.90388
01-Jan-94	9.43128	10.95276	9.77360	8.83789	8.05873
01-Feb-94	5.51595	7.96127	9.51863	8.86998	7.97191
01-Mar-94	7.41860	6.80655	8.30075	8.53093	8.10200
01-Apr-94	17.12487	13.54126	11.59185	10.70033	9.28346
01-May-94	11.96089	14.78398	12.97345	11.36755	9.44541
AVERAGE	7.25793	7.47398	7.54292	7.79813	8.43176
MAX	17.15345	15.04225	13.59036	11.36755	9.44541
MIN	2.34212	2.44773	2.67800	2.88260	6.13659
MID	9.74779	8.74499	8.13418	7.12507	7.79100

Table 5.5 Estimation of the Volatility Cone for BTP futures.

The first actual volatility estimate was generated in November 1991 when the contract was one month old. At that point there was just enough data to construct the first one month volatility estimate (based upon the daily returns and annualising this result[11]). This first volatility was estimated at 3.15117%. In December 1991, it was possible to re-evaluate the one month volatility since one more month had passed. Thus from November 1991 to the end of December 1991, the second one

---

[11]By multiplying the daily Standard Deviation by the $\sqrt{252}$, see Chapter 4 for the reason.

month volatility was 2.63920%. In addition, I had my first two month period from October to December and could estimate my first two month volatility which turned out to be 2.94384%. Then, in January, I could update both my one month and two month volatilities and add the first three month historical volatility estimate. This process rolls along as each new month allows me to create a "moving" estimate of actual historical volatilities.

By May 1994, I have an adequate number of volatilities for all my sample horizons to evaluate some statistics. At the bottom of Table 5.5, the reader will find Average, Max, Min and Mid. These are the average historical volatility for the period, the maximum volatility, the minimum volatility and the mid volatility between the max and min, respectively. When one looks at the average volatilities, one will notice that the further out in time one goes for the sample horizon, the higher the average volatility. For example, the one year average historical volatility is 8.43176% while the one month average historical volatility is only 7.25793%. If one looks at the mid volatility that should be similar to what is called the median in statistics. This number is the centre observation between the lowest and highest observations and should be equal to the average if the data series is normally distributed. However, in this case, the mid and average values are far from being equal and therefore, I conclude that volatilities are not normally distributed. Also it is interesting that these mid volatilities are decreasing through time. Therefore, it is difficult to state if the term structure of BTP historical volatilities is upward sloping or downward sloping. My guess is that it is probably upward sloping.

When one looks at the maximum volatilities and the minimum volatilities, then something quite strange happens as the sample horizon periods lengthen. The dispersion between the maximum and minimum levels becomes more compact the further out in time one goes. The widest margin for error in the historical volatility over time is for the one month sample horizon with the maximum volatility recorded at 17.15345% and the minimum volatility recorded at 2.34212%. The term "Volatility Cone" comes from plotting the maximum, average and minimum volatilities against their sample horizon periods. This can be seen in Figure 5.15 and it is not hard to see why this pattern is called the "Cone".

In the volatility cone plotted in Figure 5.15, I have also superimposed the ATM implied volatilities for the BTP future from April to May 1994 for the sake of comparison. As one can see, the ATM implied volatilities do seem to remain within the boundary of the cone reverting back to the long term average when they start approaching the upper or lower boundaries. In addition, the fact that the dispersion for longer term historical volatilities is not as extreme as for shorter term volatilities provides compelling evidence that if given a sufficiently long enough time, volatility does indeed revert back to the longer term average. Short term volatility is generally higher than the longer term volatility because the sample period is simply not long enough to achieve a large enough sample of observations to achieve stability. Going back to the example of Blackjack in the last chapter: if we only deal eight cards, it is possible that we will either obtain eight low cards or eight high cards. However, if we deal all 52 cards we are assured that we will have

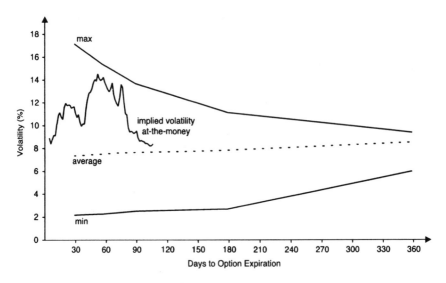

Figure 5.15 Volatility Cone for the BTP Futures.

dealt 16 "ten" cards, 4 aces and 32 low cards. The shorter the sampling horizon, the more likely that the sampled volatility will fluctuate in value due to "noise" or the fact that economic days just happened to be clumped or are absent in that particular period.

The existence of the volatility cone not only confirms that mean reversion plays a major role in the existence of the term structure effect but it also suggests that when we have to evaluate the price of long dated options, the degree of error in our volatility estimate will be relatively low. Given the incredible importance of volatility to the prices of options, this should be seen as very good news indeed!

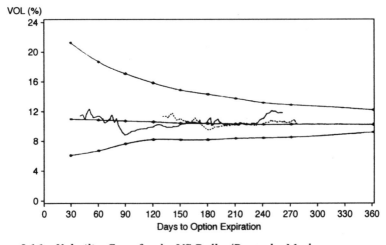

Figure 5.16a Volatility Cone for the US Dollar/Deutsche Mark.

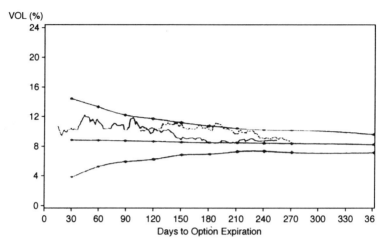

Figure 5.16b Volatility Cone for the US 20 year Treasury Bond Futures.

But does this volatility cone effect only occur for the BTP market? The answer is no. With thanks to Galen Burghardt and his team at Dean Witter in Chicago, Figures 5.16a, 5.16b, 5.16c, 5.16d and 5.16e are reproduced here. These are the volatility cones for the US Dollar /Deutsche Mark, US 20 Year Treasury Bond Futures, S&P 500 Futures, the Live Cattle Futures and for Eurodollar Futures. Almost all of the cones have been constructed using the last two years of data for the analysis of the historical volatility relationships. The exception is for the S&P 500 Futures which uses the past four years of data in the analysis. For all of these markets, the cones tighten the further out in time one goes which again confirms how important mean reversion is for all these markets.

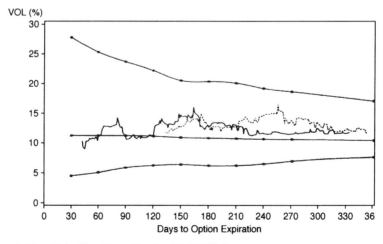

Figure 5.16c Volatility Cone for the S&P 500 Futures.

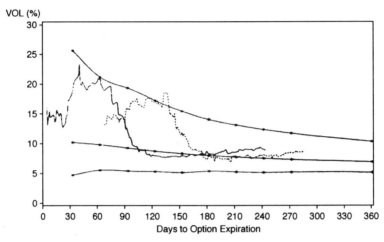

Figure 5.16d Volatility Cone for the Live Cattle Futures.

In all of these volatility cones, the implied volatilities for the ATM options are also displayed for comparison. These can be seen as the "jagged" series which tend to hover around the average historical volatility through time. Many market participants increase the accuracy of their volatility forecasts by comparing implied volatilities with historical averages. If the implied volatilities diverge significantly from the historical average, this would suggest that a correction is in the offing. This is illustrated for the Live Cattle futures in Figure 5.16d. The implied volatility briefly exceeded the boundaries of the cone to the upside and was promptly knocked back down. It is not surprising that this analysis tool has proven to be critical to the success of those who trade options and benefit from the edge it provides in predicting how implied volatilities will change.

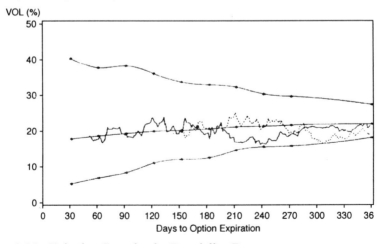

Figure 5.16e Volatility Cone for the Eurodollar Futures.

This is an appropriate point to summarise what I have discussed so far and the implications for the pricing of options. For more than 20 years, market participants have utilised the options pricing approach introduced by Black and Scholes. Due to the somewhat onerous assumptions in the original model, various adjustments were made to the approach to address dividends (Merton 1973), discrete price movements (the Binomial Approach) and the possibility that the price of an asset in the future would be different from the current asset price (Black 1976). Other approaches were attempted to address problems with the early exercise problem for puts (see Chapter 3) and for other problems that appeared over time. However, for most of these approaches, the foundation for the development of the pricing methodologies remains the assumption of some sort of price dispersion process which is lognormal with the effective variance proportional to time.

As each new pricing model evolved from an earlier version, there can be little doubt that improvements were made and some important issues had been addressed. But it is fair to say that these incremental improvements were not as earth shaking as the original Black and Scholes model had been. The gains from these new pricing models were iterative improvements approaching some perceived ideal but an ideal that became increasingly elusive. While this was the approach of the academic side, market practitioners (including myself) took another approach: the pricing models are secondary in importance relative to the most important element - volatility estimation. However, this viewpoint among those trading options day in and day out has begun to change: maybe there really is a "Holy Grail" equivalent for options pricing after all.

The entire process of modelling the implied volatilities for smile patterns and the term structure relies on the use of the flawed pricing models to derive the volatility estimates. Then, by symmetry, if the analyst inputs these implied volatilities back into the flawed option pricing model, correct prices will be obtained. This is yet another case of the dog chasing his tail. One can completely describe the circle the dog is making without really getting anywhere. However, if the biases which the smile and term structure reflect are consistent, then it may be possible to use the flawed pricing model adjusting the volatilities to reflect the errors in the assumptions and yield reasonable prices. The reader may remember my analogy that the Black and Scholes model is as accurate as a Nikon camera. I still believe it is. It will take an accurate picture of the world if the assumptions it is based upon hold. If the assumptions that underlie it are incorrect, then the prices will also be incorrect. With the camera example, if the pictures taken are not accurate (that is distorted) that does not mean that one throws the camera away. With a little skill, a photographer will modify the camera by putting a different lens on the body or filters which modify the image reflected on the film to better reflect reality. The same approach has been used in the marketplace when adjusting the Black and Scholes model to take a more accurate "snapshot" of option prices.

This approach has many merits. First of all, the same basic pricing model can be used over time for all assets. However, each market will require a different modification to the basic model to achieve accurate results. It is as if each underlying market has its own lens or filters that must be attached to the basic camera body to eliminate the distortions. Thus the need for analysis of the volatility matrix for each underlying market. But at some point, so many different adjustments have to be made to the basic options pricing methodology that the analyst has to ask himself if maybe a better and more consistent pricing approach might be taken. In the world of photography, the ultimate test of a camera is the quality of the pictures taken. For some, this is achieved through the extensive modification of the set-up of the basic camera with lens and filters to achieve satisfactory results. Obviously, this is the realm of the professional photographer. Another approach is to use the extensive technological electronic advances on run of the mill cameras that will make all of these adjustments automatically. This type of approach is more often used by most of us who are weekend photographers. Given the technology is sufficiently sophisticated, the ultimate results will be the same: excellent photographs. In the options market, a parallel process has been developed. Instead of the option analyst making all the adjustments to the basic pricing model, a new potentially Super Model is being developed that makes all the adjustments automatically. It could very well be that this promises to become the first real breakthrough in options pricing since the dawn of the Black and Scholes methodology.

THE SUPER MODEL FOR THE PRICING OF OPTIONS[12]

In 1994, three researchers from both sides of the Atlantic published research which described the development of a Super options pricing model which automatically incorporated the smile and term structure effects seen in all options markets. Bruno Dupire of Paribas Capital Markets in London and Emanuel Derman and Iraj Kani of Goldman Sachs in New York both published articles in Risk Magazine with their findings.[13] On 4 January 1994, Mark Rubinstein gave a speech to the American Finance Association in Boston with a similar finding. And this is what they came up with.

All the approaches modify the basic options pricing methodology through modification of the underlying stochastic process that is driving that particular market. To determine what this process is, they incorporate the information that the smile and term structures provide from inverting the usual Black and Scholes methodology to solve for the implied volatilities. From this they will build a model which is consistent with the smile patterns through time (and thereby include the impact of the term structure) and have a "complete" model that allows for no arbitrage opportunities to exist between theoretical and actual option prices.

The smile and term structure effects have been known for a long time and this approach directly attempts to solve both problems. Other approaches which have

---

[12]This section is drawn extensively from the Risk Magazine articles referenced below and Graham Cooper's article in the January 1994 Risk Magazine, titled "The Supermodel comes of Age". I would like to thank Peter Field of Risk Magazine for allowing me to draw upon these sources.

[13]Dupire, Bruno. "Pricing with a Smile", Risk Magazine Volume 7, Number 1 (January 1994) pp. 18-20 and Derman, Emanuel and Kani, Iraj, "Riding on a Smile", Risk Magazine Volume 7, Number 2 (February 1994) pp. 32-40.

been tried include non-traded sources of risk such as jumps[14], stochastic volatility[15] or transactions costs. However, these approaches introduce elements that can no longer be hedged away. For any pricing model, it can only be an improvement on the Black and Scholes model if it works. If the results from the pricing model are different from the actual traded market price, the model has to tell you how to create an equivalent portfolio of assets allowing you to lock in the difference between the theoretical price produced by the model and the market price. The Super Model appears to do this. In more formal terms, the model is preference free: The values of the options do not depend on investors' risk preferences but only upon arbitrage to enforce the results.

The Super Model replaces the constant volatility term in the Black and Scholes model with a volatility function obtained from market prices of normal European options and the prices of the underlying asset through time. These functions are allowed to depend upon the strike price and the time to maturity of the options. The assumed stochastic process for this can be written as :

$$dS \,/\, S = \mu(t)dt + \sigma(S,t)\,dz$$

where:

  dS/S is the return on an asset

  $\mu(t)dt$ is the drift term which is only a function of time

  $\sigma(S,t)$ is the volatility function dependent on both
        the stock price and time, and

  dz is a Wiener process with a mean of zero and a
        variance equal to dt

While other approaches try to draw from theory to find the volatility function σ (S,t), the Super Model uses the actual market implied volatility to solve for it numerically. The volatility function is entered in such a way that all the resulting theoretical options prices are identical with market prices; With only the inclusion of a single volatility input. To better describe how this works, we will move from the continuous time world of Black and Scholes to the discrete world of the Binomial approach.

The reader may recall that in Chapter 3, the Binomial approach was introduced when the price of the underlying asset is assumed to move in discrete increments. When these increments become smaller and smaller, the binomial approach will be identical to the Black and Scholes result for the same assumptions of constant

[14]Merton, Robert, "Options pricing when Underlying Stock Returns are Discontinuous", Journal of Financial Economics, Volume 3, 1976, pp 125-144.
[15]Hull, John and Alan White, "The Pricing of Options on Assets with Stochastic Volatilties", Journal of Finance, Volume 42, 1987, pp. 281-300.

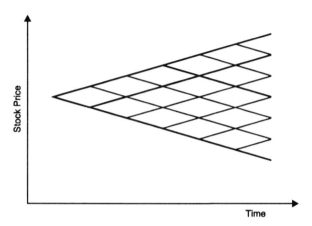

Figure 5.17 A Standard Binomial Process for Stock Prices.

volatility and so forth. This process looks like the traditional tree diagram produced in that chapter and reproduced in Figure 5.17. But Derman and Kani point out that the implied volatilities for the S&P 500 market they were examining were inconsistent with this diagram by producing both a smile graph and the term structure of volatilities (for this market as of 5 May 1993). This can be seen in Figure 5.18. Clearly, the volatilities differ both across strike prices and maturities. This is consistent with all the volatility matrices I displayed earlier in this chapter and inconsistent with the assumption of a Binomial dispersion process for the underlying S&P 500.

Now comes the interesting part: They then modify the shape of the tree diagram to take into account these volatility structures, resulting in an implied tree diagram. This can be seen in Figure 5.19. As they say, "Options prices for all strikes and expirations, obtained by interpolation from known options prices, will determine the position and the probability of reaching each node in the implied tree"[16]. Once

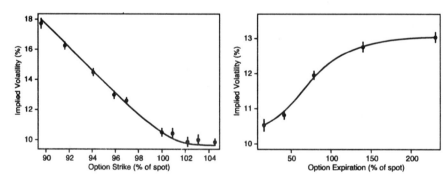

Figure 5.18 S&P 500 Smile and Term Structure Patterns as of 5 May 1993.

---

[16]Derman, Emanuel and Kani, Iraj, "Riding on a Smile", Risk Magazine Volume 7, Number 2 (February 1994) pp. 3.33.

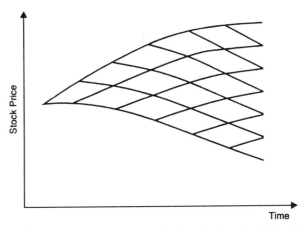

Figure 5.19 The Implied Stochastic Process Implied by the S&P 500 Smile.

the nodes of the tree diagram have been drawn for those options for which implied volatilities can be estimated, then all of the other nodes at all points in time from the final expiration of the longest dated options until today can be estimated through the construction of equivalent portfolios of standard options (which are in the tree). Furthermore, positions in either the underlying asset or risk free interest bearing securities can be included.

Once the entire implied stochastic process has become known, then not only can normal European options be evaluated but a much wider range of other contingent claims (non-standard options such as customised OTCs and American options) can now be priced correctly. In addition, the range of exotic options that will be discussed later in this book in Chapter 13 can also be priced using the implied tree. Finally, the existence of a fully unifying approach to the pricing of all contingent claims means that all options or option-like securities can be aggregated for hedging purposes. This is because all of the Greek derivatives necessary for risk management are now consistent with the same stochastic process and are therefore directly comparable. This answers one of the key problems of many financial institutions: How to hedge all their options positions in a consistent manner.

Clearly, this evolution in options pricing holds the potential of solving many of the problems this chapter has raised. The reader is urged to read the papers previously referenced for a fuller exposition of the methodology. Following my previous analogy, it can be said that this research has developed an automatic camera which can be built for each market. It is important to consider that these models all depend on the continued utilisation of the standard options pricing models to determine the implied stochastic processes. If everyone uses the Supermodel for pricing, where will the implied distributions come from to re-calibrate the Supermodel? It would then appear that the Supermodel is certainly a refinement relative to the initial Black and Scholes methodology. However, it is most likely that it will compliment rather than replace the traditional approach. A major benefit is that the Supermodel should allow analysts a better approach especially for more exotic option structures and for the comparison of European and American option prices.

In the final section of this chapter, I will discuss the estimation of forward volatilities and the implications they have for the pricing of options.

ESTIMATION OF FORWARD VOLATILITIES

While there is no doubt that the implied volatilities for options are not always the same across maturities, this very fact may lead to opportunities in the markets.

In the interest rate markets, a tremendous amount of emphasis has been placed on the term structure of interest rates. Fixed income traders and money market traders have always looked at the yield curves to identify mispriced securities and thus initiate interest rate arbitrage strategies. The types of yield curves vary given the method for calculation of the interest rates. The simplest method of yield curve estimation uses the simple yield to maturity of the instruments plotted against the maturities of the instruments associated with these yields. Another approach has been to determine the zero coupon yields associated not necessarily with a single instrument but instead with a particular point in time. These zero coupon yields are the yields associated with instruments which pay no coupons or other cash flows during their lives, only paying the principal value at the end. Thus, the purchase of the security today for the pure discounted value will offer the investor a guaranteed rate of return not muddled by the problems of coupon reinvestment. Typical zero coupon instruments are discount securities often issued by Governments for short maturities often referred to Bills. Zero coupon instruments can also be constructed synthetically by stripping the individual coupons or principal payments from more traditional instruments such as bonds and selling them individually as zero coupons. In the interest rate markets, these yields are now acknowledged as the most appropriate method to assess the interest rate return from today to a certain point in the future.

For the options markets, the term structure of volatility (the volatility from to-day to a variety of points in the future) is most similar to this zero coupon approach for interest rates. Another approach used in the interest rate markets to determine yields is the assessment of forward or future yields. Anyone who has been involved in the interest rate markets in the last ten years knows the importance of forward interest rates. They are the basis for such securities such as Forward Rate Agreements, Financial futures and Interest Rate Swaps. These derivative products based on interest rates will be discussed in some detail in Chapter 12 of this book.

The importance of forward volatilities is just starting to become important with the recent introduction of forward start options which are simply options in the future. These will be discussed in Chapter 13 in the sections on pay later and delayed options. As with the comparable interest rate forward contracts, the key element is the correct determination of the volatility in the future. As with the estimation of forward interest rates all that is needed is the zero coupon term structure which can

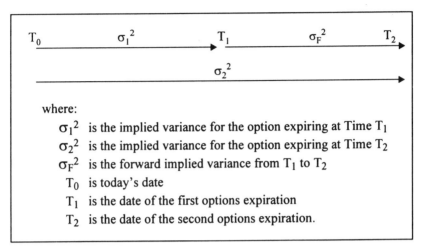

where:

σ_1^2 is the implied variance for the option expiring at Time T_1
σ_2^2 is the implied variance for the option expiring at Time T_2
σ_F^2 is the forward implied variance from T_1 to T_2
T_0 is today's date
T_1 is the date of the first options expiration
T_2 is the date of the second options expiration.

Figure 5.20 The Forward Volatility Implied by the Term Structure of Volatility.

then be used to estimate the forward interest rate. For options all that is needed is the term structure of volatility which will allow for the estimation of forward volatilities. Figure 5.20 displays the forward volatility we are attempting to estimate.

To find out what the forward volatility is, all we must do is apply a relatively simple formula which is in principle similar to that for forward interest rate agreements (see Chapter 12). Essentially, we must determine the forward variance, σ_F^2 and then take the square root. This is the formula for the determination of the forward volatility:

$$\sigma_F = \sqrt{\left[(T_2 - T_0)\cdot\sigma_2^2 - (T_1 - T_0)\cdot\sigma_1^2\right]/(T_2 - T_1)}$$

Again, let us go through a numerical example. Suppose that we are interested in the forward volatility for the BTP futures from 6 months (181 days) until one year (365 days). The six month implied BTP volatility is 7.85% and the one year implied volatility is 9.35%[17]. These numbers are plugged into the above formula to yield:

$$\sigma_F = \sqrt{\left[(365 - 0)\cdot(0.0935)^2 - (181 - 0)\cdot(0.0785)^2\right]/(365 - 181)}$$

$$\sigma_F = \mathbf{10.621\%}$$

This result of 10.621% is the forward volatility implied from the current term structure of implied volatilities. This number can then be applied to the pricing of

---

[17]The reader may recall that options on BTP futures do not trade past a 3 month expiration. However, it is possible to obtain OTC options on BTPs with longer maturities. This is how these implied volatilities have been obtained.

options on the BTP which will start in the future or can be used to spot mispricing opportunities in the volatility term structure.

One may think that since volatility is simply a measure of the risk of movement in the price of an underlying asset, that the further out in time one goes, the more risk there will be. This principle would be consistent with the assumption of non-uniformity that appears to hold for markets such as options on stock index futures and for BTP futures. This factor would not only explain why the term structure of volatility is upward sloping but would also be associated with increasing forward volatilities. Occasionally, market prices can vary from the term structure in an irrational way and it may be possible to detect this by estimating the forward volatilities from the term structure. The analyst may compare the forward volatility with the historical ranges for the same period from the historical volatility cone to see if they are consistent. If they diverge significantly, then the analyst may expect the entire term structure of volatilities to shift eventually back to their long term averages causing the forward volatilities to come back into line. This could be done using a class of trading strategies known as "calendar" or time spreads which will be discussed later in Chapter 7. While this will be discussed in some detail at that point, it makes sense to give the reader an intuitive feel for how this would work.

From our example above, the estimated six month volatility in six months time was 10.621% and average six month volatility for BTP futures from the historical cone for the BTP futures is 7.79813% (see Table 5.5). We would expect that the forward volatility should drop to this level. How can this occur? Only from a change in the shape of the volatility term structure. If one looks at the formula above for the estimation of the forward volatility then it should be evident that the only way the forward volatility can fall is if either the longer dated volatility (for one year) falls or if the shorter dated volatility (for six months) rises. Thus, the trading strategy one would employ would be to buy shorter dated volatility and sell longer dated volatility expecting the term structure to flatten out or even invert. Once this has happened, the trader would sell back the short dated options and buy back the longer dated options with an expected tidy profit.

As the reader might surmise, the existence of contingent claims based upon forward volatilities will add an entirely new dimension to the options market. Not only will option traders have a clearer viewpoint of how volatility may change in the future but increased use of forward options will allow more effective hedging of option portfolios exposed to changes in the term structure of volatility. I have little doubt that this area will become as important to the options markets as Forward Rate Agreements and Forward Foreign Exchange. These forward options are a necessary tool to "span" the markets since volatilities are clearly a function of time and such securities will allow traders to cover their exposures more completely.

As a conclusion to this chapter, it is clear that the basic Black and Scholes assumptions that the dispersion processes of underlying markets follows a simple Random Walk process are incorrect. The existence of volatility smiles and the term structure is no longer ignored by market participants but studied carefully. This has led to ad hoc modifications to the original option pricing model or to the development of the Super Model for the pricing of options. It may very well be that if a major theoretical breakthrough in the area of option pricing occurs, it will come from an even more careful consideration of the issues raised in this chapter.

6: Directional Trading Strategies

In most markets, there are only two possible strategies one can employ to earn profits: one can either buy or sell some underlying asset. To profit, you have to correctly predict which direction the market will take and when. With options, you can likewise profit from correctly predicting market direction, but in addition, you also can gain from changes in the perceptions of risk, and from the passage of time. Furthermore, options allow you to arbitrage price discrepancies easily and completely. Finally, options can be traded between related underlying markets profiting from either relative directional or volatility discrepancies. In this chapter, I will emphasise directional trading strategies that can be used with options on Crude Oil futures, while I will cover volatility strategies, arbitrage and cross market trading strategies for other underlying assets in the following three chapters.

As the reader learned in Chapter 2, the value of an option is composed of the intrinsic value and the time value. Changes in intrinsic value are associated with movement in the underlying market while changes in the time value are associated with changes in volatility and the passage of time. Therefore, when options are traded, a viewpoint must be taken on the movement of both the underlying asset and volatility. It is important to consider which volatility one must take a viewpoint upon. In Chapter 3, I mentioned that option positions can benefit from a change in both the implied volatility of the options market and from the actual volatility of the underlying market. One must be clear as to which volatility one is expecting to change for it will have a profound impact on the choice of the appropriate trading strategy. This will be evident in the next chapter on volatility trading. However, for

Trading Unit	1 Nymex crude oil future contract
Trading Months	six consecutive months
Last Drading Day	first Friday of the month prior to the delivery month
Minimum Price Movement	$0.01 per barrel ($10 per option contract)
Exercise Price Intervals	$1 per barrel (7 different exercise prices)
Trading Hours	9:45 - 15:10 (New York time)
Exercise	by 16:30, on any day up to and including the option's expiration

Table 6.1 Options on Crude Oil Futures (NYMEX)

this chapter, I will assume that a viewpoint on volatility means an identical viewpoint on both the implied and actual volatility levels.

Very few people need to take a view on time because it is always passing. When I mention taking a view, I mean choosing a specific trading strategy which earns the maximum profit from particular market and volatility movements.

Now consider the option on Crude Oil futures traded at the New York Mercantile Exchange (Nymex) which I will use for our examples in this chapter. The prices are in dollars per barrel. Table 6.1 outlines the contract specification for this underlying asset. The asset underlying the option is a Nymex Crude Oil futures contract which is the obligation to either buy or sell 42,000 Gallons of Crude Oil (1000 Barrels) in the month following the expiration of the option.

POSSIBLE VIEWPOINTS FOR THE UNDERLYING AND VOLATILITY

The three viewpoints that are possible with options are: to buy, sell, or to sit still. These three actions must be applied to both the underlying Crude Oil futures market and to volatility. For example, the trader may have the opinion that the Crude Oil market could increase, decrease, or remain the same. He could also form a similar viewpoint on volatility. With these two viewpoints, we can determine which trading strategy will be optimal under given conditions. Table 6.2 displays a trading strategy matrix that will be filled over the course of the next four chapters with all the options strategies I will present. In each cell, I will define the optimal strategy given one's viewpoint on the underlying market and volatility.

What I will do in this chapter is to help the user combine his views on the underlying market and volatility to determine the most appropriate options strategy to employ. In later chapters, I will also show the reader how to take "views" on time

Viewpoint on the crude oil market

		Buyer	Seller	Neutral
Viewpoint on Volatility	**Buyer**			
	Seller			
	Neutral			

Table 6.2 Option Trading Strategy Matrix.

decay, intra market spreads (commonly defined as a spread between different futures contract months), and to consider the liquidity of the underlying and options markets when placing these trades. As a rule of thumb, if three out of these five elements are in your favour initially and at least two of the three actually work out, then the options strategy has a high probability of success. For example, if my view on volatility is bearish then I will sell options. When selling options, time decay works for me. Hence, even if the underlying price moves against my position, I might still profit more from time decay and a decrease in volatility. Thus, the unfavourable movement in the underlying market can be offset because two of the five factors produced a greater profit.

THREE WAYS TO BENEFIT FROM AN INCREASE IN THE UNDERLYING MARKET

Concerning market direction, there are three ways to assume an equivalent buying position in Crude Oil: one can buy a Crude Oil futures contract, buy a call option on Crude Oil futures or sell a put option on Crude Oil futures. On the selling side, there are also three ways to assume a short position: one can sell a Crude Oil futures contract, buy a put option on Crude Oil futures or sell a call option on Crude Oil futures. The choice of which trade to use depends on one's viewpoint on volatility.

When you buy an option, you buy the two components of its value: intrinsic value and time value. Intrinsic value is comprised of the in-the-money amount which is the maximum difference between the strike price and the current price of the underlying Crude Oil futures or zero. Volatility is the critical element in time value, comprising almost all of the unknown elements that determine this value. If volatility increases, the time value will increase as well, all other things remaining equal.

Buying an option implies buying volatility; consequently, when you sell an option, you sell volatility. If I buy or hold a call option, my position has a buying volatility bias. When the implied volatility increases, I should make money due to the increase in the time value of the option. This has been referred to as the "vega" effect. If the actual volatility of the market increases that means the exposure of the call option will react positively both to increases and decreases in the prices of the underlying asset. This effect is known as the "gamma" effect. On the other hand, if I sell a put option, I am selling volatility, and when either the actual or implied volatility increases I expect to lose money (or at best have a limited profit). However, when volatility decreases I should make money.

Finally, consider a long position in Crude Oil futures. Volatility does not impact the prices of these contracts. The price of Crude Oil futures is determined by supply and demand and is bound by the futures pricing relationship I discussed in Chapter 2 with the estimated forward price for IBM stock. The spreads for the futures price may widen when volatility increases, but the centre price (that is midway between the bid and ask prices) is based on cash prices and holding costs. Hence, the Crude Oil futures is not determined by volatility and therefore its exposure to volatility is neutral. If volatility increases or decreases, you will not make money from that fact. You only make money if the Crude Oil market moves up or down, in other words by directional moves in the underlying Crude Oil market.

Buying a Crude Oil Futures Contract

Buying a Crude Oil futures contract is the most aggressive position for benefiting from an increase in prices. If the Crude Oil market price increases, you profit instantly and significantly. But it must be emphasised that one also assumes an unlimited risk potential if the Crude Oil market price falls. The profit/loss potential of this strategy can be seen in Figure 6.1. This position can be thought of as "long" the Crude Oil market and neutral to volatility. Therefore, if our view is to buy the underlying Crude Oil market and we have no view of volatility or expect it to be unchanged, one strategy we can employ is to buy the Crude Oil futures. In the trading strategy matrix, at the end of this chapter (Table 6.9), we would therefore place the long Crude Oil futures strategy in the cell at the lower left indicating a buying bias relative to the underlying Crude Oil market but neutral to volatility. The reader will also notice that the exposure of the long futures position relative to the price of the underlying does not vary either from a change in the price of the underlying or from a passage in time. Therefore, the only exposure we are concerned about with buying a futures contract is the exposure to the underlying asset price and in option terms, this is known as the delta. For a long futures contract the

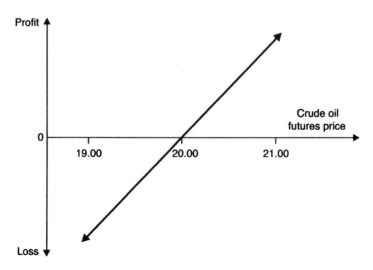

Figure 6.1 Profit/loss Profile: Long Crude oil Futures.

delta is always 1.0 and all the other "Greek" derivatives are zero. This means the change in the futures price is not a function of volatility, the level of the underlying asset price or time.

The problem with buying an underlying asset such as a Crude Oil futures contract is the unlimited loss potential. If, prior to the trading of options, you did not want an unlimited loss potential and had no viewpoint on volatility, there was not much you could have done. You would probably have abstained from involvement altogether. However, options on Crude Oil futures allow limited loss trading strategies to be established. I will now examine the two other ways of going "long" the Crude Oil market using these products. These positions include buying calls and selling puts. Let us first consider buying call options on Crude Oil futures.

Buying a Call Option on Crude Oil Futures

Suppose one buys a call option with a strike price of $20 per barrel. When the price of Crude Oil futures increases above that level, you have an unlimited profit potential. If the Crude Oil futures price decreases below $20, you abandon the call, and the most you lose is the premium paid for the option. Therefore, as indicated previously, holding calls allows you a limited loss potential. The profit/loss profile at expiration for buying a call option can be seen in Figure 6.2 as the usual "hockey stick" diagram. In addition, the profit/loss profile of the call has been reproduced at various points prior to expiration. I have included 90 days, 60 days and 30 days to expiration for the sake of comparison.

The first thing the reader will notice is that the position profits at all points in the life of the call from an increase in the price of the underlying Crude Oil futures

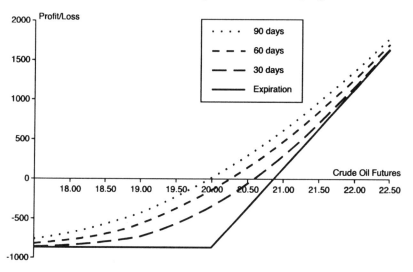

Figure 6.2 Profit/Loss Profile: Holding a Call Option.

(given the implied volatility does not change). In addition, prior to expiration the option has additional time value which is a function of volatility and the square root of time (σ√T from Chapter 2). It was shown that if volatility doubles for the at-the-money option, the time value of the option will also double. This can be seen in Figure 2.16 in Chapter 2.

In Chapter 3, I showed how important the "Greek" derivatives are in the estimation of the exposures of all options positions. Without them, the trader is flying blind. With this thought in mind, I also have estimated the major Greek derivatives for an at-the-money crude oil call option with:

- a strike price of 20,
- the underlying crude oil futures also at 20,
- 90 days until expiration,
- implied volatility of 22%, and
- short term interest rates at 4%.

The results of this can be seen in Table 6.3.

LONG CALL:
Theoretical values based upon a futures price of 20.00;
volatility 22%; rate of interest 4% and 90 days to expiration.

	PRICE	DELTA	GAMMA	VEGA	THETA
BUY 20.00 CALL	+0.865	+0.5177	+0.001812	+0.0394	-4.7288

Table 6.3 Long Call Sensitivities.

As the reader can see, the theoretical value of the call is 0.865 $ per barrel or 86.5 cents. Given that each contract is for 1000 barrels of Crude Oil, the total cost of one call option is $865. The delta is positive and equal to +0.5177. This indicates that when the price of the underlying Crude Oil futures rises, the call option price will initially rise by only 51.77% of the movement in the underlying. However, if the underlying price experiences an extreme move, the options delta will change: increasing when underlying Crude Oil futures prices rise and decreasing when the Crude Oil futures fall.

As was indicated in Chapter 3, whenever one buys an option, the gamma is positive and the reader can see in the above table indeed a positive gamma of +0.001812 is the result. This signifies how much the delta will change for every tick change in the level of the underlying crude oil futures. Since the gamma is the measure of the sensitivity of the options price to a change in the actual volatility in the underlying asset, we will benefit from increased underlying price variability because we have a positive gamma. If the reader looks back at the profit and loss profile for the option at 90 days until expiration, he will notice that the curved relationship between the options price and the underlying price is convex or half smiling. This means that if extreme movements occur in the price of the underlying, the option will automatically adapt its exposures to the benefit of the holder. So it is fair to say that the holder of the call option would want the actual volatility to increase (though it would be better if that increased price variability were associated with rising prices).

Whenever one buys an option, one is also buying the implied volatility since that is the critical factor in the estimation of the time value of the option. In "Greek" terms, this is referred to as the vega. In Table 6.3, the vega is +0.0394 and this stands for the amount the value of the option will change for a change in 1% in the implied volatility. This number is expressed relative to 1,000 US Dollars in this table. It means that if the implied volatility rises from 22% (the current level) to 23%, the premium cost of the option will rise by $39.40. Given that the original price of the option was $865, this would mean that the new price of the option should be $904.40 at a 23% implied volatility. Of course, if the volatility fell to 21%, the holder of the call would expect to lose $39.40 due to the reduction in the time value of the option.

As the reader can see, the buyer of the call benefits from increases in both the actual volatility of the underlying market because he has a gamma positive position and from the implied volatility of the options market because he is long vega.

Finally, in Table 6.3 the holder of the call option has a theta negative position of -4.7288. This measure is expressed in the number of US Dollars that will be lost from the passage of one calendar day in the options life (from 90 days to 89 days to expiration). Thus, if everything else remains constant, the holder of the call would expect tomorrow that his option would only be worth $860.27 (current price of $865 minus time decay of $4.73).

In conclusion, when you hold a call on Crude Oil futures you are buying the right to buy a Crude Oil futures contract. Therefore, you have an equivalent long position in Crude Oil futures in addition to buying both actual and implied volatilities. In summary, the Crude Oil call option holder is both a buyer of the Crude Oil market and a buyer of volatility. If one expects both the Crude Oil market to increase and volatility to increase, the best strategy is to purchase a call option. Therefore in our strategy matrix at the end of this chapter (Table 6.9), the long call option fits into the cell in the upper left corner which indicates both a buying position in the underlying Crude Oil market and a buying position in volatility.

Buying Calls versus a Stop Loss Strategy with Long Futures

Suppose that instead of buying a call option I tried to replicate the pay off diagram of a call option by buying Crude Oil futures when the futures price rose above $20 and selling the Crude Oil futures when the futures price fell below $20. In the mind's eye, this payoff should look like the intrinsic value of a call option. Unfortunately, as will be discussed in the section on Portfolio Insurance in Chapter 11, there is no guarantee that I will achieve the same result as with a call.

The way this technique would work would involve buying a Crude Oil futures contract at $20 and if the futures price rose, one would hold the position. If the futures price fell, then one would have to "stop" the loss potential by selling the Crude Oil futures hopefully at $20. To do this, one would place a "stop loss" order after buying the Crude Oil futures. If the position was "stopped out", the trader would then place another order - a limit buying order - again at $20. If the futures price then rose to this level, the trader would buy back in.

A stop loss order is an order that is triggered when a specific price is reached. When that particular price is reached, the broker has instructions to fill the trade at the best possible price. For example, if I bought the Crude Oil futures at $20 and then placed a stop loss order to sell at $19.95. When Crude Oil futures traded at $19.95, my broker would automatically sell my long futures position out at the best possible price. Unfortunately, the broker is not bound to sell at that price and the actual price of the transaction might be less than $19.95. A limit buying order instructs the broker to buy a Crude Oil futures contract if my target price is reached. Again, there is no assurance that my position will be filled at the price. If the market only trades at my target price, I am not assured a "fill". To assure I am filled, the market must trade higher than that target price.

The purpose of a stop loss order is to provide a limited loss feature to a trade previously filled in the Crude Oil futures. Therefore, a stop loss order attempts to provide the same limited loss potential as a call (or put) option. The problem with a stop loss order is that once it has been filled, the trader no longer has a position in the Crude Oil futures. If one was "stopped out" and then if the Crude Oil futures price proceeded to rise, the trader will not be able to profit from this fact, unless he buys another Crude Oil futures contract. A call option on Crude Oil futures, on the other hand, will allow the trader a limited loss and an unlimited profit potential, which trading the Crude Oil futures with stop loss orders and limit buying orders can not provide.

To create a synthetic call option by dynamically trading Crude Oil futures, one would have to sell every time the futures price fell to one's target price and have to buy every time the futures rose above the target price. Each time this would occur, the "stop loss"/"limit buy" strategy would involve transaction costs and being on the wrong side of the bid/offer spread. This means that when a trader buys or sells from a market maker, the trader must buy at the market maker's offer price and the trader can only sell at the market maker's bid price. This spread between bid and offer is typically 1 cent on the Crude Oil futures (for instance $19.94 bid and $19.95 offer). An additional cost (which is variable) is associated with the fact that with a stop loss (sell) order (or a limit buy order) there is no guarantee that you will be able to sell (or buy) at the price you want. For example, if one had the stop loss sell order outlined above, the order would become "active" when the Crude Oil futures market trades at $19.95. This "active" order means the transaction is then completed at the best current price even if the best current price were well below $19.95.

Most traders have been burnt by these kinds of orders. Inevitably, once a stop loss order (or limit buy order) is placed, the market will fluctuate sufficiently to trigger the order, resulting in a loss (or a new position). Then, as the fluctuation continues, the market will eventually rise (or fall) back to the previous level. Because of this, many traders refer to stop loss orders and limit orders as "price magnets" which seem to the unlucky trader to draw the underlying price to the level of his order only to assure that it is filled. Thereafter, as if laughing at them, the market goes back to previous levels.

If you buy a call option, you establish a position at a known strike price which gives you "automatic" sell stop and limit buying features. When you pay for a call option, you pay a premium. This premium can be thought of as (the present value of) the expected costs one would incur by replicating the payoffs of a call option using stop loss sell orders (and limit buying orders) in the underlying market. When volatility increases, time value increases because of the increased costs that would occur in a dynamic replication strategy using the underlying Crude Oil futures market. Thus, if the expected future volatility increases, it is favourable for those who have bought options because the prices of these securities rise.

Selling a Put Option on Crude Oil Futures

The third way to achieve a long position in the Crude Oil market is to sell a put option on Crude Oil futures. Consider selling a $20 put, which is the obligation to buy the underlying Crude Oil futures at $20, the strike price. When I sell the put option, I receive a premium of say $0.865, which is all that I will gain on the transaction. In terms of real money, this would result in a receipt of $865 for 1000 barrels of crude oil. This position profits if the Crude Oil futures price is stable or rises above the strike price. If the futures price finishes at $20 or above, the holder will let the option expire and I will retain all the premium. If the market finishes below $20, the put holder will exercise the option. The profit or loss to the put seller depends on how far below the strike price the Crude Oil futures market finishes and how much premium he has received. If the market loss exceeds the premium inflow, the net impact will be a loss to the put writer. The profit/loss profile for selling a put on Crude Oil futures can be seen in Figure 6.3. Once again, the profiles have been portrayed at a number of dates prior to and including the expiration of the option.

The reader will notice that the position will profit from an increase in the price of the underlying Crude Oil futures. However, this assumes that the level of the implied volatility has remained constant. If the implied volatility rose, the position would potentially be at a loss since the time value of the option had increased. Thus, if the option seller reversed his position and bought back the option, he might have to pay more for it than he received in premium when he initiated the transaction. What can save him? If time simply passes, the option value will drop from the time decay. To quantify this exposure exactly, we must again turn to the "Greeks". These have been estimated for a short position in an at-the-money Crude

Oil put option with:
- a strike price of 20,
- the underlying crude oil futures also at 20,
- 90 days until expiration,
- implied volatility of 22%, and
- short term interest rates at 4%.

The results of this can be seen in Table 6.4.

SHORT PUT:
Theoretical values based upon a futures price of 20.00;
volatility 22%; rate of interest 4% and 90 days to expiration.

	PRICE	DELTA	GAMMA	VEGA	THETA
SELL 20.00 PUT	-0.865	+0.4745	-0.001812	-0.0394	+4.7313

Table 6.4 Short Put Sensitivities.

Once again, the theoretical value of the put is 86.5 cents per barrel (the reason the put price is identical to the call is due to put-call parity). The delta is positive and equal to +0.4745. This indicates that when the price of the underlying Crude Oil futures rises, the put option price will fall by 47.45% of the movement in the underlying. *Wait a minute, Fall?* Of course, when one sells something (in this case a put), one wants the price to fall so that it can be bought back at a lower price and result in a profit. So, when the price of the underlying Crude Oil futures rises, that will benefit the put seller. However, if the underlying price experiences an extreme

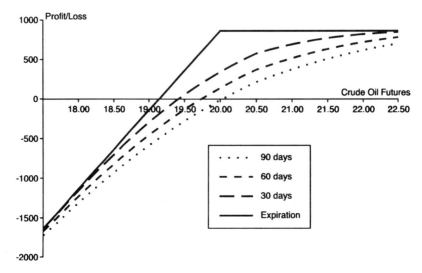

Figure 6.3 Profit/Loss Profile: Writing a Put Option.

move, the options delta will also change. For the put seller this can be catastrophic: his exposure will increase when the underlying crude oil futures price falls and decrease when the crude oil futures rises. As the reader can see from Figure 6.3, he has an unlimited loss potential which is accelerating and a limited profit potential that is decelerating. The term for this is gamma negative.

In the above table, the short put position does indeed have a negative gamma of -0.001812. This indicates: how the delta will change adversely for every tick change in the level of the underlying Crude Oil futures. If the reader looks back at the profit and loss profile for the option at 90 days until expiration, he will notice that the curved relationship between the options price and the underlying price is now concave or half frowning. This means that if extreme movements occur in the price of the underlying, the option will automatically become either the option seller's worst nightmare or at best result in a limited profit of the premium received. So it is fair to say that the seller of the put option would want the actual volatility to decrease (though it would be better if that decreased price variability were associated with slightly rising prices).

Whenever one sells an option, one is also selling the implied volatility. In Table 6.4, the vega is -0.0394 and this means the amount that the value of the option will change for a change in 1% increase in the implied volatility. This number is expressed relative to US $1,000 in this table, meaning that if the implied volatility rises from 22% (the current level) to 23%, the premium cost of the option will rise by $39.40. Given that the original price of the option was $865, this would mean that the new price of the option should be 904.40 at a 23% implied volatility. If the put option seller were to reverse his position by buying back the option, he would have to take this loss.

As is indicated by the "Greeks", the seller of the put benefits from decreases in both the actual volatility of the underlying market (gamma negative) and from the implied volatility of the options market (vega negative). In fact, the option seller will wish he was never born if the underlying market collapses and volatility increases. What he is banking on is the passage of time and the accompanying time decay that might just make him his profit.

Finally, in Table 6.4 the writer of the put option has a theta positive position of +4.7313. This measure is expressed in the number of US Dollars that will be earned from the passage of one calendar day in the option's life (from 90 days to 89 days to expiration). Thus, if everything else remains constant, the holder of the call would expect tomorrow that his option would only be worth $860.27 (current price of $865 minus time decay of $4.73). While, this may not sound like very much, the reader is reminded that this will begin to accelerate as the option approaches expiration (see Figures 2.13a and 2.13b).

Therefore, when you sell a put option on Crude Oil futures, you assume the obligation to buy a Crude Oil futures contract. You have a long position not only because you profit as the futures price increase and you lose when prices fall, but also because of this obligation to become a buyer of the Crude Oil futures. Since you sold the two components of an option's value, intrinsic value and time value, you will benefit if the Crude Oil market increases and/or when volatility decreases. Thus, in our strategy matrix in Table 6.9, the short put option position will be placed in the middle left cell which is bullish on the Crude Oil market but bearish on volatility.

If you sell put options, you must realise that the most that can be gained is the time value. The intrinsic value must be returned at expiration if the option remains in the money. Therefore, if conditions are unchanged the put writer has the intrinsic value on "loan" that must eventually be paid back. Compared to buying the Crude Oil futures or buying a call on Crude Oil futures, selling the put option provides an inflow of premium. If the Crude Oil market stays at that particular level, you will earn a superior profit compared with buying the Crude Oil futures or buying the call. This is because 86.5 cents of time value will be credited to your account if the Crude Oil futures price finishes equal to or above your strike price. This can be a greater profit than buying the Crude Oil futures which will provide no profit if the eventual settlement price is equal to the present levels. The call option will actually experience a loss if the Crude Oil market is stable because the premium paid will be lost. Therefore, for stable to slightly rising Crude Oil markets, selling a put option is the ideal strategy.

Comparison of the Bullish Strategies

Figure 6.4 compares all these bullish positions. From the directional standpoint, the most aggressive position is to buy the Crude Oil futures. A less aggressive position is to buy a call option with the limited loss potential. The best strategy if one expects the Crude Oil market to move up minimally, is to sell a put option. Which trade you choose will depend on how far you think the Crude Oil market will go, when it is going to move, and your viewpoint on volatility.

If you believe implied volatility will increase, the general rule is to buy options. Unfortunately when you buy options you are subject to time decay. Unless volatility increases immediately, time decay can quickly waste the option value. Therefore you should try to buy options with as long a maturity as possible.[1] While you will pay more for these long dated options, you can sell them if volatility rises and should make a profit not offset by time decay. In this case, you are buying high to sell higher.

If you believe that the implied volatility will fall, then you should sell options. Now you benefit from time decay, especially in the last 45 days of the options life. Therefore, if one sells short maturity options and volatility drops, the writer will

---

[1] In Chapter 2, the reader is referred to Figures 2.13a and 2.13b where we show that it is better to buy long maturity options to minimise the time decay impact. Of course, if the option buyer is looking for the maximum leverage, then, short dated options are preferable (see Figure 2.14). However, the time decay for these options is also maximised.

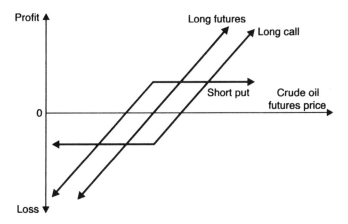

Figure 6.4 Option Strategies: Bullish Positions.

benefit from both the volatility drop and the passage of time. The problem is that if the actual volatility rises in the last 45 days, the gamma effect can bury the option seller. So once again, regardless of how we define volatility, option sellers want the risk of the market to fall to earn their profits.

The consideration of loss potential, and whether it is limited or unlimited, is another consideration important to option traders. Selling options can be lucrative but requires the ability to quickly apply "damage control" if the market starts to move against your position. Thus, option writers must watch exposed short options positions very carefully indeed. Buyers of options must also watch their positions assiduously even though they are assured of only a limited loss if things go wrong. Thus buying options is a better strategy for those with a limited taste for risk.

THREE WAYS TO BENEFIT FROM A DECREASE IN THE UNDERLYING MARKET

On the selling side, there are three ways of going short in the Crude Oil market: selling the Crude Oil futures, buying a put on Crude Oil futures, or selling a call on Crude Oil futures. When selling the Crude Oil futures, you have an unlimited profit potential and an unlimited loss potential. When the Crude Oil market decreases, you make money, because you can buy back the asset (futures) which you have sold at a higher level. Figure 6.5 displays the profit/loss profile of selling the Crude Oil futures.

When you purchase a put, you have the right to an unlimited profit potential as the Crude Oil market decreases. If the Crude Oil market rises instead, you will let the put expire with a maximum loss equal to the premium. Buying a put option, or any option for that matter, is similar to playing roulette in that the most you can lose is the chip you put down on the table. On the other hand, if you sell the call

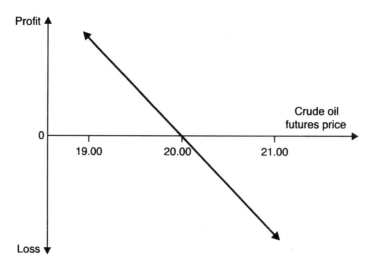

Profit

Crude oil
futures price

0

19.00   20.00   21.00

Loss

Figure 6.5 Profit/Loss Profile: Short Crude Oil Futures.

option, you are acting like the casino. You assume an unlimited loss potential less the premium paid to you and the most you can gain is the "chip" you have received.

Let us consider the volatility impacts of each of these short underlying positions. Consider a position where one sells a Crude Oil futures contract. This profits only when the price of Crude Oil falls and is not impacted by changes in volatility. When you buy a put option, you are buying both components of the option premium. The intrinsic value increases when the Crude Oil market price falls and the time value or "insurance" increases when volatility rises and decreases from the passage of time. Therefore, when Crude Oil market prices fall and volatility increases, the put option buyer gains a double benefit as long as not too much time decay has occurred.

When you sell a call option, you can benefit either from a drop in the time value or from a drop in the intrinsic value. Time value will decrease either when volatility drops or as the time passes. Intrinsic value for a call option will decrease to zero when the Crude Oil futures price falls below the strike price.

Selling a Crude Oil Futures Contract

I will now examine each of these short positions in turn and identify each strategy's sensitivity to volatility. Suppose I sold the Crude Oil futures at $20, and the market price decreases to $19.50. By selling the Crude Oil futures, my position is short relative to the underlying Crude Oil market and is neutral to volatility. Furthermore, the exposure of the short futures position relative to the price of the underlying does not vary either from a change in the price of the underlying or from a passage in time. As discussed earlier, the value of Crude Oil futures positions are independent of the implied and actual volatilities and of time. These positions only profit if the price falls. Therefore, for a short futures contract the delta is always -1.0 and all the other "Greek" derivatives are zero. If my viewpoint is neutral to volatility but I wish to be a seller of the underlying Crude Oil market, then the trading strategy I may wish to consider is to sell the Crude Oil futures. As with the long underlying position, I face unlimited loss and profit potentials. Therefore, the selection of this strategy depends on ability to assume risk. Thus, in the trading strategy matrix Table 6.9, we will place the short Crude Oil futures strategy in the lower middle cell which indicates neutrality to volatility and a bias which is short the Crude Oil market.

Buying a Put Option on Crude Oil Futures

With a put option on Crude Oil futures, you pay a premium to establish the position. It is inconsequential when you pay, as long as you pay at some point. Therefore, when you buy this option, and hold it to expiration, the maximum loss will be equal to the premium value agreed upon when the option is initially transacted. If Crude Oil futures prices fall enough to cover the cost of the premium, the put holder will break even. If it falls further, he or she will then make a net profit. Anyone buying option positions has an unlimited profit potential and a limited loss potential. If you buy a put option at a strike price of $20 and pay $0.865 for it, and the Crude Oil futures prices drop from $20 to $18.65 (a $1.35 move in the underlying futures), the net profit to the option holder would be $0.485 per barrel at expiration.

The reader will notice that the position will definitely profit from a decrease in the price of the underlying Crude Oil futures (assuming a constant implied volatility). In addition, prior to expiration the option has additional time value that is a function of volatility and time. As with the call, if volatility rises, the time value of the option will also rise proportionally. The profit and loss profile of holding a put option can be seen in Figure 6.6.

To assess the exposure of the put option prior to expiration, it is critical to calculate the "Greek" derivatives. Here they are for an at-the-money crude oil put option with:

- a strike price of 20,
- the underlying crude oil futures also at 20,
- 90 days until expiration,
- implied volatility of 22%, and
- short term interest rates at 4%.

The results of this can be seen in Table 6.5.

LONG PUT:
Theoretical values based upon a futures price of 20.00;
volatility 22%; rate of interest 4% and 90 days to expiration.

	PRICE	DELTA	GAMMA	VEGA	THETA
BUY 20.00 PUT	+0.865	-0.4745	+0.001812	+0.0394	-4.7313

Table 6.5 Long Put Sensitivities.

In this Table, the theoretical value of the put is $0.865 per barrel which implies that the total cost of one put option is $865. The delta is negative and equal to -0.4745. This indicates that when the price of the underlying Crude Oil futures falls, the put option price will initially rise by only 47.45% of the movement in the underlying. However as with the long call position, if the underlying price experiences an extreme move, the options delta will change: increasing (closer to zero) when underlying crude oil futures prices rise and decreasing (approaching minus 1.0) when the crude oil futures fall.

As with the long call position, the gamma is positive and the reader can see in the above table the long put has a positive gamma of +0.001812. If the reader looks back at the profit and loss profile for the option at 90 days until expiration, he will notice that the curved relationship between the options price and the underlying price is once again convex or half smiling (but this time smiling on the other side of the "face" compared to the call). This means that if extreme movements occur in the price of the underlying, the put option will automatically adapt its exposures to the benefit of the holder. Profits will accelerate when the underlying prices fall and losses will decelerate when prices rise. Clearly, the holder of the put option would want the actual volatility to increase (though it would be better if that increased price variability were associated with falling prices).

As with buying a call option, when one buys a put one is also buying the implied volatility. The vega is +0.0394 just like the call at the same strike price and

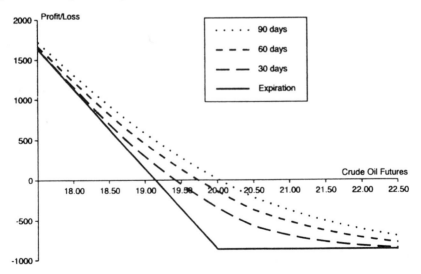

Figure 6.6 Profit/Loss Profile: Holding a Put Option.

the profit and loss implications are the same. The buyer of the put once again benefits from increases in both the actual volatility of the underlying market because he/she has a gamma positive position and from the implied volatility of the options market because he/she is long vega.

Finally, in Table 6.5 the holder of the put option has a theta negative position of -4.7313. This measure is also expressed as the quantity of US Dollars that will be lost from the passage of one calendar day in the options life. Of course, if the strike price of the long put position is different than in this example, the "Greeks" which influence option prices will also differ.

Suppose you have a situation where the put option purchased is deep in-the-money (a strike price of $22 when the Crude Oil futures price is at $20), its price will be made up of a substantial intrinsic value and a relatively small time value. In addition, since the delta of the put will approach -1.0, the change in the option price will move approximately one for one with the movement of one short Crude Oil futures position. At expiration, all in-the-money put options will be exercised into a short Crude Oil futures position and will at that point have a delta exactly equal to -1.0 for a put and +1.0 for all in-the-money calls. Once the Crude Oil futures has moved sufficiently to cover the amount paid for the put option, you have broken even and only hence can you make a profit. If the Crude Oil futures finishes equal to the strike price or higher, the put option premium is lost.

But a key point in options trading is profiting from changing volatility prior to expiration. Consider an at-the-money put option with a strike price of $20. Suppose the price of the option is $0.975 per barrel when the volatility is at 25%. Then CNN reports that IRAQ is once again massing troops on the border with Kuwait. Everyone becomes nervous and boosts the expectation of Crude Oil volatility to 30%. The put option premium will rise immediately to $1.17 per barrel. If I sold the put at that point, I would realise a profit of 19.5 cents per barrel even though the Crude Oil futures market had not yet moved. If the Crude Oil futures price happened to decrease as well, I would then achieve a double benefit from the increase in both intrinsic value and time value. Therefore, if my viewpoint is that volatility will increase as Crude Oil futures prices fall, purchasing a put option on Crude Oil futures will maximise my exposure to these two elements and provide the greatest profit if these events occur concurrently. If instead the Crude Oil futures price slowly rose as volatility fell, the put option would instead experience a double jeopardy and would in addition lose from time decay. So, in our trading strategy matrix Table 6.9, the purchase of a put option fits into the middle upper cell of the strategy matrix indicating biases of long volatility and short the Crude Oil market.

Selling a Call Option on Crude Oil Futures

The last trade that I will discuss on the short side is writing or selling a call option. For example, if we sell a $20 call, we receive a premium. For that premium, one assumes the obligation to sell. If the Crude Oil futures price decreases below $20

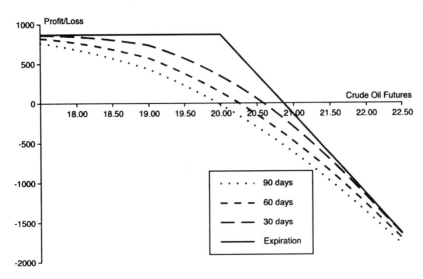

Figure 6.7 Profit/Loss Profile: Writing a Call Option.

per barrel, the call option holder will not exercise his or her option and the option seller will retain all the premium received. Unfortunately, when the Crude Oil futures price increases the option seller has to "pay back" some of the option premium he has received in the losses associated with selling the underlying position at what is now an unfavourable price. Consequently, if the Crude Oil futures price rises more than the premium the seller had received, the seller will have a net loss. However, this position is most advantageous when the Crude Oil futures price finishes at the strike price of the option or lower. Figure 6.7 displays the profit/loss profile from selling a call option.

A written call position will profit from a decrease in the price of the underlying crude oil futures. Again, this assumes that the level of the implied volatility has remained constant. If the implied volatility rises, the position is potentially at a loss since the time value of the option has increased. Thus, if the option seller reversed his position and bought back the option, he might have to pay more for it than he received in premium when he initiated the transaction. However, if time simply passes, the option value will drop from the time decay. To quantify this exposure exactly, we must again turn to the "Greeks". These have been estimated for a short position in an at-the-money crude oil call option with:

         - a strike price of 20,
         - the underlying crude oil futures also at 20,
         - 90 days until expiration,
         - implied volatility of 22%, and
         - short term interest rates at 4%.

The results of this can be seen in Table 6.6.

SHORT CALL:
Theoretical values based upon a futures price of 20.00;
volatility 22%; rate of interest 4% and 90 days to expiration.

	PRICE	DELTA	GAMMA	VEGA	THETA
SELL 20.00 CALL	-0.865	-0.5177	-0.001812	-0.0394	+4.7288

Table 6.6 Short Call Sensitivities.

By symmetry with the long call position, the premium received is equal to 86.5 cents per barrel. The delta is negative; equal to -0.5117. This indicates that when the price of the underlying Crude Oil futures falls, the call option price will fall by 51.17% of the movement in the underlying. As with the short put position, the seller of the call wants the price to fall so that he can buy it back at a lower price, resulting in a profit. So when the price of the underlying Crude Oil futures falls, that will benefit the call seller. However, if the underlying price experiences an extreme move, the options delta will also change. For the call seller, his "short" exposure will increase when the underlying crude Oil Futures price rises and decrease when the crude oil futures falls. As the reader can see from Figure 6.7, he has an unlimited loss potential which is accelerating. Again, the seller of options has a gamma negative exposure.

The amount of the exposure is -0.001812. This shows how adversely the delta will change for every tick change in the level of the underlying crude oil futures. If the reader looks back at the profit and loss profile for the option at 90 days until expiration, he will notice that the curved relationship between the options price and the underlying price is now concave or half frowning (the upside down mirror image of the long call). This means that if extreme movements occur in the price of the underlying, the option will automatically become either the option seller's worst nightmare or at best result in a limited profit of the premium received. Clearly, the seller of the call option would want the actual volatility to decrease (though it would be better if that decreased price variability were associated with slightly falling prices).

Whenever one sells any option, one is selling the implied volatility. In Table 6.6, the vega is -0.0394 and this means the amount that the value of the option will change for a change in 1% increase in the implied volatility. The profit and loss impact is exactly the same as for the short put example presented above.

As is indicated by the gamma and vega derivatives in Table 6.6, the seller of the call benefits from decreases in both the actual volatility of the underlying market (gamma negative) and from the implied volatility of the options market (vega negative).

Finally, in Table 6.6 the writer of the call option has a theta positive position of +4.7288. It is obvious that the seller of the call will gain the exact amount per day that the holder of the call will lose. As with the short put position, the call seller is depending on the time decay to accelerate and provide the profits from the strategy. Why would anyone want to sell options when such an unlimited risk potential exists?

Consider a stable market. That is the worst time for dealing because people attempt to make money out of sideways markets; often taking large positions which they get stuck with and are only disposed of at a loss (or at the very least the bid/ offer spread). Selling volatility via the options market is a better and more consistent way to make money when the market is stable compared with dealing in the futures.

If my viewpoint is that the underlying Crude Oil market is going to be stable, selling options allows me to profit from that opinion. This occurs because as Crude Oil market movements subside and risk decreases, option premiums fall. But which option should be sold, a call or a put? If I expect the drop in volatility to accompany a decrease in the Crude Oil market, the best position from that joint viewpoint is to sell the call option. In Table 6.9, since the call option seller is both a seller of the Crude Oil market and of volatility, this trade fits into our trading matrix in the centre cell.

Compared to buying a put option, the short call position has a limited gain if the Crude Oil futures market is steady or falls while the put option has an unlimited profit potential. If the Crude Oil futures market rises, the call option seller has an unlimited loss potential less the premium he has received, while the put buyer has the limited loss of his premium. The worst strategy to use when the Crude Oil market increases is a short position in the Crude Oil futures which has an unlimited loss potential without any premium to cushion these losses.

Comparison of the Bearish Strategies

Figure 6.8 displays the three positions which are bearish relative to the underlying Crude Oil market. On the downside, the most aggressive position is to sell the Crude Oil futures because you make a profit immediately. If you expect the Crude Oil market to decrease 20 or 25 cents, then you will receive all this in gain. That is your best short term trade. If you are concerned that the Crude Oil market might rise, you may not wish to have the unlimited loss potential associated with a short Crude Oil futures contract.

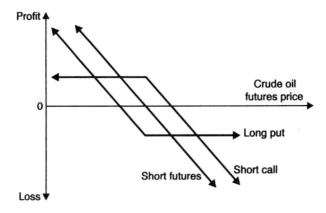

Figure 6.8 Option Strategies: Bearish Positions.

Put option buyers have a short position because they benefit when the price of the Crude Oil futures goes down. You also achieve a great deal of leverage with a relatively small amount of capital invested. Unfortunately, when you buy a put option, the Crude Oil market must drop during the life of the option otherwise the option will expire worthless. Remember, options are wasting assets. The worst drawback when buying an option is waiting while the time value steadily depletes and the market fails to move. It is like driving a car up a hill and you are hoping you make it to the top before it runs out of petrol.

The benefit for all option sellers is that they do not have to pay a premium and therefore do not suffer time decay. It works for them. They receive a premium and if the Crude Oil market is stable, they profit. As time passes they earn their income and if they sell the options near expiration, they will benefit from a very rapid time decay and inflow of income. But never forget that the most they can make is the premium paid to them, and their risk potential is unlimited. Therefore, with options one must decide if one wishes to buy an option with limited loss, or sell an option with a limited gain.

VERTICAL SPREADS

Fortunately, that is not the end of the story. With options one can use a wide variety of additional strategies by buying and selling options in combination. The strategist, by using both calls and puts of different strike prices can create new "instruments" with an infinite number of possible combinations. One of the most popular kind of combination trades which provides a directional viewpoint is the vertical spread. In these trades, you buy a call and sell a call, or you buy a put and sell a put. Both options will be on the same underlying position and with the same maturity. The twist is that one buys and sells options with different strike prices.

For example, suppose once again that you bought a Mercedes C 180 and sold a Mercedes 600 SL. What is your position versus Mercedes? You have a long position and a short position, but as I discussed in the previous chapter, the position may not be "square" relative to Mercedes. You have the obligation to take delivery and make delivery on two different models. In the options market, if I buy a call I have a long position. If I sell a call, I have a short position. Since I have varied the strike prices, they are also not direct offsets. As in the Mercedes example, I am not directly offset because the 600 SL model is worth more than the C 180. Nevertheless, even though they are not the same car, I will be able to reduce my exposure relative to the purchase of a single Mercedes Benz automobile.

The Bull Vertical Spread

If I expect the Crude Oil futures market to increase (that is, if I am bullish), then I might consider buying a bull spread. A bull spread is a vertical spread produced

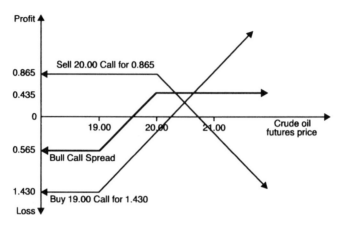

Figure 6.9 Bull Call Spread: Crude Oil Futures at 20.00.

either by the purchase and sale of calls, or by the purchase and sale of puts. However, the rule for bull spreads is to buy the lower strike price option and sell the higher strike price option. For the Crude Oil futures, let us consider a situation where there are 90 days to expiration, the volatility is 22% and the rate of interest 4%. Suppose I buy the $19/$20 bull spread, meaning I either buy the $19 call and sell the $20 call, or I buy the $19 put and sell the $20 put. This position profits when the Crude Oil futures increases. In this example, the Crude Oil futures is trading at $20.00 so the $19 call will cost me $1.430. To reduce my premium expense, I sell the $20 call option against it and receive $0.865 in premium. The net premium outflow is $0.565 which is the most I can lose.

Consider first the individual components in the bull spread. I have bought the $19 call which gives me the right to buy at $19. I have also sold the $20 call which is the obligation to sell at $20. If I bought at $19 and sold at $20, my inflow would be $1. But since I paid $0.565 for this strategy, the most I can make is the difference between these strike prices, $1, minus what I paid for the spread, $0.565, for a maximum profit potential of $0.435.

Suppose the Crude Oil futures market can finish at either $19, $20, or over $20. If the Crude Oil futures market finishes at $19, both the calls will expire worthless. My loss is equal to the $0.565 in premium I paid for the spread. Furthermore, if the Crude Oil futures market finishes at any price below $19, both options will also expire worthless and again I will lose the premium I paid. If the Crude Oil futures market finishes at $20, the $19 call will be in the money by $1 and the $20 call we sold will expire worthless. So I have an inflow of $1 less my $0.565 outflow in the initial premium expense which means I have a gain of 0.435 at that price. The same result will occur at any futures price over $20 because any additional gain I would have on the $19 call would be taken away by the $20 call which I had sold. Remember, buying the $19 call provides me the right to buy at $19 and selling the

$20 call obligates me to sell at $20. If one bought at $19 and sold at $20, the result is always the same, an inflow of $1. So I achieve both a limited loss and limited gain with this strategy.

Figure 6.9 displays the profit and loss diagram for this trade. In this diagram, we have included all the component parts as well as the combined positions. To determine the combined position, we will use our graphing rules, if we break up the profit and loss potentials into three sectors: The sector to the left of $19, the middle sector between $19 and $20 and the right sector to the right of $20. In the furthest left sector, the $19 call has a limited loss potential equal to the premium of $1.430 and the $20 call has a limited profit potential of $0.865. The rule is when you have two limited potentials, they will cancel. Therefore, the bull spread to the left of $19 per barrel has a limited loss potential of $0.565.

In the middle sector, the $19 call has an "unlimited" profit potential. That is, the profit rises one for one with the increase in the price of the Crude Oil futures. The $20 call has a limited profit potential over this range. The rule when we combine an unlimited and a limited is that the unlimited will dominate the limited. So, the combined strategy moves in the north-east direction parallel to the profit/loss profile of the $19 call option.

Finally in the right sector, the $19 call option still has an unlimited profit potential (above $20) and the $20 call option has an unlimited loss potential. The rule when we have two opposite unlimited potentials is that they cancel. So to the right of $20, the bull spread has a limited gain potential of $0.435 per barrel.

This mutated position profits when the price of the underlying crude oil futures rises. But how will the strategy perform prior to expiration? To see this, another figure has been produced which examines the value of the spread at various points in its life including 90, 60, 30 days until expiration and at expiration. This can be seen in Figure 6.10.

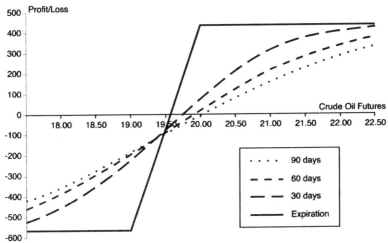

Figure 6.10 Bull Call Spread at Various Points in the Life of the Options.

As can be seen, at all points in the life of the options, the bull vertical spread has a bullish bias. The curvature of the strategy prior to expiration is fairly smooth with a tendency to flatten if the price of the underlying market moves far away from the strike prices of the options. While we are certain that the bull spread has a positive exposure to the underlying market (and a positive delta), it is impossible to assess the other sensitivities of the spread to those other factors which influence the value of the spread without looking at the "Greeks". So, once again the reader is referred to Table 6.7 for the option derivatives for each of the component parts of the bull spread and the combined exposure.

BULL CALL SPREAD:
Theoretical values based upon a futures price of 20.00;
volatility 22%; rate of interest 4% and 90 days to expiration.

	PRICE	DELTA	GAMMA	VEGA	THETA
BUY 19.00 CALL	+1.430	+0.6951	+0.001588	+0.03462	-4.0907
SELL 20.00 CALL	-0.865	-0.5177	-0.001810	-0.03939	+4.7288
BULL CALL SPREAD	**+0.565**	+0.1774	-0.00022	-0.00477	+0.6381

Table 6.7 Bull Call Spread Sensitivities.

As the reader can see, the theoretical value of the bull call spread is 56.5 cents per barrel. The total cost of one bull call spread is $565. Because a premium was paid for the spread, this type of bull spread is also known as a "debit" spread. As with any long option strategy, if a premium is paid out to establish a vertical spread, that is the most the trader can lose. The net delta of the spread is positive and equal to +0.1774. This indicates that when the price of the underlying crude oil futures rises, the bull call spread will initially rise by only 17.74% of the movement in the underlying. However, if the underlying price experiences an extreme move, the options delta will change: decreasing to zero when underlying crude oil futures prices rise sufficiently above the higher strike price for the spread and also decreasing to zero when the crude oil futures price falls sufficiently below the lower strike price of the spread.

It is interesting that the other exposures of the spread are entirely different from those previously examined for the other options strategies. For example, the net gamma position of the bull spread is almost zero at -0.00022. This means that almost no curvature exists for the spread if the underlying market price changes. This is the case because the spread contains two option positions that have opposite gamma exposures. Thus the positive gamma of the long call almost completely offsets the negative gamma of the short call. Likewise, for the vega exposure, the long call is vega positive while the short call is vega negative. When these are combined in the spread, the net vega exposure is trivial at -0.00477. In dollar terms, this means if the implied volatility rises or falls by 1%, the impact on the spread is $4.77. Whenever the vega impact is less than the cost of lunch at McDonalds, it is not worth worrying about. Finally, the time decay of the bull spread has been neu-tralised at a theta of +0.6381. This number means that we will make almost 64 cents in time decay over the next day (from 90 to 89 days). This neutralisation to the passage of time is a critical benefit to those using these spreads. For in no other options strategy does one achieve an equivalent position relative to the underlying with a limited loss without being ravaged by the effects of time decay. For this rea-son, I will consider the time decay benefits of vertical spreads in more detail.

Time Decay and Volatility Sensitivities of a Bull Spread

Why would one want to buy this? Two reasons may exist: time decay neutrality and volatility immunisation. If I buy an option outright (also known as a "naked call") my exposure to time decay is extensive. If an option is sold, then time decay works in my favour. Therefore, if I am both buying and selling options, my expo-sure to volatility and time decay is reduced and can be neutral. Figure 6.11 displays the time decay characteristics of buying a $20 call compared to a $19/$20 and a $20/$21 bull spread. If I buy the $20 call, I pay a premium of $0.865 per barrel. The time decay for this option as can be seen in the chart is rapid and accelerating. The bull spreads on the other hand do not experience such time decay because the time value of the bought option is decaying at a rate similar to the time decay of the option we have sold and thus offsets. Therefore, an advantage for vertical spreads is that they can be held for a very long time without appreciable time decay and also provide a limited loss feature. In the last 30 days, however, the reader can see that the time decay for the bull spreads is quite rapid. For example, the in-the-money bull spread ($19/$20) will rapidly decay to its intrinsic value of $1 (when the crude oil market is at $20.00) while the out-of-the money bull spread ($20/$21) will rapidly decay to its intrinsic value of zero.

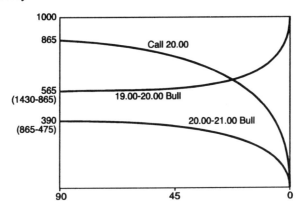

Figure 6.11 Time Decay Characteristics: Bull Spread.

Assume for a moment that it is your viewpoint that over the next six months Crude Oil futures price will increase, but you do not know exactly when. Further, you might feel that volatility may decrease over this period but you do not wish to be hurt if this occurs, and that you require a strategy with limited loss potential in case you are wrong. Finally, you want a strategy which will not be eroded by time decay. If you establish a bull spread, you will achieve all these objectives. Suppose Crude Oil futures take four months to rise. When that occurs, the bull spread increases in value due to intrinsic value gain on the lower strike price call. Because the bull spread is neutral to time decay, you have not been hurt by patiently waiting for the Crude Oil market to move. In practice, if you hold the bull spread up to 30 days until expiration and if the Crude Oil futures market still has not moved, then the spread should have approximately the same value the spread had when you purchased it and you should be able to sell it back at little or no loss. If you put on a bull spread and then have to unwind it, you may still believe the Crude Oil futures market may rise. So if your viewpoint is still bullish you can "roll" the bull spread forward in time by doing exactly the same spread in the next expiration month. This spread will also have immunity to time decay and volatility. As long as you "roll" out of bull spreads 30 days prior to expiration, you should not have any appreciable loss on the spread due to time decay. However, during the last 30 days, bull spreads can decay very rapidly which, incidentally, can be quite advantageous to sellers of these spreads. So, if you are a buyer of an out-of-the money bull spread, make sure to roll out of it by that point.

The biases of bull spreads are directionally buyers of the underlying Crude Oil market, and regarding volatility neutral because they are both buying and selling options. That is how you achieve a position with a limited loss and a negligible volatility exposure. So, if my viewpoint is that the Crude Oil market will increase and I wish to be neutral to volatility, then the bull spread is the ideal strategy to use. Thus, if we return to our Strategy Matrix in Table 6.9, the bull spread will be the cell in the lower left hand side with a long underlying bias but neutral to volatility. It is important to note that in this cell is also the long Crude Oil futures position.

The bull spread shares the same directional and volatility biases as a long Crude Oil futures contract. However the bull spread's advantage is the limited loss feature which the Crude Oil futures position does not share. In addition, if the trader wished to have the same exposure as one long Crude Oil futures contract, he can still achieve this using the Bull spread above. The only trick is to make sure the total delta position of the strategy is equivalent to that of one long futures contract (delta of 1.0). How can this be done given the delta of the bull spread is only 0.1774? Easy, put on more bull spreads. Since all the "Greeks" simply can be summed across the strategies used, to achieve a delta of 1.0, we simply put on six \$19/\$20 bull spreads and the equivalent exposure is +1.0644 (6 · +0.1774). Of course, all of the other "Greek" exposures must also be multiplied by 6, however, this will still indicate a relatively small exposure to both volatilties and time decay.

It is not difficult to understand why vertical spreads are so widely used by traders wishing to take directional viewpoints on the market. They achieve a limited loss, can assume the same directional exposure (delta) as holding the underlying with minimal exposure to volatility changes or time decay. But vertical spreads do not work just for bull markets, they are ideal trades for bearish scenarios as well.

The Bear Vertical Spread

While bull spreads benefit when the Crude Oil market increases, bear spreads benefit when the Crude Oil futures price decreases. Bear spreads are almost identical to bull spreads, except that the rule with bear spreads is that you buy the higher strike price option and sell the lower strike price option. Therefore, to create a bear spread one would buy the $21 put and sell the $20 put. However, if I buy the $21 call and sell the $20 call, that is also known as a bear spread but this trade is called a bear call spread. The bear call spread is referred to as a credit vertical spread because your account will be credited with an inflow of premium. A bear put spread is known as a debit vertical spread because one must pay out premium for it. Similar to buying options, if I pay a premium to establish a vertical spread that is the most I can lose (and if I receive a premium that is the most I can make). Now, back to the bear put spread.

If I buy a $21 put option, I might have to pay $1.47 for it: a limited loss and an unlimited profit potential, but at a dear price. To reduce this premium cost and protect myself against time decay, I also sell a $20 put option; receiving back 0.865. The net cost of this combination is equal to an outflow of 0.605 ($1.47 minus 0.865). Again, that is the most I can lose and the profit potential for this spread is $0.395 (the $1 between $21 and $20 less the 0.605 I paid for the option spread). Figure 6.12 displays a build-up profit and loss diagram for this strategy.

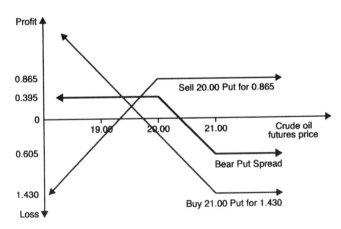

Figure 6.12 Bear Put Spread: Crude Oil Futures at 20.00.

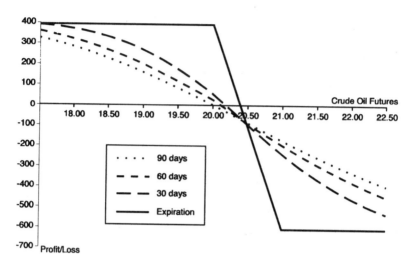

Figure 6.13 Bear Put Spread at Various Points in the Life of the Options.

Again using our graphing rules, we can break up the profit and loss potentials into three sectors. As with the bull spread, we will look at the left sector below $20, the middle sector between $20 and $21 and the right sector above $21. Below $20, the $20 put option I sold has an unlimited loss potential and the $21 put I purchased has an unlimited profit potential. Apply our graphing rules, since opposite unlimited potentials cancel, the bear spread has a limited profit over this range equal to the difference in the strike prices, $1, less the amount I paid for the spread 0.605 for a net profit of $0.395.

In the middle sector between $20 and $21, the $20 put I sold expires worthless and the $21 put I bought has an "unlimited" profit potential. Because the unlimited dominates the limited, I achieve an unlimited profit potential sloping to the north-west.

Finally in the right sector above $21, both put options expire worthless and therefore the combined position has both limited gain and loss profits. So I lose $1.47 on the $21 put I purchased and gain 0.865 on the $20 put I sold, with a net loss of 0.605. Again, like the bull call spread, I achieve a limited profit potential with the bear spread.

This mutated position profits when the price of the underlying crude oil futures falls. But how will the strategy perform prior to expiration? To see this, another figure has been produced which examines the value of the spread at various points in its life including 90, 60, 30 days until expiration and at expiration. This can be seen in Figure 6.13.

As can be seen, at all points in the life of the options, the bear vertical spread has a bearish bias. The curvature of the strategy prior to expiration is fairly smooth to the downside with a tendency to flatten if the price of the underlying market moves far away from the strike prices of the options. While it is clear that the bear spread has a negative exposure to the underlying market (and a negative delta), it is impossible to assess the other sensitivities of the spread to those other factors which influence the value of the spread without once again looking at the "Greeks". Table 6.8 displays the option derivatives for each component of the bear spread and in combination.

BEAR PUT SPREAD:
Theoretical values based upon a futures price of 20.00;
volatility 22%; rate of interest 4% and 90 days to expiration.

	PRICE	DELTA	GAMMA	VEGA	THETA
SELL 20.00 PUT	-0.865	+0.4745	-0.00181	-0.03942	+4.7313
BUY 21.00 PUT	+1.470	-0.6480	+0.00169	+0.03682	-4.3533
BEAR PUT SPREAD	+0.605	-0.1735	-0.00012	-0.00260	+0.3780

Table 6.8 Bear Put Spread Sensitivities.

The theoretical value of the bear put spread is 60.5 cents per barrel. The total cost of one bear put spread is $605. Again because a premium was paid for the spread, this is also a "debit" spread.

The net delta of the spread is negative; equal to -0.1735. This indicates that when the price of the underlying crude oil futures falls, the bear put spread will rise in value by only 17.35% of the movement in the underlying. As was the case with the bull call spread, the deltas of the bear spread will change in a similar manner: decreasing to zero when underlying Crude Oil futures prices rise sufficiently above the higher strike price for the spread and also decreasing to zero when the Crude Oil futures price falls sufficiently below the lower strike price of the spread.

Again, the other option derivatives are all close to zero. The net gamma position of the bear spread is -0.00012. The net vega exposure is once again minuscule at -0.00260. In dollar terms, this means if the implied volatility rises or falls by 1%, the impact on the spread is $2.60. This is certainly less than the price of a Big Mac, so once again we can ignore the sensitivity of the spread to changes in the implied volatility. Regarding the time decay of the bear spread, this has been neutralised with a theta exposure of only +0.3780.

The advantages of bear spreads are that one is a seller of the underlying Crude Oil market, and the exposures to volatility and time decay are neutral because the trade involves both buying and selling options. Thus, the strategy offers a limited loss and a negligible volatility exposure, and is an equivalent short position relative to the underlying Crude Oil market. As with the bull spread, the time decay characteristics are neutral. The reader is referred to Figure 6.14 which compares the time decay of holding a put option to two bear spreads, one which is in-the-money and one which is out-of-the-money. As with the comparison for the long calls and the bull spreads, the bear put spread gives the trader more time to realise his profit from a drop in the price of the underlying asset. So, if my viewpoint is that the

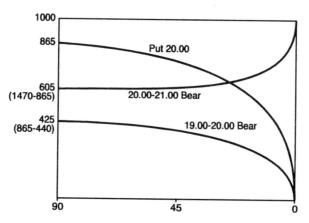

Figure 6.14 Time Decay Characteristics: Bear Spreads.

Crude Oil market will decrease, and I wish to be neutral to volatility and time decay, then a bear spread is the ideal strategy to use. In our strategy matrix in Table 6.9, the bear spread will be the cell in the lower middle. This strategy is a seller of the underlying market but neutral to volatility. As was promised earlier in this chapter, we can use options to provide the same volatility neutrality as an Crude Oil futures position but with a limited loss feature.

DIRECTIONAL TRADING STRATEGIES PLACEMENT IN THE STRATEGY MATRIX

With the completion of our discussion of vertical spreads, I have filled Table 6.9 with eight possible strategies. What I will do in the next three chapters is to examine the category of option strategies that fit into the furthest right cells of the

Viewpoint on the crude oil market

		Buyer	Seller	Neutral
Viewpoint on Volatility	Buyer	Buy call option	Buy put option	
	Seller	Sell put option	Sell call option	
	Neutral	Long futures Bull spread	Short futures Bear spread	

Table 6.9 Option Trading Strategy Matrix.

Strategy Matrix. These trades will be neutral to the underlying market but bullish, bearish or neutral on volatility. These trades include volatility strategies, options arbitrage and trading options between related markets.

7: Volatility Trading Strategies

In this chapter, I will discuss what may be the most creative of the options strategies, volatility trades. As previously explained, volatility is essentially the risk aspect of the market. It is the perception of risk that is "securitised" in the time value component of an option premium. The volatility can be implied in the options price (which includes traders' expectations of future price movements) or be based upon the actual fluctuations in the price of the asset which underlies the option. As I mentioned in Chapter 4, there are three ways to measure volatility. One method is the historical basis which measures what has happened in the past and is expressed as the annualised standard deviation of percentage changes in the underlying asset. The second method is the implied volatility which is the current volatility associated with the option's price. Finally, there is the method of volatility estimation which forecasts future volatility by using econometric techniques which incorporate both the historical and implied techniques.

Traders buy or sell volatility as their perception of future risk in the future changes. When market makers get more "edgy", they buy up volatility and when they expect stability, volatility goes down. So, the current determination of volatility is simply the supply and demand for risk and this is reflected in the fluctuations in the prices of options.

In this chapter, I will use the option on coffee futures traded at the Coffee Sugar and Cocoa Exchange (CSCE). The prices are in US Dollars and Table 7.1 outlines the contract specification for this underlying. The asset underlying the option is a CSCE Coffee futures contract which is the obligation to either buy or sell 37,500 pounds of Coffee beans.

Trading Unit	One Coffee "C" futures contract
Trading Hours	9:15 A.M. New York Time until the completion of the closing period which shall commence at 2:05 P.M.
Price Quotation	Cents per pound
Contract Months	"Regular Options": March, May, July, September, December. "Serial Options": January, February, April, June, August, October, November.
Minimum Fluctuation	1/100 cent/lb., equivalent to $3.75 per contract.

Position Limits	Options are considered part of futures positions. 2,000 net/long short any one month; 4,000 net total. Combined published "futures equivalent" ratios of options positions with futures positions. Exemptions may apply for hedge, straddle and arbitrage positions.
Strike Price Increments	Futures Contract Price All months Less than $1.00 2.5 cents Less than $2.00 5 cents $2.00 or more 10 cents
Expiration Date and Time	9.00 P.M. New York Time on the last trading day. Notification of intention to exercise must be made by an option holder to a carrying member firm by 4.00 P.M. on such day.
First Trading Day	"Regular Options": First Trading day following the last trading day of any expiring regular option month. "Serial Options": First trading day of the second calendar month preceding the serial option month.
Last Trading Day	First Friday of the calendar month preceding the contract month.

Table 7.1 Options on Coffee Futures (CSCE).

HOW TO MAKE MONEY FROM A CHANGE IN VOLATILITY

How can someone make money from a change in risk? In an earlier chapter, I provided an example of risk trading with the story about the fellow who bought insurance and was later (incorrectly) diagnosed as having a terminal disease. Because the value of the health insurance increased dramatically, the policy holder sold it back to the insurance agent and made a profit.[1] Then, when he was diagnosed correctly, as not having a terminal disease, he was able to repurchase his health insurance at a low price once again. The insurance buyer had purchased low risk and then sold higher risk, to make money. The higher the perception of risk, the greater the value of the insurance. As risk recedes, insurance premiums and options prices both drop in value. So, if you expect risk to increase, you will buy risk and if you expect risk to fall, you sell risk. In this section, I will examine how to both buy and sell risk using volatility trading strategies.

---

[1]While this may seem to be a contrived example, sadly this is not the case. Recently in the United States an entire industry has sprung up with investors buying the life insurance policies of victims of the HIV virus. The chronically ill patient receives a big cheque that he can spend now while he can still enjoy it and the buyer of the policy has unfortunately a sure payoff of which the only unknown is when it will be paid.

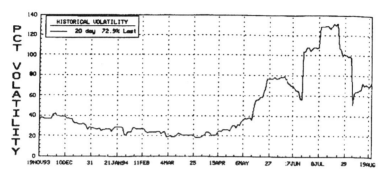

Figure 7.1a Historical Price Volatility Coffee Futures (Source: Bloomberg).

As was mentioned earlier, volatility is measured in percentage terms. How often does this perception of risk change? It can change as often as daily. Figures 7.1a and 7.1b display the historical and implied volatilities of the nearby coffee futures from 19 November 1993 until 23 August 1994. To calculate the historical volatility each day, the previous 20 days' percentage change in the nearby coffee futures prices was used. As each day passed, the 20 day analysis period was moved forward one day to achieve a rolling 20 day historical volatility.

Consequently, the standard deviation is calculated based upon daily returns. To turn it into an annualised number, one simply multiplies the daily standard deviation by the square root of the number of trading days in a year (which is approximately 260 days). Each trading day the process was repeated (using the preceding 20 days) to provide the estimate of volatility for that period. To estimate the implied volatility series, the at-the-money call option for the nearest maturity was inverted to yield an implied volatility based upon the closing price of the option on that date. This number was re-estimated for each date in Figure 7.1b.

Over the period of time shown in Figure 7.1a volatility started out at around 40%, then drifted downwards to about 20% in April 1994. Then all hell broke loose. Over May to July, frosts in South America destroyed a major portion of the

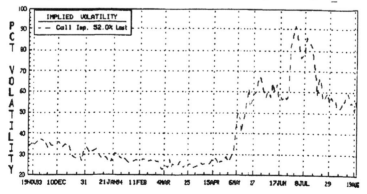

Figure 7.1b Historical Implied Volatility Coffee Options (Source: Bloomberg).

coffee crop in Brazil and the actual movement in the nearby coffee futures rose to more than 120% actual volatility. Clearly, those who had been long actual volatility (positions that were gamma positive) would have benefited over this time. After the middle of July, the air came out of the over-inflated volatility balloon, and the actual variability in the market began to stabilise. The actual volatility was still around 60% but this is substantially down on the levels experienced in June and early July. Therefore, one would have benefited from "selling" volatility in early July and taking profits later in the month when the market variability was reduced. However, this is the actual historical coffee volatility that occurred over the period. Would the implied volatility of traded options contracts also have "sky rocketed" and subsequently dropped during this period? Figure 7.1b displays the implied volatility for the same period. As the reader can see, the implied volatility did indeed start to rise at the end of April 1994 and peaked in the first week of July 1994 at an implied level of around 90% (the historical volatility peaked one week later at 120%). Thereafter, both the historical and implied volatilities collapsed to between 50% and 60% by the middle of August. While one may not necessarily predict the other, it is clear that the general trends for both the implied and actual volatilities are similar. In most markets, the historical actual volatility has a reasonably close relationship to implied volatility.

When you trade volatility, the principles are the same as when you trade any price series. You buy when it is low and sell it at a higher level or you sell it at a high level and buy it back at a lower level. For instance, over the time period represented in Figure 7.1b, one can see that volatility in coffee futures experienced a steady downtrend from November 1993 until April 1994. During that period, traders would have benefited by selling options volatility. After April 1994, volatility was certainly a "buy" until the first week of July when the implied volatility was running out of steam. At that point, it would have made sense to sell volatility once again, perhaps taking profits at the end of July. Of course, hindsight is always 20/20. However, this does not preclude the fact that some traders (perhaps using the techniques presented in Chapters 4 and 5 of this book) had identified opportunities to exploit the changes in the volatilities of coffee futures.

Upon closer scrutiny of Figure 7.1a and 7.1b, the reader will observe that volatility seems to move like any other price series. It will rise and fall and then rise again. This can occur because the perception of risk changes over time. When new information comes into the market, people revise their opinions of risk and thereby change the prices at which they are willing to buy or sell options, which are after all insurance policies on that risk. Ceteris Paribus (that is everything else remaining the same), if volatility increases, option prices rise and if volatility decreases, option prices fall. Therefore, one buys options when the perception of risk rises and one sells options when risk is presumed to fall.

The ideal way to trade volatility is to maximise the exposure to both kinds of volatility (actual and implied) and minimise the exposure to the other factors which influence option prices, such as small movements in the underlying market and if possible time decay. This is done by using the "Greeks" to assess the exposure the trading strategy has to all the variables which drive options prices. To benefit from a change in the actual volatility of the market, the trader will concentrate on establishing a gamma positive or negative position. Likewise, to benefit from a change in the implied volatility, the trader will focus on his vega exposures. For the other derivatives such as delta, theta and rho, he will minimise his exposure to these elements if possible, by driving the level of these "Greeks" to zero. By doing so, the trader can focus his viewpoint on volatility alone. Then, one can trade volatility as though it was a simple price series. When one is completely neutral to the underlying market and is just trading volatility, it is termed pure volatility trading. In addition to pure volatility trading, one can establish trading strategies that are initially neutral to the underlying market but can become an equivalent long or short position if the underlying market price moves to a particular level. These trades I will call leaning volatility trades. In this chapter, I will examine in detail both pure and leaning volatility strategies.

Option prices (the time value component) are nothing more than risk channelled into a security. As risk increases it will increase the value of the security or the option derived from it. Sometimes, the increase in time value can be so extreme as to offset and even dominate changes in the intrinsic value. Figure 7.2 provides such an example of how this can occur.

In this example, when the underlying market price is at 135 cents per pound, the 135 call with 90 days to go has a price of 6.375 cents if volatility is at 24% and the rate of interest is 4%. Suppose the market price goes down to 130 cents per pound. If the volatility remains at 24%, the call option price will fall from 6.375 cents to 4 cents. But what happens if the market goes down because something dramatic happened in the coffee market? If the fall in the market is concurrent with a volatility increase to 36%, the option would then be worth 7 cents even though

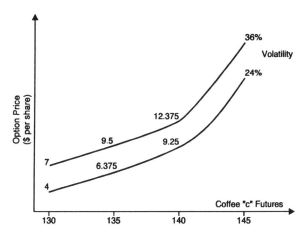

Figure 7.2 Volatility impacts for a 90 day call option.

the underlying market price has fallen. Therefore, one was able to make money buying the call option even though the underlying market price fell. In this case, the impact of volatility was more substantial than the other factors influencing the option price. Let us assume my view is that volatility will increase and the market will also increase, and therefore I buy the call option. Given that both events occur, I will make a substantial gain on this trade. Suppose the market increases to 140 cents per pound and volatility goes up to 36%, I will nearly double my investment of 6.375 cents in the call. This is because I could then sell the call for 12.375 cents. As I demonstrated above, if volatility increases and the market is stable or falls I can still make a profit from the purchase of the call.

Volatility is so important that in some circumstances one may wish to trade the volatility separately because its impact is so critical to option premiums. To isolate for the volatility impacts, we must immunise the exposure to the underlying market. To do this, we will combine various options or underlying positions so that in combination, the strategy is immune to changes in the value of the underlying asset (as measured by the delta). Thus, the position will experience neither profits nor losses if the price of the underlying asset changes. The reader may recall that in Chapter 3, I mentioned that long equivalent positions offset short equivalent positions. So, in volatility trading, we will establish positions which have opposite and equivalent exposures to the underlying market to achieve this immunised position. These strategies will all initially have a delta exposure of zero and are often referred to as delta neutral strategies.

THE "PURE" BUYING VOLATILITY STRATEGIES

Suppose one purchased a call option which is an equivalent long position. As demonstrated above if volatility increases one will profit. If the same person also bought a put option which is an equivalent short position, in combination with the long call what would he have? The put option has an opposite exposure to the underlying market, in other words, short, but will also benefit if volatility increases. So in combination, these two trades can be combined in such a way that they will be neutral to the underlying market but one will still be holding two options both of which have a long volatility bias. That is how you go "long" volatility; by buying options. If one buys both a call and a put and adjusts carefully for the delta exposure of each, then the position can be neutralised to the underlying asset and will then be purely a volatility trade. Depending on which strike prices you choose, this combination trade is called either a straddle or a strangle.

Buying a Straddle

A long or buying straddle is achieved when you buy a call option and a put option both at the same strike price (generally both at-the-money). The call option you purchase is a long position relative to the underlying market and the put option is a short position relative to the underlying. The total exposure of these two in combination will cancel out relative to the underlying position. Suppose we buy both options which are at-the-money, both options have deltas of approximately 0.50. In our case, a long call has a delta around positive 0.50 and a long put has a delta close to -0.50. If we combine the +0.50 delta with the -0.50 delta, the net delta position is 0.0 or neutral to the underlying. This means that if the price of the underlying asset changes up or down and this change is sufficiently small, there will be no impact on the combined values of the options positions. The gains in one will exactly offset the losses in the other.

Even though you are neutral to the underlying asset, you are still holding two options having paid two premiums. Thus, for both options you are long volatility. One establishes this trade on the same underlying position, the same maturity and at the same strike price. Suppose when the underlying market is trading at 135 cents per pound I bought a 135 cents call option on coffee futures, the most I can lose is the premium paid but I have gained an unlimited upside potential. When I purchase the 135 cents put, I also have a limited loss potential and an unlimited profit potential to the downside. Figure 7.3a displays the two positions plotted together. To the left of 135 cents, we have an unlimited profit potential for the put and a limited loss potential for the call. The graphing rule for the combination of an unlimited profit potential and a limited loss potential says that the unlimited profit potential will dominate the limited loss potential. Therefore, the combination has an unlimited profit potential to the left of the strike price. To the right of 135 cents, we have an unlimited profit potential on the call and a limited loss potential on the put. Once again, the unlimited profit potential dominates the limited loss potential, and the combination will have an unlimited profit potential over this range. So, if

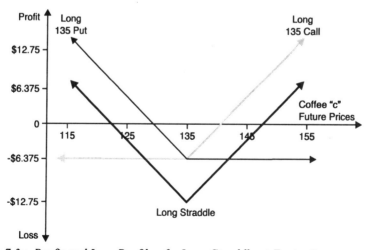

Figure 7.3a Profit and Loss Profile of a Long Straddle at Expiration.

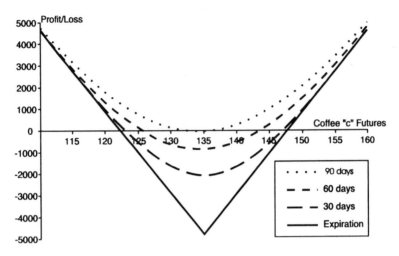

Figure 7.3b The Profit and Loss Profile of a Long Straddle over time.

you combine these two positions, the overall strategy looks like a big "V". You gain an unlimited profit potential to the left of 135 cents and an unlimited profit potential to the right of 135 cents. This strategy fails when the market stays level at 135 cents and both option premiums are lost.

If the straddle is purchased with 90 days until expiration, the position is flat at the current price of the underlying asset which is 135 cents. This can be seen in Figure 7.3b, where the value of the straddle is displayed at various points in its life and at expiration. If the price of the coffee futures moves sufficiently up or down, immediate profits will be generated. However, if time simply passes, the straddle will lose value if the underlying coffee futures price stays at 135 cents.

While it was shown that if volatility doubles for the at-the-money option, the time value of the option will also double. The straddle has two such at-the-money options, thus the trader is doubling up the exposure to changes in the implied volatility.

The only way we can quantify these effects is to examine the "Greek" derivatives for each element of the strategy and in total. This has been done for the long coffee straddle assuming:

- a strike price of 135 cents,
- the underlying coffee futures also at 135 cents,
- 90 days until expiration,
- implied volatility of 24%, and
- short term interest rates at 4%.

The results of this can be seen in Table 7.2.

LONG STRADDLE:
Futures 135; volatility 24%; rate of interest 4%; 90 days to expiration.

	PRICE	DELTA	GAMMA	VEGA	THETA
BUY 1 135 PUT	+6.36	-0.47256	+0.000246	+0.09978	-13.061
BUY 1 135 CALL	+6.36	+0.51972	+0.000246	+0.09970	-13.054
LONG STRADDLE	**+12.72**	+0.04714	+0.000492	+0.19948	-26.115

Table 7.2 Long Straddle Sensitivities.

As the reader can see, the theoretical value of the long straddle is 12.72 cents. Given that each contract is for 37,500 pounds of coffee, the total cost of one straddle is $4,770. The delta is slightly positive at +0.04714. But this is trivial. Generally, all delta positions which are ±0.10 are considered delta neutral. Essentially, this delta level indicates that when the price of the underlying coffee futures moves, the value of the straddle will initially change in the same direction by only 4.714% of the movement in the underlying. However, if the underlying price experiences an extreme move, the options delta will change: both increasing when underlying coffee futures prices rise and also when the coffee futures prices fall.

From the last chapter, the reader will remember that whenever one buys an option, the gamma is positive. In the case of the straddle, we have bought two options and thus have a double gamma effect. In the above table, the gamma for the straddle is +0.000492. While this number appears to be slight, that is because it is expressed in the impact on the delta from a one tick movement in the coffee futures which is 1/100th of a US cent per pound. If we look at a movement of 10 cents per pound, this will imply that the delta will change by ±0.4920 ($10·100·.000492$). Since the gamma is the measure of the sensitivity of the options price to a change in the actual volatility in the underlying asset, we will benefit from increased underlying price variability because we have a doubly positive gamma. If the reader looks back at the profit and loss profile for the option at 90 days until expiration, he will notice that the curved relationship between the options price and the underlying price is fully smiling. This means that if extreme movements occur in the price of the underlying, the option will automatically adapt its exposures to the benefit of the holder in both directions. So it is fair to say that the holder of the straddle would want the actual volatility to increase and would be indifferent if the market prices rose or fell.

Whenever one buys an option, one is also buying the implied volatility. For the straddle, the sensitivity to this factor is again doubled. In Table 7.2, the vega is +0.19948 and this means the amount that the value of the straddle will change for a change in 1% in the implied volatility. This number is again expressed relative to US $1,000 in this table. Therefore, if the implied volatility rises from 24% (the current level) to 25%, the premium cost of the option will rise by $199.48. Given that the original price of the straddle was $4770, this would mean that the new price of the option should be $4969.48 at a 25% implied volatility.

Finally, in Table 7.2 the holder of the straddle has a negative theta position (of -26.115). This measure is expressed in the amount of US Dollars lost due to the passage of one calendar day in the option's life (from 90 days to 89 days to expiration). Thus, if everything else remains constant, the holder of the call would expect tomorrow that his option would only be worth $4743.885 (current price of $4770 minus time decay of $26.115).

If this position is initiated when the underlying coffee futures is at 135 cents, it will be delta neutral. This is because the positions bought are at-the-money options with delta exposures that approximately offset. While you have no exposure to the underlying market, this trade will be extremely sensitive to volatility. Purchasing at-the-money options, which have the greatest time value, gives you the greatest absolute volatility sensitivity. Unfortunately, these options are also extremely sensitive to time decay. Thus, very few traders can afford to maintain these strategies for long periods or until expiration; most traders rather trade them for a short time period and take off the spread when and if the volatility increases. Often, these are effective strategies to establish prior to the release of government trade figures or other news events that tend to cause volatility or market uncertainty to change.

Prior to expiration, both options will have substantial time value. As with the call option trade discussed previously, the value of each can increase dramatically from any increase in volatility. Straddles essentially double the exposure to volatility compared to the purchase of a single option. This means a doubling in the straddle value for the same increase in the rate of volatility. Here is an example.

If the volatility is at 24%, we may pay 12.75 cents for the at-the-money 135 cents straddle, each option valued at 6.375 cents. Now, what happens if volatility goes up five percent to 29%? If the market price remains at 135 cents, both the call and the put premiums will now be worth 7.75 cents or a total of 15.5 cents for the straddle. If the straddle is sold at the now higher volatility, we have made 2.75 cents per contract just from the 5% increase in volatility. The market is still sitting at 135 cents, it has not moved. But because the volatility rose, we were able to realise an immediate profit with the straddle. Unfortunately, if nothing occurs and both volatility and the market are stagnant, the trade will erode due to the time decay. That is the reason most dealers rarely buy straddles for more than a few days. They use them as a short term trade expecting an immediate increase in volatility to occur. If that occurs, they will immediately close out the straddle, take their profits and run. These trades are often traded and quoted as spreads: buying the straddle at 12.75 cents and then selling it at 13.25 cents for example.

Buying a Strangle

A variation on this theme is the strangle which costs less that the straddle to establish. With the strangle you are buying a call and a put on the same coffee futures position for the same maturity, but at different strike prices. As before, the equivalent long position and the equivalent short position will offset each other relative to the underlying market. Generally, strangles are established with out-of-the-money

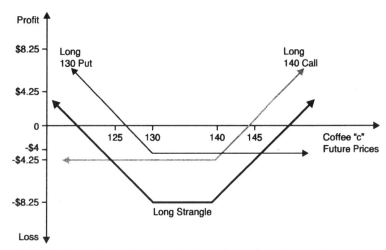

Figure 7.4a Profit and Loss Profile of a Long Strangle at Expiration.

options. If they are established with in-the-money-options, they are often referred to as "guts" positions. So, you are going to buy an out-of-the-money call and an out-of-the-money put. With the market trading at 135 cents, you would buy the 140 call (price 4.25 cents) which is out-of-the-money. At the same time, you will buy a 130 put (price 4 cents) which is also out-of-the-money. In Figure 7.4a both of these trades are displayed and we will apply our graphing rules to see what the profit and loss profile of this combination will be.

To the left of 130 cents per pound, we have an unlimited profit potential on the long put option and a limited loss potential on the call option. The graphing rule states that an unlimited profit potential will dominate the limited loss potential, so the strangle will have an unlimited profit potential below 130 cents. Between 130 cents and 140 cents, the 130 put has a limited loss potential and the 140 call also has a limited loss potential. In this case, they do not cancel but instead combine. Nevertheless, the loss potential is limited to the total premium cost. To the right of 140 cents, the 140 call has an unlimited profit potential and the 130 put has a limited loss potential, so the rule is that the unlimited profit potential dominates the limited loss potential and the strangle will have an unlimited profit potential over this range.

If the strangle is purchased with 90 days until expiration, the position is even flatter than the straddle at the current price of the underlying asset which is 135 cents. This can be seen in Figure 7.4b. Once again, if the price of the coffee futures moves sufficiently up or down, profits will be generated. However, if time simply passes, the strangle will lose value especially if the underlying coffee futures price remains between $130 and $140.

While I have said elsewhere in this book (Chapter 3) that a picture is worth a thousand words, it may be somewhat difficult to compare the straddle and strangle

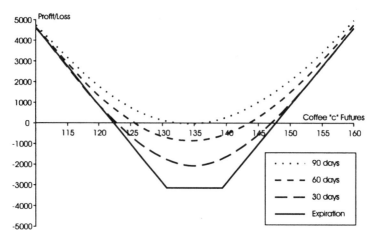

Figure 7.4b The Profit and Loss Profile of a Long Strangle over time.

by looking at Figures 7.3b and 7.4b. The only way we can quantify the differences between the strategies is to examine the "Greek" derivatives for each strategy. This has been done for the long coffee strangle assuming:

> - a strike price of 130 for the put and 140 for the call,
> - the underlying coffee futures at 135 cents,
> - 90 days until expiration,
> - implied volatility of 24%, and
> - short term interest rates at 4%.

The results of this can be seen in Table 7.3.

LONG STRANGLE:
Futures 135; volatility 24%; rate of interest 4%; 90 days to expiration.

	PRICE	DELTA	GAMMA	VEGA	THETA
BUY 1 130 PUT	+4.08	-0.35052	+0.000229	+0.09292	-12.234
BUY 1 140 CALL	+4.30	+0.39977	+0.000238	+0.09673	-12.735
LONG STRANGLE	+8.38	+0.04925	+0.000468	+0.18965	-24.969

Table 7.3 Long Strangle Sensitivities.

The theoretical value of the long strangle is 8.38 cents with the total cost of one straddle equal to $3142.50 (8.38 cents · 37,500 pounds). The delta is again slightly positive at +0.04925 and will be considered delta neutral for all practical purposes. The gamma exposure for the strangle is positive equal to +0.000468. If the reader looks back at the profit and loss profile for the option at 90 days until expiration, he will notice that the curved relationship between the options price and the underlying price is fully smiling. This means that if extreme movements occur in the price of the underlying, the option will automatically adapt its exposures to the benefit of the holder in both directions. So it is fair to say that the holder of the strangle would want the actual volatility to increase and would be indifferent if the market prices rose or fell. Comparing the strangle to the straddle, it is not clear from the graph which is smiling more. If we look at the gammas, then these indicate that for 90 days until expiration, the straddle with the higher gamma has the bigger "grin". If the underlying market stays at 135 cents, then as the both strategies approach expiration, the gamma for the at-the-money options that make up the straddle will rapidly rise. At the same time, the out-of-the-money options which make up the strangle will decrease to zero. Therefore, not only at the current moment (90 days to expiration) but throughout time, the straddle will always have a higher gamma than the strangle and will therefore be more appropriate for those traders who are betting on an increase in the actual volatility of the market.

Whenever one buys an option, one is also buying the implied volatility. For the straddle, the sensitivity to this factor is again doubled. In Table 7.3, the vega is +0.18965 and this means the amount that the value of the straddle will change for a change in 1% in the implied volatility. This number is again expressed relative to 1,000 US Dollars in this table, therefore, if the implied volatility rises from 24% (the current level) to 25%, the premium cost of the option will rise by $189.65. Given that the original price of the strangle was $3142.50, this would mean that the new price of the option should be $3332.15 at a 25% implied volatility.

Finally, in Table 7.3 the holder of the strangle has a negative theta position of -24.969. This measure is expressed in the number of US Dollars that will be lost from the passage of one calendar day in the options life (from 90 days to 89 days to expiration). Thus, if everything else remains constant, the holder of the call would expect tomorrow that his option would only be worth $3117.804 (current price of $3142.50 minus the time decay of $24.969).

Since with the strangle you are buying out-of-the money options, you are paying a smaller premium compared to the straddle and you are not going to have the same amount of money exposed to time decay, because you have purchased less time value.[2] In this example, the 130 put price would be worth 4 cents and the 140 would also be priced at 4.25 cents. Therefore, the strangle price would be 8.25 cents. With the strangle, you are no longer maximising your exposure to time value or to volatility. But you do have a position that does not cost as much to establish and therefore has a smaller loss potential. These trades can be established for perhaps a longer time period than the straddle, but you still will want to take them off within 7 to 10 days if market volatility has failed to change. The other major benefit of the strangle is that it is constructed using out-of-the-money options which experience a greater percentage increase in their value from a change in volatility. The reader is referred back to the end of Chapter 2 (Table 2.4) which demonstrated that when an option is at-the-money, it will experience the greatest absolute in-

---

[2]Although the rate of time decay for the strangle may actually be greater than for the straddle for various periods prior to expiration, the quantity of money that will be lost is less.

crease in price from a change in the implied volatility but that the out-of-the-money options will have the greatest percentage impact. So the strangle is preferred by those traders who wish to bet on increases of the implied volatility while the straddle traders are betting on both an increase in the actual volatility (gamma effect) and the absolute impact of the implied volatility (vega effect).

While there are numerous other strategies one can establish to buy volatility, most traders will keep things simple and buy either the straddle or the strangle when trying to initiate a pure volatility strategy, because these strategies are the most sensitive to changes in volatility and are relatively simple to initiate and unwind.

Where Long Straddles and Strangles Fit in the Strategy Matrix

With both straddles and strangles, the viewpoint is neutral to the market and long volatility. So, if we return to our trading strategy matrix at the end of this chapter (Table 7.12), we will place the long straddle and long strangle into the upper right cell which is neutral to the underlying market but with a buying bias to volatility. These trades work when one is uncertain where the underlying market is going but one believes that volatility will increase over the short term and before time decay erodes the value of the position.

When establishing any of these trades, it is critical that the trader remains disciplined: He must place the trades as a spread and take the trades off as a spread. If one starts looking at each component separately and trades them not as a spread but one at a time, things can get very dangerous. Remember that the viewpoint with these trades is neutral to the underlying position: I do not care whether the market goes up or goes down, I will buy it and sell it as a spread because my initial viewpoint was to make money on the increase in volatility. The disciplined trader remembers that he has "bought" volatility at a low level expecting to sell it at a higher level, ideally in two or three days before the spread starts experiencing heavy time decay. What may occur is that the coffee market jolts one way or the other and he will be very tempted to take off only one side of the spread. For example, let us consider we bought a straddle and the market collapsed, one might want to take off the call and let the put "ride". What usually happens is that then the market will rally and you lose on both the call and the put. This kind of trading technique is called "legging".

To understand the risks of legging I will use the analogy of a cowboy in the Old West facing the problem of crossing a barbed wire fence. The cowboy on his horse rides up to the barbed wire fence and plans to cross over the fence and change onto another horse on the other side. He will raise one leg at a time keeping one leg astride his first horse and at the same time trying to place his free leg on the other horse on the other side. Now as he is suspended over the barbed wire fence in the process of switching horses, what happens if one of the horses takes off? He is probably going to be badly hurt. Legging trades are essentially like this. If you decide not to trade these strategies as a spread but instead try to take off one leg at a time hoping the other one will move in your favour, the results can be calamitous in case the market fails to accommodate your technique. When one does this one is no longer purely trading volatility but attempting a foolhardy trading technique. Whenever you trade, remember what your objectives are. More good trades go wrong when traders try to change position in midstream because they forget why they established the position in the first place. The spread trader would be well advised whenever he considers legging a trade to remember the old Wall Street adage: "Bulls make money, bears make money, but pigs get slaughtered". Remain disciplined, greed can cost you dearly!

Straddles and strangles are referred to as pure volatility trades because when you initially establish them, the positions are delta neutral and the trader profits equally if the market goes up or down. With both strategies, the unlimited profit opportunity is equal on both sides. What the straddle and strangle buyer is concerned about is that something happens quickly; either the market moves or volatility increases.

LEANING VOLATILITY BUYING STRATEGIES: RATIO BACK SPREADS

There are other ways to buy volatility that do not have the same balanced viewpoint on the underlying market and these trades are called leaning volatility trades. These trades start out as delta neutral, but as the market moves, they will develop a bias on the movement of the underlying asset. The two most common of these trades are known as call-back spreads and put-back spreads.

Call Ratio Back Spreads: the Call-Back

Call-back spreads are also referred to as call ratio back spreads, but I prefer to call them call-backs. With the call-back, you buy two or more higher strike call options, and you sell one lower strike price call option or any other combination which leaves you delta neutral. How can this be neutral to the underlying market? Remember that when one buys call options these positions provide positive deltas and when one sells call options these positions provide negative deltas. What we must do is balance the deltas so that in combination they equal zero.

Suppose I buy two out-of-the-money call options which have a strike price higher than the prevailing market price. Suppose each option has a delta of 0.25. If I buy two of them, my total delta position will be a positive 0.50. If I then sold an at-the-money call, that would give me an equivalent short position with a delta of -0.50. Remember, at-the-money options always have a delta of 50/50. In combination, the two options I have purchased give me a delta position of +0.50 and the short call at the money gives me a delta of -0.50. Consequently, the overall delta

241

position is zero and therefore is delta neutral. This position is "long" volatility because you are buying more options than you are selling. Thus, this position profits as volatility increases because the two options we have purchased are more sensitive to volatility changes than the single option we sold. As I will demonstrate, you are going to have a limited gain potential if the market falls and an unlimited gain potential if the market rises.

To show how this works, I will separate the components of the spread into trades already discussed. If I buy one out-of-the-money call and sell an at-the-money call what is that? The answer is a bear call spread. Let us assume I have a bear call position and if the reader refers back to our trading strategy matrix Table 6.9 in the last Chapter, he will see that the bear spread is bearish on the market and neutral to volatility. I will split our two long calls in the call-back into two sets of one apiece and combine one of these with the short call to create our bear spread. Then I will add another long call option to the bear call spread. What will be the net effect? Since buying a call has a bullish bias on the underlying position and the bear spread has a bearish bias, in combination the bias relative to the underlying would be neutral. Regarding the volatility exposure, the long call is a buyer of volatility while the bear call spread is neutral. So in combination, the spread will be a net buyer of volatility. Thus, the call-back spread will be neutral to the market but long volatility.

It would appear that the call-back spread is purely a volatility spread because it is neutral to the market and long volatility. Why then am I calling this a "leaning" volatility strategy? The reason is that at expiration the payoff profile will not be symmetrical as it was with the straddle or the strangle. The call-back will profit more from the market going one way than the other. To see this better, the reader is referred to Figure 7.5a which is the build-up diagram for the call-back spread.

We start off by combining a 140 cents call we have purchased with the 130 cents call we have sold. Suppose that when this trade was established, the underly-

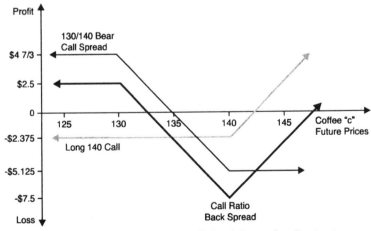

Figure 7.5a Profit and Loss Profile of a Call-Back Spread at Expiration.

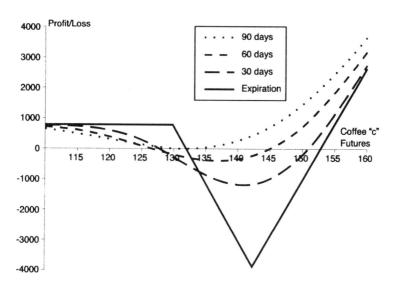

Figure 7.5b The Profit and Loss Profile of a Call-Back Spread over time.

ing coffee futures market was at 135 cents, there were 42 days to expiration and volatility was 24%. So the 130 call we wrote is in-the-money and the 140 call we bought is out-of-the-money. To determine the exposure now, I must either view the current profit and loss profile or look at the deltas. Consider first the delta values. The 130 short call has a delta of -0.69 when its price is 7.25 cents and the 140 long call has a delta of +0.34 associated with a price of 2.375 cents. In combination, the bear spread has a delta position of -0.35. When we add the second long 140 call, we pick up another +0.34 delta. Thus, our overall exposure to the underlying coffee futures will approach zero because the size of the positive and negative delta positions are approximately offsetting. For this reason, the call-back spread starts out as delta neutral at the current levels.

Let us consider another example, where the call-back spread is established with 90 days to expiration. It is constructed by selling two 142.5 calls (receiving 3.48 cents for each) and by buying one 130 call (paying 9.04 cents).The profit/loss of this trade at expiration is displayed in Figure 7.5b and also indicated are the profit and loss profiles of the trade at various points prior to expiration.

If the call-back spread is purchased with 90 days until expiration, the position is extremely flat at 135 cents which is the current price of the underlying asset and will remain so until a price of 130 cents is reached. Once again, if the price of the coffee futures moves sufficiently up or down, profits will be generated. However, the strategy is leaning to the upside as the profit potential is unlimited there and limited only if the underlying coffee price falls. Again, if time simply passes, the call-back spread will lose value with a maximum loss if the underlying coffee futures price finishes at 142.5 cents which is the higher strike price of the options in the strategy. To quantify the exact exposures of the call-back spread we must assess the "Greek" derivatives for each component of the strategy. This has been done for the coffee call-back spread assuming:

- a strike price of 130 cents for the lower strike call we sold,
- a strike price of 142.5 cents for the higher strike price calls we bought,
- the underlying coffee futures at 135 cents,
- 90 days until expiration,
- implied volatility of 24%, and
- short term interest rates at 4%.

The results of this can be seen in Table 7.4.

CALL-BACK SPREAD:
Futures 135; volatility 24%; rate of interest 4%; 90 days to expiration.

	PRICE	DELTA	GAMMA	VEGA	THETA
BUY 2 142.5 CALLS	+2·3.48	+0.6879	+0.000455	+0.18438	-24.322
SELL 1 130 CALL	-9.04	-0.6420	-0.000230	-0.09339	+12.115
CALL-BACK SPREAD	**-2.08**	+0.0459	+0.000225	+0.09099	-12.207

Table 7.4 Call-Back Spread Sensitivities.

The theoretical value of the call-back spread is minus 2.08 cents. This means that we will actually receive a premium from this strategy and the total receipt for the call-back spread is $780 (2.08 cents · 37,500 pounds). The delta is slightly positive at +0.0459 which is within the range of ±0.10 so this qualifies as delta neutral. The gamma exposure for the call-back is positive equal to +0.000225. If the reader looks back at the profit and loss profile for the option at 90 days until expiration, he will notice that the curved relationship between the options price and the underlying price is smiling in a sort of crooked way. This means that if extreme movements occur in the price of the underlying, the option will automatically adapt its exposures to the benefit of the holder especially in a rising underlying market scenario. The holder of the call-back spread would want the actual volatility to increase to realise the benefits of having a gamma positive position.

Whenever one buys more options than one is selling, one is generally a "net" buyer of the implied volatility. For the call-back spread, this can be assessed by examining the vega. In Table 7.4, the vega is +0.09099 and this means the amount that the value of the straddle will change for a change in 1% in the implied volatility. This number is again expressed relative to US $1,000 in this table, therefore, if the implied volatility rises from 24% (the current level) to 25%, the total premium value of all the options will rise by $90.99. Given that originally the call-back spreader would have received $780 upon the initiation of the trade, he would realise an additional profit of $90.99 if the implied volatility rose.

Finally, in Table 7.4 the call-back spread has a negative theta position of only -12.207. While this loss of $12.21 is minimal for one calendar day, it will begin accelerating especially if the underlying coffee market slowly rises to 142.5. At that point, the greatest time decay effect will occur.

If one compares the call-back profit/loss profile to that of either the long straddle or the strangle, one will notice that while the price volatility strategies are balanced to underlying movement profiting equally, the call-back spread is "leaning" to the upside.

So, the call-back is a spread which is initially neutral to the market and a buyer of volatility. If, however, the market moves up, the call-back has an unlimited profit potential and if the market falls the call-back has a limited profit potential. What the call-back spreader is hoping for is a dramatic increase to the upside. If he is wrong and the market crashes, he will still make some profits. The worst thing that could happen is that the market slowly rises and then stays put until the expiration of the option. The next example is another "back" spread which will also provide both an unlimited gain potential on one side and a limited gain potential on the other side. The difference is that this "back" spread will be the mirror image of the call-back spread.

The Put Ratio Back Spread: The Put-back

This leaning volatility spread is the put-back spread. The put-back is established when you buy two or possibly more puts and you sell one put, so that the combination is delta neutral. In this example, let us assume the coffee futures price is currently at 135 cents, there are 50 days until the coffee options expire, the options volatility is 24% and the short term interest rate is 4%. You buy two puts at a strike price of 130 and pay 2.625 cents for each (5.25 cents in total). These puts are out-of-the-money with a delta of -0.318. Then, you sell one put which is in-the-money with a strike price of 140 and receive back 7.75 cents. The 140 put is in-the-money and when we sell it has a delta of +0.640. The total negative delta exposure is once again approximately equal to the positive delta exposure so the overall position is almost delta neutral. This position profits as volatility increases because once again you are buying more options than you are selling. Secondly, you have a limited gain potential on the upside and an unlimited gain potential on the downside.

To see how this is created, we will once again break the spread into trading strategies I have previously examined and see how in combination the spread evolves. We split the two long 130 put options into two sets of one put each and combine one of the long 130 puts with the 140 put we have sold. By selling the higher strike price put option for 7.75 cents and buying the lower strike price put option at 2.625 cents we have constructed a bull put spread. This is a credit bull spread as we will receive 5.125 cents in premium back and this maximum profit will occur at prices 140 cents or higher. The biases of a bull spread are neutral to volatility and bullish on the underlying market. Then we buy an additional put op-

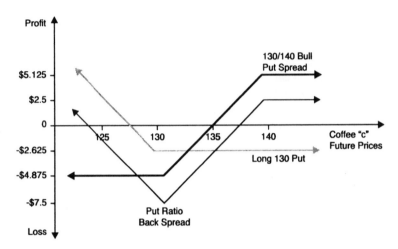

Figure 7.6a Profit and Loss Profile of a Put-Back Spread at Expiration.

tion at the 130 strike price and again have to pay 2.625 cents for it. This trade is a bearish position relative to the underlying market and bullish to volatility. In combination, the put-back will be neutral to the market and bullish on volatility. But since the spread is almost delta neutral, how can it be a leaning strategy? Like the call-back spread, the put-back gains more on one side than on the other. In the case of the put-back spread, this will occur on the downside. To see this, we must again view the strategy at expiration. In Figure 7.6a, another put-back spread is displayed using current prices for the options on the coffee futures.

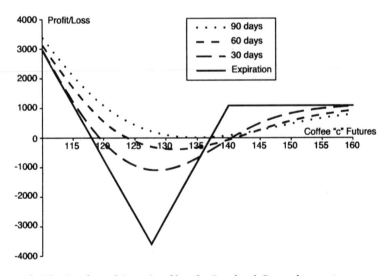

Figure 7.6b The Profit and Loss Profile of a Put-back Spread over time.

To see how the profit and loss profile of the spread changes through time, let us consider another example with real numbers. Suppose, I have purchased two 127.5 puts and sold one 140 put. If the put-back spread is purchased with 90 days until expiration, the position is extremely flat at the current price of the underlying asset which is 135 cents and will remain so over a range from 130 cents to 140 cents. This can be seen in Figure 7.6b. Once again, if the price of the coffee futures moves sufficiently up or down, immediate profits will be generated. However, the strategy is leaning to the downside as the profit potential is unlimited there and limited only if the underlying coffee price rises.

Again, if time simply passes, the put-back spread will lose value with a maximum loss if the underlying coffee futures price finishes at 127.5 cents which is the lower strike price of the strategy. To quantify the exact exposures of the put-back spread we must assess the "Greek" derivatives for each component of the strategy. This has been done for the coffee put-back spread assuming:

- a strike price of 140 cents for the higher strike put we sold,
- a strike price of 127.5 cents for the lower strike price puts we bought,
- the underlying coffee futures at 135 cents,
- 90 days until expiration,
- implied volatility of 24%, and
- short term interest rates at 4%.

The results of this can be seen in Table 7.5.

PUT-BACK SPREAD:
Futures 135; volatility 24%; rate of interest 4%; 90 days to expiration.

	PRICE	DELTA	GAMMA	VEGA	THETA
BUY 2 127.5 PUTS	+2·3.16	-0.5849	+0.000425	+0.17238	-22.742
SELL 1 140 PUT	-9.26	+0.5927	-0.000230	-0.09738	+12.633
PUT-BACK SPREAD	**-2.94**	+0.0078	+0.000185	+0.07500	-10.109

Table 7.5 Put-back Spread Sensitivities.

The theoretical value of the put-back spread is again negative (-2.94 cents). This means that once again we will receive a premium from this strategy and the total receipt for the put-back spread is $1,102.50 (2.94 cents · 37,500 pounds). The delta is very slightly positive at +0.0078 which is well within the range of ±0.10. The gamma exposure for the put-back is positive equal to +0.000185. If the reader looks back at the profit and loss profile for the option at 90 days until expiration, he will notice that the curved relationship between the options price and the underlying price is also smiling in a sort of crooked way. This means that if extreme movements occur in the price of the underlying, the option will automatically adapt its exposures to the benefit of the holder especially in a falling underlying market scenario. The holder of the put-back spread would want the actual volatility to increase to realise the benefits of having a gamma positive position.

In Table 7.5, the vega is +0.07500 and this means the amount that the value of the put-back spread will change for a change in 1% in the implied volatility. This number is again expressed relative to US $1,000 in this table, therefore, if the implied volatility rises from 24% (the current level) to 25%, the premium cost of the option falls by $75.00. Given that originally, the put-back spreader would have received $1,102.50 upon the initiation of the trade, he would realise an additional profit of $75 if the implied volatility rose.

Finally, in Table 7.5 the put-back spread has a negative theta position of only -10.109. While this loss of $10.11 is also minimal for one calendar day, it will begin accelerating especially if the underlying coffee market slowly falls to 127.5 cents. At that point, the greatest time decay effect will occur.

Quite often these spreads are created over time. Suppose I have purchased a bull spread, either a bull call or a bull put spread. The market moves up and I have a profit. I could simply take my profit and consolidate. But if my viewpoint has now changed and my bias is now bearish on the market and bullish on volatility, I can protect the profit in the bull spread and change the bull spread into a put-back spread by simply purchasing another put. At that moment, I am delta neutral which means my exposure to the underlying position has been covered. In addition, the trade is now long volatility and if the market really collapses as volatility rises, the put-back will profit where the bull spread would show a loss.

Where Back Spreads Fit in the Strategy Matrix

Call-backs and put-backs are somewhat difficult to categorise. Are they volatility trades or directional trades? The correct answer is that they are both. They are initially neutral to the underlying market but they can become a buying or selling position depending on how dramatically the market moves. They are net buyers of volatility because you are buying more options than you are selling, so they are definitely bullish on volatility. We might be inclined to put them into our trading strategy matrix in the neutral volatility category. But we should instead review when a trader might use these trades rather than the long straddle or strangle. Traders would use a call-back, for instance, when their viewpoint is that the market will rise and they also wish to be buyers of volatility but do not want to pay any premium as would be required for an outright call option. In fact, the back spreaders will receive a premium. Because the call-back spread precisely meets this viewpoint, it makes more sense to place the call-back into the strategy cell which is long on the market and long on volatility. So, if the reader refers to our updated strategy matrix at the end of the chapter (Table 7.12), he will see that I have placed the call-back spread in this cell. The put-back spread by a similar argument would be classified as a bearish directional viewpoint with a long volatility bias. So, we will put it into the same cell as the long put option. Thus, if traders have a bullish volatility bias and can form some sort of directional viewpoint, the call-back can substitute for the purchase of a call option and the put-back can substitute for a long put option.

This ability to evolve one type of strategy into another by adding an option or two is one reason why options markets provide such tremendous flexibility to the investment strategist. The addition of one simple trade can change the whole characteristic of an existing strategy to meet a trader's revised views on both the underlying market and volatility. With these two trades I will conclude volatility buying strategies.

THE "PURE" SELLING VOLATILITY STRATEGIES

Strategies which benefit from quiet times and static markets are probably the most common use for options in volatility trading. Many option trading professionals make money from selling options. Since options are securitised risk, some people think of them in a similar light to a casino. Strictly speaking, this is not correct. Risk in an underlying market existed prior to the introduction of options. On the other hand, casinos create risk that did not previously exist in order to provide a vehicle for gambling. Nevertheless, gambling does provide an insight when considering the selling of options. In casinos, the consistent winners over time are the gambling houses which sell the bets. In options, this can also be the case. Option sellers will win over time if they have the "edge". The edge is an important consideration in option trading and deserves a slight digression at this point.

The "edge" is the difference between theoretical option values and actual option prices. For example, consider the following gamble: Someone throws a die. You will receive from the gamble one Dollar times whatever is on the top face of the die when it comes to rest. If it lands with one dot up you will receive one Dollar and if it lands with 6 dots up you get six Dollars. What is the theoretical value of the gamble? To determine this, we multiply the possible payoffs by each payoff's probability of occurrence and then add these together. So, in this case, ($1 · 1/6) + ($2 · 1/6) + ($3 · 1/6) + ($4 · 1/6) + ($5 · 1/6) + ($6 · 1/6) = $3.5. The theoretical price is $3.5 but the house may wish to sell the gamble for $4. That means the casino would have an "edge" of 50 cents on each toss. Thus over time, the difference between the amount the casino receives in bets and the amount it has to pay out will average to a profit of 50 cents. Of course, if the buyer of the gamble was able to buy it for $3 then he would have the edge of 50 cents and that would be the amount he would expect to make on average if he repeated the gamble an infinite number of times.

In option dealing the same principle applies: The option seller attempts to sell options at prices higher than their theoretical value and option buyers do the reverse. In volatility selling strategies, trades are established to maximise the edge from over-valued market prices for options. The key element in the determination of the theoretical value of the option is an accurate estimation of future volatility. Suppose a trader, using the techniques outlined in Chapters 4 and 5, determines that the future volatility for coffee options should be 20% while the current implied volatility in the market is 25%. To gain the edge, he will select those strategies which would profit from the implied volatility falling from 25% to 20%. In essence, he will select those strategies which have a negative vega. This means that the change in the value of the position will be inversely related to changes in the levels of the implied volatility. Therefore, if the implied volatility eventually falls (as the trader is forecasting), then the vega negative strategies will generate a profit.

The volatility selling (and vega negative) strategies in this section will include straddles, strangles, butterflies, and condors. Options sellers benefit from selling a volatility level which is currently higher than they believe it should be. When sellers do this, they are gaining a theoretical edge.

Selling the Straddle

To understand selling volatility, the reader should follow the same steps we took for the buying volatility strategies. Consider the individual that sells a call option. He will have a short (delta) position relative to the underlying market. He also sells a put option that is a long (delta) position relative to the underlying market. So, if he combines these two trades, he will have a position that can be neutral to movements in the underlying market. The purest of the selling volatility trades is the straddle where one simply does the exact opposite of those trades which make up the long straddle. With the short straddle, I sell a call option and I sell a put option both on the same underlying position and maturity and with the same strike price, generally both at-the-money. Why do we sell at-the-money options? The simple reason is that the greatest time value for an option is when that option is at-the-money. Furthermore, the time value is the insurance component of the option premium and that is the amount the option writer expects to earn. At-the-money options are entirely composed of this insurance component.

Option sellers make money in the same way as insurance companies do, by selling insurances. Insurance companies receive a premium by assuming a risk for the policy holder. Such companies generally make a lot of money by collecting premiums and investing the proceeds. However, they can only sell their insurance against one side of the market. For example, they can sell insurance to pay if you die, or to protect against one's house burning down. The insurance companies cannot sell an insurance policy against your not dying or against your house not burning down. But with options, you can sell somebody the right to sell and sell somebody the right to buy and by definition these two trades will offset each other to some degree. Options sellers therefore have an advantage when compared to insurance underwriters who can only sell insurance policies on one side of the market. Consider for a moment the short straddle. By selling both a call and put option at the same strike price, at least one of these options has to expire worthless, and potentially both could expire worthless.

Let us look at an example: Suppose you sell a 135 call option on coffee futures. The most you can make is the premium received and you have an unlimited loss potential. A short call is an equivalent short position that makes money when the

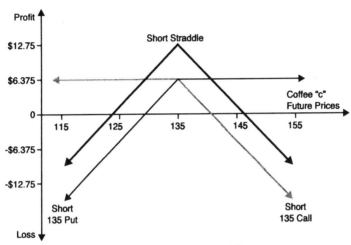

Figure 7.7a Profit and Loss Profile of a Short Straddle at Expiration.

market goes down and loses money when the market goes up. In this case, you also sell a 135 put option.

Again, the most you can make is the premium you received when the market rises and you have an unlimited loss potential when the market falls. What will these options look like in combination? If we apply our graphing rules, it will look like the opposite of the long straddle. To the right of 135 cents, one has a limited gain on the put and an unlimited loss potential on the call. To the left of 135 cents, one has a limited gain on the call and an unlimited loss potential for the put. What is the graphing rule when you have an unlimited loss and a limited profit together? Unlimited is going to dominate the limited, so the short straddle will have an un-limited loss potential on both sides. However, you are going to make a substantial amount of money if the market finishes right at 135 cents, the strike price for the options. The profit/loss profile for the short straddle can be seen in Figure 7.7a.

If the straddle is sold with 90 days until expiration, the position is flat at the current price of the underlying asset which is 135 cents. If the price of the coffee futures moves sufficiently up or down, losses will be generated assuming no change in the implied volatility component of the options. However, if time simply passes, the straddle will lose value if the underlying coffee futures price stays at 135 cents. This is what will provide the profits to the seller of the straddle. To see this better, Figure 7.7b has been drawn that shows the profit and loss profile of the short straddle at various points in time prior to and including the expiration.

In addition, the seller of the straddle has sold two at-the-money options which means the position has a "double" exposure to changes in the implied volatility. To quantify how much the short straddle could make from these effects, the option derivatives have been estimated assuming:

      - a strike price of 135 cents,
      - the underlying coffee futures also at 135 cents,

- 90 days until expiration,
- implied volatility of 24%, and
- short term interest rates at 4%.

The results of this can be seen in Table 7.6.

SHORT STRADDLE:

Futures 135; volatility 24%; rate of interest 4%; 90 days to expiration.

	PRICE	DELTA	GAMMA	VEGA	THETA
SELL 1 135 PUT	-6.36	+0.47256	-0.000246	-0.09978	+13.061
SELL 1 135 CALL	-6.36	-0.51972	-0.000246	-0.09970	+13.054
SHORT STRADDLE	-12.72	-0.04714	-0.000492	-0.19948	+26.115

Table 7.6 Short Straddle Sensitivities.

The numbers in this table are the exact inverse of those for the long straddle found in Table 7.2. The theoretical value of the long straddle is -12.72 cents which indicates that for each spread we sell we will receive $4,770. The delta is slightly negative at -0.04714. But it is once again within the acceptable range to be classi-fied as delta neutral. If the underlying price experiences an extreme move, the op-tions delta will change: with devastating effects both when underlying coffee fu-tures prices rise or fall.

The short straddle also has a double gamma effect. In this case it is negative (-0.000492). For a movement of 10 cents per pound in coffee futures prices, this will imply that the delta will change adversely by ±0.4920 (10·100·.000492). Since the gamma is the measure of the sensitivity of the options price to a change in the

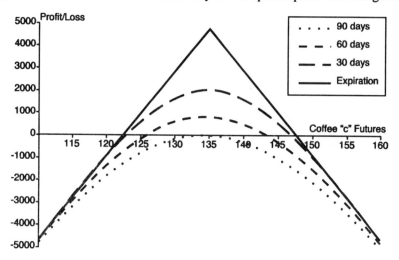

Figure 7.7b The Profit and Loss Profile of a Short Straddle over time.

actual volatility in the underlying asset, the short straddle will benefit from decreased underlying price variability. This can be seen vividly in the profit and loss profile for the option at 90 days until expiration. You will notice that the curved relationship between the options price and the underlying price is extremely unhappy; a frown if I ever saw one. This means that if extreme movements occur in the price of the underlying, the short straddle will experience severe losses in both directions. The closer to expiration the short straddle is taken, the more unhappy the graph looks and the more extreme the negative gamma effect will impact the position.

Whenever one sells an option, one is also selling the implied volatility. For the short straddle, the sensitivity to this factor is again doubled. In Table 7.6, the vega is -0.19948 and this means the amount that the value of the straddle will change for a change in 1% in the implied volatility. This number is again expressed relative to US $1,000 in this table, therefore, if the implied volatility rises from 24% (the current level) to 25%, the premium cost of the option will rise by $199.48. Given that originally, the straddle was sold for $4770, this would mean that if the seller of the straddle covered the position at the new price of the option, he would have to pay $4969.48 for it at a 25% implied volatility and realise a loss of $199.48.

Finally, in Table 7.6 the seller of the straddle has a positive theta position (of +26.115). This measure is expressed in the number of US Dollars that will be earned from the passage of one calendar day in the options life (from 90 days to 89 days to expiration). Thus, if everything else remains constant, the straddle seller would expect tomorrow that the spread would only be worth $4743.885 (current price of $4770 minus time decay of $26.115) and that this daily time decay profit would accelerate through time.

This ability to profit from market prices staying in a range is unique to options trading. How many people have heard a dealer say "I do not know where the market is going but, I tell you what, I guarantee that it is going to be between 130 cents and 140 cents over the next month?" How can someone make money from this view? With the short straddle, you can profit if the market stays within a given range. It is a very effective strategy for making money in stable markets. It is like roulette, when someone bets on the reds and someone bets on the blacks. At least one of them will lose and the house will profit from that fact.

So, you receive premiums from both buyers. If both options are priced at 6.375 cents you will receive a total of 12.75 cents inflow, and you are going to make money anywhere in the range from 122.25 cents to 147.75 cents (plus or minus 12.75 cents from 135 cents). Your maximum profit is going to be 12.75 cents per pound if the market finishes at 135 cents. The best thing about selling straddles is that one earns so much from time decay. As Figure 7.7b indicates, the time decay is accelerating with the greatest gain occurring over the last 30 days. Volatility sellers often try to sell straddles during this time period of heaviest time decay. Prior to this time, for example 60 days, the time decay is much less and given the risk the straddle seller must assume, it is often not worth considering.

Selling the Strangle

Another way to sell volatility, which I personally prefer to selling the straddle, is to sell a strangle. Straddles are problematic because they are only delta neutral at one point. If I am trying to maintain a delta neutral position with the straddle, when the market starts moving around, I have to constantly re-adjust my position to remain hedged. This has proven to be the number one cause of grey hair in options dealers. Many dealers prefer a position which may not make as much money but is easier to manage. That is, positions which remain delta neutral over a wider range and do not require the same degree of revision. The strangle provides these kind of benefits. My maximum profit is spread over a much wider range.

A short strangle is easy to understand if you recall the buying strangle and consider we will do the exact opposite transaction. You sell the out-of-the-money call which is a short position and you sell an out-of-the-money put which is a long position. You establish this trade on the same underlying, the same maturity, and at strike prices which are out-of-the-money options, equidistant from the prevailing underlying market price. Suppose the underlying market is trading at 135 cents, the first thing I will do is sell the 140 call. I receive 4.25 cents for it. Then, I will sell a put option against it to balance the exposure to the underlying position. I will sell the put option at 130 and receive 4 cents for it. Because these options are equally distant from the current futures price, they are going to have roughly the same premium and the same delta. The total premium received is 8.25 cents per pound.

How will the combined position look? Using our graphing rules we would say that to the left of 130 cents, the 140 call has a limited gain potential and the 130 put has an unlimited loss potential. So, the unlimited loss potential will dominate. Between 130 cents and 140 cents, we have a limited gain on both the options, so they

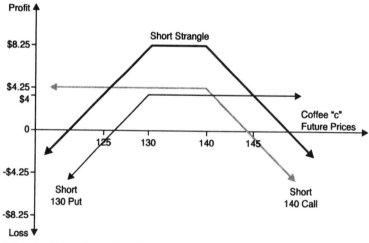

Figure 7.8a Profit and Loss Profile of a Short Strangle at Expiration.

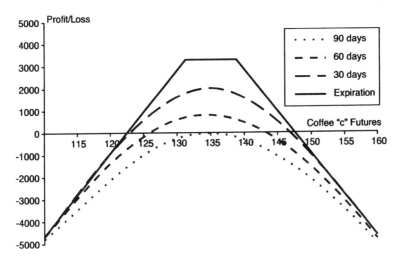

Figure 7.8b The Profit and Loss Profile of a Short Strangle over time.

add up for a limited gain. Above 140 cents, the 130 put has a limited gain and the 140 call has an unlimited loss potential. In combination, the short strangle has an unlimited loss potential. As the reader can see in Figure 7.8a, the strangle seller will earn his maximum profit of 8.25 cents per pound if the market finishes anywhere between 130 cents and 140 cents. Suppose the market ends up at 135 cents.

Both the 130 put and the 140 call expire worthless and the strangle seller will retain the entire premium inflow. In fact, they will expire worthless anywhere over the range. So, between the strike price levels, I will have a flat return. Above 140 cents, I have an unlimited loss potential and below 130 cents another unlimited loss potential.

The example of the short strangle is again exactly the opposite profit and loss profile as the long strangle. If it is sold with 90 days until expiration, the position is even flatter than the straddle at the current price of the underlying asset which is 135 cents. Furthermore, the profile remains flat as we approach expiration due to the fact that the gamma effect will be falling. In addition, the profile will flatten to the plateau shape if the underlying coffee market is anywhere between 130 cents and 140 cents. However, if the price of the coffee futures moves sufficiently up or down, substantial losses may be realised. This can be vividly seen in Figure 7.8b. at a number of points during the life of the trade.

What will earn the profit for the strangle seller is the passage of time or a drop in the implied volatility of the options which have been sold. To properly quantify the differences between the short volatility strategies it is necessary to compare the "Greek" derivatives at the initiation of the trade and during the duration of the strategy. This has been done for the short coffee strangle assuming:

    - a strike price of $130 for the put and $140 for the call,
    - the underlying coffee futures at 135 cents,

- 90 days until expiration,
- implied volatility of 24%, and
- short term interest rates at 4%.

The results of this can be seen in Table 7.7.

SHORT STRANGLE:

Futures 135; volatility 24%; rate of interest 4%; 90 days to expiration.

	PRICE	DELTA	GAMMA	VEGA	THETA
SELL 1 130 PUT	-4.08	+0.35052	-0.000229	-0.09292	+12.234
SELL 1 140 CALL	-4.30	-0.39977	-0.000238	-0.09673	+12.735
SHORT STRANGLE	**-8.38**	-0.04925	-0.000468	-0.18965	+24.969

Table 7.7 Short Strangle Sensitivities.

The seller of the strangle receives the 8.38 cents premium from the buyer with a total inflow of $3142.50 (8.38 cents · 37,500 pounds). In the case of the short strangle, the delta is slightly negative at -0.04925 which is insignificantly different from zero. The gamma exposure for the short strangle is negative equal to -0.000468. This negative gamma effect can be seen clearly from Figure 7.8b as a characteristic frown. This means that if extreme movements occur in the price of the underlying, the strategy will accumulate substantial losses. Clearly, strangle sellers want the actual volatility in the market to be subdued as long as they maintain the strategy. As with all short volatility strategies, the degree of discomfort that will be felt from varying underlying market prices can be ascertained from the gamma. The more negative the gamma, the more the position will be hurt if extreme movements occur in the underlying market. Comparing the short straddle and strangle, it is clear that the short strangle will cause less anxiety to the volatility seller than the straddle. This is because it has a smaller gamma negative exposure (-0.000486 versus -0.000492). This only seems like a small difference, because the comparison of the gamma derivatives is at 90 days to expiration. As we move closer to the expiration of the options, the gammas for the at-the-money options (135 in this case) will rise dramatically, while the gammas for the out-of-the-money options will fall to zero. Of course, the price of this peace of mind is a lower profit potential associated with the strangle, since less premium is received.

By selling two options the strangle seller is also taking a viewpoint on the implied volatility of the options market. In Table 7.7, the vega is -0.18965 which reflects the profit that will be realised from a drop of 1% in the implied volatility.

Finally, in Table 7.7 the seller of the strangle has a positive theta position of +24.969. This measure is expressed in the number of US Dollars that will be gained from the passage of one calendar day in the options life (from 90 days to 89 days to expiration). Thus, if everything else remains constant, the seller will accrue an increasing amount of time decay as the options approach expiration.

Generally, when you are trying to sell volatility, one of the most important considerations is to remain delta neutral. A major problem with deltas is that they change. Back in the chapter on advanced option pricing I discussed this and introduced the concept of the gamma which measures how much the delta changes. For both the straddle and the strangle, the initial slope of the position is zero which implies that the delta is also zero. But at expiration, the straddle can only be delta neutral if the market finishes right at 135 cents. The strangle, on the other hand, has a slope of zero anywhere from 130 cents to 140 cents per pound. So, the strangle is both delta neutral and relatively gamma neutral, especially as the options approach expiration. With strangles, because they are more gamma neutral than are straddles, you do not have to continually revise the position to remain delta neutral. However, if the underlying market moves up or down close to your strike prices, things may start getting a little bit painful.

The time decay characteristics of the strangle can be seen in Figure 7.8b. While the amount you earn will be less, the rate of decay for out-of-the money options is more linear than the rate of decay for at-the-money options (see Figure 3.5). Quite often in a systematic volatility selling program, one will first sell strangles at about 60 days until expiration and then when one reaches 30 days to go, buy back the strangles and sell straddles to get the maximum benefit from time decay over both periods. In essence, we will choose which strategy to sell depending on which one has the greatest relative benefit of time decay for that particular period.

The good thing about selling straddles and strangles is that you make money from volatility decreasing and from time decay. If both occur you will have a double benefit. Time decay can become so important especially as you approach expiration that it can "save" your position even if volatility increases. The time decay is so rapid that the increased volatility may not have time to be realised by an actual movement in the underlying asset. Often by the time the market has moved, the options may have expired.

The major problem with both of these trades is the unlimited loss potential. A large group of individual option traders made quite a good living for many years by selling option volatility via straddles and strangles. Like the gambling house, they won almost all the time. But the probabilities are against them winning all the time. I have personally known people who have made money on almost every expiration for five years selling straddles and strangles. Then, during one expiration, the unexpected happened and they lost all the money they had made during the previous five years. Remember, there was once a man who broke the bank at Monte Carlo and had a song dedicated to his feat (he later proceeded to lose it all!). Therefore, if one assumes an unlimited risk potential for a long enough period, eventually one will realise that loss.

Many conservative and low capitalised traders may still wish to sell volatility but can only do so if they can limit their loss potentials. How is this achieved? The answer can be found with our graphing rules. The only way to cancel an unlimited loss potential is with an unlimited profit potential. I am now going to show you two more kinds of volatility selling strategies called butterflies and condors that allow you to limit your loss potential when selling volatility by applying this rule.

Buying a Butterfly Spread

With a butterfly, you sell at-the-money options that have the highest time value, and you buy out-of-the-money options as disaster insurance. Thus, you are selling the options with the greatest amount of time value and you are buying options with very low time value to eliminate the unlimited loss potentials on both the upside and the downside. The spread is known in America as a long or bought butterfly even though a net premium is received at the established of the strategy.

To construct the butterfly, we will combine strategies I have already discussed. You start off with a short straddle. That is created by selling the 135 call option on coffee futures and the 135 put option on coffee futures. Figure 7.9a displays what this looks like. Suppose I am unable to accept the unlimited loss potentials on the downside and upside. The only way to cancel an unlimited loss potential is with an unlimited profit potential. Therefore, I will buy options both on the downside and the upside to provide me with protection against the unlimited loss potentials. Suppose I buy a 130 put and a 140 call. To the left of 130 cents, the 135 put I sold has an unlimited loss potential and the 130 put I purchased has an unlimited profit potential. If we use our graphing rules, we can see that these two will cancel, yielding a limited loss potential for the combined trade.

Between 130 cents and 135 cents, the 130 put has a limited loss and the 135 put has an increasing profit, so the increasing profit will beat the limited and the combined trade over this range will profit up to 135 cents per pound. Between 135 cents and 140 cents, the 135 call has an sloped profit potential while the 140 call

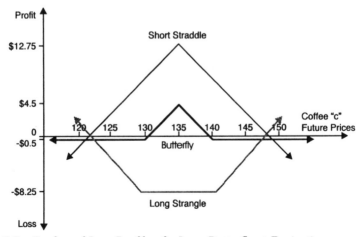

Figure 7.9a Profit and Loss Profile of a Long Butterfly at Expiration.

we purchased will expire worthless with a limited loss. Again, the sloped profit potential will dominate the limited, so the combination has a sloped profit potential over this range. Finally, above the 140 strike price, the 140 call has an unlimited profit potential and the 135 call we sold has an unlimited loss potential and both puts will expire worthless. So, the unlimited profit potential and the unlimited loss potential cancel each other.

For many new to the options market, this profit and loss profile of the butterfly can be quite confounding. It is unlike any of the earlier simpler strategies I have shown you. Upon closer inspection, the strategy is really a combination of simple strategies already discussed.

For example, on the left side of the butterfly, the loss is limited and rises to top out at the higher strike price. Going back to the description of how the strategy is constructed, this is due to the fact that we purchased a put option with a lower strike price (130) and sold a put option at higher strike price (135). From the last chapter, the reader will recall that when we buy a put (or call) at a lower strike price and sell a put (or call) at a higher strike price, this is simply a bull spread. Because the spread was done with puts, we receive more premium than we pay and this bull spread is referred to as a credit spread. What about the right side of the butterfly? We purchased a call option with a higher strike price (140) and sold a call option at lower strike price (135). Wait a minute, is that not a vertical spread as well? The reader will recall that when we buy a call (or put) at a higher strike price and sell a call (or put) at a lower strike price, this is simply a bear spread. Because the spread was done with calls, we receive more premium than we pay and this bear spread is once again referred to as a credit spread. Thus, for both vertical spreads we have received premiums and have a limited loss. Putting the two together, the butterfly is the mutated result.

One of the most fascinating features of options markets is the fact that combinations of simple strategies can easily be done to construct wholly new strategies with entirely different biases on market conditions. It is almost as if the individual options are building blocks and the trader is putting them together not unlike a small child to create new things. One may not be surprised, that a number of authors refer to this process of strategy building with options being similar to children playing with LEGO™ toys. Consider once again the butterfly above: We have constructed it using a bull put spread and a bear call spread. But could not the same thing be constructed using a bull call spread and a bear call spread? The answer is yes. Furthermore, the same spread could be constructed using a bull put spread and a bear put spread. If any divergences in the values of these equivalent structures exist, there is an easy arbitrage strategy called the box which will be discussed in the next chapter.

Finally, my approach to the construction of the butterfly presented above is only one of many equivalent combinations that will produce the characteristic profit and loss profile. Instead of looking at my combination as the merging of two vertical spreads, let us look at it in another way. Recalling the previous butterfly construction, I sold an at-the-money call and an at-the-money put (both at 135),

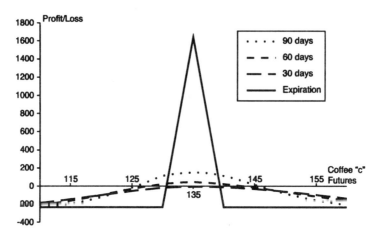

Figure 7.9b The Profit and Loss Profile of a Long Butterfly over time.

and that is simply a short straddle. I also bought an out-of-the-money call and an out-of-the-money put, which is a long strangle. Putting these together yelded the butterfly profile seen in Figure 7.9a. Regardless of what I called the building blocks used in constructing the strategy, the outcome will be the same. In the markets, this approach for the construction of the butterfly is known as an "Iron Butterfly" after the popular 1960s rock group. But regardless of whether the butterfly is made of "iron" or is constructed solely of calls or puts, the payoff must be the same or an arbitrage opportunity will exist.

If the butterfly is established with 90 days until expiration, the position is the flattest profile yet encountered. This can be seen in Figure 7.9b.

Furthermore, the profile remains flat as we approach expiration due to the fact that the overall gamma effect seems to be self hedging. However, in the last 30 days, the profit will rise rapidly to the peak value if the underlying market finishes right at the middle strike price. If the underlying market finishes above the higher strike price or below the lower strike price, the strategy will experience a limited loss (just like one of the vertical spreads that make it up). But why does the butterfly move so dramatically in the last 30 days? We must first look at the "Greeks" and see if the answer lies there. This has been done for the long coffee butterfly assuming:

- a strike price of 130 for the put we bought,
- a strike price of 135 for the put we sold,
- a strike price of 135 for the call we sold,
- a strike price of 140 for the call we bought,
- the underlying coffee futures at 135 cents,
- 90 days until expiration,
- implied volatility of 24%, and
- short term interest rates at 4%.

The results of this can be seen in Table 7.8.

LONG BUTTERFLY:

Futures 135; volatility 24%; rate of interest 4%; 90 days to expiration.

	PRICE	DELTA	GAMMA	VEGA	THETA
BUY 130 PUT	+4.08	-0.35052	+0.000229	+0.09292	-12.234
SELL 135 PUT	-6.36	+0.47256	-0.000246	-0.09978	+13.061
SELL 135 CALL	-6.36	-0.51972	-0.000246	-0.09970	+13.054
BUY 140 CALL	+4.30	+0.39977	+0.000238	+0.09673	-12.735
LONG BUTTERFLY	**-4.34**	+0.00209	-0.000025	-0.00983	+1.1460

Table 7.8 Long Butterfly Sensitivities.

The long butterfly provides an inflow of 4.34 cents at the establishment of the position. This means the trader will receive $1,627.50 (4.34 cents · 37,500 pounds). The delta is only slightly positive at +0.00209 which is for all practical purposes zero. Interestingly, the gamma exposure is also extremely close to zero at -0.000025. This neutral gamma effect can be seen from Figure 7.9b by the fact that the profit and loss profile at 90 days until expiration is almost completely flat. Therefore, if extreme movements occur in the price of the underlying, the strategy will be totally immunised to the actual movements of the underlying coffee market.

By selling options which have the greatest time value and the highest vega and covering the risks by buying options with less time value and a lower vega, the net exposure to the implied volatility remains negative. This can be seen in Table 7.8 with the overall vega derivative equal to -0.00983. While this means that the long butterfly only makes $9.83 from a 1% fall in the implied volatility, it still indicates a selling bias of volatility. This strategy really shines with the impact of time decay, especially over the last 30 days of the options life.

This can be seen in Table 7.8 from the theta derivative. At 90 days until expiration, the theta is only $1.1460 per day. But when one looks at Figure 7.9b, one can see that this changes. Almost all the profits earned are reaped over the final 30 days of the options life. So the "Greeks" are not really telling us why the last 30 days are so important. But if we look at the butterfly as the combination of two vertical spreads, we may find the answer.

In the last chapter, I demonstrated that one of the best features of vertical spreads was that they are relatively immune to time decay prior to about 30 days to expiration. This can be see in Figure 6.11 for bull spreads and Figure 6.14 for bear spreads. After the 30 day point, the time decay accelerates. While this is not the ideal time to hold a debit vertical spread, it may just be the ideal time to sell the vertical spread (credit spread) receiving a premium which will be earned rapidly if the underlying market remains stable. The good thing about the butterfly is that because we have combined both a bull and bear spread, we are no longer taking a viewpoint regarding the movement of the underlying market but our viewpoint is centred on the reduction of the actual volatility in the underlying market during the last 30 days of the options life.

In summary, the butterfly strategy has a limited loss to the left of 130 cents, a north-eastern sloping unlimited profit potential up to 135 cents, and a north-western sloping unlimited profit potential from 135 cents to 140 cents, and a limited loss potential to the right of 140 cents per pound.

A butterfly is a short volatility strategy that makes money from volatility decreasing but mostly from time decay. In this case, the most you can lose is determined at the initiation of the strategy thus giving it a limited loss potential. Butterflies are superb trades for under-capitalised traders who wish to sell volatility but cannot accept the unlimited loss potential associated with straddles and strangles. The profit potential has been reduced because the disaster insurance options had to be purchased, but if the market does move dramatically, these small traders will suffer a limited loss instead of being wiped out.

Consider October 1987, the great stock market crash: The people who did not come back after the crash were the people who sold straddles. They had risked the unlimited loss potential for the chance of a little extra profit. Many of those who survived were individuals who remained disciplined and continued to establish strategies with limited loss potentials like the butterfly trade. Whenever you have small dealers or speculators selling strangles or straddles, they are asking for big trouble. I have seen the proverbial "market wise" dentists lose everything by establishing positions with unlimited loss potentials. Straddles and strangles should only be undertaken by market professionals who can withstand the possible loss potentials.

Butterfly spreads are also brilliant from a time decay standpoint, especially in the last 30 days. They decay at an extraordinarily rapid pace in the last 30 days. So, these trades are ideal to reap the rewards of heavy time decay without having to assume an unreasonable amount of risk. Figure 7.9b displays the time decay characteristics of the butterfly. I would highly recommend that you trade butterflies when you first start selling volatility until you become more comfortable with the risks of an unlimited loss potential strategy.

Buying a Condor Spread

The last pure volatility selling trade I am going to discuss is a variation on the same theme. This trade is called the condor. With a condor, you are selling options near the prevailing underlying price and buying options further out-of-the-money to protect yourself, similar to the butterfly. The difference is that you are selling the first out-of-the-money put option and the first out-of-the-money call option rather than the at-the-money options. As with the butterfly, to protect against the unlimited loss potentials, you are buying a deeper out-of-the-money put and a deeper out-of-the-money call. If you balance it correctly with the same underlying position and maturity, the positions should be approximately delta neutral.

To show you how the condor is constructed I will once again use trades previously discussed. Suppose you start with an 130/140 short strangle. That means you

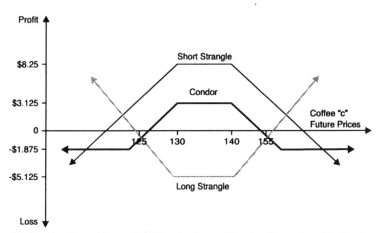

Figure 7.10a Profit and Loss Profile of a Long Condor Spread at Expiration.

sell the 130 put and the 140 call with the market trading at 135 cents. Then, to off-set the unlimited loss potentials, you purchase options which provide unlimited profit potentials. So, you are buying deeper out-of-the-money options at strikes of 125 (put) and 145 (call). That is, you are buying the further out-of-the-money strangle. Figure 7.10a displays the build-up profit/loss graph for this combination trade.

Below 125 cents, we have an unlimited profit potential on the 125 put and an unlimited loss potential on the 130 put and because unlimited profits and losses cancel, the combination will have a limited loss potential. Between 125 cents and 130 cents, the 130 put has a rising profit potential and the 125 put has a limited loss, so the rising profit dominates here. Between 130 cents and 140 cents, all the options expire worthless, providing a limited gain overall. Between 140 cents and 145 cents, the 140 call has a sloping profit potential and the 145 call has a limited loss potential, so the sloping potential dominates the limited potential. Finally, above 145 cents, the 145 call has an unlimited profit potential and the 140 call has an unlimited loss potential and they will offset leaving the condor with a limited loss potential.

Perhaps the reader is experiencing a degree of deja vu? In the condor profit and loss profile above, one can easily see the two vertical spreads. Clearly to the left, is a bull spread and coming from the right is a bear spread. Due to the fact, that they no longer share the middle strike price (which is the case with the butterfly), the two distinct components are easier to see.

If the condor is established with 90 days until expiration, the position starts out almost as flat as the butterfly. However, as time passes, the "larger wings" of the condor "flap" much more than the butterfly's. This is because of the wider disper-sion of the strike prices involved in the strategy. This can be seen in Figure 7.10b.

The overall gamma effect is not as self hedging for the condor as the butterfly. However, once again in the last 30 days, the profit will rise rapidly to it maximum

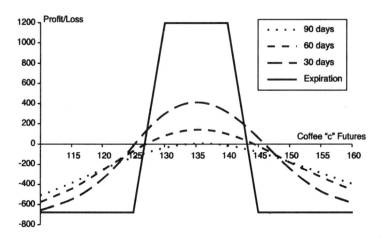

Figure 7.10b The Profit and Loss Profile of a Long Condor over time.

value if the underlying market finishes anywhere between the middle strike prices. If the underlying market finishes above the highest strike price or below the lowest strike price, the strategy will experience a limited loss (again just like one of the vertical spreads that it consists of). At this point, let us compare the sensitivities of the condor to the butterfly at 90 days until expiration. I will assume that the coffee condor is evaluated under the following conditions:

 - a strike price of 125 for the put we bought,
 - a strike price of 130 for the put we sold,
 - a strike price of 140 for the call we sold,
 - a strike price of 145 for the call we bought,
 - the underlying coffee futures at 135 cents,
 - 90 days until expiration,
 - implied volatility of 24%, and
 - short term interest rates at 4%.

The results of this can be seen in Table 7.9.

LONG CONDOR:
Futures 135; volatility 24%; rate of interest 4%; 90 days to expiration.

	PRICE	DELTA	GAMMA	VEGA	THETA
BUY 125 PUT	+2.40	-0.23832	+0.00019	+0.07768	-10.266
SELL 130 PUT	-4.08	+0.35052	-0.00022	-0.09292	+12.234
SELL 140 CALL	-4.30	-0.39977	-0.00023	-0.09673	+12.735
BUY 145 CALL	+2.79	+0.29218	+0.00021	+0.08608	-11.373
LONG CONDOR	-3.19	+0.00461	-0.00006	-0.02589	+3.3306

Table 7.9 Long Condor Sensitivities.

The long condor spreader will receive a premium of 3.19 cents when establishing the position. This is an inflow of $1,196.25 (3.19 cents · 37,500 pounds). The delta is slightly positive at +0.00461 but still within the range which is defined as delta neutral. The gamma exposure remains low at -0.00006 but is almost three times as great as the gamma of the butterfly. Clearly, this neutral gamma effect can be seen from Figure 7.10b by the fact that the profit and loss profile at 90 days until expiration is almost completely flat. Relative to the butterfly, the condor does have more of a gamma effect from changes in the price of the underlying asset. It must be remembered that the sensitivities of options change continuously, requiring constant monitoring of the "Greeks". What may be relatively gamma neutral at 90 days to expiration may no longer be neutral with 10 days to expiration.

By selling options which have relatively more time value and higher vegas and covering the risks by buying options with less time value and a lower vegas, the net exposure to the implied volatility will remain negative. This can be seen in Table 7.9 with the overall vega derivative equal to -0.02589. While this means that the long butterfly will earn $25.89 from a 1% fall in the implied volatility, indicating a selling bias of volatility. Compared to the butterfly, this is more exposed to changes in the implied volatility at 90 days to expiration. This strategy also shines over the last 30 days of the options life due to the impact of time decay.

This can be seen in Table 7.9 from the theta derivative. At 90 days until expiration, the theta is only $3.3306 per day. But when one looks at Figure 7.10b, one can see that this changes. As with the butterfly, almost all the profits that are earned are reaped over the final 30 days of the options life.

Condors are one of my favourite short volatility trades because they are a position which is both delta neutral and extremely gamma neutral with a limited loss on both sides. The problem with condors is that you rarely make any money with these trades because the out-of-the-money options you are selling seldom bring in much premium. This is compounded by the fact that very elaborate condors can become what are known as "crocodile" spreads. These are trades with so many elements that the brokers take their many pieces of flesh in the form of bid/offer spreads. As a result the condor could be eaten piecemeal by a crocodile.

Condors are often evolved over time and are not established at the same moment. Unfortunately, this involves the risks of legging as discussed before. But legging here is different from the legging techniques previously discussed. This trading technique is not based on greed but rather on a disciplined approach to risk reduction. Condors are usually either established by market makers who do not have to give up the bid/offer spreads when establishing the positions or by traders who build the position over time establishing each component at levels which will produce a reasonable profit.

The way condors generally evolve starts with first selling a strangle. Suppose you sell it at 60 days prior to expiration and it works fairly well and at 30 days to expiration you decide that instead of taking off the strangle at that point, you will limit your losses by buying the further out-of-the-money options, which should be very inexpensive at that point. Then, for the last 30 days you will experience extremely rapid time decay on any remaining time value in the options, all with a limited loss. The time decay characteristics of the condor can be seen in Figure 7.10b. So, unless you are a market maker, setting up a condor is essentially an evolutionary process. Thus, condors are as much an example of a disciplined trading routine as they are a trading strategy. One should always take the opportunity to limit one's loss potentials whenever possible. Only when your loss potentials are limited can you get to sleep at night knowing that the morning will not bring dreadful positions with dreadful losses.

Comparison of the Pure Volatility Selling Strategies

With the condor, I conclude the strategies one can use for pure volatility selling. At this point, I will compare the profit and loss profiles of all four strategies I have discussed. The reader can see these displayed in Figure 7.11.

The straddle offers the maximum return from selling premium with the profit peaking at the strike price of both options, in this case 135. The straddle has an unlimited loss potential on both sides. Our strangle provides a flat maximum return between 130 cents and 140 cents but also has an unlimited loss potential on both sides. The 130/135/140 butterfly provides a peaked return like the straddle, however, the maximum profit is reduced due to the purchase of the out-of-the-money options which are required to limit the loss potential. So the butterfly is essentially an evolution of the straddle. The condor is in the same way an evolution of the strangle. The condor has a flat pattern of maximum returns with limited risks on both sides and it makes the smallest maximum profit. Obviously, if you are trying

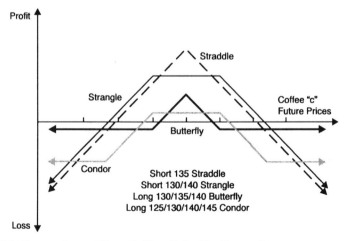

Figure 7.11 Comparison of Pure Selling Volatility Strategies.

to earn the highest possible profit, you sell a straddle but the market must finish exactly at your strike price. Strangles are the second best money maker and will make their money over a very wide range but unfortunately they also have an unlimited loss potential on both sides. The butterfly has the next highest profit potential but again you have to have the market finish exactly at the middle strike price. But if you are wrong, the butterfly's potential is a small price to pay for cutting off the unlimited loss potentials. Finally, the lowest money maker is the condor which gives you a wide range for the maximum profit and a limited loss.

For a disciplined, systematic volatility selling program, the sequence might be like this: start off by selling a strangle 60 days to expiration. At 30 days either turn it into a condor or sell the butterfly for the last 30 days. If you really have courage, over these last 30 days you could also sell the straddle.

Where Pure Volatility Selling Strategies Fit into the Strategy Matrix

These positions are all initiated as delta neutral positions. That is, you do not know whether the market will go up or down. You would prefer that over the period it goes nowhere, if possible. Because you are receiving premium, you have a position which will also benefit as volatility decreases. So, we can go to our trading matrix Table 7.12 and place these strategies in their appropriate spot. Since these trades are neutral to the market and sellers of volatility we will put them into the middle right cell of the strategy matrix. For all these trades, time decay works in your favour and so does a decrease in volatility.

Which of these strategies should be used depends on whether you can accept a limited or an unlimited loss potential. These trades are pure volatility trades because they are neutral to the underlying market when they are established and they will get hurt equally if the market goes up or down. They are not leaning in any way, shape or form: they are essentially neutral. One is simply trying to benefit from a decrease in volatility and an increase in time decay with these trades.

LEANING VOLATILITY SELLING STRATEGIES: THE RATIO SPREADS

Volatility selling trades called "leaning volatility selling trades" have a bias or preference for the direction of market movements. The most common of these short volatility trades are known as put ratio spreads and call ratio spreads.

The Put Ratio Spread

A put ratio spread is the exact opposite of the put-back spread I discussed previously. The put-back spread is created when you buy two or more puts and sell one at a lower strike price. As the reader will recall, the put-back is initially delta neutral but long volatility because you are buying more options than you are selling. With the put ratio spread one will sell more options than one is buying. If the exact opposite of the put-back spread is done, then one will sell two or more put options and buy one put. As with the put-back spread, there is a preference for where the market will go. With the put-back (which is the opposite of this strategy), the trader has an unlimited profit potential on one side and a limited profit or bias on the other side. The put-back buyer loses the most if the market finishes in the middle. Since the put ratio spread is on the opposite side, he will have exactly the opposite profit/loss payoff. He will have a limited profit or loss on one side and an unlimited loss potential on the opposite side, and the maximum profit if the market finishes in the middle. Because we are selling more options than we are buying, the put ratio spread is a position that will benefit if volatility decreases. To demonstrate why the position has limited loss if the market goes up and an unlimited loss potential if the market goes down, we will once again combine option strategies (and the premiums) I have previously examined and use our graphing rules to determine the profit/loss profile of the combined position.

Let us go back to our previous example with the put ratio spread. If I am selling this spread, I am selling two of the 127.5 put options and buying one of the 140 puts. Again, I will split the two puts we have sold into two sets of one each. When you combine a short 127.5 put option with a long 140 put, this position is a vertical spread. When one buys the higher strike option that means that the spread is a bear spread. As the reader will recall, a bear spread is a bearish position relative to the underlying coffee futures market and neutral to volatility. Then, I sell another put option at the strike price of 127.5. What are the viewpoints when one sells a put? Short put positions are bullish on the underlying coffee futures market and sellers of volatility. So in combination with the bear spread, we will have a position which is neutral to the underlying position and bearish on volatility. This trade is used

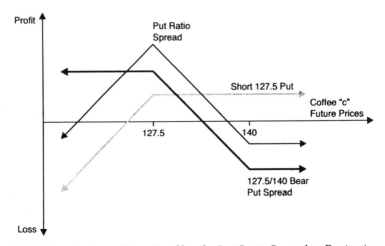

Figure 7.12a The Profit and Loss Profile of a Put Ratio Spread at Expiration.

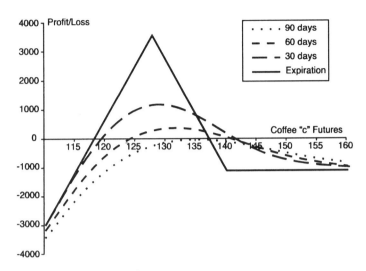

Figure 7.12b The Profit and Loss Profile of a Put Ratio Spread over time.

when one's viewpoint is that volatility is going down and the market is going to be stable. Why is this trade a leaning trade? While it is initially delta neutral the pay-offs of the strategy at expiration are not symmetrical. On one side you find a limited loss and on the other side an unlimited loss potential. So the put ratio spreader would prefer that the market moves one way rather than the other. The best thing would be for the market to remain stable. But if things go wrong, the put ratio spreader is not indifferent to where the market goes. He wants the market to rise rather than fall. This is best seen in the payoff diagram of the put ratio spread at expiration in Figure 7.12a.

To the left of the lower strike price, 127.5, the combination has an unlimited loss potential. Between the 127.5 and the 140 strike prices, the put ratio spread looks similar to the profile of a short straddle. Above 140 cents, all the options in the spread expire worthless and the spread has a limited loss.

In this example, I have sold two 127.5 puts and purchased one 140 put. If the put ratio spread is estiablished with 90 days until expiration, the position is extremely flat at the current price of the underlying asset which is 135 cents and will remain so over a range from 130 cents to 140 cents. This can be seen in Figure 7.12b. Once again, if the price of the coffee futures moves sufficiently up or down, the trade will experience losses. However, the strategy is leaning to the upside as the loss potential is limited there and unlimited if the underlying coffee price falls. Again, if time simply passes, the put ratio spread will profit with a maximum profit if the underlying coffee futures price finishes at 127.5 cents which is the lower strike price of the strategy.

To quantify the exact exposures of the put ratio spread we must assess the "Greek" derivatives for each component of the strategy. This has been done for the coffee put ratio spread assuming:

   - a strike price of 140 cents for the higher strike put we bought,
   - a strike price of 127.5 cents for the lower strike price puts we sold,
   - the underlying coffee futures at 135 cents,
   - 90 days until expiration,
   - implied volatility of 24%, and
   - short term interest rates at 4%.

The results of this can be seen in Table 7.10.

PUT RATIO SPREAD:
Futures 135; volatility 24%; rate of interest 4%; 90 days to expiration.

	PRICE	DELTA	GAMMA	VEGA	THETA
SELL 2 127.5 PUTS	-2·3.16	+0.5849	-0.000425	-0.17238	+22.742
BUY 1 140 PUT	+9.26	-0.5927	+0.000230	+0.09738	-12.633
PUT RATIO SPREAD	+2.94	-0.0078	-0.000185	-0.07500	+10.109

Table 7.10 Put Ratio Spread Sensitivities.

  The theoretical value of the put ratio spread is a positive 2.94 cents. This means that we must pay a premium for this strategy and the total cost for the put ratio spread is $1102.50 (2.94 cents · 37,500 pounds). The delta is very slightly negative at -0.0078 which is well within the range of ±0.10 delta neutral range. The gamma exposure for the put ratio spread is negative equal to -0.000185. If the reader looks back at the profit and loss profile for the option at 90 days until expiration, he will notice that the curved relationship between the options price and the underlying price is now frowning in a sort of crooked way which is opposite to the put-back spread in Figure 7.6b. This means that if extreme movements occur in the price of the underlying, the overall strategy will experience losses, especially in a falling underlying market scenario. Thus, the put ratio spreader wants the actual volatility of the underlying coffee futures to decrease.

  In Table 7.10, the vega is -0.07500 and this stands for the amount the value of the put ratio spread will change for a change in 1% in the implied volatility. This number is again expressed relative to 1,000 US Dollars in this table, therefore, if the implied volatility rises from 24% (the current level) to 25%, the premium cost of the option combination will rise by $75.00. Given that originally, the put-back spreader would have paid $1102.50 upon the initiation of the trade, he would real-ise an additional profit of $75 if the implied volatility fell.

  Finally, in Table 7.10 the put ratio spread has a positive theta position of +10.109. While this gain of $10.11 is small for one calendar day, it will begin ac-celerating especially if the underlying coffee market slowly falls to 127.5 cents. At that point, the greatest time decay effect will occur.

  Overall, the put ratio spread has an unlimited loss potential to the downside; makes the greatest profit if the market is stable; and has a limited loss on the upside. Because we are selling more options than we are buying, we make money from volatility going down. If we are wrong and the market fails to remain stable, we hope that if it moves, it moves to the upside where we have a limited loss potential. This trade is "leaning" because we do care where the market goes; we want it to go up if it moves at all. Therefore, the put ratio spread, while initially neutral to the underlying market, is leaning to the upside. But the ideal situation for the put ratio spread is for time decay and a decrease in volatility to accompany underlying market stability.

The Call Ratio Spread

The other leaning volatility selling strategy is the call ratio spread, which is the opposite of the call-back spread. What you do here is to sell two or more higher strike price calls and buy one lower strike price call, to balance the number of options to delta neutral. Like the put ratio spread, I achieve a volatility selling strategy which is initially delta neutral but has a preference for market movement. In this case, the call ratio spread has a limited loss potential to the downside and an unlimited loss potential on the upside.

To be able to see these characteristics, I will display how the call ratio spread is created graphically in Figure 7.13a.

Again, we create the spread by selling two call options and buying one. As with the put ratio spread, we separate the two short calls into two sets of one and combine one with the long call. By buying the lower strike price call and selling a higher strike price call, this will give us a bull call spread. The bull call spread has a bullish bias on the underlying market and is neutral to volatility. Then, we sell an additional call option at the higher strike price. When we sell a call, the viewpoint

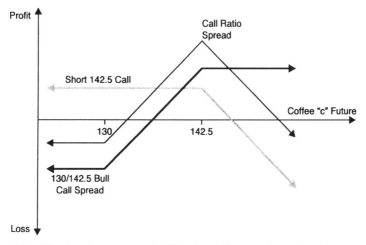

Figure 7.13a The Profit and Loss Profile of a Call Ratio Spread at Expiration.

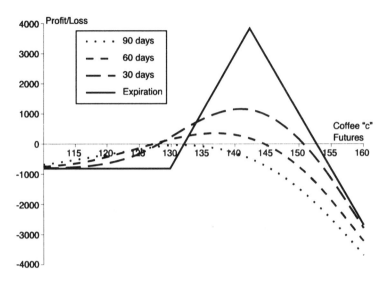

Figure 7.13b The Profit and Loss Profile of a Call Ratio Spread over time.

is bearish on the market and also bearish on volatility. Therefore, in combination with the bull call spread, the call ratio is now neutral to the market but bearish on volatility.

If the call ratio spread is established with 90 days until expiration, the position is extremely flat at the current coffee futures price of 135 cents. This can be seen in Figure 7.13b. It will slowly lose value if the price falls below 135 cents. As with the put ratio spread, if the price of the coffee futures moves significantly, losses will occur. However, the strategy is leaning to the downside as the loss potential is limited there and unlimited if the underlying coffee price rises. As time passes, the call ratio spread will gain from time decay with a maximum profit if the underlying coffee futures price finishes at 142.5 cents which is the higher strike price of the options in the strategy.

To quantify the exact exposures of the call ratio spread we must again assess the "Greek" derivatives for each component of the strategy. This has been done for the coffee call ratio spread assuming:

- a strike price of 130 cents for the lower strike call we bought,
- a strike price of 142.5 cents for the higher strike price calls we sold,
- the underlying coffee futures at 135 cents,
- 90 days until expiration,
- implied volatility of 24%, and
- short term interest rates at 4%.

The results of this can be seen in Table 7.11.

CALL RATIO SPREAD:
Futures 135; volatility 24%; rate of interest 4%; 90 days to expiration.

	PRICE	DELTA	GAMMA	VEGA	THETA
SELL 2 142.5 CALLS	-2·3.48	-0.6879	-0.000455	-0.18438	+24.322
BUY 1 130 CALL	9.04	+0.6420	+0.000230	+0.09339	-12.115
CALL RATIO SPREAD	**2.08**	-0.0459	-0.000225	-0.09099	+12.207

Table 7.11 Call Ratio Spread Sensitivities.

The theoretical value of the call ratio spread is positive 2.08 cents. This means that one would have to pay a premium to establish this strategy and the total cost would be $780 (2.08 cents · 37,500 pounds). The delta is slightly negative at -0.0459 which is within the range of delta neutral. The gamma exposure for the strangle is negative (equal to -0.000225). If the reader looks back at the profit and loss profile for the option at 90 days until expiration, he will notice that the curved relationship between the options price and the underlying price is frowning in a sort of crooked way. This profile is characteristic of asymmetrical gamma negative strategies like the ratio spreads. The call ratio spreader wants the price variability of the underlying market to subside with the price slowly rising to the higher strike where the calls have been sold. If the price finishes exactly equal to (in this case) 142.5 cents, the spread will make the maximum profit.

Whenever one sells more options than one is buying, one is generally a "net" seller of the implied volatility. For the call ratio spread, this can be assessed by examining the vega. In Table 7.11, the vega is -0.09099 and this stands for the amount that the value of the straddle will change for a change in 1% in the implied volatility. This number is again expressed relative to US $1,000 in this table, therefore, if the implied volatility rises from 24% (the current level) to 25%, the premium cost of the options will fall by $90.99. Given that originally, the call-back spreader would have paid $780 upon the initiation of the trade, he would realise a loss of $90.99 if the implied volatility rose.

Finally, in Table 7.11 the call-back spread has a positive theta position of +12.207. While this gain of $12.21 is rather small for one calendar day, it will begin accelerating especially if the underlying coffee market slowly rises to 142.5 cents. At that point, the greatest time decay profit will be earned.

The establishment of the call and put ratio spreads are very often mutations of more simple strategies. For example: I put on a bull spread and the market has gone up and I have made my profit objective. Now my viewpoint has changed and I want to benefit from the market retracing to the downside and from volatility decreasing. If I sell the higher strike price call option, I will achieve both objectives and turn the bull spread into a call ratio spread. The simple addition of the short call caused the bull spread to be transformed into another and totally divergent strategy: One that now would prefer the markets to remain stable (or if movement occurs to the downside) and which benefits from a reduction in volatility. In addition, the call ratio spread also benefits from time decay. This is yet another positive element which should help the trade turn a profit. The optimal event would be for the market to remain at the current level and time decay to earn the profit. This is the perfect way to get the remaining profit out of a bull spread in the last 30 days prior to expiration when time decay is at its greatest.

However, there is no law requiring you to keep the unlimited loss potential for this trade indefinitely. Often traders will turn a bull spread into a call ratio spread and then if the market falls a little, buy another call at an even higher strike price, above the higher strike previously purchased. By adding this long call, that has cancelled the unlimited loss potential on the upside and in combination, the trade has now become a butterfly. If the trader is disciplined, he might be able to create a butterfly which has no loss potential and therefore no risk. But this once again requires legging the spread over time and can be extremely risky until all the trades are in place. But once the trades are placed, the combination can potentially be risk-free.

Where Ratio Spreads Fit into the Strategy Matrix

Ratio spreads are initially neutral to the underlying market but the extra short call or put positions can turn the ratio spread into either an adversely buying or selling position. They lean one way or the other, with a preference for where the market might go. With ratio spreads, you believe that if the market does move it will move to one side rather than to the other. With this viewpoint, you cut off the unlimited loss potential on that one side. The reason why professional traders use this trade frequently is because it is often possible to build up strategies like condors or butterflies for a more reasonable risk/reward trade-off if you start with simple trades and add more positions at opportune moments. Traders use ratio spreads because with these trades they are not giving up all the theoretical edge initially (and the bid/offer spreads). They are assuming the risk that if they are wrong it will be on one side. Of course, this entails the assumption of risk. But professional option dealers make their money from assuming intelligent risks and covering them quickly if they are wrong. Ratio spreads are ideal trades for this kind of trading philosophy.

In conclusion, call ratio spreads for the reasons outlined above, start out initially neutral to the underlying market but have a directional bias to the downside rather than to the upside. Therefore we will assign these trades a bearish bias on the underlying and because we are selling more options than we are buying, the call ratio spread is also bearish on volatility. Thus in our strategy matrix (Table 7.12), we will place call ratio spreads in the middle cell of the table along with the short call option. By a similar argument, we will categorise the put ratio spread as an equivalent "long" underlying position with a selling volatility bias. Therefore, it will be placed in the same cell of the strategy matrix as the short put. With this final entry, we have filled up eight of the nine cells in our matrix. The only cell that is left to fill is the lower right hand cell when the trader has both a neutral viewpoint on the underlying market and on volatility. I will cover these trades in the next two chapters.

Viewpoint on the Coffee Market

		Buyer	Seller	Neutral
Viewpoint on Volatility	Buyer	Buy call option Call Back Spread	Buy put option Put Back Spread	Buy Straddle Buy Strangle
	Seller	Sell put option Put Ratio Spread	Sell call option Call Ratio Spread	Sell Straddle Sell Strangle Buy Butterfly Buy Condor
	Neutral	Long Futures Bull spread	Short Futures Bear spread	

Table 7.12 Option Trading Strategy Matrix.

As was indicated at the beginning of the last chapter, options trading allows the strategist a tremendous amount of flexibility in his choice of strategies to use. In a typical market, only three things can be done: buy, sell, or sit still. But with options, applying these three possible viewpoints on all the factors which determine an options' prices will allow the strategist an almost infinite number of trading strategies. In the strategy matrix, I have expanded the realms of the possible to 18 and I am not finished yet. There is in fact no limit to the possible trades that can be created using options.

THE DIFFERENCE BETWEEN TRADING FUTURES AND OPTIONS

The principal difference between option trading and trading an underlying futures or spot market is that trading the underlying market is more like guerrilla warfare. You buy and sell quickly. In guerrilla warfare, you kill one guy at a time and sometimes he kills you. Options trading is more like a well thought out military strategy. You develop a campaign plan, deciding what you want to do and when to do it. Then you will decide how best to achieve the objectives arising from your viewpoints and develop contingency plans for revising the strategy if things do not work out the way you planned. Once you have established the strategy, you sit back, leave it and let it work. These strategies will work as time decay, volatility movements, and the spreads change. Once the market has moved, you can do one simple transaction and evolve the strategy into something else. So the difference between guerrilla warfare and a long term military strategy is rationale and discipline. Options dealing, especially with volatility strategies, allows you to use these virtues to their best effect.

8: Option Arbitrage

This section discusses option arbitrage, the last category of option trading strategies where one has a neutral view on the underlying market and on volatility. In most markets, this would preclude any activity, but with options, opportunities may still exist to profit. These opportunities include calendar spreads, "delta neutral" trading, put/call parity arbitrages like conversions, reversals, and box trades and jelly roll spreads.

In this chapter, I will use the option on Eurodollar futures traded at the International Monetary Market of the Chicago Mercantile Exchange (IMM). The futures prices are actually an index level which is calculated by subtracting from 100.00 the expected annualised three month London InterBank Offer Rate (LIBOR) for U.S. Dollar time deposits in London on the expiration date of the futures contract. So, if the expected 3 month LIBOR is 5.5%, then the Eurodollar futures price is equal to 94.50 (which is 100 - 5.5). The underlying value of the contract is $1,000,000 in a hypothetical deposit and the minimum movement in the value of the futures contract is 0.01 points (or 1/100th of an interest rate percentage point). This minimum movement ("a tick") is worth $25 because 1/100th of a interest rate percentage point for a $1,000,000 deposit with a three month time horizon will equal this amount (0.0001 · $1,000,000 · 90 days/360 days = $25) Table 8.1 outlines the contract specification for this option contract. The interesting factor about this contract is that it moves exactly inversely to the movement in interest rates. For example, if LIBOR rises, then the Eurodollar futures price will fall (and vice versa).

Trading Unit:	1 Eurodollar time deposit futures contract
Contract Months:	March, June, September, December. Serial, nearest two 2-year Mid-Curve & nearest two 5-year Mid-Curve quarterly months.
Last Trading Day:	2nd London business day before 3rd Wednesday of contract month.
Minimum Price Movement: (tick size)	0.01 (1 basis pt) ($25/pt) ($25.00) cab = $12.50
Trading Hours:	7.20 A.M. - 2.00 P.M. (New York Time)
Exercise Price Intervals:	0.25 Intervals (e.g. 95.00, 95.25)
Exercise:	Any trading day. The futures position is effective on the trading day following exercise, and is marked-to-market to the settlement that day.

Table 8.1 Contract Specification of Options on Eurodollar Futures.

The options on Eurodollar futures allow the buyer or seller to deal in what amounts to interest rate insurance. They can pay a premium to assure either borrowing insurance (a put on Eurodollar futures) or investment insurance (a call on Eurodollar futures). This highly successful contract has led to the development of similar futures and options contracts on deposits in Deutsche Marks, Sterling, Yen, Lira, French Franc and a wide variety of other currencies. The simple index format has also proven to be a winner as the general format has been copied world-wide. The cash settlement feature of the Euro futures and options has made settlement easy and free from manipulation. Thus, the option on Eurodollar futures is ideal for explaining option arbitrage.

THE TYPES OF ARBITRAGE STRATEGIES

Arbitrage in the purest sense is buying and selling the same thing for a differential in price at the same moment. It has to be exactly the same thing, not a spread, not slightly different, not a "relative value" trade. You buy gold and you sell gold; the same purity of gold from two different people at two different prices and at the same point in time. That is arbitrage. In options, arbitrage includes trades which fit this definition and are referred to as pure arbitrage trades. Other option strategies fall under the category of arbitrage without having the risk-free element that arbitrage implies.

These kinds of "arbitrage" are either isolating for the time decay element in an option or buying and selling mispriced volatility. The pure arbitrage strategies involve creating synthetic positions that are dealt against the actual positions to lock in any price discrepancies. In this chapter, I will examine all these kinds of trades beginning with the less "pure" strategies and finishing with the purest of the arbitrage trades.

CALENDAR SPREADS

The first category of "arbitrage" I will examine is the calendar spread which is not really a pure "arbitrage" strategy but is instead a way to benefit from relative discrepancies in the levels of implied and actual volatilities. In addition, these trades allow the trader to benefit from time decay in a rather clever way.

Calendar spreads are similar to vertical spreads in that you buy a call option and sell a call option or buy a put option and sell a put option. But this time, both options have the same strike price. How can this be? If you buy a call option and then sell the same strike call option then will you not have wiped out your position? That is true; it is a complete offset if you buy and sell the same option series. In a calendar spread, one will buy and sell options with the same strike price but for different maturities.

Long Calendar Spreads

If I buy a call for December Eurodollar futures and then sell a call for September Eurodollar futures at the same strike price, then I have a position that is offsetting to some degree relative to the underlying Eurodollar time deposit market, but it is in a position that will benefit from various factors, not the least of which is time decay. If I buy a long dated option, over the period of its life the time value will initially decay slowly and then accelerate as it approaches expiration.

Suppose on 21 June 1994, the September is trading at 94.50 and the December Eurodollar futures is also trading at 94.50 and I buy a 94.50 December call option. Over the time period from 21 June to 19 September (the expiration of the September Eurodollar option), the time decay for the December call option will be relatively slow and then from 19 September to 19 December, it will accelerate. Then, suppose on 21 June, I also sell a September 94.50 call. For the time period between then until the September expiration (19 September), the time decay will be very rapid. At the expiration of the September contract, the September 94.50 call will have no time value at all, its value will only consist of its intrinsic value. In this case, if I buy options which have a very slow time decay and sell options with a rapid time decay over that same time period, I should be able to benefit simply from this time decay discrepancy. When one does this, it is called buying or going long the calendar or time spread.

Let us look at an example with numbers. On 21 June, the December 94.50 call I bought might be worth 0.38. If the Eurodollar futures market remains at the current level of 94.50 by 19 September 1994, the December call should then be worth about 0.27 (at that point, the option will have 91 days remaining to expiration). The loss on this call from time decay would therefore be 0.11. If I sold the September 94.50 call for 0.25, and the market finishes at 94.50, the option will be worth nothing. So by selling the September 94.50 call, I am essentially playing the time decay game expecting stable markets to exist but purchasing the longer dated December option to limit my loss potential. The time decay loss of 0.11 on the December call will be more than offset by the time decay profit of 0.25 on the September call yielding an expected overall profit of 0.14. Therefore, if I buy long-dated options before they experience rapid time decay and sell short dated options during the period of their most rapid time decay, I can gain from the passage of time if markets remain static.

This sounds too good to be true. How can this be? Well, on 19 September, the December call option I bought will still have the two components of an options price, intrinsic value and time value. This means that the option price relative to the underlying Eurodollar futures market price will have a curved slope leading up to the north-east. If I sell a September call option against it, this call option will have no time value in September. Its price will be made up entirely of intrinsic value. Hence, its profit/loss profile will be the typical "hockey stick" diagram for an option value at expiration.

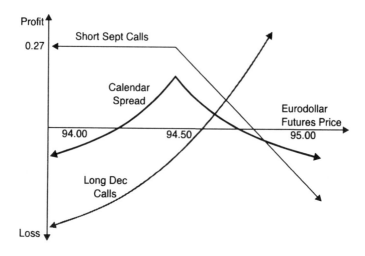

Figure 8.1 The Profit & Loss Profile of a Calendar Spread at the first expiration.

On the 19 September, both 94.50 call options values will contain intrinsic value, but the December call will additionally have time value. Thus, relative to the Eurodollar futures price, the unlimited intrinsic value profit potential on the December call should offset the unlimited intrinsic value loss potential on the September call. The combined position should flatten out. Figure 8.1 displays the profit and loss diagram for this trade at expiration.

As the reader can see, when you combine the two call options you will get a payoff that looks similar to a curved butterfly at expiration. It is curved with a limited loss on the downside and curved with a limited loss on the upside and will make money if the market remains at the current level. The pure effect of time decay earns the profit. The reader may also notice that the profit/loss profile for this trade looks remarkably like the time value graph in the option pricing chapter (Figure 2.11b). That is because this trade is isolating for the time value of the December option. If the market finishes at 94.50 and both calls are at-the-money, then the total profit will be 25 - 11 or 14. That is the expected amount you make from this trade. The loss potential is 13 which is the premium outflow when you bought the spread (38-25). So, you are risking 13 to make 14, which is a risk/reward of slightly better than 1 to 1 in the best case. The reader will note that this is not a pure arbitrage trade because the trade can experience losses. A true arbitrage involves no risk. The calendar spread is really a fairly low risk trade that attempts to benefit from the different rate of time decay that occurs for long dated and short dated options. By both buying and selling the same kind of options (calls or puts), the loss potential from the movement of the Eurodollar futures is limited and the volatility exposure is less than that of a single option purchase or sale. However, this spread has additional benefits prior to expiration that might lead a trader to consider implementing this strategy. To see this, we must consider the profit and loss profiles of the calendar spread prior to expiration. This is displayed in Figure 8.2.

If the calendar spread is purchased with 90 days until expiration, the position is flat at the current price of the underlying asset which is 94.50. If the price of the Eurodollar futures moves sufficiently up or down, losses will occur. However, if time simply passes, the calendar spread will earn profits if the underlying Eurodollar futures price remains at 94.50. This is due to the fact that the time decay (or theta) for the September call will be much larger than for the December call. The volatility sensitivity of the calendar spread is not that obvious. The reader will remember that at-the-money options have the greatest time value. If the volatility doubles for the at-the-money option, the time value of the option will also double. However, in the case of the calendar spread we have both bought and sold two at-the-money options with different expiration months. Given that the more the time, the more the time value, the December call we have purchased will have even more time value than the September call we sold. Since the implied volatility sensitivity is directly related to the absolute level of the time value in the option, then one would expect the overall vega exposure to be positive. This is because the option we purchased for December should have a higher vega than the September option. What about the gamma exposures? The gamma, which is the measure of the exposure to a change in the actual volatility of the underlying market, is highest for at-the-money options. Again, we will have a position which both buys and sells at-the-money options. However, the gamma is also a measure of how close one is to the expiration of the option. The closer the time to expiration, the higher the gamma value of the at-the-money option. We would therefore expect the September call to have a higher gamma than the December call option. Given we have sold the September call, we would predict our gamma exposure would overall be negative. While this is our hypothesis, the only way to make sure if they are cor-

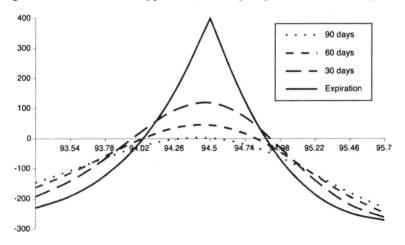

Figure 8.2 The Profit & Loss Profile of a Long Calendar Spread over time.

rect is to examine the "Greek" derivatives for each element of the strategy and in total. This has been done for the long Eurodollar calendar spread assuming:
- a strike price of 94.50 for both September and December options
- the underlying Eurodollar futures is also at 94.50 for both,
- 90 days until expiration of the September contract,
- implied volatility of 25%, and
- short term interest rates at 4%.

The results of this can be seen in Table 8.2.

LONG CALENDAR SPREAD:
Futures 94.5; volatility 25%; rate of interest 4%;
90 days to expiration of the September contract.

	PRICE	DELTA	GAMMA	VEGA	THETA
BUY 94.50 CALL DECEMBER	+0.38	+0.45747	+0.004057	+0.03817	-2.5311
SELL 94.50 CALL SEPTEMBER	-0.25	-0.47159	-0.005790	-0.02709	+3.6949
CALENDAR SPREAD	**+0.13**	-0.01412	-0.00173	+0.01107	+1.1638

Table 8.2 Long Calendar Spread Sensitivities.

As the reader can see, the theoretical value of the long calendar spread is +0.13. Given that each contract is for a $1,000,000 three month deposit and the value of each tick is $25, the total cost of one calendar spread is $325. The delta is slightly negative at -0.01412. Unfortunately, this is difficult to interpret. If both options were for the same delivery months, one would say that this position is for all practical purposes delta neutral. However, the delta of the September call is relative to the September futures and the delta of the December call is relative to the December futures. All we can say is that if both the September and December futures move exactly in the same way, the overall position will be delta neutral. What this spread is telling us is that we are short 47.159% (delta) of one September Eurodollar futures and long 45.747% of one December Eurodollar futures. This is known as an intra-market spread between the two futures months and we will benefit if the price of the September futures drops relative to the December futures. This is not an insubstantial risk and must be considered carefully. Later in this book (Chapter 14), I will show the reader how to eliminate this intra-market risk, but for this example, we will assume the two futures contracts move in a parallel fashion.

If the underlying futures price experiences an extreme move, the options delta will change: decreasing when underlying Eurodollar futures prices rise and also when the Eurodollar futures prices fall. Whenever one buys an option, the gamma is positive and whenever one sells an option, the gamma is negative. In the case of the calendar spread, we have sold one call option with a large gamma effect and bought another call option with a lower gamma. In the above table, the overall gamma for the long calendar spread is -0.00173. While again this number appears to be slight, that is because it is expressed in the impact on the delta from a one tick movement in the Eurodollar futures which is 1/100th of an interest rate percentage point. If we look at a movement of 0.5 a percentage point in the U.S. three month interest rates to 5% (futures price of 95.00) or to 4% (futures price of 94.00), this still implies that the delta will change by only ±0.0865 (50 ticks times -0.00173). Thus, at 90 days until the expiration of the September futures, the impact of the change in the underlying market price is still fairly small. If we assume parallel movements in both Eurodollar futures, the position will remain within a delta neutral range for all movements ±50 ticks overnight. If the reader looks back at the profit and loss profile for the option at 90 days until expiration, he will notice that the curved relationship between the options price and the underlying price is indeed fairly flat. However, this situation may not stay this way. As the September option approaches expiration, the gamma effect will rise and the reader should see this effect by comparing the profit and loss profile at 60 days an at 30 days when the "frowning" pattern of a gamma negative position becomes more apparent. However, the gamma impact switches at the first expiration to became gamma positive. This is because as the first option expires, the negative gamma of that option will also disappear. The only remaining gamma exposure will be positive for the long option still hold. So it is fair to say that the holder of the calendar spread would want the actual volatility to decrease, especially as we approach the September expiration. Thereafter, his gamma viewpoint would change.

Whenever one buys an option, one is also buying the implied volatility. The more time value that the option has, the greater the impact on the options price from a change in the implied volatility. Since for the long calendar spread we paid more premium than we received, the net effect is that we are vega positive. In Table 8.2, the vega is +0.01107 and this means the amount that the value of the long calendar spread will change for a change in 1% in the implied volatility. This number is again expressed relative to U.S. $1,000 in this table. This says that if the implied volatility rises from 25% (the current level) to 26%, the premium cost of the option will rise by $11.07. Given that the original price of the long calendar spread was $325, this would mean that the new price of the option should be $336.07 at a 26% implied volatility. At first glance, this may seem to be insubstantial. But if we look at the impact as a percentage of the original price of the spread, the effect reflects more than a 3% change in the value ($11.07/$325) for a change of only 1% in volatility. Furthermore, as the September option approaches expiration, the time value (and the vega effect) for this option will decrease. At the September expiration, the only remaining vega exposure will be for the December option and it should be at a level around +0.030. Thus, the spread will become more and more exposed to the implied volatility (higher vega) through time.

Finally, in Table 8.2 the holder of the long calendar spread has a positive theta position (of +1.1638). This measure is expressed in the number of U.S. Dollars that will be gained from the passage of one calendar day in the spread's life (from 90 days to 89 days to expiration). Thus, if everything else remains constant, the holder of the calendar spread would expect tomorrow that his spread would now be worth $326.16 (current price of $325 plus the time decay of $1.1638). While this may not seem like a lot, it is better than losing time value and will accelerate as the September option will begin to experience heavier time decay loss.

The long calendar spread is unique when compared to the other volatility strategies discussed in the previous chapter, in that for the first time the exposures of the gamma and the vega are opposite. In all the spreads using the same expiration period the gamma and vega exposures are of the same sign. But calendars are a different animal altogether. It is also interesting to note that for the first time, we can both gain from time decay and benefit from an increase in the implied volatility. The only fly in the ointment is that the gamma effect is detrimental. We want the actual volatility of the September futures to decrease and at the same time the implied volatility of the December futures to rise. If the volatilities fail to change in the manner predicted by the trader, there is still a chance the spread may work due to the profits accruing from time decay or from favourable intra-market spread changes.

Let us consider the impacts of the implied volatility in a little more detail. A disadvantage of calendar spreads is that while initially the strategy is spreading actual versus implied volatility, the initial exposures to the gamma and vega are slight (as can be seen in Table 8.2). As time passes, these exposures will change requiring the trader to hold the strategy only if the viewpoint on the relationship between the actual and implied volatilities has remained unchanged. Otherwise adjustments have to be made. For example, as we approach 19 September, you will start becoming "long" volatility (positive vega) as the short dated option approaches expiration. The reason is that the December option will still have a positive volatility exposure when the September option expires with no volatility exposure at all. Therefore, your position will be exposed to the level of December volatility at the September expiration when you will have to sell back the December option. If the market is stable and volatility has not fallen, then you should make the 14 ticks from the time decay. As calendar spreads benefit most from this time decay, most traders establish calendar spreads in the 30 days preceding the short dated option's expiration expecting stable underlying markets but perhaps increased implied volatility. Even with these complications, long calendar spreads can be an alternative to a long butterfly since they provide an even greater benefit from time decay. However, the spreader must be cognisant that relative to the butterfly spread, the implied volatility exposure is positive, while both share negative gamma exposures and positive theta.

The long calendar spread can go wrong if the actual volatility of the September futures rises or if the implied volatility for December options falls. Consider the situation where the implied volatility falls. If the implied volatility decreases, the December option will be worth less than the expected 27 and the profit from the trade would be less than the 14 ticks expected. Fortunately, a common market effect may preclude this from occurring. Increases in volatility often occur when traders roll their long call option positions from the shorter maturity to the longer maturity to continue their directional viewpoint. As traders do this, the demand increases for the longer dated options and their prices increase. This higher demand, which means higher prices, will be reflected as a higher implied volatility in the longer dated options. Thus, a long calendar spread can be a very good strategy to bearing in mind near the point where people roll their buying positions, usually within the last 30 days before expiration. Calendar spreads, because they are composed of both buying and selling options, limit the loss to the net premium paid out. They also benefit from time decay and will profit from volatility either remaining stable or increasing.

Another potential problem for option calendar spreads as was indicated above is the intra-month spread relationship between the September and December futures. If you are going to establish calendar spreads with options, you must make a prediction on what will happen to the price relationship between the September and December underlying futures markets. For instance, if you buy a call in December and the December futures price increases, you make money from that fact. If September happens to fall at the same time, then the call option you sold will also profit. However, if the opposite occurs and the September contract rises as the December futures falls, the change in the intra-market spread will hurt this long call options calendar spread. Generally, this spread is determined by subtracting the price of the deferred futures contract (December) from the price of the nearby futures contract (September).

To take advantage of this change in the intra-month spreads, you can construct a calendar spread with either calls or puts depending on what you project will occur to the intra-month spread relationship. You buy longer maturity puts and sell shorter maturity puts, when you expect that either the spreads will remain constant or will widen out (the nearby futures price minus the deferred futures price). To benefit from the spread falling, one could buy the deferred call and sell the nearby call. Call calendar spreads and put calendar spreads possess a similar profit/loss profile. But, the call calendar spread benefits more from a drop in the intra-month spread and vice versa for the put calendar spread. Therefore, in the analysis of calendar spreads, the trader must have a view on the underlying Eurodollar futures market, volatility and the intra-market spreads. As always, time decay and the liquidity of the options markets must also be considered.

Another consideration when establishing calendar spreads is that the prices for the deferred and nearby futures may not be the same. Suppose that in our above example, the December and September futures prices were not at the same level, this will complicate the establishment of the calendar spread. The standard technique for implementing a calendar spread is to buy and sell at the same strike price. However, when the underlying Eurodollar futures prices are different, a better technique is to choose strike prices which are the same relative to each Eurodollar futures price. If I sold the at-the-money September call option, that means I would sell the 94.50 call because the September Eurodollar futures was trading at around that level for this period. But the 94.50 call strike price may not be the at-the-money call for the December underlying futures because the December futures might be trading at 94.00. Therefore, for the December option series, it makes more sense to buy the 94.00 call option which is the at-the-money option for that particular Eurodollar futures position. Likewise, if I sold the first out-of-the-money September call option, then I would go to the next contract month, December and buy the first out-of-the-money call option. Often, and especially in the share market, calendar spreads are established at the same strike price. For options on Eurodollar futures, you should establish the calendar spreads not necessarily at the same strike price but at strike prices which have the same relationship to the prevailing Eurodollar futures market. Frequently, the December Eurodollar futures price will be different from the September Eurodollar futures price, so the strike prices to choose in the calendar spread should also be different.

Short Calendar Spreads

If I sell a call for December Eurodollar futures and then buy a call for September Eurodollar futures at the same relative strike price, then I have a position that is also offsetting to some degree relative to the underlying Eurodollar time deposit market. In this case, the strategy will be hurt by time decay. If I buy a short dated option, over the period of its life the time value will decay rapidly, while the option I have sold will experience a reduced time decay.

Suppose on 21 June 1994, the September is trading at 94.50 and the December Eurodollar futures is also trading at 94.50 and I sell an 94.50 December call option. Over the time period from 21 June to 19 September (the expiration of the September Eurodollar option), the time decay for the December call option will be relatively slow and then from 19 September to 19 December, it will accelerate. Then, suppose on 21 June, I also buy a September 94.50 call. For the time period between then until the September expiration (19 September), the time decay will be very rapid. At the expiration of the September contract, the September 94.50 call will have no time value at all, its value will only consist of its intrinsic value. In this case, if I sell options which have a very slow time decay and buy options with a rapid time decay over that same time period, I should be hurt from this time decay discrepancy. When one does this, it is called selling or going short the calendar or time spread.

The example for this is the opposite of the long calendar spread discussed above. On 21 June, the December 94.50 call I sold would be worth 0.38. If the Eurodollar futures market remains at the current level of 94.50 by 19 September 1994, the December call should then be worth about 0.27. The gain on this call from time decay would therefore be 0.11. If I bought the September 94.50 call for 0.25, and the market finishes at 94.50, the option will be worth nothing.

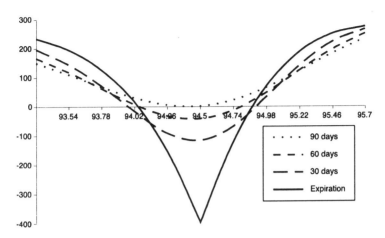

Figure 8.3 The Profit & Loss Profile of a Short Calendar Spread over time.

This may appear to be a sure loser. However, this may not be the case, if the trader does not plan to hold the position all the way to expiration he may not thus realise the entire impact of the time decay. Further, if his viewpoint is that the actual volatility of the September futures may rise while the implied volatility of the December futures might fall the short calendar can make sense. Let us look at the profit and loss profiles of the short calendar spread throughout its life and at expiration. Figure 8.3 displays this.

On the 19 September, both 94.50 call options values will contain intrinsic value, but the December call will additionally have time value. Thus, relative to the Eurodollar futures price, the unlimited intrinsic value profit potential on the September call should offset the unlimited intrinsic value loss potential on the December call. The combined position will be represented by a profit and loss profile which is opposite to the long calendar spread.

As you can see, when you combine the two call options you will get a payoff that looks similar to an upside down curved butterfly at expiration. It is curved with a limited profit on the downside and curved with a limited profit on the upside and will lose money if the market remains at the current level. The effect of time decay generates this loss. If the market finishes at 94.50 and both calls are at-the-money, then the total loss will be the same as the profit for the long calendar spread or 14 ticks. The profit potential is 13 ticks which is the premium inflow when you sold the spread. It would appear that you are risking 14 to make 13, which is a risk/reward ratio of less than 1 to 1 in the best case. While this is not an ideal risk/reward ratio, this spread has additional benefits prior to expiration that might lead a trader to consider implementing this strategy.

If the calendar spread is sold with 90 days until expiration, the position is relatively flat at the current price of the underlying asset which is 94.50. If the price of the Eurodollar futures moves sufficiently up or down, profits will occur. However, if time simply passes, the calendar spread will be hurt if the underlying Eurodollar futures price remains at 94.50. The volatility sensitivity of the calendar spread is what makes it an interesting strategy. Suppose, that the trader feels that the implied volatility is much higher than the actual volatility he expects will occur in the market. This situation was pointed out in Chapter 4 when I examined a forecasting technique for estimating the actual volatility using economic days. In that example for options on BTP futures, the implied volatility was considerably higher than the actual volatility that occurred over the subsequent period. Therefore, such a result would suggest that one would initiate a vega negative strategy (selling volatility) to realise profits. However, in a market as unpredictable as the Italian Bond market, it really takes courage to sell the volatility outright. The trader may wish to buy the actual volatility (by being gamma long) and sell the implied volatility (vega short) to protect himself against the gyrations in that market. For him, the short calendar spread may be the best alternative. To assess, the sensitivities of the short calendar spread one again requires examination of the "Greek" derivatives for each element of the strategy and in total. This has been done for the short Eurodollar calendar spread assuming:

> - a strike price of 94.50 for both September and December options
> - the underlying Eurodollar futures is also at 94.50 for both,
> - 90 days until expiration of the September contract,
> - implied volatility of 25%, and
> - short term interest rates at 4%.

The results of this can be seen in Table 8.3.

SHORT CALENDAR SPREAD:
Futures 94.5; volatility 25%; rate of interest 4%;
90 days to expiration of the September contract.

	PRICE	DELTA	GAMMA	VEGA	THETA
SELL 1 94.50 CALL DECEMBER	-0.38	-0.45747	-0.004057	-0.03817	+2.5311
BUY 1 94.50 CALL SEPTEMBER	+0.25	+0.47159	+0.005790	+0.02709	-3.6949
CALENDAR SPREAD	-0.13	+0.01412	+0.00173	-0.01107	-1.1638

Table 8.3 Short Calendar Spread Sensitivities.

The theoretical value of the short calendar spread is still at 0.13. However, in this case the trader will receive a premium of $325. The delta is slightly positive at +0.01412, but once again is difficult to interpret due to the fact that the options are for different delivery months.

If the underlying futures price experiences an extreme move, the options delta will change: both increasing when underlying Eurodollar futures prices rise and also when the Eurodollar futures prices fall. In the case of the short calendar spread, we have bought one call option with a large gamma effect and sold another call option with a lower gamma. Thus, the overall gamma for the short calendar spread is +0.00173.

Whenever one buys an option, one is also buying the implied volatility. The more time value that the option has, the greater the impact on the option's price from a change in the implied volatility. Since for the short calendar spread we received more premium than we paid, the net effect is that we are vega negative. In Table 8.3, the vega is -0.01107. So this strategy would benefit from a drop in the implied volatility relative to the actual volatility associated with the variability in the underlying market.

The price for this implied versus actual volatility spread is a negative theta. The seller of the calendar spread will lose $1.1638 from the passage of one calendar day in the spread's life. This loss will accelerate as the September option will begin to experience heavier time decay loss coming into expiration.

The short calendar spread is also unique when compared to the other short volatility strategies discussed in the previous chapter, in that again the exposures of the gamma and the vega are opposite. This trade can gain both from a decrease in the implied volatility for December options and an increase in the actual volatility of the September futures. If the volatilities fail to change in the manner predicted by the trader, the spread will lose from time decay. Therefore, as was stated above, this strategy may not be held until expiration but will be unwound as soon as the implied volatility falls back to levels more consistent with the actual variability in the underlying markets. Of course, this assumes that there is some relationship between the actual volatility in September futures and the implied volatility in December futures. While these two estimates of volatility may not be directly tied, it is probably safe to infer the relationship between the two by examining the term structure relationship between the two periods. This was discussed in Chapter 5.

In that chapter, we also showed you the "Volatility Cone" method of estimating volatilties. In these graphs, one saw that the historical volatility range is more extreme for underlying assets with a short time to expiration. In addition, the implied volatilities can be compared to the "Cone" to assess if they are relatively expensive or cheap. When the implied volatility is well above the historical average volatility and may be at the upper boundary of the cone, the trader may wish to sell the longer dated implied volatility and buy the short term actual volatility since the "Cone" indicates that a much greater deviation in the short term actual volatility does seem to occur. In this scenario, the short calendar spread may be the best strategy to use with the proviso that when the implied volatility changes, the trader unwinds the strategy.

COMPARISON OF ALL THE VOLATILITY SENSITIVE STRATEGIES

With the coverage completed for the calendar spreads, we can now summarise all the exposures for the volatility sensitive strategies discussed so far. This can be seen in Table 8.4.

STRATEGY	DELTA	GAMMA	VEGA	THETA
Long Call	+	+	+	-
Short Put	+	-	-	+
Long Put	-	+	+	-
Short Call	-	-	-	+
Long Straddle	0	+	+	-
Long Strangle	0	+	+	-
Short Straddle	0	-	-	+
Short Strangle	0	-	-	+
Long Butterfly	0	-	-	+
Long Condor	0	-	-	+
Long Calendar Spread	0	-	+	+
Short Calendar Spread	0	+	-	-

Table 8.4 Comparisons of the Volatility Sensitive Strategies.

In this table, I have indicated a positive exposure to the "Greek" derivative with a "+" and a negative exposure with a "-". The reader may notice that some of the pluses or minuses are larger than others. The strategies with larger pluses or minuses indicate a greater relative impact from the derivative than might be the case for other strategies. For example, the long straddle has a bigger plus for gamma than the long strangle, this is because the straddle (which is constructed with at-the-money options) is more sensitive than the strangle to changes in the actual volatility. Likewise, the long strangle has a lower theta than the long straddle because it has less time value to decay. For those strategies which sell volatility, the butterfly and condor, have less of a gamma or vega sensitivity relative to the short straddle or strangle, but make most of their money on time decay in the last 30 days. Finally, for the calendar spreads, we can see that the long calendar spread is a buyer of the implied volatility (vega positive) and a seller of the actual volatility (gamma negative). The short calendar spread is inverse. Regardless of the strategy available, there is no possibility of both being gamma positive and theta positive. The reason for this lies in the foundation of options prices presented in Chapter 2. If the reader peers back to Figure 2.14, he will see the trade off between the gearing of an option (gamma) and the time decay (theta). This effect implies that there is no free lunch in the option markets: Whenever one achieves high gearing, the cost will be time decay.

Having just stated this, the reader may be puzzled as to what I will discuss in the remainder of this chapter on arbitrage, which is the financial market's equivalent of a free lunch. When opportunities for arbitrage exist that simply means that someone has made a mistake. Mistakes that can occur include incorrect levels of implied volatility relative to the actual volatility for the same underlying asset, simple "goof ups" in the pricing of options and misvaluations of options for different maturities. I will show the first of these mistakes and how to exploit it. In doing so, I will address divergences between actual and implied volatility. This strategy is known as delta neutral trading.

DELTA NEUTRAL TRADING

The second category of options arbitrage that I will discuss is again not a "pure" arbitrage but a technique for profiting from an incorrect estimation of the market's volatility. This category of volatility "arbitrages" is known as delta neutral trading. When Black and Scholes and others developed their pricing models, a critical assumption they had to make was that equilibrium options prices could only exist if no arbitrage was possible. For example, if you could hold a position which provided an equivalent pay off to an option contract by borrowing money to buy the underlying asset, then the value of this equivalent portfolio should be equal to the price of the option. If this is not the case, someone can create a risk-free strategy by borrowing to buy the underlying asset and selling options against it or selling stock short, investing the proceeds in interest bearing securities and buying options.

One of the major breakthroughs in the Black and Scholes findings was the determination of the proper hedge ratio to use to create a risk-free strategy. This hedge ratio, later christened the delta, determined the proper amount of underlying positions one needed to hold that would be "equivalent" to an options position. While a number of their fundamental assumptions seem erroneous, such as the assumptions that no transaction costs exist, and that markets moved perfectly, the Black and Scholes formula remains remarkably robust. Furthermore, it allows traders not only to identify divergences existing between options markets and the underlying markets, but also allows traders the tools (in the form of deltas) necessary to benefit from these discrepancies. Reliance on such pricing models is the essence of delta neutral trading.

As a review[1], option deltas are variable. Their value depends on whether the option is an equivalent long position or a short position and what the relationship of the option strike price is to the underlying market price. For equivalent short positions, deltas vary from minus one for options which are deep in-the-money to zero for options which are deep out-of-the-money. For equivalent long positions, they can also vary between zero and positive one. At-the-money options always have deltas of approximately 0.50/-0.50. Deltas are the measures of relative risk to the underlying asset position which the volatility arbitrageur will use to hedge both underlying and options positions.

To create the hedge ratio from the delta, you simply divide the number of the underlying asset positions you intend to trade by the delta. If a delta for a particular

---

[1]We will recover ground here that we have previously covered in Chapter 3. In that chapter, the emphasis was on the theoretical foundations of the option markets. In this chapter, we have chosen to use similar examples as in Chapter 3, however in this chapter the emphasis is on practical applications of the concepts discussed previously.

option is 0.67 and you intend to hedge using one of the Eurodollar futures position, you divide 1 by 0.67 and get 1.5. This indicates that for every one Eurodollar futures you would require 1.5 of that particular strike price option to establish a risk-free position. Since one cannot trade half an options contract, you have to round up until both the number of Eurodollar futures trades and options are integer numbers, assuming that the ratio stays the same. If we multiply this hedge ratio by two then we will get three and this means that we would require three options for every two trades in the underlying market, that means still a ratio of 1.5. If an option has a delta of 0.33, one underlying position divided by 0.33 gives a hedge ratio of three. This indicates that you must trade three options for every Eurodollar futures contract to create a hedged portfolio. Therefore, one technique to determine the hedge ratio is to divide one by the delta and find the nearest integer mix that is equal to that ratio.

Now that the review is over, let us look at a few practical examples of these theoretical concepts. Suppose I bought 10 contracts of the Eurodollar futures, the delta position overall would be positive 10. To hedge the position, I would have to acquire offsetting negative deltas. Suppose I chose to use at-the-money call options. With a volatility of 25%, 90 days until expiration, and the current Eurodollar futures price at 94.50, each 94.50 call would result in an inflow of 27 ticks. Moreover, if I sell call options, they will provide me with offsetting negative deltas and, in this particular case, the exposure of each option is equal to -0.471. So, how many calls must I sell? Ten underlying positions divided by 0.471 yields about 21. Therefore, selling 21 at-the-money call options would result in a delta neutral position. As we have seen when I sell the calls, the call buyer pays me a premium of 27 per option. In total, I would have received 567 ticks in time value for the sale of the options (short 21 options each providing a premium of 27 ticks). In real money this would yield a premium inflow of $14,175 (567 ticks times $25 per tick). The profit/loss profile for this strategy can be seen in Figure 8.4 at various points in time prior to the expiration of the options.

If this position is really a hedged position, then any losses or gains on the call option side will be the same amount I gain or lose on the futures side. Suppose that after one day the price of the Eurodollar futures goes down to 94.40, then I will lose 10 points on my 10 long Eurodollar futures contracts for a total loss of 100 points. The option price will drop from 27 points when the market was at 94.50 to 22 points now that it is at 94.40. Thus, I have a gain of 5 points times 21 contracts yielding an overall profit of 105 on the option side. Since I have a loss of 100 on the Eurodollar futures and a gain of 105 on the options on Eurodollar futures, the total position is approximately neutral to changes in the price of the underlying asset. In this instance, I actually make a small profit. As this example illustrates, for small changes in the price of the underlying market, a delta neutral position is indeed immunised.

The problem with deltas is that they change as the price of the underlying market changes. So, at the new price of 94.40, the 94.50 call options are no longer at-

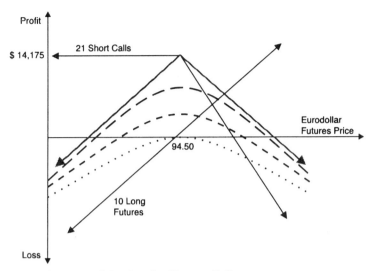

Figure 8.4 Delta Neutral Trading by Writing Calls.

the-money but are now out-of-the-money. Thus, their delta has risen above -0.471. At the new price of 94.40, the short 94.50 call options now have a delta of -0.414. The exposure of the position has now changed from being an overall delta of zero to *positive* 1.306 deltas. This is estimated by multiplying the new call option delta of -0.414 times 21 contracts which is equal to -8.694. When this is added to the +10 deltas of the ten long futures, the net result is +1.306. The strategy will now act as if one were holding 1.306 long futures contracts and thus we are no longer delta neutral. To return to delta neutrality, we have two alternatives:

• Sell out 1.306 of the futures position, or
• Sell more call options with a total delta of 1.306.

The first alternative has a logistical problem: It is not possible to sell less than an integer amount of a futures contract, that is we cannot sell 0.306 of a futures. We could only sell 1 or 2 futures contracts. The other alternative would be to sell more call options. To determine how many we would have to sell we must determine the new hedge ratio to retain our risk-free position. The 10 futures contracts divided by 0.414 will now yield a hedge ratio of 24.15 options. Since we are unable to sell 0.15 of an option, we must round to the nearest integer which indicates that we will sell 3 additional call options at the new price of 22 ticks. These extra call options will bring us back approximately to delta neutral. In total, that will give us 24 short call options against the 10 long futures. In addition, we have more premium to work with since an additional 66 ticks of premium has been paid to us. That now means that we have $15,825 in the pot (the original $14,175 plus a 3 additional short calls worth in total 66 ticks or $1,650).

But suppose the price of the Eurodollar futures market then shot up to 94.65. What is now the effect on the rebalanced delta neutral position? You originally bought the 10 futures contracts at 94.50. With the market at 94.65, you make 15 ticks on each of the 10 contracts for a total profit of 150 ticks. You are short 24 options, 3 were sold at 22 ticks and 21 were sold at 27 ticks. At 94.65, the 94.50 call option is now worth 35 ticks, so the call options we sold for 22 ticks have a loss of 13 ticks, and the 21 we sold at 27 ticks will lose 8 points per option. In total, we lose 207 ticks on the short option position. This overall position now has a net loss of 57 ticks because the loss on the adjusted option position exceeds the profit on the underlying Eurodollar futures position. The actual dollar loss is $1,425 (57 ticks times $25 per tick).

One might ask: What is the problem? I have received $15,825 in total premium and I have only lost $1,425. Does not this imply that I have kept more than I would have to pay away? The answer is yes if this is the only time in the entire life of the strategy that the underlying Eurodollar futures price moved. In reality, everyday the futures will move and every time the delta neutral spreader rebalances his position, he will realise losses. This strategy will only work if the actual volatility in the underlying Eurodollar futures market requires less rebalancing losses than was originally received in option premium. Said another way, this strategy will only work if the actual volatility in the market is less than the implied volatility associated with the options that were sold. This process is not unlike the problem one faces when on a camping holiday.

Suppose, you took a holiday in the woods. Given you are "roughing it" you can not take all the luxuries you may normally consider part of your daily life. But one thing you can not do without is water. So here you are in the "boondocks" and you need some water. Unless it is provided by the heavens above (which always seems to happen on my camping trips), you will have to fetch it from a lake or stream. How? In a bucket of course. For some reason, these buckets always seem to leak. Very often by the time you have returned to camp with the bucket all the water has trickled out, simply watering the path you took from the water source. While you could try again and run back to the camp as quickly as possible, now as you speed along the water will slosh around and again you will lose a major portion of your H_2O.

Consider the bucket of water as the premium initially received when selling the options. Over time, readjustment will imply that the premium inflow will leak out. If before the expiration of the options, all the premium has leaked away, the trade was a failure. Often, at that point when all the premium has been lost, the trader will close out the position with no profits and lots of transactions costs. If the market is especially volatile, then that is like the situation of running with the bucket, the premium just gets sloshed away. The difference between the water bucket and selling options in the delta neutral strategy is that if I lose all my water I will just be thirsty, if I lose all the premium I received and more, I could be bankrupt.

Therefore, as one can see from this example, the problem with delta neutral trading is that when the Eurodollar futures price changes, the hedger must continually re-adjust his position to remain neutral. The delta neutral hedger had to sell additional 94.50 call options at 94.40 and then as the market went back up he should have bought them back at 94.50. Furthermore, as the futures market continued to rise, additional calls should have been bought back at a loss to remain neutral.

A burning question for most market makers that employ the delta neutral technique is: When to rebalance the position. Essentially three methods are used. The first requires a rebalancing decision to occur once a day typically at the same time each day. The second approach rebalances the position back to zero if the aggregate delta amount exceeds some pre-defined delta levels such as ± 0.50. The third technique uses the daily standard deviation principle. The trader will convert the annual volatility he has predicted by $\sqrt{260}$ (trading days in a year to assess the daily volatility (standard deviation). This is then multiplied by the current level of the underlying to determine the number of ticks this represents for that market. Once the underlying market varies by more than this range, the trader will then rebalance back to delta neutrality. In practice, most experienced market makers use all off these methods in combination.

In conclusion, the problem with delta neutral trading is that you will have mismatches whenever the market price changes unless you continually revise your hedged position. Thus, delta neutral hedging only works for very small price changes in the underlying position and requires continuous revision of the hedged position. However, if the Eurodollar futures market stays in a fairly tight range, delta hedging will work. If you continuously rebalance the hedged portfolio, then and only then you can achieve a delta neutral hedge which is immune to movements in the underlying Eurodollar futures markets. Such continuous rebalancing is impractical. Therefore, if the Eurodollar futures market rallies up, you rebalance and then the market proceeds to collapse, you are going to have losses instead of profits because the hedge will now be unbalanced. However, if you have strong instincts for where the market will eventually settle, you may decide to run these positions with the original hedge ratio. This strategy contains the implicit acceptance of an overall position which may become mismatched but might be neutral at expiration.

Given the problems in remaining delta neutral, why would anyone do this? One reason is that you expect the actual market volatility to be less than the volatility implied in the options price. So you sell the implied volatility because you consider it to be overvalued but wish to remain hedged to overall movements in the underlying market price. You are "arbitraging" volatility by gaining more from the drop in the volatility embedded in the options time value than you are giving up in the expected rebalancing costs to remain delta neutral. So this is not a true risk-free arbitrage but is rather a volatility trade with a risk that the actual volatility may increase more than the level of the implied volatility which has been sold.

Theoretically, this should work. However, the assumption this strategy is based upon does not hold in the real world. For example, the Black and Scholes pricing model and the delta hedge ratio assume continuous markets that allow instantaneous revisions to the number of underlying or options positions all held with no transactions costs. The basic problem is that the deltas for these two kinds of assets (underlying markets and options) do not behave the same as the price of the underlying market changes. The underlying Eurodollar futures contract always has a delta of 100% which does not change. Option deltas are more fluid and variable. Many delta neutral traders who combine the underlying Eurodollar futures market with options often find that it is like trying to hit a bowl of jelly with a hammer. As the fixed hammer hits, the jelly simply squirts away. Because of this, many "volatility" arbitrageurs hedge their option positions with other options which also have fluid deltas. This often reduces the "gamma" risk, which is the change in deltas. Unfortunately, a reduction of the expected profit from the "volatility arbitrage" may occur because option premiums must be paid for to achieve this neutrality.

Delta neutral positions occur whenever the overall deltas of the equivalent long positions are equal to the overall deltas of the equivalent short positions. With a number of strike price series available, the possible combination of options and underlying assets which will be delta neutral is almost infinite. Since all delta neutral strategies have a net delta equal to zero, these strategies also have a slope in their profit/loss diagrams which for instantaneous changes in time will be near zero. When the position is initiated, the delta neutral position profits solely from either a change in volatility or from time decay. To remain absolutely neutral to the underlying market is critical, for only then can one isolate the volatility and time decay factors.

If we return to our delta neutral strategy of buying 10 Eurodollar futures and selling 21 calls, we find that, at expiration, we make our maximum profit if the market ends up at the option strike price and the slope of the trade will no longer be zero. This can be seen in Figure 8.5. In fact, the final profit/loss profile of this delta neutral spread resembles a short straddle. How can this be? We have sold 21 call options and bought ten of the underlying position, and an option straddle is produced when we sell (eleven) 94.50 calls and (ten) 94.50 puts.

We know that in this delta neutral strategy we have sold ten calls as well as another eleven calls which means that we have 21 short calls. It is easy to spot the short eleven calls, but where do the short ten puts come from? For the answer, we must return to put-call parity:

$$C - P = F - E$$

Now if we combine a long position in the Eurodollar futures market with a short call we have a trade known as a covered call write. If the reader refers back to the chapter on advanced option pricing (Chapter 3), he will remember that this position is equivalent to a short put. By selling ten call options and buying ten Eurodollar futures contracts, we achieve exactly the same payoff as selling ten put options. Therefore, by buying ten futures and selling 21 calls, we have a position equivalent to selling eleven calls and selling ten synthetic puts which has the same payoff as a delta neutral short straddle.

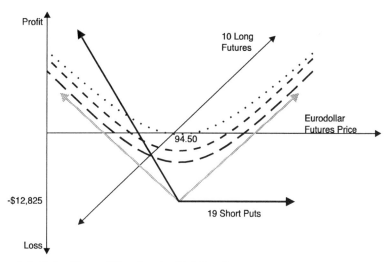

Figure 8.5 Delta Neutral Trading by Holding Puts.

It is easy to see that this position is delta neutral. In fact, the put options at 94.50 (with 90 days to expiration and volatility of 25%) have a delta of 0.520. The overall position is therefore: $11 \cdot 0.471 - 10 \cdot 0.520 = -0.019$ (approximately delta neutral).

Another method of achieving a delta neutral position might be to buy ten of the underlying Eurodollar futures at 94.50 and pick up negative deltas by buying put options. To determine the correct number of puts to hedge, we divide the number of Eurodollar futures by the delta of the put options. Suppose we use the at-the-money 94.50 put options, which, as we have seen, have a delta of -0.520. If we buy these puts each one provides a negative delta position of -0.520. Suppose, we have purchased ten of the underlying Eurodollar futures, by dividing these by -0.520 our hedge ratio turns out to be 19 options. Suppose we buy them at a price of 27 ticks. At the prevailing market price of 94.50, we will also have a position that is delta neutral. However this time, we have established a position which benefits from volatility increasing.

Essentially, we are buying low implied volatility and selling expensive actual volatility. Every time we rebalance our position, we will be realising profits. Consequently, we will suffer from time decay. If we establish this trade with 90 days until expiration and volatility does not increase or the market price fails to move within 30 days, we should lose about $125 in time value per option. If nothing happens by expiration, we expect to lose the entire $675 in premium we have paid per option (27 ticks x $25 per tick). Therefore, we want the actual market volatility to be higher in this period than the volatility implied in the option. If this occurs, we will make money from this volatility discrepancy by gaining rebalancing profits for the put options which would exceed the price we paid for them.

Initially the profit/loss of the strategy is flat (a slope of zero) at the current market price of 94.50. However, the strategy does bend to the north-east as prices rise and bends to the north-west as prices fall. In fact, it looks like a big "smile". At expiration, the strategy resembles something quite different. It looks identical to the long straddle I discussed in the last chapter.

The reason that this payoff resembles a long straddle is because we have once again created a synthetic position. The logic is similar to the one used for the creation of the synthetic short straddle we discussed above. As before, we can separate the 19 long puts into two sets of ten and nine. We then combine the long ten Eurodollar futures with ten of the long put options. Applying put-call parity, we know that long underlying positions combined with long puts produce synthetic long call options. Therefore, we have bought nine actual put options and purchased ten synthetic call options which gives us the same payoff as a long straddle. So, this delta neutral position is really just a long straddle in disguise.

Why trade a synthetic straddle when you could trade the actual straddle? Let us say you want to buy a straddle and no one is making a market in calls, but a number of market makers are offering to sell puts. Since it is impossible to buy calls, you could still buy your straddle by buying ten of the underlying Eurodollar futures and buying 19 puts. You are able to purchase a synthetic straddle which you were unable to establish in the normal way. This ability to create synthetic option strategies is critical in assuring that fair option pricing exists; otherwise arbitrage would take place. These trades help keep option prices in line.

Two practical considerations in doing these delta neutral volatility "arbitrages" are the liquidity in the Eurodollar futures and options markets and the transactions costs involved in the implementation. Very often, these trades can be difficult to establish. Both the options and futures trades must be filled at the same moment and in practice this does not always occur. In addition, when the delta neutral trader is establishing the trades, he must give up the bid/offer spread on both the futures and the options. Not surprisingly, this can result in the reduction of the total profit of the trade.

PURE ARBITRAGE STRATEGIES

Finally, there is the category of trades that are pure arbitrages. These allow the arbitrageur to profit from options being mispriced. These trades have "locked in" returns which offer you a risk-free return. The ability to create synthetic options positions implies that if at any time options prices become mispriced, the trader will buy the underpriced position and sell the equivalent overvalued position; these trades are truly arbitrage trades.

In this final section, I am going to examine how to create synthetic positions with options, compare them to actual positions, and if any discrepancies exist, show how to lock in these deviations to make a risk-free return. Although the next few pages will review what we previously discussed in Chapter 3, I believe that it is worth the reader's while. The essence of true options arbitrage is contained in the put-call parity equation and only with a clear understanding of this can the reader truly grasp option arbitrage.

Let us first consider how to create a synthetic long futures position. When I buy a call I secure the right to buy. If I sell a put, I am obliged to buy. If I combine these two, what do I get? Remember in the first chapter I claimed that to create options, all you need to do is take a long position in any underlying market and split that position into two parts, a good part and a bad part. In this case, if we utilise options from the underlying Eurodollar futures, all we have to do to create a synthetic long Eurodollar futures position is to recombine the options. So, by buying a call on Eurodollar futures and selling a put on Eurodollar futures (both at the same strike price), we will produce the same profit and loss profile as buying the actual Eurodollar futures.

In the United States, this technique is often used to create synthetic futures contracts for markets where only options contracts exist. I did this to create Ginnie Mae (Government National Mortgage Association) futures on a particular security. These were created on an over-the-counter basis when I bought a call on the particular security and sold a put on that same security at the same strike price. The combination was a futures contract on the specific security. In any market, if calls and puts are available, it is possible to create futures contracts. By buying the call option and selling the same strike price put option a long futures position has been produced. The reader is referred back to the discussion in Chapter 3 on put-call parity for a more thorough coverage of why this is the case.

Now that we have identified the synthetic long underlying Eurodollar futures position, we will also identify the synthetic strategies which are equivalent to the long call and the short put. Assume we want to purchase a call option. We may want to evaluate if it is fairly valued. One way to check this is to examine the price of the actual call and compare it to the price of a synthetic call with the same strike price. First of all, we must determine what a call option is equal to. We find the answer with the put-call parity formula, $C - P = (F - E)$. If we add a P to both sides of this equation, it will now read:

$$C = (F - E) + P$$

Thus, the call price must be equal to buying the underlying Eurodollar futures market and buying a put option. How would we create a synthetic short put? Essentially, we are asking what is a minus P equal to? If we subtract a C from both sides of the put-call parity equation, which implies selling a call, we get:

$$-P = (F - E) - C$$

So, a synthetic short put has to be equal to buying the underlying market and selling a call option. Whenever a call or put option price gets out of line, you can create a synthetic option that will provide exactly the same payoff and can be used to deal against the mispriced option to lock in the discrepancy.

What are synthetic selling positions? To create synthetic short positions all you need do is take our put-call parity equation and multiply it by minus 1. The new equation now reads:

$$-C + P = -(F - E)$$

If you sell a call option and buy a put option, the position is equivalent to selling the underlying Eurodollar futures. Thus, when you combine the right to sell and the obligation to sell, that produces a short position in the underlying futures.

To create a synthetic long put you take the negative put-call parity formula and simply add a C to both sides, in other words, buy a call option. The equation now reads:

$$P = -(F - E) + C$$

That implies that if you are short the underlying futures and buy a call, you will have a position which must be equal to the price of the put option. The most you can lose if you buy an option is the premium paid. So, what is the most you can lose on the purchase of a synthetic put option? It is equal to the premium paid for the actual put option. If the actual put option premium and the synthetic put option premium ever diverge, you can close the differential by buying the actual option and selling the synthetic. Therefore, for "no arbitrage" to exist, there must be no difference between the prices of synthetic puts and actual puts.

Finally, how do we create a synthetic short call? With the negative put-call parity equation, we subtract a P from both sides of the equation. That cancels the +P on the left and adds a -P on the right. The new equation reads:

$$-C = -(F - E) - P$$

This implies that if we are short the underlying position and short a put, I will have exactly the same position as being short a call.

Practical Applications of Synthetic Transactions

If a particular trader buys a Eurodollar futures and then buys a put option to protect it, what is the net effect of this transaction? The answer is a synthetic long call. Suppose he establishes this trade and the price of the futures rises. He may then wish to close out his position and take his profits. One way he could do this would be to sell back the put and sell the underlying Eurodollar futures. An alternative, which is much simpler, is to sell a call at the same strike price as the put and he has closed out the position without having to sell the underlying position. In the put-call parity equation it would then read:

$$0 = (F - E) + P - C$$

In literal form: zero is the difference between buying the underlying Eurodollar futures, buying a put and selling a call.

Consider instead the trader who implements a cover call write. In this trade, he buys a Eurodollar futures and sells a call against it. Suppose he also decides he wants to cover the position. He will have to buy back the call and the liquidity for this option may have "dried up" (especially if it is deep in-the-money). However, the put option which at that point is deep out-of-the-money may still be trading. By purchasing the put option, the position will be completely covered:

$$0 = (F - E) - C + P$$

These synthetic transactions add considerable flexibility to hedgers. For market makers and arbitrageurs, these same transactions are referred to as conversions, reversals, and box trades, rather than as synthetics. These trades are essential to efficiency in the options market. The first of the strategies I will examine is the conversion.

When people trade options as market makers, to facilitate fair pricing and arbitrage, many dealers refer to sheets of theoretical option prices. These sheets provide the fair value of options for a given set of strike prices and for a given range of underlying Eurodollar futures prices. These sheets allow the market maker an overview of all option prices for a given volatility and for a given interest rate factor. Table 8.5 provides an example of such a worksheet.

For example, one can read across from the current market price of 94.50 on the left column and down from the strike price of 94.25 to see that the 94.25 call option is worth 42 ticks when the Eurodollar futures price is at 94.50. What happens if the futures price rises to 94.60? One can read across from 94.60 on the further left column to see that the 94.25 call should rise in value from 42 to 48 ticks. This is a change of 6 ticks, which implies a delta of about 60% (60% of the movement in the Eurodollar futures price). One will also notice that below the call premium on the sheet (at a price of 94.50) is a delta of 0.612. Thus, the option price did change roughly in line with the delta's prediction. We can also look at the 94.50 options which are at-the-money. The 94.50 put option will have a theoretical price of 27 ticks when the Eurodollar futures market is trading at 94.50. If the market moves up or down, how much should the option price change? Below the price of 0.27 one can see that the delta is 0.520. If the market price falls from 94.50 to 94.40, the new value of the put will be 32 ticks. So, the theoretical option price has risen from 27 to 32, which is a profit of 5 ticks. As predicted by the delta, for a market move of 10 ticks, the option only moved by five ticks which is 50% of the movement in the underlying Eurodollar futures.

With these price sheets in hand, market makers can review at a glance what is happening to all the available option series. Many dealers will also have three or four different sheets with different volatilities in case the volatility changes during the day. On the Eurodollar futures, it would be reasonable to have three separate sheets at 26.5%, 27%, and 27.5% volatility to complement a trader's market making activities. Basically, what a market maker does during a typical trading day is to use his price sheets as an indication of what theoretical option values should be at certain levels. They are constantly comparing the theoretical values on the sheets to actual market prices to both revise their volatility estimates and spot arbitrage opportunities.

Eurodollar September 1994						
Days To Expiration = 77						
Volatility = 27%						
Rate = 5.25%						
Futures		Strike Prices				
		94.00	94.25	94.50	94.75	95.00
94.40	Call	0.53	0.36	0.23	0.13	0.06
	Delta	(0.685)	(0.556)	(0.414)	(0.278)	(0.163)
	Put	0.13	0.21	0.32	0.47	0.66
	Delta	(0.308)	(0.436)	(0.577)	(0.715)	(0.831)
94.45	Call	0.56	0.39	0.25	0.14	0.07
	Delta	(0.710)	(0.584)	(0.442)	(0.302)	(0.181)
	Put	0.11	0.19	0.30	0.44	0.62
	Delta	(0.283)	(0.408)	(0.549)	(0.690)	(0.812)
94.50	Call	0.60	0.42	0.27	0.16	0.08
	Delta	(0.734)	(0.612)	(0.471)	(0.328)	(0.201)
	Put	0.10	0.17	0.27	0.41	0.58
	Delta	(0.239)	(0.380)	(0.520)	(0.664)	(0.792)
94.55	Call	0.63	0.45	0.29	0.17	0.09
	Delta	(0.757)	(0.639)	(0.500)	(0.355)	(0.222)
	Put	0.09	0.15	0.24	0.37	0.54
	Delta	(0.236)	(0.352)	(0.491)	(0.637)	(0.770)
94.60	Call	0.67	0.48	0.32	0.19	0.10
	Delta	(0.780)	(0.667)	(0.530)	(0.383)	(0.245)
	Put	0.08	0.13	0.22	0.34	0.50
	Delta	(0.213)	(0.325)	(0.462)	(0.609)	(0.747)

Table 8.5 Minerva Consulting Eurodollar Option Evaluations September 1994.

The Conversion Arbitrage Strategy

If you looked on the screen and spotted a bid on the 94.50 Eurodollar futures call at 27 and an offer on the 94.50 Eurodollar futures put at 25, the trader would glance at his sheet and see that both should be at 27 when the market is offered at 94.50. The call is fair valued and the put is undervalued. What do you do if something is undervalued? You buy it. But then you have a position exposed to changes in volatility and sensitive to time decay. So, let us close up the trade and eliminate all risk. Since we have bought the actual put, we must sell a synthetic put. This is accomplished by selling a call and buying the underlying Eurodollar futures. This trade is commonly known as a conversion.

You have to do all three trades in the batting of an eye: buy the 94.50 put, sell the 94.50 call and buy the Eurodollar futures. Otherwise others will see it and close the discrepancy, taking the profit themselves. It is as if you saw a 20 dollar note on the ground. You had better pick it up quickly before someone else sees it and grabs it.

But is this trade truly an arbitrage? Let us see what could happen at expiration. If you have truly closed the trade, you can then consolidate it, knowing that irrespective of where the market price finishes, you will make the arbitrage profit. What are the three things that could possibly happen by the expiration date? The answer is: the market could fall, rise, or stay the same.

Let us first assume that the market falls to 94.00 at expiration. You bought the underlying market at 94.50, it is now worth 94.00. Therefore, you are going to lose 50 ticks on that. But remember you purchased the put option which gives you the right to sell at 94.50. With the market at 94.00, you will exercise your put with an inflow of 50 ticks. That exactly offsets the 50 ticks that you lost on the position in futures. So, no loss or gain here. What about the call option you sold? With the market at 94.00, the call option buyer will let his option expire worthless. You are therefore going to receive the entire 27 ticks for the call option. Then you must deduct the 25 ticks you paid for the 94.50 put. The net effect if the market finishes at 94.00, is an inflow of 27 ticks in option premium minus your payment of 25 ticks plus a flat position which has no profit or loss (futures/put offset). This sums up to two ticks in profit.

What happens if the Eurodollar futures market ends up at 94.50 at expiration? The put option is the right to sell at 94.50, and if the market is also at 94.50, the put will expire worthless and you will lose the 25 ticks you paid. The short call option is the obligation to sell at 94.50, and if the market is sitting at 94.50 the call also expires worthless. In this case, providing an inflow of 27 ticks in premium. Finally, the underlying futures market is also at 94.50 and you could sell it back at that level with no profit or loss. The net inflow is equal to two ticks. That seems to work if the market finishes at 94.50, but could it not finish higher than 94.50?

Suppose the market does finish above 94.50. You have bought the underlying Eurodollar futures at 94.50 and the market is now at 95.00, so your profit on this trade is 50 ticks. What about the 94.50 put option you purchased? With the market at 95.00, you will abandon the put option allowing it to expire worthless losing the 25 ticks you paid for it. But the call holder has the right to buy at 94.50, and with the market at 95.00, will exercise it. Since you are obligated to sell it to him at 94.50, you will lose 50 ticks exactly equal to the 50 ticks you made by buying the underlying futures. However, you will still earn the premium of 27 ticks the call buyer paid to you less the 25 ticks in premium you paid, so once again the net profit from the arbitrage will be 2 ticks. Whenever options prices get out of line, one can knock them back into line using the put-call parity principles underlying the conversion.

What you have done with this conversion is to create a synthetic short underlying Eurodollar futures position by purchasing the put option and selling the call at the same strike price, and you covered the synthetic by buying the actual underlying Eurodollar futures market. We will now see how these arbitrages are produced using our graphing rules. In Figure 8.6, all the positions involved in the arbitrage are displayed. To the left of 94.50, there is an unlimited profit potential for the long put option and a limited gain potential for the short call option. What is the rule? Unlimited dominates limited, so the combination gives me an unlimited profit potential. To the right of 94.50, you have an unlimited loss potential on the short call option and a limited profit potential on the long put option, so what is going to happen? The unlimited loss on the call is going to overwhelm the limited loss on the put and we end up with a position that has an unlimited loss potential. Overall, this is the same payoff as selling a Eurodollar futures contract. All we need to do to eliminate all risk is to establish an offsetting trade which has exactly the opposite profit/loss profile. The opposite trade is obviously to buy the underlying Eurodollar futures market. The arbitrage occurs because you are buying the natural underlying position at a fair price and selling the synthetic at an overvalued price locking in a risk-free return as demonstrated above. This profit is "locked in" no matter where the market price finishes at expiration.

These transactions, as one might imagine, do not happen very often and when they do, they exist only momentarily. But the same thing can be said about finding a $20 note on the street. It does not happen very often, but when you see it lying there, you will surely pick it up.

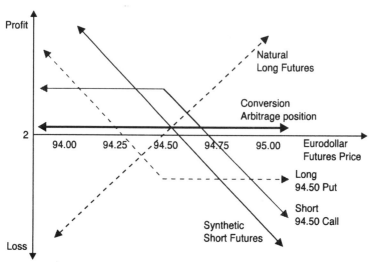

Figure 8.6 The Conversion Arbitrage.

But will these trades work in an illiquid market? If you can complete all three components of this transaction the answer is yes. That is, once you lock these trades in, you do not have to trade again to realise your profits. Liquidity becomes irrelevant.

As the reader may begin to see, arbitrage keeps market prices efficient. Options arbitrageurs are basically the "fair price police" that step in and keep prices in line. Without them, options markets would be no better than a free-for-all and option pricing theory would become unmanageable.

The Reversal Arbitrage Strategy

The second kind of arbitrage trade we will discuss is known as the reversal (which is also known as a reverse conversion). In this trade, suppose that a 94.50 call option is offered at a price of 24 ticks, the 94.50 put is bid at 27 ticks and the Eurodollar futures is bid at 94.50, what are you going to do? Buy the undervalued call, sell the fairly valued put, and finally sell the underlying Eurodollar futures. Now that is done, let us see what can happen to the combination of trades at expiration. As before, if the arbitrage profit is earned no matter where the underlying Eurodollar futures market finishes, we can declare this trade to be risk-free.

Let us assume that the market remains unchanged at 94.50. The call and the put both have strike prices of 94.50, and since the market is also at 94.50, both options expire worthless. The profit and loss on the underlying Eurodollar futures is also zero because it is unchanged from the level where you sold it previously. The only cash flows that occur are the 24 points you paid for the call option and the 27 ticks you received back from the put option you sold. So, if the market finishes at 94.50, you are going to collect the three ticks differential between the option prices.

What happens if the market goes down? If the market goes down to 94.00 and you sold the Eurodollar futures at 94.50, you can buy it back at 94.00 realising a profit of 50 ticks. Unfortunately, someone has purchased a put option from you which allows them the right to sell the underlying to you at 94.50. With the market at 94.00, the put holder will exercise and you have to pay the put holder the 50 ticks right back. What about the call you purchased? Since you possess the right to buy at 94.50, and the market is below that, you are going to abandon it, allowing it to expire worthless. So once again, the futures profit covers the option's loss and you paid 24 ticks for the call and received 27 for the put. Thus, you are also going to earn those three points even when the market price falls.

The last thing that can possibly happen is that the market finishes above my strike price. If it goes above my strike price, finishing at 95.00, and you have sold the underlying Eurodollar futures market at 94.50, you are going to have a loss of 50 ticks. The put option holder will let the option expire worthless because it is out-of-the-money. Finally, the call you have bought gives you the right to buy at 94.50. When the market is at 95.00, you will have an inflow of 50 ticks which covers the

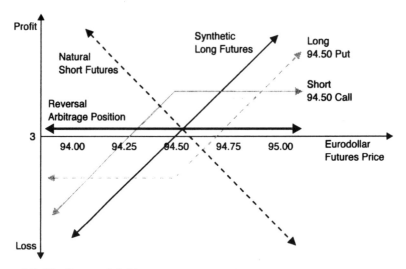

Figure 8.7 The Reversal Arbitrage.

outflow on the futures position. Again, you have a premium outflow of 24 ticks on the call and a premium inflow of 27 ticks from the put. Since the intrinsic value is covered, you still earn the three points which were the initial divergence in the option premiums.

In this example, I have shown how to create a synthetic long Eurodollar futures by buying a call and selling a put. Because the options were mispriced, this allowed us to create a synthetic long position that was cheaper than an actual long position in the Eurodollar futures market. To eliminate the risk from holding this position on an outright basis, we hedge our exposure by selling an actual Eurodollar futures contract. In combination, these positions are risk-less producing a three tick arbitrage profit. Figure 8.7 displays how this trade is formed and why it is risk-less. This trade is known as the reversal.

The Box Arbitrage Strategy

But what happens if it is impossible to trade the underlying Eurodollar futures market? This can occur when you do not have Eurodollar futures markets or if a Eurodollar futures market does exist but it is illiquid.[2] As long as there are other option strike prices trading, you can employ options alone to close the arbitrage and this trade is referred to as a box trade.

---

[2]While illiquidity is not a problem with Eurodollar futures, in certain markets such as shares it is not possible to trade futures on these assets directly. Thus, box arbitrage opportunities are more often exploited for options on shares.

So back to our price sheet in Table 8.5. I will now concentrate on both the 94.50 and the 94.00 strike price options on Eurodollar futures. At the 94.00 strike, the call option value is 60 ticks when the market is at 94.50 and the put is valued at 10 ticks. The 94.50 strike price call and put options are both priced at 27 ticks. With these sheets in hand, you look at the screen and notice somebody has made a mistake, offering the 94.50 put option at 23 ticks when it should be worth 27. So, you buy this put for 23 ticks and sell the same strike price call at its fair price of 27 ticks. As outlined above, this will produce a synthetic short Eurodollar futures position. Now to close the arbitrage, you need a long underlying Eurodollar futures position. If no long Eurodollar futures position is available, you can simply create a synthetic long position by buying another call and selling another put. But instead of using the 94.50 strike prices, you will use the 94.00 strike price options to create the synthetic long Eurodollar futures position. By doing this trade with options at different strike prices, you will have four separate trades which will lock in an arbitrage, assuming that only the 94.50 put is mispriced.

Suppose you bought the 94.00 call and sold the 94.00 put, with both the right to buy and the obligation to buy at 94.00. You have created a synthetic long futures position at 94.00. By buying the 94.50 put and selling the 94.50 call, with both the right and obligation to sell at 94.50, you have a synthetic short position at 94.50. If you bought the futures at 94.00 and sold it at 94.50, you would have a gain of 50. So, with this trade, you are guaranteed a 50 tick inflow. Now, you must determine how much it has cost to establish this trade. By selling the 94.00 put for 10 ticks and selling the 94.50 call for 27 ticks you have a premium inflow of 37 ticks. For the 94.00 call, you must pay 60 ticks and for the 94.50 put you must pay 23 ticks. This is a total outflow of 83 ticks. The net outflow is therefore 46 ticks (83 - 37 ticks) for the box and you expect to receive 50 ticks back.

Do you really lock in the four ticks of arbitrage? Again, what could happen at expiration? The markets could finish below the lower strike price, at the lower strike price, in between the strike prices, at the higher strike price or higher than the higher strike price. I will now go through all five possible situations at expiration and prove that the profit of four ticks will be earned in each possible case.

If the market price finishes below the lower strike price, say at 93.75, you have bought the 94.00 call and sold the 94.50 call, both of which expire worthless. What about your two put options? You bought the right to sell at 94.50 and when the market finishes at 93.75, you will exercise this option receiving 75 points back. Unfortunately, someone else has purchased a 94.00 put from you which gives him the right to sell at 94.00. With the market at 93.75, you will have to pay out 25 ticks. The difference between these cash flows is an inflow of 50 points. This minus what you paid for the spread initially, 46 points, yields a profit of four points. So, in the first case, you do indeed make your four ticks.

What happens if the futures market finishes right at 94.00? Again both calls expire worthless and the put you sold at the 94.00 strike price also expires worthless. However, the put you purchased at the 94.50 strike price is worth 50 ticks which is an inflow. This less the 46 ticks you paid for this spread is a net inflow of 4 ticks. Therefore, in the second situation, you also earn your expected profit.

What about the third case? Suppose the market finishes between the 94.00 and 94.50 strike prices at 94.25. You bought the right to buy at 94.00 and you also have bought the right to sell at 94.50. If the market is at 94.25, you will exercise both the 94.00 call and the 94.50 put you purchased, and pull in 25 on each or a total inflow of 50 ticks. What about the options you sold? One is the right to buy at 94.50, and because that call is out-of-the-money, it will expire worthless. The other option is the right to sell at 94.00, and this put option is also out-of-the-money, expiring worthless. Therefore, you have an inflow of 50 points less the 46 points you paid or a profit of four points once again. So in the third case, you also earn your expected arbitrage profit.

In the fourth circumstance, the futures market finishes at 94.50. In that case, both the 94.00 and the 94.50 put options expire worthless. In addition, the 94.50 call option you sold is also worthless so you have no inflow or outflow on that option. But the 94.00 call you purchased, is in-the-money by 50 ticks which is an inflow of 50 ticks on this trade at expiration. Since your initial premium outflow was 46 ticks, the profit of four ticks is again earned.

Finally, when the futures market finishes above 94.50, the reader can rest assured the arbitrage works here too. If the market finishes at 95.00, you have the right to buy at 94.00 which you will exercise to realise an inflow of 100 ticks. However, you also sold a call option at 94.50. With the market at 95.00, the holder will exercise, calling away from you the underlying asset for a loss of 50 points. So, the net inflow is 50 points. As far as the put options go, at 95.00 both puts expire worthless. Since the spread cost me 46, and you have a 50 points inflow on the options, the net profit is four points in this final situation. Therefore, no matter where the market finishes at expiration, you will earn the four ticks of the "locked in" arbitrage.

The box demonstrates that it is not necessary to deal in the underlying Eurodollar futures market to arbitrage option prices. However, one must be sure of sufficient liquidity in the options market to place all these trades simultaneously.

We will now look at the box spread graphically. The reader will notice that I will examine the box trade in terms of the equivalent option strategies previously discussed. This can be seen in Figure 8.8.

If you sell the 94.00 put at 10 and buy the 94.50 put at 23, this is simply a vertical spread. In Figure 8.8 we can see this. When one establishes a vertical spread by buying the higher strike price put option, this strategy is known as a bear put spread. On the call option side, you bought a 94.00 call at 60 and sold a 94.50 call at 27. When one establishes a vertical spread by buying the lower strike call option that is a bull call spread. This can also be seen in Table 8.5. What happens when you combine a bear spread with a bull spread at the same strike prices? To the left of 94.00 the limited profit potential on the bear spread and the limited loss potential on the bull spread cancel. Between 94.00 and 94.50, the unlimited profit potential

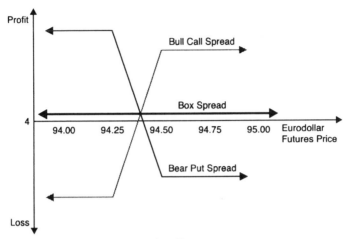

Figure 8.8 Box Spread with Bear and Bull.

on the bear spread and unlimited profit potential on the bull spread cancel. And finally above 94.50, the limited loss potential on the bear spread and the limited profit potential on the bull spread also cancel. So, the whole position is exactly offsetting: you earn the arbitrage profits no matter what happens to the price of the underlying Eurodollar futures market.

Some complications do exist for this trade if people exercise early. At the IMM, early exercise can occur and cause problems if option contracts and the underlying assets do not expire on the same day. If such exercises occur (most commonly in the share market) these positions must be financed until expiration (which is where bankers come in). But because everything at the IMM does settle at the same moment and cash settlement occurs, financing of option premium is minimal and the box trade is a relatively pure extension of put-call parity.

JELLY ROLL ARBITRAGE STRATEGIES

The final arbitrage strategy I will cover in this chapter, consists of a synthetic long futures position in one expiration month versus a synthetic short futures position in another expiration month. While this kind of strategy is not often used in futures options markets (such Eurodollars), where it is easy to buy or sell actual futures, this strategy is often used in stock option markets to profit from divergences in the cost of carry relationship implied in the future. The reader may recall that we discussed forward prices of stocks in Chapter 2 with the example of the forward stock price of IBM. As a brief review, the price of the stock in the future is defined by the equivalent portfolio (to a futures contract) of buying the stock today, financing the stock until the future date and the borrowing costs are reduced by any dividends that are received. Since the pricing of options on stocks take into account these factors (see Chapter 3, the Merton adjustment to the Garman/Kohlhagen model), then if one buys a European call and sells a European put with the same exercise price and expiration, that will mimic a futures contract on that asset. This is the same principle as the one I indicated above which was used to create synthetic Ginnie Mae futures.

The same procedure can be applied to create a synthetic short futures contract by selling a European call and buying a European put. If one were to do this for the same maturity and all the strike prices were the same, the position would be simply a scratched trade. If the strike prices for the synthetic long and short were different, then a box trade would have been constructed similar to the one described above. When the strike prices are the same but the synthetic long position and synthetic short position have different expirations this is known as a Jelly Roll spread. The term originated from the Chicago Board Options Exchange, where stock options are traded. The story goes that a particularly rotund trader who had a taste for the American pastry known as a Jelly Roll was the originator of this trade. The "floor" had decided to "nickname" the trader after his favourite food and by association the same name was applied to his "pet" trading strategy. This is how it works.

Suppose we have a stock with a current price of $100 per share. Call and put options are available for trading with expirations in 3 months and 6 months time. The options do not require payment of the premium today but are margined with payment or receipt of premium at the expiration (see Chapter 3 or Chapter 15 for explanation of futures style margining for options). The current volatility for both the 3 month options is 27.5% and the volatility for the 6 month options is 29.6. A dividend will be paid in 100 days time after the expiration of the first option. The dividend is expected to be $2.50 per share. The prices of the $100 strike price calls and puts for both expirations are presented in Table 8.6 as is the implied future price of the share.

Assumptions	Stock Price $100 ; rate of interest 4%;
	volatility of 27.5% for the 3 month options
	volatility of 29.6% for the 6 month options;
	90 days and 180 days until expirations, and
	a dividend of 2.5$ is expected to be paid in 100 days.
	$100 3 month Call Price $6
	$100 3 month Put Price $5
	Implied 3 month Futures $101
	$100 6 month Call Price $8
	$100 6 month Put Price $8.5
	Implied 6 month Futures $99.5

Table 8.6 Prices of Call & Put Options for Evaluation of Jelly Roll Strategy.

The first question is whether or not the option prices are consistent with the fair price for the stock futures. To evaluate this, we apply the following formula:

> Futures price = Spot price · (1+rt) - D
>
> where:
>   r is the interest rate for the period
>   t is the time period in percentage of a year, and
>   D is the amount of dividend that would be paid.

Applying this to the 3 month expiration date, we will obtain:

$$\$101 = \$100 \cdot (1+0.04 \cdot .25) - 0$$

This implies that at an interest rate of 4% for one quarter of the year and the fact that no dividends will be paid during this period, the fair price of the future stock price from the equivalent cost of carry arbitrage should be $101. From Table 8.6, we see that this is consistent with the options prices and put-call parity (assuming futures style margining for the options):

$$C - P = F - E$$

$$\$6 - \$5 = \$101 - \$100.$$

In the instance that the options are not margined but require payment up front, then the arbitrage future price would be determined using an alternative formula:

> $$C - P = (F - E) \cdot e^{-rt}$$
>
> where:
>   e is the exponential function for continuous interest
>   r is the interest rate over the period
>   t is the time in % of a year until expiration.

Plugging in the call and put prices from above, the fair futures price is now slightly lower at $100.99. This can be seen from this result:

$$\$6 - \$5 \neq (\$101 - \$100) \cdot e^{-(.04 \cdot .25)}$$

$$\$1 \neq \$0.99.$$

Thus, if the option prices were actually $6 for the call and $5 for the put, there would be an arbitrage opportunity of 1 cent. Anyway, we are not going to worry about this because I have assumed futures style margining.

If we then apply the same procedure to the six month expiration period, we will obtain:

$$\$99.50 = \$100 \cdot (1+0.04 \cdot .50) - \$2.50$$

This implies that at an interest rate of 4% for one half of the year and the fact that a dividend of $2.50 will be paid in 100 days[3], the fair price of the future stock price from the equivalent cost of carry arbitrage should be $99.50. From Table 8.6, we see that this is consistent with the options prices and put-call parity (assuming futures style margining for the options):

$$C - P = F - E$$

$$\$8 - \$8.50 = \$99.50 - \$100.$$

Now I will assume that the trader believes the actual dividend will not be $2.50 but will actually be $3.50. With this information, he will initiate a Jelly Roll strategy by synthetically buying a three month futures and simultaneously selling a synthetic six month futures via the options listed in Table 8.6. He is assuming the following price relationship:

SYNTHETIC EXPOSURE

Synthetic Long	-	Synthetic Short	=	Expected	-	Cost of Carry Interest
3 month futures		6 month futures		Dividend		3 versus 6 months
$101	-	$99.50	=	$2.50	-	$1.00
			=	**$1.50**		

Table 8.7a Synthetic Futures Price Relationships at Initiation of Jelly Roll Spread.

One interesting feature of the Jelly Roll strategy, is that it can be seen as a combination of a synthetic long futures position and synthetic short futures position or as a combination of a short call calendar spread (long the nearer term option and short the longer term option) and a long put calendar spread (short the nearer term option and long the longer term option). The synthetic futures combination can be seen in Table 8.7b by comparing the four strategies vertically. If we only look at the 3 month expiration column, this is clearly a synthetic long futures position (long the $100 call and short the $100 put). Likewise, if we concentrate on the 6 month expiration column, this is a synthetic short futures position (short the $100 call and long the $100 put). If we look at the trades in Table 8.7b horizontally, we

---

[3]Strictly speaking, we should take into account that this dividend could be reinvested for the remaining period of the six month period, but this will have a trivial effect and I have chosen to ignore it.

ACTUAL OPTIONS TRADES				
3 month expiration		6 month expiration		
Long $100 Call	$6.00	Short $100 Call	$8.00	=	-$2.00
Short $100 Put	$5.00	Long $100 Put	$8.50	=	+$3.50
	+$1.00	+	+$1.50	=	**$1.50**

Table 8.7b Option Transactions which Comprise the Jelly Roll.

see the calendar spreads. For the calls, we are long a three month $100 call and short a six month $100 call. For this spread, we receive $2.00. For the puts, we are short a three month $100 put and long a six month $100 put for a net premium outflow of $3.50. In total, the combinations of calendar spreads (as will the results of the synthetic futures) will require a premium payment of $1.50.

When I discussed the calendar spreads earlier for the options on the Eurodollar futures, I suggested that the values of the put and call calendar spreads should be similar. This will be the case when the levels of the futures for both the expirations are the same. In the situation where the futures prices for the two expirations are different, then the values of the put and call calendar spreads will also differ in a manner similar to the example presented above. If the deferred Eurodollar futures price is lower than the nearby Eurodollar futures, then the put calendar spread will be worth more than the call calendar spread. In that instance where the deferred Eurodollar futures price is higher than the nearby Eurodollar futures, then the call spread will be worth more than the put calendar spread. To say the very least, if this is not the case, then traders will make use of the Jelly Roll trade to arbitrage the differences. Let us return to our example of the Jelly Roll with the $100 stock.

Suppose at the end of the life of the first option (in three months), the stock has remained at a price of $100 and the dividend has not yet been declared. The relationship between the current stock price and the longer dated option which now has three months to expiration would be:

SYNTHETIC EXPOSURE AT FIRST EXPIRATION				
Long Stock	- Synthetic Short	= Expected	- Cost of Carry Interest
Position	3 month futures	Dividend	on 3 month futures
$100	- $98.50	= $2.50	- $1.00
		= **$1.50**	

Table 8.8a Synthetic Futures Price Relationships at Expiration of First Options in the Jelly Roll.

Because the stock has remained at $100, the first set of options will have expired worthless. The previously held 6 month options now have only three months to go and the call price has fallen to $6.00 while the put is traded at $7.50 which is consistent with the arbitrage relationship in Table 8.8a. This is summarised in the next table:

OPTIONS TRADES AT FIRST EXPIRATION ASSUMING $2.50 DIVIDEND					
first expiration		3 month expiration			
Long $100 Call	$0.00	Short $100 Call	$6.00	=	-$6.00
Short $100 Put	$0.00	Long $100 Put	$7.50	=	+$7.50
	+$0.00	+	+$1.50	=	**$1.50**

Table 8.8b Option Transactions which Comprise the Jelly Roll at First Expiration.

As the reader can see from Table 8.8b, the value of the Jelly Roll strategy has remained unchanged from the initiation (see Table 8.7b). Then suppose that the dividend of $3.50 is declared. The price of the synthetic short three month futures will drop by $1.00. This will mean that the put-call parity relationship will now imply a $2.50 differential between the call and put prices. Let us say the new price of the call is $5.50 and the put is $8.00 consistent with this differential. Then the profit and loss associated with this result can be seen in the following table:

OPTIONS TRADES AT FIRST EXPIRATION WITH ACTUAL $3.50 DIVIDEND					
first expiration		3 month expiration			
Long $100 Call	$0.00	Short $100 Call	$5.50	=	-$5.50
Short $100 Put	$0.00	Long $100 Put	$8.00	=	+$8.00
	+$0.00	+	+$2.50	=	**$2.50**

Table 8.8c Option Transactions which Comprise the Jelly Roll at First Expiration with $3.5 dividend.

In Table 8.8c, the reader can see that the jelly roll spread is now worth $2.50. Since the spread was originally purchased for $1.50, this will result in an overall profit of $1.00 to the spread trader due to the unexpected increase in the dividend.

Another interesting feature of the Jelly Roll strategy is that it also will allow the trader to benefit from changes in the short term interest rates between today and the expiration of the two options contracts. Consider the situation that immediately after the initiation of the Jelly Roll strategy outlined in Table 8.7b, the level of the short term interest rate rises from 4% to 8%. This will have a profound impact both on the levels of the synthetic futures and of the option prices. Consider Tables 8.9a and 8.9b for these impacts:

SYNTHETIC EXPOSURE					
Synthetic Long	- Synthetic Short	= Expected	- Cost of Carry	Interest
3 month futures	6 month futures	Dividend	3 versus 6 months	
$102	- $101.50	= $2.50	- $2.00	
		= **$0.50**		

Table 8.9a Synthetic Futures Price Relationships Assuming Interest Rate of 8%.

The reader will notice that both the theoretical futures prices have risen due to the increase in the interest rate from 4% to 8%. However, the 6 month futures price has had a greater impact due to the longer period that the increased interest will impact the cost of carry relationship. The value of spread relationship has now dropped from $1.50 to $0.50. How is this reflected in the value of the options in the Jelly Roll? The impacts can be seen in Table 8.9b.

ACTUAL OPTIONS TRADES					
3 month expiration		6 month expiration			
Long $100 Call	$6.50	Short $100 Call	$9.00	=	-$2.50
Short $100 Put	$4.50	Long $100 Put	$7.50	=	+$3.00
	+$2.00	+		=	**$0.50**
			$1.50		

Table 8.9b Option Transactions which Comprise the Jelly Roll Assuming Interest Rate of 8%.

The Jelly Roll has dropped in value by the same amount predicted above in Table 8.7a. What has caused the loss of $1.00 is the fact that the both the call prices have risen from the initiation of the trade due to the increase in the value of the stock synthetic futures price and in addition, the puts have dropped as well. The greatest proportion of the loss is coming from the 6 month expiration options with a loss from the increased value of the call and a reduction in the value of the put.

315

Thus, the Jelly Roll spread is also sensitive to changes in the short term interest rate. In this case, if a Jelly Roll is established by creating a synthetic long nearby futures contract and synthetic short deferred futures contract, the spread will lose money if interest rates rise. To profit from this occurrence, the trader would simply reverse the Jelly Roll strategy, creating a synthetic short nearby futures position and a synthetic long deferred futures position.

In conclusion, the Jelly Roll strategy is often used for dividend plays, trading changes in interest rates and when the prices of calendar spreads deviate away from their theoretical values. While this strategy may seem to have a limited scope for options on futures, they are popular strategies for equity options and commodity options.

WHERE THE ARBITRAGE STRATEGIES FIT IN THE STRATEGY MATRIX

So in conclusion, option "arbitrage" strategies are neutral to the underlying market and for the most part neutral to volatility with the exception of calendar spreads which become long volatility at the expiration of the short dated option and delta neutral trading. Delta neutral trading is not a pure arbitrage trade but is usually an extension of volatility trading which is why many people consider it as "volatility arbitrage". So back to our trading strategy matrix that has been filled by now. In Table 8.10, all these trades will be placed into the cell in the lower right corner.[4]

Viewpoint on the Eurodollar Market

		Buyer	Seller	Neutral
Viewpoint on Volatility	Buyer	Buy call option Call Back Spread	Buy put option Put Back Spread	Buy Straddle Buy Strangle
	Seller	Sell put option Put Ratio Spread	Sell call option Call Ratio Spread	Sell Straddle Sell Strangle Buy Butterfly Buy Condor
	Neutral	Long Futures Bull spread	Short Futures Bear spread	Calendar Spread Delta Neutral Trading Conversions, Reversals Box Arbitrage Jelly Roll

Table 8.10 Option Trading Strategy Matrix.

---

[4]We could just as easily put delta neutral trading in the long or short volatility cells in the strategy matrix. But since these trades are really long or short straddles, they are already in those cells. We chose to include delta neutral trading in the arbitrage cell because it is based on volatility "arbitrage" and in reality effective delta neutral trading is simply maximising the trader's theoretical edge.

If you have no viewpoint on the market, and you have a neutral viewpoint on volatility, the categories of trades that you might wish to consider include calendar spreads, delta neutral trading (if you think that the volatility is mispriced), jelly rolls and pure option arbitrage. This last category of strategies works most effectively when prices get out of line.

As promised, options provide the dealer with a tremendous amount of flexibility. If one can form viewpoints on both the underlying market and volatility, then the use of our trading matrix should assist the trader to find that particular trade which will maximise his expected profits given the dual viewpoint on the underlying market price and volatility. All the trader needs to do is to refer to the strategy matrix in Table 8.10 which identifies the appropriate strategy for a given set of viewpoints.

In the next chapter, I will strike out on new territory by examining the trading of options not on the same underlying instrument but on options between related underlying markets. Thus, as I will show, the range of what is possible in options trading is truly unlimited.

9: Trading Options Between Markets

In this last chapter on options trading strategies, I will examine a set of strategies which to my knowledge has not been thoroughly discussed in any book on the topic. These strategies examine trading options between different underlying markets and are known as Inter-Market trading strategies.

INTER-MARKET TRADING STRATEGIES IN FUTURES MARKETS

It is curious that option inter-market trading strategies have not been examined in more detail for these strategies are of prime importance in other derivative markets. In the futures markets, strategies which spread futures between different markets have been utilised for years. The rationale for trading between markets is that when one buys one market and sells another, the risk can be substantially less when compared to an outright "naked" long or short position in one market. In addition, the prices of related markets can and do deviate from their fair or long term relationships and the spread trader makes his profits from exploiting such discrepancies. For example in the fixed income markets, spread strategies have been extensively studied and are used every day. At the Chicago Board of Trade, the entire complex of U.S. Government Debt Futures contracts are spread against each other. One of the most well known of these strategies is the 10 Year Note vs. the 20 Year Bond futures which is universally referred to as the NOB spread (notes over Bonds). In the short term interest rate futures market at the Chicago Mercantile Exchange (International Monetary Market division) spread trading has been going on for years between the 90 day U.S. Government Treasury Bill futures and the 3 month Eurodollar Time Deposit futures which is known affectionately as the TED spread. In those financial futures markets with a wider range of products, often offered across different currencies, spreading has become a lifeblood of trading activity. At the London International Financial Futures Exchange, various long term (generally 10 years) Bond futures and short term deposit are offered in U.S. Dollars, Sterling, Deutsche Marks, Lira, Swiss Franc and ECU. The LIFFE has completed extensive research of the range of possible trading strategies that could be constructed based upon either a perceived mispricing in the relative relationships between these markets or upon a viewpoint about how the spread relationships between markets will change.[1]

---

[1]One of the best studies in this area was done by the LIFFE and is titled "A Guide to Cross Currency Spread Trading"

In the commodity markets, inter-market (which means between different markets) spread trading is extremely active and sometimes even makes sense. At the New York Mercantile Exchange where petroleum products are the most successful products, traders construct "paper refineries" by buying crude oil futures and then selling gasoline and heating oil futures which are the end products of the input commodity (the crude oil). These trades are done when the inter-relationships between the markets are expected to change. Also at the Chicago Board of Trade, the soybean complex is often involved in inter-market spread trading as traders will buy the soybean futures and then sell the soybean meal and oil futures which are the end products of the raw soybeans. This spread is known universally as the "soybean crush" spread. These spreads make sense logically because the trader knows that these markets are inter-related. Of course, that does not keep traders from initiating inter-market spreads where no apparent relationship exists. For example, at the IMM in Chicago, trading strategies have existed between the commodity futures and financial futures for many years. Some traders will buy the British Pound futures and simultaneously sell Live Cattle futures (the Beef Wellington spread) or buy Japanese Yen futures and sell Gold futures (the Golden Toyota spread). As one might expect, these spreads sound funny in more ways than the name. There is practically no relationship between these markets and essentially the trader is simply taking a viewpoint on two totally unrelated markets. The fact that it is has been identified as an inter-market spread strategy is in name rather than in fact.

When does such a spread deviate from having a solid economic basis for consideration to having none at all? The answer depends on how inter-related the two markets are and this can be determined by using a statistical technique known as correlation.

MEASURING THE RELATIONSHIP
BETWEEN MARKETS - THE CORRELATION COEFFICIENT

Correlation is a statistical measure of how closely two markets move together. It is a standardised measure of the variability of two assets to each other. Whenever we mention the word variability in the options market, the first thought that should spring to mind is volatility. That being the case, then, this correlation measure must have some relationship to the volatility we have discussed extensively in this book and indeed it does. The formula for the correlation of two assets is provided below:

$$\rho = \frac{\dfrac{1}{n}\sum_{i=1}^{n}(X_i - \chi)\cdot(Y_i - \psi)}{\sigma_x \cdot \sigma_y}$$

where:

    ρ is the correlation coefficient between X and Y

    X_i is each observation of X's asset returns

    χ is the average return of asset X in the Period

    Y_i is each observation of Y's asset returns

    ψ is the average return of asset Y in the Period

    σ_x is the Standard Deviation of X in the Period

    σ_y is the Standard Deviation of Y in the Period

As the reader can see, when comparing this formula to the one on page 102 in Chapter 4, there is indeed some resemblance. The top part of the equation somehow looks hauntingly familiar: we add up (that is what the Σ stands for) the differences between the average return we observe and each return over a period. The difference is that in the previous equation this result is then squared so that all the observations are positive. Here, we are examining the relative relationship of how both assets deviate away from their average observation at each point. Said in a simpler way: how does the second asset differ from its average return when the first asset is higher or lower than the average return? When the assets vary from what we expect to observe, do they vary together? The formal name for the top part of the above equation is the Covariance. In some ways, it is similar in principal to the variance discussed in Chapter 4 and shares some of the similar problems in interpretation.

The reader may recall that the variance (which is the standard deviation or volatility squared) is like a squared Deutsche Mark and has no meaning in the real world. To obtain a number that we can compare to the current level of markets (or returns), we must standardise the variance and this is simply done by taking its square root to yield the standard deviation or what we call the volatility. In a similar fashion, the above equation must be standardised to allow for interpretation and this is done by dividing the covariance by the standard deviations of both assets multiplied by each other. The resulting number, which is the correlation coefficient, tells us in a standardised way the manner that these two markets move together (or not). Table 9.1 demonstrates how this covariance and correlation coefficient is estimated for the Long Term Gilt and 10 Year German Bund futures contracts traded at the LIFFE (by using Excel™).

For the period from 4 January to 4 May 1994, the correlation between the Gilt and Bund futures markets was estimated to be 0.658757 or a positive 65.9% relationship. This means that these markets tend to move in the same direction (when deviating from what one would expect) 65.8% of the time. However, it is clear that the movements between these two markets are far from perfect. This can be seen in Figure 9.1 which demonstrates a scatter plot of the daily returns for both markets plotted against each other.

Daily Return %		Daily Return %	
Bund Futures		Gilt Futures	
Mean	-0.084234	Mean	-0.172719
Standard Error	0.050007	Standard Error	0.075259
Standard Deviation	0.461041	Standard Deviation	0.693851
Variance	0.212559	Variance	0.481429
Sum	-7.159852	Sum	-14.681090
Count	85	Count	85
Covariance	0.210732		
Correlation	0.658757		

Table 9.1 Covariance and Correlation for the Long Gilt and the 10 Year Bund.

In the centre of the graph is a big "+" of which the vertical line is the average return for the Gilts for this period and the horizontal line is the average return for the Bunds. Each dot represents a single day's observed Gilt and Bund return. The reader can see that this plot of dots tends to be bunched in the south-west and north-east quadrants of the diagram. This indicates that when the Gilt returns are lower than what we expect (the average) the Bund returns also tend to be lower than what we expect. When the Gilt returns are higher than their average, the Bund returns are also higher than we expect and this is associated with the dots in the north-east sector of the graph. When dots fall in the other sectors (north-west and south-east) this means that the two markets have moved exactly in an opposite way

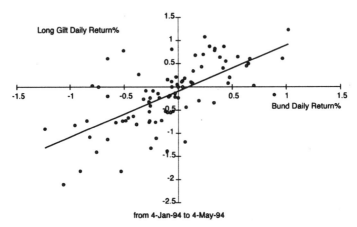

from 4-Jan-94 to 4-May-94

Figure 9.1 Scatter Plot of the Daily Returns for Gilt and Bund Futures Markets.

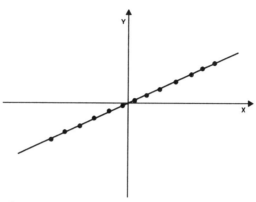

Figure 9.2a Correlation = 1.0.

on that day. The correlation coefficient of 65.9% simply tells us that these markets move together about two thirds of the time and one third of the time they move differently. Of course, this relationship is different for different kinds of assets. Figures 9.2a, 9.2b and 9.2c display sample scatter plots for assets that have a positive 100% correlation, no correlation at all (0%) and a perfectly negative 100% correlation.

As one can see, a positive 100% correlation is a straight line going through the average values for both assets. This line goes from the south-west to the north-east. For the 0% correlation relationship in Figure 9.2b, the dots are spread all over the chart indicating no fixed relationship between the two markets. The negative 100% correlation chart (Figure 9.2c) indicates that the two markets move exactly opposite to one another. In this case, again there is a straight line relationship between the two markets but it goes from the south-east to the north-west. These markets move in the same way as one's reflection moves in a mirror, exactly opposite.

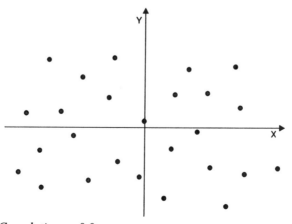

Figure 9.2b Correlation = 0.0.

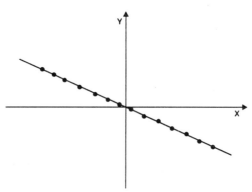

Figure 9.2c Correlation = -1.0.

In reality, few markets move perfectly together or diametrically opposed. Table 9.2 is a correlation matrix between the fixed income futures markets traded at the LIFFE. In this analysis, data from 4 January 1994 until 4 May 1994 was used to estimate the correlations. This type of matrix is useful in that we can see at a glance all the inter-relationships between the markets. For example, the highest correlation between markets in this period was between the Bund futures and the BTP futures with a correlation of 0.80515. The next highest correlation was between the Bund futures and the Gilt futures at 0.65875. It is not surprising that the Japanese Government Bond future (JGB) displayed almost no correlation with the Gilts, BTPs or the Bunds. In fact, when correlations between assets are less then 0.15, this would indicate that these markets moved (for all practical purposes) in-dependently over this period.

CORRELATION MATRIX ON DAILY RETURNS %				
	from 4 Jan 94 to 4 May 94			
	Bund	Gilt	Jap.Gov. Bond	BTP
Bund	1			
Gilt	0.65875	1		
Jap. Gov. Bond	0.12009	0.00582	1	
BTP	0.80515	0.55048	0.08956	1

Table 9.2 Correlation Matrix for Bond Futures at the LIFFE.

Why are these numbers so important to inter-market spread traders? The answer is that the correlation coefficients indicate the degree of inter-relationships that exist historically between the assets and this indicates whether trading these mar-kets against each other has some logical basis. In the earlier example, one would expect the markets that make up the "Paper Refinery" (that is Crude Oil, Gasoline and Heating Oil) to be highly correlated and the markets that make up the "Beef

Wellington" (British Pound and Live Cattle) spread to have no correlation. Indeed, this is the case for both spreads. Thus, the measure of correlation is the critical element is determining whether or not an inter-market spread strategy will make any sense at all.[2]

What does this have to do with options trading? Everything! First of all, there are significant opportunities for trading between markets via options as a substitute for trading futures or other underlying assets. Secondly, it is clear that the correlation relationship has something to do with volatility since both the top and bottom of the formula for correlation have elements which are related to volatility. It is clear, from the bottom of the equation, that both the volatilities of the markets are direct inputs. On the top of the equation, the summation of each observation minus the average return is one of the steps in the calculation of the historical volatility of a series of data. It seems obvious that the correlation measure is the simply another way of expressing volatility of asset prices, but in this instance relative to another asset. Since this is the case, why have options inter-market strategies not been more widely used? The answer is most probably that traders have had their hands full trying to estimate the volatilities of individual markets. The additional complication of how volatilities move together in different markets was well beyond what most traders were willing to consider. However, this situation has begun to change recently as an entirely new class of exotic options have been gradually introduced that are called "correlation dependent options".

In this chapter, I will discuss what the correlation relationships are between markets both from the movements of the underlying assets and from the relationships between the volatilities of options on these underlying assets. This will allow us to use options as tools to implement directional trading strategies between markets, trade volatility relationships and to price and trade spread options. Finally, I will present examples which exploit the correlation relationships between currency markets and will also examine the relationship between the volatilities of individual stock options and the volatility of the stock index that these stocks are contained within.

The best news of all is that all of this can be achieved using concepts I have previously discussed such as volatility estimation in Chapter 4, the formula for correlation described above and a simple generalised form of the Black and Scholes model outlined in Chapter 2. With these three basic concepts under your belt, you will be amazed how simple inter-market options trading can be.

INTER-MARKET DIRECTIONAL STRATEGIES USING OPTIONS

One reason why speculating on inter-market spreads is more often implemented with futures as opposed to options is that most traders only want to concentrate on

---

[2] Correlation is also a critical element whether or not one can use a derivative market to hedge a position in the cash market. The international accounting rule to allow such a strategy to qualify for Hedge Accounting treatment is that a minimum correlation coefficient of 70% or higher is required. See Chapter 16 for more information.

the relative price relationships between markets without having to worry about volatility changes or the time decay of the options. But those who hold to this view are missing out on significant opportunities that options offer to the inter-market spread trader.

Consider the currency markets.[3] Let us go back a few years to the time of the Gulf War. During that period, the U.S. Dollar displayed considerable strength as the uncertainty of that time induced a flight of capital to security. If a trader had taken a long position on the U.S. Dollar versus let us say, the Japanese Yen, the trader would have done quite well initially. The curious result was that after the conclusion of the conflict, the U.S. Dollar resumed its long term downwards trend and actually experienced an accelerated depreciation. Those who had maintained their long U.S.$ position would have eventually been buried. The temporary winners during both the war and the post war periods were the British Pound and the Swiss Franc. The Pound probably benefited from the perceived independence of the UK economy on Middle East oil. The Swiss Franc attracted funds because skittish Middle East investors started withdrawing their funds (generally in U.S. $) prior to the War, parking it in Switzerland. During such uncertain periods a trader might not be willing to bet directly for or against the U.S. Dollar. He or she may decide a safer bet would be to trade the currency relationship between two European currencies that were expected to react differently to the conflict in the Gulf. For example, a trader might consider an inter-market spread trade between the Swiss Franc and the Deutsche Mark: buying the Swiss Franc and selling the Deutsche Mark.

While this can be done on an OTC basis from a major bank, traders can utilise standard exchange traded currency options on U.S. $/Swiss Franc and U.S. $/Deutsche Mark to create a synthetic position. If the investor expected the Swiss Franc to appreciate, they could initiate any of our three equivalent long positions outlined in Chapter 6. That is, they could buy the underlying (futures), buy a call or sell a put. In this example, we would buy a slightly out-of-the-money call on the Swiss Franc (put on the U.S. Dollar). To benefit from the relative underperformance of the Deutsche Mark, the trader would have sold the Deutsche Mark. Given the choice of a short underlying (futures) long put or short call, the investor would sell a slightly out-of-the-money call on the Deutsche Mark (put on the U.S. $). So, it appears that the U.S. Dollar drops out because one is both long and short a put on the U.S. Dollar. Unfortunately, it is not that simple.

Back in 1985, when I was working with Harris Bank and Trust Company of Chicago, our chief currency dealer wanted to create a "synthetic cross option" between the British Pound and the Deutsche Mark. The assumption was that the U.S. Dollar exposure would be eliminated. This was not the case for two reasons. Firstly, the standardised contract sizes on the exchanges (the CME for example) are all worth a different amount of U.S. $. So the position is not exactly balanced.

---

[3]This section is based upon an article, "'Spreading' currency options" that appeared in the November, 1990 edition of Futures Magazine and was written by Jon Stein.

Secondly, if the movements of the two currencies are not perfectly 100% correlated then as the initial spread relationship between the currencies changes, the U.S. Dollar value of the underlying futures contract also changes and the exposure is no longer flat. To show you how this happens let us return to our example on the Swiss Franc/Deutsche Mark spread and put in some numbers.

On 1 August, 1990 right before the invasion of Kuwait, the December Deutsche Mark Futures was trading at 0.6285 (1.5911 in European Terms) and the Swiss Franc December Futures was trading at 0.7357 (1.3268 in European Terms). The implied cross rate between the Swiss Franc and the Deutsche Mark was 1.1706 (0.7357/0.6285) Deutsche Marks to each Swiss Franc. The spread of the Swiss Franc over the Deutsche Mark December futures contracts was 0.1072 (0.7357 - 0.6285). Suppose a trader wanted to bet on the Swiss Franc rising relative to the Deutsche Mark. The first thing he would need to do would be to construct a position that would be immunised to the U.S. Dollar. Let us suppose that on 1 August, our trader was considering buying the October 0.7500 Swiss Franc call for 0.0078 and selling the October 0.6400 Deutsche Mark call for 0.0061. What would be his U.S. Dollar position given the values of each contract? The 0.7500 Swiss Franc call is for 125,000 Swiss Francs and this is provides the buyer of the call the right to buy 125,000 Swiss Francs at 0.7500 and to sell 93,750 U.S. Dollars (125,000 · 0.7500). The .6400 Deutsche Mark call is also for 125,000 Deutsche Marks and this obligates the seller of the call to sell 125,000 Deutsche Marks at 0.6400 and to buy 80,000 U.S. Dollars (125,000 · 0.6400) if exercised upon. Thus, if the trader buys one Swiss Franc call and sells one Deutsche Mark call against it, he will have an uncovered U.S. Dollar position of $13,750. In fact, he should sell more Deutsche Mark calls than the number of Swiss Franc calls, otherwise his position will be unbalanced. The correct hedge ratio to remain flat to the U.S. Dollar would be:

The Value of the US Dollar Equivalent for the 0.7500 Swiss Franc call

The Value of the US Dollar Equivalent for the 0.6400 Deutsche Mark call

Which is: $\dfrac{\$93,750}{\$80,000}$ and is equal to 1.17188

To remain neutral to the U.S. Dollar the trader would buy 100 0.7500 October Swiss Franc calls and sell 117 0.6400 October Deutsche Mark calls. The price of the 0.7500 October Swiss Franc calls on 1 August was 78 ticks (or 0.0078) and the price of the 0.6400 October Deutsche Mark calls was 61 ticks (or 0.0061). Since both contracts are in U.S. Dollar terms, each tick is in 100ths of U.S. cents so a .0001 (tick) for 125,000 is worth $12.50 for both contracts. Thus, for the 100 0.7500 Swiss Franc calls the trader would have paid $97,500 (100 · $12.50 · 78) and received back on the sale of the 117 0.6400 Deutsche Mark calls $89,212.50 (117 · $12.50 · 61). The net outflow for the trader would have been $8,287.50. In addition, the trader would have been required to post margin on the exchange to cover the short calls position which would have been around $1890 per short call or $221,130. However, this margin could have been met by depositing Treasury Bills with the Clearing House of the exchange and is not really a out of pocket cost to the trader.

On 23 August, the spread had indeed widened out between the two futures contracts as the Swiss Franc December Futures price rose to 0.7950 and the Deutsche Mark December Futures price rose to 0.6469. The spread difference was now 0.1481 which is an increase of 409 ticks from the spread of 0.1072 on 1 August. The new cross rate of Swiss/Deutsche Mark is now 1.2289 Deutsche Marks to every one Swiss Franc. The 0.7500 October Swiss Franc call was now trading at 0.0472 ticks and the Deutsche mark 0.6400 call was trading at .0152 ticks. The net result is that the trader made a profit of 394 ticks on the 0.7500 Swiss Franc calls and a loss of 91 ticks on the 0.6400 Deutsche Mark calls. The net effect is an overall profit from the strategy of $359,412.50, which is made up of a $492,500 profit on the long 100 Swiss Franc calls and a $133,087.50 loss on the short 117 Deutsche Mark calls.

If the trader had simply used the December futures contracts instead of the options, he would have realised a profit of 593 ticks for Swiss Franc futures he had purchased (sold out at 0.7950 and bought in at 0.7357). For one long December futures contracts this would have resulted in a profit of $7,412.50. On the December Deutsche Mark position he would have lost 184 ticks per contract (bought in at 0.6469 and sold originally at 0.6285). For one short December futures, he would have experienced a loss of $2300. Using the same hedge ratio as was used for the options this results in an overall profit of $472,150 for the strategy (profit of $741,250 on the long 100 Swiss Franc futures and a loss of $269,100 on the short 117 Deutsche Mark futures). So why use options when the futures trading strategy would have been more profitable?

One possible reason is that with the futures spread strategy, the trader has an unlimited loss potential for both contracts and must rely on stop-loss orders to control his risk. For the options strategy, he at least faces a limited loss scenario from the Swiss Franc leg. Only the short call on the Deutsche Marks face the unlimited loss potential that would have to be stopped out. Another reason, is that the strategy has an unusual profit or loss payoff depending upon the relative performance of the Swiss Franc versus the Deutsche Mark. In Figure 9.3, a three dimensional graph is produced that shows the relationship of the options strategy to the movements in the U.S.$ versus the Swiss Franc, the U.S.$ versus the Deutsche Mark and the Swiss Franc versus the Deutsche Mark.

As the reader can see: If the U.S.$/Deutsche Mark price ends at 0.6400 and the U.S.$/Swiss Franc price ends at 0.7500 at the expiration of the October options, there is a loss which is equal to the premium paid of $8,287.50. However, if the Swiss Franc appreciates while the Deutsche Mark stays the same or depreciates, the spread will profit. Of course, if the opposite occurs, the spread will lose money and this can be seen in this graph. So by using options, the spread will provide an un-

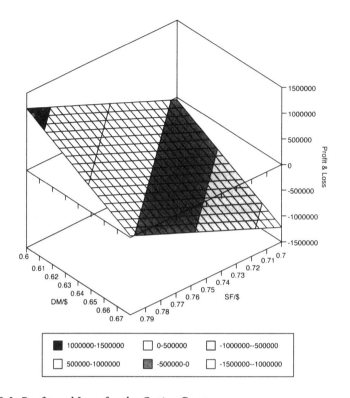

Figure 9.3 Profit and Loss for the Option Strategy.

usual profit or loss profile depending on the relative price relationship between the Swiss Franc and the Deutsche Mark changing over the investment horizon.

The most important benefit from this strategy is that prior to the expiration of the options, there can be the opportunity to benefit from a change in the volatilities of the two markets relative to each other. Even if the Swiss Franc/ Deutsche Mark spread had remained unchanged over the period, there was still an opportunity to profit from an increase in Swiss volatility relative to Deutsche Mark volatility. Next, I will discuss the volatility relationship that occurs between related markets.

THE INTER-MARKET VOLATILITY RELATIONSHIP

Normally, when comparing the relative values of markets one will assess how these markets are bound through arbitrage. This fundamental ability to knock prices back into line if they diverge is critical to the pricing of many kinds of assets and particularly so in options.

When comparing volatilities across different markets, it is rarely possible to find such opportunities for riskless "arbitrage" profits because these markets are not identical. Furthermore, the degree of inter-relationship, defined by the correlation between these markets, may also be changing through time. Having said this, opportunities for profit may still be uncovered through careful study of the relationships between volatilities in different markets. Inter-market volatility trading is simply the establishment of a trading strategy which will profit from those situations where volatilities for related markets have diverged beyond their historical equilibrium relationship and the trader believes the current deviant relationship will revert to the long term average.

Let us return to the currency markets once again to examine how the mechanism of arbitrage maintains parity across currencies and why such an arbitrage mechanism is not available for currency options. Consider the following relationship in the spot foreign exchange markets:

> U.S.$/Deutsche Mark 1.6400
> U.S.$/Yen   104.00
> Deutsche Mark/Yen   63.00.

Are these prices correct and if not, is there an opportunity for arbitrage? Figure 9.4 displays the triangular arbitrage relationship and what the trader would do to exploit the mispricing in the Deutsche Mark/Yen exchange rate. The trader will receive U.S. $1,000,000 and pay 1.64 million Deutsche Marks in the spot market. He will then pay U.S. $1,000,000 to receive 104 million Japanese Yen. Finally, with the Yen he has, he will pay 104 million Yen and receive 1.65 million Deutsche Marks. At the end of the operation, the trader has made 10,000 Deutsche Marks (or $6,098) with no risk since at no time did he use his own money, he simply transferred other people's money around between two other counterparties to lock in a no risk arbitrage profit.

Clearly, in the currency markets, these opportunities seldom arise because of the ease in completing the arbitrage trades which will immediately realise the arbitrage profit. What about in the currency options market?

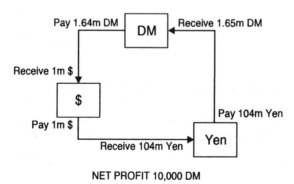

NET PROFIT 10,000 DM

Figure 9.4 Spot Currency Arbitrage.

Consider the following relationship in the foreign exchange options markets:

U.S.$/Deutsche Mark ATM* Volatility 10%
U.S.$/Yen ATM Volatility   10%
Deutsche Mark/Yen ATM Volatility   8%.

*ATM stands for at-the-money

Is there an opportunity? It would appear so at first glance. The U.S.$/Deutsche Mark and U.S.$/Yen ATM volatilities are exactly the same at 10% while the Deutsche Mark/Yen ATM volatility is only 8%. The trader might be inclined to do a similar strategy to what we suggested above for the Swiss Franc and the Deutsche Mark. He would buy a U.S.$/Deutsche Mark Call at 10% volatility, buy a U.S.$/Yen put at 10% volatility and sell a Deutsche Mark/Yen call at an 8% volatility with the logic that the two options he purchased would hedge out both his U.S. Dollar exposure and would have a net volatility exposure of zero. This strategy is outlined in Figure 9.5. Unfortunately, things are not as simple as they seem.

To evaluate the performance of the strategy it is not simply possible to do so by looking at the movement in one currency exchange rate, we must look at all three simultaneously. Once again, this requires the use of a three dimensional graph to get a grip on where the strategy will make or lose money. The first graph is portrayed in Figure 9.6.[4]

In this graph, a little explanation is warranted. The vertical dimension is the value of the overall options strategy which here is called the "option cluster". On the lower horizontal dimensions, one axis is the $/Yen spot rate where 150 reflects a strengthening of the U.S.$ and 115 reflects a weakening of the U.S.$ (stronger Yen). The other axis displays ranges of the $/Deutsche Mark spot rate. Again, if the exchange rate goes to 1.90 that means the U.S.$ has strengthened and at 1.55, the U.S.$ has weakened. The shape of the curve is most curious, it looks like a saddle.

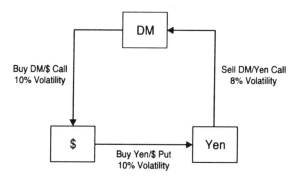

Figure 9.5 Cross Market Volatility Relationship.

[4]The next two charts were kindly supplied by Martin Cooper of Chase Manhattan Bank, London.

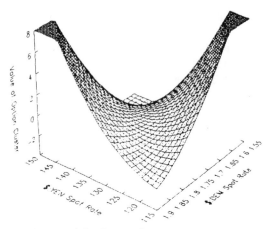

Figure 9.6 Profit and Loss of the Option Strategy.

The maximum profits occur if the U.S. Dollar strengthens or weakens equally versus the Yen and the Deutsche Mark. For example, when the $/Yen rate is 150 and the $/Deutsche Mark is at 1.90, a profit of "8" is realised. This will also occur if the U.S. Dollar weakens versus the Yen to 115 at the same time the U.S. Dollar weakens versus the Deutsche Mark to 1.55. Thus, if the Deutsche Mark and the Yen exchange rates move exactly the same way versus the U.S. Dollar, the trade will profit. If the exchange rate remains at the current spot rate of 130 $/Yen (this example is not drawn from data in 1994 but reflects market conditions in the early 1990s) and 1.75 $/Deutsche Mark, the position breaks even. If, however, the Yen and Deutsche Mark exchange rates move in the opposite directions, the strategy loses money. That is, the Yen and Deutsche Mark are negatively correlated. This graph assumes that the implied volatilities of all the options remain the same and only the spot exchange rates change, but what happens to the strategy if the implied volatilities change?

In Figure 9.7, the volatility sensitivity of the options strategy is once again plotted in three dimensions. On the vertical axis we find the value of the entire position which again is referred to as an "option cluster".

On the horizontal axes are both the implied volatilities for $/Yen and $/Deutsche Mark options. In this case, we do not get a saddle shape but more of a curved plane which indicates that if the implied volatilities of both the $/Yen and $/Deutsche Mark options fall, the strategy will be a big loser. However, if the implied volatilities for both options rise, the strategy will be profitable. Essentially, we are long both $/Yen and $/Deutsche Mark volatilities and at the same time "long" the correlation between the markets. If the correlation in the spot rates is highly positive, this means that as the U.S. Dollar value changes, it will change in identical ways for both currencies. As Figure 9.6 demonstrates, we will profit. From Figure 9.7, we are also long both implied volatilities. Thus, from these graphs it is easy to see that there is no "arbitrage" relationship between the individ-

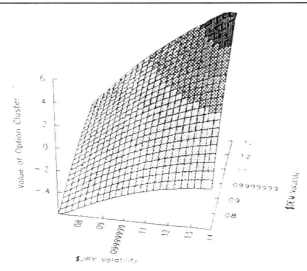

Figure 9.7 Volatility Sensitivity of the Option Strategy.

ual $/Deutsche Mark and $/Yen options and the cross Deutsche Mark/Yen option. If the strategy were an arbitrage, then the profits would be locked in, regardless of what could possibly occur in the market. However, as these two figures indicate, the profits of the strategy depend both upon the relative movement of the two currencies involved in the cross options and the changes in their volatilities.

Therefore, the problem of the estimation of cross options and the evaluation of inter-market options trading strategies are one and the same problem. Clearly, when evaluating inter-market option trading strategies, analysis tool must be different from the normal tools required for evaluating option strategies on the same underlying asset. For the same underlying asset, we have our trusty options pricing model such as the Black and Scholes which will allow us to run projections of the performance of the strategy. Clearly, this simple methodology is inappropriate for options on two different underlying assets, or is it not? What we really require is a new approach which considers the co-movement of two assets which can be exchanged for one another. Fortunately, this approach was outlined and solved only five years after Black and Scholes.

A PRICING MODEL
FOR ASSESSING INTER-MARKET OPTIONS RELATIONSHIPS

Shortly after Black and Scholes found their answer to the problem of pricing a European call option, another academic, Bill Margrabe, wished to apply the same approach to solving a different problem.[5] His goal was to find a model which

---

[5]Margrabe, William, "The Value of an Option to Exchange One Asset for Another", Journal of Finance, 33 (March 1977), pp. 177-186.

would price an option to exchange one asset for another. After tinkering around, he found a closed form solution for both a European and American style option to exchange one asset for another. This is:

Margrabe Exchange Option Model

$$CALL = X_1 \cdot N(d_1) - X_2 \cdot N(d_2)$$

where:

$$d_1 = \frac{\ln(X_1 / X_2) + (\sigma^2 / 2) \cdot t}{\sigma \cdot \sqrt{t}}$$

$$d_2 = d_1 - \sigma \cdot \sqrt{t}$$

$$\sigma^2 = \sigma^2_{X_1} + \sigma^2_{X_2} - 2 \cdot \rho_{X_1,X_2} \cdot \sigma_{X_1} \cdot \sigma_{X_2}$$

$\sigma^2_{X_1}$ = variance of First Asset

$\sigma^2_{X_1}$ = variance of Second Asset

σ_{X_1} = square root of variance, i.e. volatility of first asset

σ_{X_1} = square root of variance, i.e. volatility of second asset

$\rho_{X_1 \cdot X_2}$ = correlation between First and Second Assets

t = time to expiration % of a year

X_1 = Price of First Asset

X_2 = Price of Second Asset

$\ln$ = natural logarithm function

e = exponential function

$N(\ )$ = cumulative normal density function

Before, the reader rolls his/her eyes and says "What another formula!", let me assure the reader that this is almost identical to the Black and Scholes model. The only real differences are that the strike price is no longer fixed and has been replaced by X_2 which is the price of the second asset and the volatility input is now a little more complicated. This volatility input is the key element both in this model and in assessing the risks of inter-market option trading strategies. Because of this, I will focus now on this new volatility factor:

$$\sigma_{X_1/X_2} = \sqrt{\sigma^2_{X_1} + \sigma^2_{X_2} - 2 \cdot \rho_{X_1,X_2} \cdot \sigma_{X_1} \cdot \sigma_{X_2}}$$

What the new volatility factor says is that the total variance of the option to exchange one asset for another is a function of the variances of both assets minus two

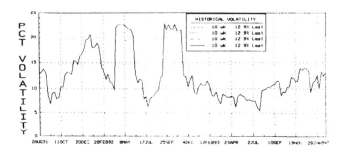

Figure 9.8a Historical Price Volatility for the FTSE 100.

times the covariance of the two assets.[6] Of course, in the options markets, we are interested in the square root of the variance or the standard deviation for our volatility input. To determine the volatility input for an option to exchange one asset for another, we simply need to take the square root of the entire variance function. But consider the following: If the variance of the second asset is zero (that is riskless) and therefore earns the risk free rate of return and we plug this into Margrabe's model, what do we get? The answer: the Black and Scholes model. The volatility will only depend on the variance of the first asset since both the 2nd and 3rd element in the Margrabe volatility drop out (see for yourself, set σ_2 to zero and see what happens) and the other asset price X_2 becomes a fixed amount discounted by the risk free interest rate which in my choice of variables is $E \cdot e^{-rt}$. So, we had the answer all along and just did not see it!

Another nice feature of the Margrabe model for options to exchange one asset for another is that the European and American option prices are identical and a proof of this appears in his paper for those who may be interested.

Anyway, let us get back to the importance of the volatility input to the Margrabe model. While it is clear what is meant by the volatility of each of the markets, it may not be clear as to what the correlation is and how it can be estimated. The good news is that the correlation can be estimated in the same way that volatility is estimated. In fact, as we demonstrated in the earlier formula for the correlation coefficient, the volatility (standard deviation) input is critical to the estimation of the correlation. But to make things a little easier, let us consider the inter-market relationship between the volatilities of the FTSE and the S&P indices. Figures 9.8a, 9.8b and 9.8c display the historical price volatility for the FTSE, the S&P 500 and the correlation between the FTSE and the S&P 500 from August 1991 to February 1994.

In these graphs, both the volatilities and the correlations are calculated on a rolling 10 week basis using weekly data. What one can see, is that not only do the

---

[6]As a technical point, the reader may wish to go back in this chapter to the definition of the correlation coefficient and if he/she multiplies both sides of the equation by both standard deviations, the result will show that the immediately preceding equation is indeed equal to the covariance.

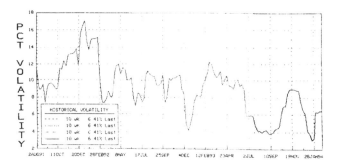

Figure 9.8b   Historical Price Volatility for the S&P 500.

volatilities not follow the same patterns but the correlations between the returns on the FTSE and the S&P 500 are not stable over time. In Figure 9.8c, the correlation between the returns for these markets at one point is almost as high as 90% and at one point is almost 0%. Clearly, the spread moves around, and what those who are trading inter-market volatility are doing is essentially trading this correlation relationship. How do changes in the individual volatilities and the correlation affect the inter-market spread relationship? To find the answer, we must return to the Margrabe volatility estimate for the option to exchange one asset for another.

The Margrabe formula, $\sigma_{X_1/X_2} = \sqrt{\sigma_{X_1}^2 + \sigma_{X_2}^2 - 2 \cdot \rho_{X_1/X_2} \cdot \sigma_{X_1} \cdot \sigma_{X_2}}$, has been modified to reflect the square root function. The resulting volatility of the exchange option (and therefore of the inter-market spread relationship) is compared for three different levels of the correlation. With an implied volatility of 20% for the FTSE and 15% for the S&P 500, the overall volatility of the inter-market relationship depends solely on the impact of the correlation. In the first case, if the correlation is perfectly 100% negative, then the risk of the spread trade is simply the sum of the

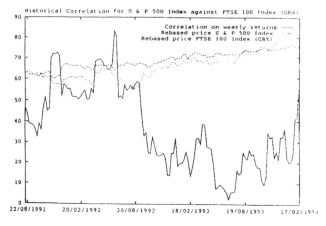

Figure 9.8c   Historical Correlation of the FTSE 100 vs. S&P 500.

two volatilities of the diverse markets. This is because the markets are moving exactly opposite and the option represents the right to buy one asset and sell the other asset. If they move exactly the opposite way, then the volatility effect is additive. Essentially, it is as if one were doubling up. If the correlation is zero, then the composite volatility is greater than the volatility for either of the individual markets but is less than the sum of the volatilities. If, however, the correlation between the FTSE and the S&P 500 returns is 100% perfectly correlated (in a positive way), then the risk of the inter-market volatility spread is simply the difference between the volatilities for the FTSE and the S&P 500. This reduction in the volatility is due to the fact that by having an option to buy the FTSE and to sell the S&P 500 (given that they move in exactly the same way) is self hedging. The risk that is left is due to the fact that the FTSE movement relative to the S&P 500 can vary somewhat more. The implications of this formula for inter-market options spread relationships are:

(1) If the volatility of either the first or second market rises, the volatility of the inter-market option spread will rise.

(2) If the correlation between the returns for the two assets rises, the volatility of the inter-market option spread will fall.

So the inter-market spread trader is once again trading volatilities, he buys volatility implicit in the spread between option markets if he expects either the implied volatilities of the individual markets to rise or for the correlation between the markets to fall.

THE CONCEPT OF THE IMPLIED CORRELATION

When one is trading options on the same underlying asset, the implied volatility is the key element in the changes in the time value of the strategy. Chapter 7 of this book is devoted to showing the reader how to benefit from changes in the implied volatility of the market he was trading. In trading options between markets, the critical factor in the changes in the spread relationships is a similar concept, that of the implied correlation.

In many markets such as foreign exchange, it is possible to have options which allow a variety of assets to be exchanged for other assets. For example, let us return to the earlier example with the U.S.\$/Deutsche Mark, U.S.\$/Yen and Deutsche Mark/Yen options. As the reader may recall, both the U.S.\$/Deutsche Mark and the U.S.\$/Yen options had an implied volatility of 10% while the Deutsche Mark/Yen implied volatility was 8%. With these numbers in hand, it is possible to determine the implied correlation that had to exist for the Deutsche Mark/Yen volatility to be 8%. This is done simply by modifying the Margrabe composite volatility equation:

$$\sigma_{DM/Yen} = \sqrt{\sigma^2_{\$/DM} + \sigma^2_{\$/Yen} - 2 \cdot \rho_{DM/Yen} \cdot \sigma_{\$/DM} \cdot \sigma_{\$/Yen}}$$

Substitution of the above implied volatilities in the formula will produce the following:

$$8\% = \sqrt{0.10^2 + 0.10^2 - 2 \cdot \rho_{DM/Yen} \cdot 0.10 \cdot 0.10}$$

By turning around the equation to solve for the $\rho_{DM/Yen}$, we generate the new implied correlation formula:

$$\rho_{DM/Yen} = -\left[\left(\sigma^2_{DM/Yen} - \sigma^2_{\$/DM} - \sigma^2_{\$/Yen}\right) / \left(2 \cdot \sigma_{\$/DM} \cdot \sigma_{\$/Yen}\right)\right]$$

Which using the numbers above will yield:

$$0.68 = -\left[(.08)^2 - (.10)^2 - (.10)^2\right] / (2 \cdot .10 \cdot .10)$$

This result of 0.68 is the implied correlation between Deutsche Marks and Yen which when expressed as a percentage is $+68\%$. What does this number mean and how can traders make money from it?

Essentially, traders employ inter-market spreads with options when they believe that the actual correlation relationship between the markets will diverge from the correlation implied in the cross option volatility. In most option markets such as equities or bonds, these techniques are used for evaluating trading strategies between related markets or for pricing exotic options that either pay off the return of a basket of securities or the best performing asset among diverse markets. This will be discussed in more detail in Chapter 13. However, in the currency options market, this technique is the mainstay of those that trade in non-standard cross option contracts.

APPLICATION OF THE CORRELATION COEFFICIENT IN PRICING CROSS CURRENCY OPTIONS

A frequent problem faced by major banks when pricing cross currency options is the estimation of the appropriate volatility to estimate a fair price. Often, the historical volatility is the only method that can be used for the estimation of the volatility input and, as was discussed in Chapter 5, this is fraught with danger especially for short dated options. One may remember that a problem with using a historical volatility estimate is that the actual realised volatility can be different. The variability of using the volatility cone for shorter estimation periods suggest that widest margin for error exists for the estimation of short dated volatility. An alternative technique would be to use other options from which implied volatilities can be estimated and then using the above Margrabe composite volatility formula, an estimated "cross" implied volatility can be generated.

For example, let us say that a major Italian bank wishes to determine the volatility to price an Italian Lira vs. Japanese Yen currency option. This is not exactly the most liquid market and it would be impossible to directly determine an implied volatility with which to price the option. However, it is possible to obtain an implied volatility for a U.S.$/Lira option and for a U.S.$/Yen option: The Bank has done a historical analysis of the correlation between U.S.$/Lira and U.S.$/Yen and found the relationship relatively stable. Here are the current market conditions:

> U.S. Dollar/Yen implied volatility   14%
> U.S. Dollar/Lira implied volatility   15.5%
> Lira/Yen Historical Correlation   30%

Then the trader simply plugs these numbers into the Margrabe Composite Volatility formula:

$$0.17494 = \sqrt{0.14^2 + 0.155^2 - 2 \cdot 0.30 \cdot 0.14 \cdot 0.155}$$

Which means that a 17.494% volatility would be used to price the cross option of Lira for Yen using a standard options pricing model. The price could be enforced through a delta hedging strategy using the correct amounts of Lira/Yen Forward contracts. Alternatively, the Bank could use the Margrabe formula and use two deltas [N(d1) and N(d2)] from the model to determine the appropriate amount of U.S.$/Lira and U.S.$/Yen options that would need to be held (respectively) to hedge the position. Yet, once again the trader would have to be careful to maintain a flat U.S. Dollar position over time.

While this is all very interesting, it does appear that we have lost our way given that this chapter is discussing inter-market trading strategies with options. To return back to the track, the next example will apply a slight twist on the correlation technique to assess the volatility relationships between options on individual stocks and options on the Stock index that contains these stocks.

TRADING THE VOLATILITIES OF STOCK OPTIONS AND STOCK INDEX OPTIONS

In the equity markets, the concept of correlation is well established and often referred to. This measure is fundamental to Portfolio Theory and to the Capital Asset Pricing Model (CAPM). Both of these concepts will be discussed in detail when I discuss the portfolio applications of options in Chapter 11. In portfolio theory, the correlation measures if a particular security diversifies the risk of a portfolio. This will occur whenever that asset's returns have a correlation less than a positive 100% to the returns of the portfolio. In CAPM, the correlation (and the covariance) are critical elements in the determination of the relative risk of a stock to that of the market portfolio of which the individual stock is a part. In most markets, a surrogate measure of the "market portfolio" will be a capitalisation weighted stock index like the S&P 500 or the FTSE 100. Again, the magic word has to be mentioned: risk. If a model like CAPM does relate the relative risk of the stock to the stock index, then there should be some relation to the volatilities of both the stock and the stock index. The technique for assessing this relationship is called the R squared method and as the reader will soon see this is intimately related to the correlation relationship previously discussed.

THE R SQUARED METHOD
FOR COMPARING STOCK AND STOCK INDEX VOLATILITIES

In this technique, the analyst reviews the amount of variance in the movement of the stock that is explained by the movement in the stock index. This ratio is derived from the statistical technique known as regression and the formula for this is:

$$\Delta S / S = \alpha + \beta\, \Delta M / M + \varepsilon$$

where:
$\Delta S/S$ is the Return of the stock
$\Delta M/M$ is the Return of the Market (Stock Index)
α is the constant Return of the Stock which occurs regardless of the returns of the Market
β is the relative risk of the Stock to the Market
ε is the residual random variation of the Stock which is expected to be zero and is indipendent of the Market

For many traders involved in the equity markets this formula should be familiar. If not, then at least the concept of the Beta (β) will be known. Beta indicates how much the stock will move for a given movement in the overall market measured by the stock index. If the Beta is 1.0 then when the market moves 10%, the stock will also move 10%. When the Beta is 0.50, the stock will move 50% of the move of the market. In some ways, the reader can think of the Beta of a stock like the delta of an option. But as we know the delta is bounded by -1 and +1, while a Beta can possess any value both negative and positive.

Because the Beta measures the relative risk between two assets, then it must have some relationship to the correlation and indeed it does. What follows is the formula for the Beta of a stock to the market:

340

$$\beta = \frac{1/n \cdot \sum (X_1 - \chi)(Y_1 - \psi)}{\sigma_X \cdot \sigma_X}$$

where:

β is the Beta between stock Y and market X
Y_1 is each observation of stock Y's returns
ψ is the average return of stock Y in the Period
X_1 is each observation of market X's returns
χ is the average return of market X in the Period
σ_X is the Standard Deviation of X in the Period
n is the number of observations for the analysis

If the reader compares the formula for the Beta to that for the correlation coefficient expressed earlier in this chapter, he will notice that they are almost identical apart from a slight difference in the lower portion of the formula. The difference is that for the correlation coefficient the upper portion of the equation is divided by ($\sigma_y \cdot \sigma_x$). For the Beta formula, the upper portion of the equation (which is identical to the correlation) is divided by ($\sigma_x \cdot \sigma_x$). What does this difference in the denominators imply?

The correlation coefficient is a standardised measure of the inter-relationship between markets because it is standardised for the risk of both securities. The Beta is only the relative relationship between one security (the market) and the other security (the stock). Furthermore, the ($\sigma_x \cdot \sigma_x$) term is simply the volatility (standard deviation) of the market multiplied by itself and this is referred to as the variance of the market. The correlation will tell the analyst if the two markets are related, while the Beta will tell the analyst how much one asset will move given the other asset has moved.

The regression analysis produces a very useful statistic that indicates the amount of the variation in the movement of the stock that is explained by movements in the market. This statistic is called the R squared and the formula for this is:

$$R_H^2 = \beta \cdot (\sigma_X \cdot \sigma_X) / (\sigma_Y \cdot \sigma_Y)$$

where:

R_H^2 is the Historical R squared Relationship
β is the Historical Beta relationship
($\sigma_x \cdot \sigma_x$) is the Variance of the Market (Stock Index)
($\sigma_y \cdot \sigma_y$) is the Variance of the Individual Stock

This formula indicates that the relationship of the (squared) volatilities of the stock and the stock index are related to the Historical Beta relationship of the two assets. When comparing individual stock option volatility to the volatility of the stock index that stock comprises, this Historical R squared statistic is compared to the current levels of implied volatilities in the market. The assumption is that if divergences are observed to occur, then they will return to their historical relationship over time.

As we look at the above equation, we will immediately notice that the volatility terms (σ_x and σ_y) both appear. To compare the historical R squared relationship between these assets, we must substitute today's implied volatilities for the historical volatilities in the formula to derive an implied R squared relationship. This is done in the following formula:

$$R_I^2 = \beta \cdot (\sigma_X \cdot \sigma_X) / (\sigma_Y \cdot \sigma_Y)$$

where:
R_I^2 is the Implied R squared Relationship
β is the Historical Beta relationship
$(\sigma_x \cdot \sigma_x)$ is the Squared Implied Volatility of the Market (Stock Index)
$(\sigma_y \cdot \sigma_y)$ is the Squared Implied Volatility of the Individual Stock

While this may appear to be a totally different methodology when compared to the implied correlation technique I introduced earlier, in fact it is not. The R squared is simply the correlation coefficient multiplied by itself and is therefore for all practical purposes measuring the same thing.

To aid understanding, I will lead you through an example using two stocks in the UK market on which options are traded and compare their R squared relationships to the options on the most popular UK Stock Index, the FTSE 100. The two stocks I have selected are British Telecom (telecommunications) and Prudential (financial services and insurance). For both of these stocks, I took historical data of daily returns from May 1992 until May 1994 and determined the rolling one year Beta relationship and the historical R squared relationship. For every week in time, I re-estimated these statistical relationships always maintaining a one year period for analysis. Next, I took the implied volatilities for the ATM options for the individual stocks and for the FTSE stock index for the near term expiration and determined an implied R squared using the past one year's historical Beta. Then, the historical and implied R squares were plotted against each other. This can be seen in Figure 9.9a for British Telecom and Figure 9.9b for Prudential.

Two interesting things pop out from these figures. Firstly, the Historical R squared relationship (labelled as Actual R squared) represented by the dotted line is remarkably stable from May 1993 until May 1994. For British Telecom, the his-

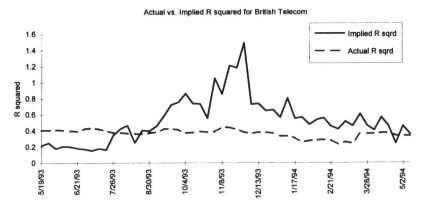

Figure 9.9a Historical and Implied R squared for British Telecom.

torical R squared tends to be at around 40% and for Prudential, the historical R squared starts out at around 50% and slowly decreases over the period. However, such stability is not shared by the implied R squared series that exhibits extreme variability. Often, the series exceeds the mathematical limit of the R squared which is 100% (of the variance of the stock explained by the movement in the market). Secondly, the reader will notice that at certain times, the two time series cross. It is as if the options markets swing back to their fair relationship and then wander away again.

Having seen these graphs, I decided to back track and try some simple trading strategies to see if profits could be generated. My hypothesis is that if the implied R squared deviates significantly from the historical R squared it must return back to the parity relationship eventually. If, for example, the implied R squared is too high relative to the historical R squared, it must fall. Given that the Beta is assumed to be constant, then the only way this can occur is if the implied volatility of the FTSE

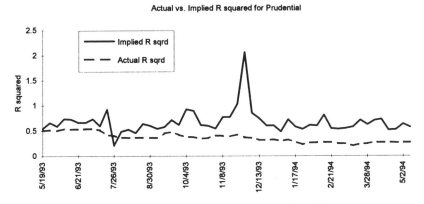

Figure 9.9b Historical and Implied R squared for Prudential.

343

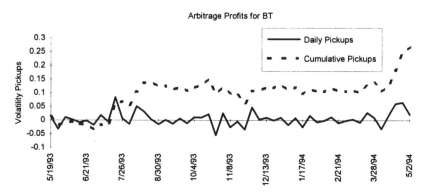

Figure 9.10a Daily and Cumulative Pickups in Volatility Percentage for British Telecom.

100 falls or the implied volatility of the individual stock rises. This can be inferred from the above formula for the implied R squared relationship. The trading strategy is simple: I would buy the implied volatility of the individual stock and sell the volatility of the FTSE.

Let us consider the alternative situation where the implied R squared is below the historical R squared. For the implied R squared to rise back to its parity value, the volatility of the FTSE would either have to rise or the volatility of the individual stock would have to fall. Again, the trading strategy is simple, I would then buy the implied volatility of the FTSE and sell the implied volatility of the stock.

The logistics of both strategies are as follows. For both the stock and the FTSE, I would buy or sell at the money straddles making sure the positions were exactly delta neutral. Secondly, I will hedge the theta risk by making sure the amount I was losing on the long straddle was offset by the gains on the short straddle and finally the gamma was adjusted to be neutral by assuming the gamma effect of the stock option was a function of the historical Beta relationship between the stock and the stock index. In this way, the position was only concentrating on the vega (or implied volatility) sensitivities of both the stock and the stock index.

Using these simple trading rules (and ignoring transactions costs), I re-ran the data to see how the rules performed. Figure 9.10a displays the daily and cumulative pickups in volatility percentage terms for the trading rules for British Telecom versus FTSE options. While, it does appear that the daily pickups (solid line) hover around zero, the cumulative profits shoot (dotted line) up during the month of August 1993. Thereafter, this profit remains relatively stable until May 1994 when another jump in profits occur. Regardless, the overall profit achieved in one year from this trading strategy is more than 25% in volatility terms.

To explain why the profits are not spread evenly over the year but only really occur at two points in time, we must return to Figure 9.9a to see what is happening between the implied and historical R squared time series for British Telecom. It would appear that every time the implied R squared series crosses through the historical R squared time series, the volatility relationships between the implied volatilities of the British Telecom and FTSE come back into line rather abruptly. When a significant divergence occurs between the time series, then no profits appear to be generated. Thus the historical record would suggest that at these "cross over" points between the implied and historical relationships, the markets do react to the mispricing relationships.

What is the evidence for Prudential versus the FTSE using these simple trading rules? In Figure 9.10b, the results are presented for both the daily and cumulative pickups from the spread in volatility percentage terms over time. Again, there is only one point at which the strategy performs well. This is in July 1993 when a cumulative profit of almost 20% in volatility terms is realised. After that, the cumulative profits hover around this level. Again, referring back to Figure 9.9b, one can see what has happened. On only one occasion did the implied R squared time series cross through the actual R squared time series and that occurred around the middle of July 1993. At this point, the option market makers then revised their relative volatilities for the two markets and they swung back into line. Thereafter, no further profit could be earned from the simple trading rule. Thus, it would not have been advisable to make any further cross market volatility trades unless the two series once again intersect.

An interesting question is that since most evidence suggests that markets are relatively efficient, how could this apparent anomaly still exist? The definitive answer may never be known but one possibility that I can offer is that we are comparing two diverse approaches to how assets are valued in the capital markets. The first model assumes that asset prices will approach an equilibrium value which will depend on the consensus of the entire market. The other model allows asset prices to be determined through arbitrage. That is, if the prices of the asset vary from their fair value, an equivalent portfolio of other fairly priced assets will be put together that will exactly mimic the payoffs of the mispriced asset. Then the arbitrageur will

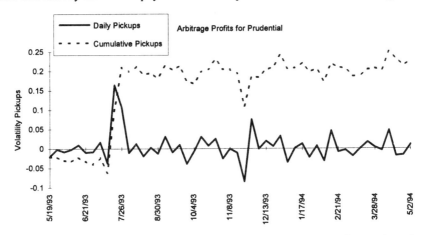

Figure 9.10b Daily and Cumulative Pickups in Volatility Percentage for Prudential.

buy (or sell) the mispriced asset and sell (or buy) the fair priced equivalent portfolio, locking in a profit for no risk. Clearly, these two models depend on different mechanisms for their enforcement. In options pricing, arbitrage is what keeps the prices in line.

The range of arbitrage strategies were covered in the last chapter. If prices diverge from their fair value, there is a well defined strategy which will return the prices to fair levels at no risk. In the Capital Asset Pricing Model, the mechanism that keeps prices in line is known as equilibrium theory. That is, over time, if people spot mispriced assets, they will start to sell the overvalued security and buy the undervalued security until prices return to their equilibrium values. However, this is the key point: this mechanism is not a risk free arbitrage because the two assets are not perfectly correlated. If you have any doubt, simply return to Figures 9.9a and 9.9b where actual R squared levels are at best 50% for Prudential and 40% for British Telecom. Expressed in correlation terms, Prudential has at best a 70% correlation with the FTSE ($\sqrt{0.5}$) and British Telecom has a 63% correlation with the FTSE ($\sqrt{0.4}$). Given the lack of perfect co-movement between these assets, a return to an equilibrium will occur but this may be associated with a significant amount of variability along the way. Often, when they do return to equilibrium, this means that things have moved out of line to such a degree that everyone becomes aware of the blatant discrepancy and the levels (in this case of the volatility) jump back into line.

An analogy I like to think of, when comparing equilibrium pricing and arbitrage pricing, is how a car and a caravan (a trailer) move together on the highway. If the car is towing the caravan and the tie between the car and the caravan is fixed (i.e. it is properly bolted on to the trailer hitch), the two vehicles will move exactly together. This is similar to the process in a capital Markets model which is based upon arbitrage. If, on the other hand, the car and the caravan are linked together with a spring, then the two vehicles will also tend to move together, but if the car suddenly accelerates or turns sharply, the caravan will pause before it dramatically springs to catch up with the car. This is similar to the process in Capital markets for a model based upon equilibrium. As one can appreciate, the second process will also get both vehicles from A to B, but the relationship will not be as stable with the possibility of disastrous results for both the car and caravan.

Perhaps by using the CAPM (an equilibrium) model for the evaluation of relative volatilities of options (priced using arbitrage), one would expect sudden swings would occur that would return stock option and stock index options volatilities to parity. While these findings do point out an interesting result, caution is advised. Any of my readers intending to implement this kind of cross market volatility strategy should carefully examine the historical record for the markets they may wish to apply this technique to and to stick to any trading rule that works.

The final area I will examine in this chapter will look at an entirely new area in options markets, that of options on spreads between markets. These spread options are becoming more and more prevalent. The good news is that the principles that underlie the evolution of these products have already been introduced in this chapter.

OPTIONS ON THE SPREADS BETWEEN MARKETS

In recent years, many market participants have been effected by the spreads which occur between related markets. For example, the spread between crude oil prices and gasoline prices is critical to both oil producers and consumers. In the interest rate markets, hedgers who are cross hedging instruments, such as Mortgaged Backed securities with standardised financial futures, based upon Government Bonds, have always been exposed to a concept called basis risk and for many of these users, there were no instruments to manage this risk. One solution to these problems has been the development of options on the spreads between markets.

Two of my colleagues (and friends), Dr. Michael Selby and Les Clewlow have completed considerable research on spread options and were kind enough to allow me to refer to their work for this section of Options Explained[2].[7] The motivation for their research is that it is becoming increasingly obvious that the spread in price between related commodity futures markets is important to both producers and consumers of the products which underlie the futures contracts. In addition, spread options would allow hedgers to avoid the risk associated with rolling hedged positions from one contract month to another and could assist in the recovery of storage and inventory financing costs.

They examined a number of Spread relationships of which spread options could potentially be offered. These included what they call Interdelivery Spreads and Intercommodity Spreads.

They defined Interdelivery spreads as the spread between two futures with different maturities on the same underlying commodity. An example of this would be long March corn futures and short July corn futures. This spread is called an intra-market spread in this book (see Chapter 8 for calendar spreads). What they call an intercommodity spread is what I have referred to as an inter-market spread. Once again, these are defined as the difference between the prices of futures contracts on two closely related commodities such as raw and white sugar futures, crude oil and heating oil futures and gold and platinum futures.[8]

The aim of their work was to solve the appropriate pricing model for the pricing of spread options using a variety of techniques. However, what I will draw from this research is the empirical analysis they completed on their models using actual market data comparing two inter-market spreads between the London Commodity Exchange futures contracts on raw and white sugar and the International Petroleum Exchange (London) futures contracts on crude oil and gasoil (the British term for Heating Oil). But before this, let us look at their pricing model for spread options.

---

[7]This section is based upon a Financial Options Research Centre of the Warwick Business School working paper by Les Clewlow and Michael Selby that was presented in October 1993.

[8]They also referred to another kind of spread between the same futures contract with the same maturity traded in two different markets. An example of this would be London and New York silver which they call an inter-market spread. I have footnoted this to avoid confusion with my use of the term: inter-market spread which is the spread between different underlying markets.

After looking at simple single factor models following either geometric Brownian or arithmetic Brownian motion and a more complicated two factor model, they determined that the most appropriate model for spread options was the two factor model. What interested me was the solution they derived for the volatility of the spread, which is expressed in the following formula.

$$\sigma_S^2 = \frac{\left(\sigma_1^2 \cdot F_1^2 + \sigma_2^2 \cdot F_2^2 - 2 \cdot \rho_{F1,F2} \cdot \sigma_1 \cdot F_1 \cdot \sigma_2 \cdot F_2\right)}{S^2}$$

where:

σ_s^2 is the variance of the Spread
σ_1^2 is the variance of the first futures in the spread
σ_2^2 is the variance of the second futures in the spread
F_1 is the first futures price
F_2 is the second futures price
$\rho_{F1,F2}$ is the correlation coefficient between futures F_1 and F_2
S^2 is the square of the Spread between futures prices F_1 and F_2

Of course, when we take the square root of the spread variance we obtain the volatility input we would put into the pricing model. The interesting test was to see how the estimated volatility worked relative to the actual volatility relationships that existed in the markets during a certain period.

To obtain a theoretical volatility of the spread, they applied the function of the two futures prices (see above equation) and graphed the result onto a regular grid of futures prices. Under their assumptions for the futures price series, the correlation was originally assumed to be a constant. With this they could assess the theoretical volatility function. This can be seen in Figure 9.11 and the three dimensional graph is a nice smooth plane for the comparison of the volatilities for the spread between the LCE raw and white sugar futures. If the raw sugar futures contract price rises as the white sugar futures price falls, the volatility of the spread will rise.

This volatility increase is associated with the spread of white minus raw sugar prices falling. If, instead, the raw sugar futures price falls as the white sugar futures price rises, then the spread increases with a prediction that the volatility would decrease. The reason that this occurs can be explained in two ways: an intuitive explanation and a mathematical explanation.

The intuition is that when a constant level of volatility is applied to a decreasing spread level, the proportional impact of the volatility on the smaller spread level is greater. For example, a 20% volatility for a spread of only 20 ticks will cause a greater proportional impact on the changes in the spread when compared with a

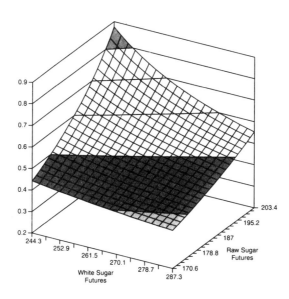

Figure 9.11 Theoretical Volatility Function (May '92).

spread of 120 ticks. A useful analogy can be drawn once again from the world of physics. If we have a quantity of gas (the spread volatility) and that gas is compressed into a smaller and smaller space, the temperature and pressure of the gas rises. If instead, the gas is placed into a larger space, the temperature and pressure of the gas falls. Thus, in the spread option, a similar principle is occurring, when the volatility is compressed over a increasingly smaller spread, the proportional impact rises.

The mathematical explanation for the increase in the volatility of the spread comes directly from the above equation for the spread volatility. The reader will notice that the volatility is a function of the level of the spread. On the top of the equation, the formula looks similar to the Margrabe composite volatility formula only both the variances and volatilities (standard deviation) are multiplied by the price of the underlying futures that make up the spread (or these prices squared). On the bottom of the equation, it is divided by the level of the spread squared. If the level of the spread decreases, then the equation says that the variance (or the volatility) on the top of the equation is being divided by a smaller and smaller number which will cause the theoretical result to rise. Thus, as the spread decreases, the spread volatility increases. Of course, the whole formula blows up if the spread is zero but this model obviously considers this a remote possibility.

Whenever a theory is developed, it is critical to test that theory with real data. This had been done by comparing this theoretical volatility relationship to the actual volatility that occurred over rolling 30 day periods. The actual volatility rela-

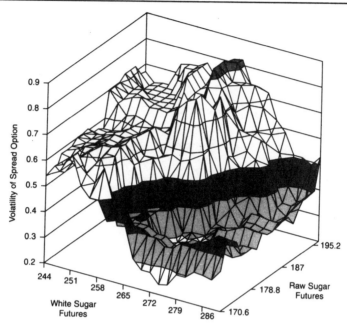

Figure 9.12 Actual Historical Volatility (May 1992).

tionship can be seen in Figure 9.12 and should be compared to the theoretical relationship in Figure 9.11.

In Figure 9.12, the shape of the actual volatility experienced over the period
from January 1991 to December 1992 is not smooth at all but extremely rugged.
However, the general relationship does seem to hold that when the spread widens
the volatility decreases and when the spread comes in the volatility rises. But why
is the actual volatility surface so different from the predicted volatility surface? The
answer is that the correlations are not constant but continuously changing through
time. Figure 9.13 displays the 30 day correlation between Raw and White sug₋

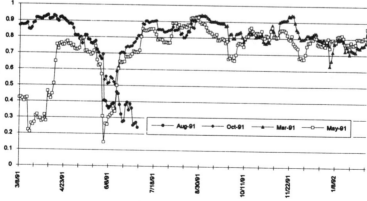

Figure 9.13 Raw-White Sugar Correlation (30 day).

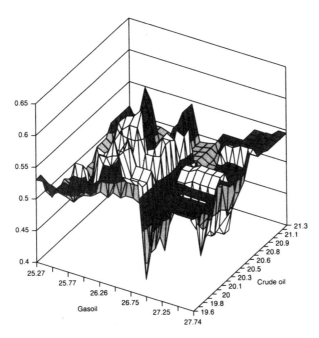

Figure 9.14 Historical Volatility (30 day) Function (Nov '92).

futures contracts for a variety of futures expirations from March 1991 to February 1992.

As the reader can see, the correlations are anything but stable and in the period from May to July 1991, the correlation relationship seems to break down from the normal 70% to 80% level to a 20% to 30% level. Thus, once again the key element to assess and to trade these spread options is the correlation between the assets.

Selby and Clewlow also examined the spread relationship between the IPE Crude Oil and Gasoil futures between May 1992 to November 1992. Once again the volatility surface for the spread was not smooth and flat but extremely unstable as can be seen in Figures 9.14. These figures present the actual volatility relationships for the November futures delivery month. Once again, the reason why the volatility relationship is so unstable is because of changes in the correlation relationship between the Crude Oil and Gasoil markets (which can be seen in Figure 9.15).

These innovative products reconfirm the importance of the inter-market relationships between related markets. The key factors in trading options on different markets are not just the volatilities of the individual markets but more importantly the correlation (or R squared) between the two underlying markets.

While it may be too early to guess, I predict that correlations will become an important element in the trading of not only options markets but of all derivative product markets by the turn of the millennium. For those of you who wish to ride

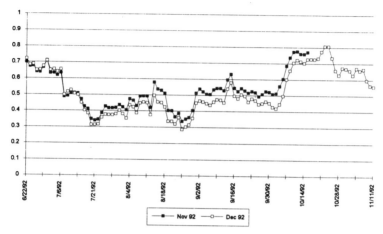

Figure 9.15 Crude Oil - Gasoil Correlation (30 day).

the next wave should carefully consider correlation dependent options and option inter-market spreads as the topics at the top of the list.

Where would these inter-market option spreading strategies be categorised relative to our trading matrix? Relative to the volatility of the underlying asset, it is a difficult call. The inter-market option spreads can both be buyers or sellers of the volatility of an individual asset as indeed they can assume a viewpoint on the movement of each of the underlying assets. Given this conundrum, I will decide that these trades fit into the same category of strategies as options arbitrage. In a way they are semi-arbitrage transactions benefiting from the mispricing of two related option markets. The reader is referred to Figure 9.16 for the final trading matrix of this book.

Viewpoint on the Underlying Market

		Buyer	Seller	Neutral
Viewpoint on Volatility	Buyer	Buy call option Call Back Spread	Buy put option Put Back Spread	Buy Straddle Buy Strangle
	Seller	Sell put option Put Ratio Spread	Sell call option Call Ratio Spread	Sell Straddle Sell Strangle Buy Butterfly Buy Condor
	Neutral	Long Futures Bull spread	Short Futures Bear spread	Calendar Spread Delta Neutral Trading Conversions, Reversals Box Arbitrage, Jelly Roll Inter-Market Option Spreads

Figure 9.16 Option Trading Strategy Matrix.

With this, the trading sections of Options Explained[2] are completed. In the next few chapters, I will examine the use of options in reducing the risks of investment and for portfolio applications. Thereafter, we delve into the worlds of interest rate options, exotics, risk management and then organisational issues.

10: Option Hedging Strategies

In this chapter, I will examine the applications of options for hedging fixed income securities. Across the world, futures and option contracts on Bonds, Gilts, or Bundesanleihen have proven to be among the most successful of all derivative products. In this chapter I will examine one of the first and certainly the most successful of the Government Fixed income derivative markets: the U.S. Treasury Bond futures and options markets traded at the Chicago Board of Trade (CBOT).

Let us review the T-Bond futures and the option on T-Bond futures which are traded at the CBOT. The price of the T-Bond futures will be in percentage of the par value for a hypothetical 20 year U.S. Treasury Bond with a face value of $100,000 and coupon of 8%. The quotations are in full points ($1000) followed by thirty-seconds (1/32). For example, if the futures price equals 80-16 that indicates that the value of the contract is 80 % of $100,000 (or $80,000) plus 16/32 of a % which is 0.5% of $100,000 (or $500). So the monetary volume of one contract would be 80,500 U.S. Dollars. The option on T-Bond futures is quoted in a similar fashion, except that in addition to the full points for the option premium, the following numbers after the "-" are in sixty-fourths (1/64). So, if a particular option is quoted at 1-40, that means the cash cost for the option is 1% of $100,000 (or

Trading Unit:	1 CBOT U.S. Treasury bond futures contract (face value $100,000 or multiple thereof).
Contract Months:	Front month of current quarter plus next three contracts of the regular quarterly cycle (March, June, September and December).
Minimum Price Movement:	1/64 of a point ($15.625).
Exercise Price Intervals:	2 points per T-Bond futures contract (80, 82, 84 etc.).
Trading Hours:	Daytime hours: 7.20 - 14.00 Evening hours: 17.00 - 20.30 or 18.00 - 21.30 daylight savings time
Exercise:	Any business day prior to expiration by 18.00 Chicago time. Automatic exercise occurs in on the last trading day, the option in I-T-M by at least 2 points.
Expiration:	10.00 A.M. on the first Saturday following the last trading day.

Table 10.1 Options on U.S. T-Bond Futures (CBOT).

$1000) plus 40/64 of 1% which is 0.625 of 1% (or $625). In this example, the total price for the option would be $1,625. Furthermore, the tick size (the minimum value of the movement) for the futures is $31.25 (1/32% · $100,000) and for the option on T-Bond futures is $15.625 (1/64% · $100,000). Table 10.1 outlines the contract specification for the options on T-Bond futures.

The ultimate asset underlying the option is a U.S. Treasury Bond that is closely tied to the T-Bond futures contract and the option represents the obligation to either buy or sell this U.S. Treasury Bond in the month following the expiration of the option.

THE BASIC CONSIDERATIONS IN DESIGNING A HEDGING STRATEGY

When considering how to construct an effective hedging strategy, a helpful analogy is a scale. Consider the old fashioned scales with plates on the opposite sides of a fulcrum. The scale operates by balancing weights on the two sides. To balance the scale, whatever is on one side must be matched with an equal weight on the other side. When hedging, the first thing to do is to find which "side" one is on (either a long or short position), and one must also determine the size of the exposure. Then, on the opposite side, one establishes a position which offsets it with an equivalent exposure. The goal of the hedged portfolio is to neutralise the original exposure or to restructure the pattern of returns. Therefore, when the original position loses money the hedging position gains a profit of exactly the same amount. Furthermore, when the hedging position loses money the original position earns exactly the same amount. Thus, as the price of the original asset changes, the hedged portfolio will experience no profit or loss and is considered risk-less.

In hedging, three points must be established:

(1) The size of the exposure

(2) Whether the exposure is long or short

(3) A position in the intended hedging instrument
(which is exactly opposite to points 1 and 2)

For example, suppose I am long a physical T-Bond on one side of my "scale". To hedge the risk of this position I must either sell short physical T-Bonds, sell T-Bond futures or utilise options strategies which have a selling equivalency to the underlying market. Similarly, hedgers may have a short position relative to the underlying U.S. Treasury Bonds market and will require equivalent long positions in derivative products to manage these risks.

Early in this book, I have identified the two kinds of options equivalent short positions and the two kinds of equivalent long positions. This chapter will examine when a hedger might use all of these options strategies in a hedging programme.

Specifically, I will show you how the purchase of calls or puts will reduce the risk of an exposure to the U.S. Treasury Bonds market. I will also cover when a hedger might sell calls or puts to increase yields and cushion his or her loss potentials. In addition, one of these examples will compare and contrast in some detail an options hedge to a futures hedge. The aim of this chapter is to show the reader the realm of the possible so that it will be possible to determine when hedging with options would be most appropriate to the situation.

CASH MARKET CONDITIONS (11 July 94)				
Securities	**Price**	**Yield**	**C. Factor**	**Decimal** **Gross Basis**
UST 7.5 11/15/16	97-12	7.746	0.9486	35.9
UST 7.25 05/15/16	94-28	7.738	0.9236	37.1
UST 8.75 05/15/17	110-18	7.753	1.0777	39.8
UST 8.875 08/15/17	111-30	7.755	1.0908	40.2
UST 9.25 02/15/16	115-21	7.743	1.1265	43.3
UST 9.875 11/15/16	122-04	7.740	1.1892	46.6

FUTURES PRICES & DELIVERY DATE
SEPTEMBER
T - BOND FUTURES
CURRENT PRICE: 101-15
DELIVERY DAY: 30/9/94 (81 DAYS)

OPTIONS ON FUTURES PRICES
SEPTEMBER T-BONDS FUTURES EXPIRATION

PRICES		PRICES	
96.00 SEPT. CALL 5-35		96.00 SEPT. PUT	0-06
98.00 SEPT. CALL 3-50		98.00 SEPT. PUT	0-21
100.00 SEPT. CALL 2-19		100.00 SEPT. PUT	0-54
102.00 SEPT. CALL 1-14		102.00 SEPT. PUT	1-48
104.00 SEPT. CALL 0-35		104.00 SEPT. PUT	3-05

WITH 40 DAYS UNTIL EXPIRATION OF THE OPTIONS (ON AUGUST 20th).
A 4.25% INTEREST RATE AND 11% VOLATILITY.

Table 10.2   U.S. Treasury Bond Market Conditions; Cash, Futures and Options, 11 July 1994.

MARKET CONDITIONS: 11 JULY 1994

To compare and contrast the hedging strategies mentioned above, I will take a particular point in time, present a set of market conditions, and show the reader how hedgers with different objectives might choose the most appropriate hedging strategy. The market conditions as of 11 July 1994 is presented in Table 10.2. In this table, the current September T-Bond futures price is 101-15/32 and the current prices and yields are presented for a variety of U.S. Treasury Bonds. In addition, I have included a few statistics that are critical in determining the relationship of these U.S. Treasury Bonds to the T-Bond futures and options markets. Shortly, I will examine these numbers in more detail to allow the reader an overview of how the cash, futures and options markets are integrated. Also in Table 10.2, there is a variety of T-Bond call and put options with strike prices of 96, 98, 100, 102 and 104 and these will be the universe of tools I will apply to the various hedging situations.

THE RELATIONSHIP BETWEEN U.S. TREASURY BONDS AND T-BOND FUTURES

While the reader is studying the table, he may be curious as to what the numbers in the table under the headings *C. Factor* and *Decimal Gross Basis*. These numbers provide an insight into what the relationship is between each of the five U.S. Treasury Bonds and the T-Bond futures. To understand the relationship between these markets, I must explain the conceptual framework for T-Bond futures. Options on T-Bonds futures are derived from the underlying T-Bond futures market as we have previously discussed. In the case of T-Bond futures, they are derived from the U.S. Treasury Bonds market.[1]

In Table 10.2, five deliverable U.S. Treasury Bonds are listed. The reader may ask, "But which one underlies the T-Bond futures?" The answer to this question is, the U.S. Treasury Bond which is cheapest to purchase and subsequently to deliver into the T-Bond futures (at the expiration of the T-Bond futures in September). To determine which U.S. Treasury Bond is cheapest to deliver, we will need to digress slightly and examine the mechanics of T-Bond futures.

To simplify matters, let us only consider two of the U.S. Treasury Bonds in Table 10.2, the 7.5 per cent coupon T-Bond maturing on 15 November 2016 (hereafter referred to as the 7.5%) and the 7.25% coupon T-Bond maturing on 15 May 2016 (called the 7.25% in the text, hence). The reader will notice that the 7.5% is priced at 97-12/32 and the 7.25% is priced at 94-28/32.[2] The concept of "Cheapest to deliver" means that when there is a choice between a number of U.S. Treasury Bonds for delivery into a T-Bond futures contract, the one which is cheaper to purchase and ultimately deliver will underlie the futures. At first glance, the one that might appear cheaper is the 7.25% because its price is lower. However

---

[1]By definition then, Options on T-Bond futures are a derivative of a derivative.

[2]When a 32nd price for a Treasury Bond has either a "-" or a "+" associated with it, that means that the price is midway between that 32nd and the next lower or higher 32nd. For example, a price of 85-18+/32 means 85% of the par value plus 18.5/32. This is also equal to 37/64s. If the price were 85-18-/32, then this would be equal to 85% of par plus 17.5/32. Thus, 17+/32s is equal to 18-/32s and is also equal to 37/64s. The convention is to not use "-"s in the quotes but rather "+"s or 64ths.

logical this may seem, this is not necessarily the case. Cheapest to deliver is defined by the net cost. The net cost is equal to what you actually receive when you sell the U.S. Treasury Bond via the futures market minus the price you had to pay to purchase the T-Bond. Obviously, if you delivered instruments into the futures market with low coupons, the price would be low as well. Unfortunately, what you receive back upon delivery is also low. If cheapest to deliver simply means the most inexpensive to purchase, then the U.S. Treasury Bond underlying the T-Bond futures would always be the one with the lowest coupon. However, this is not the case.

To correct for the fact that the range of deliverable U.S. Treasury Bonds may all have different coupons, the CBOT provides a conversion factor system to make all these securities equivalent to the 8% coupon standard of the futures contract. To make all U.S. Treasury Bonds of the maturity range equally attractive to deliver into the T-Bond futures contract, an adjustment is made to the T-Bond futures price to take into account that the coupon of the U.S. Treasury Bond delivered might be different from the 8% which is the basis of the T-Bond futures contract. This adjustment is achieved by multiplying the T-Bond futures price by a conversion factor which is provided by the CBOT. The reader can see that these factors are listed in Table 10.2 for a variety of deliverable U.S. Treasury Bonds under the column titled *C. Factor*. For example, the 7.5% conversion factor is 0.9486, while the 7.25% a conversion factor is 0.9236. This means that the 7.5% instrument is roughly 5.14% (1.0 minus 0.9486) less valuable than a 8% 20 year maturity T-Bond futures and that the 7.25% instrument is about 7.64% less valuable. To determine the cheapest to deliver, we must consider what will be the net cost of buying a particular U.S. Treasury Bond and then delivering it into the futures. What we receive upon delivery (at the futures expiration) is the closing futures price times the conversion factor and what we pay is the current price of the U.S. Treasury Bond.

As of 11 July 1994 what would be the net costs for these two T-Bonds if we purchased them and then delivered them into the September futures at the current futures price of 101-15/32? If we bought the 7.5%, the price would be 97-12/32% of par. Since the par value underlying the T-Bond future is $100,000, the amount we would have to pay to deliver this U.S. Treasury Bond into one T-Bond futures contract would be $97,375 (97-12/32% of $100,000). At the T-Bond futures delivery, if the current futures price remained unchanged, we would be paid 101-15/32% multiplied by $100,000, multiplied by 0.9486. This would result in a payment of $96,253.25 upon delivery of this security into the T-Bond futures. A loss would result equal to $1,121.75. This loss can also be expressed in terms of T-Bond futures prices (as a percentage of the par value) which for the 7.5% T-Bond is equal to 35.9 ($1,121.75/$31.25 per basis point). If the reader refers to Table 10.2, he will see that under the column *Decimal Gross Basis*, the number 35.9 appears for the 7.5% coupon U.S. Treasury Bonds. This corresponds exactly to our 35.9 calculated above. What about the 7.25% T-Bonds? If we purchased this security, the current cost is 94-28/32% of par. By selling the T-Bond via the futures market, we agree to receive 101-15/32% multiplied by $100,000 and 0.9236 (at the futures delivery date of 30 September). This translates into a cash inflow of $93,716.54 minus today's price for the 7.25% T-Bond of $94,875, which results in a net loss of $1,158.46. In price terms, this is equal to 37.07 ($1,158.46/$31.25 per basis point). Again in Table 10.2, under the *Decimal Gross Basis* column, the number 37.1 corresponds to this loss for the 7.25% T-Bond. In conclusion, the 7.5% T-Bonds loses $1,121.75 and the 7.25% T- Bonds loses $1,158.46 by purchase and subsequent delivery into the September T-Bond futures. It is easy to see that between these two securities, the 7.5% T-Bonds are cheaper to deliver because of their smaller loss. A brief overview of this example is provided by Table 10.3.

EXAMPLE							
Security	**Cash Price**	**Futures Price**	x	**Conversion Factor**	=	**Adjusted Futures Price**	
UST 7.5 of 11/15/16	97-12	(101-15	x	0.9486)	=	96.25	96-08+
UST 7.25 of 05/15/16	94-28	(101-15	x	0.9236)	=	93.716	93-23
	Cash			**Adjusted**			
Security	**Price**	-	**Futures Price**	=	**Basis**		
UST 7.5	97-12	-	96-08+	=	35.9/32		
UST 7.25	94-28	-	93-23	=	37.1/32		

Since 35.9 < 37.1
The UST 7.5 % T-BOND is Cheaper to Deliver

Table 10.3 Cheapest T-Bond to Deliver Determination.

The "cheapest-to-deliver" U.S. Treasury Bond is determined by using this methodology for each of the potentially deliverable T-Bonds. The security, which has the smallest loss upon delivery into the futures contract, or in some cases which provides the largest profit, is the "cheapest to deliver" U.S. Treasury Bond. Under the column *Decimal Gross Basis* this loss is standardised in basis points. Therefore, the cheapest to deliver T-Bond also has the smallest decimal gross basis. In Table 10.2, the cheapest to deliver U.S. Treasury Bond is the 7.5% coupon of 11/2016 (35.9) followed closely by the 7.25% coupon of 05/2016 (37.1) and then the 8.75% coupon of 15/2017 (39.8).

On 11 July 1994, the September futures price was at a price of 101-15/32. The basis values indicate the number of basis points which the T-Bond futures is at a discount to these deliverable U.S. Treasury Bonds. This means that when we adjust the futures price for the coupon of a particular U.S. Treasury Bond, say the 7.5% T-Bond, the actual futures price of 101-15/32 is lower than the 7.5% T-Bond price adjusted to the 8% standard. Furthermore, the current T-Bond futures price is below all of the futures adjusted cash prices.[3]

---

[3]To determine the future price equivalent of a particular US Treasury Bond, one simply applies the following formula: Current US Treasury Bond Price/Conversion factor.

Why would anyone buy a U.S. Treasury Bond and then sell futures to hedge if the net effect is a loss? The reason is that when one hedges a U.S. Treasury Bond with a short T-Bond futures contract, the combination of transactions provides a new pattern of returns that is fundamentally different from the initial position in the U.S. Treasury Bond. What we need to do is not compare the hedged position with the unhedged U.S. Treasury Bond but rather compare the hedged position with some other security which has exactly the same cash flows. Only in this way, we can assess the true performance of the hedged position. When we sell T-Bond futures to hedge our holdings in U.S. Treasury Bonds, we agree to sell that security in the future. In this example, if we do deliver the security into the futures market in 81 days time (11 July to 30 September), the period of time for holding the T-Bond is only for this period. If we hold the U.S. Treasury Bond unhedged, our expected return is equal to the current yield of the Bond. However, this depends on holding the security until its final maturity in 2016 and yield to maturity also assumes that the coupons received will be reinvested at the same yield. Furthermore, this means that we are willing to accept the risks of holding that security for 22 years. Suppose instead that our exposure to U.S. Government debt was only for 81 days', as it is the case with the short T-Bond futures hedge, we would no longer expect to make the yield associated with 22 year securities but rather the yield for a 81 day maturity security. When we sell our U.S. Treasury Bonds using the T-Bond futures market, at delivery, we will actually surrender the security and will be paid cash for it. If we consider the period of exposure, we have reduced our exposure to U.S. Government interest rates to 81 days. Therefore, the short T-Bond futures hedged position has cash flows which are identical to investing in a short term U.S. Government paper with a maturity of 81 days. If the short term U.S. Government interest rates from 11 July to 30 September is lower than the yield for the longer maturity U.S. Government instruments (which it was for this period equal to 4.25%), we would also expect to have a lower yield on a short T-Bond futures hedge since it provides exactly the same pattern of cash flows. Thus, relative to the original investment in the U.S. Treasury Bonds, we are surrendering a portion of our yield. The way the reduction in yield occurs is for the cash equivalent T-Bond futures price to be lower than the current cash market prices. Thereby, the hedger is selling the T-Bond futures at a level that is lower than the current (adjusted) prices in the cash market. This loss of, for example, 35.9 basis points for the 7.5% T-Bond, simply equilibrates the 22 year securities' return with that of a 81 day investment. The amount of the futures discount is a function of the short term interest rate for 81 days, the coupon rate for the instrument, and the current price for the cheapest to deliver security.

HEDGING EXAMPLE 1: BUYING T-BOND FUTURES VERSUS BUYING CALL OPTIONS TO HEDGE A U.S. TREASURY BOND PURCHASE

Our first hedging example compares the use of futures contracts and call options to hedge an anticipated purchase in the U.S. Treasury Bonds market. Our scenario involves a money manager in the U.S. who has offered his services to a corporate pension fund. $10,000,000 is in the pension fund and the corporation has stipulated that it wants a minimum yield of 7.6% for 22 years. The money manager has identified the 7.25% U.S. Treasury Bonds maturing in May 2016 as the instrument that would be most appropriate. This security can be seen in Table 10.2. At the time of the scenario, July 1994, this instrument had a 7.738% yield. However, the pension fund will not choose who will manage the money before the board of directors will meet in two weeks. The money manager is concerned that within the two weeks yields may have dropped below the target. A problem arises because he may have agreed to provide a rate of 7.6% and if yields have decreased by the time the board meets and agrees to retain him, he might be unable to provide this yield at that point. The money manager has identified two kinds of risk he is facing:

(1) The underlying market risk from a possible drop in yields;

(2) The contingent risk that he may not be chosen by the pension fund directors in two weeks' time.

His market risk is one-sided, that is, that yields might fall below the 7.6% return he has agreed to provide. The contingent risk is that he may not be awarded the funds. Thus, he needs one-sided protection that will only pay off if yields fall, and he also needs to be able to cancel his protection if his services are not retained.

Hedge Ratio Determination

The first problem our money manager has is to determine the size of his exposure. Given the situation outlined above he knows that the money he might be responsible for is $10,000,000. The second problem he has is to find out which side of the market his exposure is on. The easiest way to determine this is to see what happens to his profits and losses as the price of the securities at risk changes.

In this scenario, if yields increase and the price of U.S. Treasury Bonds falls, the money manager will be better off, assuming of course that he is awarded the funds to manage. For example, if the yields for the appropriate T-Bonds rise to 8.5% and he has promised to provide a 7.6% yield, then the money manager will be able to pocket this difference. However, if yields fall and U.S. Treasury Bonds prices rise, the money manager could be in trouble. Consider the situation where the yields drop to 7.25%. The money manager has promised to provide a 7.6% yield and can only purchase securities which offer a 7.25% yield. Unless he can find another security with a higher yield, he will be losing 0.35% per year for 22 years which would be unacceptable. When the T-Bond market falls, he makes an additional profit and when the T-Bond market rises, he will experience losses. This position is equivalent to a short position in the U.S. Treasury Bonds market. To hedge this exposure, the money manager must establish a long position in T-Bond futures or an equivalent long position using options on T-Bond futures.

So far, I have spoken about short T-Bond futures hedges. When one is holding a U.S. Treasury Bond and is selling T-Bond futures to protect the value, the return for the hedge is equal to the short term interest rate. As I discussed, a basis loss occurs for the short futures hedge which reduces the yield on the U.S. Treasury Bonds holding to equal the yield of short term U.S. Government paper. What about the individual who places a long T-Bond futures hedge? He is buying T-Bond futures which are at a discount to the cash T-Bond market. So, he expects to have a profit as the T-Bond futures rises to be equal to the cash market at expiration. In conclusion, in a normal yield curve environment, where longer maturity yields exceed shorter maturity yields, the long T-Bond futures expect to make a profit from the convergence of the futures to the cash market. This is exactly opposite to the situation of the short T-Bond hedge I discussed previously.

However, the final problem that our money manager faces is the determination of the proper number of futures or options to use for his hedge. There exist many methodologies for the estimation of hedging ratios. These run the range from the simple, such as simply using the par values of the securities, to the esoteric, such as multi-factor duration techniques. For our purposes, I will choose a "middle" approach, which is to divide the par value of the hedged instrument by the par value of the underlying futures and multiply it by the conversion factor, which equates the value of that security to the 8% hypothetical T-Bond futures. While this technique is a "rough and ready" approach, it is fairly accurate when applied to the cheapest-to-deliver T-Bonds that a short future contract holder would presumably select to deliver. If the reader finds the 7.25% T-Bond in Table 10.2, he will see that the decimal gross basis is only 37.1 which is slightly higher than the cheapest to deliver (the 7.5% T-Bond at 35.9). Therefore, both T-Bonds are practically equal in terms of attractiveness for delivery and the money manager can treat the 7.25% T-Bond as though it was the cheapest to deliver, applying the conversion factor hedge ratio scheme outlined above.

The actual hedge ratio he will use is determined by dividing $10,000,000 by the par value of the T-Bond futures, which is $100,000 and then multiplying this result by the conversion factor of the 7.25% T-Bond which is 0.9236. This will result in a hedge ratio of 92 T-Bond futures to cover his exposure.

T-Bond Futures Hedge Result

What will be the effect of his hedge of buying 92 T-Bond futures? As yields go down and the T-Bond futures prices rise, the 92 September T-Bond futures will provide profits which will offset the loss incurred by the increased price he will have to pay for the U.S. Treasury Bond. Essentially, he will have locked in the prevailing yield of 7.738% for the 7.25% T-Bond, plus a profit from the futures basis converging from its current discount up to the cash market. If the market remains at present yields, the futures price should slowly converge to the level of the cash market and at expiration the basis should be zero. But during the two week time horizon for the hedge, the money manager will not expect to earn the entire basis but a proportion of the basis which is related to the number of days the hedge is maintained. This will amount to an expected profit of 6.41 basis points in the futures price for the two week period.[4] In terms of yields, this amounts to an additional profit of 0.02% which will make it even easier to meet his 7.6% target on his cash T- Bonds.[5] If the yields increase by 27 basis points on 25 July, he will be able to get a higher 8.00% rate (7.73% plus 27 basis points) on the 7.25% T-Bond. Unfortunately, this will be erased by the loss on the long futures contracts, for the T-Bond futures market will fall when yields rise. Furthermore, if the yields decrease instead, he will have a loss on the U.S. Treasury Bond position which will be exactly offset by the profits on the T-Bond futures and will "lock in" the 7.758% yield that is equal to the prevailing yield for the security at the beginning of his hedge plus the convergence profit on the futures basis he expects to earn over the period. The money manager has therefore created a position that will be immune to changes in yields for his U.S. Treasury Bonds. The logic of the futures hedge is that when one side makes money, the other side loses exactly the same amount. Thus, his achievable yield expected to be at 7.758%, plus or minus any divergences in the cash/futures basis relationship. Table 10.4 displays the hedged results by buying futures as a substitute for buying the 7.25% U.S. Treasury Bonds and assumes that the money manager is awarded the management of the entire $10,000,000. If yields fall to 7.2% the money manager has to pay $565,577 more for the purchase of the T-Bonds. The futures hedge makes $583,242. The money manager will close out the 92 long futures contracts (by selling 92 September T-Bond futures) and this cash amount will be credited to his account. He will then withdraw these funds and apply them to the purchase price of the T-Bonds. The hedge position was able to cover the increased cost of the T-Bond purchase plus provide an additional profit of $17,665.[6] So the long futures hedge protected the position when a decrease in yields occurred.

Unfortunately, if yields rose to 8.25%, the money manager would have been able to buy the T-Bonds at a price which was $493,433 cheaper but the long futures position has a loss of $471,640 which wipes most of this out. In this case,

---

[4]Since the basis for the 7 1/4% T-Bond is 37.1 basis points and this should converge to 0 basis points in 81 days, he can do a simple linear extrapolation to see how much the basis should have dropped in 14 days. The specific formula would be basis/days to futures delivery times the number of days for the hedge. In this example 37.1/81 days times 14 days equals 6.41 basis points.

[5]To determine the yield effect of the 6.4 basis point convergence profit on the futures, we determined the yield for a futures contract with a 8 per cent coupon, a maturity of 20 years and at a price of 101-15. The yield was 7.85%. Then, we changed the futures price to 101-21/32 (including the 6.4 basis points in convergence gain) and re-evaluated the yield. The new yield was 7.83%. Note that when yields go down prices will rise.

[6]This result is mostly due to the positive convergence of the T-Bond futures of 6.4 basis points over the two weeks period. If one multiplies 6.4 x $31.25 x 92 the result is $18,400.

when the money manager closed out the 92 futures contract, he would have to pay the $471,640 to settle his account. As the reader can see, at all yields from 7.2% to 8.25%, the futures hedge achieves a yield equivalent close to the money manager's expected rate of 7.758% and in this rate is the profit between $17,665 and $21,793 from the futures convergence.

Assuming the Manager is Chosen and Purchases the 7.25% T-Bond Profit and Loss Table on 11 July 1994					
Yields on 25/7	7.2	7.45	7.739	8	8.25
Market Price of 7.25% on 11/7	94 28/32	94 28/32	94 28/32	94 28/32	94 28/32
Market Price of 7.25% on 25/7	100 17/32	97 27/32	94 28/32	92 10/32	89 30/32
Change in Price from 11/7	-5 21/32	-2 31/32	-0	2 18/32	4 30/32
Loss on $10,000,000	-$565,577	-$296,941	$0.0	$257,218	$493,433
Sep T-BOND Futures 25/7	107 26/32	104 29/32	101 22/32	98 29/32	96 11/32
Sep T-BOND Futures Price as of 11/7	101 15/32	101 15/32	101 15/32	101 15/32	101 15/32
Change in Price from 11/7	6 11/32	3 14/32	7/32	-2 18/32	-5 4/32
Number of Contracts	x 92	x 92	x 92	x 92	x 92
Futures Profit/Loss ($31.25 per Point)	$583,242	$315,654	$20,024	-$236,346	-$471,640
Overall Hedge Result	$17,665	$18,713	$20,024	$20,872	$21,793
Yield Equivalent	7.756%	7.757%	7.758%	7.759%	7.760%

Table 10.4 T-Bond Futures Hedge.

T-Bond Call Options Hedge Result

Let us now consider a simple option hedge that entails buying call options with a strike price of 100-00/32, instead of buying futures. The same hedge ratio of 92 is used for the options because the asset underlying the option is a T-Bond futures. In order to achieve the limited loss payoff and unlimited profit potential we are look-ing for, we always use the same hedge ratio as we would with the underlying asset.[7]

Purchasing calls provides a "floor" price assuring the money manager that he will be able to buy his T-Bonds at a price which will provide the yield he is looking for. Consider the cash side, when yields increase, the physical T-Bonds will be cheaper to buy. Because futures move in lockstep with the cash market, the futures would also be cheaper, probably below the options strike price. Thus, the call op-tions would then be out-of-the-money. If it were expiration they would expire worthless and that would be the end of the story. If yields decrease, the 7.25%

---

[7]A thorough discussion of why one uses the same hedge ratio for the options as one would with T-Bond futures will follow in the next chapter with the section which discusses the falacy of delta weighting a hedge ratio.

T-Bonds becomes more expensive and the futures prices also increase potentially above the strike price of the call. In that case the call options would then be in-the-money and the proceeds from selling them would offset the increased cost for the T-Bonds. If the date of consolidation was at the options expiration, the options position would provide the same profits as buying 92 T-Bond futures contracts at a price of 100-00/32 and this is a fully covered hedge. However, we are not holding the options until expiration and will remove the hedge in only two weeks' time. At that point, the proceeds of the options hedge will depend upon the option price. On 25 July, there will be 26 days remaining until the expiration of the option. At that point, the 100-00/32 options price will contain both intrinsic value and time value. Thus, the results of the hedge will depend not only on what happens to the underlying T-Bond market but also what happens to volatility and the time decay impact on the time value component of the option's price.

As with all options strategies, the premium must be carefully considered. In this example, we must pay 2-19/64 points (see Table 10.2). This limited premium expense implies that when the T-Bond market falls, we can walk away from the option with a fixed and known loss. If the drop in the market is accompanied by an increase in volatility, then it might actually result in a profit (most certainly a reduction of the loss). The reader is referred back to the explanation of Figure 2.16 which describes how this could occur. Nevertheless, the hedger knows the worst case scenario. In combination with the unlimited gain potential on the physical T-Bond position, the known and fixed premium loss allows the hedged position to

Assuming the Manager is Chosen and Purchases the 7.25% T-Bond Profit and Loss Table on 25/7/94					
Yields on 25/7	7.2	7.45	7.739	8	8.25
Market Price of 7.25% on 11/7	94 28/32	94 28/32	94 28/32	94 28/32	94 28/32
Market Price of 7.25% on 25/7	100 17/32	97 27/32	94 28/32	92 10/32	89 30/32
Change in Price from 11/7	-5 21/32	-2 31/32	-0	2 18/32	4 30/32
Loss on $10,000,000	-$565,577.2	-$296,941.7	$0.0	$257,218.2	$493,433.2
Sep T-BOND Futures 25/7	107 26/32	104 29/32	101 22/32	98 29/32	96 11/32
Price of 100.00 Call Option on 25 July	7 52/64	4 62/64	2 13/64	45/64	9/64
Price of 100.00 Call Option on 11 July	2 19/64	2 19/64	2 19/64	2 19/64	2 19/64
Change in Price from 11/7	5 33/64	2 43/64	- 6/64	-1 38/64	-2 10/64
Number of Contracts	x 92	x 92	x 92	x 92	x 92
Options Profit/Loss ($31.25 Per Point)	$507,438	$245,813	-$8,625	-$146,625	-$198,375
Overall Hedge Result	-$58,140	-$51,129	-$8,625	$110,593	$295,058
Yield Equivalent	7.681%	7.688%	7.730%	7.849%	8.039%

Table 10.5 T-Bond Options Hedge.

have an unlimited gain potential to the downside (for prices) and this is reflected in Table 10.5. The logic behind this is that if the 7.25% T-Bond is cheaper in the market, the hedger will not need the insurance offered by the call. However, if T-Bond prices rise, he will use the insurance benefits of the call to allow him to purchase the T-Bond at an acceptable level.

Table 10.5 displays the hedged results achieved by buying the 92 call options and assumes that the money manager is awarded the management of the entire $10,000,000. If yields fall to 7.2%, the new price for the 7.25% T-Bond would be much higher, equal to 100-17/32 , and the September T-Bond futures price would also have risen to 107-26/32. The 100-00/32 call option is deeply-in-the-money and is worth 7-52/64. The mechanics of the hedge would require the money manager to sell his call options on 25 July receiving the premiums listed in the table. He would include the proceeds (or losses) from the sale of the options to the $10,000,000 awarded by the pension fund and he would then purchase the 7.25% T-Bonds. If he sold the 100-00/32 call for 7-52/64, then after deducting the initial premium payment of 2-19/64, his net profit is 5-33/64 points for the 92 options or a gain of $507,438. The increased cost for the 7.25% T-Bonds of $565,577 is substantially covered by the option's gain of $507,438. However, the options missed the mark of a perfect result by $58,140. The options contracts failed to keep pace with the movement in the T-Bonds because of two factors:

(1) the time decay occurred over this period for the options;
(2) the fact that option price movements will be less than 100%
    of the price change in the underlying because of the delta factor.

If yields had increased instead, the price of the T-Bonds the money manager intends to purchase will be cheaper. Unfortunately, the options prices will have fallen as well. So he would once again sell the options back to the market and get what he can. The difference between what he paid for the options and what he can sell them for is deducted from the savings of the cheaper T-Bonds to provide him his profit. If yields rise to 8.00%, the 7.25% T-Bond is $257,218.2 cheaper and the loss on the option premium is $146,625. So, he can still provide the yield he promised and pocket the difference of $110,593. If instead he decided to pass all these gains to the pension fund, then the realised yield could be increased to a 7.849% yield. Furthermore, if yields rise to 8.25%, the 7.25% T-Bond will be $493,433.2 cheaper with the options position losing almost all its premium value. However, even with the $198,375 options premium loss, the money manager is ahead by $295,058. Again if he passes this along to his client, the yield would be increased to 8.039%. If the money manager had instead sold T-Bond futures at these levels, he would have locked in a yield of approximately 7.758%. Therefore, in two weeks' time, the options hedge will allow the money manager a "floor" yield of 7.681% and the chance to make significant profits if yields rise and the T-Bond is cheaper to purchase. The comparison of the T-Bond futures and options hedges can be seen graphically in Figure 10.1.

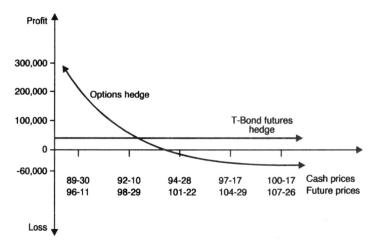

Figure 10.1 Hedge Comparison; T-Bond Futures versus T-Bond Options.

So far, we have only looked at the hedge, assuming that the pension fund capital would be awarded to the money manager. If we examine the hedged positions with the assumption that the board of directors rejects the services of the money manager, then we shall see a very different picture.

Comparison of T-Bond Futures and Call Options Hedges if the Cash Market Exposure does not Materialise

Suppose the contract is not awarded on 25 July. The money manager would have to lift the hedged position and depending upon the prevailing yields and the hedging strategy he chose, the money manager would have a profit or loss on the strategy.

The Impact of the Open T-Bond Futures Contracts
The hedge which is now unmatched is equivalent to an exposed open position in either T-Bond futures or options. Let us consider the implications of not being awarded the pension plan funds for the futures hedged position he has established. If he bought the futures at 101-15/32 and the underlying T-Bond market did not change, then his now exposed position will experience a slight gain from the convergence. He can get out of his position with a small profit. But if the futures market increases, he will make a substantial profit of perhaps $583,242 on the futures contract if yields drop to 7.2% (at that point the T-Bond futures price would be 107-26/32). If the market goes the other way, he will face equally substantial losses. This can be seen in Table 10.6 (this table contains the same numbers as Table 10.4 without the impact of the 7.25% T-Bond).

Assuming the Manager is not Chosen Profit and Loss Table on 25/7/94					
Yields on 25/7	7.2	7.45	7.739	8	8.25
Sep T-BOND Futures 25/7	107 26/32	104 29/32	101 22/32	98 29/32	96 11/32
Sep T-BOND Futures Price as of 11/7	101 15/32	101 15/32	101 15/32	101 15/32	101 15/32
Change in Price from 11/7	6 11/32	3 14/32	7/32	-2 18/32	-5 4/32
Number of Contracts	x 92	x 92	x 92	x 92	x 92
Futures Profit/Loss ($31.25 per Point)	$583,242	$315,654	$20,024	-$236,346	-$471,640

Table 10.6 T-Bond Futures Hedge without underlying Cash Purchase.

In the worst case, he will suffer a loss of $471,640 for a 51 basis point increase in yields for the T-Bond market (at a 8.25% yield the T-Bond future price would be 96-11/32). Since he has an unlimited loss potential and an unlimited gain potential with the futures contract, he faces a significant exposure to interest rates and changes in T-Bond futures prices.

The Impact of the Open Call Option Positions
Let us now compare this to the call option hedge. If the contract to manage the funds is cancelled two weeks later, he can simply sell the call option back to the market, like cancelling an insurance policy and receiving the outstanding premium back. When he sells it, he will be paid the two components of an option's value: the intrinsic value and the time value. Table 10.7 displays the value of the call options in this circumstance (Again, like Table 10.6, Table 10.7 has the same numbers as the earlier Table 10.5. The only difference is that the cash flows for the 7.25% T-Bond have been removed). To determine how much cash he will receive back, the value of the call is multiplied by 92 (contracts) at each appropriate futures price

Assuming the Manager is not Chosen Profit and Loss Table on 25/7/94					
Yields on 25/7	7.2	7.45	7.739	8	8.25
Sep T-Bond Futures 25/7	107 26/32	104 29/32	101 22/32	98 29/32	96 11/32
Price of 100.00 Call Option on 25 July	7 52/64	4 62/64	2 13/64	45/64	9/64
Price of 100.00 Call Option on 11 July	2 19/64	2 19/64	2 19/64	2 19/64	2 19/64
Change in Price from 11/7	5 33/64	2 43/64	- 6/64	-1 38/64	-2 10/64
Number of Contracts	x 92	x 92	x 92	x 92	x 92
Options Profit/Loss ($31.25 per Point)	$507,438	$245,813	-$8,625	-$146,625	-$198,375

Table 10.7 T-Bond Options Hedge without underlying Cash Purchase.

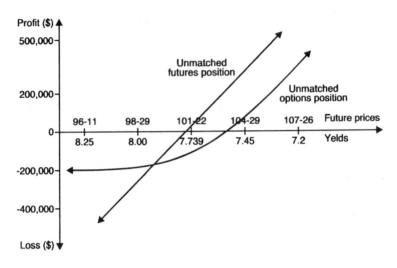

Figure 10.2 Unmatched Futures Position.

level. Since he initially paid $211,312.5 (92 contracts · $15.625 per 1/64 point · 147⁸ of the 1/64s), his net profit or loss on the options hedge will be the amount he retrieves back less this amount that he paid on 11 July. If yields increase to 8.25% or decrease to 7.2% the profit/loss on the option is in a range between a $507,438 profit and a $198,375 loss. As can be seen in the preceding Table 10.6, the uncovered futures hedge has a much larger gain and loss potential with a loss at the 8.25% yield at $471,640. On the other side, when yields fall to 7.2%, the futures position picks up $583,242 which is $75,804 more than the options position at the same level ($583,282 - $507,438). In fact, the option losses start levelling out very quickly to a loss amount limited by the premium expense.

Figure 10.2 displays graphically the profits and losses of both the T-Bond futures hedge and the T-Bond options hedge if the manager is not chosen to manage the funds. Therefore, if the money manager's services are not retained and he used an options hedge, he faces a maximum loss potential of $198,375 while the futures position could lose more than four times this amount in the worst case scenario.

Comparison of T-Bond Futures and T-Bond Options Impacts

One can see that the options hedge does not only have a limited loss and unlimited gain potential, but also does not experience as much of a profit or loss compared with hedging with the T-Bond futures. An unmatched T-Bond futures position has an unlimited loss potential while an unmatched option position has a limited loss potential. Thus, a priori, the money manager should prefer options over futures for this hedging situation, since effective hedging defined as is the minimisation of the

⁸The reason why it is 147 64s is that 2-19/64 is equal to 128/64 + 19/64 which equals 147/64.

expected change in net wealth. Clearly, in this case, the options strategy minimises the risk for the money manager.

Quite often, options are ideal for reducing the risk of contingent situations. For example, currency options are often used when a corporation is bidding on a project abroad. These options provide protection in case the project is not secured and no foreign exchange receipts result. If the project is awarded, the option has insured the value of the foreign exchange position. Another contingent application is for corporations that purchase or sell raw materials without knowing the exact quantity of raw materials required. They may use futures to lock in the amount they know they will need, and use options for the remainder. Whenever a contingency is involved in a hedging situation, the hedger should look at options as the appropriate hedging tool. Alternatively, the hedger could investigate purchasing an option to buy another option which will be discussed in Chapter 13 in the section on compound options.

HEDGING EXAMPLE 2: BUYING A PUT OPTION ON T-BOND FUTURES TO PROTECT THE VALUE OF A U.S. TREASURY BOND

Another example of when it is appropriate to buy options to hedge is to protect the value of underlying assets already held. Suppose I have purchased a U.S. Treasury Bond and I want to protect its value. What I need is an insurance policy on the price of the security. As we discussed in Chapter 1, purchasing an option is similar to an insurance purchase. Furthermore, buying a put option can be thought of as "selling price" insurance. So, buying put options can be an effective tool to protect a long T-Bond position against a decrease in its price by providing the right to sell at an appropriate level.

What would one expect the profit/loss profile of the put hedge to resemble? At the end of Chapter 3, I combined a long position in $/£ forward (same as futures) with a long put option. The result was a new synthetic security. To jog the reader's memory, I determined the composition of this synthetic security by applying the Put-Call Parity formula. I was were able to prove that when combining a long underlying position (F-E) with a long put (+P) the resultant payoff is identical to a long call (+C). So, when one hedges the holding of an asset with a put option, the payoff should resemble a long call with the maximum loss potential occurring when the underlying market price is equal to or less than the strike price. Therefore, the break-even point is the price in the underlying futures equal to the strike price of the put plus the put option premium. At that point, the increase in the value of the underlying futures is sufficient to offset the cost of the put option and above that is an unlimited profit potential. Let us go through a simple example.

Suppose the T-Bond futures is trading at 100-00/32 and we have purchased one futures contract. If we also bought a 100-00/32 put option and paid 1-29/64s for it, what would the payoff of this put hedging strategy be at the expiration of the option? If the T-Bond futures market finishes at 99-00/32, the futures position will have lost 1 full point and this will be exactly offset by the 1 full point in intrinsic value for the put. After the 1-29/64s premium has been taken into account, the net effect of the hedge is a loss of 1-29/64s in premium. If the T-Bond futures market remains at 100-00/32, there will be no profit or loss on the futures and the put option will also expire worthless. Again the net effect of the hedge is a loss of the put option premium of 1-29/64s. If the T-Bond futures ends up at 101-15/32, then there is a profit of 1-15/32s on the long futures contract and again the 100-00/32 put option will expire worthless. After the 1-29/64s premium (which is equivalent to 1-14+/32) has been deducted, the net result of the position is that the put option expense has been covered by the movement in the underlying asset. This price is known as the break-even point for the put hedge. If the T-Bond futures market rises to 102-00/32, then the long futures contract will have a profit of 2 full points, the put expires worthless and after deducting the put option premium, the net profit is 35/64s which is equivalent to 17+/32s. The reader will recognise that this is exactly the same payoff as a long 100-00/32 call.

Complications of Using Options on T-Bond Futures to Hedge a U.S. Treasury Bond

When one hedges a U.S. Treasury Bond with options on T-Bond futures, the situation becomes more complicated. The hedge involves the use of a derivative of another derivative. That is the underlying for options on T-Bond futures is the T-Bond futures and the underlying for the T-Bond futures is a U.S. Treasury Bond (which we may be interested in hedging). Therefore, to properly evaluate a T-Bond futures option hedging strategy, we must first compare the option strategy to its underlying (the T-Bond futures) and adjust that comparison for the relationship between the T-Bond futures and the underlying U.S. Treasury Bond.

Suppose we are holding $10,000,000 in par value of the 7.5% U.S. Treasury Bonds maturing in 2016. Again it is 11 July (the prices for this security can be seen in Table 10.2) and the 7.5% U.S. Treasury Bond also happens to be the cheapest to deliver into the futures market with a current yield of 7.746%. Suppose we believe that the yields will increase by 20 August (the expiration of the September T-Bond futures options for the September 1994 delivery) and that we expect the value of these T-Bonds to decrease by then. However, we are unsure when the yields may increase and are concerned that an increased volatility in the T-Bond market may occur instead. If this is the case, then it is possible that yields might fall instead of rising. In a highly volatile and uncertain market, we might want to limit our exposure and still be able to profit if the T-Bond market happens to rally. Thus, we purchase put options to establish a floor value for the T-Bond position and still retain the upside potential.

Since the options we can use (in Table 10.2) are offered at five separate strike prices, we have the opportunity to vary the degree of protection we want to receive and the price we will have to pay for it. For example, suppose you purchased colli-sion insurance for your car and you could choose between policies with no excess or one with a large excess (also known as a deductible). The one with no excess will cost more because the entire risk is passed off to the insurance broker. If in-stead you chose the insurance with a large excess, you are assuming part of the risk. Therefore, the insurance with an excess would be less expensive. A similar situation occurs when one is deciding which strike price to choose when hedging. Purchasing an at-the-money strike price put option is like purchasing an insurance policy with no excess and the out-of-the-money strike price put options are more like purchasing an insurance policy with an excess. The more risk one assumes, the lower the cost of the insurance or of the option.

Choosing At-the-Money or Out-of-the-Money Puts

Referring back to Table 10.2, I will concentrate on the 100-00/32 and 102-00/32 put options. The premium for the 100-00/32 put is 54/64s and the 102-00/32 put is priced at 1-48/64s. Let us consider what these options offer us. One is the right to sell at 100-00/32 and the other is the right to sell at 102-00/32. The market is pres-ently trading at 101-15/32. If I buy the right to sell at 100-00/32, then I do not get any protection until the futures market falls below 100-00/32. Therefore the "excess" on this put "insurance" will be almost one and a half bond points. If I buy the 102-00/32 put, there is no excess. This is because the 102-00/32 is in-the-money and if the T-Bond futures price falls, the intrinsic value of this put option will thereafter increase one for one. Hence, the 102-00/32 put provides an imme-diate coverage (relative to the T-Bond futures). This is the reason why it is more expensive than the 100-00/32 put which has a 1-15/32 point excess. Which option would I choose? Given the expectation that T-Bond futures are more likely to fall, I will be more conservative and purchase the put option with no excess. That would be the 102-00/32 put.

Hedge Ratio Determination

Since I have decided to purchase the 102-00/32 put option to hedge the exposure, I must now determine the proper hedge ratio. To determine the hedge ratio for the 7.5% T-Bond, I would divide the par value of the holding - which is $10,000,000 - by $100,000 and multiply this result by the conversion factor of 0.9486. The result is a hedge ratio of 94.86 contracts. Unfortunately, I cannot purchase 0.86 of an op-tion contract, so I must either buy 94 puts or 95. The choice of which number to use will decide upon my view of whether it is more likely for the market to fall or rise. Since the viewpoint is that it is more likely prices will fall for T-Bonds and that volatility may increase, I will choose to buy 95 puts and be slightly over hedged. The total premium cost would be 166,250 U.S. Dollars (1-48/64 · $1000 · 95).

Conversion of the Option on T-Bond Futures
to an Option on the U.S. Treasury Bond

Having determined the hedge ratio, I will determine where the maximum loss occurs for the hedge and where the hedge breaks even. Since the ultimate underlying security is the 7.5% T-Bond, I must then convert all our prices from the 8% T-Bond futures standard to the levels of the 7.5% U.S. Treasury Bond. To convert the put option on T-Bond futures to the level of the 7.5% bond, I simply multiply the strike price by the conversion factor for the 7.5% bond. When I do this, the 102 strike price is equivalent to a price of 96-24/32 for the 7.5% U.S. Treasury Bonds (102 · 0.9486).

It is interesting to note that the 102-00/32 put option is in-the-money relative to the September T-Bond futures (which is currently at 101-15/32). However, when I convert the 102-00/32 put option into an equivalent 7.5% T-Bond price, the strike price of the option is now out-of-the-money. That is because the 102-00/32 strike price for the T-Bond futures is equivalent to a 96-24/32 strike price for the 7.5% T-Bond and with the current 7.5% T-Bond price at 97-12/32, the put is out-of-the-money relative to this security. The reason why this has occurred is that the underlying T-Bond futures is at a discount to the cash U.S. Treasury Bonds market, because short term interest rates are lower (4.25%) than the yields for the U.S. Treasury Bonds (7.746%) on 11 July. As discussed earlier, the short T-Bond futures hedger gives up this convergence loss so that the proceeds of the hedge are equal to the equivalent investment in short term U.S. government paper. Since the put option is a substitute strategy for selling the T-Bond futures, it will also be exposed to this convergence loss. Therefore, the put hedger will not only lose the premium he must pay, but he will also lose an additional amount equal to the price differential between the T-Bond futures underlying the put and the 7.5% instrument to be hedged.

To determine the break-even for the put hedge in terms of the 7.5 bond price, we simply add the price of the put (1-48/64s) to the current price of the 7.5 bond (97-12/32). When this is done the break-even price for the hedge is 99-4/32s.

Hedge Results of the Put Purchase

Having converted the put option on T-Bond futures to a 7.5% equivalent, I can now examine the profit/loss profile of this hedge at the expiration of the put. Figure 10.3 displays the payoffs for the put and the profit and loss profile for the 7.5% T-Bond on an unhedged basis. To assist the reader in comparing the levels of the 7.5% bond and the T-Bond futures I have included both the prices for the 7.5% bond and the equivalent in the T-Bond futures (the numbers directly above the x axis represent prices for the 7.5% and the prices underneath are the T-Bond futures prices).

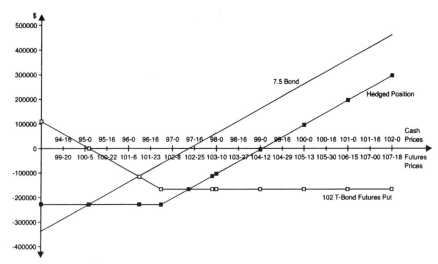

Figure 10.3 Hedging with a Put Option.

The reader can see that the put option hedging provides protection only below a price of 96-24/32 for the 7.5 bond. This is due to the fact that the 102 T-Bond put option is out-of-the-money relative to this instruments. Below this level, the hedge has a limited loss of $228,750. This loss is due to the basis relationship of the current price of the 7.5 bond (97-12/32) and the equivalent price of the 102 strike price for the T-Bond futures (96-24/32). This out-of-the-money amount is 20/32 which for a $10,000,000 nominal amount is equivalent to $62,500. When this is added to the premium cost of $166,250, the resulting maximum loss is $228,750. The break-even is at a 7.5% price of 99-4/32 and the profit potential thereafter is unlimited. The hedged position, as expected, looks similar to a long call option. I forego some of the upside potential by paying an option premium, but the most I can lose is the premium paid.

When the market price of the 7.5% T-Bond decreases, I have an unlimited loss potential if the position is unhedged. This can be seen in Figure 10.3. However, the put options allow me to sell the market at a fixed price and thereby limit the loss for my holding of the 7.5% T-Bond. Thus, I am limiting the risk of falling markets without sacrificing the "risks" of rising markets.

HEDGING EXAMPLE 3: SELLING CALL OPTIONS ON T-BOND FUTURES AGAINST A U.S. TREASURY BOND TO REDUCE RISK AND ENHANCE YIELDS.

Having discussed hedging positions with short T-Bond futures and long put options, I will examine another strategy for protecting a long position in U.S.

375

Treasury Bonds and that is to sell call options against the position. This is probably the most popular option hedging strategy used by institutional investors world-wide. This strategy is commonly called covered call writing because you sell a call option and at the same time, you are holding the assets needed in case the option is exercised against you.

In this example, let us suppose an American institutional investor is holding $25,000,000 in the 8.875% T-Bond maturing on 15 August 2017. The price for this security is 111-30/32 (which can be found in Table 10.2). The basis for this security is 40.2 which is only slightly higher than the basis for the cheapest to deliver 7.5% T-Bond (at 35.9). Therefore, once again, the investor might consider this security to have a similar relationship to the underlying T-Bond futures as does the 7.25% T-Bond and for his purposes, consider it to be a relatively cheap to deliver T-Bond. The prevailing yield of this T-Bond is 7.755%.

This time, the holder of the 8.875% T-Bond expects the T-Bond market to be stable over the period from 11 July to 20 August. Since his view differs from the one taken in the previous example, another strategy has to be employed. Suppose the investor's objective was to enhance the yield on his holdings and reduce the risk caused by an increase in yields. Since he has a long U.S. Treasury Bonds position on one side, he must establish a short position on the other side. Of the three alternative short positions, the long put would be inappropriate given the investor's objectives. This also applies to a short futures hedge because it would reduce his risk but also reduce his yield (remember on 11 July, the futures is at a discount). So the only hedging strategy left is to sell a call option. The investor knows that he will be paid a premium and that if the call expires worthless, it will enhance his yield. Furthermore, if he is expecting the T-Bond market to be stable over the summer period, the chances that the call will be exercised are fairly small, especially if its strike price is currently out-of-the-money. Referring to the investor's viewpoint, selling a call would meet his objectives.

The Choice of the Call Option Strike Price to Sell

With the T-Bond futures market trading at 101-15/32, the hedger looks at the four available call options in Table 10.2 and asks himself: "Which one should I sell?" If he is correct in his predictions, market stability occurs and he sells the 100-00/32 call, he can be fairly certain that he will be exercised upon and will either have to offset the position in the T-Bond futures market or ultimately deliver his T-Bond. But he may not want to sell his T-Bond. He may only want to increase its yield over this period. If this is the case, the 100-00/32 strike price call would not meet his needs. What about the 102-00/32, 104-00/32 and the 106-00/32 strike price calls? The 102-00/32 call will provide a premium inflow of 1-14/64s, the 104-00/32 call would provide an inflow of 35/64. So, it would appear that if his goal is to maximise his yield, then the 102-00/32 call might be his best choice.

Unfortunately, things are not always as simple as they appear. The hedger must once again convert the strike price of 102 for the T-Bond futures to an equivalent strike price for the 8.875 bond he is holding. The strike of 102 is equivalent to a strike on the 8.875 bond of 111-8/32. This is done by multiplying the strike of 102 by the conversion factor of 1.0908 (see Table 10.2).

If the hedger sells the 102 T-Bond futures call it is actually in-the-money relative to the 8.875 bond he is holding. This is once again due to the basis relationship (of 40.2 basis points) between the T-Bond futures price and the 8.875 bond.

To reduce the potential for being exercised, the hedger might consider selling the 104 call. Relative to an equivalent strike price for the 8.875 bond (113-14/32) and the current price of the bond (111-30/32), this option is indeed out-of-the-money. However, the investor must be aware that he gives up all the profit potential above the strike price of the option when he sells a call option against his T-Bond. That means, if the call is exercised, he will experience losses that will directly offset any gains achieved by a favourable change in the price of his T-Bond. The choice of the strike price is quite simple, the investor must choose a strike price that is equal to where he believes the market will end up on the expiration date of the option. In this example, the investor really expects no movement in the market and that the futures will finish at the current levels or slightly higher. Considering this, he decides to sell the 104-00/32 call option and receives a premium of 35/64s per option.

Hedge Ratio Determination

So far, the investor has determined the most appropriate strategy and which strike price to use. Now he needs to estimate the correct hedge ratio. Once again, the 7.5% and the 8.875% T-Bonds are almost equally cheap to deliver. This allows him to determine the hedge ratio using the simple conversion factor formula. The correct hedge ratio is the par value of the T-Bond holdings ($25,000,000) divided by the par value of the T-Bond futures ($100,000) and multiplied by the conversion factor for the 8.875% T-Bond which is (1.0908). This will result in a hedge ratio of 272.7 call options. Again, it is not possible to sell 0.7 of one option, so the investor will round to the nearest integer and sell 273 of the 104-00/32 call options. With each option worth 35/64s, he will have a total premium inflow of $149,247 (273 contracts x $15.625 per 1/64th x 35 64s).

Result of the Covered Call Hedging Strategy

If the T-Bond futures market ends up equal to or less than 104-00/32 in 40 days, he will retain all the premium as income. If the T-Bond futures market increases above 104-00/32, his income will depend on how much the futures price will have risen. If the T-Bond futures rises to 104-17+/32 (35/64s), he will break-even on the hedge relative to his unhedged position. Above that, he will have a maximum income equal to the call option premium he was paid and will have a yield lower than the one he would have achieved without hedging. Again, this goes back to the basics of options discussed in Chapter 1. Figure 10.4 presents the profit/loss profile for the covered call writing relative to a long position in the 8.875% T-Bond at the expiration of the options. In this table, the prices above of the x axis are again the equivalent 8.875% prices with the associated T-Bond futures prices immediately below in the parentheses.

Suppose the long position in U.S. Treasury Bonds was established when the T-Bond futures was trading at 101-15/32. You have sold a call option and bought the underlying bond at an equivalent futures prices of 102-20/32[9]. As prices fall, the unlimited loss potential of the underlying T-Bond dominates the limited gain potential of the call option. Thus, the net effect is an unlimited loss potential for both positions. If prices rise the covered call write position has a limited gain potential with the most you can gain on the hedge being equal to the premium paid to you for the call. In summary, the hedged position makes money when the futures market increases and loses money when the market decreases with a limited gain potential and an unlimited loss potential. Upon careful consideration of the hedged position's payoff diagram, the reader might wonder how a short call option could end up looking "backwards". The reason is that the combined portfolio has an identical payoff structure to that of selling a put, which also makes money when the market increases and loses as the market falls. In fact, it is hardly surprising if one recalls the put-call parity formula discussed in Chapter 3.

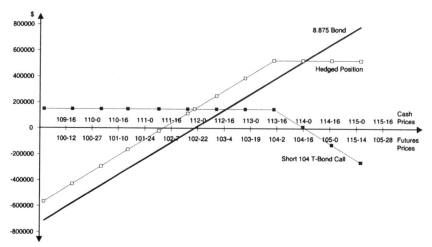

Figure 10.4 Covered Call Writing Results.

[9]This is simple estimated by dividing the current price of the 8 7/8 bond (111-30/32) by the conversion factor (of 1.0908).

The Risks of the Covered Call Hedging Strategy

With the covered call writing strategy considerable risk still exists. One might step back at this point and say "but I thought the objective in hedging was to eliminate the loss potential". Since covered call writing still retains an unlimited loss potential how can it be considered hedging? Well, is the covered call position any worse than holding the underlying U.S. Treasury Bonds position unhedged? Both have an unlimited loss potential. The difference is the covered call hedge brings in a premium which serves as a buffer to losses as prices fall.

For example, suppose the 8.875 bond price drops from 111-30/32 to 111-12+/32. The position has lost 17+/32 on the underlying 8.875 Treasury. As the market goes from 111-30/32 to 111-12+/32, the call options that were sold against the position expire worthless and the inflow of 35/64s in option premium will exactly offset that loss. If the market decreases further, you continue to lose on the underlying position but by selling the call you are 35/64s better off than you would have been otherwise. The cost of this buffer is the foregone opportunity if the market instead increases. However, because there might be up to six actively traded T-Bond option strike prices that one can choose from when selling the calls, the hedger has an equally wide range of possible payoff structures that can emphasise downside protection or upside opportunities. Figure 10.5 displays the possible payoffs to a covered call writing programme using out-of-the-money, at-the- money, and in-the-money call options.

Performance of the Covered Call Hedging Strategy

How would this strategy perform? When these options were sold, the 8.875% T-Bonds were at a yield of 7.755%. Let us suppose that yields had actually increased slightly to 7.770% at the expiry of the options in the middle of August 1994. The prices of the T-Bonds therefore remain basically unchanged (111-24/32).

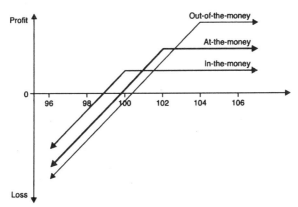

Figure 10.5 Alternative Covered Call Writing Results.

The futures market converged to the cash market with a final price of 102-14/32. This means the 104-00/32 calls have finished out-of-the-money.

Since they have expired out-of-the-money, the options will not be exercised and the hedger will earn the premium of 35/64s. He has also experienced a small loss of 6+/32s on the cash position. Consequently, if the T-Bond holder had remained un-hedged, he would have achieved a 7.755% yield. By selling the 104-00/32 call options against his holdings he was given the opportunity to increase his realised yield. The formula to estimate this return is as follows:

$$\text{Return} = \text{Interest} \pm \text{Bond Return} \pm \text{Option Return}$$

$$= \frac{\$243,150.7 - \$46,875 + \$149,297}{\$27,984,375} \cdot \frac{365}{40}$$

$$= 11.27\%$$

In this formula, the return for a covered call writing strategy is calculated by first estimating the interest received on the particular instrument. In our case, it is for 40 days on a 8.875% coupon for $25 million or ($243,150.7). The next step is to subtract the loss on the U.S. Treasury Bonds position (how it actually changed in value) of $46,875 and then add the option premium retained at expiration which equals $149,297. Finally, this sum is divided by the value of the underlying U.S. Treasury Bonds holdings at the beginning of the period. By converting it to an annualised basis (365 days divided by 63) one finds that a 11.27% yield has been achieved for the holding period.

The way this strategy works is similar to the way casinos make money. Those who are selling call options against their holdings are basically providing a "bet" to speculators. These speculators are paying for the right to possess what they do not have. However, over the long term, does the casino or the gambler make more money? The casino, of course because the casino has what the gambler wants: money. So if you hold the assets, you can act like the casino and speculators will pay you for the chance of the big payoff. Considerable research has shown that you can consistently increase your returns and reduce your risk by writing call options against your holdings.[10]

The research on covered call writing strategies have also pointed out that one must be careful when comparing the results of a covered call writing strategy with an unhedged position in the underlying asset. Consider the following table reproduced from Futures magazine (see footnote for reference). In Table 10.8, results are presented for the annual returns to investors from simply holding the S&P 500 index (including the receipt of dividends), the Ryan index which is an index of the additional return provided by those funds which write call options against their holdings and the total return of call writing strategies from 1987 to 1993.

---

[10]A good review of the covered call writing process for equities is Miriam Bensman's article, "No free lunch?", *Futures*, March 1994, pp.48-50.

S&P 500 w/dividends		Ryan Index*	Total return
1987	5.09	0.17	5.26
1988	16.53	1.82	18.35
1989	32.73	-2.31	30.42
1990	-8.19	3.50	-4.69
1991	30.40	-5.05	25.35
1992	7.57	1.47	9.04
1993	10.07	-0.37	9.64

Table 10.8 Comparison of S&P 500 Returns and Gains from Covered Call Writing.

When we look at the total returns in every year, it appears that when the underlying market rises sharply, the total return using covered calls is reduced. In the years, 1989, 1991 and 1993, writing calls reduced the return relative to simply holding the underlying S&P index. When the underlying market had a bad year (such as 1990) or a flat performance (such as in 1987 or 1992), the covered call writing strategy added value. This is as one would expect. Covered call writing strategies benefit from flat to slightly bullish market conditions. However, consider 1993 when the addition of a covered call writing strategy would have reduced the return relative to doing nothing. One might believe that the covered call writing strategy under performed. Fortunately this seemingly obvious conclusion may be incorrect. Perhaps we are not comparing equivalent investments after all.

Consider what we know from options theory. If we hold an underlying asset, the delta, or risk relative to the underlying, is one. When the benchmark for risk measurement is the standard deviation (volatility) then we can say the risk is measured by 100% times the standard deviation of the underlying. What happens if we hedge 50% of the underlying exposure? Then, the expected risk of the holdings will be 50% of the standard deviation. This is similar in principle to the process of portfolio insurance that will be discussed in the following chapter. With this thought in mind, consider what happens to the risk of an underlying position (in delta terms) if we sold an at-the-money call option against the position. Since the delta of the at-the-money call is approximately 0.50 (or 50%) and we have sold the option, we have reduced the exposure of the underlying to 50% of the previous level of risk (as measured by the standard deviation). The reader may recall that if we perfectly hedge a Treasury Bond with T-Bond futures, the new position will no longer act like the underlying asset but instead a short term instrument. The same holds true with the covered call writing strategy. Thus, the equivalent portfolio risk that is achieved when one sells call options against a position in the underlying asset is by definition less than the risk of the outright position in that asset. The basis for comparison for the call write hedging strategy cannot be the underlying asset but an equivalent risk portfolio which would be 50% in that risky asset and 50% in a risk free asset. Only in this way, can the performance of covered call writing strategies be properly compared. When this is done, the covered call writing strategy does indeed show impressive results.

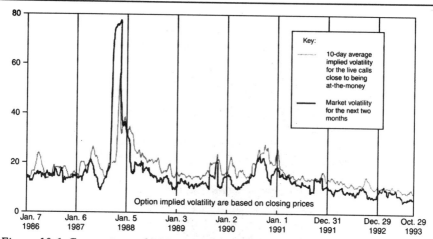

Figure 10.6 Comparison of S&P 500 Implied and Actual Volatilities: 1986-1993.

If this is the case, then covered call writing strategies actually may over per-form. Does not this imply that option prices are above their theoretical values? One would expect from options pricing theory that buyers and sellers of options would break-even over time. That is because options pricing theory is based upon a zero sum game. While this a key stone of options theory, the evidence suggests that op-tions prices are significantly above their theoretical value and that is why covered call writers have an edge. In most markets, the implied volatility of options is greater than the actual volatility that occurs subsequently in the underlying asset. Given that the covered call writer is selling the implied volatility but his perform-ance will depend on the actual realised volatility, covered call writers should over perform. In Chapter 4 of this book, I examined how to forecast historical volatility using economic days. In that example, it was shown that the implied volatility of the options market was significantly above the actual volatility that subsequently occurred. This also occurs in other option markets such as those on stock indices. In Figure 10.6, a table has been reproduced from Morgan Stanley Equities Analytical Research, which displays the relationship between the implied volatility for the S&P 100 index options (OEX) and the subsequent actual realised volatility for the underlying index over the next 2 months.

The reader can see that the options markets do not necessarily hold to the as-sumptions of the theoretical options pricing models.[11] The implied volatility tends over time to be consistently higher than the actual volatility that occurred over the future period the implied was attempting to estimate. Apart from the 1987 crash period, when the actual volatility line crossed the implied volatility, option sellers seem to have the edge. According to Morgan Stanley, since 1983 the gap between the theoretical values of S&P 100 options and their market prices has averaged two to three volatility points and this has not disappeared through time. Thus, it appears

---

[11]Most probably the reason why the implied volatility is systematically higher than then the subsequent actual volatility is due to the substantial transaction costs required to arbitrage the discrepancy.

that there may be something in my casino example after all regarding the added value covered call writing strategies can provide to the hedger.

HEDGING EXAMPLE 4: SELLING PUT OPTIONS IN ANTICIPATION OF THE PURCHASE OF A U.S. TREASURY BONDS

In this final section of Chapter 10, I will discuss another possible hedging strategy which is to sell put options against an anticipated purchase of an asset. This is considered a hedging strategy when the investor has a short position in the T-Bond market. As it was the case with the call buyer, the investor may not actually have sold short the security but might have a position where he will profit or lose from market movements as if he were short. The classic example of this is someone who anticipates buying a U.S. Treasury Bond at some point in the future. When he sets his cash aside in anticipation of a purchase and sells put options to protect himself, the hedging strategy is referred to as cash secured put writing.

Imagine the following situation. The yield for the 9.25% U.S. Treasury Bond is currently at 7.743% on 11 July and you are interested in buying this T-Bond. However, you believe that the yields will improve to 8.27% shortly. If you bought this bond today and yields did increase, you would experience a capital loss on your investment. Therefore, you decide not to buy now but to wait. One thing you could do is put in an order with your broker to buy the T-Bond for you when the yields rise to 8.27% and keep you money in deposits until the time your order is filled. But suppose instead, you decided to make use of the T-Bond options market to achieve your 8.27% yield. With a few calculations, it is easy to determine that at a 8.27% yield the T-Bond futures price should be around 96-00/32. So you could place an order to buy the T-Bond futures at 96-00/32 (with the current price at 101-15/32) and hope for the best. However, this is the equivalent to placing a limit order to buy the cash market. Another thing you could do is assume the obligation to buy the T-Bond futures at 96-00/32 and if you play your cards right, someone will pay you a premium for agreeing to do so. Is this too good to be true? Well, no. You have just sold a 96-00/32 put option. Remember that when you buy a put option, you pay a premium and receive the right to sell. The put seller receives this premium and is obligated to buy from the put buyer upon exercise. If you are certain that you wish to buy at a 8.27% yield (or a futures price of 96-00/32), then the short put can be a clever alternative to placing your purchase order.

Results of the Cash Secured Put Writing Hedging Strategy

The profit/loss profile for this strategy can be seen in Figure 10.7. The reader will see that the payoff for the cash secured put writing strategy looks remarkably like the payoff for selling a "naked" call (that is an uncovered call). You will see that the combination of a short put with a short position in the underlying will provide the same payoff as selling a call option.

383

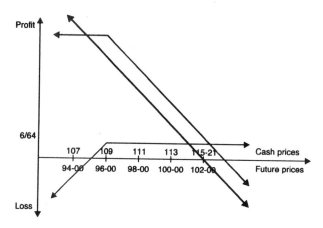

Figure 10.7 Cash Secured Put Strategy.

Cash secured put writing works particularly well when the yield curve environment is inverted. That means short term interest rates are higher than longer maturity yields. Let us look at a hypothetical situation in the U.S. Suppose an investor could receive a 9.00% return on short term money market instruments. At the same time, the best he could achieve in the longer end of the T-Bond market would be a 7.755% yield.

He may not wish to invest in long term debt that only offers an 7.755% return at this time, but he might be willing to buy T-Bonds if he could receive a 8.27% yield. Furthermore, suppose he feels the yields for the T-Bond market will rise for a while but will eventually drop. Therefore, he would invest all of his funds in the money markets and then enhance the yield on his short term instruments by selling the 96-00/32 put options. If rates increase above the 8.27% threshold, the put options he has sold will be exercised and he will have to buy the U.S. Treasury Bonds at the target yield of 8.27%. On the other hand, if yields remain below that 8.27% level, his investment will earn 9% for the investment period plus an additional 6/64s for each put option he sells (see Table 10.2 for the 96-00/32 put price).

As long as the yield curve remains inverted, the short term investment will be preferred. However, if the yield curve returns to its normal shape that will probably be associated with an increase in longer maturity yields. His put options will obligate him to purchase a long term T-Bond with a very attractive yield with the additional benefit of the put option premium income. Therefore, he can receive money for agreeing to buy the underlying at the yield in which he was interested in the first place.

While it is certainly possible for this strategy to be used for any underlying market where an investor is obligated to purchase an underlying asset, the most obvious application for institutions is in the stock market, where covered put writing strategies are used to synthetically underwrite stock purchases. It works like this[12].

---

[12]This section is based upon an article which appeared in Futures Magazine. The title is "Selling Puts Gives Life to Grim Repos", by Laurie Kaplan, *Futures*, August 1993, pp. 18-20.

Suppose a company would like to buy back its shares if the price fell to a certain level, for example $5 per share with the current share price at $7.50. The sale of the put options obligates the firm to buy back its shares at an attractive price and it receives a premium for doing so. Writing put options to offset the cost of a stock repurchase programme effectively guarantees that the company will be able to repurchase its stock at the strike price if the stock closes below the strike at expiration. If the stock does not fall below the strike, then the proceeds can be used to reduce the cost of an open market purchase of the stock at whatever the prevailing stock price turns out to be. Why would a firm do this?

Two reasons come immediately to mind. The first is that the company may feel its shares are undervalued and it wishes to build up its holding of treasury stock. Another reason is that the company may have initiated an employee stock option compensation plan and buying in shares via the put option sale would reduce any impact of dilution if the employees exercise their calls.

When one thinks about it, the company can hardly lose. The strategy makes so much sense that the only potential problem is that (as with most good ideas) regulators would not allow this to be done. Fortunately, in the United States, the Securities and Exchange Commission (SEC) which regulates the trading of stock options has arrived at the insightful conclusion that companies can sell put options against their own stock.[13] While this only applies to exchange traded stock options and not OTCs, the ruling clearly states what must be done to comply with SEC rules. Another potential problem as always is the accounting treatment of these transactions. Fortunately, this has been worked out in the following way: the premium received from the sale of the options on a company's stock is deemed a capital transaction and thus not subject to income taxes. This means that the inflows of premium and any subsequent purchase of the shares can be included in the accounts as a straight forward repurchase of stock.

Given that such companies as Intel and IBM have made use of this strategy, there is little doubt that firms world-wide will become more active in underwriting the purchase of their own shares using the covered put writing strategy.

SUMMARY

The purpose of this chapter has been to show the reader how to utilise a variety of hedging objectives to choose the most appropriate futures or options hedging strategy. I have presented detailed examples of hedging by purchasing both call and put options and how investors can sell options to increase yields and reduce risks. While it is possible to construct other hedging strategies using combinations of different option strike prices, these four basic hedging strategies should be enough to get the hedger ready to use options to reduce the risks of dealing in any underlying market.

---

[13]The SEC position is outlined by a no-action letter dated 16 February 1992 and addressed to Andrew Klein of Schiff, Hardin & Waite, solicitors to the Chicago Board Options Exchange.

11: Option Portfolio Application

This section discusses potential portfolio applications of options. It differs from the previous chapter in emphasis. The last chapter examined options in a tactical light. I examined how one could use call options as substitutes for the purchase of an underlying asset (a US Treasury Bond); how to buy puts to protect against declines; how to sell call options to enhance yields by expecting volatility to decrease; and how to write cash-secured put options in anticipation of a better price in the underlying market. In this chapter, I will place more emphasis on the strategic applications of options in portfolio management. The options contracts I will use to explain these concepts include the Standard & Poors 100 (S&P 100 or OEX) Stock Index option traded at the Chicago Board Options Exchange (CBOE) and options on the Standard & Poors 500 (S&P 500) Stock Index futures traded at the Index and Options Market (IOM) of the Chicago Mercantile Exchange. In addition, I will also examine the use of the S&P 500 Stock Index futures also traded at the IOM. The contract specifications for all these contracts can be seen in Tables 11.1a, 11.1b and 11.1c.

When one thinks of portfolio management, probably the underlying assets which will come to mind are shares since most of the breakthrough research on portfolio theory applied to stocks[1]. The conclusions of these seminal papers was

Trading Unit	$ 100 times the current value of the index
Expiration Months	Each of the four nearby months
Expiration Date	First saturday following the third friday of the expiration month
Premium Quotations	Dollars and fractions per unit of the index. each premium point represents $100. The minimum fraction is 1/16 (for series trading in first 4 nearby months) and 1/8 for all other long maturities.
Exercise Price	Five point intervals to bracket the current value of the index.

Table 11.1a S&P 100 Index Options (CBOE).

---

[1] The first of the major papers on Portfolio Theory was Markowitz, Harris M. "Portfolio Selection", Journal of Finance, March 1952 #7, pp. 77-91. In addition, the reader is referred to the ground breaking work on the Capital Asset Pricing Model (CAPM) by William F. Sharpe, "Capital Asset Prices: A Theory of Market Equilibrium under Conditions of Risk", Journal of Finance, September 1964 #19, pp. 425-442 and J. Linter, "The Valuation of Risk Assets and the Selection of Risky Investments in Stock Portfolios and Capital Budgets", Review of Economics and Statistics, February 1965 #47, pp. 13-37.

Trading Unit	One S&P 500 futures contract
Expiration Months	All twelve calendar months
Last Day Of Trading	March, June, September, December: Thursday prior to the third Friday. Other 8 months: the third Friday.
Minimum Price Movement (tick size)	0.05 index points = $ 25.00 per contract
Exercise Price Intervals	5.00 points
Trading Hours	8:30 - 15:15 (Chicago time)

Table 11.1b Options on S&P 500 Index Futures (CME).

Trading Unit	$500 times the current value of the index
Expiration Months	March, June, September, December
Last Day Of Trading	Thursday prior to the third Friday of the contract month
Minimum Price Movement (tick size)	0.05 index points = $ 25.00 per contract
Exercise Price Intervals	N/A
Trading Hours	8:30 - 15:15 (Chicago time)

Table 11.1c S&P 500 Index Futures (CBOE).

that the best way (in terms of expected risk and return) to invest in stock markets was to buy the entire market. To facilitate the measurement of the movement of the entire stock market, Stock Indices were constructed which measured either the entire stock market or a representative subset of that market. To understand why Stock Index futures and options are among the most actively traded of all derivative products, we must first understand the concepts of index construction and later I will examine the basics of portfolio theory that underlie these products.

BASICS OF STOCK INDICES²

A Stock Index is a measure of the value of a group of stocks. Stock indices are complied and published by various sources, including securities markets. An index may be designed to be representative of the stock market as a whole, of a particular broadly based sector, or of a particular industry. A Stock Index is ordinarily standardised relative to a "base" period when the index was first created. For example, suppose a new "value-weighted" index were created today with the total value of the component stocks (market prices times the number of shares outstanding) being equal to $25 billion. The publisher of the index will assign an arbitrary index level

---

²This section draws extensively from the publication, "Characteristics and Risks of Standardised Options", published by the Options Clearing Corporation, pp. 32-34.

of say 500. He does this by dividing the value of the stock portfolio today ($25 billion) by the value at the base period which is also today ($25 billion) and multiplies this result by 500. If the market value of the component stocks in the index rose tomorrow by 2.5% to be worth $25.625 billion, then the new value of the index would be $25.625 billion/$25 billion x 500 or a new level of 512.50. Thus the index level would rise by the same amount (2.5%) as the value of the underlying portfolio.

This base may be adjusted from time to time to reflect such events as changes in the capitalisation or to maintain continuity as stocks are added or deleted from the index group. These changes are generally done to assure that any changes in the index level will result only as a result of price changes occurring from trading.

There are a variety of ways of calculating Stock Indices. The most popular indices referred to by institutional investors (like the Standard & Poors Stock indices), are "value weighted" indices. This means that the market prices of the stocks included in the index are each multiplied by the number of shares outstanding. Because of this method of calculation, changes in the stock prices of larger corporations will generally have a greater influence on the level of the index compared with the price changes of smaller corporations.

Another popular method for index construction is the "price weighted" index. These indices simply sum the prices of the component shares and divide by the value of the shares in the base period. Popular price indices include the Dow Jones Industrial Average, the Nikkei Dow Index and the Major Market Index (which trades as a futures and options contract at the Chicago Board of Trade and elsewhere). These price indices allow each Stock in the index to have more or less equal impact on the level of the index and are often preferred to the "value weighted" indices by traders who place more importance on price changes.

The final kind of Stock Index construction is known as a "geometric weighted" approach. These indices are based upon the percentage changes in either the "value" or the "prices" of the component shares in the index. The percentage changes of each of the components is summed and then multiplied by the level of the index in the previous period to provide the index value today. These have proved to be the least popular of the Stock Indices used by either institutional investors or traders. The Deutsche Aktien Index (DAX) which underlies futures and options contracts at the Deutsche Terminbörse (DTB) and Value Line index (which underlies futures and option contracts at the Kansas City Board of Trade) are examples of "value" weighted geometric indices and the Financial Times 30 is an example of a "price" weighted geometric index.

STOCK INDEX FUTURES CONTRACTS

The most popular of the Stock Index futures contracts on US equities is the Standard & Poors 500 Stock Index futures traded at the IOM. At the beginning of 1994, 69 Stock Index futures or options contracts were offered in 22 countries (30 of which trade in the US). This contract is equal to $500 times the futures price of the S&P 500 Stock Index. For example, with a price of 440.5, the value of one futures contract would be $500 x 440.50, or $2202.50. At the expiration of the futures contract, the final futures settlement price is set equal to the level of the cash S&P index on that day. The S&P 500 futures price will generally follow the movement of the underlying index, but the level will usually be different until the final day when they are exactly equal. The advantage of participating in the stock market with S&P 500 Stock Index futures rather than the actual stocks is that the position can be established in the futures market with only a margin payment and the excess funds can remain in more liquid assets such as deposits. Furthermore, the transaction costs involved in trading futures can be as little as 5% of the cost in purchasing (or selling) an equivalent amount in the cash market.

On the final settlement date for the S&P 500 futures, no delivery of shares occurs but rather there is a cash transferral equal to the difference between the level of the cash index and the level at which the futures contract was originally established. This procedure called "cash settlement" assures liquidity and efficient settlement of the contracts. Compared with the physical delivery of the T-Bond futures discussed in the last chapter, there is no "cheapest to deliver" into the Stock Index futures. The only underlying the hedger or trader need consider is the Stock Index itself. The contract specifications for the S&P 500 futures can be seen in Table 11.1c.

OPTIONS ON STOCK INDEX FUTURES CONTRACTS

Also traded at the IOM are options on S&P 500 Stock Index futures. These contracts are the right but not the obligation to buy or sell an S&P 500 futures contract any time before the option expires. Exercise of the option prior to expiration will result in an S&P 500 futures contract position being assigned to the holder on the next business day (and the writer will be assigned an opposite position in the S&P 500 futures). This was discussed in detail in Chapter 1 with the COMEX gold option. At the expiration of the option contract, cash settlement also occurs as it does for the futures contract. The cash inflow for the call option holder will be equal to the amount the cash S&P 500 Index is above the call's strike price (if the Index is equal to or less than the call strike price, no cash is transferred). The cash inflow for the put option holder will be equal to the amount the S&P 500 Index is below the put's strike price (if the Index is equal to or greater than the put strike price, no cash is transferred). The contract specifications for the option on S&P 500 futures is displayed in Table 11.1b.

OPTIONS ON STOCK INDICES

Index options are very similar to stock options and are traded in essentially the same manner. The most popular of the options on a US Stock index is the S&P 100

Stock Index option traded at the Chicago Board Options Exchange (CBOE). The underlying index is similar to the S&P 500 index. The S&P 100 index includes the stocks of those corporations which are roughly the 100 largest corporations in the S&P 500. The major difference between stock options and Stock Index options is how exercise is handled. When the S&P 100 Stock Index option is exercised, the settlement is made by the payment of cash and not by the delivery of stock. The assigned writer is obligated to pay the exercising holder cash in an amount equal to the difference between the current level of the S&P 100 Stock Index and the exercise price of the option times $100. The difference between options on Stock Indices and options on Stock Index futures is that upon exercise, the holder of the option on the Stock Index receives cash and the holder of the option on the Stock Index futures receives a position in the futures market. The contract specifications for S&P 100 Stock Index option can be found in Table 11.1a.

Now that I have introduced the products, I will later devote considerable time to the concept of risk and return and the rationale for Stock Index trading generally. In addition, I will examine how options and futures on Stock Indices allow the portfolio manager to restructure the patterns of his portfolio returns and control his risks. In addition, I will explain some of the most popular portfolio applications of options on Stock Indices namely the 90/10 money market and the 90/10 plus strategies, zero cost options, portfolio insurance and delta neutral strategies. Then I will examine how options impact the risks of equities portofolios. Finally, I will conclude the chapter with examples of possible portfolio payoffs associated with the most popular futures and options hedging strategies. The first topic I will discuss is a popular call option buying strategy, known as 90/10.

THE 90/10 MONEY MARKET STRATEGY

The 90/10 strategy is the name often applied to an investment in interest bearing securities (typically short term) and the purchase of option contracts in some underlying market. The expression "90/10" comes from the convention of allocating 90% of the investor's asset in risk-free money market instruments and 10% in options. These are also known as guaranteed return funds.

Consider, a US. portfolio manager who finds that short term rates are particularly attractive in the current environment and who believes the stock market is poised for a rally. He may wish to invest in short term money market rates which are presently high and at the same time benefit if the stock market stages a dramatic increase. The objective is to earn the high short term interest rates, but also to have the option to benefit from the potential capital gain associated with an increase in the value of the stock market.

Suppose that he has $10,000,000 to invest on 15 June, the yield on six month money markets is at 6% and the price of the cash S&P 500 Stock Index is 444.72. The December S&P 500 futures is trading at 451.40 and a variety of options are where the 440 call is priced at 23.96, the 445 call is priced at 21.23, the 450 call is priced at 18.71, the 455 call is priced at 16.42 and the 460 call at 14.32. These five options give him the right to buy the December futures at prices of 440,445,450,455 and 460 respectively (Table 11.2).

As discussed before, the rationale for this strategy is to benefit from the expectation that the stock market will rally dramatically in the next 6 months. However, because short term interest bearing securities are presently more attractive than the dividend yield for the S&P 500 stocks (about 3%), the investor will place the bulk of his funds there. Thus, the portfolio manager would place 90% of his $10,000,000 on the money market at 6% rate in a deposit which matures in six months on 15 December. With the remaining 10%, he would purchase call options on December S&P 500 futures.

6 MONTH MONEY MARKET RATE	6.00%
S&P STOCK INDEX	444.72
DEC S&P 500 FUTURES	451.40
VOLATILITY	14.50%
	PRICES
DEC 440 CALL	23.96
DEC 445 CALL	21.23
DEC 450 CALL	18.71
DEC 455 CALL	16.42
DEC 460 CALL	14.32

Table 11.2 90/10. Market Conditions (15 June).

Suppose that he chooses to purchase call options with a strike price of 455. With the $1,000,000 allocated to the purchase of options, he could purchase 121 options giving him the right to purchase $27,527,500 worth of S&P 500 futures (the strike price of 455 · $500 · 121). The investment of $9,000,000 in a 6% money market security will provide a return to the investor of the $9,000,000 plus interest which in total is $9,270,000 in six months. The worst that can happen to the calls is that they expire worthless. So the investor knows the minimum value his portfolio can have in this worst case. He could vary the allocation mix to be somewhat different from 90 per cent/10 per cent. Suppose, he places 97.09% of his funds in money market deposits and the remaining $291,000 he purchases the 455 call options. He can still purchase 35 options which give him the right to buy $7,962,500 worth of S&P 500 futures (the strike price of 455 · $500 · 35). In this case, the money market security will provide a cash inflow of $10,000,000 on 15 December and no matter what happens to the Stock market, he will have guaranteed to recoup his initial investment. In addition, he would have the right to hold a position which represents 79.6% of the magnitude of what he would hold by placing all of his funds in Stocks in the S&P 500. By varying the allocation ratio devoted to options from 10% to 0%, he can achieve a minimum payback on this investment strategy from between $9,270,000 and $10,300,000.

The 90/10 Plus Strategy for Options with Futures Style Margining

At a number of exchanges (for example the LIFFE and Sydney Futures Exchange), the ability to margin the call options purchase means that the 90/10 strategy is even more advantageous and I will rename it the 90/10 money market plus strategy. In a traditional 90/10, 90% of the assets are placed in a money market instrument, and 10% remains. At the exchanges with futures style margining of option premium, the option is not paid up front, but the position is margined and one pays the premium ultimately at expiration. These exchanges allow you to use a variety of interest bearing securities as the basis for margin. These instruments generally include short term Government paper and sometimes Government bonds. Theoretically, one could place the entire $10,000,000 in one of these instruments and leave it at the exchange as the basis for purchasing the options. For example, he could invest all of the US Dollars in one of these instruments that matures in 6 months and provides a 6% yield and would know with certainty that on 15 December $10,300,000 would be returned. The clearing house treats this as an initial margin payment and it will guarantee the position. Therefore, because all of the money is in a 6% investment, he can simply use the interest he earns to purchase options and can leave the principal of $10,000,000 untouched.

With the $300,000 in interest earned he can buy even more options. For example, if such futures style margining were available at the IOM, the price for a single option would have been 16.78. Therefore, the number of 455 call options that could be purchased would have been 36 (one additional option), equivalent to $8,190,000 worth of S&P 500 futures. In the worst case, if the options expire worthless, the investor gets back his $10,000,000.

If the stock market actually rallies, the S&P 500 futures price will increase and the call options will provide 81.9% of the profits associated with a holding of 10 million in actual shares. Any profit from this would be added to the investors holdings. As, at the futures style margined exchange, the option premium is ultimately paid at expiration when the instrument pays its interest, the portfolio manager knows a priori his cash flows. So, the investor looking to implement a 90/10 strategy should see if the exchange he is dealing on allows this extra bonus. However, for the IOM this feature is not possible, so we will return to the original strategy of the 90/10.

Result of the 90/10 Call Option Buying Strategy

If the investor decides that he wants to apply the 90/10 strategy but guarantee that his initial endowment is returned, he will not use a 90%/10% allocation ratio, but will choose instead a 97.09 per cent/2.91 per cent allocation ratio. As was shown above, this will assure that $10,000,000 will be returned regardless of what happens to the stock market by December. The result on 15 June is that the investor is guaranteed the preservation of his capital and irrespective, will recover his $10,000,000. In addition, he has the chance to buy the S&P 500 index at a price of 455 for 35 contracts. These 35 contracts would be equivalent to $7,962,500 US Dollars worth of S&P 500 futures. The profit/loss profile for this strategy can be seen in Figure 11.1. As you can see in this graph, regardless of what happens to the stock market, the portfolio will be worth $10,000,000.

However, consider that the stock market does rally above 455, which implies that the options are in-the-money. Since the options are in-the-money and thus have a delta close to 1, he has the equivalent of $7,962,500 million US Dollars worth of S&P 500 futures. This is a fair amount of leverage, since his capital is guaranteed.

What else could the investor do to achieve a similar position? On the other hand, he could have chosen the strategy of buying the equivalent in S&P 500 futures and also placing a US government security with the clearing house of the IOM for his margin requirement (futures contracts can be margined with such securities). Again, this position would provide the $300,000 in interest and no option premium would be required. But he would face an unlimited loss potential from an unfavourable move in stock prices; if stock prices decrease, the S&P 500 futures will also decrease and his loss potential is unlimited. In Figure 11.2, this strategy is compared with the 97.09/2.91 strategy. The reader can see that the futures strategy is better off by the $300,000 interest earned but the loss potential is unlimited and the futures is more geared.

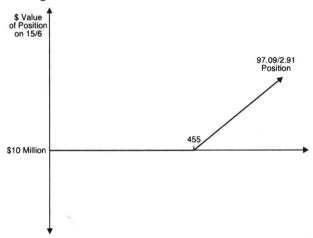

Figure 11.1 Profit/Loss Profile of Guaranteed Capital Fund.

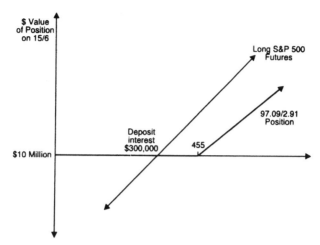

Figure 11.2 Long S&P 500 Futures versus Capital Fund.

What about the strategy of simply placing the investment in the Stock Market? In this case, if the dividend rate is only 3.0%, then the investment will earn over the period $150,000 in dividends. Once again, the loss potential is substantial, similar to that of the S&P 500 futures.

Suppose the investor is willing to take some risk and implements the 90/10 strategy instead. With this strategy $9,270,000 will be returned regardless of what can happen to the stock market by December. Moreover, the investor can buy the S&P 500 index at 455 for 121 contracts. This is equivalent to the purchase of $27,527,500 worth of shares if the underlying S&P 500 index rises above 455. Figure 11.3 shows the comparison between this position and the strategy of buying the equivalent in S&P 500 futures (obtaining also the $300,000 in interest).

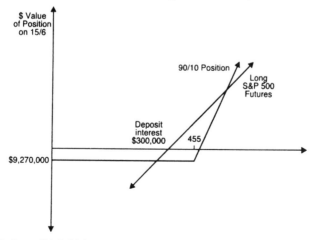

Figure 11.3 Long S&P 500 Futures versus 90/10 Geared Fund.

395

The reader can see that the 90/10 strategy is highly levered. If the underlying S&P 500 market increases, the position has 2.753 times more "punch" than simply purchasing the S&P 500 Stock portfolio (with the 97.09/2.91, the leverage would have been only 0.796, but the initial investment of $10,000,000 would have been assured regardless of any decrease in the stock market). If the market remains at the same level, buying the underlying instrument and receiving the dividends, or just buying the futures contract and leaving the endowment in deposits earning (6% or $300,000) would be the more profitable alternatives. But with the levered position of the 90/10 strategy, this strategy will only win if the underlying market rises. If the stock market falls by 15 December, the investor lets the options lapse, but must realise the loss of $730,000 (his original investment of $10,000,000 minus the return of the 90% on deposit which will return $9,270,000). However, it may very well be that the reason the stock market fell was an increase in short term interest rates. Thus, the investor may be able to reinvest his $9,270,000 at the higher money market rate which may allow him to make up for the loss in the first period of the strategy. If he had instead employed the alternative strategy of buying the S&P 500 stock index and the market had fallen precipitously then the loss might be much larger than $730,000 and the option strategy would be preferable. If the stock market rallies, the investor has a position that is 2.753 times the size of his initial investment and will profit from the advantageous movement in this same multiple. Thus, the 90/10 strategy provides him with a maximum loss potential and increased leverage. Therefore, it is easy to see why this strategy is extremely popular among portfolio managers world-wide.

Most investment funds will go for the no loss of capital approach (in our example 97.09% in deposits and 2.91% in options) as opposed to the more risky 90/10 allocation ratio. The reader may surmise that for this product to both offer sufficient gearing and capital security, two elements must occur simultaneously in the market:

- Short Term Interest Rates must be relatively high, and
- Call Option Premiums must be relatively low.

These elements are both required because the cost of the options must be generated from the interest received on the deposit. If the interest that can be earned is higher, then given the price of the option (and the implied volatility) remains at the same level more gearing can be achieved for the same guaranteed return of capital. Suppose the interest rate in the above example was 7.50% instead of 6%. The investor would only have to put $9,638,554 on deposit for 6 months to return $10,000,000. With the remaining $361,446 he could buy 44 of the 455 call options ($361,446/$500 · 16.42) which would provide equivalent full exposure to the S&P 500. This is because 44 call options at a strike price of 455 are equivalent to $10,010,000 worth of the index (455 · 44 · $500). Unfortunately, it is unlikely that if interest rates rise the implied volatility of the stock market will remain the same.

Generally, speaking the higher the short term interest rate, the lower the stock market. Furthermore, there is evidence that the lower the stock market the higher the implied volatility of the options. Therefore, for the guaranteed return fund to work, there must be some combination of high interest rates and low stock market volatilities to provide the sufficiently attractive level of gearing with a capital preserving floor. For marketing purposes, funds must provide at least 100% of the increases in the underlying market with a guaranteed return of capital to be attractive. In addition, investors prefer having their money back as soon as possible, so the additional target of a short time horizon is seen as an added benefit. However, it is rare that all the conditions are just right to meet all of these demands which is why such guaranteed funds are often offered at the same moment or none are available at all. Many fund management houses create the basic structure of the guaranteed return fund and then shelve it waiting for the market conditions for such a gearing/guarantee trade-off to be sufficiently attractive and then immediately launch the funds.

Still, one can find guaranteed return funds available even when the market conditions would seem not to be able to provide sufficient interest income to pay for the required number of options. This is done by varying the time horizon of the fund until the interest income finally covers the payment of a sufficient number of options to provide 100% coverage. But how can a 6% level of interest ever pay for a 14% level of implied volatility? Would not one simply achieve lower and lower gearing the further out in time one goes? This would appear to be the case, until one remembers that the income from interest investments is a function of the time the money is on deposit while the impact of volatility on an options price is a function of the square root of time of the options life. Thus, as a approximation, the fund manager can offer a guaranteed investment fund with full protection of capital and 100% of the movement in the underlying asset by solving the following equation for the time horizon, t:

$$r \cdot t = \sigma \cdot \sqrt{t}$$

where:
    r is the interest rate for the period t
    t is the time period of the fund
    σ is the implied volatility of the options

Using the above numbers and solving for t, we find that 6% interest for 5.4444 years will pay for a 5.4444 year option at a 14% volatility. This number is estimated by dividing the volatility squared (σ^2) by the interest rate squared (r^2). In this example, it is (0.14 · 0.14) or 0.0196 divided by (0.06 · 0.06) or 0.0036, which yields 5.4444.

Of course, if some way could be found to increase the interest rate return or to reduce the cost of the option, either the gearing could be increased or the time horizon could be shortened. Recently, a number of extremely successful funds³ have been launched in the United Kingdom, applying this technique for a 5 year time horizon with an exotic equity option substituted for a normal option. The exotic option used is known as an Asian option which in volatility terms is about 57.7% of the cost of a normal option. It is therefore hardly surprising that this fund offered 100% gearing and a guaranteed return of £120 at the end of the five years for every £100 invested. Why this Asian option is so much cheaper will be explained in Chapter 13 of this book. If we analyse this product using the formula displayed above and assume a five year time horizon with a 7.25% interest rate and a 12% five year volatility, we can see where the extra £20 comes from solving the revised equation for the excess payout:

$$r \cdot t - (\sigma \cdot 0.577) \cdot \sqrt{t} = \text{excess payout}$$

Substituting the numbers above into this equation, we obtain:

$$7.25\% \cdot 5 - (12\% \cdot 0.577) \cdot \sqrt{5} = \text{excess payout}$$

$$36.25 - 15.48 = 20.77.$$

In the real world, compound interest would be used as would actual option prices, but the logic is sound. The fund was able to pay out £20 pounds in addition to the initial investment because there was more than sufficient interest to pay for the option, and after deducting 0.77% for the fund manager, the investor was able to receive the £20 bonus. Clearly, the success of funds like these will expand their use in fund management. However, I must reiterate, these funds are extremely sensitive to the levels of interest and the volatility of the underlying asset market. So, do not be surprised that when interest rates rise again and the stock market volatility is low, your mail box will be jammed with guaranteed return fund prospectuses from your investment advisor.

THE ZERO COST OPTIONS HEDGING STRATEGY

Another important and interesting use of options in portfolio management is to create profit/loss payoffs which are flat for certain levels of the underlying asset and fully exposed for other levels. One example of this kind of contingent hedge is the popular zero cost option. A zero cost option is a combination of two options. The primary selling point of this strategy is that people do not pay any premium to

---

³The fund I am referring to is the Foreign Colonial HYPO five year FTSE fund which attracted more than £500,000,000 in funds from private clients.

pick up the limited loss benefits of a long option hedging strategy. To do that, they must give up something and what they give up is the unlimited profit potential by selling another option. This technique involves buying and selling options in such a way that the premium inflow and the premium outflow offset each other. These strategies are also known as hedge wraps, collars, range forwards, or cylinders.

I learned of a situation where this trade occurred when I was trading options in London. A certain Japanese institution was concerned about its exposure to the US Dollar. They were interested in purchasing a currency option to cover this risk but were loath to pay a premium. They called their favourite currency broker and asked for help. The Japanese indicated a concern that the exchange rate for Yen for US Dollars might fall below 125 Yen per US Dollar. The current exchange rate was 130 Yen per US Dollar. So, the broker determined the price for a 125 Yen/US Dollar put option and informed the Japanese institution of the cost. The broker could tell from his client voice that the cost of the option was prohibitive. Being a smart broker, he suggested that the cost of the option could be reduced if the Japanese were willing to "give up" some of the unlimited profit potential if the US Dollar strengthened. The suggestion fell on responsive ears and he asked the Japanese clients what the upper limit was that they believed that Yen per US Dollar could be within the life of the option. They felt that 135 Yen/US Dollar was an acceptable ceiling. With this bit of information and the request by the Japanese client to reduce the premium expense as much as possible, the broker set to work.

His proposed strategy was to sell a 125 put option to his client and purchase back from the client a 135 call option. This would reduce the cost of the put options for the client, because the positive cash flow from selling the call option would be credited back to the Japanese client's account and would offset to some degree the cost of the put option.

After calculating the fair values for the put and call and calling a market maker to verify that deals could be done at those levels, the broker found to his delight that the call option was worth $75,000 more than the put. If we purchased the 125 put and sold the 135 call, the market maker would pay the broker this amount.

The broker then called back the Japanese client and informed him that not only could the cost be reduced, but that the cost of both transactions would exactly offset and the Japanese client could get the 125 put option "for free". The delighted client agreed at once to the transaction and the broker consummated the trades.

What occurred was that the Japanese client was so eager to reduce his premium expense that he actually accepted a hedging strategy that was a $75,000 "loser". The broker, on the other hand just pocketed the $75,000 and made his first down payment on a new Porsche.

This situation is not uncommon. These strategies of premium reduction often are most advantageous to brokers or market makers and can be disadvantageous to the client. Nevertheless, if a client can determine the fair prices of the options and makes sure that the broker gives him these prices, this type of strategy can make a lot of sense.

Suppose you are long a diversified portfolio of stocks that tracks the S&P 100 index underlying the options at the CBOE and you decide to purchase a S&P 100 put option to protect yourself. Of course, that will cost you a premium. To reduce the cost of the put, you could sell a call option against it. Generally, these trades are done with strike prices that are out-of-the-money. The zero cost hedger must simply find which strike prices have options with equal premiums. The net effect of this strategy is that the hedger will hedge his downside risk by limiting his upside potential. Let us go through an example with the S&P 100 options to see how this might work.

Zero Cost Option Hedging Strategy with Options on the S&P 100

Suppose on 13 June 1994, an investor wishes to protect his holdings of $5 million worth of US stock. The current price for the S&P 100 index is 418.70. The short term interest rate is 4.30% and the dividend yield for shares in the S&P 100 is equal to 3.0%. As I discussed in Chapter 3, the critical price is not the current price but the expected forward price. To determine the arbitrage free forward price on the last trading day of the options (20 August 1994), one simply multiplies the current Stock Index level by:

$$1 + (\text{interest rate} - \text{the dividend yield}) \cdot \frac{\text{number of days}}{365}.$$

This will provide a forward price for the S&P 100 Stock Index on 20 August of 419.71. The portfolio manager wants to protect himself with options on the S&P 100 but he must find two series of puts and calls that have exactly the same premium. Table 11.3 shows the range of S&P 100 options available on 13 June. He finds that the 410 put is offered at 6 and the 430 call is priced at 6 as well. He decides to purchase an out-of-the-money 410 put option to protect himself. It is out-of-the-money by about 8.70 index points relative to the current index and 9.71 index points relative to the estimated forward price. This option will cost him 6 index points in premium per option. The number of options he should purchase will be equal to the size of his holdings $5,000,000 divided by the contract value of this option. Each option allows him the right to sell the index at a price of 410 and the contract multiple is $100. Therefore, each 410 put option gives him the right to sell $41,000 worth of stock. In total, we divide $5,000,000 by $41,000 and come up with a hedge ratio of 122 options he must purchase. His total premium expense is 6 x $100 x 122 contracts or $73,200. In order to fund that cash outflow, he sells the August 430 call which is trading at 6. The hedge ratio for the number of these he should sell is determined by dividing $5,000,000 by $43,000 and this yields 117 contracts. The total amount of money he receives back is equal to $70,200. So in fact, the zero cost option in this example has produced a small outflow of $3,000.

With this strategy, the hedger expects either a dramatic drop in the stock market or a slow increase in the market, the latter being the more likely case. Figures 11.4a and 11.4b represent all the transactions plotted individually and the composite result. As the reader can see in Figure 11.4a, the 410 put option will offset the loss potential of the underlying stock portfolio when the market falls below 410. Above 430, the profit potential for the stock portfolio is "cut off" by the sale of the 430 call. In between these strike prices, the stock portfolio is unaffected by the options. The net effect represented in Figure 11.4b looks remarkably like the bull spread I discussed in Chapter 4.

MARKET CONDITIONS (JUNE 13)	
S&P 100 INDEX	418.70
SHORT TERM INTEREST RATE	4.30%
DIVIDEND YIELD (SHARES S&P 100)	3.00%
S&P 100 FORWARD PRICE	419.71
AUG 410 PUT	6
AUG 415 PUT	8
AUG 420 PUT	10 3/8
AUG 425 PUT	13 1/8
AUG 430 PUT	16 1/4
AUG 410 CALL	15 5/8
AUG 415 CALL	12 5/8
AUG 420 CALL	10
AUG 425 CALL	7 7/8
AUG 430 CALL	6

Table 11.3 Zero Cost Options Strategy.

This strategy has cut off the upside profit potential in exchange for cutting off the downside loss potential. On the other hand, if the hedger had used a short S&P 500 futures position to hedge, then he would have locked in the current level without any chance to profit if prices rose. Thus, the zero cost option strategy enables the hedger to choose a trade off between being completely hedged if the price of the stock market falls and unhedged in the range between the lower strike price to the higher strike price.

Comparison of the Zero Cost Options Hedge with a Futures Hedge

Let us compare in more detail the zero cost option hedge with S&P 100 options to a S&P 500 futures hedge. The futures hedge will have no loss potential and no gain potential, because it is an instantaneous and a fully hedged position. The futures

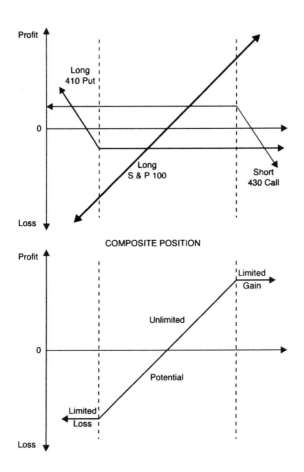

Profit

Long
410 Put

0

Long
S & P 100

Short
430 Call

Loss

COMPOSITE POSITION

Profit

Limited
Gain

Unlimited

0

Potential

Limited
Loss

Loss

Figures 11.4a & 11.4b Construction of Zero Cost Options Edge.

hedge is established with only a margin payment that can be established with interest bearing securities. Thus, I will claim that a futures hedge is also "zero cost". For the zero cost option strategy, I will also have no cost but with this hedging strategy my limited loss potential only occurs at levels at or below the strike price of the option I have purchased. My position is unhedged above that level until the underlying market price reached the level of the strike price for the option I have sold. Therefore, this strategy has a little downside risk and a little upside potential. If the market does drop dramatically I will still retain a fully hedged position.

If one expects a dramatic decrease in the stock market to occur and an equally dramatic drop in the S&P 100 or S&P 500 indices to occur, then the best hedging strategy is to sell S&P 500 futures. In case you expect a major rally in the stock market to occur, then the best course is not to hedge at all. However, as I have stated earlier, clairvoyance is not one of the pillars of modern financial theory, so given there is risk what is the best thing to do? With the zero cost option, the position is hedged at the level of 410 for the S&P 100 or below. Between 410 and 430, you retain the good and bad features of your underlying stock market portfolio. Should the stock market slowly drift up then you make money on this position, and should it dramatically fall one has a predetermined maximum loss potential.

If you wish to use this strategy, it is critical that you must determine what the fair prices are for the options. The aim is to cover what you plan to pay in premium with what you will receive back. Remember the story about the Japanese client. Many brokers make considerable money with this strategy by relying on their clients naiveté. Many clients who do not fully understand how options work will refuse to pay a premium. The broker will then provide the client with this kind of strategy for "free" when the client should have been paid a premium. The brokers will instantly cover their position and make a risk-free profit.

PORTFOLIO INSURANCE

The next topic I will discuss is portfolio insurance. I will examine both a dynamic asset allocation portfolio insurance method using a dynamic trading strategy in a stock portfolio and S&P 500 futures and compare this to purchasing put options on S&P 500 futures.

Basic Concepts In Portfolio Theory

To properly discuss portfolio insurance and to understand the rationale for Stock Indices, we need to go back to the basics of portfolio theory: the trade-off between risk and return.[4] The classical risk/return trade-off assumes that the more risk you take the more return you will expect. Furthermore, the risk of a particular investment will be defined by its variance of return, which is the square of the standard deviation.[5] Finally, with a portfolio of more than one asset, the risk of the portfolio will be defined by the proportion invested in each asset multiplied by its particular risk and the correlative relationship that asset has with other investments in the portfolio. Suppose, the capital market is composed of two kinds of assets: risky assets (like the stock market) and risk-free assets (like short term pure discounted Government paper) and we are interested in assessing the risk of this two asset

---

[4] In some ways, this was covered in Chapter 9 when I introduced the concept of Beta which allows the investor to compare the volatilities of stocks with the volatilities of the stock indices these stock comprise. In this section, we will address the foundations of the theory which the Beta concept is based upon and in this way is a compliment to Chapter 9.

[5] If one assumes the Capital Asset Pricing Model, then the risk of a particular asset is its risk relative to the portfolio of all assets and this is called the Beta. For a thorough and simple introduction to these concepts, the reader should read Brealey, Richard and Stewart Myers, Principles of Corporate Finance, 4th Edition, 1993, McGraw-Hill, Chapters 7,8 and 9.

portfolio. The formula for the expected return for this combination is the proportion invested in each asset multiplied by each assets expected return. For example, let us assume we have as our two assets a stock portfolio which we expect to make 12.5% on in the investment horizon and a risk-free US government Treasury Bill yielding 7% and we decide to invest 50% in each. Then the expected return will be 0.50 x 12.5% + 0.50 x 7% for an overall expected portfolio return of 9.75%.

The risk as stated above will depend on the risk of each security, the proportion invested in each and their correlations. The formula for the standard deviation of this two asset portfolio is:

$$\sqrt{x_1^2\sigma_1^2 + x_2^2\sigma_2^2 + 2x_1x_2\rho_{12}\sigma_1\sigma_2}$$

In this formula, the x_1 is the proportion invested in the risky stock portfolio, the x_2 is the proportion invested in the risk-free deposit, σ_1^2 and σ_2^2 are the variances of each of these assets. Respectively, σ_1 and σ_2 are the standard deviations for these assets and ρ_{12} is the correlation coefficient which indicates how these assets' returns move together.

Now imagine a portfolio investment strategy which is 50% in the risky stock portfolio and 50% in the risk-free assets. Given that the σ^2 (variance) of the risk-free asset is zero, what is the risk of the entire portfolio? If one looks at the above formula for the portfolio standard deviation, one will see that the σ_2 (or the σ_2^2) appears in both the second and third term. If this value is set to zero, then the total portfolio risk is simply defined as $\sqrt{x_1^2\sigma_1^2}$. Once one takes the square root, the equation reads in English: the portfolio risk is equal to the proportion invested in the stock portfolio multiplied by its standard deviation. Unfortunately, the expected return for the stock portfolio is not that easy to estimate; however it is possible to determine the expected return for the stock market by looking at historical returns or by subscribing to the numerous forecasting services. In this example, my trusty investment advisor provided the input of 12.5%. Where does one get the expected standard deviation? If the reader goes back to Chapter 4 and looks again at the concept of implied volatility, he will see that this is the expected standard deviation for the underlying asset. Therefore, the options market plays a critical role in providing expectations of what risk will be over a particular investment horizon (until the expiration of the options contract). With these bits of information, we can determine easily what we expect to gain on this simple portfolio and what the risk is expected to be over its life.

The Foundations of Portfolio Insurance

As the investor changes the allocation percentages between the risk-free asset and the risky asset, he can either reduce his risk and hence his expected return or increase both. When he has invested 100% in the risk-free asset, his standard deviation or volatility is zero and his expected return is 7%. If he invests 100% of his asset in the stock portfolio his expected return is 12.5% and his standard deviation can be estimated by the implied volatility for the stock portfolio options that expire at the date of his investment horizon. Let us assume that this implied standard deviation (volatility) is 15% per year. With these numbers, we can estimate the price of the risk. By being fully invested in the stock portfolio as opposed to the risk-free asset, he picks up an additional 5.5% in yield. For this pickup, he must assume an additional 15% risk, so the "price of risk" is 5.5%/15% or 0.37 percentage points in return for each 1% in additional risk he takes.

These concepts were fundamental to the development of the hedging strategy known as portfolio insurance. Basically, how portfolio insurance works is that the portfolio manager will dynamically shift his asset allocation mix between the risk-free asset and the risky asset as the price of the risky asset changes. When the risky asset's price rises, the investor places more of his investment there. Conversely, as the risky asset's price falls, the investor shifts his investment to the risk-free investment. Simply said, this implies that when the stock market rises, you buy more of it (using the proceeds of selling a proportion of your risk-free asset) and when the market falls, you sell out of the stock portfolio (putting the proceeds into the risk-free asset). This strategy is an attempt to achieve downside portfolio protection and provide for an unlimited profit potential as the value of the stock portfolio rises. Let us stop here and consider what the portfolio manager is trying to achieve. He wants a limited loss potential and an unlimited profit potential. What does that sound like? It is exactly the same rationale as that for purchasing an option.

Thus, as the market starts to go up, you shift your allocation base to those riskier assets and as markets are falling you shift out of them and into risk-free assets where you are guaranteed a risk-free rate. How does this strategy actually work? Generally, the investor starts out with 50% in risky assets at a current market price and 50% in the risk-free asset, such as short term deposits. As the market for risky assets starts to fall, the investor will at certain predetermined points, commonly referred to as trigger points, sell a percentage of his stock portfolio and place the proceeds on deposit. For example, if the market price of the stock portfolio drops from its current level by 5%, the portfolio manager may sell 20% of his stocks. Then his allocation percentages would be 40% in stock and 60% in the risk- free asset. If the stock market falls another 5%, again he would sell another 20% of his stocks, at that point 30% of his holdings would be in stock and 70% in the risk-free asset. This process continues as the stock market falls until at some point he would be completely out of stock and completely invested in the risk-free investment. Figure 11.5 displays the profit/loss profile for this dynamic allocation strategy as the price of the stock market falls. As the reader can see, the loss potential is limited at some point. However until the position is fully hedged, the portfolio will incur losses from having to wait for the trigger points at which the portfolio insurer will sell the falling stock.

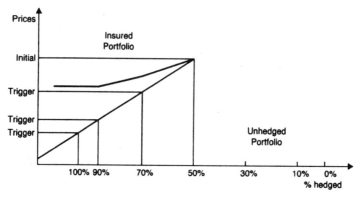

Figure 11.5 The Dynamic Allocation Strategy as the Stock Market Falls.

If, on the other hand, the stock market rises, the process is reversed. For example, imagine that stock prices rise by 5%. The portfolio manager will sell a proportion of his holdings in the risk-free security and use the proceeds to buy more stock. At that point, his allocation percentages will be 60% in stock and 40% in the risk-free asset. Again as the stock market continues to rise, this process is repeated until he has invested entirely in stock. The profit/loss diagram for this strategy when the stock market rallies is shown in Figure 11.6.

Finally, let us combine these two graphs to see how the strategy would appear over the entire range of possible stock market prices. This is done in Figure 11.7. The reader can see that the profit/loss profile for this strategy looks remarkably like that of a call option prior to expiration. It is a call option with both intrinsic and time value. The reader who reviews the original Black and Scholes paper will realise that this is the expected outcome. For the Black and Scholes model was solved

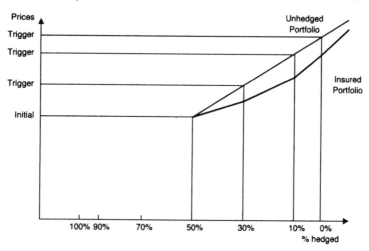

Figure 11.6 The Dynamic Allocation Strategy as the Stock Market Rises.

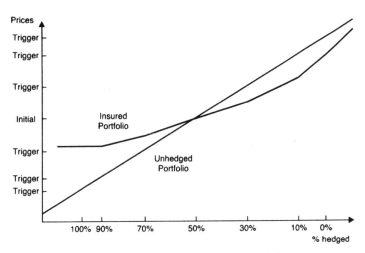

Figure 11.7   The Expected Profit & Loss Profile for Portfolio Insurance versus the Profit & Loss of an Unhedged Stock Market Portfolio.

using a similar allocation process to determine the fair value of the call option. By shifting between the risky asset and the risk-free asset, they were able to create a portfolio which mimicked the payoff of a call option. Since they were able to determine the values for the risky asset and the risk-free asset in their "equivalent" portfolio, they were also able to determine the call option's price. Their fundamental problem was to determine the amount of each asset to hold in order to create that equivalent portfolio. Here enters the heat transfer equation which provided them with the proper hedge ratio to create that equivalent portfolio. We now know this statistic as the delta.

Going back to our example, our portfolio insurer initially invested 50% of his investment in the risky stock portfolio. The reader may recall that, in Chapter 3, 50% figured quite prominently with the delta concept. When an option is at-the-money, the delta is approximately 50%. This is not simply an accident that the asset proportion for the risky stock is also 50%. Consider the case where the underlying stock price falls. In the portfolio insurance scheme, the hedger will systematically reduce his holdings (and the associated exposure) in the stock portfolio. This is exactly what happens to the delta of the call option. The call option's relative exposure (which is the delta) to the underlying stock market will also fall as the price of the stock market falls. Furthermore, at some point, the call option's delta will be zero as will the holdings in the stock market be for the portfolio insurer. When the underlying stock prices rise, the delta of the call will also rise. Likewise, the insured portfolio will increase its exposure in the stock portfolio until there is a 100% exposure in this risky asset. Essentially, portfolio insurance is the creation of a synthetic call option on the risky asset, in our case a well diversified US stock portfolio, by dynamically trading the underlying stock market.

The Relationship between Portfolio Insurance and Options

Basically, that describes the manner in which portfolio insurance is supposed to operate. But what happens in practice? To see if the technique actually fulfils its promise, we should review the assumptions the strategy is based upon. As I stated earlier, the aim of portfolio insurance is to replicate a Black and Scholes call option. Since this is the case, the assumptions underlying portfolio insurance and Black and Scholes call options are the same. Therefore, we will review the assumptions of the Black and Scholes options pricing formula to understand the potential flaws of portfolio insurance better.

Two of Black and Scholes most fundamental assumptions are that markets trade continuously (without transaction costs) and that the market variance is constant. Since portfolio insurance is based upon these same assumptions, these conditions must also hold for portfolio insurance to work. Are these assumptions correct? In the US stock market (and almost all other markets except foreign exchange), the market does not trade around the clock (although selected stocks like IBM do). Furthermore, we know that the risk of the stock market (measured by the volatility) is not constant. So it is clear that these assumptions are incorrect.

The important question becomes: What are the implications for portfolio insurance (and indeed option markets) if the fundamental assumptions underlying it are violated? For instance, suppose you wanted to apply portfolio insurance to a particular US stock portfolio. This would require shifting your asset allocation between short term US money market instruments and the stock portfolio continuously. To truly work, the transaction costs involved would have to be extremely low and the portfolio manager must have access to these markets on a 24 hour basis. We know that this is not the case. The high transaction costs alone would quickly reduce the profit potential for this strategy. In addition, the volatility of the stock markets is certainly not stable. The reader can verify this fact by looking at Figure 2.15 in Chapter 2 for the IBM stock. In that table, we will see that stock volatility does vary considerably over time. Why then do so many portfolio managers world-wide use portfolio insurance when the two most fundamental assumptions underlying its use are flawed?

Reasons for the Use of Portfolio Insurance

There are a number of possible reasons for the use of this strategy in portfolio management. I believe that at least three reasons are pre-eminent. Initially, this potentially dangerous strategy is veiled behind the term "Portfolio Insurance" and insurance has the connotation of risk reduction. Therefore, an aggressive portfolio manager might be able to have the strategy approved by the investment committee of his financial institution by claiming that this strategy will "insure" the portfolio. Secondly, portfolio insurance is a technique for trading volatility. If one expects the actual market volatility to be less than the volatility implied in options prices, one can create an "option-like" position for a smaller expected cost. In addition, if the market fails to move at all (implying that the realised volatility is much lower than was expected), then the insured portfolio will not lose anything. If this occurs for the purchase of an option the portfolio manager will suffer the loss of the premium. Finally, the introduction of alternative securities which have greater liquidity and lower transaction costs (compared with the cash stock portfolio) might make this strategy feasible. With the introduction of the S&P 500 futures at the IOM, such an alternative security became available. With S&P 500 futures, the portfolio insurer simply substitutes a short S&P 500 futures position instead of selling the stock portfolio. He will also buy the S&P 500 futures when he wants to increase his exposure to the risky stock market.[6]

Portfolio Insurance with Stock Index Futures

Even when using S&P 500 futures, one is still attempting to create a synthetic call option. It is most probable that this will require a large number of transactions in S&P 500 futures to work. Imagine that a particular S&P 500 futures contract became illiquid at the IOM or perhaps that the stock market moved when the IOM was closed. This could be disastrous to the portfolio insurance strategy because in these cases it would be impossible to continuously rebalance the portfolio mix. In addition, even if the IOM was open and fairly actively trading, if other portfolio managers were using the same strategy at the same trigger prices, they would join you, doing the same trades at the same time. So, when the market rises, you are buying with everybody else, and when the market falls, you will be selling with everybody else. Even with only 15% of futures trading volume associated with this kind of strategy (as is the estimates with the S&P 500 Stock Index futures in the US) this "lemming" effect could be destabilising. For example, whenever the market falls, portfolio insurance strategies would then by definition sell more, causing the market to fall further and, thus triggering more portfolio insurance selling until the whole process spirals out of control. While the jury is still out on the causes of the 1987 stock market crash, there can be little doubt that these kinds of dynamic "hedging" strategies played a role.[7] Thus, in some markets, it appears that portfolio insurance is a key element of the market dynamics and this has certainly proved to be the case with the US stock market. Nevertheless, while the liquidity is adequate on the IOM, the coverage cannot extend around the clock and the risks of overnight moves in the stock market may make this strategy unsuitable. This has spurred the

[6]For a good introduction to the use of futures in hedging a Stock Portfolio, the reader is referred to Kolb, Robert W. "Understanding Futures Markets", Scott, Foreman Co., 1988.

[7]For an interesting review of the effect of Portfolio Insurance and other kinds of Programmed Trading strategies on the 1987 stock market crash the reader is referred to: Well Fargos Investment Advisors, "Anatomy of a Decline: The Role of Index-Related Trading in the Market's Records Fall" 9, November 1987.

Chicago Mercantile Exchange (and a number of world-wide exchanges) to set up a 24 hours market which has been christened GLOBEX. This new development may substantially reduce the risk of overnight moves in the stock market for portfolio insurers.

However, why should the investor consider dynamic portfolio insurance given its chequered track record (the crash of 1987 is just one example). Since the allocation ratio in the dynamic strategy is defined by the delta of a hypothetical option, why try to replicate an option using a dynamic asset allocation strategy when one could go directly to the options market? Let us now see how put options on S&P 500 futures can provide a purer insurance protection to the portfolio manager.

Portfolio Insurance with Put Options on S&P 500 Futures

In the options market, when you buy a put option you purchase the guaranteed right to sell at a specific price level. The put option hedge has a limited loss and an unlimited profit potential. Therefore, like portfolio insurance, you can eliminate the risk of your stock position when the market goes down. When the stock market goes up, the option is ignored, allowing you to have an overall position that is similar to the insured portfolio. In fact, this portfolio is truly insured. You pay your "stock insurance premium" to achieve a hedged position. The profit/loss profile for the put option "portfolio insurance" can be seen in Figure 11.8.

If one thinks about it logically, the Black and Scholes fair value of the put is the cost of the equivalent portfolio which tries to synthetically recreate it being something like a portfolio insurance scheme. Given the high transaction costs in the US. stock market and the fact that the US stock market and S&P futures and options contracts do not trade 24 hours, it is best to leave this kind of synthetic options

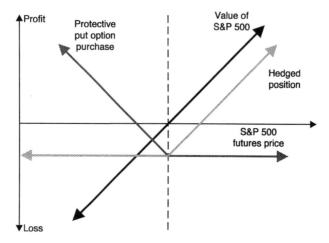

Figure 11.8 Portfolio Insurance with a purchased Put Option.

creation to those arbitrageurs who are best able to do it. The individual portfolio manager could be doomed to failure by attempting to create his own synthetic put option.

	PERCENT OF STOCK PORTFOLIO
REAL PUT OPTIONS	
- 2% ONE WAY COMMISSION	
- 1% ONE WAY SPREAD GIVE UP	0.48%
- 6 TRADES PER YEAR	
SYNTHETIC PUT OPTIONS	
A) FUTURES	
- $30 ROUND-TRIP COMMISSION PER CONTRACT	0.18%
- $25 SPREAD GIVE-UP	
- TURNOVER OF 2.5 TIMES PORTFOLIO VALUE	
B) CASH/STOCK TRANSACTIONS	0.56%

Table 11.4 Comparison of Portfolio Insurance Costs.

If the portfolio manager does try to insure his portfolio using the put option, at least he will know what the additional cost would be. Nevertheless, before deciding on a put option to insure his portfolio, he should compare the cost of the put option to the expected costs of the dynamic cash or futures strategy. In a study completed by Salomon Brothers in 1985, these costs were compared. Table 11.4 displays the costs for hedging a US stock portfolio with a variety of portfolio insurance schemes.

Cost Comparisons of Various Portfolio Insurance Techniques

The traditional method of dealing in the cash market to implement a portfolio insurance strategy had the greatest cost of 0.56% of the stock portfolios value per year. The second most expensive was the purchase of put options on Stock Indices which cost 0.48% and the cheapest alternative was using Stock Index futures contracts which only cost 0.18%. However, the reader must be careful when drawing conclusions about future performance. The 1987 crash and the 1989 mini crash demonstrated just how vulnerable the dynamic strategy can be.

THE FALLACY OF DELTA HEDGING A STOCK PORTFOLIO

In this section I will discuss delta hedging with options. This strategy can be considered an extension of the concept of portfolio insurance I have just discussed. The difference between these two techniques is that portfolio insurance is the dynamic trading of futures contracts in an attempt to replicate an option, while delta hedging is the dynamic trading of options to attempt to replicate the strategy of selling Stock Index futures.

Returning to Chapter 3, the reader will recall that the delta is the hedge ratio of the options relative to its particular asset. For options on Stock Index futures like the S&P 500 traded at the IOM the underlying asset is the S&P 500 futures. If, for example, the delta of a particular option on a S&P 500 futures is 0.60, when the futures rises by 10 basis points, the option will only rise by 6 basis points. The implication for the hedger seems obvious. If the hedger buys one option to hedge his exposure of a $2,000,000 cash stock portfolio and the market price fell, then he will be underhedged. Assuming that the stock portfolio moves exactly like the S&P 500 futures, if the cash stock portfolio drops in value by $10,000, the options profit will not necessarily be equal to that amount. If the option's delta is 0.5, then the gain will only be $5000. The only way that the option would provide "full" protection was if the delta of that option was 1.0.

Some authors (and a lot of brokers) use this fact to argue for increasing the number of options in the hedge ratio to take into account the delta factor. However, I find this logic to be fundamentally flawed and will attempt to prove this presently.

Suppose that a hedger decided to hedge a particular stock portfolio and he was considering the available alternative instruments. He could go short S&P 500 futures, buy put options or sell call options on the S&P 500 futures. However, the hedger wishes to have a limited loss potential and an unlimited gain potential because he is uncertain about where the market may go. Of the two bearish options strategies, the long put hedge will fit the bill. As a hedger, buying the put is the more conservative strategy. In fact, hedging by buying options as I have said is in many ways comparable to buying asset price insurance.

Suddenly, the hedger faces a dilemma. He remembers that the put option will not offset gains or losses of his underlying stock portfolio exactly because of the delta and therefore he considers delta-weighting the hedge ratio. This seems logical, especially since many people, myself included, refer to the delta as "the hedge ratio". *Beware!* Do not fall into the common trap of misinterpreting the delta and its appropriateness to the hedger. The delta tells you how many options you must have to replicate a single S&P 500 futures position. So, by delta-weighting your hedge ratio of put options, you have simply created a "short" futures equivalent position. The delta weighted put options position will benefit (or lose) from a drop (or rise) in the futures price exactly as if it were a short futures position.

For example, if you have an at-the-money option the delta will be approximately 0.5. So, you would need two of these options to get the same effect as one future contract. Our hedger, would therefore need to buy two at-the-money put options to equal one short futures. If the hedger needed 10 short futures contracts to hedge his cash market position and instead he decided to create the equivalent hedge by buying puts, he would have to buy 20 put options. These 20 put options will mimic 10 short futures contracts both when the market falls and when it rises.

Surely the reader can see that this is madness. The delta neutral hedger must not only pay twice as much transaction costs to establish the hedge but must also pay the premiums for the 20 options. These premiums will most probably be extremely expensive. If the hedger sold the 10 S&P 500 futures contracts, his transactions costs would be cut in half and there would be no option premium to pay. In addition, as I discussed above (with portfolio insurance) the futures hedge can be considered costless since only a margin is required (and the funds used for margin can earn interest). This fact alone begs the question: Why pay so much in option premium to duplicate what is essentially an almost costless futures contract? The answer is that one should shy away from this kind of hedging technique. You should use options in a hedging programme because you want the option to act like a futures contract when you need protection and act like nothing when you do not need protection. Options allow the hedger insurance benefits only if the hedger uses them correctly. Use the options for their own unique protection characteristics; do not try to dynamically reconstruct a futures contract with them.

So, what is the correct hedge ratio that should be used when using option contracts? The answer is to use the same number of options contracts as one would use if they used the S&P 500 futures underlying the option contracts. In this example, since we would use 10 short S&P 500 futures contracts to hedge, we should also buy 10 put options on S&P 500 futures if we decided to hedge.

The reader may still be wondering what his profit and losses will be if the underlying market falls and he is only holding 10 put options. It is true that the option profits will not completely offset his loss in the underlying asset initially. However, at the expiration of the option contract, he will be fully hedged if the market has fallen below the strike price of the option and fully unhedged if the market price is above that level. The key concept is to compare the options hedge over the long term, that means at the expiration day of the option. The hedger will have paid a premium but that is simply the cost of insurance. The delta neutral strategy outlined above can double this insurance cost. Therefore, delta neutral hedging can be thought of as a short-term hedging strategy. Clearly in the long run, it does not make sense and can actually increase the risk. Taking the example outlined above, if my true underlying exposure is 10 S&P 500 futures (equivalent) and I buy 20 put options, at expiration, my position could potentially be overhedged by a factor of two if the options finish in the money. Options are not the ideal instrument for short term hedging except when a contingent situation is involved. If one wishes to cover a short term exposure with complete coverage, futures contracts make much more sense.

HOW OPTIONS IMPACT THE BETA OF A PORTFOLIO

In Chapter 9, the concept of the Beta was introduced. As a brief review, the Beta is a measure of the relative risk of a stock to the market as a whole. In most instances,

413

a stock index is used as a surrogate for the overall market exposure. Most equity fund managers have a good working knowledge of Betas and thus, I will not spend an inordinate amount of time on this concept. However, apart from referring the reader to the previous chapter and the references in the footnotes of this chapter, I will concentrate on the application of the Beta in fund management instead of the theory.

In the last chapter, I discussed the determination of the hedge ratio for hedging US Treasury Bonds with futures or options. The basic formula for determining the appropriate number of contracts to use to hedge the exposure was:

$$\frac{\text{Nominal Value of Cash Position}}{\text{Nominal Value of Derivative Position}} \text{ times Risk Adjustment Factor}$$

For the Treasury Bond examples, it was relatively straight forward to determine the ratio of the nominal values of the two positions. If we held $10,000,000 nominal value in Bonds and the futures nominal value was $100,000, then this ratio would say we would have to buy or sell 100 contracts in the derivative products (futures or options) to eliminate our exposure. The problem is that this ratio must be multiplied by a risk adjustment factor which takes into account the different sensitivities of the two assets to changing market conditions. For the US Treasury Bond market, the conversion factor was used as the risk adjustment factor for those bonds that were either the cheapest to delivery or were near cheapest to deliver in that futures contract.[8]

In the same way, the appropriate number of stock or stock index derivatives can be estimated for the minimum variance hedged position. This is done adapting the above formula for the US Treasury hedging ratio and including the Beta as the factor adjusting for the relative risks of the two markets:

$$\frac{\text{Nominal Value of Cash Position}}{\text{Nominal Value of Derivative Position}} \text{ times Beta of the Cash position to the Asset underlying the Derivative Market}$$

Let us go through a simple example using the data in Table 11.2 of this chapter. Suppose a fund manager wishes to eliminate the overall stock market risk of his holdings of US equity by selling futures on the S&P 500. The December futures is trading at 451.40 and the S&P cash index was at 444.72. From historical data, the fund manager was able to determine the statistical Beta relationship between the returns on his portfolio and the returns of the S&P 500 cash index, and this was determined to be 1.20. That means that if the S&P 500 index drops by 10%, his portfolio would drop by 12%. To estimate the number of futures he would have to sell to eliminate his risk to the overall stock market (as measured by the S&P 500

---

[8]Although other methods can be used to determine this risk adjustment. These include the Basis point value technique, comparisons of the Modified Durations of the two instruments or the estimation of the historical Beta relationship which assesses the past relationship between the movement of the two assets.

index), he would simply apply the above equation plugging in the following numbers:

$$\frac{\$10,000,000}{444.72 \cdot \$500} \text{ times } 1.20 = 53.97 \text{ futures contracts.}$$

The reason for using the cash index level and not the futures price to determine the nominal value of the S&P 500 futures is to be consistent with the Beta which is estimated relative to the cash market index. You can also look at it from a different angle: If the position is held to expiration, then the S&P futures will be exactly equal to the S&P cash index. At that point, the hedger would be interested in how the S&P cash index had changed (since the futures must be equal to it at that point in time). The hedger would therefore have to sell 54 December futures to reduce his risk to the stock market. What would be the net exposure of the investor to the stock market? By definition, it should be zero. This can be expressed in a more quantifiable way using the Beta measure, and also in terms of the delta of the total composite position.

Total Beta of Hedged Position	=	Beta of Cash Position		Beta of Futures Position
(0.0)		(+1.20)	-	(1.20 · 1.00).

Total Delta of Hedged Position	=	Delta of Cash Position		Delta of Futures Position
(0.0)		(+1.20 · 45)	-	54.

The result is the same; an exposure of zero. For the delta exposure, we must be consistent with the definition of the delta as the change in the value of the overall position for a change in the movement of the price of the underlying asset. For the cash portfolio of $10,000,000 in nominal value, this is equivalent to approximately 45 underlying futures contracts ($10,000,000/444.72 · $500 = 44.97). Since the portfolio moves 20% more than the underlying S&P 500 index, the equivalent delta position of this portfolio is 20% larger. Thus, the delta of the portfolio is 1.20. Using this methodology, we can now include options in a hedging program and correctly estimate the exposure of the hedged position.

Now, suppose a fund manager wishes to reduce the overall stock market risk of his holdings of US equity by selling call options on the S&P 500. For this example, we will assume that the hedger chooses the 450 call from Table 11.2 which was trading at 18.71. The December futures is trading at 451.40 and the delta of the call was 0.5250. To estimate the number of call options he would have to sell to reduce his risk, to the overall stock market (in an appropriate manner, not adjusting for the delta as outlined above), he would simply apply the above equation plugging in his numbers:

$$\frac{\$10,000,000}{450.00 \cdot \$500} \text{ times } 1.20 = 53.33 \text{ options contracts.}$$

The strike price of the S&P 500 option is now used instead of the cash index level because that represents the amount of stock he would be obligated to sell at the level of the strike price. The hedger would therefore have to sell 53 December 450 call options to reduce his risk to the stock market in the appropriate manner. What would be the net exposure of the investor to the stock market now? This can be ascertained once again using the Beta and delta measures of the total composite position. First we must estimate the easy one, delta, and then infer the more difficult one, which is the Beta.

Total Delta of Hedged Position	=	Delta of Cash Position		Delta of Option Position
(26.175)		(+1.20 · 45)	-	(53 · 0.5250).

As the reader can see, in delta terms, the risk of the position has been halved and this is consistent with the covered call writing exposures discussed in the previous chapter. The risk expressed in Beta terms must be proportional to the delta risk. The only difference is how these measures are expressed. So, to determine the new Beta we simply apply the following simple proportional relationship:[9]

$$\frac{\text{Initial Delta}}{\text{Initial Beta}} = \frac{\text{Final Delta}}{\text{Final Beta}}$$

and putting in the numbers for this example, to solve for the Final Beta, we get:

$$\frac{1.20 \cdot 45}{1.20} = \frac{26.1750}{\text{Final Beta}} \text{ or a Final Beta} = 0.5817$$

This can now be input into the Beta exposure formula as:

Total Beta of Hedged Position	=	Beta of Cash Position		Beta of Option Position
(0.5817)		(+1.20)	-	(0.6183).

The Beta of the options position is equal to -0.6183. This can also be estimated with the following simple formula:

$$\frac{\text{Number of S\&P Futures in the Hedge}}{\text{Number of 450 Call Options to Hedge}} \cdot \text{Beta of Portfolio} \cdot \text{Delta of the Option}$$

$$-0.6183 = 54/53 \cdot 1.20 \cdot -0.5250.$$

The result is the same; an exposure which is approximately one half the level it had been initially. Both a delta measure and a beta measure will provide the hedger with equivalent measures of the remaining risk of the portfolio.

---

[9]This formula is drawn from "Converting betas to deltas", by Robert A Strong, Futures Magazine January 1993, pp. 46-48.

This section has examined the impact of hedging with options on the Beta of a stock portfolio, but options have their own Betas relative to the market. This measure is extremely easy to understand.

When one remembers that the Beta is simply the measure of how a stock will move in percentage terms for a percentage movement in the underlying market, then if one applies the same measure to an option contract one must be cognisant that options are geared instruments. Suppose, I have the same 450 call option on the S&P 500 index with a current price of 18.71 with the underlying December futures trading at 451.40. The delta of the option is 0.5250. Then, the underlying futures moves up by 1% in value. Would you expect the option to rise also by 0.5250% in value? Let us see:

Asset	Original Price	New price 1% higher	Change in Price	%Change in Price
Futures	451.40	455.91	4.51	1%
Call Option	18.71	21.08	2.37	12.67%

So the option did not change by 0.5250%. It did move in delta terms 52.5% of the absolute change in price of the underlying (2.37/4.51 = 52.5%) but not in percentage terms. This is because of the levered nature of the options market. The reader may remember that in Chapter 3, we discussed a "Greek" derivative which does measure this levered nature of the option which was called lambda. This measure tells us the percentage change in an options price for a percentage change in the price of the underlying asset. This is simply calculated by multiplying the delta of the option by the ratio of the underlying price divided by the price of the option. The formula for the lambda is:

$$\Delta \cdot \text{Underlying price/Option Price.}$$

If we apply the formula to the above example we obtain:

$$0.5250 \cdot 451.40/18.71 = 12.67 \text{ or } 12.67\%.$$

Given the Beta of the S&P 500 is by definition 1.0, then the Beta of the 450 call on the S&P 500 is 12.67. Thus, the formula for the Beta of a call relative to the market portfolio is simply:

$$\beta_{option} = \lambda_{option} \cdot \beta_{underlying\ asset}$$

where:

λ_{option} is the Lambda of the option, and

$\beta_{underlying\ asset}$ is the Beta of the asset which underlies the option

COMPARISON OF ALTERNATIVE HEDGING STRATEGIES FOR HOLDER OF STOCK PORTFOLIO

In this final section, I will compare the alternative hedging strategies available to the portfolio manager. These hedges include: remaining unhedged (which really is not a hedging strategy but most portfolio managers seem to do this), buying puts on Stock Indices, selling calls on Stock Indices or hedging with Stock Index futures. For this analysis, we assume that the stock market can do one of three things: it could fall, stay the same or rise. Given these possible states of the world, we will compare the three most popular hedging strategies and rank them in terms of hedging effectiveness.

Assume that one is holding a well diversified US. stock portfolio which has a high correlation to the S&P 500 Stock Index and that the near month S&P 500 futures is trading at 450. If a decrease in stock prices occurs what are the results of the three hedging strategies? With an S&P 500 futures hedge, the protection is immediate and the hedging costs are trivial. Remember that you can establish a margin with interest bearing securities and when futures prices fall your margin account will always have a positive cash balance. So, the value of the stock portfolio is maintained at the level at which the S&P 500 futures contract was sold. This can be seen in Figure 11.9 on the left side of the diagram. The put option hedge provides a "floor" level of protection but is only effective if the stock market drops dramatically. The short call position has a limited profit potential and in case the market decreases by more points than the premium received, the losses start to mount. Finally, the unhedged position has the worst performance of all with an immediate loss potential that exceeds the previous three hedging strategies.

Rankin			
	BEARISH	NEUTRAL	BULLISH
SELL FUTURES	1	2	4
BUY PUTS	2	4	2
SELL CALLS	3	1	3
UNHEDGED	4	3	1

Table 11.5 Comparison of Alternatives for Portfolio Protection.

We will rank the efficiency of these strategies as follows: the best in a bearish market is to sell the S&P 500 futures; the second best alternative is to buy the put option on either the S&P 500 futures or on the S&P 100 Stock Index, the third choice is to sell the call option on either of these indices; while in dead last place is to remain unhedged. This ranking can be seen in Table 11.5.

What about the situation of market stability? If you have this expectation, you might be inclined to remain unhedged. If you did that, then your profit would be equal to the dividends you were paid for that period and you would have no ad-

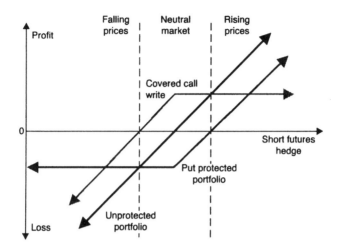

Figure 11.9 Comparison of Potential Hedging Strategies for Holders of Stock.

verse impact from price changes. If instead you sold the futures, there would be no benefit from a movement in the market price. For this hedge, your return would be equal to the short term interest rate needed to "carry" the stock portfolio until the futures delivery.[10] If the short term interest rate is substantially higher than the dividend yield, then the futures hedge would be superior to simply holding the cash and your return is equal to a short term money market instrument.

If instead of these strategies you sold a call option on a Stock Index (or the futures) then you would receive a premium in addition to the dividend income on the stock portfolio. This profit is maximised over a range extending from the current market price to slightly higher. To the downside, the covered call strategy will still profit until that point where the premium received has been exhausted and the hedge then displays the same profit and loss profile as the short futures hedge. What about the put option purchase? In the stable state of the world, the premium is lost and the net position has the worst performance. The profit/loss profiles for these hedging strategies can be seen in the centre of Figure 11.9.

The ranking for these four alternatives in a stable market is as follows: the best strategy is to sell the call option on the Stock Index; when interest rates are higher than dividend yields, number two is to hedge the stock portfolio with a short S&P 500 futures contract; the third best choice is to remain unhedged; (where the dividend yields are higher than the returns on the interest bearing security, remaining unhedged is superior to the S&P 500 futures hedge); and the worst alternative is to buy the put option on the S&P 100 Index or on S&P 500 futures. These rankings can also be seen in the centre column of Table 11.5.

---

[10]The reader is referred to Darrell Duffies', "Futures Markets", Prentice-Hall, 1989, for a thorough discussion of the expected gains that accrue from a short Stock Index futures hedge.

Finally, if the market rises dramatically, what are the comparative results from these four strategies? If one remained unhedged and the market rallied, then this position would do best of all. Unfortunately, the portfolio manager must be cognisant that he is taking an unlimited risk position. If he protects the stock portfolio by buying a put option on an S&P index, he is still going to enjoy an unlimited profit potential but will only realise a profit after the movement in the market has been sufficient to cover the premium paid. Now consider the covered call position. When he sold the call option, the most he can ever make is the premium paid. Therefore, when the market rises the covered call hedge has a limited participation. Finally, what about the short S&P 500 futures hedge? In this situation, this is the worst choice because he cannot participate at all in the profits associated with the market increase. Once again, the profit/loss profiles for these strategies when the market rises can be seen in the right hand portion of Figure 11.9. In our ranking of these strategies, in a rising market we will choose being unhedged as the best alternative, the put option purchase is second, the covered call writing strategy is third and the short futures hedge is the least promising. Table 11.5 lists on the right hand column this final ranking for the possible approaches.

The reader might find it interesting that in none of the possible states of the world will the put option purchase be the best alternative. Why does anyone purchase a put option to hedge an asset? The reason is that people cannot be certain that the market will fall, remain stable or rise. Therefore, in a world dominated by uncertainty, insurance exists to provide protection against the unforeseeable. Puts are also ideal if you anticipate that markets will go down and then come back over a given period of time. You might then want to establish a minimum acceptable level to protect yourself and still benefit if eventually the market rises to higher levels. In an uncertain world where you expect a high degree of volatility, then a put option will give that floor to your potential losses (see Figure 11.9) and allow you to benefit if the market does rally above current levels. If one buys a put and the market remains stable you lose the premium. Is that any reason for not buying a put? If it is a valid reason, then the same logic could be applied to your home fire insurance. If one knew with certainty whether one's house was going to burn down in any given year, then the optimal strategy would be simple: either go uninsured if you know your house will not catch fire or sell the house before it burns down. If the world were so contrived, insurance has no purpose. However, with house fires and market prices, uncertainty does exist and that is why option contracts exist.

I would like to finish this chapter, by providing a few guidelines to stock portfolio managers who may wish to include Stock Index futures and options in their risk management strategies. The first step in designing a hedging programme with either futures or options is to determine what the long-term objectives of the portfolio manager are. These could include maximising return, assuring the stability of the principal or perhaps increasing the cash flow over an investment period. Secondly, the portfolio manager must make some judgements about what will happen to the stock market in general to interest rates and finally to the volatility of the market. Next, given this viewpoint, he must construct an optimal strategy using combinations of cash, futures and options to benefit most from these viewpoints. Thereby, he should place special attention to the fact that if his viewpoints are uncertain, options may be the appropriate instrument to use (see the first example in Chapter 10). Finally, the portfolio manager must evaluate the performance of his hedging strategies over time, making sure to evaluate the performance relative to his initial assumptions and viewpoints. As his viewpoints change, he must revise his portfolio strategy accordingly.

The portfolio manager who is allowed to use Stock Index futures and options will face a situation similar to that of a carpenter who is first introduced to a drill or a keysaw. It is true that it was possible to make the hole in a piece of wood before the advent of the drill or keysaw, for example with a hammer, but the introduction of these tools has made the job more efficient and accurate. Thus, the use of Stock Index futures and options will provide a similar benefit to the astute stock portfolio manager.

12: OTC Interest Rate Options

So far in this book, I have discussed only options that are traded at organised markets. In the 1980s a whole new option market developed to address the unprecedented interest rate, commodity and currency risks that were associated with a variety of economic shocks. These products were not offered at an organised marketplace but were instead offered directly by financial institutions to clients. These products became known as Over the Counter (OTC) options. The principal differences between exchange traded options and OTCs are that exchange-traded options are more actively traded but not very flexible (a restricted range of maturities and strike prices) while OTCs offer tailor-made terms but often with a lower liquidity or at a higher cost. In this chapter, I will examine only interest rate OTCs. In the next chapter, the coverage of OTCs will cover all the major financial markets with the discussion of exotic options.

These products were particularly popular in the management of interest rate risks and they include OTC option on fixed income instruments (like Bonds), Interest Rate Guarantees, Interest Rate Ceilings, Floors and Collars and Options on Interest Rate Swaps (Swaptions). In this chapter, I will discuss each of these in turn and show the reader how these customised products relate to the concepts I have previously discussed in this book. The first OTC option I will consider is the OTC option on Bonds.

OTC OPTIONS ON BONDS

Of the available interest rate OTC options, options on fixed income securities, portfolios, or loans have been among the most popular. Of course, options have long been associated with fixed income securities with the embedded call features that many Bonds possess. A call feature typically gives the issuer of the Bond the right to buy the Bonds back from the holders at a price specified at the issuance of the Bond and for a certain period. The holder of a callable Bond essentially has a position which is "long" a Bond and "short" a call option on that Bond. If the reader refers to Example #3 in Chapter 10, he will note that when one combines a long position in a Bond with a short call the payoff to the portfolio is identical to a short put option.[1] Thus, the issuer of the callable Bond, by symmetry, must have a position which is similar to buying a put option on Bonds.

---

[1] See section titled "Hedging Example 3: Selling Call Options on T-Bond Futures Against a US Treasury Bond to Reduce Risk and Enhance Returns", page 375.

Quite often, these call (or put) features will be decoupled from the underlying Bond and sold separately as OTC Bond options. One recent example of this technique has been in the German market where the German Government issued Bundesanleihen (Government Bonds) which are called Schuldscheindarlehen and include a put feature allowing the buyer to sell the security back to the German Government after one, two and three years. A number of investment banks purchased these securities and then stripped off the put option feature, selling them into the market as OTC Bundesanleihen options (actually as Swaptions, which I will discuss later in this chapter).[2] This technique was also applied in the Italian market where the Republic of Italy issued Certificati di Credito del Tesoro Con Opzione (CTOs) which also include an embedded put option to sell the bond back to the Government at fixed dates. Again, a number of Italian investment banks have stripped this option and sold it into the market as a Lira swaption. There is no risk to the investment bank since the swaption (put on the bond) sold is set exactly equal to the terms of the option in the CTO. Once again, the investment banks apply the simple Put-Call parity rules described in Chapters 3 and 8 to lock in a risk-free transaction (at a profit of course). The option stripping technique is now done in almost all fixed income markets and has proven a solid money maker for a number of Investment Banks. The key element in the success of these operations is determining the "fair" value of the option which is embedded in the complex structured product. One goal of this chapter is to show the reader how these options are fairly priced.

In addition, to the creation of OTC Bond options by stripping embedded options away from an existing Bond, many market makers have also offered "new" options by writing the options and hedging the risks with the underlying security. What exactly is an OTC Bond Option? Typical conditions for an OTC Bond option can be seen in Table 12.1. An OTC Bond option is a negotiated (sometimes called "bespoke") option flexible with regards to the terms of the contract. The terms that can be negotiated include the underlying instrument (i.e. a particular fixed income

Size	Subject to minimum of $1,000,000 nominal Bonds
Put or Call	These can also be either "European" or "American style"
Strike Price	Any price is available expressed in terms of clean price of the Bond
Exercise/Expiry Date	with a duration up to 5 years
Settlement	This can either be for delivery of the specific Bond or for The Cash difference, in which case the settlement price will be that of the cash market fixing on the day of exercise

Table 12.1 Conditions for an OTC Bond Option.

---

[2]For a good introduction to how this was done, the reader is referred to "Strip Mining", in Risk Magazine, Vol. 4, No. 2 (February 1991), pp. 20-24.

instrument), the size of the underlying amount (subject to a minimum amount), puts or calls with either European or American (or a variety of other) exercise features, a completely flexible maturity (generally out to one year) and settlement that can be either by physical delivery or cash settlement upon exercise.

Why would one want to deal with an OTC Bond option when exchange traded options on Bonds are so liquid? The answer is flexibility. The terms of an OTC Bond option are totally negotiable while the exchange traded option on Bond futures (or on a physical Bond) are not. Therefore, the OTC Bond option allows the user an instrument which will exactly meet his trading or hedging needs without having to incur the risks of "cross-hedging" an exposure with another instrument and taking on what is known as the "basis risk".[3] Furthermore, the hedger will not have to accept yield curve or the risks of hedging a time period which is mismatched with the maturity of an exchange traded option.

Examples of Applications for OTC Bond Options

I will now examine a number of applications of OTC Bond options for customers. Let us say that an investor plans to buy a particular Bond (perhaps a new issue) and has a particular level where he would wish to sell it out. This being the case, he can initiate a Buy-Write strategy, where he buys the Bond and writes a call option on that Bond to the Bank at a strike price equal to the level the investor wishes to sell the Bond. Then, if the Bond price rises to his level, the investor will sell his Bond via the option exercise and if the market fails to rally, he will be able to retain the OTC Bond option premium. In addition, an investor can use OTC Bond options as substitutes for the purchase of a particular security. As the reader will recall from Chapter 10, this was discussed in Example #1 of that chapter. The difference with the OTC Bond option is that the buyer knows which security he will actually purchase upon exercise. With options on T-Bond futures, he will receive upon exercise a T-Bond futures contract which at delivery will allow him to buy the "cheapest-to-deliver" US Treasury Bond which may not be the instrument he wishes ultimately to purchase. The third example is for the foreign investor who might wish to benefit from the movement in the US Treasury market but does not want to place the bulk of his available funds in US Dollars. The OTC Bond option will allow him for a small premium payment a chance to choose exactly the security he wishes to purchase (or sell) with a minimum exposure to the US Dollar. Furthermore, if the exchange rate between his currency and the US Dollar moves in his favour (as does the level of the US Treasury security), then he will have a double benefit amounting to a combined fixed income option and a currency option. The final example

---

[3]The basis risk is the risk that the relationship between the instrument to be hedged with the instrument used in the hedging strategy diverges overtime. This was discussed extensively in Chapter 10 and the reader is referred to that chapter for a discussion of the basis relationship between US. Treasury Bonds and the T-Bond futures.

for customer use of OTC Bond options is for those traders who may want to be short a particular Bond but for various reasons are unable to borrow that particular Bond to sell short. By buying OTC put options and selling OTC call options on that same security at the same strike price, they will have created a synthetic short selling position in the security.[4]

Pricing of OTC Bond Options

The pricing of interest rate options is easily the most difficult topic I will address so far in this book. This is mainly because the ultimate underlying factor driving the value of Bonds or other interest bearing securities is the interest rate itself. While stocks or commodities can be assumed to follow a random walk, interest rate movements are much harder to model. In addition, a Bond price will not be just a function of one interest rate but as many interest rates as that Bond has cash flows. For example, a 10 year US Treasury Bond will pay coupons biannually and after 10 years the principal. So in total, the Bond has 20 dates where cash is paid to the holder. To determine the value of the Bond today, we simply take all these future payments and discount them back to present value, sum them up and we have the Bond price. The problem is which interest rate or rates underly the option. If one argues that a coupon Bond is simply a set of (in this example 20) pure discount Bonds, then each of the 20 cash payouts should be discounted to present value by their own particular interest rate. Quite often this is called the "Zero Coupon" interest rate because each of the 20 cash flows can be thought of as a series of single Bonds that pay no (and thereby Zero) coupon.

We determine each of the interest rates for the individual cash flows and probably find that they are at different levels. This is generally the case and the term academics have for this effect is "the Term Structure of Interest Rates". Most practitioners call this effect the (zero coupon) yield curve. The problem with pricing options on Bonds is that one is not pricing a derivative security (an option) of just one underlying security but rather an option on a portfolio of underlying securities (the individual cash flows) and each of these 20 "sub-securities" may have a different underlying level, volatility and life time. So, to price the option on the portfolio of cash flows (the coupon Bond), one must provide a lot more information than would be required for a simple option that could be priced by the Black and Scholes model. In fact, one needs to incorporate the entire term structure of interest rates and assess somehow how this could change over the life of the option. Furthermore, the Bond price itself will change over time as it moves closer to its maturity. Consider the following: the volatility of a Bond is simply some sort of summation of the volatilities of each of the individual cash flows that are part of it. As these cash flows are paid up (coupon payment dates) these elements of uncer-

---

[4]The construction of synthetic underlying positions using short calls and long puts was discussed extensively in Chapter 8 as the conversion trade.

tanly drop from the Bond's volatility because they are no longer uncertain (they are already sitting in your pocket). So as one would expect, a Bond's volatility slowly drops over time as it approaches maturity.

To address these issues and obtain a price for a Bond option, basically two approaches have been proposed. The first adapts the basic Black and Scholes model and tries to incorporate the changing Bond variance as the Bond approaches its final maturity. These models include Merton's Debt option model, the "Brownian Bridge" model of Ball and Torous and the Schaefer and Schwartz Duration model. The other approach is to tackle the problem by trying to estimate the movements in the overall term structure of interest rates and the most famous of these models is the Ho and Lee model.

The Black and Scholes model is immediately thrown out of the running because it assumes a constant volatility and while that might make sense for one security, it certainly will not work for a portfolio of different securities each of which most certainly has a different volatility. Returning to the analogy of the Black and Scholes model in Chapter 2, the basic model is as good as a Nikon camera, but the problem with Bond options is one would need a "movie camera" to record a number of pictures almost simultaneously and not just a single frame. The first model which tried to take in a "broader picture" was supplied by Robert Merton in 1975.[5] The solution Merton found to the problem of pricing Bond options entailed specifying the Bond (return) volatility which included the average expected volatility over the life of the option along with a correlation term between short term interest rates and long term rates. Later, in this chapter, I will present another model which essentially does this for the pricing of Options on Swaps.[6]

The second revision of the Black and Scholes model for Bond options came from Ball and Torous in 1983.[7] They questioned the Black and Scholes assumption about Brownian motion. They argue that a Bond price cannot just wander around aimlessly (like the random walk of a drunk). We know that when a Bond is first issued if the coupon is equal to the prevailing yield for comparable Bonds of the same maturity, its initial price will be 100 (par) and at maturity it will also be at 100 (par) as the last payment of the principal is made. Between these dates, however, the Bond prices can vary. Their term for this is called a Brownian Bridge. This can be seen in Figure 12.1. In that graph, the Bond starts at 100 (on one side of the "river") and varies around until it returns to 100 (on the other side of the "river") at maturity. With this revised assumption for how Bond prices move, they essentially used the Black and Scholes approach to price Bond options. The prob-

---

[5]Merton, Robert C., "On the pricing of corporate debt: The risk structure of interest rates"; Journal of Finance, Vol. 29, pp. 449-470.

[6]At that point, I will reintroduce the Margrabe model to exchange one asset for another. If one substitutes a Bond for the first asset and a short term interest security for the second asset and finally includes the "average volatility" for the Bond over the life of the option, one will get the Merton model.

[7]Ball C., A. and W. Torous, "Bond price dynamics and options", Journal of Financial and Quantitative Analysis, Vol. 18, No. 4, pp. 517-530.

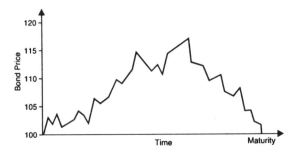

Figure 12.1 Brownian Bridge Dispersion Process for a Bond.

lem with the Brownian Bridge approach is that it also assumes a constant proportional variance overtime. As the bond approaches maturity, the volatility can increase to infinity and we know that exactly the opposite thing happens as the number of cash flows (that cause the Bond volatility in the first place) are increasingly paid (and cease to add to the total volatility of the Bond).

The next approach I will discuss for pricing options on Bonds by adjusting the Bond's volatility was the Schaefer and Schwartz Duration Model.[8] Schaefer and Schwartz decided to assume that the risk of a Bond is related to its duration.[9] The problem with this model is that duration is like an option's delta; it can change when interest rates change. Furthermore, the duration concept assumes that the term structure of interest rates can only change in one way: the same amount for the maturity of each interest rate. So, if interest rates rose by 1% from 7% to 8% for the 90 day interest rate, then they would also change by the same 1% for the 20 year interest rate from perhaps 9% to 10%. If interest rates fail to follow this pattern, then the approach will not work. For those readers unfamiliar with the concepts of duration and convexity, I will introduce both of these concepts later in this chapter and discuss how options impact these measures of bond price risks.

To take into account the fact that interest rates do not always change by the same amount across the term structure, another approach was tried: that of trying to model the possible changes in the whole term structure of interest rates. The first of these models was presented by Ho and Lee.[10] Rather than try to model the volatility of one or more interest rates to determine the term structure of interest rates, they begin with the term structure as it is (at the point when they have to price the option) and ask how could the entire thing change? By assuming that the term structure is that way for a reason; that the market has determined it should look that way (and that no arbitrage trades are possible), they simply try a variety of differ-

---

[8]Schaefer, Steven M. and Edwardo S. Schwartz, "Time dependent variance and the pricing of bond options," Journal of Finance, Vol. 42, No. 5, pp. 1113-1128.

[9]Duration is a measure of the average life of a bond and when divided by 1+yield for the bond will predict how much a bond's price will change for a given movement in interest rates.

[10]Ho, Thomas, S. Y. and S.B. Lee, "Term Structure Movements and Pricing Interest Rate Contingent Claims," Journal of Finance, Vol. 41 (December 1986), pp: 1011-29.

ent term structure patterns and see what happens. The way they do this is to apply the Binomial approach outlined in Chapter 3. Overtime, the term structure can twist upwards or downwards or become flatter with certain probabilities. With the expected movement in the term structure taken into account, then it is a simple matter to evaluate each of the individual sub-bonds in the overall coupon Bond and the sum of all these mini-options is the price of the option on the coupon Bond. Unfortunately, one of the problems with the Ho and Lee model is that their assumptions allow the possibility for negative nominal interest rates (which is clearly impossible). Given this problem for the Ho and Lee model, other approaches have been developed which do not share this problem of possible negative interest rates. Essentially, there are three popular option pricing models used to solve for the term structure of interest rate problem (which is really an assumption of the mean reversion of interest rates). The three models include: the Black, Derman and Toy Model[11], Hull and White Model[12], and the Heath, Jarrow and Morton Model[13]. In Table 12.2, the stochastic dispersion process assumptions are presented for all of these models. The Ho and Lee model is also included for comparison.

Ho and Lee Model

$$dR = \theta t\, dt + \sigma\, dz$$

where:

    dR is the Absolute Change in an Interest Rate

    θt is the mean of the dispersion process as a function of time

    dt is the change in time

    σ is the Volatility of the Absolute Interest Rate Change

    dz is a standard Wiener Process with z a function of $\sqrt{t}$

Black, Derman and Toy Model

$$dR / R = \theta t\, dt + \sigma\, dz$$

where:

    dR/R is the Proportional Change in an Interest Rate

    θt is the mean of the dispersion process as a function of time

    dt   is the change in time

    σ is the Volatility of the Proportional Interest Rate Change

    dz   is a standard Wiener Process with z a function of $\sqrt{t}$

---

[11]Black, Fischer, Emanuel Derman and William Toy, 1990, "A One-Factor Model of Interest Rates and its Application to Treasury Bond Options", Financial Analyst Journal (January-February 1990), pp. 33-39.

[12]Hull, John, and Alan White. "Pricing Interest-Rate-Derivative Securities. "The Review of Financial Studies, Vol. 3, No. 4 (1990), pp. 573-592.

[13]Heath, David, Robert Jarrow and Andrew Morton, 1990, "Bond Pricing and the Term Structure of Interest Rates: a New Methodology for Contingents Claims Valuation", Journal of Financial and Quantitative Analysis 25 (December 1990), pp. 419-440.

Hull and White Model

$$dR = \left[\theta t + a(t)\cdot(b-r)\right]dt + \sigma\,dz$$

where:

    dR is the Absolute Change in an Interest Rate

    θt is the mean of the dispersion process as a function of time

    a(t) · (b-r) is an adjustment constant returning to long term Rate r

    dt is the change in time

    σ is the Volatility of the Absolute Interest Rate Change

    dz is a standard Wiener Process with z a function of $\sqrt{t}$

Heath, Jarrow and Morton Model

$$dR(t,T) = a(t,T) + \sum \sigma(t,T)\,f(t,T)\,dz(t)$$

where:

    dR   is the Absolute Change in an Interest Rate which is a function of the time of the option t and of the maturity of the underlying asset typically a Bond of T maturity

    a(t,T) is the mean of the dispersion process as a function of time

    dz   is a standard Wiener Process with z a function of $\sqrt{t}$

    (t,T) f (t,T) is the Volatility of the Absolute InterestRate Change which is a Function of the Underlying Maturity T and of time t, wich is the expiration of the option.

Table 12.2 The Stochastic Dispersion Processes for Mean Reversion Models.

While I normally do not shy away from showing the reader the complete pricing models, in this case I will make an exception because of the complexity of these four models. However, it will suffice to show the reader the assumed stochastic dispersion process to demonstrate what the various models are doing. For all of these models, the result is essentially the same. The Mean Reversion is effected by either an adjustment to the mean (or drift) term or to the volatility term. The first three models adjust the mean term and the last model adjusts the volatility term. These adjustments allow the statistical dispersion of the terminal asset price (in these cases interest rates) to be dampened and rendered no longer simply proportional to the time to expiration.

It is as if one fires the shotgun and the pellets fail to hit the target on the barn door due to the effects of gravity pulling the heavy shot downwards. What is the solution? Either point the shot gun high enough to offset the effects of gravity (adjust the mean of the dispersion process) or get a shotgun with a longer barrel such that the dispersion of the pellets is reduced and more focused on the target (by adjusting the volatility). But as the reader might surmise these models have been specifically developed only to handle the mean reversion problem and mean reversion may not be the only reason why the term structure of volatility is not flat. Therefore, the models may be limited in correcting for all the factors causing the term structure to be sloping instead of flat.

So, with so many models to choose from, which one should the practitioner choose to price options on Bonds? Of the approaches outlined above, the Ho and Lee or the Hull and White models seem to be currently in vogue but they are very complicated and assume the trader can feed in variables about the expected movements in the term structure. Another simpler approach has already been presented in Chapter 3. In the discussions of the correct pricing model for currency options, I presented the argument of Mark Garman that all options can be seen as options on the future price of the asset. If this is so, then it is a simple matter to determine the future price of the Bond and then apply the trusty Black (1976) model for options on futures. In a recent book[14], it was shown that there is almost no difference between the result of the Ho and Lee model and the Black (1976) model for options on future Bond prices. Essentially, all these complicated option formulae are trying to estimate what the Bond price will be at the expiration date of the option (the future price) and then they determine the option price at that point. To determine the option price today, this result is simply the present value of the expected option price at expiration. As with the currency options in Chapter 3, why not just estimate the forward price of the Bond yourself and then apply a simple model to determine just the option's time value component? For many traders (including myself), simplicity seems to win out and they will estimate their own future price for the Bond and then apply the Black (1976) model to price the option on a Bond.

Estimation Of The Volatility Input For Options On Bonds

A key issue in the pricing of any option is the estimation of the volatility input into the pricing model of choice. There are special problems in the volatility input for bonds which I will address in this section. So far, when we discuss the volatility input for the options pricing models, the volatility is a measure of the price variability of the underlying instrument. When this is done for a share, currency or a futures contract this is appropriate given the underlying instrument is basically the same over time. For example, an option on one futures contract will always be on that same futures contract until the expiration. Not so for a bond.

Consider the situation where we have a one year call option on the price of a five year bond. In six months' time, the underlying asset will no longer be a five year bond but will have been transformed into a four and one half year bond. As

---

[14]Figlewski Stephen, William L. Silber and Marti G. Subrahmanyam, "Financial Options: From Theory to Practice" Business One Irwin, Homewood, Illinois, 1990. pp. 337-338.

was indicated above, a four and one half year instrument will be less volatile than a five year instrument, so the input of price volatility is clearly inappropriate for the pricing of options on bonds. Therefore, the difference in the dispersion processes between shares and bonds requires another input for the volatility which is not influenced by the changing nature of the bond through time. The best alternative measure of bond volatility is to base the volatility on changes in yields rather than prices.

The advantage of yield volatilities is that they are not dependent on the maturity of the underlying bond. Yields can be compared throughout the life of the underlying fixed income instrument. However, the impact of the yield volatility on the price of the bond and the option will depend on the remaining life of the underlying instrument. The translation of yield volatility to price volatility will depend on the sensitivity of the bond price to a change in yields. The most common measures of a bond's price sensitivity to a change in yields are known as duration and convexity which will be discussed in a subsequent section of this chapter.

Unfortunately, there exist major problems with using yield volatility as the input into the bond options pricing models. One problem is that as the bond approaches maturity, the yield volatilities will tend to rise. This does not reflect a "volatility" buying opportunity but is a function of the mean reversion problem all interest rate options face. This can once again be seen in the volatility cones for fixed interest instruments and for the US Dollar interest volatility matrix portrayed in Chapter 5. Another problem is that a pricing model that values options by converting prices into yields is inconsistent with Put-Call parity and would therefore suggest prices which may be able to be arbitraged. Finally, yield to maturities are universally recognised to be a flawed measure of the actual returns one receives from the investment in bonds. Thus, the use of yields as the time series for the estimation of the volatility is at best an approximation of how the price of the bond will change. However, for most applications, the degree of error is sufficiently small to allow the analyst to use yield volatility as his input into the pricing model, as long as the underlying asset has more than one year to maturity after the expiration of the option.

Issues In The Pricing Of OTC Options On Bonds

Steps Involved in Pricing an OTC Option on Bonds
As with the pricing of any OTC option, the analyst must take the following steps to assure a reasonable price is obtained. These steps and their sequence are:

- The choice of the Pricing Model
- Determination of the Underlying Asset Price or Yield
- Assessment of the other Variables to input into the Model
- Estimation of the Volatility
- Comparison of the Theoretical price to Actual prices if possible

The choice of the appropriate option pricing model for the option on a bond will depend on the exercise style of the option (European versus American) and whether the option is a standard option or an exotic (see the next chapter for an overview of exotic option types). Assuming the option is a standard one and the exercise style is European, then as I indicated above, the most efficient approach is to estimate the forward price of the underlying bond and apply the Black (1976) model for pricing options on forwards. This will also apply to American options if no possibility of early exercise exists. For American options where early exercise may be rational (for some price level of the underlying asset, for example puts), then the analyst will input the spot price of the underlying bond and choose the Ho and Lee model or one of the variants presented above.

The next step is to determine the underlying asset input. While it generally will not make a great deal of difference, if the trader is intending to sell the call, he would have to buy the underlying bond to hedge the position, so he will look at the offer side of the current bond price. On the other hand, if the trader intends to buy the call option, he will input the bid side of the current bond price into his pricing model. For put options, the input of the bid or offer price for the underlying is reversed. If the trader will make an offer on the put, he will input the bid side of the cash market and will input the offer side of the cash market into the model if he intends to bid for the put.

If we suppose that most OTC options are either European style or American style where early exercise would not make rational sense, then we could apply the simple approach of determining the forward price of the underlying asset on the expiration date of the option and use the simple Black (1976) model. As was discussed previously in this book (Chapter 3 for example), all options pricing models are implicitly determining the forward price of the underlying in any case. Thereafter, the option price is determined by working backwards to today. The simple approach I propose, supersedes the internal "forward pricing" element in the options pricing model and substitutes in a "real" forward price that the analyst could actually deal at.

The estimation of the forward price of an asset has been discussed extensively in this Book. The formula for the forward price of bonds is similar in spirit to the formulae for individual stocks (presented in Chapter 2) and stock indices (presented in Chapter 11). It is simply:

Theoretical Forward Price	=	Cash Price	+	Repo Rate	-	Coupon Income	-	Reinvestment of all Price Coupons Received From now until the the Future Date

The variables required for the forward price estimation include: the dirty price of the bond,[15] the interest rate at which the bond can be financed (known as the repurchase or repo rate), the income from holding the bond (accrued coupon interest)

---

[15]Clean price plus accrued interest at bond purchased or sold today.

and any additional income that would be earned by receiving coupons over the interim period from now until the future date and reinvesting the coupons until the future date. Once again the approach is to determine the equivalent portfolio in the cash market to the price of a bond futures contract (which was discussed previously in Chapter 10). Once the forward price is determined using real market prices or rates, the trader must then find the rest of the variables that must be inputted into the options pricing model.

The strike price is fixed for a standard option, so there will be no problem there. However, for some OTC exotic options, the strike prices can be variable and require a more complex pricing model to deal with. Time to expiration should also be straight forward. It must be entered as either the number of calendar days until the expiration of the option or the trader simply puts the expiration date of the option and the computer figures out the number of days until expiration automatically. Care must be taken if the expiration date falls on coupon payment dates or on non-business days (such as weekends or bank holidays) and either the forward price of the underlying must be adjusted (for the previous problem) or the time input must be adjusted (for the latter problem).

A big problem for many OTC option market makers is the determination of the appropriate interest rate factor to be used in the options pricing model. Should a repo rate, lending rate, coupon rate or yield to maturity for the bond or perhaps the cost of capital inside the bank be used as the input. The probable answer comes from examining what the interest rate factor is doing when one uses the Black (1976) model for example. In that model, all the interest rate factor does is to take into account the opportunity cost associated with paying (or receiving) the option premium. Said another way, if the premium were placed on deposit what could be earned by the expiration date of the option. Thus, theory would say that some risk free deposit rate should be used. Practically speaking, most market makers would park any excess funds in the interbank money markets, so this rate would be more realistic. Another approach is based upon the premise in options theory that says whenever one buys or sells an option, the expected rate of return is the risk-free rate. For many financial institutions the benchmark interest rate for the evaluation of investments may not be the risk-free interest rate but an internal cost of capital within that institution. If this is the case, it may make sense to input the cost of capital into the options pricing model to justify to top management that the expected return on the operations is at least equal to the internal costs. In most cases, the interbank deposit rate will be sufficient.

However, as was indicated previously, the most important input into the options pricing model is the volatility. While there is a strong case for using volatilities based upon yields, there are alternative approaches which may work just as well assuming the option is European style and the Black (1976) model is used for pricing. Even if we do decide to use the yield volatility input, where does it come from?

The determination of yield volatility is really no different than the estimation of price volatility. It can be estimated historically, from the implied volatility of related markets or forecasted in the future using the same techniques as were presented in Chapters 4 and 5. The only difference for the historical estimation is that instead of taking the difference between the natural logarithm of prices, we simply take the difference in the natural logarithm of yields. For the implied volatility, it is unlikely that we will have other yield based options available which are similar enough to the option we are pricing to find a meaningful number. The forecasted technique may be the best alternative for OTC bond option volatility estimation since these products tend to have a longer term to expiration than standard exchange traded options on bond futures for example. The best alternatives are to compare yield volatilities using the volatility cone technique presented in Chapter 5. With all these variables determined and plugged into the appropriate pricing model, we now have the theoretical OTC options price. Then, this may need to be adjusted to reflect our actual bid or offer price which is presented to the market.

Why Actual OTC Option Prices Differ From Theoretical Values

The factors which would cause the actual option price to deviate from the theoretical price include:

- Basis Risks
- Illiquidity in the Underlying or Options market
- Transactions Costs
- Volatility Mis-estimation
- Instability of Interest Rates
- A Higher than the Risk-free required rate of return
- Credit Risks

Considerable risk exists when one buys or sells an OTC bond option and then hedges the delta exposure with securities which differ from the bond which underlies the option. Typically, OTC option market makers will use exchange traded derivative products to hedge their exposures. This risk is known as the basis risk and is the same concept as we discussed in Chapter 10 for the futures and options on T-bonds. To measure this risk, one should run a regression of the historical price or yield relationships between the bond underlying the option and the instrument we are using to hedge the options risks. The percentage amount that the R^2 falls below 100% should be then added or subtracted to the theoretical value of the option.[16] As an example, suppose we are offering an OTC bond option on the US Treasury Bond 7.5% of 11/15/16 and intend to hedge the risk of this position using T-bond futures or option. For a one year call option with an at-the-money strike price, the cost of the option is 3.5 percentage points. When a regression is run between the changes in the price of this bond to changes in the price of the T-bond futures, the

---

[16]For a full explanation of the R squared, the reader is referred to Chapter 9 of this book.

regression indicates that 90% of the risk of the 7.5% bonds is explained by the T-bond futures (the R^2 is 0.90). This means that 10% of the variation in the bond which underlies our option is independent from the T-bond futures (or options) which we may be using to hedge with. Thus, the theoretical price of the option will be adjusted by 10%. The new offered price for this option would be 3.85% and the new bid would be 3.15%.

If instead the OTC option market maker were to hedge the option with a position in the underlying bond, the bid and offer spreads must be considered when adjusting the theoretical value of the option. The user must recognise that the assumptions of most pricing models do not include the bid and offer spreads. The more illiquid the underlying bond and/or the options market, the more the trader should add (or subtract) from the theoretical price when making a "real" market quote.

In a similar vein, the market maker may make use of options pricing theory to estimate the number of revisions he may have to make to remain hedged. As the costs of dealing in different markets can vary, this must be taken into account when adjusting the theoretical price of the OTC option. This becomes even more critical when there are substantial costs involved in short selling the instrument underlying the option.[17]

When adjusting for the mis-estimation of volatility, the trader must recognise that in many cases the underlying asset may not yet exist. This occurs when OTC options are offered on when issued bonds. These are bonds that an issuer has indicated will be issued at some defined point in the future, but the exact conditions including the coupon and amount is to be determined by market conditions when the bonds are actually issued. Furthermore, in most cases, OTC options will not have other options with which the implied volatility can be estimated for comparison. Often the bid/offer spread around the theoretical price of the option will widen to reflect the lowest possible volatility and the highest possible volatility that would be expected to occur. This can be determined using the volatility cone in yield terms for that maturity bond with the appropriate time to expiration for the option (see Chapter 5).

Regarding interest rate variability, for longer dated OTC bond options the interest rate sensitivity of the option is much greater than for short dated options. As I indicated earlier for most of the option markets covered in this book, the rho effect is negligible and was almost totally ignored. This can not be done with long dated OTCs. For certain kinds of options, the rho factor will become as important as the vega factor. Again, to adjust the theoretical price of the option, the highest and lowest historical interest rates could be input into the pricing model to assess the bid and offer prices of the option. Remember, the theoretical option price should only be the mid price between the bid and offer prices. It is the price at which the option market maker would not buy above or sell below. The actual market prices must be adjusted for the risks the OTC option dealer is taking.

---

[17]Hodges Stewart, Les Clewlow, "Optimal Delta Hedging Under Transactions Cost", Financial Options Research Centre Pre-print, University of Warwick.

Finally, many trading operations will require that a minimum level of expected return be achieved for all activities. This is of particular importance to the trading of OTC options since the risk can be so substantial. That is why so many institutions will not offer theoretical values for deep out-of-the-money options. When the premium received is amortised over a long lived option, the rate of return given the risk will simply be insufficient. This fact would lead to the offer prices for OTC options being substantially above their theoretical values.

In practice, an OTC options market maker will take into account all of these factors when making his bids and offers for the options. The theoretical value is simply a starting point from which real prices can be determined. A final issue which must be considered whenever dealing in OTC markets is that of the credit risk of the counterparty. This is so important, that it warrants an own section.

Credit Risk Implications of OTC Options

One of the crucial advantages of exchange traded options is that the Clearing House of the Exchange guarantees the performance of all the participants.[18] When dealing in the OTC markets, the only guarantee is the creditworthiness of the counterparty. However, the credit risk only exists on one side of the options market. If a market maker sells an option to a counterparty and the counterparty pays the premium upfront, then there is no additional credit risk from the standpoint of the market maker. The most the counterparty could lose is the premium and this has already been paid. However, in that instance where the market maker buys an option from the counterparty, then there is the credit risk that the counterparty will default when the market maker's option is in-the-money and holder is owed money. Thus, the impact of counterparty credit risk for market makers is only on the bid side. The offer side will be unchanged since at this price, the market maker will have received the option premium from the counterparty and no credit risk exists (after the premium has been paid).

For counterparties with poor credit risk, the marker maker must automatically lower his bid price to take into account the possibility of default. In many cases, if the credit risk is sufficiently poor, the market maker will not make a bid price at all to these potential counterparties. What can these poor credit risk counterparties do to have someone make them a bid? There are basically four methods that are used in the markets to improve a poor credit. These include:

- Posting the underlying bond or cash
- Maintaining a Margin Account
- Establish the Credit Lines, or
- Signing Binding Contracts.

---

[18]For a complete discussion of the function of the Clearing House and how it guarantees the performance of all counterparties, the reader should review the first few sections of Chapter 15.

The first approach requires the counterparty to post the underlying bond (in the case of a written call) on the value of the strike price in cash (in the case of a written put) to the market maker or an agreed intermediary for safe keeping. This will assure the performance for the short option position. Very often, as an alternative, margin accounts are established and run not unlike margin accounts at exchanges. The option seller must maintain a minimum balance in the account with the market maker and top it up if the options contract value has moved adversely for the counterparty. If the credit of the counterparty is relatively good, the market maker may be willing to loan him the money via credit lines to assure his performance. Finally, for all counterparties, regardless of their credit quality, it is essential that a binding contract be drawn up and signed prior to the dealing of any transaction. Examples of such contracts can be obtained from any of the OTC option dealing houses or are available from the International Swaps and Derivatives Association (ISDA).

While credit risk of derivatives and OTC is both interesting and important, I will not dwell on it further in this book. However, there are a number of very solid books currently in print which the reader should obtain if he is interested specifically in these issues.[19]

The final issue in OTC options on Bond relates to how the risks of options can be compared to the most prevalent measures of risks for the underlying bonds themselves.

Impacts of OTC Bond Options on Bond Duration and Convexity

For those involved in the fixed income market, the concepts of duration and convexity should be familiar. For those new to these concepts, I will only provide an overview to what the concepts mean and how they are used. The concepts are once again sufficiently important to warrant an entire book in themselves. However, there do exist some very good books the reader may wish to consult when requiring more detail on these concepts.[20]

For all bonds, the ultimate factor which drives their prices is changes in the levels of interest rates. In some ways, one might think of a bond as a derivative product where the fundamental underlying factor is interest rates. With options, we are also interested in determining the impacts on these derivative products to changes in the underlying factors which make up their prices. Most of Chapter 3 of this book examined these sensitivities and the result was a collection of Greek letters. For every variable which could influence the options price, another "Greek" had to be estimated. Since bonds can also be seen as a kind of derivative of interest rates, the sensitivity of the bond price for a change in the interest rate can also be estimated. When this is done, the relative sensitivity of the bond price to a change

---

[19]Banks, Erik, "The Credit Risk of Complex Derivarives", Macmillan 1993.

[20]Bierwag, Gerald, "Duration Analysis, Managing Interest Rate Risk", Ballinger Publishing Company, 1987.

in interest rates is known as the duration (or more properly the modified duration). Since the only factor which causes bond prices to change is interest rates, then only this risk factor need be estimated. In some ways, the duration of the bond can be thought of in a similar manner to the delta for an option. As delta measures the relationship between changes in the options' price for a change in the price of the asset which underlies that option, duration measures the relationship between changes in the bonds' price for a change in the yield to maturity which underlies the bond.

The problem with the delta is that when the price of the underlying market changes, the delta will also change. The same effect occurs for the duration of a bond. As yields change, the duration will also change. How is this effect addressed in the options market? Through the estimation of the gamma, which is the change in the delta for a change in the price of the underlying market price. For the duration, this effect is addressed through the estimation of the second derivative of the bond price with respect to the yield and this is known as the convexity. The convexity indicates how much the duration will change for a change in yields. Its option equivalent is obviously the gamma. Since, it would be foolhardy to try to trade options without knowing the delta and gamma of the positions, it is equally unwise to manage bond positions without knowing the duration and convexity of the holdings.

Thus, when OTC options on bonds are held by those who normally look at their risks in terms of duration and convexity it is critical to express the risks of the options in these terms. The principle is similar to what was done in the last chapter of expressing options on stock in terms of the Beta risk of that option for equity fund managers. When a fixed income investor has a portfolio of bonds and options on those bonds, to estimate the overall risk in terms of duration and convexity the following three steps must be followed:

(1) All the OTC options in the portfolio must be estimated relative to that bond which underlies those particular options.
(2) For each of these bonds (including options), the duration risk must be aggregated by simple summation, and
(3) For each of these bonds (including options), the convexity risk must then be aggregated again by simple summation.

In Table 12.3, the formulae for the duration and convexity of options on bonds are presented.

$$\frac{Duration\ of\ OTC}{Bond\ Option} = \frac{Bond\ Price}{Option\ Price} \cdot \frac{Delta\ of}{Option} \cdot \frac{Duration}{of\ Bond}$$

$$\frac{Convexity\ of\ OTC}{Bond\ Option} = \frac{Convexity}{of\ Bond} \cdot \frac{Delta\ of}{Option} + \frac{Price\ of}{Bond} \cdot \frac{Gamma\ of}{Option} \cdot \left(\frac{Duration}{of\ Bond}\right)^2$$

Table 12.3 Duration and Convexity Formulae for Options on Bonds.

As one would suppose, the duration of the option depends on the gearing the options provide, the delta of the option, and the Duration of the bond which underlies the option. Likewise, for the Convexity of an option both the delta and the gamma of the option are required along with the duration and convexity of the bond underlying the option.

With this final topic covered, we will leave OTC options on bonds and discuss other OTC options on interest rates. However, instead of the long term interest rates associated with bonds, we will examine OTC options on short term interest rates, and structured products based upon these options on short term interest rates.

INTEREST RATE GUARANTEE AGREEMENTS

Interest Rate Guarantee Agreements are simply interest rate insurance policies for a single floating rate interest rate exposure. IRGs generally come in two varieties: borrower and lender options. In this market, the equivalent of a put option on rates is called the Lender option (LO) as it benefits as rates fall and the Borrower option (BO) is the equivalent of a call option on rates as it benefits as rates rise. The underlying asset for this contract can either be an interest rate such as the Prime Rate or the London InterBank Offer Rate (LIBOR) or a forward contract on interest rates. These forward contracts on interest rates are essentially OTC futures contracts and they are universally known as Forward Rate Agreements (FRAs).

An FRA is an arrangement between a financial institution and a client that allows the client to fix interest costs (or investment returns) for a specific future period. The interest rate to be paid on a nominal deposit of a specified maturity on that future date is agreed upon at the consummation of the transaction. At the maturity of the FRA, if rates have risen above the agreed rate, the seller of the FRA will pay an amount in cash that will remedy the buyer for his increased interest expense. If rates are below the agreed rate, then the buyer will have to compensate the seller. With the FRA, no principal is exchanged, only the difference between the agreed upon rate and the interest rate on the maturity date. As the reader may see, an FRA is almost identical to a Eurodollar futures contract. The differences are: a Eurodollar futures contract is standardised for dates (IMM dates) and amounts ($1,000,000 contract size) and the FRA is customised; a Eurodollar futures price is 100 minus the interest rate level, while the FRA is simply the interest rate level and finally, Eurodollar futures must be margined every day and FRAs generally have no such margining requirement.

Therefore, if FRAs are simply OTC Eurodollar futures, then Interest Rate Guarantees (which are options on FRAs) must simply be OTC options on Eurodollar futures. Since this is the case, the pricing of these products must be identical to that of the option on Eurodollar futures. The major difference in the pricing of Interest Rate Guarantees are that they tend to have a European exercise feature. Thus, the method for estimating the theoretical price for European Interest

Rate Guarantees is determined by using the simple Black (1976) model for futures with the underlying price equal to the FRA rate for the expiration date of the Interest Rate Guarantee. If the Interest Rate Guarantee is American style, the Binomial Approach could be used. The reader is referred back to Chapter 3 (Table 3.13) for the actual formulae for these models.

OTC interest rate options like Interest Rate Guarantees are based upon the annualised interest rates rather than upon price indices like Eurodollar futures options. The premiums for these options are also in terms of annualised percentage terms and as with futures options the cash price for the option is equal to the price in percentages (basis points) times the value of each 0.01% point (1 basis point). Because most OTC interest rate options cannot be exercised early (European style), there is no problem associated with what is actually delivered upon exercise. At the final maturity date of the option (a lender option for example), the writer of the option will simply pay the holder of the Interest Rate Guarantee in cash the difference between the strike "rate" for the IRG and the market reference rate. This will only occur if the reference interest rate (like LIBOR) is below the strike "rate". If the reference interest rate is higher no cash is paid and the option expires worthless.

An example of the use of an Interest Rate Guarantee application would be for a borrower who must insure his next rollover of his floating rate funding. He would choose to purchase a Borrower Option (BO) to protect himself. Table 12.4 outlines the current market dynamics for the hedger.

Option Type:	European
Underlying Interest Rate:	6 Month $ LIBOR
Expiration Date:	9 Months (274 Days)
Strike Level:	6.5%
Face Value:	$20,000,000
Current 6 Month $Libor Interest Rate:	6.5%
Cost Of Option	0.50%

Table 12.4 Interest Rate Options.

He finds that the current 6 month LIBOR is 6.5% and he wishes to lock in this rate in 9 months' time. The strike rate is 6.5% and the amount of the exposure is $20,000,000. Since the BO is an European style option, it is important to determine what the expected 6 month LIBOR is in 9 months' time (the forward rate) and this can be determined with a 9 vs. 15 FRA. This quote format for FRAs indicates that the beginning of the borrowing or lending exposure begins in 9 months' time and finishes in 15 months' time. Thus, this would represent a 6 month borrowing in 9 months' time. This rate is 6.75%. To better see when the exposures occur, Figure 12.2 displays the period of exposure the option covers and the actual borrowing period.

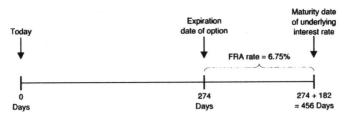

Figure 12.2 Exposure Period of Interest Rate Option and Underlying Exposure.

The cost of the option is 0.50% or $50,000 (50 basis points · 50$ per 6 month LIBOR basis point per $1,000,000 · $20,000,000). At the expiration of the BO, the holder receives either nothing if the 6 month LIBOR is below 6.5% or the difference between the current 6 month LIBOR and 6.5% · 182/360 · $20,000,000. Suppose that on the expiration date, 6 month LIBOR is equal to 8%. Then, the Holder of the BO will be paid $151,667 (8% - 6.5%) · 182/360 · $20,000,000. Then the borrower must actually borrow in the market at 8% at that point, however the $151,667 he has been paid by the BO writer will reduce his interest payment accordingly.

The net effect of the BO hedge will be an interest expense of $808,889 borrowing at 8% (8% · 182/360 · $20,000,000) minus the inflow on the BO of $151,667 plus the premium he had to pay upfront for the BO of $50,000. In total, his interest expense is equal to $707,222 ($808,889 - $151,667 + $50,000) or a rate of 7% 6 month LIBOR ($707,222/$20,000,000 · 360/182). As expected, his worst case result is equal to his strike rate of 6.5% + the 0.50% in premium he paid for the BO.

INTEREST RATE CEILING, FLOOR AND COLLAR AGREEMENTS[21]

The extreme interest rate variability in the early 1980s led many borrowers and investors to seek protection for their streams of floating rate payments. A perfect product for these needs was the Interest Rate Cap Agreement which would limit either the variable rate interest expense of a borrower or the variable rate of return for an investor. This OTC product thus "capped" the exposure and hence the name "Cap Agreement". An Interest Rate Cap Agreement is a contractual arrangement where the Grantor (seller) of the Agreement has an obligation to pay cash to the Holder (buyer) if a particular interest rate exceeds or is less than a mutually agreed upon level at some future point in time.

The two most basic forms of the Interest Rate Cap Agreement are Floor and Ceiling Agreements. The Ceiling Agreement allows the Holder to establish a maximum interest rate level for borrowing (on a floating basis) over a given period. If interest rates rise above the Ceiling rate, the holder receives cash to exactly

---

[21]This section is heavily drawn upon a paper written by this author and published as, "The A to Z of Caps", in Risk Magazine, Vol. 2, No. 3 (March 1989), pp. 21-24.

offset the additional interest expense incurred at the now higher interest rate. If rates fall, the Holder will be able to borrow at a rate below the Ceiling rate. In this case, he receives nothing from the Grantor. He might regard the Agreement as an interest rate insurance policy that has simply lapsed unused. The Floor Agreement allows the Holder to establish a minimum invesment rate level for his floating rate deposits over a given period. If interest rates fall below the floor rate, the Grantor makes good the Holders interest income shortfall. If rates exceed the floor rate, the Holder receives nothing from the Grantor, but can place his deposit at the higher prevailing market rate.

Collars (sometimes known as fences) are simply a combination of these two transactions. Collars allow the Holder to establish a maximum (or minimum) interest rate level for borrowing (or investing) over a given period. In addition, the Holder has sold a Floor Agreement which limits the gain from any fall in interest rates. If Interest rates exceed the Ceiling rate, he receives cash from the Grantor which (in cash flow terms) allows him to borrow at that rate. If interest rates are below the Ceiling rate, then he can borrow at the more favourable rate until rates reach the level of the Floor Agreement he sold. At that rate and below, he must pay cash to the Grantor (which in cash flow terms) estblishes a minimum borrowing rate. The reason why Collars are popular is because the cost can be substantially less than for a Ceiling Agreement. Basically, the rationale for the Collar is exactly the same as the Zero Cost Option strategy outlined in Chapter 11. The premium cost is reduced by giving up the unlimited profit potential.

By far, the most popular of the Interest Rate Cap Agreements are the Ceiling Agreements. Therefore, Interest Rate Caps are used mostly by those who borrow at variable rates and are at risk that rates will have changed by the time they rollover their borrowing. Take the example of a borrower funding himself for a three year period at three-month LIBOR (the London Interbank Offer Rate in this case for US Dollars). He may be concerned that over the next three years, when he must rollover his borrowing in three month increments; rates will rise. He may also have in mind a target LIBOR which, if exceeded, could cause him major problems. For this borrower, the appropriate Interest Rate Cap Agreement would be a Ceiling.

An increasingly important use of Ceiling Agreements for hedgers is for private individuals who have floating rate mortgages and wish to protect themselves from an increase in the floating rate determinant of their mortgage payments.

During the turbulent 1970s and 1980s, levels of interest rates fluctuated wildly. During most of this period, interest rates rose and for those financial institutions which had lent money at the lower fixed rate interest levels of the 1960s, financial ruin was assured. No category of financial institutions were hurt more than the Savings and Loan Associations in the United States. These institutions had lent money at fixed interest rates to homeowners to mortgage their homes. Often these loans extended out for 20 or 30 years. To raise the money for these loans, the S&Ls borrowed essential on an overnight basis from passbook holders, who could demand their money back immediately or at very short notice. To assure the cost of funds was below the interest earned on the mortgage loans, the rates of interest paid on the passbooks were very low indeed. Then, when interest rates rose in the early 1980s, the passbook savers were offered higher rates of interest by money market mutual funds and they withdrew their funds in droves. To avoid insolvency, the S&Ls also had to access the money markets for their funding. Given the rates of interest paid were much higher than what the S&Ls received on their mortgage loans, the S&Ls began haemorrhaging money.

The rest as they say is "History". After the Junk Bond salesmen were finished with them and interest rates continued gyrating, the S&L industry was devastated. Those who did survive, decided that either they would no longer offer fixed rate mortgage loans or would sell off all fixed rate mortgages into the market as soon as possible. With this development, mortgage backed securities were born. But that is another book at another time. The key element is that S&Ls would no longer accept the risks of fluctuating interest rates. They either passed them on to investors or made those taking out the mortgage assume the risk through a variable interest loan.

Of course, this was nothing new for the United Kingdom, where until recently almost all home mortgages were paying variable interest. This meant that many home owners lost their hearths as interest rates rose to double digit levels in Britain during the late 1980s. Then, out of the blue, insurance brokers began selling insurance policies which capped the variable rate interest these home owners would have to pay on their mortgages. These were simply the Interest Rate Ceiling Agreements repackaged and sold to "pools" of private individuals. These products have been a booming success in Britain and have now expanded into many markets world-wide where for the first time the private individual had access (albeit indirectly) to OTC option products.

For the other kind of Cap Agreement, a potential user of a Floor Agreement would be a Bond portfolio manager wishing to limit his down-side exposure on a floating-rate Bond portfolio to falling interest rates. He could either switch to a fixed-rate investment or purchase a Floor as an investment insurance policy.

When a Cap Agreement is purchased by the Holder, a premium must be paid to the Grantor. Thus, an Interest Rate Cap Agreement is similar to an option in this way. And as with an option, the Holder of the Agreement pays the premium to enjoy its beneficial conditions and not be bound by the detrimental facets.

On the other side, the Grantor is unsure when the Agreement is reached whether or not a payout will occur. However, assuming that interest rate "returns" are distributed comparably to other asset returns, he can use standard option pricing methodologies to help him determine the value of the Agreement, gain an indication of the probability of payout, and quantify the risk of the position.

Given that Cap Agreements are similar to options, would this Ceiling Holder be buying a three year option on interest rates? The answer is yes and no. What he is buying is a strip of European options (similar to Interest Rate Guarantees) that expire on the day each quarter during the three year period that he rolls over his bor-

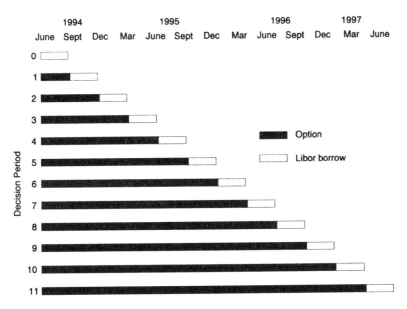

Figure 12.3 Structure of a 3 Year LIBOR Cap-Rate Ceiling Agreement.

rowing at the then prevailing LIBOR. Essentially, the Ceiling Agreement guarantees him a maximum rate for all his LIBOR rollovers.

Figure 12.3 outlines this process. It also shows that the buyer of a three-year Ceiling Agreement starting in June 1994 actually acquires eleven (11) options on 3 month LIBOR.

The open boxes to the right of each decision period that have LIBOR BORROW associated with them indicate the periods of his actual borrowing. The filled boxes to the left of the borrowing period represent the term for each rollover option. The price he must pay for the Ceiling Agreement is simply the sum of the premiums for each of the eleven options.

Pricing of the Ceiling Rate Agreement

Payouts of a Ceiling Rate Agreement on three month LIBOR are determined by the levels of three month LIBOR at a specific future point in time. To value the Cap Agreement today, we must somehow determine the projected future levels of three month LIBOR. In other words, we need futures prices of three month LIBOR for the duration of the Cap Agreement.

If the term of the Cap Agreement is ten years or less, and if the dates on which the Cap payout is determined correspond to the maturities of LIBOR futures contracts (Eurodollar futures) traded in Chicago, Singapore and London, all one has to do is subtract the Eurodollar futures price from 100 to determine expected LIBOR for the Cap Agreement. If the Cap Agreement is for a longer term (over 10 years), or payouts are determined on a day other than the maturity of the futures, one must consult the Forward Rate Agreement market or do a forward/forward calculation using long-dated LIBOR deposit rates to determine the expected three month rate. Returning to our example of three year Cap Agreement starting in June 1994, let us assume that payout is determined on the expiration of the Eurodollar futures. Table 12.5 displays actual (LIBOR) Eurodollar futures prices as of 15 June 1994 and the implied LIBOR rates (100 minus futures price).

	1994	1994	1995	1995	1995	1995	1996	1996	1996	1996	1997
Options expiration period	Sep	Dec	Mar	June	Sep	Dec	Mar	June	Sep	Dec	Mar
Days to Maturity	91	182	273	364	455	546	637	728	819	910	1001
Eurodollar Futures Price	94.84	94.14	93.91	93.61	93.36	93.12	93.08	92.98	92.89	92.74	92.72
Implied Eurodollar Rate	5.16	5.86	6.09	6.39	6.64	6.88	6.92	7.02	7.11	7.26	7.28
Strike Price	7.00	7.00	7.00	7.00	7.00	7.00	7.00	7.00	7.00	7.00	7.00
Risk-free Interest Rate	4.40	4.50	4.63	4.75	4.75	4.88	5.00	5.13	5.25	5.38	5.50
Volatility (%)	19.00	19.00	19.00	18.20	18.20	17.90	17.50	17.50	17.50	17.25	17.00
Option Premium	0.001	0.04	0.12	0.23	0.37	0.52	0.57	0.66	0.74	0.84	0.87
Delta Factor		0.003	0.10243	0.21623	0.32904	0.4197	0.48886	0.4988	0.52168	0.5391	0.56576	0.56589

Quarterly Cap Price = 4.961
Quoted Cap Price = 1.24025

Table 12.5 Example of Pricing of a 3 Year Cap-Rate Ceiling Agreement.

We can use these futures rates as elements in determining the value of our individual LIBOR options that by summation make up our Ceiling Rate Agreement price. But first we must determine the other variables that we will need to price the individual options. The variables depend upon which option pricing model we select.

We have established that, since the separate LIBOR options can only experience cash flow from the Grantor to the Holder on a single day (expiration) they can be thought of as European options. We have also established that the expected future LIBOR will be equal to 100 minus the Eurodollar futures price. To price these LIBOR options therefore, we will use Black's (1976) model for pricing European options on futures.

This model requires five variables to be supplied: time to expiration (or payout determination date); the price of the underlying futures (or expected future

LIBOR); the strike or exercise price (Cap Rate level); the risk-free interest rate for the time period of the option; and the variance of the return on the underlying (or the square root of this variance which is the "volatility").

Table 12.5 displays these variables for each of the eleven options that comprise the value of our Ceiling. We have assumed that the buyer wanted a Ceiling with a strike price of 7%. The price of the Ceiling Rate Agreement is the sum of the individual LIBOR option premiums. In this case, 496 (three-month) LIBOR basis points, or $12,400 per million Dollars borrowed. Generally these products are quoted in annual interest rate terms and this is determined by simply dividing the quarterly price (of 496) by 4 (for a quoted price of 1.24025). In our example, the Ceiling Rate Agreement was for a $20,000,000 worth of borrowing and would have cost $248,050.

Hedging a Ceiling Rate Agreement with Eurodollar Futures and Options

The Holder of the Ceiling Rate Agreement is paying the Grantor to assume his interest rate risk. A critical element in the price the Grantor makes is how the string of OTC options will be hedged. How does the Grantor hedge the risk of interest rates rising? In our example, if three-month LIBOR is above 7%, the Grantor could hedge by then taking an opposite position in Eurodollar futures or LIBOR FRAs, with a 1:1 hedge ratio. In this case, selling $20,000,000 worth of Eurodollar futures at 93.00 for each LIBOR rollover would do the trick (or buying $20 million worth of FRAs for each of the 11 dates).

However, if LIBOR at any rollover point is less than 7.00%, no futures or FRAs are required, implying a hedge ratio of zero. Thus the Grantor cannot tell a priori if he needs to hedge or not. Because the hedge/no hedge decision is based upon probabilities, he can only be sure that the proper hedge ratio is somewhere between 0 and 1.

So, how does the granter arrive at a precise calculation of the hedge ratio he requires? In our estimation of the value of the Ceiling Rate Agreement, we used the Black (1976) futures options pricing model. In Chapter 3, at page 76 we can find the formula and Table 3.6 shows a few of the partial derivatives of the model. Since we used the Eurodollar futures as the underlying price input - or rather 100 minus Eurodollar futures - we can, through differentiation determine how the value of the individual option changes for a given change in the futures price. If we know this relationship, we can adjust the number of futures (or FRAs) in our hedge to exactly offset gains of losses in the value of the options comprising our Ceiling Rate Agreement (for a given change in underlying LIBOR rates).

The derivative we want is dc/dF, commonly referred to as the delta. The delta derivatives of the Black model for both calls and puts appear in Table 3.6. As Black points out on page 177 of his 1976 paper, "[this delta derivative determines] the size of the short position in the futures that makes the combined position risk-less". Thus, the proper hedge ratio for each Eurodollar futures month (or FRA) is the delta for that LIBOR (component of the Ceiling Rate Agreement) that expires at the expiration of the particular Eurodollar futures month. This hedge ratio can be seen in the delta factor row of Table 12.5.

For example, if our Ceiling Grantor were to hedge the Agreement with futures, he would sell December 1994 Eurodollar futures equal to 10.2% of the principal amount of the Ceiling Rate Agreement then remaining (because the delta for that single option is 0.10243). So, if the principal amount at the time to be rolled over was $20,000,000, then the Grantor would now sell approximately two December 1994 Eurodollar futures to hedge the value of the Agreement from changes in the expected LIBOR interest rate for that date. (Actually he would sell 2.0486 futures if that were possible.) He would repeat this technique for each Eurodollar futures contract month that corresponds to a particular LIBOR option. If perfect divisibility of futures contracts existed, the Ceiling Rate Agreement Grantor could achieve a risk-less hedged position with futures (relative to changes in the present levels of interest rates). This hedging strategy using deltas is what I have previously referred to as delta neutral hedging.

Risks of The Hedged Positions

Traditional wisdom states that hedging involves the exchange of price (or interest rate) risk for basis risk. The basis risk, or the relationship of the changes in the cash price and futures price, is generally less than price risk, especially if the cash and futures prices move together (often measured by a correlation statistic). Since this basis risk has now become the primary risk of a futures/cash hedged position, the hedger manages his hedge by managing the basis risk. However, when hedging interest rate Cap Agreements or options with futures, there are additional risks beside the basis risk. These additional risks can be summarised as the risk of the deltas and the risk of changing variance in the underlying market.

A major problem of hedging options or option-like instruments with futures is that the magnitude of an options position varies while the futures (or FRA) magnitude is fixed. The delta-neutral hedged position is only "hedged" at a single point (as I discussed in Chapters 3 and 8). If the underlying futures price (or interest rate) changes, the risk dimension of the options can become larger or smaller relative to the futures while the risk of the futures position is unchanged. As these option deltas change, the "hedge" no longer exists and revisions must be made to the number of futures sold for the position to remain neutral. Thus, the hedger faces an additional risk of changing deltas.

This risk can also be quantified through the differentiation of the Black model. It is simply the second derivative of the option price relative to the underlying, commonly referred to as the gamma. The formula for this derivative is also given in Table 3.6. Because the risk dimension of the futures is impervious to such changes in the levels of the underlying markets, an effective futures hedging strategy must include monitoring and revision. This will involve transaction costs that must be considered by the hedger.

Another alternative for hedging options on LIBOR is to use other options on LIBOR - exchange traded options on Eurodollar futures, other Interest Rate Cap Agreements, or Interest Rate Guarantee Agreements.

The intuition behind this approach is that it is best to cover a contingent liability (or asset) with another equally contingent asset (or liability). In reality, the only truly perfect hedge for a Cap Rate Agreement is to cover it with exactly the same Cap Rate Agreement. However, this reduces the Grantor to the role of a broker and limits his profit potential accordingly. If the Grantor chooses to hedge his risk by purchasing options, he must pay a premium, but he will offset underlying market risk and minimise the impacts that the market dynamics have on deltas. Thus, with options, the hedger can achieve both delta neutrality and gamma neutrality, but at a price.

Another advantage of options (relative to futures) for hedging Interest Rate Cap Agreements concerns the effect that changing market variances have on the value of these Agreements. Cap Agreements and options increase (or decrease) in value when the variance of the underlying increases (or decreases), while futures values are not effected by changes in the variance. Again, hedging option-like instruments with futures creates a mismatch that implies the risks of changing variances remain uncovered.

This variance risk can also be quantified through differentiation of the Black model; this derivative appears in Table 3.6 as vega. The only way to offset variance risk is to hedge with assets whose value is sensitive to changes in the level of variance in exactly the opposite way. Thus, buying options for the same maturity, strike price and underlying asset will be the only exact hedge for the variance risk (and delta/gamma risk) associated with selling options.

Unfortunately, if the Grantor of the Ceiling Rate Agreement decided he wished to do this by using the options on Eurodollar futures market, he would find it impossible because options failed to trade out as far as March 1997 (in June 1994). In fact, past the first two contract expirations, no options are actively traded. So, how can the Ceiling Grantor hedge a string of LIBOR option risk extending out eleven quarters with only the first 2 nearby (September 1994 and December 1994) Eurodollar options? The answer entails making all the various options positions directly comparable to one standard.

In Table 12.6, additional derivatives for the Black (1976) model are presented that make the deltas and gammas equivalent to either a spot price or a nearby futures. Therefore, to hedge multiple option maturities with a single option maturity, one must make all the deltas in the multiple maturity options equivalent to the single maturity and these modified derivatives will do it for you.

DELTA DERIVATIVES

To make delta equivalent to spot, Sp

$$\alpha C / \alpha Sp = \exp^{-rt} \times \exp^{ht} \times N(d_1)$$

$$\alpha C / \alpha Sp = \exp^{-rt} \times \exp^{ht} \times \left[N(d_1) - 1\right]$$

to make delta equivalent to nearby futures

$$\alpha C / \alpha NF = \exp^{-rt} \times \exp^{h\left(t - t\,\text{nearby}_\text{futures}\right)} \times N(d_1)$$

$$\alpha C / \alpha NF = \exp^{-rt} \times \exp^{h\left(t - t\,\text{nearby}_\text{futures}\right)} \times \left[N(d_1) - 1\right]$$

where h = the implied holding cost rate from
today to the expiration of the futures

GAMMA DERIVATIVES

$$\text{Calls \& Puts} = \exp^{-rt} \times \exp^{(-d_1^2/2)/(F \times S \times \sqrt{2\pi t})}$$

to make gamma equivalent to spot, Sp

multiply above by $\exp^{(2ht)}$

Table 12.6   The Black (1976) Commodity Option Pricing Model.
Derivatives Relative to Spot and the Nearby Futures.

In these modifications the volatility derivative, vega, is not affected since it is assumed to move to the same degree across time. Unfortunately a new risk emerges: the spread risk between the maturities. When comparing nearby futures (or spot) to deferred futures, we must assume that the holding cost relationships remain unchanged. But if these holding cost relationships do change, they will introduce another component of risk for the hedging strategy. The holding cost defines the implied relationship between spot prices and futures prices and also applies between futures months. The holding cost adjusted derivative (rho) can also be seen in Table 3.6. This measures the intra month risk that will be discussed in Chapter 14 and the hedging of which will be addressed at that point.

To come full circle, when hedging cash markets with futures markets, one exchanges price risk for basis risk; when hedging options with futures, one exchanges price risk for gamma risk and volatility risk; and when hedging multiple maturity options with single maturity options, one exchanges price risk, gamma risk and volatility risk for spread risk.

The advent of Eurodollar (and deposit on other currencies) futures and options has provided the fundamental building blocks financial engineers require to develope OTC option products. The Interest Rate Cap Agreement is a classic example of how this has occurred.

OPTIONS ON INTEREST RATE SWAPS[22]

A Swaption is the right, but not the obligation, to assume a position in an underlying Interest Rate Swap. Swaptions came about (as almost all OTC option products have) when financial institutions perceived that a derivative product niche existed that had not yet been filled, and that by offering these new products a reasonable profit might be made. Moreover, the first to market Swaptions would probably earn much more than just prestige. Unfortunately, any introduction had to wait until those intending to offer Swaptions could determine a "fair" price that would adequately cover any risk assumed, and still provide a reasonable profit.

The Structure Of Swaption Agreements

Before we can examine in depth how these OTC options work, it is necessary to define terms and clarify what Swaptions are: what do they promise and when. What is promised is a conditional acceptance of a position in an Interest Rate Swap of a predetermined maturity. It is important to remember that an Interest Rate Swap is an exchange of a fixed rate stream of payments (like a fixed bond rate) for a floating rate stream of payments (like a floating rate bond). The buyer of the Swaption has the right, but not the obligation, to accept the Interest Rate Swap and will rationally exercise the right only if doing so would be beneficial. If, relative to the strike "rate"(instead of strike price) of the Swaption, the buyer would exacerbate a loss, the Interest Rate Swap Agreement is not taken. For this right, buyers pay sellers a premium. It is not surprising that when Swaptions are reduced to their most basic form, one discovers that they are simply options on Interest Rate Swaps.

The question, "What is actually exchanged: a floating rate stream or a fixed rate stream?", is a source of confusion for many potential users of Swaptions. A comparable conundrum exists in foreign exchange options where a similar "mirror" effect exists. For example, the right to buy Deutsche Marks (calls) for US Dollars is exactly the same transaction as the right to sell US Dollars (puts) and receive Deutsche Marks. In Swaptions, the right to pay the fixed component of an Interest Rate Swap is identical to the right to receive the floating component (and vice versa). To simplify matters, in general, the Swaption market quotes on the FIXED rate component of Interest Rate Swaps. Swaptions (as most options) come in two varieties. Instead of calls (the right to buy) and puts (the right to sell), Swaption varieties are offered as RECEIVER Swaptions (the right to receive a fixed interest rate) and PAYER Swaptions (the right to pay a fixed interest rate). However, we must remember that a RECEIVER Swaption on the fixed component is the same as a "payer" Swaption on the floating side (and vice versa).

---

[22]This section is drawn heavily from a paper written by this Author and appeared as "Behind the Mirror", in Risk Magazine, Vol. 2, No. 2 (February 1989), pp. 17-23.

A RECEIVER Swaption allows the purchaser the right, but not the obligation to receive the fixed rate side of an Interest Rate Swap. The buyer of the RECEIVER Swaption benefits as interest rates fall because he guarantees the receipt of a fixed rate above the prevailing rate (funding it at what now is a lower rate). As interest rates rise, the Swaption buyer will ignore the Swaption because he can choose to receive a higher fixed rate in the market (that offsets his higher floating rate expense). The seller of the RECEIVER Swaption is obligated to pay the fixed rate of the Interest Rate Swap and receive the floating rate. This type of instrument will produce a payoff structure similar to a simple put on interest rates (or a call on a fixed income instrument).

A PAYER Swaption allows the buyer the right, but not the obligation, to pay a fixed rate and receive the floating rate for an Interest Rate Swap. In contrast to the RECEIVER Swaption, as interest rates rise, the buyer can lock in an attractive fixed rate and when fixed rates fall (below the Swaption strike) the buyer can let the Swaption expire worthless. The seller of the PAYER Swaption is obligated to receive the fixed side of the Interest Rate Swap and pay the floating. PAYER Swaptions will produce a payoff structure similar to call options on rates (or put options on fixed income instruments).

Now that we know what is promised, it is important to ask when does the exchange of the fixed for the floating actually occur, given the buyer wishes to exercise the Swaption? For most Swaption Agreements (hereafter referred to as "standard" Swaptions) the "clock" on the Interest Rate Swap begins at the point of exercise. This "starting gun" feature allows the buyer to define the exact term of the Swap and the dates of interest exchange.

For example, a 1 year Swaption on a 5 year Swap, would allow the buyer upon exercise to establish a fixed for floating position on a 5 year Swap, beginning immediately. Future coupon exchange dates would be set relative to this exercise date. So, if a PAYER Swaption exercised the contract for a five year Swap on 1 April , he would be obligated to pay a fixed coupon (the strike "rate" of the Swaption) every 1 April (or an appropriate business date near it) for the next 5 years and would receive floating interest payments on dates set relative to 1 April. If the Swaption buyer exercised instead on 15 April, all payments of fixed for floating interest would be on dates relative to 15 April. Therefore, at initiation of the Agreement, both participants in the Swaption know they are dealing with a hypothetical Swap with a 5 year term but it is possible that neither know at the inception of the Swaption which dates the payments will occur or if the Agreement will be used at all.

As one might surmise, if buyers could exercise Swaptions at any date prior to expiration, the sellers of the Agreements may have to accept an undesirable Interest Rate Swap with "broken dates". These "broken dates" can present a problem because the non-standardisation of dates makes secondary trading of the underlying interest Rate Swap Agreements difficult (and subsequent laying off of the Swaption's risk) relative to Swaps exchanging coupons on dates that are standard.

Typically, standard dates are those dates on which a significant number of financial institutions rollover floating rate obligations. Often the settlement dates of Eurodollar Futures represent such standardised dates as hedgers roll hedged positions into the cash market.

This particular uncertainty leads most sellers of Swaptions to not allow buyers the ability to exercise Swaption Agreements early (American exercise feature). The vast majority of options offered by sellers only allow exercise on a single date (European exercise feature) which would mean that if the buyers exercise, the resulting Interest Rate Swap Agreement would have not only a known maturity, but would also exchange interest payments on standard dates. I estimate that "standard" Swaption arrangements with European exercise features comprise almost 90% of all Swaption transactions. The remaining 10% of Swaption transactions are primarily "reversible" Swaptions.

Reversibles are based upon an existing Interest Rate Swap where the terms of coupon exchange, as well as the maturity of the Swap, are established at the inception of the Swaption. These differ from "standard" Swaptions which are based on a hypothetical Interest Rate Swap. We find that reversible Swaptions are more likely to have an American exercise feature since the dates of exchange are predetermined and early exercise would not result in broken dates. However, European exercise features seem to be more prevalent for reversibles as well as standard Swaptions.

Swaptions vs. Interest Rate Cap Agreements

Swaptions and Cap agreements are both option derivatives of underlying interest rate markets. The Swaption allows the holder the right to pay (or receive) a specific fixed rate and receive (or pay) a floating rate for an agreed upon term. The Swaption can only be exercised once into the underlying Interest Rate Swap. A Cap Agreement is the right to fix a series of individual interest payments. As was outlined above, the Cap Agreement is really a string of options for each borrowing point. Thus, the Cap agreement tends to be more expensive because the holder has multiple exercise dates and during the life of the Agreement can benefit if rates fall and limit his loss potential if at any point interest rates have risen.

The Logic Underlying Swaption Pricing

The theoretical pricing of Swaptions is remarkably simple, after one gets over the initial hurdle that the instrument is "a derivative of a derivative". Derivative markets imply that their tradable instruments are derived from some other market and that they are "substitutes" several steps removed from it. For example, an ultimate underlying "market" could be the term structure of interest rates. Unfortunately, interest rates cannot themselves be traded directly. Securities such as fixed and floating rate bonds provide a market surrogate for trading this "time value of money". Interest Rate Swap Agreements are second order derivatives because they are not directly tied to the underlying term structure, but rather they reflect the relative price of fixed verses floating rate bonds (which are one step closer to the ultimate term structure). Swaptions are one step further removed because they are derived from the Interest Rate Swap. In essence, Swaptions allow the buyer the right to "bet" on the relationship between fixed and floating rate bonds, rather than on interest rates (or bonds) directly.

The initial challenge in any option pricing problem is to determine what underlies the option. If you exercise the option, what do you get and when do you get it? Once this problem has been answered, the theoretical pricing problem is greatly simplified. As was outlined earlier, a Swaption allows the buyer the right to receive or pay the fixed rate on an Interest Rate Swap. So the first step is to identify the particular features of the underlying Interest Rate Swap and determine its rate.

In an interesting article on Interest Rate Swaps,[23] the authors suggest that the Swap rate has three components: forward interest rates, transaction costs, and the credit risk inherent in the Swap transaction. Essentially they show that a Swap contract is "fundamentally a series of forward contracts" (p.28).

To determine the fixed rate associated with an Interest Rate Swap, the forward rates for floating rate assets are treated like a string of cash flows and discounted back to present value using a methodology not dissimilar to a yield to maturity calculation. This "yield" is the fixed rate in the Interest Rate Swap. In other words, Interest Rate Swaps reflect an equilibrium rate that would equate a floating rate stream of payments (bond) with a fixed rate stream of payments (bond) at the present date.

In addition, to assess the Swap rate, the market maker in the Swap must then take into account the prevailing bid/offer spread (determined by the supply/ demand for liquidity) and incorporate any credit risk of the intermediary and/or the counterparties. As is common knowledge to most credit officers, this credit issue potentially opens a nasty can of worms.

One might suppose that options on Swaps would require all these elements to be considered plus additional option related variables. Luckily, this is unnecessary because the rate associated with the Swap already includes these elements. If the option took into account the yield curve impacts, transactions costs and credit risk, that would then amount to double counting. The Interest Rate Swap already has these elements embedded in the rate. Our principal task is to determine the appropriate stochastic process driving the underlying Interest Rate Swap market. Once this is accomplished, a Swaption price can be determined by applying an appropriate option pricing model with the rate on the Swap as the "underlying market" input into the model.

---

[23]See Smith, Clifford W. Jr., Charles W. Smithson, and Lee M. Wakeman, "The Evolving Market for Swaps", Midland Corporate Finance Journal, Winter 1986, pp. 20-32.

Another significant issue must be considered: when do you actually acquire the Interest Rate Swap? Consider a Swaption with a European exercise feature (as is the convention for the vast majority of Swaptions). The actual underlying asset for the Swaption is not the present Interest Rate Swap rate, but rather the "forward" rate of the Interest Rate Swap for the expiration day of the Swaption. Now we have the problem of determining the "forward" rate of an Interest Rate Swap. As pointed out above in our discussion on option pricing, the "forward" rate of a Swap need not include all the elements necessary for the evaluation of the present Interest Rate Swap rate. All that is required is to apply a simple time value of money "arbitrage" formula that is often used to determine forward/forward rates. In the Interest Rate Swap market, these transactions are commonly and referred to as forward Interest Rate Swaps.

Having determined the forward Interest Rate Swap rate, it might appear that the Black (1976) model for pricing options on forwards would be most appropriate, and indeed most market participants utilise this formula. However, it must be recognised, that the Black (1976) model applies to commodity (futures) markets where the option contract allows for the exchange of CASH for some commodity at a future date and the model assumes that interest rates are constant. In Swaptions, the option contract allows the exchange of a floating rate "bond" for a fixed rate "bond" and therefore, the use of the Black (1976) model is inappropriate as the model explicitly assumes that interest rates must be constant. It seems that a more appropriate approach to the Swaption pricing problem is to determine the value of an option to exchange one asset for another. Margrabe has already solved this problem and has determined a closed form solution for estimation of European options.[24] The reader may remember that Margrabe's model figured prominently in Chapter 9 when I discussed the trading of options between markets. To save having to refer back to this chapter, the Margrabe model for pricing an option to exchange one asset for another is presented again in Table 12.7.

The reader can once again see that this option pricing model is almost identical to the Black and Scholes formula. The only difference this time is that there is no interest rate component (so we do not have to assume that interest rates are constant) and the strike price "E" has now been replaced by B2. B1 is the value of a "fixed" stream of payments and B2 is the value of a "floating" stream of payments. Thus with the Margrabe model, both the "underlying" asset (B1) and the strike price (B2) are allowed to vary. The only trick to the Margrabe model is the volatility input. Here, because both assets can vary, the variance of both is important to the overall volatility of the Swaption. To determine the volatility input, one must assess the volatilities for both the assets and subtract from this the covariance between them (multiplied by 2). Thus, the reader will see that the formula for volatility in Table 12.7 looks remarkably similar to the formula for the risk of a portfolio presented in Chapter 11. This is no accident because the Margrabe model (and in-

[24]Margrabe, William, "The Value of an Option to Exchange One Asset for Another", *Journal of Finance*, 33 (March 1977), pp. 177-186.

deed all option pricing models) are based upon the concept of equivalent portfolio positions. For example, the Margrabe model for Swaptions assumes that one could create a portfolio with a stream of "fixed" payments and another stream of "floating" payments that would provide the same instantaneous return as would an option on an Interest Rate Swap. So, the worlds of portfolio theory and options pricing are much closer than one would at first think.

$$CALL = B_1 \cdot N(d_1) - B_2 \cdot N(d_2)$$

where:

$$d_1 = \frac{\ln(B_1 / B_2) + (\sigma^2 / 2) \cdot t}{\sigma \cdot \sqrt{t}}$$

$$d_2 = d_1 - \sigma \cdot \sqrt{t}$$

$$\sigma^2 = \sigma_{B_1}^2 - 2\sigma_{B_1} \cdot \sigma_{B_2} \cdot \rho_{B_1 \cdot B_2} + \sigma_{B_2}^2$$

$\sigma_{B_1}^2$ = variance of Fixed Coupon Bond

$\sigma_{B_1}^2$ = variance of Floating Coupon Bond

$\rho_{B_1 \cdot B_2}$ = correlation between Fixed and Floating Bonds

σ = square root of variance, i.e. volatility

t = time to expiration % of a year

B_1 = Value of Fixed Coupon Bond

B_2 = Value of Floating Coupon Bond

$\ln$ = natural logarithm function

e = exponential function

$N(\ )$ = cumulative normal density function

Table 12.7 The Margrabe Model Applied to SWAPTIONS.

Present Market Conventions For Swaption Pricing

Suppose, we decide to follow market convention and use the Black (1976) formula, this assumes the "correct" underlying asset for European pricing is the forward rate for the Interest Rate Swap. Now all we need to do is to gather the other data required by the formula to proceed.

These data include the strike "rate" of the Swaption, the time until expiration, the government (risk-free) interest rate for the Swaption expiration and the volatility of the forward Interest Rate Swap. All of these variables are directly observable, except the volatility (and we will explain how the reader might be able to estimate it). Assuming the trader has all these inputs, he can simply plug the variables into the Black equation to determine a theoretical European Swaption's price.

What of American style Swaptions? In options theory, if the possibility of early exercise exists, things can be complicated. If early exercise is not a rational strategy, than the value of an American Swaptions will equal that of European Swaptions. In stock options, the element that makes early exercise rational for calls is generally the payment for dividends (although as was discussed in Chapter 3, Merton has shown that put options have other aspects that can justify early exercise, see the reference to Merton 1973 in that chapter).

How does this relate to Swaptions? The problem of early exercise (and the American exercise feature) has simply been avoided by most Swaption participants. For those that offer American style Swaptions, they must recognise that the element possibly causing early exercise could be some positive cash flow (i.e. accrued interest) that would induce the buyer of the Swaption to exercise to obtain it. For standard Swaption transactions this is irrelevant because the term of the Swap begins at the point of exercise and, therefore, cannot involve any cumulative cash flows to that point.

For reversible Swaptions, however, the buyer of the American RECEIVER Swaption could have an incentive to exercise if floating rates were significantly below the fixed rate (or for the PAYER Swaption if floating rates were significantly higher than the fixed rate). Nevertheless, this "payment" is not really like a dividend, but is in fact the "in the money amount" for that one segment of the overall Interest Rate Swap Agreement, and would already be embedded in the Swaption price.

Further, if the Swaption is exercised, it may result in a cash flow immediately, but the buyer must consider the rest of the Interest Rate Swap Agreement cash flows that will be deferred into the future. Even so, it is conceivable that a reversible Swaption could potentially be exercised early if the present value of the deferred cash flows is below that of the immediate cash flow. For reversible Swaptions this potential value of early exercise implies that an American Swaption price must be greater than or equal to the European Swaption price for the same maturity. To value the American Swaption, some valuation model that accounts for early exercise would be more appropriate. The Binomial approach (Cox, Ross, Rubinstein discussed in Chapter 3) and the Schaefer and Schwartz's formula (presented earlier) that incorporates the term structure of interest rates are two approaches that market participants are applying to the problem of pricing American Swaptions. However, many market participants approximate the American Swaption price by using a method similar in spirit to Fischer Black's approximation for valuing American call options on dividend paying stock.

This approximation is:

American price = MAXIMUM(Intrinsic Value, European price).

Hence, one can avoid the computational complexity associated with using the other approaches. Anyway, as most option dealers will tell you, the choice of models may be important, but the determination of the volatility to input into the model is of greater importance.

If Swaption prices are already available, then it is a simple matter to determine the implied volatility by an iterative process. However, if Swaption prices are unavailable, the determination of the projected volatility for the forward Interest Rate Swap requires, in theory, historical analysis. Past Interest Rate Swap data must be collected either for "spot" Interest Rate Swap rates or for forward Interest Rate Swap rates. Generally it is easier to get "spot" Interest Rate Swap rates (especially as a spread over treasuries). If the analyst does use "spot" rates, he must convert these to "forward" rates using, in theory, the appropriate government (risk-free) rate. However in practice, what is used to calculate the forward Swap rate is the appropriate deposit rate that the analyst's institution could invest at. With the synthetic or actual forward Interest Rate Swap rate data in hand, the projected volatility is determined by assuming that proportional changes in the interest rates are normally distributed. With this assumption in hand, the projected volatility is determined using the (historical volatility) methodology in the usual manner or applying the "cone" technique discussed in chapter 5.

After all these steps are completed and the data are input in the pricing model, there is one final adjustment to be made to the theoretical prices. This adjustment is required because the "prices" of Swaptions are expressed in annualised interest rate terms. Quite often the underlying Interest Rate Swap can extend beyond 1 year and the Swaption price must reflect the fact that the intrinsic value (a positive interest rate spread) increases with the maturity of the Swap. To account for this effect, the intrinsic value of the Swaption must be multiplied by a factor that measures the present value of the positive interest spread extending over the term of the Interest Rate Swap (and then express this at an annual rate).

CONCLUSION FOR OTC OPTIONS ON INTEREST RATES

By some estimates, the customised OTC market for options and other derivative products dwarfs the exchange traded markets in terms of the volume and underlying exposure these contracts represent. There is little doubt that if interest rates continue the pattern of extreme variability that has been seen in the last 20 years, OTC options on interest rates will continue to flourish.

It is clear that most financial markets have displayed variability just as extreme over the two last decades. For these markets, OTC options are as important as they are for interest rate options and for some markets, such as foreign exchange, OTC options represent 98% of the total trading in options (including exchange traded options such as those presented in Chapter 3). The major factor in this success has been the customisation that OTC options provide to the end user. This flexibility knows almost no bounds as more and more bizarre OTC option products are introduced every day. Thus, I have devoted the entire next chapter to the realm of the unusual or as they are appropriately referred to, exotic options.

13: Exotic Options

In the financial world, no other product provides as much flexibility as is offered by option contracts.[1] If one reviews the chapters on trading strategies, it will again become apparent that options provide few limitations to traders when devising strategies. It is not surprising that options have become a staple in the capital markets because they provide benefits that no other products can provide. For hedgers, options can allow for guaranteed returns in volatile markets and enhanced yields when prevailing rates of return are low. Indeed, there seems to be almost nothing that cannot be constructed using these innovative products. As further proof of this statement, in the last five years, financial analysts have begun to use the fundamental concepts in options theory to "engineer" entirely new products some of which have never existed before. The fruition of human creativity combined with an extremely flexible product such as the option has led to an entirely new field in financial markets to emerge. This area of contingent claims analysis includes those securities which are known as exotic options.

Since options have such an intimate tie to the world of higher mathematics and physics (see Chapters 4 and 14 for the history of the evolution of options theory from these disciplines), it is not a surprise that innovations in these fields have been transferred to the realm of options. For the pure scientists, options markets provide the outlet for the practical application of their theories and at the very least, earn real money for the theorists. However, this interaction between the pure sciences and the financial markets (via options) is not a new phenomenon. The breakthrough began in the early 1970s as another field which required pure scientists began to breakdown.

As almost everyone over 30 will remember, the summer of 1969 saw a profound event occur in human history. The US managed to land men on the surface of the moon and return them to earth safely. The Apollo space program drew upon the very best of the pure scientists to achieve in only a decade what was previously thought impossible. Unfortunately, once there, it quickly became apparent that there was nothing of value on the moon, no gold, diamonds or even crude oil. Therefore, once the goal had been reached, no one was interested in the moon any more. The US Government decided that it made little sense to spend billions of dollars to bring back more rocks which were more or less homogeneous with the

---

[1]I would like to thank Les Clewlow and Stewart Hodges of the Financial Options Research Centre of the University of Warwick for their invaluable contributions on the theoretical pricing issues discussed in this chapter.

461

ones collected on the first mission. Thus, thousands of these "rocket scientists" were thrown out of work. Given that these individuals had such a specialised training and experience, it seemed they were out of luck. The universities simply did not have the capacity to absorb all these out of work theoreticians with impressive resumés. So a number of these individuals went to Wall Street and offered their services to the Investment houses. At least they could add and subtract numbers accurately to track the profit and losses of trader's positions. At this same time, Black (trained in Higher Maths) and Scholes (trained in Physics) published their paper on options pricing. Every investment bank quickly realised that they had to have some expertise in the worlds of the pure sciences or otherwise they would fall behind. At these investment houses (often in the back office) the "rocket scientists" were patiently biding their time. These individuals were immediately transferred to a new analytic department and given the brief to come up with new and innovative products based upon the theories they knew so well. The most successful investment banks in America such as Goldman Sachs and Salomon Brothers vied for the best of these rocket scientists and the rest is history. It is interesting to note that both Fischer Black (now at Goldman Sachs) and Myron Scholes (now at Salomon Brothers) have left academia to work at what are now the finest finance departments in the world. Interestingly, these are no longer found at universities but centred in the financial districts of New York, London and Tokyo.

The range of new OTC option products that have been and are currently being developed are truly mind boggling. These exotic options differ from the conditions of standard options in several ways offering products for almost every possible risk managment problem. The variations of these products can be grouped into four broad classifications:

- Options which allow the holder to buy or sell another Option
- Options which vary the standard terms of normal options
- Path-dependent options, where the payoff of the options depends on the behaviour of the price of some underlying asset during the life of the option and not solely the price at the expiration of the option, and
- Multi-factor options where the final payoff depends upon the prices of two or more underlying assets.

In this chapter, I will introduce each of these areas and provide the reader with an overview of the key issues involved in the products. For each product, I will define what the product is, suggest a few applications and examine key issues in the pricing of that particular product. When it will add to understanding, a profit and loss profile of the product will be presented. It would be inappropriate to devote the same degree of detail to these products as I have provided to simple options as this would require space warranted for another book. However, throughout this chapter, every product will have references for further reading for those interested in the detail of each product. Before I can discuss the theoretical pricing issues involved with exotic options, I must introduce the general approaches used for pricing these products.

GENERAL APPROACHES TO PRICING EXOTIC OPTIONS

When discussing the pricing of exotic options, the methods utilised to find a solution are way and above the complexity of anything yet encountered in this book. There are essentially three methodologies that can be used to estimate the price of an exotic option. I will only briefly introduce the concepts so that the reader will be able to better understand the discourse that follows. The three approaches include:

(1) The Analytic Models
(2) The Numerical Models
(3) Monte Carlo Simulation Models

The Analytic Models

This class of models are those where there is a "closed-form" solution to the partial differential equation the formula is attempting to solve. In simpler terms, a unique formula exists which will produce a single fair option price based upon the input variables. The Black and Scholes model is the best known example of a closed form solution among the analytic models. For exotic options, we will find a number of situations where a closed form solution exists. As the reader will learn, simple compound options, the Quanto, Power options, All or Nothing Digital options and Choosers options all have closed form analytic solutions. These are the "cleanest" solutions to solving the problem of exotic options pricing but as the reader will learn can also be extremely complicated.

The Numerical Models

This approach requires a path to be drawn which is a model for the dispersion process of the underlying asset. The most commonly known of these models is the binomial technique introduced by Cox, Ross and Rubinstein, which was discussed extensively in Chapter 3. Other approaches have expanded the binomial process to a trinomial process with the asset moving up, down or remaining the same. In addition, the Supermodel introduced in Chapter 9, is a numerical model that builds the shape of the tree depending upon the smile patterns for ordinary European options. As I discussed in those earlier chapters, all the possible outcomes for the option are estimated at the expiration date. These are weighted by the probability of each outcome occurring and the sum of all these elements will be the expected value of the option at expiration. To determine the value of the option today, this terminal value is simply discounted back to present value using the appropriate discount interest rate. Apart from simple American options, Bermudan options and the family of exotics which include Ratchet, Ladder and Shout options depend on this method for their pricing.

Monte Carlo Simulation Models[2]

Sometimes it is impossible to apply either the analytic or numerical approaches to price a particularly difficult options pricing problem. This technique essentially involves simulating how an underlying asset price could move over time by including the assumptions in a computer and rerunning the simulation perhaps thousands of times. As this is done, an estimated distribution function for that asset will be generated. At each trial, the final payoff for the option of interest will also be estimated. Once this is done, a distribution of possible option values can be examined and the average result will be the one which will determine the exotic option's price. Clearly, the most critical element in the application of this technique is getting the initial conditions for the underlying asset correct. This technique is most often used with option with "open boundary" conditions where the simple stochastic dominance arguments laid out in Chapter 2 do not apply. This type of situation occurs for "barrier" options such as knock out and knock in options discussed in this chapter. Also, this technique is used for the "one touch" digital option.

The first category of exotic options I will cover will include options which allow the holder to buy or sell another option.

OPTIONS WHICH ALLOW THE HOLDER
TO BUY OR SELL ANOTHER OPTION

These options are known universally as compound options. They allow the holder the right but not the obligation to buy another underlying option. For example, it may be possible to buy a call option that allows the holder the right to buy another call having a longer life than the compound. In this case, the underlying asset of the compound option is a simple option. The four possible types of compound options are presented in Table 13.1.

In this matrix, the horizontal dimension is the underlying option and the vertical dimension is the compound option. For example, in the upper left quadrant of the matrix, you will find a compound call on a normal call. This provides the holder the right but not the obligation to buy another call. Immediately below this is the put on a call which allows the holder the right but not the obligation to sell another call and so forth for the compound call and put on the underlying put option.

---

[2]Kemna, A. G. Z., and A. C. F. Vorst, "A pricing Method for options Based on Average Asset Values" Journal of Banking and Finance, 14 March 1990, pp. 113-124.

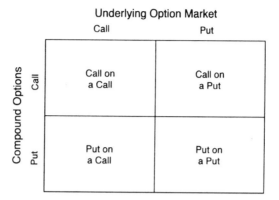

Table 13.1 *The Possible Types of Compound Options.*

As with all options structures, it is always helpful to examine the profit and loss profiles of the instruments.[3] Often, seemingly complex structures resemble one of the option strategies previously discussed in Chapters 6, 7, 8 or 9. Figures 13.1a, 13.1b, 13.1c and 13.1d display the values of all the possible compound options with 90 days to expiration and at expiration. For all of these graphs, we assume an underlying asset price of 100 and the option which underlies the compound option has a maturity of three months at the expiration of the compound option and a price of 3. The compound options themselves all cost 1.

It is apparent that both compound call options most resemble simple call or put options. The major difference is that the compound options cost less (one third in this example) compared to the price of the option they underlie. The compound put options do appear to have a unique profit and loss profile when compared to simple option strategies discussed so far. However, they do seem to resemble one side of

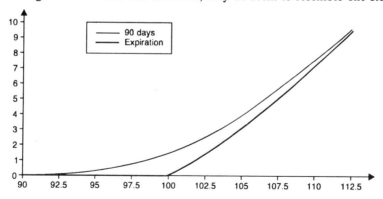

Figure 13.1a *Profit & Loss Profile of a Call on a Call over time.*

---

[3]These Profit and Loss Profiles were modified from diagrammes kindly supplied by Brian Thomas of Bank of America, London.

the short calendar spread profile discussed in Chapter 8. In more ways than one, the compound option can be thought of as a variation of a calendar spread and this will be discussed later in the immediately following sections. First of all, let us examine those situations where compound options may be required.

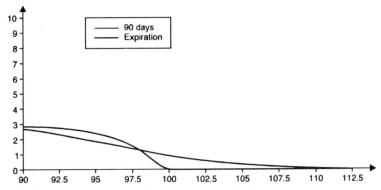

Figure 13.1b Profit & Loss Profile of a Put on a Call over time.

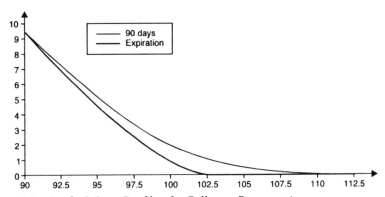

Figure 13.1c Profit & Loss Profile of a Call on a Put over time.

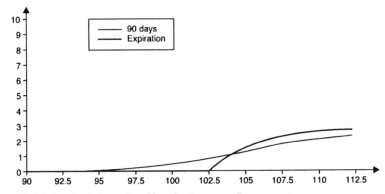

Figure 13.1d Profit & Loss Profile of a Put on a Put over time.

Compound Options On Cap Rate Agreements Captions And Floptions

For a number of contingent hedging situations, a client may not require an option but rather an option to buy an option. This situation was outlined in some detail in the first hedging example presented in Chapter 10. To review that example, a money manager had to submit a bid to a pension fund to provide his investment services and had to offer a particular rate to the client. He was at risk that if the market rates (for a long dated US Treasury Bond) changed, he could be in trouble. Furthermore, he had a contingent risk that his services might not be selected at all. In that example, it was shown that an option hedge was superior to a futures hedge if the bid was rejected. This situation occurs quite often in the foreign exchange markets and has led a number of financial institutions to offer a whole new kind of option contract which is an option on an option. As always, these institution have come up with clever names for these options on options. Typical names for foreign exchange compound options include the EXTRA (by Hambros Bank), the TTC (the Tender to Contract option by Barclays Bank) and the SCOUT (a Midland Bank product). Of course many other names exist for these products and perhaps the more exotic the name the more the bank can charge the customer for that option.

In the interest rate risk management area, the most popular of the compound options are the options to purchase a Ceiling Agreement or to buy a Floor Agreement. The option to purchase a Ceiling Agreement is known as a Caption (a Marine Midland trademark name) and the option to purchase a Floor Agreement is known either as a Floption or a Floortion. These products were created for those hedgers that faced a contingent interest rate risk and are uncertain whether or not an interest rate exposure would occur.

A classical example of such a contingent interest rate risk would be for the firm which begins a friendly take-over bid for another firm. To purchase a sufficient quantity of the target firms shares, money would have to be borrowed. However, the take-over firm is uncertain if the regulators will allow the take-over process to proceed. During the period awaiting the regulators' decision, the firm intending to initiate the take-over would be exposed to a rise in interest rates. To protect itself against the rise in interest rates and to address the risk that the take-over bid might not be allowed, an option on a Ceiling Agreement (a Caption) would be the ideal solution. However, Captions and Floptions can also be useful for firms with existing borrowing or lending exposures.

For example, Chicago and Northwestern Transportation Company wanted to protect itself against a rise in dollar interest rates on a two-year $800 million loan extension being used for project financing. The company was concerned that rates would rise, but if instead rates declined, the firm would have missed an opportunity for interest savings. Thus, Chemical Bank, New York was able to put together a Caption that provided the greatest flexibility for the company. In September 1989, Chicago and Northwestern executed a strip of European-style options with Chemical Bank to run over the two-year loan extension period. The strike levels were set at 10% and 11% against six-month US Dollar LIBOR and every six months from the beginning of September 1990, the company could elect to execute the Cap Agreement. The Caption was structured in two parts, with an upfront fee to purchase the Cap in the futures at today's prices and then the exercise price if the company elected to exercise the option. Overall, the caption premium amounted to 35-40% of the value of the underlying Cap Agreement.[4]

While options pricing is difficult at best, the reader might imagine that the pricing of options on options would be doubly difficult. This is not necessarily the case. The first academic to crack the problem of pricing compound options was Robert Geske of the University of California, Berkeley.[5] Geske examined compound options on stock.

The equity in a levered firm (that is a firm that borrows money) can be viewed as a call option on the value of the firm. Just like a call option, the most you can lose is the amount you pay for the security and your profit potential is unlimited. The only difference between a stock price and an option price is that the stock's "term to maturity" is assumed to be infinite (or at least for a very long time). Geske supposed that the value of firm could be estimated as "V" and that the face value of the outstanding debt was "A". We will substitute "V" for the price of the stock "S" in the Black and Scholes formula and substitute "A" for the strike price of the option "E". So if the value of the firm (like the stock price) is below the amount of money borrowed (the strike price of an option), the firm is worthless and bankrupt (and the option is out-of-the-money and also worth nothing).

Prior to expiration (or closing down of the firm), time value must be added and this is done using a formula very similar to the Black and Scholes formula. This formula for the Geske model on compound options can be seen in Table 13.2.

Geske uses the value of the firm "V" instead of "S" and he assumes that the volatility of the firm's value (σ_V) is constant. Furthermore, he assumes that the amount of debt "A" does not vary (like the strike price E never varies). Finally, and this is the critical point, the volatility of the stock price S is negatively correlated with the value of the firm "V". That means that when the firm value decreased and it looks like the firm will go bankrupt, the volatility of the stock price will increase. Of course, the reverse would occur when the firm value increases.

In Table 13.2, "V" is the value of the firm, "A" is the amount of debt held, "E" is the exercise price of the option and the M() function is a cumulative probability of a bivariate normal distribution (that takes into account both the distributions of the stock price and the value of the firm and the correlation between the two). Essentially, the Geske model first evaluates the price of the stock (the option-like feature in the two left terms) minus the exercise price for the option in the furthest right term.

---

[4]The source for this example is Chemical Bank, New York and is drawn from the article "Insurance against the Unknown", in Risk Magazine, Volume 2, Number 9, October 1989, pp. 20.

[5]Geske, Robert, "The Valuation of Compound Options", Journal of Financial Economics, Vol. 7 (1979), pp. 63-81.

$$C = VM\left(a_1, b_1; \sqrt{\frac{t_1}{t_2}}\right) - Ae^{-rt_2}M\left(a_2, b_2; \sqrt{\frac{t_1}{t_2}}\right) - Ee^{-rt_1}N(a_2)$$

where:

$$a_1 = \frac{\ln(V/V^*) + (r + 1/2\sigma_v^2) \cdot t_1}{\sigma_v \sqrt{t_1}}$$

$$b_1 = \frac{\ln(V/A) + (r + 1/2\sigma_v^2) \cdot t_2}{\sigma_v \sqrt{t_2}}$$

$$a_2 = a_1 - \sigma_v \sqrt{t_1}$$

$$b_2 = b_1 - \sigma_v \sqrt{t_2}$$

$$t_1 = T - t$$

$$t_2 = T^* - t$$

V = Underlying asset price

A = Strike price of underlying option

E = Strike price of the compound option

M = Bivariate normal distribution

T = Expiration of compound option

T^* = Expiration of the underlying option

t = Today's date

r = Risk - free interest rate

σ_v = Volatility for underlying asset

V^* is the stock price such that the compound option will be At-The-Money at expiration relative to the underlying option.

Table 13.2 Geske Compound Option Pricing Model.

How does this all relate to Captions, Floptions and other compound options? Simply by substituting the value of the underlying option (or string of options like a Ceiling Agreement) for "V", the strike price (or rate) of that underlying option for "A" and then include the strike price of the compound option for "E", the Geske approach will easily evaluate the theoretical value for a compound option with an early exercise feature.[6]

The most important input into the compound options pricing model is (as always) the volatility. In the instance of the compound option, the volatility input is not the spot volatility but is the forward volatility from the expiration of the compound until the expiration of the underlying option. To determine the forward volatility, one simply applies the forward/forward volatility calculation presented in the final sections of Chapter 5.

Another way to look at Caption pricing is as the expected change in the time value of the underlying Cap agreement over the life of the compound option. For example, the reader is referred back to the graphs of time decay in Chapter 2. In Tables 2.13a and 2.13b, the time decay expected for two particular option buying strategies is presented. Basically, a Caption is similar to the situation in Table 2.13b

---

[6]Many thanks to Dr. Michael J.P. Selby of the Cambridge University for his advice on how the Geske model applies to Captions. For what may be a more interesting paper on compound options, the reader is referred to: Selby, Michael J.P. and Stewart D. Hodges, "On the Evaluation of Compound Options", Management Science, Vol. 33, No. 3, March 1987, pp. 347-355.

or to the payoff from a calendar spread. In that case, one buys a long dated option (or a string of options in the Ceiling Agreement) and then sells the option back well before the expiration of the option.

The expected value of the Caption should be equal to the time decay (that would occur over the life of the Caption) for the underlying option contract. In Table 2.13b, the expected loss is equal to 2-1/2 US Dollars and would also represent the expected cost of the option on that option. Unfortunately, the graphs in Tables 2.13a and 2.13b will only look that way if all the other variables are constant. The rationale for the compound option pricing model is to take into account the fact that the shape of the curves in Tables 2.13a and 2.13b could deviate if the price of the underlying asset or volatility changes.

OPTIONS WHICH VARY THE STANDARD TERMS
OF NORMAL OPTIONS

Bermudan Option

These options are as they sound: somewhere between a European and an American option. A Bermudan style option allows the holder only to exercise the option on specific dates during an options life. For example, the option may have three years to expiration but can only be exercised for a month period at the end of each of the three years.

Applications Of The Bermudan Option

Applications of the Bermudan style option are often associated with the fixed in-come markets where a bond may be putable or callable at various points in its life. If the buyer of the bond wishes to eliminate the impact of the call feature or to sell off the put feature (see the last chapter for an example of this), the Bermudan structure is the only way to achieve this. Suppose, a holder of a callable bond has three such windows at which the Bond will be called away. The bond is maturing in 2004 but can be called at par (or 100) in years 2001, 2002 and 2003 during the month of September. The holder of the bond may be interested in replacing the bond if it were called away during any of these periods but would only exercise his options during these three (month long) "windows". A Bermudan style option ex-piring at the end of September 2003 would fit the bill with expiration periods avail-able in that month and the two preceding Septembers. Of course, even if the bond holder did not wish to buy the Bermudan style option, it would be important to evaluate its fair price to assess if the pickup in yields (by buying the callable bond compared to buying a non-callable bond of the same maturity) was sufficient to cover the price of the call option he had implicitly sold.

Pricing Of The Bermudan Option

The pricing of the Bermudan option is essentially no different than that employed for American options that was covered in Chapter 3. In that Chapter, the concept of the binomial tree approach was introduced. All one needs to do is evaluate the option at those nodes in the binomial tree when the possibility of exercise could occur. If the options value at any of these points is lower than the intrinsic value at that price, the option is assumed to be exercised. Once all the values of the Bermudan option are estimated for all the possible underlying prices, these are then discounted back to today's probability weighted value for the option.

Digital / Binary Options[7]

Binary options are among the simplest kind of exotic options. They are a straight bet that an underlying market will finish above or below the strike price at expiration. The payoff of this event occurring is a fixed amount regardless of the level of the underlying asset. If one remembers the payoff at expiration for a standard call option, it is equal to:

$$MAX\ (0, S - E)$$

where:
    S is the price of the underlying asset at expiration, and
    E is the strike price of the standard option.

For a digital option, the payoff is slightly different:

$$MAX\ (0, P\ |\ S > E)$$

where:
    P is the payoff from the Digital option
    | means given that
    S is the price of the underlying asset at expiration, and
    E is the strike price of the standard option.

The payoff for this option is presented in Figure 13.2. As the reader can see, this exotic looks like a step on a staircase.

---

[7]Rubinstein, Mark, "Unscrambling The Binary Code", Risk Magazine, Oct 1991, pp. 75-83.

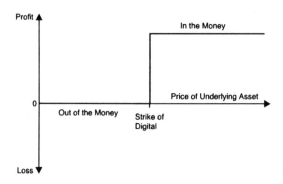

Figure 13.2 The Profit & Loss Profile of a Digital Call Option at Expiration.

This kind of instrument is also known as a all-or-nothing call. When one looks at the payoff from the digital option, one might find that the profit and loss profile looks remarkably similar to another combination of simple options presented elsewhere in this book. If one returns to Chapter 6, and closely examines the Bull vertical spread, one will see a similar pattern. In fact apart from the fact that the profit and loss profile is rising at a 45° angle from the lower strike price to the higher strike price and the digital rises vertically (at a 90° angle), the strategies appear to be similar. These digital options come in two basic varieties:

-All or Nothing, and
-One Touch

The All or Nothing digital option only pays out if the underlying asset finishes in- the-money at the expiration of the option. The one touch digital will payout as long as at some point in the life of the option, the underlying price was at any time higher than the strike price of the option. For the one touch, the payout can either be made immediately when the underlying asset is in the money or deferred until the expiration of the option. The one touch thus depends upon the path the underlying asset will take over the life of the option and discussion of this kind of option and the related exotics will be covered later in this chapter. In this section, I will only concentrate on the all or nothing digital option.

Applications Of The Digital Option
Probably the most famous use of the digital option has been in the construction of Supershares proposed by Nils Hakansson of the University of California, Berkeley[8]. A supershare is a security, which on its expiration date entitles the

---

[8]The reader is referred to "The Purchasing Power Fund: A New Kind of Financial Intermediary", by Nils Hakansson which appeared in Financial Analysts Journal, 32 (November-December 1976), pp. 49-59.

owner to a given dollar value which is proportional to the assets of a fund, provided that the value of those assets on the expiration date lies between a lower and upper value. Otherwise, the supershares are worth nothing. Of course, another kind of supershare could exist that will pay off at any level above the strike price as well.

As Cox and Rubinstein show in their book[9], the real beauty of these hybrid digital options lies in providing customised portfolio payoffs for investment managers. For example, if the investment objectives are to meet specific liability requirements which are tied to the performance of an underlying asset market, then a portfolio of supershares can be constructed which will exactly meet those requirements. In this way, the portfolio of supershares is guaranteed to meet its obligations while simply investing in the underlying asset may not.

Pricing Of The Digital Option
Of the two types of digital options, the easiest to price (by far) is the all or nothing digital. The one touch is far more complicated to value as they involve a "barrier" and this requires the estimation of the appropriate "barrier" probability density function. For the all or nothing digital, the pricing can be seen as a direct extension of the Black and Scholes approach adjusted for dividends:

$$CALL = S \cdot N(d_1) \cdot e^{-dT} - E \cdot N(d_2) \cdot e^{-rT}$$

where:

$$d_1 = \frac{\ln(S/E) + (r - d + \sigma^2/2) \cdot T}{\sigma \cdot \sqrt{T}}$$

$$d_2 = d_1 - \sigma \cdot \sqrt{T}$$

T = time to expiration % of a year
E = exercise price of option
r = risk free interest rate of period T
d = dividend yield of stock over period T
ln = natural logarithm function
σ^2 = variance of the rate of return
S = share price
e = exponential function
σ = square root of variance, i.e. volatility
N = cumulative normal density function

---

[9]John C. Cox and Mark Rubinstein, "Options Markets", Prentice-Hall, 1985, pp. 458-468.

What we are interested in pricing with the all or nothing digital is the expected value of the asset (for the asset or nothing call) or of the cash value of the strike price (for the cash or nothing call). Thus, the Black and Scholes model already tells us what these values are. The incredibly simple result for all or nothing digital options is :

$$\text{Asset or Nothing Call} = S \cdot N(d_1) \cdot e^{-dT}$$
$$\text{Cash or Nothing Call} = E \cdot N(d_2) \cdot e^{-rT}$$

Pay Later Options[10]

These are options for which no premium must be paid unless the option is exercised. However, the option must be exercised if the underlying asset is equal to or greater than the strike price of the option, even if that means the intrinsic value received is less than the premium that must be paid. The profit and loss profile of this strategy is presented in Figure 13.3.

As the reader can see, this also resembles another strategy we discussed in this book. If the reader turns back to Chapter 7 on volatility trading strategies and finds the profit and loss profile for the call-back spread, he will immediately notice the similarity. The key advantage of the pay later option to the option buyer is that no premium is ever payable if the option expires out-of-the-money. However, the reader may recall that when doing an equivalent call-back spread, he can actually receive a premium which is foregone with the pay later option. In addition, the pay later option drops vertically at the strike price of the option down to the maximum loss potential while the call-back spread slowly drops again reaching the maximum loss potential at the higher strike price of the spread.

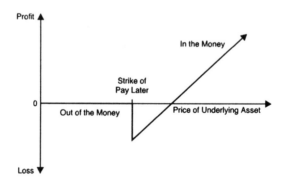

Figure 13.3 The Profit & Loss Profile of a Pay Later Call Option at Expiration.

---

[10]Turnbull, Stuart, "The Price Is Right", Risk Magazine, Apr 1992, pp.56-57.

Applications Of The Pay Later Option
The principal targeted client for pay later options are those which hate paying option premium when hedging. As we discussed in Chapter 11 on portfolio applications, this has also led to the development of other option strategies such as zero cost options which are trying to achieve the same goal: limited protection for no cost. The difference is that if the market finished at the exercise price, the holder of the pay later option will experience a loss from the premium having to be paid. In some ways, he will be worse off than simply buying a call option. The pay later option can be thought of as the equivalent portfolio to buying a standard call option and selling an all or nothing digital option where the digital premium is set equal to the premium of the standard option. Therefore, the pay later option seller has sold the equivalent of a digital option when he buys the pay later option.

Pricing Of The Pay Later Option
The pricing of the pay later option as was indicated above is simply the price of a standard Black and Scholes call option minus the price of an all or nothing digital option. The formulae for both these options appear above and if one combines these one can solve for the pay later option the result is:

$$\text{Pay Later Call} = [S \cdot N(d_1) \cdot e^{-dT} - E \cdot N(d_2) \cdot e^{-rT}] - (R \cdot [S \cdot N(d_1) \cdot e^{-dT}])$$

where:

$R =$ the quantity of the "asset or nothing" option that is sold such the premiums of the ordinary call and the asset or nothing option are identical

All other variables are the same as above.

Delayed Option

This kind of option allows the holder to receive at the expiration date another option with the strike price set equal to the underlying asset price at that future date. This product can be thought of as a compound option with a zero strike price but where the strike price of the underlying option is only determined at the point the compound option is exercised. These options are also known as Forward Start options.

Applications Of The Delayed Option
The possible applications of the delayed option are similar to that of the compound options previously discussed. However, in my experience, these options have a

special benefit to fund managers who are creating guaranteed return funds. When the 90/10 or guaranteed investment fund was presented in Chapter 11, the process entailed placing a majority of the investment on deposit and buying call options with the remainder. When standard options are purchased, they only provide coverage for a fixed period. Very often, these funds may be rolled over into another 90/10 strategy upon maturity assuming the clients are satisfied so far. However, it is unknown what percentage of clients will choose to roll over the investment . The purchase of a delayed option would allow the fund to offer not only a one period target gearing but also gearing levels for subsequent periods. This would be extremely attractive to a longer term investor. Furthermore, as was indicated in Chapter 11, the success of the guaranteed fund depends upon certain market conditions existing. The short term interest rate must be sufficiently high to provide the interest to buy the options and the volatility of the options market must be relatively low. In the situation, where the fund manager finds himself with extraordinary low volatilities for the options market, he may wish to lock in this low volatility not only for the first period but for subsequent periods when the funds may be rolled over. Since, he is uncertain about the amount which will be rolled over, he purchases the delayed option. Because he is buying it today, he is locking in an attractive level of volatility and knows that upon the rollover of the funds, the current strike price will be equal to the prevailing level of the market on that date.

Another application of the Delayed option is for employee stock incentive schemes, where the option will only be offered to the employee if he remains at the firm until some point in the future, when his or her option will actually exist.

Pricing Of The Delayed Option

The pricing of this exotic is also relatively straightforward. On the grant date t, the value of the forward-starting option on an at-the-money call which then has time to expiration τ will be :

$$C(S_t, S_t, \tau)$$

Since multiplying both the asset value and the strike by the same factor (St) is the same as increasing the number of options by that factor, we can rewrite this as:

$$S_t \cdot C(1,1,\tau)$$

This is simply a constant amount times the future share price S_t. The current market value of the stock on the grant date in the future (S_t) is simply the current stock price S, adjusted for any dividends paid over the period from the grant date t to today. This has been done with the e^{-dt} function as before.[11] Thus arriving at the current value of the Delayed option:

---

[11]The only assumption needed to infer that the market value today of S_t at time t is $S \cdot e^{-dt}$ is that the dividend yield is constant and equals d.

$$S \cdot e^{-dt} \cdot C(1,1,\tau)$$

Finally, using the same trick of changing the asset price and the strike by the same ratio (S), we get:

$$e^{-dt} \cdot C(S,S,\tau)$$

Thus, the delayed start option is worth the same amount as an at-the-money option of the same maturity, but with the quantity adjusted for the effect of the dividend yield.

Chooser Option[12]

This mutation of standard options allows the holder to choose at the expiration whether the option he has purchased is a call or a put at the same exercise price. This option is very similar to a straddle but is considerably cheaper because after the holder has made his choice, he can only have that one type of option. Furthermore, because these strategies are OTC, the possibility of obtaining prices prior to expiration is limited when compared to exchange traded options. Thus, the principle rationale for the purchase of the straddle, that of volatility trading, is lost due to the inability to trade the chooser option in a liquid market prior to expiration.

Applications Of The Chooser Option
The natural user of the chooser option would be speculators who are betting on an extreme movement in the underlying asset at the expiration with no objective of trading changes in the implied volatility in the interim. Another application could be for investment managers trading in the shares of a company that is experiencing a hostile take-over bid. If the bid is accepted at a supposedly higher level, the call element of the chooser option will be selected. If the company successfully beats off the hostile bid by consuming a "poison pill" which implies a corporate restructuring that makes the entire company unpalatable to any potential suitor, then the market may react negatively to the company sending its shares reeling. In either case, as the results of the success of the bid become known a major source of uncertainty will be removed from the market regarding the stock price of the targeted company and the implied volatility should fall. Thus, the chooser option would allow for the directional viewpoint of the change in the stock price to be realised without the same degree of implied volatility exposure as would be associated with a straddle.

---

[12]Rubinstein, Mark, "Pay Now, Choose Later", Risk Magazine, Feb 1991, p. 13.

Pricing Of The Chooser Option

The first step in solving for the price of a Chooser option is to write down what the payoff will be at the choice date. This is simply:

$$MAX\left(C_t(E,T-t),P_t(E,T-t);t\right)$$

where:
C_t is the payoff of a call with exercise price E
P_t is the payoff of a put with exercise price E
T_t is the time to expiration for both options
t is the time to the choice

Using simple put-call parity, this can be written as:

$$MAX\left(C_t,(C_t-S_t\cdot e^{-d(T-t)}+E\cdot e^{-r(T-t)});t\right)$$

$$=C_t(E,T-t)+MAX\left(0,E\cdot e^{-r(T-t)}-S_t\cdot e^{-d(T-t)};t\right).$$

This means that we receive the best of a call or a put. Since (from put-call parity) the put is just a call minus a forward contract, we can also express the above payoff as a call plus a (zero strike put) option on the forward.

Using simple put-call parity, this can be written as:

$$P_t=C_t+E\cdot e^{-r(T-t)}-S\cdot e^{-d(T-t)}$$

When this is substituted into $MAX\left(C_t,P_t\right)$, we obtain:

$$=C_t+MAX\left(0,E\cdot e^{-r(T-t)}-S_t\cdot e^{-d(T-t)}\right).$$

This implies that the payoff from a Chooser option will be the same as the payoff from:

• Buying a Call with an underlying asset price of S, Strike Price of E and Time to Expiration T, and

• Buying a Put with an underlying asset price $S\cdot e^{-d(T-t)}$, Strike Price of $E\cdot e^{-r(T-t)}$ and Time to Expiration of t.

The value of the standard Chooser Options is simply:

$$CALL = S \cdot N(x) \cdot e^{-dT} - E \cdot N(x - \sigma\sqrt{T}) \cdot e^{-rT}$$

$$-S \cdot N(-y) \cdot e^{-dT} + E \cdot N(-y + \sigma\sqrt{T}) \cdot e^{-rT}$$

where:

$$x = \frac{\ln(S \cdot e^{-dT} / E \cdot e^{-rT})}{\sigma\sqrt{T}} + \frac{1}{2}\sigma\sqrt{T}$$

$$y = \frac{\ln(S \cdot e^{-dT} / E \cdot e^{-rT})}{\sigma\sqrt{t}} + \frac{1}{2}\sigma\sqrt{t}$$

Alternatively, the analysis could have been done the other way around by substituting the put-call parity equivalent for the call:

$$C_t = P_t + S \cdot e^{-d(T-t)} - E \cdot e^{-r(T-t)}$$

In this case, the Chooser option is worth:

$$= P_t + MAX(0, S_t \cdot e^{-d(T-t)} - E \cdot e^{-r(T-t)}).$$

This implies that the payoff from a Chooser option will be the same as the payoff from:

- Buying a Put with an underlying asset price of S, Strike Price of E and Time to Expiration T, and

- Buying a Call with an underlying asset price $S \cdot e^{-d(T-t)}$, Strike Price of $E \cdot e^{-r(T-t)}$ and Time to Expiration of t.

The results should come out the same if put-call parity holds.

Power Option

These options allow the holder the payoffs of a standard option but with the value of the underlying asset raised to some power. For example, the payoff at expiration from a standard call is simply:

MAX (0, S - E)

where:
S is the price of the underlying asset at expiration, and
E is the strike price of the standard option

A Power call option would instead provide a different payoff at expiration:

MAX [0, (S^2 - E)]

where:
S is the squared price of the underlying asset at expiration, and
E is the strike price of the Power option.

In this case, the holder of the option gets the value of the underlying at expiration squared minus the Power option strike price. Suppose the Power option was on a share with a strike price of $100. If the underlying asset finishes at $10 or lower, the option is worthless. In the case that the underlying asset finishes at $20, the payoff is $300 (which is $20 squared minus $100) and if the underlying asset finishes at $25, the payoff is $525. Figure 13.4 displays the profit and loss profile of the Power call option compared to holding ten standard call options with a strike price of $10 (equivalent to a $100 strike price).

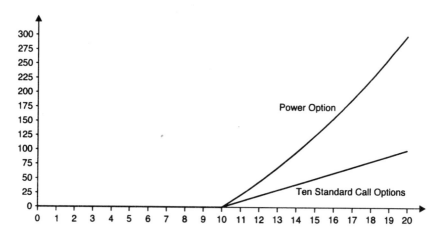

Figure 13.4 Profit & Loss Profile of a Power Call Option vs. ten Standard Calls.

Application of the Power Option
Clearly, Power options are for those wanting to maximise their gearing to the movement of the underlying market. For those investors who are trying to maximise their gamma or lambda exposures to an underlying asset, the Power option may be the best alternative.

Pricing Of The Power Option
The pricing of the Power Option is actually quite simple. This is because when we square the price of the underlying asset (S^2), this remains lognormally distributed if the underlying asset price is assumed to be lognormally distributed. This being the case, we can simply square the assumed stochastic process of the underlying asset.

Simple Stochastic Process for Asset

$$dS = \mu \cdot Sdt + \sigma \cdot Sdz \,^{13}$$

Stochastic Process for Square of Asset

$$d(S^2) = 2 \cdot S \cdot (\mu \cdot Sdt + \sigma \cdot Sdz)$$
$$+ \frac{1}{2} \cdot 2 \cdot \sigma^2 \cdot S^2 dt$$

By solving through this equation and simplifying terms, the result is:

$$d(S^2) = (2 \cdot \mu \cdot \sigma^2)S^2 dt + (2 \cdot \sigma) \cdot S^2 dz$$

Then, all one needs do to price the Power option is to substitute the new drift term, $(2 \cdot \mu \cdot \sigma^2)$ and volatility term $(2 \cdot \sigma)$ into the Black and Scholes formula and one will have their answer in a risk neutral world.

PATH-DEPENDENT OPTIONS

A key feature of OTC options is the ability to customise the transactions to meet individual client's needs. Examples of how far Investment Banks will go to meet a client's needs are best represented by options known as path-dependent options. Of these, the Average Rate (Asian style) Options and the Maximum/Minimum (Look back) Options have come into prominence in the last few years.

---

[13]If one divides both sides by S, then the result is: $\frac{dS}{S} = \mu \cdot dt + \sigma \cdot dz$ which is the same equation I have presented previously.

481

Average Rate Options - The "Asian" Style Options[14]

In the field of exotic OTC options, Average Rate options (also known as Asian options) have a broad appeal for corporate users. An Asian option, when exercised, pays out the difference between the strike rate (or price) and the average interest rate (or underlying asset price) for the period of the option.[15]

Asian options tend to be much cheaper than other kinds of options and are particularly well adapted to the needs of borrowers who are uncertain as to the timing and quantity of their exposures. These options tend to have a European exercise feature and are generally cash settled. The term "Asian" option comes from the fact that Bankers Trust was the first to offer these products out of their Tokyo office. The maturity for these options is typically in the one to two year range, however it is not uncommon for these options to have maturities as long as three years.

Applications Of The Average Rate Option
The most obvious interest rate application of Asian options is for firms that have uncertain borrowing needs over the year. If for example, a firm can not easily identify exactly when its borrowing needs will be or their quantity, then the Average Rate option will provide a hedge against the overall levels of interest rates that occur for that period.

As was discussed above, the most attractive selling point of the Average Rate option is the fact that the premiums can be substantially lower than the premiums for conventional options. Most Asian options are priced at 60% to 65% of the value of a conventional OTC interest rate option. While the concept is fairly simple in its construction, the pricing of Average Rate options is not.

Pricing Of The Average Rate Option
Average Rate options pricing is complicated by the fact that their values depend on how the price of the underlying asset moves over time and not simply on the level of the underlying asset. The only economically useful Average Rate options are based upon the simple arithmetic average of the prices of the underlying asset. Which can be written as:

$$A = \left[S(t_1) + S(t_2) + \ldots + S(t_N) \right] / N$$

To date no (closed form) solution to the problem has been found for options on a simple arithmetic average. The only Average Rate option that can be valued ex-

---

[14]This section is drawn heavily from "Asian Elegance" by Krystyna Kryzak in Risk Magazine, Vol. 3 (December 1989 - January 1990), No. 1, pp. 30-34,49.

[15]Asian options also are available on currencies, commodities and stock indices, allowing the holder an average price for the period at risk.

actly depends on the geometric average of the prices. Which is simply:

$$G = \sqrt[N]{S(t_1) \cdot S(t_2) \cdot \ldots \cdot S(t_N)}$$

The reason for this is that the Black and Scholes methodology only works for log normal dispersion processes and while the geometric average is log normal, the arithmetic average is not.

A number of approaches have been tried to solve for this problem. The simplest of these assumes that the distribution of the geometric average will be similar to that for the arithmetic average and to evaluate the Average Rate option, the geometric average is entered into the Black and Scholes model. The error from this approach is in the range of 0.20% per year with the Average Rate call options being undervalued and the Average Rate put options being overvalued. A better approach which has been suggested adjusts the strike price of the Average Rate option by the difference between the geometric and arithmetic averages. In this case, the error drops to less than 0.05% per year. To reduce the error further, one must apply a Wilkinson-Levy approximation which attempts to directly assess the distribution of the arithmetic average.[16] It can be shown that the error can now be reduced to about 0.02% per year for the price of the Average Rate option.

While some institutions do use these techniques, most banks, which offer Asian options, have come up with an approximation for the price of these securities by either applying a Binomial approach (similar to what I presented in Chapter 3) or by adjusting standard option pricing models for the reduced volatility associated with the average rate of the underlying asset.

When using the standard options pricing models, the adjustments include treating the average interest rate for the period as though it were an ordinary interest rate and reducing the volatility input into a Black and Scholes type model to take into account the reduced volatility. The rule of thumb is that the volatility of the average rate should be $1/\sqrt{3}$ (57.7%) of the ordinary underlying volatility. According to John Hull of the University of Toronto this is not too bad an approximation provided that the number of points used in the averaging is sufficiently frequent and the volatility is not too high.[17] However, the big problem with using Black and Scholes or a modification of this model remains the assumption that the distribution of the underlying asset is lognormal. When one combines a series of assets each of which are distributed lognormally (as one would do with the estimation of an average), the result may no longer be lognormal (especially if the assets are correlated).

Surprisingly, while banks have difficulty in pricing the Average Rate options, the hedging is less problematic. These Asian options can be delta-hedged in the cash market in a manner similar to standard options (the reader is referred to

---

[16]Levy, Edmond, "Asian Arithmetic", Risk Magazine, May 1990, pp. 7-8.

Levy, Edmond, "Average Intelligence", Risk Magazine, Feb 1992, pp. 53-9.

[17]"Asian Elegance" by Krystyna Kryzak IBID., page 49.

Chapter 8 for a discussion of delta hedging). The only difference is that it makes much more sense for a bank to have a portfolio of these Asian options on their books. Otherwise the transaction costs involved in maintaining a delta neutral hedge can become excessive. Fortunately, the risk to a bank of an Asian option decreases over its life because the uncertainty of what the average rate will be decreases. The maximum risk is at the beginning of the Asian option's life. That means that near the expiration of the Asian option, the Bank is fairly certain what the average rate will be and can more accurately calculate the exposure.

Average Strike Option[18]

These options are similar to the Asian style options discussed above, both kinds of options depending on the underlying price over the life of the option to be averaged. The difference for the average strike price option is that strike price of the option is set to this average price and the payout is the difference between this averaged strike and the asset price on the expiration date. To aid the reader in seeing the differences between these average options and normal call options, we will compare the payouts of all three at expiration:

Standard Call Option

$$MAX (0, S - E)$$

where:
　　S is the price of the underlying asset at expiration, and
　　E is the strike price of the standard option

Average Rate Call Option

$$MAX (0, S_a - E)$$

where:
　　S_a is the average price of the underlying asset
　　　　throughout the period of the option
　　E　is the strike price of the option

---

[18]Coward, Martin, "When Average Can Be Good", Risk Magazine, Jul 1988, pp.42-43.
　Curran, Michael, "Beyond Average Intelligence", Risk Magazine, Nov 1992, pp. 60-61.
　Levy, Edmond, "Average Intelligence", Risk Magazine, Feb 1992, pp. 53-9.

Average Strike Call Option

MAX $(0, S - E_a)$

where:

  S   is the price of the underlying asset at expiration, and

  E_a is the strike price of the option which is equal
     to the average price of the underlying asset at a
     predetermined period of the option's life

The difference between the two average options are best addressed by looking at those situations in which each would be more appropriate.

Applications Of The Average Strike Option

Let us consider the hedging problems faced by a major British pharmaceutical firm with substantial business in Italy. This firm has three types of foreign exchange exposure to its Italian operations. Firstly, it will have one off transactions with an Italian customer for bulk purchases of drugs. Secondly, it will have a steady flow of business of existing products to a range of Italian customers. Finally, since business is so good in Italy, it has established a new subsidiary in Italy which will not turn a profit in Lira before one year is over. In the first example, the large deals are fixed as to the time of delivery and the amount of Lira that will be paid. The British firm could either lock in the sale of the Lira for Sterling using forward foreign exchange contracts or simply buy a put option on Lira/call option on Sterling. Standard products will do here.

For the second problem of a steady inflow of Lira per month, the Average rate option would be the ideal solution, since the British firm is interested in locking in the average exchange rate over the period for the total amount of projected sales.

The third problem is a little more complex. For the coming 10 months the subsidiary in Italy has been financed locally in Lira for the start-up. The cost of the interest will be funded by a lump sum of Sterling that have been converted at the current spot rate as seed money by the British firm. In months eleven and twelve, the subsidiary will be on its feet and start earning Lira which at that point must be converted back into Sterling to pay back the initial investment. In this case, the British firm is not exposed to the exchange rate risk throughout the year but only in months 11 and 12. Thus, they would buy a one year Average Strike option with the strike set as the average rate which occurred over months 11 and 12.

Comparison of Average Rate and Average Strike Price Options

To see the differences more clearly between the Average Rate and the Average Strike Price options, the reader is referred to Figure 13.5. In this figure, the actual

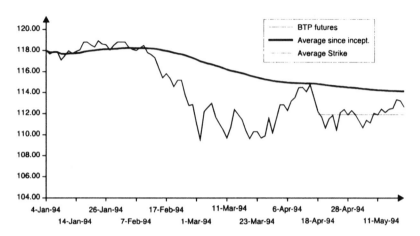

Figure 13.5   Determination of Average Rate and Average Strike Price for the BTP Futures from January to May 1994.

closing prices for the nearby BTP futures from January to May 1994 are displayed. In addition, the average rate is displayed over the entire period as is the setting of the average strike price. The simple arithmetic averaged price for the BTP futures is the relatively smooth line which reduces the gyrations of the underlying market. The average strike price can only be determined at the expiration date of the option in May and therefore a single value for that final one month period. This is why it is a flat line over the last month.

Maximum/Minimum Options - The "Look Back" Option[19]

The concept of the Maximum/Minimum option was built upon the classic customer complaint that they were not able to get the best price possible over the period. The Maximum/Minimum option (also known as a "look back" option) gives the holder the right to purchase or sell the underlying asset at the best price attained in the option's lifetime. For a call option, this means the minimum price (or rate) for the period and for a put option this means the maximum price (or rate). For example, consider a Borrower option with this Minimum/Maximum feature. Suppose the Holder of the Borrower option held it for a 6 month period. At expiration, he could "look back" over the preceding 6 month period and exercise the option at the lowest borrowing rate which occurred for the period. This feature provides the holder a "no-regrets" result: the best interest rate (or price level) is never missed.

---

[19]This section is drawn heavily from "Recollection in Tranquillity", a paper by Mark Garman which appeared in Risk Magazine, Vol. 2 (March 1989), No. 3, pp. 16-19.

Potential Uses For "Look Back" Options

Obviously, the potential users of "look back" options are the same clients who would be interested in ordinary options on interest rates or any underlying asset. The difference is that the clients which go for "look back" options want to achieve the very best rate. Examples of potential users include: investors in Floating Rate Note Bonds who would like to assure that the rate they achieve on their floating rate investment is maximised, borrowers who wish to minimise their floating borrowing expense in highly volatile markets and traders who combine "look back" options with ordinary options to create a "zero-cost" hedging strategy. The final example, a "zero-cost" hedging strategy will resemble the example I presented in Chapter 11 with the difference that the maximum profit potential would not be bounded as it was with an ordinary option (assuming the hedger bought the "look back" option and sold an ordinary option).

Pricing Of "Look Back" Options

While this is great for the customer, the institution which must price and hedge this "look back" option has a much greater problem figuring out the value. To determine the theoretical price of the "look back", the usual assumptions in option pricing must be made. One must assume that the interest rates underlying the option are distributed lognormally, the volatility for the interest rate is known and that the market for the interest rate underlying security trades 24 hours and continuously.

With these assumptions in hand, Goldman, Sosin and Gatto[20] were able to create an equivalent portfolio of other securities which would provide exactly the same payoffs as a "look back" option. Since they could price the components of the equivalent portfolio, they were able to both price the "look back" and hedge it by dealing in the "look back" and doing exactly the opposite trades in the equivalent portfolio.

Let us consider what their equivalent portfolio looks like. Suppose that a financial institution has written the interest rate "look back" option outlined above. To hedge the risk fully, they would have to immediately purchase a 6 month ordinary Borrower option with exactly the same terms as the Borrower option they sold to the client. They will hold that option until a new minimum rate occurs and then at that point, will immediately sell the Borrower option they purchased back into the market and repurchase a new (ordinary) Borrower option with a strike rate equal to the new minimum rate. They will continue this process whenever a new minimum rate is established until the expiration of the option they sold to the client. This strategy is referred to as a "rollover" strategy and will produce exactly the same payoffs of the "look back" option at expiration.

Unfortunately, this "rollover" strategy will always involve selling the Borrower option with a higher rate when the new minimum rate is established and then buy-

---

[20]Goldman, M. B., H. Sosin, and M. Gatto, "Path Dependent Options: "Buy at the low, sell at the high"", Journal of Finance, Vol. 34, No. 5, pp. 1111-1127.

ing a new Borrower option which is then at-the-money. This will always require a cash outflow (i.e. a loss) because the premium of the at-the-money option one must now pay will most probably be greater than the amount of money received for the previously purchased Borrower option which is now out-of-the-money. Then it becomes clear that the "look back" option has two sources of cost to the writer: one is the cost of buying the ordinary Borrower option and secondly the accumulated losses from having to roll the Borrower option down to assure the minimum rate. This second element is called a "strike-bonus option".[21] These two factors imply that the price for an interest rate "look back" option is equal to the sum of the value of an ordinary interest rate option with a strike price at the minimum level for the period of the options life plus the value of the "strike-bonus option".

Pricing The "Strike-Bonus Option"
The next problem is how to estimate the values of these two components of the "look back" option? The first element is easy: It is simply the value of an ordinary interest rate option and one could use the forward price for the interest rate, the minimum achieved interest rate as the strike price and the Black (1976) model to estimate the price. The problem is the value of the "strike-bonus option". Essentially to solve the problem, one will apply the same logic that applies to the Black and Scholes formula. This formula is presented in Table 13.3.

$$V_{sb}(F,L,t,\sigma,r) = \frac{F}{\tau}e^{-rt}\left[\left(\frac{F}{L}\right)^{-\tau} n\left(y_L + 2r\sqrt{t}/\sigma\right) - N\left(y_L\right)\right]$$

where:

    F = Forward interest rate
    L = Achieved minimum(*low*)
    t = Time remaining to option maturity
    σ = Volatility of F
    r = Interest rate for period
    $\tau = 2/\sigma^2$ = The "speed" parameter
    $N(.)$ = Cumulative normal density function

$$y_L = \frac{-\ln(F/L)-(\sigma^2/2)t}{\sigma\sqrt{t}}$$

Table 13.3 "Strike Bonus" Option Pricing Model for Look Back Options.

[21]See "Recollection in tranquillity" by Mark Garman in Risk Magazine, Vol 2 (March 1989), No. 3, p 16.

As the reader can see, this model for the "strike-bonus option" looks somewhat different than the Black and Scholes formula. In reality the only major difference is that no specific underlying price (S) or exercise price (E) is multiplied by the cumulative normal distribution functions (N). Instead, the ratio of the current price (S) for the interest rate and the minimum interest rate (L) is used as the underlying input. Finally, the τ is what Mark Garman calls the "speed" factor.[22] So, the value of a "look back" option is simply the value of an ordinary Borrower option with a strike price equal to the minimum interest rate for the period and the value of this "strike-bonus option", the formula of which I have just presented.

With these pricing models in place, it is a simple matter to determine the "look back" options sensitivities to the level of the underlying interest rates. Just as is the case with any option, the delta and gamma can be estimated to determine the proper hedging ratios for a risk-less hedge. The problem with the delta hedging of "look back" options is that while the deltas are typically smaller, the gammas are generally higher, compared to ordinary options on interest rates. Furthermore, the gamma risk is one sided (it only occurs when a new minimum rate is reached). Nevertheless, research has shown that while these Maximum/Minimum options must be monitored more closely than regular options, historical data seem to indicate it is possible to effectively hedge them.[23]

One would expect that "look back" option premiums would have to be more expensive than ordinary interest rate options simply because another option is thrown in. Indeed, this is the case. Sometimes, the "strike-bonus" option price can be as large as the price of the ordinary interest rate option. Therefore, it is not unreasonable to use as a rule of thumb that a "look back" option price will be twice as expensive as the price of an ordinary interest rate option.

Cliquet Or Ratchet Option

These exotic options were first developed in France and are based upon the CAC 40 stock index. Since that time they have spread world-wide to be used especially by equity fund managers. The ratchet option starts out like a normal call option with a fixed strike price, but the strike is reset to be equal to the underlying asset price on a set of dates that have been predetermined. When the strike price is reset, any positive intrinsic value is locked in. If the underlying asset price at the next reset date is below the previous level, nothing happens except that the strike price has been reset at a lower strike price which is equal to the underlying asset price.

For example, let us suppose that on 31 December, a one year ratchet call option is purchased on the CAC 40 starting at a strike of 2100. The reset dates for the option's strike price is the end of the quarters, 31 March, 30 June and 30 September. On 31 March, the CAC 40 settles at 2250 and the option's intrinsic value of 150

---

[22]Ibid., page 17.
[23]Ibid.

points is locked in. In addition, the new strike of the ratchet is set to 2250. On 30 June, the CAC 40 drops to 2080. There will be no additional payment, nor will the initial gain of 150 points be touched. Once again the strike is reset at 2080. On 30 September, the CAC 40 rallies to 2190 and once again the intrinsic value of 110 points is credited to the account of the ratchet holder. On this date, the strike price is set at 2190 for the remaining three months of the option's life. At this point forward, the ratchet behaves like a normal option. If at 31 December the CAC 40 ends the year at 2300, another 110 points is added to the cumulative intrinsic value in the ratchet (2300 minus the last strike of 2190). Thus, in total, the holder of the ratchet has received 370 points from the option. If instead, he had simply purchased an ordinary 2100 call option, at the end of the year he would only have received 200 points in intrinsic value.

Essentially, one can think of the ratchet option as a series of forward start or delayed options such as those discussed above.

Applications Of The Ratchet Option

For portfolio managers, ratchet options are like a dream come true. In many instances, the performance of fund managers is evaluated at the end of each quarter and results are then presented to clients.

One age old complaint of investors is that when a fund has performed well in the past it usually loses all the profits in one particularly bad patch. When this occurs, the investors (if not the fund manager himself) will ask the question: Why didn't you take profits when you had them? If the dates for the evaluation of the performance can be determined before hand, the ratchet option may be a solution for the problem of variable performance in funds.

Pricing of the Ratchet Option

The Ratchet option is priced by simply summing the values of a portfolio of Delayed (or Forward Start) Options which form the equivalent portfolio to the Ratchet. Formally, this can be written as:

$$MAX\,(S_{T_1} - E, 0) \cdot e^{r(T_n - T_1)} + MAX\,(S_{T_2} - S_{T_1}, 0) \cdot e^{r(T_n - T_2)} + ... + MAX\,(S_{T_N} - S_{T_{N-1}}, 0)$$

Ladder Option

Ladder options work in essentially the same manner as the ratchet and are similar in some ways to Look Back options discussed above. With the ladder option whenever the underlying asset reaches a preset higher price in a series of predetermined prices for the underlying asset, the intrinsic value is locked in and a new strike is established at that level. When comparing this to the ratchet option, the ratchet option will only be reset on certain dates regardless of the level of the underlying market on that date. Compared to look back options, the ladder will only be reset if certain higher prices are reached. For the look back, every higher price implies a new reset of the strike price. As an analogy, the ladder differs from a look back in the same way as a staircase differs from a moving inclined walkway.

Applications Of The Ladder Option
As with the ratchet option, ladder options are ideal for the fund manager. In the case of the fund manager, the preference of the ladder to the ratchet option depends on how the performance of the fund manager is measured. If the investors evaluate the performance every day and set price levels at which profits should be realised, then the ladder option will be the ideal vehicle to achieve this. The problem with both the ratchet and ladder options is that they can be very expensive.

Pricing Of The Ladder Option
In this case, a figure will be helpful to understanding the key issues involved in pricing the ladder option. In Figure 13.6, the impact of the increasing strike prices on the ladder is displayed.

On the vertical (y) axis is the price of the underlying asset, S_T, the initial strike price of the ladder, E, and a variety of ladder strikes, L_1 to L_4. On the vertical access is the passage of time from today (t) to the expiration of the ladder (T). The jagged line represents the price history of that asset which underlies the Ladder option. As the underlying asset price reaches a higher ladder strike level, this will replace the initial strike price E. As the reader can see, the underlying market has only risen sufficiently to trigger L_1 and L_2 ladder strikes.

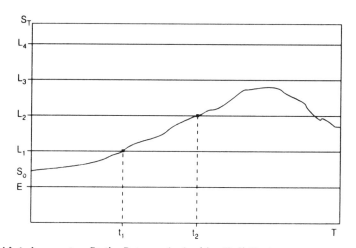

Figure 13.6 Increasing Strike Prices of a Ladder Call Option.

The payoff from the ladder in this example is:

$$MAX\,(S_T - MAX\,(L_i\,|S_T > L_i\,)) + (L_1 - E)\cdot e^{r(T-t_1)} + (L_2 - L_1)\cdot e^{r(T-t_2)}$$

If the cash is paid out immediately upon reaching the rungs of the ladder, this will be the solution. The problem of pricing Ladder options is simplified if this is not the case but the cash is paid out at the end of the life of the Ladder. In that instance, the solution for the payoff at expiration would be:

$$MAX\,(S_T - MAX\,(L_i\,|S_T > L_i\,)) + (L_{MAX} - E)$$

At present, there does not appear to be closed form solution for pricing a Ladder option, however, once again one could apply the Supermodel (modified Binomial approach) which was outlined in Chapter 9 or use a Monte Carlo simulation to obtain a fair price.

Shout Option[24]

Shout options are a further twist on the ratchet and ladder concepts. With the ratchet, the strike price is reset at certain dates which have been established in the contract terms of the option. For the ladder option, the strike price is reset once previously agreed price levels have been reached by the underlying asset. For the shout option, the reset of the strike price is neither pre-determined by certain dates or at any level of the underlying but occurs when the buyer of the option wants to reset the strike. At this point, he "shouts" to the option seller to reset the strike at a level he feels will ultimately be most advantageous. Suppose, one bought a one year shout option on the CAC 40 with a strike price of 2100 instead of the ratchet option. The strike will remain unchanged until the buyer decides he wants to lock in that new level. If the CAC 40 rose to 2280 in only one month, the holder could "shout" the option and receive an intrinsic value receipt of 180 points by the end of the year no matter what happens subsequently.

Applications Of The Shout Option
As with the ratchet and ladder options, shout options have been developed for fund managers. In that instance, where the fund manager would require more discretion in the selection of the levels at which profits are taken, the shout option may be his choice. In addition, relative to the ladder option, the shout may be cheaper due to the fact that the investor must make the decision when to reset the strike rather than having the strike automatically set at each new pre-determined higher price.

[24]Dewynne, Jeff, "Partial To The Exotic", Risk Magazine, Mar 1993, pp. 38-46.
  Garman, Mark "Recollection In Tranquillity", Mar 1989, pp. 16-19.

Pricing Of The Shout Option

The evaluation of the Shout option begins with finding the payoff of the option at expiration and then working backwards to today to find its fair price. In this case, the payoff depends on at what price level the holder "shouts". To price the Shout, the holder is assumed to only do so in an optimal manner.[25] With this assumption, the payoff at expiration can be written as:

$$MAX\,(S_{t_s} - E, S_t - E, 0) = MAX\,(S_t - S_{t_s}, 0) + (S_{t_s} - E)$$

where:
S_{t_s} is the optimal exercise level for the holder,
S_t is the level of the underlying asset at time T, and
E is the initial strike price level of the Shout option.

Once this payoff is determined, one simply works backwards along the binomial tree to today's date and discounts the sum of all the possible payoffs at expiration back to their present values to determine the price of the Shout option.

Barrier / Knockout Option[26]

The final path dependent option I will cover is the Barrier option which is one of the oldest of the exotic options. In a barrier option, after the initial strike price is set, another level is established at which, if the underlying asset reaches that price, the option is cancelled. Generally, when this occurs the option holder is paid some agreed amount of his premium back. This kind of barrier option is called a knock-out because the option ceases to exist. Another kind of barrier option exists which is called a knock-in. For this option, the option does not exist until the underlying asset price reaches some level and when this occurs the option is created with a pre-determined strike price.

For call options, the barrier level is generally set below the current market price and strike price of the options. Thus, these types of options are known as Down-and-out calls for the knockouts or Down-and-in calls for the knockins. Likewise for put options, the barrier level is generally set at a price above the current market price and strike price of the options. Therefore, these types of options are know as Up-and-out puts for the knockouts and Up-and-in puts for the knockins.

---

[25]To determine the optimal point for exercise of the option, the reader is referred for further details to Bryan Thomas's article "Something to Shout About", Risk Magazine, May 1993, pp. 56-58.

[26]Benson, Robert, "Up, Over And Out", Risk Magazine, Jun 1991, pp.17-19.

Heynen, Robert, "Crossing Barriers", Risk Magazine, June 1994, 46-51.

Hudson, Mike, "The Value In Going Out", Risk Magazine, Mar 1991, pp. 29-33.

Reiner, Eric, "Breaking Down The Barriers", Risk Magazine, Sep 1991, pp.28-35.

Applications Of The Knockout Option

A logical question one might have is why anyone would want such an option. The primary reason for buyers is that they are significantly cheaper than normal options. But the real fans of knockout options are OTC option writers especially in the bond markets. I once had a long conversation with an old bond option trader from New York who enlightened me as to the usefulness of the knockout feature for OTC options. As the reader may remember when I discussed delta neutral trading in Chapter 8, the key element in success was continually rebalancing positions in the underlying asset and options markets to remain delta neutral. In exchange traded markets, this is relatively easy since both products trade with sufficient liquidity to make rebalancing possible. However, in the world of OTCs this may not be possible. Consider the situation where an OTC option market maker sells a call option to a client. To hedge his position, he will buy the delta amount of the underlying bond. If subsequently, the price of the underlying bond falls, he will have a loss on the bond and a theoretical gain on the call option. If he has correctly balanced his delta exposures, then he should have no gain or loss. One problem is that his bond can be marked to market with an unrealised loss while the gain from the reduction in the call price can only be estimated theoretically. The other problem is that he must rebalance his position to remain delta neutral. To do this it is not possible to deal in the option since the client is still holding it, so the OTC option market maker must realise a loss on the bond. If subsequently, the bond market rises, he will once again have to buy more of the bond to remain hedged. In the situation of very "choppy" market conditions, the option dealer can easily find his rebalancing costs getting out of control and his losses accumulating to more than the premium received for the option. The knockout option prevents this from occurring due to the fact that when the market falls to the barrier level, the theoretical gain on the option is realised by being knocked out. What he will pay to the knockout holder is the difference between the premium initially received less his rebalancing costs to that point. Often, in the early days, nothing was paid back to the option holder due to the uncertainty regarding the balancing costs of the hedged position. Even though the knockout would appear to be more ideal for the seller of the option, there can be applications for buyers as well.

Consider an investor who is trying to pick the bottom of the stock market. The FTSE 100 is currently at 3100. From his repertoire of technical analysis tools, he perceives that the current level of the share market should provide what is called "minor" support. This means that there should be sufficient buying interest to keep the market steady at this level. If the price starts to fall, the buyers will turn timid and the market should fall to 3000 where everyone will once again buy into the market. The term in technical analysis for this is "major" support. Regardless of other conditions, this investor would buy at 3000. He may be interested in a knockout call with a strike of 3100 and a barrier of 3000. Why? First of all, the option will be significantly cheaper. Secondly, if the market falls to 3000, he knows exactly what will be rebated on the knockout, so he is not concerned about de-

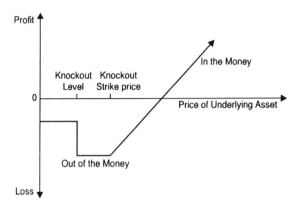

Figure 13.7 Profit & Loss Profile of a Knockout Call.

creases in the time value of the option due to the passage of time or decreases in implied volatility. Finally, at that level, he would be a buyer of the market anyway. So at that point, he would probably simply buy a futures contract on the FTSE 100. In this way, he can use the knockout option to exactly match his expectations of minor support at the current level and major support 100 points lower. In addition, his premium cost will be lower and he knows with certainty what he will receive if the option is knocked out. The profit and loss for this position can be see in Figure 13.7.

Pricing Of The Knockout Option
While these options are one of the oldest of the exotic options, they are also among the most difficult to determine a fair price. The simple reason is that when a barrier exists (such as the knockout or knockin price), the distribution is no longer continuous allowing for differentiation to find the solution. Instead of a nice smooth function like the normal or lognormal distribution, it is as if some maniac took his axe and chopped the lognormal distribution into two parts at the boundary level. It is possible to find these "barrier" distributions and build a formula for these options. However, it would require at least four pages of partial differential equations, the final results of which are neither straightforward or immediately obvious as to what is happening. Therefore, I have decided that by listing these proofs it would add a tremendous amount of bulk without adding understanding to this book. However, for those interested in finding the solution to the "barrier" distribution problem, there does exist a full explanation of the process and the reader is referred to this work.[27]

---

[27] The Reader should contact the Financial Options Research Centre at the University of Warwick and ask either Professor Stewart Hodges or Les Clewlow, for their working paper on Exotic Options. In that excellent work is the complete proof for the "barrier" distribution problem for the entire family of "barrier" options.

MULTI-FACTOR OPTIONS

These options have payoffs which depend upon the prices of two or more underlying assets. The principles which these products are based upon are the same as was discussed in Chapter 9 when I covered the trading of options between markets. In that chapter, the key element was the correlation between markets. For multi-factor options, this concept of correlation dependent options has been taken to its logical conclusion: the development of customised contingent claims based both upon volatilities and correlations.

Rainbow Option[28]

The first multi-factor exotic option I will discuss goes by the colourful name of the Rainbow option.[29] For this option, the payoff to the holder is determined by the highest price achieved at the expiration date by two or more underlying assets. The payoff of this option at expiration can be written as:

Rainbow Option

$$MAX\ [0, (S_1, S_2, S_3, ... S_n - E)$$

where:
S_1 to S_n is the price of a number of underlying assets at expiration
E   is the strike price of the standard option

An example of such a Rainbow option would allow the investor to receive the highest interest rate from among all the European countries with the strike price E being expressed as an interest rate strike.

Applications Of The Rainbow Option
Buyers of Rainbow options are trying to achieve the best performing asset in some category. It is a dream of active fund managers to be able to select that security which provides the best rate of return compared with alternative investments. Fund managers could package a rainbow option with a deposit to create a broader guaranteed investment fund. The investor would receive whatever was the best investment possible.

---

[28]Rubinstein, Mark, "Somewhere, Over The Rainbow", Risk Magazine, Nov 1991, pp. 63-66.
[29]I suppose if one buys the Rainbow option on an over the counter basis, this is known as an Over the Rainbow option or a Judy Garland option.

Pricing Of The Rainbow Option

The complexity of pricing the rainbow option depends on the number of assets in the comparative portfolio. For two assets, the solution is simply the Margrabe equation presented in Chapters 9 and 12. When more assets are added, a closed form solution is unable to be solved and the pricing of these options is most commonly achieved through the use of a Monte Carlo simulation.

Basket Option[30]

Basket options are a variation of the rainbow option, the difference being that the payoff in this product is a weighted average of the prices within the basket of underlying assets. These are created for those investors with investment portfolios which diverge from exchange traded standardised portfolios (like stock indices) or bonds.

Applications Of The Basket Option

The major application of Basket options is for investors with customised portfolios that require the hedging protection offered by an option. It is a well documented fact that an option on a portfolio will be cheaper than a portfolio of options.[31] So, instead of buying options on each instrument in the portfolio, the investor protects his portfolio as a whole.

Pricing Of The Basket Option

The key element in the pricing of the Basket option is the estimation of the volatility. For this one will apply the formula presented in Chapter 11 for the volatility of a portfolio of assets. To save the reader searching back, I have reproduced it here:

The formula for the standard deviation of a portfolio of assets is:

$$\sqrt{\sum_{i=1}^{N} x_i^2 \sigma_i^2 + 2\sum_{i=1}^{N} \sum_{j=1}^{N} x_i x_j \rho_{ij} \sigma_i \sigma_j}$$

In this formula, the x_i is the proportion invested in each of the assets i in the portfolio, σ_i^2 represents the variances of each of these assets i. The σ_i is the standard deviation of each asset i and ρ_{ij} is the correlation coefficient between each of the assets i and j. The single summation sign adds up all the weighted variances from the first to the Nth asset and the double summation sign adds up all the

---

[30]Gentle, David, "Basket Weaving", Risk Magazine, Jun 1993, pp. 51-52.

Patel, Parvez, "Protective Basket", Risk Magazine, Feb 1990, pp. 25-28.

[31]See Cox and Rubenstain book "Option Markets", Prentice-Hall, 1985, pp. 454-456.

weighted covariances between all the assets in the portfolio. This is simply the variance of a portfolio as determined by portfolio theory.

The pricing of the basket option is straightforward after this. One simply applies the Black and Scholes formula for European options and the binomial approach for American options.

Spread Option

The payoff of the spread option is the difference between the prices of two assets. In Chapter 9, I outlined this process in some detail for Crude Oil versus Gasoil and Raw Sugar versus White Sugar. The reader is referred to this chapter for more details.

Quanto[32]

For a quanto option, the payoff depends both upon an underlying price and the size of the exposure as a function of that underlying price. The name is an abbreviation for a quantity-adjusted option. In most cases, quanto options are associated with the purchase of an asset which is in another currency, the holder wishing to have the return of that asset expressed in his home currency. Let us look at a current example using a quanto on the Deutsche Aktien Index (DAX) which measures the movement in the German stock market for a United Kingdom investor.

Suppose the DAX is currently at 2100 and the UK investor buys a quanto call on the index. If the DAX finishes at 2200, instead of receiving 100 points in Deutsche Mark terms, the investor will receive 100 point in pounds sterling at an exchange rate fixed at the initiation of the option. The currency risk has been completely eliminated. There are four basic versions of the quanto:

(1) A foreign equity call struck in the foreign currency
(2) A foreign equity call struck in the domestic currency
(3) A fixed exchange rate foreign equity call, and
(4) An equity linked foreign exchange call

Applications Of The Quanto
In the United States and in Europe, considerable interest has been shown by fund managers in investing internationally. One of the major problems when investing outside your country has been the currency risk. Certainly, derivative products such as exchange traded options and futures have made the process easier by only tying up a relatively small amount of premium in the case of the option or initial margin

---

[32]Reiner, Eric, "Quanto Mechanics", Risk Magazine, Mar 1992, pp. 59-63.
  Jamshidian, Farshid, "Corralling Quantos", Risk Magazine, Mar 1994, pp. 71-75.

in the case of the futures. However, when either the options become in-the-money or futures prices change requiring cash topping up of the margin account, the investor will face currency risks. The quanto has been developed to eliminate the currency risks associated with foreign investments.

Pricing Of The Quanto

For the final exotic option that will be discussed in this chapter, the reader will be pleased to know that the pricing is among the simplest of all the exotics. When pricing the first type of quanto which is a foreign equity call struck in the foreign currency, the pricing is easy. This structure allows an investment in the foreign equity with protection against the price of the equity falling but no protection against foreign exchange risk. The payoff of this most basic of quanto options is:

$$C = X \cdot MAX(0, S' - E')$$

where:

X   is the current exchange rate
S' is the price of the Share in the foreign currency
E' is the strike of the option in the foreign currency

As far as the option writer in the foreign country is concerned, he is indifferent between an option which pays off in another currency; all he knows is that someone has bought a stock option from him which is denominated in his home currency. At the final payoff, the proceeds of the option will simply be converted to the currency of the holder at whatever the prevailing exchange rate is on that date. The value of this most simple of quanto options is simply the value of a standard call option (which could be estimated using the Black and Scholes formula) multiplied by the current exchange rate.

When pricing the second type of quanto which is a foreign equity call struck in the domestic currency, the pricing is also relatively straightforward.. This structure allows an investment in the foreign equity with protection against the price of the equity falling and some protection against foreign exchange risk. The payoff for the holder of this quanto option is:

$$C = MAX(0, [S' \cdot X] - E')$$

where:

X   is the current exchange rate
S' is the price of the Share in the foreign currency
E' is the strike of the option in the foreign currency

Of course, the seller of the quanto would have a different payoff which is:

$$C = MAX\,(0,S^{'} - [E^{'} \cdot X])$$

While, this quanto is a little more complicated than the first one (which is simply Black and Scholes), the problem is one of exchanging $E^{'}$ units of the domestic currency for one unit of the foreign stock, $S^{'}$. Once again, our problem is determining the value of an option to exchange one asset for another. The solution is the Margrabe formula presented in Chapters 9 and 11 (once again).

For the third type of quanto, which is a fixed exchange rate foreign equity call, the pricing becomes a little more difficult. This structure also allows an investment in the foreign equity with protection against the price of the equity falling and some protection against foreign exchange risk. The payoff for the holder of this quanto options is:

$$C = X_0 \cdot MAX\,(0,S^{'} - E^{'}) = MAX\,(0,[S^{'} \cdot X_0] - E)$$

where:
X_0 is the current exchange rate
S' is the price of the Share in the foreign currency
E' is the strike of the option in the foreign currency and
E   is the strike of the option in the domestic currency

The seller of this quanto would have a different payoff which is:

$$C^{'} = X_0 \cdot X^{'} \cdot MAX\,(0,S^{'} - E^{'})$$

where:
X' is the exchange rate at the option's expiration

Here, it is not simply possible to use Margrabe as above. One must first assess if the equity and the exchange rate are uncorrelated. If so, we can take expectations of the products separately and add them together to estimate the value of the quanto; otherwise, we have to adjust for the exchange rate if correlated.

For the final type of quanto, the equity linked foreign exchange call, pricing is simple again. Consider what this type of product is providing to the holder: this will provide an investment in the foreign equity, with no protection against the downside risk of the equity but complete protection against the downside risk of the exchange rate. The holder's payoff of this quanto expiration is simply:

$$C = S' \cdot MAX\,(0, X - E)$$

where:

  X is the current exchange rate
  S' is the price of the equity in the foreign currency
  E is the strike of the currency option

The seller of the option in the foreign country would see the payoff as:

$$C' = S' \cdot MAX\,(0, 1 - E \cdot X') = E \cdot S' \cdot MAX\,(0, \tfrac{1}{E} - X')$$

This type of quanto is exactly analogous to a fixed exchange rate foreign equity put with the roles of the equity and exchange rate interchanged. In this way we can simply use the results from the previous quanto.

CONCLUSION

The same principles underlying all of these exotic options have been applied to other markets such as currencies, commodities and equity products. The driving force for innovation has been the customer's needs. It is not dependent on the technological expertise of the market. The recent work in the academic world (just a few examples of these papers were referenced in this chapter), have given financial engineers the tools necessary to price almost any kind of contingent claim. So, the reader can expect that this explosion of innovation will most probably continue and spread to other markets. Regardless of the structure of option-like securities yet to be created, it is safe to assume that any of these innovations will most probably be based upon the concepts presented either in this chapter or earlier in this book (Chapters 2,3,4,5 and 9). So, no matter what kind of option the reader must evaluate, remembering the basic principles outlined in this book should suffice to address the problem.

14: Risk Management of Options

In this section, I will address the risk management of options dealing and using a popular computer risk analysis programme, help the reader see how option market makers evaluate and control the risks of their portfolios. In addition, I will show the reader how to use the analytics generated by risk analysis programmes to choose the best options trading strategy.

A BRIEF HISTORY OF OPTIONS MARKETS

Options are among mankind's oldest instruments for managing risk. For example, there are references to option contracts in ancient Greece. Aristotle indicated in Politics that a certain philosopher named Thales the Milesian "gave deposits for the use of all the olive presses in Chios and Miletus, which he hired at a low price because no one bid against him. When the harvest time came, and many wanted them all at once and of a sudden, he let them out at any rate which he pleased, and made a quantity of money."[1] Throughout ancient times, options were struck between merchants mostly for the management of commodity price risk. In the Middle Ages, although many Italian banks were offering option-like products, options became particularly infamous from their association with the Dutch tulip bulb mania. After this time, more abuses of options occurred in London and later in the US where "bucket shops" specialised in offering unsecured options.[2] While most of these abuses were due to the lack of financial backing, fundamental problems also existed in the pricing of these securities and the risk management of those who underwrote the contracts.

Why Options Markets Have Grown Exponentially Since The 1970s

Though financial options of various type have been in use for a long time, it is only since the mid-1970s that they have become actively traded on a large scale. Their surge in popularity has occurred primarily for three reasons.

---

[1] Aristotle's Politics, Book one, Chapter 11, Jowett translation. This example of early Greek options was first referred to in Gary Gastineau's Book, The Stock Options Manual.
[2] See Gastineau's Book for a lively description of the stock options markets prior to the 1970s.

503

First, Professors Fischer Black and Myron Scholes (then at the University of Chicago) developed a formula for pricing options that not only allowed people to determine a particular option's fair values, but also to regulate those values through arbitrage. While Black and Scholes are "household" names in the financial world, it is a little known fact that a much of the groundwork for their model was based upon work done by Louis Bachelier in 1900.[3] Unfortunately, this brilliant Frenchman was unable to a consolidate his work into a comprehensive, all-encompassing formula which actually worked. If he had done so, Paris might very well now be the centre for the trading of world options instead of Chicago.

The second reason was the security provided through the introduction of options contracts on regulated exchanges where the contracts had the financial backing of the Clearing House. The inauguration of the Chicago Board Options Exchange in 1973 meant that for the first time, option contracts were standardised, regulated and could easily be purchased or sold by the general public through stock brokers. This revolution was so successful that in less than 20 years fifty-four exchanges have opened world-wide to trade option contracts (see appendix 1).

The third reason that the level of options trading has grown so dramatically since the 1970s is due to the strident advances made through computerisation in the business world. Computers and computer programmes are essential to option trading because of the complexities involved in dealing with simultaneous multiple option contracts and the constant needs to analyse, change and update complicated trading positions.

Apart from dealing, the computer is vital to the formulation of market strategies, and is especially essential in maintaining an integrated approach to risk management. There has been a proliferation of risk management computer software systems over the last few years to meet this need. For our purpose of understanding options risk management, I have chosen to use the Risk Analysis Programmne (commonly known by its acronym, RAP) written by Dr. David Emanuel[4]. I have used this programme since its introduction in 1984 and I have used the latest revisions of RAP (2.84) for the analytical illustrations in this chapter.

AN OPTION RISK ANALYSIS COMPUTER PROGRAMME

With any risk analysis package, the primary task must be to evaluate the overall risks of all positions held in the underlying asset as well as for all options on this asset. The ideal system should not only determine the implied volatilities of a position, but also compare actual option prices with their theoretical values, evaluate

---

[3]Bachelier, Louis, "Theorie de la Speculation," Annales de l'Ecole Normale Superieure, 17 (1900), pp. 21-86. English translation by A.J.Boness in The Random Character of Stock Market Prices, ed. Paul H. Cootner, pp.17-78. Cambridge, Mass.: MIT Press, 1967 (thank goodness for the translation)
[4]David Emanuel worked as an economist at the Chicago Mercantile Exchange in 1984-1985, the experience of which he used in developing RAP. Apart from this programme, Dr. Emanuel is well know for his expertise in the field of warrants.

time decay, and assess all potential exposure, especially the volatility, for the period of the trade. The system should also be flexible enough to permit the creation of a custom designed contract modeled on both exchange traded instruments and over-the-counter instrument such as rights issues or warrants. Since RAP posseses all of these functions, it is ideal for demonstrating how computerized risk evaluation is done.

In this chapter, I will examine the risk management of option contracts using Live Cattle futures and options traded at the Chicago Mercantile Exchange (CME). First, we need to understand what these contracts represent. The price of the Live Cattle futures is the number of US dollars per hundred pounds of Live Cattle delivered at various points in the midwest of the United States. The quantity delivered per one futures contract is equal to 40,000 pounds of Live Cattle. The minimum price change for the futures is 2.5 cents per hundred pounds (or 0.025 cents per pound) or a dollar equivalent of $10.00 (0.025 cents x 40,000 pounds). Thus if the price for the Live Cattle futures is 66.25, then this means that the contract value is equal to $26,500. The option on Live Cattle futures is quoted similarly, except that it is in cents per pound instead of dollars per hundred pounds.

Trading Unit:	One live cattle futures contract (40,000 pounds).
Contract Months:	February, April, June, August, October, December.
Last Trading Day:	Last Friday that is more than 3 business days prior to first business day of delivery month.
Minimum Price Movement:	0.025 cents per pound ($10 per contract) (tick size)
Exercise Price Intervals:	1 cent per pound (e.g. 62, 63, 64 etc.)
Trading Hours:	9.05 - 13.00 (Chicago time).
Exercise:	By 19.00 up to and including the last trading day.

Table 14.1 Options on Live Cattle Futures (CME).

The minimum tick size for the option is also 0.025 cents per pound. Table 14.1 outlines the contract specification for the options on Live Cattle futures. The ultimate asset underlying the option is a futures contract which requires the receipt or delivery of 40,000 pounds of Live Cattle in the month following the expiration of the option.

Contract Definitions in the Program

For the futures and options seminars I present, the RAP is an integral part of our risk management module. For this purpose, I have created a contract in the RAP specifically for CME Live Cattle contracts. This contract file can be seen in Table 14.2. To analyse options on Live Cattle futures, I first need to define this product in the programme. This requires us to include all the elements in the Live Cattle options contract definitions. This includes how the underlying is quoted, what the underlying size is and how the margining system functions.

```
Quote format for futures (cash or OTC BOND) price is              DDD.DDD
Editing contract for LIVE CATTLE
Quote format for option price is                                  DDD.DDD
Quote format for strike price is                                  DDD.D

Quoted futures (or cash) price is actual futures price times            1
Quoted option price is actual option price times                       1
Quoted strike price is actual strike price times                       1

Currency for contract denomination. Type 1 for Dollar, 2 Lira 1
3 Pound, 4 Yen, 5 D-Mark, 6 Franc, 7 Peseta, 8 S-Franc
Futures (or cash) contract value is actual futures price times       400
Option contract value is actual option price times                   400
Premiums are paid up (Chicago) or margined like futures (LIFFE)  Premium (Chicago)
Interval (decimal) between adjacent strikes (can be ignored)       is 2

Option pricing model for this contract is                        American
Prices come from SLOW BINOMIAL or FAST ANALYTIC Pricing Model  ANALYTIC(Black etc)
BINOMIAL REQUIRED for IMBEDDED options (Analytic ignores them)
This contract is based on (Futures or Physical security)          Futures
Dividend(or convenience) yield in percent per year                     0
This only has relevance for Physical security options

Annual volatility of underlying contract: in percent               27.1
Range of annual percent volatility changes(+ or -) to scan            1

$ range in value of 1 futures(cash)contract to scan + or -          600
You might want to use the contract margin for these ranges
$ range in intermonth spread relationship to scan + or -            420
```

Table 14.2 Contract Definitions for Live Cattle Options in the RAP.

In Table 14.2, the first few lines determines how the Live Cattle futures and options will be quoted. These contracts are both listed in decimal format with DDD.DDD indicating that prices can have a maximum of three numbers to the left of the decimal point and three numbers to the right. The string of three "1"s indicates that each Live Cattle futures and options contract is for only one underlying. For both the Live Cattle futures and options contracts, their value is actually 400 times the prices quoted in the market ($ per 100 pounds). Therefore the contract value of the August Live Cattle futures is really equal to the price per 100 pounds x 400 which is equal to cents per pound x 40,000 pounds of Live Cattle. Consider the following example: the Live Cattle futures price is $66.0. To determine the contract value, we simply multiply $66.0 by 400 to give us the actual value of $26,400. The next line down indicates that the premiums for Live Cattle future options are based upon the Chicago system where one must pay the premium for an option upfront. This is important for the pricing and risk evaluation of Live Cattle futures and options. The Live Cattle options strike prices are quoted in cents per pounds 1 cent intervals between the strike prices. Therefore, at the bottom of the first page of the contract definition, there is a line for increments of the option strike prices and this is 2. This allows for the strike prices to have 2 cents intervals (although as RAP indicates, this can be ignored).

In the lower portion of the contract definition the more technical elements of the contract definition are found. It indicates that the option has an American-style option feature, meaning it can be exercised any time until maturity. The next line indicates that all analytic theoretical evaluations will be done using an ANALYTIC pricing approach such as the Black (1976) pricing model. Why this model? Because the option is based upon a Futures contract and this appears in the next line. Since the Live Cattle options on the CME are not on a physical security, the underlying asset (futures) pays no interest, coupon or dividend yield which is why the dividend or convenience yield is set to 0. If instead you were evaluating options on physical Live Cattle, then you would have to include a convenience or dividend yield for Live Cattle (i.e. Calves).[5] The annual volatility is a default value that we can change later in our analysis. For the Live Cattle contract I have set the default volatility to 27.1% for the August contract, 19% for the October and 16.5% for the December contract. The next line allows us to set the size of the possible volatility movements that could occur in a single day. When evaluating options risk analysis we want to know what can happen for a particular overnight movement in volatility of perhaps 1%. So, I enter into RAP a figure of 1% as the range of how much the market volatility could move overnight. Thus, if the current Live Cattle futures volatility is 27%, then we want to know what could happen if tomorrow the volatility either increased to 28% or decreased to 26%.

The next line down allows us to determine a US Dollar range of possible Live Cattle futures price movements that could occur overnight. The figure $600, for the range of the futures (cash) to scan + or -, indicates that when we do our risk management, we will assume that the underlying Live Cattle futures market can move at most $1.50 overnight. This $1.50 range is calculated by dividing the $600 by the contract multiple of 400 which gives us 1.5. This means that if the Live Cattle futures contract is trading at $66.0, the RAP assumes that for risk management purposes, the market cannot move below $64.5 or above $67.5 in a single day. Finally, the bottom line of the second page of the Live Cattle futures contract definition indicates how much the spread could change between Live Cattle futures contract months. For example, if we purchased August 1994 Live Cattle futures and sold October 1994 Live Cattle futures, we have a risk that these contracts will not move together. The spread relationship could change overnight. In the RAP, all positions and all maturities, are combined into a single risk analysis. To do this, it is unwise to assume that the various maturities will always change in the same degree. Therefore, the $420 indicates the amount that the relationship between various Live Cattle futures months could change overnight. The $420 translates to a change of $1.05 in a single day ($420/400). For example, let us say that the August 1994 Live

---

[5]Ha, Ha got you! Cattle don't pay dividends or coupons, the only time this feature is used is for option on physical stock, or Bonds.

Cattle futures is trading at $64.15 and the October 1994 Live Cattle futures is trading at $68.25. At these levels, the spread between these contracts is a positive $4.1. RAP assumes that if the spread changes overnight it cannot fall below plus $3.05 or rise above plus $5.15. These amounts for the overnight movements on the Live Cattle futures and the spreads are drawn from the margin requirements for the Live Cattle futures position ($600) and a Live Cattle futures spread ($420) established at the CME as 30 June 1994.

Adding Expiration Dates and Strike Prices into the Programme

Once we have defined our Live Cattle futures and options contracts in the programme, the next step is to add the maturities for these futures and options contracts. This can be seen in the bottom of Table 14.3.

```
Strikes (decimal) in spreadsheet for this contract(Max # is 25)are:
62.00000000     63.00000000    64.00000000 65.00000000
66.00000000     67.00000000    68.00000000

LIVE CATTLE Hypothetical date is 30 Jun 1994

Contract          Options     Days until    Futures    Days until
                  Expire    (Expiration)    Expire    (Expiration)
         22 Jul 1994 (       22)      5 Aug 1994 (      36)
         23 Sep 1994 (       85)      7 Oct 1994 (      99)
         25 Nov 1994 (      148)      2 Dec 1994 (     155)
```

Table 14.3 Maturities and Strike Prices.

Since the eventual settlement of the Live Cattle futures contract requires physical delivery of cattle, the underlying futures is considered a physical security underlying. As was discussed in Chapter 1, when this occurs, option contracts on these kinds of underlying assets often expire in the month preceding the expiration of the underlying futures. This can be seen in this table with the option contracts expiring approximately two weeks prior to the futures. After this step, we now need to add the strike prices against which we wish to evaluate the options. These values also appear at the top of Table 14.3. With these steps completed, we can now enter the futures and options positions on a spreadsheet and do our risk analysis simulation.

A Live Cattle Option Sample Trade Entry Spreadsheet

Table 14.4 displays a sample Live Cattle futures and options spreadsheet for a position entered on 30 June 1994. Let us take a few sentences to describe what the spreadsheet is showing us. Listed at the top of the sheet are the maturities for the

Live Cattle futures. Notice that only August 1994, October 1994 and December 1994 contracts are available. The maturity dates actually say 5 August '94, 7 October '94 and 2 December '94. These reflect the maturity dates of the underlying Live Cattle futures.

```
LIVE CATTLE POSITIONS
FUTURES          5 Aug 94        7 Oct 94        2 Dec 94
  QTY
  PRC            64.150          68.250          69.220
STRIKES        CALL    PUT    CALL    PUT    CALL    PUT    CALL    PUT
62.0 QTY
     PRC       2.950  0.800          0.550          0.600
     ------------------------------------------------------------------
63.0 QTY
     PRC       2.350  1.200
     ------------------------------------------------------------------
64.0 QTY
     PRC       1.800  1.650  5.125  0.925          0.925
     ------------------------------------------------------------------
65.0 QTY
     PRC       1.325  2.175
     ------------------------------------------------------------------
66.0 QTY
     PRC       0.950  2.800  3.750  1.525          1.350
     ------------------------------------------------------------------
67.0 QTY
     PRC       0.675  3.500  3.150  1.925
     ------------------------------------------------------------------
68.0 QTY
     PRC       0.463  4.313  2.700  2.450  3.525  2.300
     ------------------------------------------------------------------
```

Table 14.4 Sample Live Cattle Futures Options Spreadsheet.

The reader can see in Table 14.1 that the options on Live Cattle expire on the last Friday that is more than three business days prior to the first business day of the delivery month of the underlying futures contract. As the reader can appreciate, this is very complicated and fortunately this is already taken into account in the programme and a quick review of Table 14.3 shows this has been incorporated. Below the maturities, the reader sees that series of *"Call Put"* are repeated across the spreadsheet. These display the available calls and puts for each of the entered maturities. On the left side of the matrix, one sees the word *Futures* and below that *QTY* and *PRC*. These show the quantity of various futures contracts held and the respective prices of those instruments. Below these lines, the reader will see *Strikes*. These represent the strike prices for the options we will be evaluating. The first strike, immediately below the word *Strikes*, is 62.0. To the immediate right and below, the reader will see again *QTY* and *PRC*. Again this means that all 62.0 options, both calls and puts, will be in this row along with the quantity held and the price associated with the relevant transaction. Below these lines the sequence is repeated for 63.0, 64.0, until 68.0. These will be all the options and futures contracts necessary to build our sample market maker's portfolio. Since our spreadsheet is

509

now established, we can travel around the spreadsheet and enter the actual market prices or quantities held for the various kinds of assets.

Entry of a Sample Portfolio of Live Cattle Options into the Spreadsheet

Table 14.5 shows a sample portfolio duly entered. Suppose that the nearby Live Cattle futures is trading at a price of 64.150.[6] We have sold ten (-10) of the 64.0 August calls and bought 15 of the 66.0 August puts. So the reader should read down from "5 Aug 94" and "CALL" until on the left he sees 64.0. Immediately to the right of the "QTY" he will see -10 and below it a 1.800. This shows that the quantity held is minus ten, which means ten have been sold, at a price of 1.800. If once again, he reads down the "5 Aug 94" "PUT" column until on the left he sees "66.0" and "QTY". He will see a 15 here and below it the price of the option of 2.800.

LIVE CATTLE POSITIONS								
FUTURES	5 Aug 94		7 Oct 94		2 Dec 94			
QTY								
PRC	64.150		68.250		69.220			
STRIKES	CALL	PUT	CALL	PUT	CALL	PUT	CALL	PUT
62.0 QTY								
PRC	2.950	0.800		0.550		0.600		
63.0 QTY								
PRC	2.350	1.200						
64.0 QTY	-10			-10	5			
PRC	1.800	1.650	5.125	0.925	0.925			
65.0 QTY								
PRC	1.325	2.175						
66.0 QTY		15	15	-15	-25			
PRC	0.950	2.800	3.750	1.525	1.350			
67.0 QTY								
PRC	0.675	3.500	3.150	1.925				
68.0 QTY			35		-15			
PRC	0.463	4.313	2.700	2.450	3.525	2.300		

Table 14.5 Sample Portfolio.

As the reader scans the spreadsheet in Table 14.5, he will see that a wide variety of positions are held. For example, in the October Live Cattle futures we have purchased 15 of the 66.0 call (at a price of 3.750) and 35 of the 68.0 calls (at a price of 2.700). We have also sold 10 of the October 64.0 put options at 0.925 and 15 of the 66 put options at 1.525. The current price of the August Live Cattle futures is 64.15

---

[6]These prices are actual CME prices as of 30 June 1994.

and the October Live Cattle futures is 68.25. In the December maturity, we have sold 15 of the 68.0 calls (at a price of 3.525), bought 5 of the 64.0 puts at 0.925 and sold 25 of the 66.0 puts at 1.350. In addition, all the closing prices for the options are listed. An empty QTY (quantity) cell shows that we have no positions there and where we have entered numbers, we actually hold positions. Again, the numbers below each quantity are the prices at which we bought or sold each particular instrument.

Comparison of Market Prices with Theoretical Prices

After entering the prices we will do a comparison of the theoretical prices versus actual market prices and see if there are any discrepancies. For this purpose, the RAP programme displays a spreadsheet that shows the market prices and the theoretical prices. This can be seen in Table 14.6. It also determines the deltas (which is the relative risk of the option to a full long position in the underlying market) and the gammas (which informs you how the delta will change when the underlying market price varies).

Variable Sigma & Interest Rate LIVE CATTLE 30 Jun 1994						
	64.150		68.250		69.220	
	5 Aug 1994		7 Oct 1994		2 Dec 1994	
STRIKES	CALL	PUT	CALL	PUT	CALL	PUT
62.0 Mkt	2.950	0.800		0.550		0.600
Theory	2.958	0.812	6.656	0.450	7.652	0.515
Delta	.705959	-.29201	.858902	-.13596	.858977	-.13348
Gamma	.002011	.002009	.000894	.000869	.000781	.000736
63.0 Mkt	2.350	1.200				
Theory	2.319	1.172	5.840	0.629	6.836	0.692
Delta	.618602	-.37929	.816342	-.17757	.821796	-.16888
Gamma	.002227	.002225	.001054	.001036	.000897	.000861
64.0 Mkt	1.800	1.650	5.125	0.925		0.925
Theory	1.773	1.623	5.074	0.856	6.064	0.910
Delta	.526170	-.47170	.767625	-.22558	.780204	-.20911
Gamma	.002327	.002326	.001209	.001195	.001010	.000982
65.0 Mkt	1.325	2.175				
Theory	1.319	2.167	4.363	1.138	5.339	1.174
Delta	.433697	-.56419	.713429	-.27927	.734560	-.25371
Gamma	.002300	.002301	.001347	.001337	.001114	.001093
66.0 Mkt	0.950	2.800	3.750	1.525		1.350
Theory	0.955	2.801	3.712	1.479	4.665	1.487
Delta	.346011	-.65193	.654817	-.33754	.685457	-.30205
Gamma	.002157	.002159	.001459	.001453	.001205	.001190
67.0 Mkt	0.675	3.500	3.150	1.925		
Theory	0.672	3.516	3.122	1.882	4.044	1.853
Delta	.267013	-.731012	.593155	-.39899	.633679	-.35331
Gamma	.001923	.001927	.001538	.001534	.001278	.001267
68.0 Mkt	0.463	4.313	2.700	2.450	3.525	2.300
Theory	0.460	4.302	2.597	2.349	3.477	2.273
Delta	.199242	-.79895	.529996	-.46206	.580150	-.40652
Gamma	.001634	.001639	.001578	.001577	.001328	.001322

Table 14.6 Option Market Prices and Theoretical Prices.

These functions are most useful in options risk management software for they show whether the options dealt are over-valued or under-valued relative to their theoretical value. This is an important theoretical edge RAP can give to those dealing.

The reader may refer to the chapter on volatility trading (Chapter 7) for a more extensive discussion of how to use this theoretical advantage. To determine the theoretical value, we input our volatility estimates for the different expirations. In this case we input 27.1% for August option, 19% for October option and 16.5% for December option. For the October 64.0 put option that we sold at a price of 0.925, its theoretical price and market price are divergent. This can be seen by reading down from the "7 Oct 1994" & "PUT" column and across the 64.0 row. The actual market price is 0.925 in the table but immediately below it is the theoretical price of 0.856. Therefore, if our volatility estimate (of 19%) is correct, we expect to make a profit from mispricing of at least 0.069 cents per pound. The delta for this option is -0.22558 and thus giving it the same risk as being short 22% of one futures contract. Since, we sold this put, we have a negative position in this spread-sheet (-15) and this is multiplied by the negative delta value of -0.22558 to provide us with a positive delta exposure for this position of +3.38370 (-15·-0.22558). Its gamma, the amount by which the delta will change for a given one basis point move in the underlying, is 0.001195. Again, since we sold the put options, the negative holding position (-15) time the positive gamma value (0.001195) provides the overall gamma exposure of this position. For this position, the total gamma exposure is -0.01793 (-15·0.001195). This number indicated how the total delta exposure of the position will change for a 1 tick movement in the price of the underlying Live Cattle futures.

Since the minimum tick change is 0.025 cents per pound, this is a fairly small amount. If for example, the current August Live Cattle futures price is 64.15 cents, the minimum price change would be to either 64.175 cents or 64.125 cents. If this would occur, the delta exposure of the short fifteen October 64.0 puts would change to +3.36578 (+3.38370-0.01793) or +3.40163 (+3.38370-[-0.01793]) respectively. Given that the gamma is relatively stable for movements in the underlying asset, then if the underlying October Live Cattle futures moved by 10 ticks this change would be multiplied by ten (-0.1793 deltas). However, this October 64.0 put option is out-of-the-money and (as was stated in Chapter 3) the gamma for an out-of-the-money option should be fairly low. To see if this is the case, we must compare this gamma to the gamma values for other options in the spreadsheet.

Comparison of Gamma Values Across Strike Prices and Maturities

The highest gamma values are for options that are at-the-money and closest to maturity. If the reader looks carefully at Table 14.6, he will notice that the highest gamma values are associated with options on the August futures; those that are closest to maturity. Furthermore, if he compares the August options across the strike prices, it is evident that the highest gammas are for the 64.0 calls and puts. Given that the price of the August Live Cattle futures is at 64.15, these options are the closest to the current underlying price and would be identified as the at-the-money options. These gamma values are 0.002327 and 0.002326. If one remembers that gamma is simply a measure of how close the option is to its strike price and maturity date, then the concept of gamma is a snap. The closer it is to the strike price, and the closer it is to maturity, the higher the gamma. The reader will also notice that some of the deltas in the table have positive values and some have negative values. RAP assigns a minus sign to the deltas of put options (because they are short positions), and a plus sign to the deltas of call options. This is consistent when one recalls the relative exposure one has to the underlying market when buying put or call options.

However, the reader will recall that when one sells put or call options, the exposure is reversed. To take this into account, RAP applies a simple mathematical rule to assure that buying a put (or selling a call) is a short position and that selling a put (or buying a call) is a long position. This is achieved in a two step process in the programme. Initially, if a position is purchased then the quantity bought will be entered in the QTY cell in the spreadsheet as a positive number. Furthermore, if a position is sold then the quantity sold is represented by a negative number in the appropriate QTY cell. To determine the exposure of each position, RAP will multiply the quantity in that QTY cell by the delta for that option. For example, the exposure of a single short put is estimated by the product of -1 that is entered in the QTY cell and the negative delta factor estimated by the programme. Thus, the exposure of the short put becomes positive relative to the underlying market because a negative number multiplied by another negative number results in a positive number. So, if we sell three put options with a delta of -0.5, the relative risk is -3 x -0.5 or a +1.5 delta.

Determination of the Implied Volatilities

The RAP programme can also determine the implied volatility for every option that has been entered into the spreadsheet. At any point in time, in this case the 30 June 1994, RAP simply synthesises the option's prices, their individual striking prices and the current price of the underlying market to calculate instantaneously the implied volatility for each option. Table 14.7 displays the implied volatilities for the Live Cattle futures options in the spreadsheet. The layout is similar to the spreadsheet in Tables 14.4 and 14.5, with PRC (price) replacing QTY (quantity) and VOL (implied volatility) replacing what was previously PRC. The PRC (price) in this table is the market price for that particular option series and VOL is the implied volatility associated with that price.

```
LIVE CATTLE 30 Jun 1994 FUTURES PRICE
        64.150              68.250           69.220
        5 Aug 1994          7 Oct 1994       2 Dec 1994
STRIKES CALL      PUT       CALL      PUT    CALL      PUT
62.0 PRC  2.950   0.800               0.550           0.600
     VOL  26.96  26.88               20.35           17.37
63.0 PRC  2.350   1.200
     VOL  27.62  27.58
64.0 PRC  1.800   1.650     5.125   0.925           0.925
     VOL  27.54  27.53    19.51   19.69           16.62
65.0 PRC  1.325   2.175
     VOL  27.19  27.22
66.0 PRC  0.950   2.800     3.750   1.525           1.350
     VOL  27.01  27.08    19.32   19.38           15.59
67.0 PRC  0.675   3.500     3.150   1.925
     VOL  27.15  26.78    19.22   19.34
68.0 PRC  0.463   4.313     2.700   2.450   3.525   2.300
     VOL  27.16  27.34    19.80   19.78   16.79   16.66
```

Table 14.7 Implied Volatilities.

For example, RAP assesses that the 64.0 call and put options for the August Live Cattle futures the call has an implied volatility of 27.54% and the put has an implied volatility of 27.53%. These numbers are in reality the same but small rounding errors lead to the difference. When we examine the 64.0 option series for October futures they have lower volatilities of 19.51% for the call and 19.69% for the put. As the reader can see, the volatilities do vary across the strike prices. Generally, the out-of-the-money options have a higher implied volatility (as examples, the October 68.0 call and put and the December 62.0 put). In addition, the further in time the maturity of the option, the lower the implied volatility. There can be several possible explanations for these effects which were discussed extensively in Chapter 5. As a brief review of the conclusions of that chapter: First, these out-of-the-money options do not trade as actively as the at-the-money options and market makers do not have the same high degree of liquidity to offset these out-of-the-money options. Therefore, they charge more for these options because of that liquidity risk. Another explanation is that if the market did decrease or increase to the level of the out-of-the-money strike prices, then the volatility probably would have increased. To counter this potentiality, some market markers use the volatility they would expect to have if the market moved to the level of their strike price. Finally, it could be that the assumptions underlying the popular option pricing models such as Black and Scholes are violated. There is considerable evidence that the returns for many markets can not be characterised by a lognormal distribution but follow a bizarrely shaped distribution called leptokurtic. This means that dramatic upward or downward movements in markets occur more often than predicted by a lognormal distribution.[7] My feeling is that all these factors are relevant in explaining why volatility differs across strike prices. The important question then be-

---

[7]See: Larson, A. "Measurement of a Random Process in Futures Prices". Food Research Institute Studies, Vol.I, No 3 (November 1960), pp. 313-24.

comes what is the use of theoretical pricing models if these discrepancies occur? The answer to this question was covered extensively in Chapter 3. If the reader recalls the aeroplane analogy, option pricing models programmes such as RAP are the gauges which provide information and they should not be used as exclusive substitutes for looking out of the window. The option market maker recognises that volatility, and hence option prices, do not always conform to theory. However, theory does allow a framework within which he can recognise obvious deviations and thus take advantage of them.

Evaluating the Risks of the Option Portfolio

The next thing we need to determine is the risks inherent in an entire portfolio of Live Cattle futures and options. As was pointed out in Chapter 3, to see the entire picture it is necessary to look at the net delta, gamma, vega, and theta positions consolidated for all the trades in our options portfolio. Table 14.8 displays a print-out with just these statistics. As one looks at the table, in the upper half on the left he will see Net FUTURES and below that Net # Calls and Net # Puts. Immediately to the right of Net FUTURES, he will see 0 (no position). Below that he will see a -10 for the net number of August calls and 15 for the net number of August puts.

LIVE CATTLE 30 Jun 1994 FUTURES PRICE			
	5Aug94	7Oct94	2 Dec94	AllMths
Net FUTURES	0	0	0	0
Net # Calls	-10.	50.	-15.	25.
Net # Puts	15.	-25.	-20.	-30.
Net Delta	-15.040	35.6911	-2.1963	18.4541
Net Gamma	.009123	.043386	-.04477	.007736
Net Zeta	.98581	1.43561	-2.3012	-.76701
Net Theta	59.6702	155.418	-124.54	90.5464
FUTURES PRC	64.150	68.250	69.220	
DAILY SIGMA	1.100	0.821	0.723	
ANNUAL SIGMA	27.100	19.000	16.500	
INTEREST RATE	4.125	4.375	4.500	

Table 14.8 Delta, Gamma, Vega and Theta Table.

As I stated in Chapter 3, option risk is not only defined by the number of contracts purchased or sold; another critical factor is the delta. The reader can see the net delta impact of all these positions, if he looks further down the table to the immediate right of Net Delta. Here, he will see that the net delta of all the August positions is -15.040. Thus, relative to August Live Cattle futures, the overall impact of the trades he has established has the same underlying price risk as being short 15 August Live Cattle futures. Below this is the gamma for the August position and it is 0.009123. This indicates how much the delta for the entire August position will

515

change if the price of the underlying Live Cattle futures changes by 1 tick of 0.025 cents. The reader will note that in this case the gamma is positive, indicating that when the market rises, the delta of the overall position will also become more positive or less negative and when the Live Cattle futures price falls, the overall exposure to the underlying market will become less positive or more negative.

Below the gamma value for the August futures and options portfolio, one can see more numbers. The first is the Net Zeta. This is the same derivative that we call the vega. The numerical value for the zeta (vega) is 0.98581. This indicates the amount of $1000 that will be earned or lost for every 1% increase or decrease in volatility. With the present level of volatility at about 27%, if it increased to 28% and everything else remained unchanged, one would expect to earn $985.81 on the August trades. The number below this is the net theta. This indicates how much one will make or lose on the position from time decay as a single day passes. In our previous definition of theta, we indicated that when one is gamma positive they will also be theta negative. However, in this table, both the gamma and theta derivatives appear as positive numbers. The reader may ask: Can this be correct? The answer is yes, but the RAP program is simply portraying the theta in an inverse way to market conventions. When the RAP displays a positive theta value, that means this is the amount which will be lost in one calendar day. When the theta is negative, this indicates the amount which will be gained from the passage of one calendar day. Thus, for the August Live Cattle futures and options positions, we expect to lose $59.67 from 30 June to 1 July (a minus sign means we profit and a plus sign means a loss). Finally, below the "Greeks" are some useful statistics. These include: the futures price used in the estimation, the daily sigma (standard deviation) for the futures, the annual sigma (the volatility) used in the analysis.

The reader will recall that we also have positions in our options "book" (another name used by market makers for their option portfolio) which should be evaluated relative to the October Live Cattle futures. Thus, in the middle column of Table 14.8, we can see the same net positions, deltas, gammas, zetas and thetas for the October expiration. The overall delta for October is (a positive) 35.6911. This shows that, in total, the options we have dealt with a October expiration have the same risk as buying almost 36 October Live Cattle futures contracts. The gamma here is again positive, at 0.043386, indicating that the changes in the delta of the position will be positively related to the movement of the October futures. Finally, the zeta (vega) and the theta are both positive (at 1.43561 and 155.418 respectively). The interpretation of this is that we are net buyers of volatility in October but will lose from time decay.

In addition, we also have trades for the December expiration. Thus, in the third column of Table 14.8, we can see the same net positions, deltas, gammas, zetas and thetas for the December expiration. The overall delta for December is -2.1963. This shows that, in total, the combination of options we have dealt with a December expiration have the same (delta) risk as selling 2 December Live Cattle futures contracts. The gamma here is -0.04477 indicating that the changes in the delta of the

516

position will be inversely related to the movement of the December futures. Finally, the zeta (vega) and the theta are both negative (at -2.3012 and -124.54 respectively). The interpretation of this is that we are net sellers of volatility in December and will benefit from time decay.

The column furthest to the right indicates the exposures across all months. The exposures of the August contracts will either be additive or offsetting when combined with the October and December positions. Therefore, the delta exposure of 18.4541 indicates the combination of August, October and December deltas; the reader will no doubt notice a slight mathematical deviation, this is due to small rounding errors in adding the deltas (the simple sum of the deltas is 18.4548). This number indicates that the entire portfolio of transactions will have the same gains and losses from movements in Live Cattle futures as holding approximately eighteen Live Cattle futures. As the reader can also see, the rest of the "Greeks" are aggregated in this column as well. In conclusion, this analysis tool measures the relative risks both generally and specifically within each month.

A critical point to remember is that if one is short 20 calls or even 1000 calls, neither is the real measure of the risk. The real measures of risk are the "Greek" derivatives. For example, relative to Live Cattle futures the delta position is the true exposure to the underlying market. By adding the deltas for all the months, we can determine the total risk of the "book" relative to a given underlying futures contract.

Back again, what is our volatility risk for the entire position? The answer is the zeta (vega). This gives us a measure of the amount of dollars we will make in thousands from a 1% move in the volatility of the market. If the volatility moves up 1% and we are short in it, we will lose $767.01 (-0.76701 x $1,000). Conversely, if volatility moves down by 1% we will make an expected profit of $767.01.

What will happen to the future and options portfolio as time passes? The theta will project the amount of time decay that will occur. Since, we are overall theta negative (remember RAP presents this as a positive number), from today until tomorrow, we expect to lose $90.5464.

Graphing The Risks Of The Option Portfolio

All these numbers are extremely helpful in assessing the risk of a portfolio of derivative products. However, to really get a grasp on the situation, nothing beats a graph. Let us examine a graph of all the risks at once. With the RAP, we can take a 5 dimensional risk management problem (delta, gamma, vega, theta and intra month spreads) and reduce it to a simple 2 dimensional graph. Essentially, what the programme does is to re-evaluate our entire portfolio of derivative products, including different maturities, as though the portfolio was composed of only transactions in the futures contract month closest to expiration, which is August. This is done by simply discounting the deltas of the October and December options by the appropriate interest rate between August and October or December respectively.

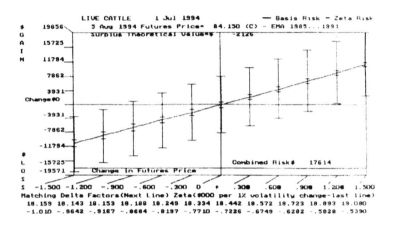

Table 14.9 Risk Analysis Graph.

This process was discussed extensively in Chapter 12 when I discussed how to compare long term Interest Rate Cap option deltas to the deltas of nearby Eurodollar options. The reader is referred to Table 12.7 for the formula which achieves this comparability among deltas of different maturities. With this accomplished, the entire portfolio can be compared to a single underlying standard: that of the nearest term futures contract. This can be seen in Table 14.9.

The total risk analysis graph is a plot that indicates the exposure relative to the nearest futures contract of the entire portfolio. Furthermore, it measures what our position expects to make overnight if the market stays at present levels or if the nearest futures contract either rises or falls (up to our maximum amount of $1.50). What the reader sees is a graph that may look not dissimilar to a rectangular gun scope. Usually, when one aims a rifle with a telescopic sight, the sight is a round image with a cross hair. Where the "cross hair" meets is where the shootist aims the rifle. In this Table, the cross hair can clearly be seen. At the point of intersection, this indicates the current level of the August Live Cattle futures (of which all the exposures of the options in the "book" are now expressed in). If one looks at the vertical cross hair and runs one's finger to the top, they will see the number "64.150". To the left of this number, the text indicates that we are indeed comparing the sensitivities of the option's portfolio to this futures contract ("5 Aug 1994 Futures Price="). Above this phrase, the date of "1 Jul 1994" appears. This indicates that the analysis completed today (30 June 1994) will examine the overnight exposures of the entire option's portfolio. Thus, the profit and loss of the portfolio will be estimated not for today but for tomorrow (which is the 1 July).

If one now runs one's finger down the vertical "hairline" until one reaches the bottom of the graph, they will see a line which is angled to the left. Under this line "0" appears. This simply implies that the vertical line is associated with the value of the portfolio for no change in the price of the August Live Cattle futures (of 64.150) from 30 June to 1 July. To the left and right of the "0" just mentioned, the reader will see other numbers from -1.500 to (positive) 1.500 in increments of 0.300. This indicates possible changes that could occur in the price of the August Live Cattle futures from 30 June to 1 July. For example, the number -1.500 would mean that the August Live Cattle futures price would have fallen by this amount from today until tomorrow. The actual price would be 62.65. Likewise, all the other numbers in this row would be associated with similar changes in the overnight price of the August Live Cattle futures. Let us now return to the point where the hairs cross in the middle of the graph.

One should now run his finger along the horizontal "hairline" to the left until one reaches the left boundary of the graph. At that point, one's finger will meet a vertical line. To the left of this point, the reader will see the phrase "Change $0". This means that the horizontal "hairline" represents the division between either profits or losses for the portfolio. Above this "hairline" profits will be earned and below it losses will be theoretically assumed. This can be seen with actual numbers along the furthest left vertical boundary of the graph. Clearly the terms "$GAIN" and "$LOSS" require no further explanation. Thus, when we consider what this graph is telling us, it indicates the profits or losses that will accrue to the entire portfolio of options (vertical axis) for a change in the price of the August Live Cattle futures (horizontal axis) from today until tomorrow.

The pattern contained within the graph which is plotted against these axes, represents the overnight potential profits or losses of the entire options portfolio. This figure may not be, at first sight, very clear. There is a straight line which goes from the lower left portion of the graph to the upper right and a series of "I"s which bracket this line. To explain what this overnight profit and loss figure is telling us, I will discuss each of these elements in turn. First, I will explain what the straight line means.

This line represents the change in the value of the entire option's portfolio that would be associated solely with the change of the August futures prices which are at the bottom of the graph. If one concentrates only on this line, one can see that this portfolio has a profit and loss profile that looks remarkably like buying a futures contract. In fact, if you return to Chapter 1 and review Figure 1.2, you will be hard pressed to see any difference. If the price of the August futures remains at the same level tomorrow, the projected change in the value of the options portfolio will be approximately zero. From Table 14.8, we know that this is not really the case given the theta is negative for this portfolio (a projected loss of $90.5464 from today until tomorrow). However, this impact has been considered by the RAP and if the plot could be magnified sufficiently, this small loss from the time decay could be seen. However, given the extreme changes in the value of the options portfolio that could occur overnight from other factors, the scaling of the graph makes it difficult to see the theta effect. For instance, if the market starts rallying, this position will make substantial profits. In fact, if the August Live Cattle futures price goes

1.50 higher, which would then be 65.65, they would make around $11,000. This is seen at that point in the graph where the solid line meets the right boundary of the graph. If the reader runs his or her finger to the left of the graph (where the "$GAIN" phrase appears), he or she will see that this point is associated with a profit around $11,000. Unfortunately, if Live Cattle futures price falls by 1.50, then worth 62.65, the portfolio would lose almost $11,000 and the career of our market maker would probably be over forthwith.

Remembering that the delta is the slope of an option or a portfolio of options, relative to the underlying market, the angle of the curve is therefore equal to the delta at that point. To aid analysis, the reader will find the deltas for this portfolio in the line of numbers at the bottom of the plot immediately below the line which reads "Matching Delta Factors(Next Line)". At the current price for August Live Cattle futures, in the middle of the line, the delta is 18.334. This means that if the current price of 64.150 prevails tomorrow, the overall risk of the portfolio will be slightly greater than eighteen August Live Cattle futures. The reader will note that this number is slightly divergent from the delta figure for all months which appeared in Table 14.8 (18.4541). This is because to be able to compare deltas for different maturity periods to the same underlying asset, the deltas for the October and December futures had to be discounted back to August deltas. The process for this was discussed above and as would be expected the overall delta for the portfolio (expressed in terms of August Live Cattle futures deltas) is slightly less than the simple sum of the individual deltas for all the months in Table 14.8. However, this difference is not really worth worrying about. The delta of 18.334 indicates that the position will experience the same profits and losses as would be associated with buying eighteen August Live Cattle futures contracts (at the current price of 64.150). Unfortunately, a problem with deltas is that they can change (see the gamma section Chapter 3 for more detail). So if one looks at the furthest left and the furthest right delta factors in this line, one sees the delta will then be equal to 18.159 deltas if the market falls by 1.50 and be equal to 19.08 deltas if the markets rises by 1.50 by tomorrow. The fact that the delta changes in a positive manner (becoming smaller when the market falls and larger when the market rises) means that we are gamma positive. If the reader refers back to Table 14.8, he will see that we are indeed gamma positive and this graph provides the pictorial evidence for that fact. While I stated earlier that gamma is relatively stable for changes in the price of the underlying asset, this is not true for extreme movements in the price of the underlying asset. One possible solution to this problem would be to evaluate another "Greek" for a change in the gamma for a change in the price of the underlying asset. Fortunately, the existence of programmes such as RAP render this exercise unnecessary. The delta and gamma values are re-estimated at each of the price levels indicated at the bottom of the graph and can be seen directly in the plotted profit and loss line. Furthermore, for reasons of simplicity, these types of plots are the only way to determine accurately what the impact of changing gamma will be.

Throughout this book, I have repeatedly stressed how important volatility is to the pricing of options. It is also consistent to stress that measuring the volatility exposure is equally important in the risk management of these securities. To reflect this factor, any risk evaluation of a portfolio of options must also display the volatility risk of the portfolio. This is done by the RAP but in a very subtle way. If the reader looks closely at the profit and loss line for the portfolio, he will notice little "I"s that appear which bracket it. This result is especially marked on the left side of the diagram. What these little "I"s indicate is the positive and negative range within which the portfolio value could lie given a change in the implied volatility by 1% up or down. If the volatility remained at the current levels, then the change in the portfolio's value would simply be a function of the movement in the underlying market price (including the time decay) and would therefore lie on the line. If, however, the volatility happens to move in your favour, then that result be beneficial to the position or at least have an ameliorating impact on the effects of a falling futures price. Again, as with the deltas, the volatility sensitivity numbers are listed in the line below the delta exposures at the very bottom of the plot. These zeta (vega) numbers indicate the thousands of dollars one would gain or lose from a 1% move in the level of volatility at each price level for the underlying August futures price tomorrow. Notice that the volatility impact is also not constant but changes as the underlying market price moves. At the current futures price of 64.15, the zeta (vega) exposure is -0.7710. This means that if volatility falls by 1% by tomorrow, the theoretical value of the portfolio should fall by $771. Given that we are short the zeta (vega), that would mean we would realise a profit if we unwound all the transactions in the portfolio at the prices the RAP assumes would then exist. However, if the market drops by 1.50 cents, the zeta (vega) would rise to -1.010. This indicates that at that price of the August Live Cattle futures, you would lose $1,010 for every 1% increase in the implied volatility. Again, the minus sign indicates that the position is short. When you consider what would probably happen to volatility if the market did fall 1.50 cents overnight, you would be safe to bet that such a market move would most probably be associated with a dramatic increase in the implied volatility of the options market.

Finally, do we not have positions in different months as well? By making everything equivalent to August Live Cattle futures, is not the RAP programme making an assumption that the October and December Live Cattle futures and options will move in a lockstep manner with August futures. The answer to both of these questions is yes. So to examine this risk, another "I" is added and it is the larger "I" that brackets both the "delta" plot and the bracketing volatility "I". This risk measure indicates that if the spread between August, October and December Live Cattle futures changes by the maximum amount we have specified (1.05 cents per pound) what would be the incremental effect on the profit or loss of the portfolio. If the change in the spreads helps us, this will be treated as an additional profit. This would occur if the August Live Cattle futures fell, the October futures price rose and the December futures also fell. How can this be seen? In Table 4.8, the deltas for each contract month appears. For the August futures, the delta of -15.040 is equivalent to selling fifteen August futures and thus, we would wish this contract price would fall. Likewise, the +35.6911 delta aggregate position for October futures indicates we would want the price of the October futures to rise.

The lower portion of the "I" indicates an adverse move in the spread. So, in review, the little "I" is the ±1% volatility range and the bigger "I" indicates the incremental impact from the spreads also changing in the most extreme manner and in addition to the maximum implied volatility change. Therefore, when one looks at the lower left hand corner of the plot in Table 14.9, this is the worst case scenario. The loss of $19,571 (-19571) occurs when "Murphy's Law" applies; the market has fallen by the maximum amount, volatility has risen by 1% and the spread between August, October and December Live Cattle futures has also moved in the worst possible way against the strategy.

We now have our delta positions at various market levels and our exposure to volatility. We can also see clearly when we make and lose money and if everything goes wrong, what our maximum loss potential would be. The number in the lower right quadrant of the plot is titled the Combined Risk. This number for the portfolio is $17,614. This designation was devised by the Chicago Mercantile Exchange to determine the margin they would require for the trader to maintain these positions with the Clearing House. The Combined Risk is basically a 95% confidence interval on everything going wrong. While the Combined Risk figure does not tell you the absolute worst case scenario, it is useful because at a 95% level these number provides us with a workable general risk measure. The final number in the graph that has not yet been explained is the "Surplus Theoretical Value". This number indicates the theoretical edge the portfolio has over the theoretical prices for the futures and the options trades we have established. In this example, the portfolio has a loss of $2,126 (-2126) relative to the theoretical prices of the securities in that portfolio. This can be seen at the top of the graph immediately below the upper boundary.

APPLICATIONS OF COMPUTER RISK ANALYSIS PROGRAMS TO THE MANAGEMENT OF OPTION PORTFOLIOS BY MARKET MAKERS

Daily Risk Management Issues

The reader may be interested in how this applies to the real day to day management of an options "book". When I set up two dealing operations, I had to determine from the management control standpoint how the traders were going to be monitored and controlled. The manager must have an accurate risk management system that will help him determine the risk limits for his traders. Ideally, he should get a simple graph or table that measures the maximum amount a trader could lose overnight and what the maximum exposure or delta position would be. The manager could then determine how far the market could move overnight, how much volatility could change and how the spread between futures months could affect the strategy. With these initial parameters set, back office staff would then update the system daily with current market data from the day's transactions. Reports then would be generated for both the individual trader's accounts and in consolidation. In our department, both traders and their managers received a copy of these reports. Traders then would be restricted to trading within prescribed limits for loss potential and deltas (sometimes gammas and vegas too). When I traded, my limits were 5 deltas (futures) long or short overnight and a maximum loss potential of no more than $15,000. Within these constraints, I could construct any combination of trades that I saw fit.

Risk Control of Option Books

Let us pretend, that this sample Live Cattle options "book" was my personal portfolio and that I had the same limits as when I traded in Chicago. The steps I would take to hedge the position would be to consider first what possible trades would bring me back within limits and reduce my risks. Since the position is extremely "long" and exposed to the spreads between months, I would have to acquire a negative delta position to offset the delta risk and would also have to cover the intramarket risks. Well, what are the possible equivalent short positions? These equivalent short positions include short futures, buying puts or writing calls. The choice of which strategy to use would depend upon my viewpoint on volatility (this was discussed extensively in Chapter 7).

Suppose that my viewpoint on volatility was neutral. If the reader returns to the strategy matrix, at the end of Chapter 7, he will find two potential strategies which are both short on the underlying market (negative delta) and neutral to volatility (vega zero), short the underlying futures and a bear spread. Upon flipping a coin, I decided to use the futures market. From Table 14.8, the delta exposures for each month can be found. To eliminate both the delta and intramarket spread risks, I would deal in futures contracts. The number which I would buy or sell would be the same as the delta equivalent exposures in Table 14.8. Of course, to hedge the risk I would have established opposite positions. This required me to buy fifteen (15) August Live Cattle futures, sell thirty five (35) October Live Cattle futures and buy two (2) December Live Cattle futures contracts. The reason why I simply did not sell eighteen August (or October) Live Cattle Futures is because I also wanted to reduce my spread risk. By reducing the delta risk in each maturity to as close to zero as is possible, my overall delta is still zero and the risk within each maturity is zero as well. By doing this, my net futures contracts sold still equals eighteen short futures but the risk between months has also been minimised. In addition, I purchased one August 63.0 put option just to tidy things up. Table 14.10 displays the risk of this new portfolio.

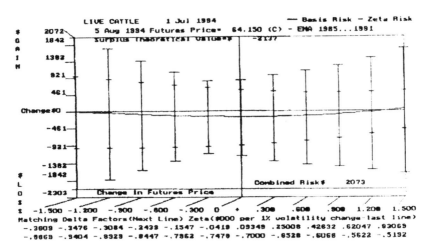

LIVE CATTLE   1 Jul 1994   — Basis Risk — Zeta Risk
5 Aug 1994 Futures Price= 64.150 (C) - EMA 1985...1991

Table 14.10 Risk Analysis Graph of the New Portfolio.

The first thing the reader should notice is that the plot has flattened considerably. Only when the market moves up or down by more than 0.30 cents or so does the position deviate from my criteria for delta neutrality (±0.10 deltas). What about the loss potential and the delta limits?

The reader can run his finger across the delta line at the bottom of the plot and see that at no point does the position exceed a delta of 0.83069, so this is now within the limits. What about the loss potential? The Combined Risk factor is now only $2,073. Therefore, this position is now within limits. Still the position has considerable risk. If this were my own portfolio, I would try a wider range of hedging strategies until the loss potential is minimised especially regarding the inter-month spread and implied volatility risks.

Regardless of the computer systems one chooses, it is critical to realise the computational complexity in dealing options. In this chapter, I have demonstrated one system which provides "gauges" critical to option risk management. Without some system to price and manage the risks of options, I highly recommend the reader to abstain from active option dealing.

Using Computer Risk Analysis Programs To Choose The Best Strategy

For option traders, possessing such a system has additional benefits. When a system shows him or her both the theoretical edge the strategy has (relative to market prices) and the potential overnight risks, it can be an invaluable tool when choosing which is the best strategy among a pool of those available. In Chapters 7 and 8, we discussed both volatility trading and option arbitrage. When the trader is comparing volatility trading strategies, calendar spreads or arbitraging implied volatility versus actual volatility, he or she must be able to assess what the potential profit of the strategy is. The RAP supplies this in the calculation of the surplus theoretical value. The estimation of the edge will simply depend on the trader entering his or her volatility forecast which would be different from the implied volatility in the markets. With surplus theoretical edge estimated, it can then be compared to the combined risk of the portfolio number RAP estimates to allow the trader to assess the risk/reward trade-off of the strategy. With this estimation of the risk/return trade-off of all the possible strategies, the trader can then easily select the best volatility strategy given his viewpoint of future volatility.

Suppose a trader believes that the actual volatility of the Live Cattle futures will be 15% and as one can see from Table 14.7, the implied volatilities for all the options are significantly above this level. The trader would wish to profit from his volatility forecast by selling options and establishing vega negative positions. To identify which strategies may be appropriate, he could refer to Table 8.4 from Chapter 8 where all the "Greek" exposures of the trading strategies can be found. Assuming the trader had no viewpoint on the movement of the underlying Live Cattle market and was only establishing volatility trades, then he would select delta neutral positions (delta of zero). In that Table, the strategies which are vega negative and delta neutral include:

- Short Straddle
- Short Strangle
- Long Butterfly
- Long Condor
- Short Calendar Spread

The trader could simply input his volatility estimate of 15% in the program with the actual market prices for the options already entered. This was done and can be seen in Table 14.11.

A quick look at the comparison of the market prices and the theoretical prices for the options in this Table indicates which options were most overvalued relative to the theoretical value.

For example, the August 64.0 call had a market price of 1.800 but only a theoretical price of 0.995 (at the 15% implied volatility). Thus, if the trader sold the August 64.0 call for 1.800, we would have a theoretical edge of 0.805. In monetary terms, the value of the August 64.0 call was $720 (1.800 cents for 40,000 pounds) but the trader estimated it was only worth $398 (0.995 cents for 40,000 pounds). Thus, for each August 64.0 call option he sold, he would have a theoretical edge of 322 US Dollars ($720 - $398).

Once the mispriced options had been identified, the trader would go to the position spread sheet and enter a "dummy" position which was associated with all the potential vega negative strategies. For all of these strategies, the trader would enter only "one lot" position sizes (that is dealing in one contract) and then evaluate the risk graph to assess the theoretical edge of the strategy and its overnight risk.

STRIKES	CALL	PUT	CALL	PUT	CALL	PUT
Variable Sigma & Interest Rate LIVE CATTLE						**1 Jul 1994**
					FUTURES PRICES	
	64.150		**68.250**		**69.220**	
	5 Aug 1994		**7 Oct 1994**		**2 Dec 1994**	
62.0 Mkt	2.950	0.800	0.550		0.600	
Theory	2.354	0.208	6.407	0.196	7.517	0.377
Delta	.831511	-.16680	.912607	-.08453	.881549	-.11249
Gamma	.002714	.002705	.000835	.000786	.000779	.000721
63.0 Mkt	2.350	1.200				
Theory	1.597	0.449	5.527	0.313	6.674	0.527
Delta	.697420	-.30063	.870975	-.12437	.844004	-.14776
Gamma	.003769	.003765	.001076	.001041	.000916	.000871
64.0 Mkt	1.800	1.650	5.125	0.925	0.925	
Theory	0.995	0.845	4.699	0.479	5.876	0.720
Delta	.532019	-.46594	.819234	-.17484	.801016	-.18902
Gamma	.004298	.004298	.001332	.001307	.001055	.001020
65.0 Mkt	1.325	2.175				
Theory	0.562	1.410	3.930	0.705	5.127	0.960
Delta	.363211	-.63480	.757579	-.23562	.752853	-.23589
Gamma	.004059	.004062	.001577	.001560	.001187	.001161
66.0 Mkt	0.950	2.800	3.750	1.525	1.350	
Theory	0.286	2.132	3.231	0.999	4.432	1.253
Delta	.219532	-.77866	.687285	-.30534	.700143	-.28766
Gamma	.003200	.003207	.001787	.001776	.001303	.001285
67.0 Mkt	0.675	3.500	3.150	1.925		
Theory	0.130	2.975	2.609	1.368	3.794	1.603
Delta	.116746	-.88185	.610602	-.38168	.643826	-.34334
Gamma	.002123	.002137	.001937	.001931	.001397	.001385
68.0 Mkt	0.463	4.313	2.700	2.450	3.525	2.300
Theory	0.053	3.896	2.066	1.818	3.215	2.011
Delta	.054474	-.94486	.530487	-.46166	.585076	-.40170
Gamma	.001195	.001221	.002011	.002010	.001462	.001455

Table 14.11 Option Market Prices and Theoretical Prices at an Implied Volatility of 15%.

The first potential vega negative strategy that could be implemented is the short straddle. For this, the trader would enter in his spreadsheet -1 in the QTY cell above the prices for both the August 64.0 call and put. Then, the risk graph was evaluated. This can be seen in Table 14.12a. In the graph, the reader can clearly see the "frowning" shape of the gamma negative short straddle. The strategy has a surplus theoretical value of $644 and an overnight combined risk of $169. These are the numbers we are interested in and will form the basis for the comparison of all the potential strategies.

The second potential vega negative strategy that would profit from the implied volatility falling to 15% would be the short strangle. For this, the trader returns to the spreadsheet (removing the previous straddle position) and would enter in his spreadsheet -1 in the QTY cell above the prices for both the August 65.0 call and

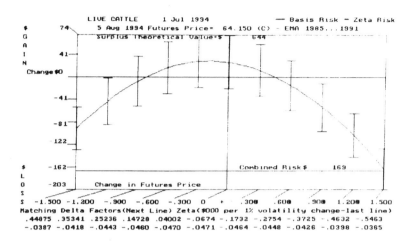

Table 14.12a Risk Analysis Graph of a Short Straddle.

the 63.0 put. The risk graph for the short strangle appears in Table 14.12b. Again, the short strangle is a vega negative and gamma negative position. The short strangle has a surplus theoretical value of $605 and an overnight combined risk of $156.

Next, the trader would return to the spreadsheet and replace the positions in the short strangle with the trades for the long butterfly. In this example, an iron butterfly was input which meant both the August 64.0 call and put were sold while the August 63.0 put and August 65.0 call were purchased. When the risk graph was drawn, the trader found that the long butterfly only had a surplus theoretical value of $38 but a very low combined overnight risk of $13. This can be seen in Table 14.12c.

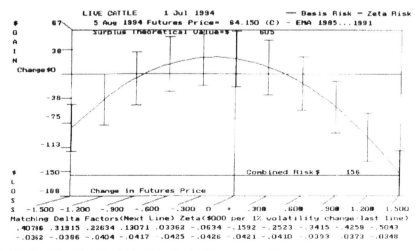

Table 14.12b Risk Analysis Graph of a Short Strangle.

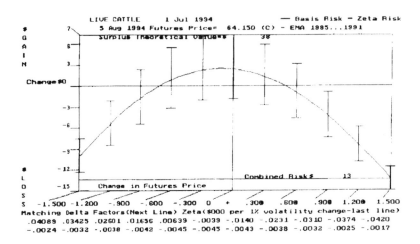

Table 14.12c *Risk Analysis Graph of a Long Butterfly.*

Following on this analysis, the trader then substituted a long August condor for the previously input long butterfly in the spreadsheet. When this risk graph was evaluated, the trader found that the condor seemed to do better than the butterfly. The surplus theoretical value as $103 with a risk of $34. This can be seen in Table 14.12d.

For all of these strategies, the shape of the risk graph is more or less the same. All of these trades are flat at the current level and curving downwards both when the market price rises or falls. In addition, from today until tomorrow at the intersection of the cross hairs in the risk graph, the strategies all produce profits at the current market price. This is due to the time decay gains all the strategies receive

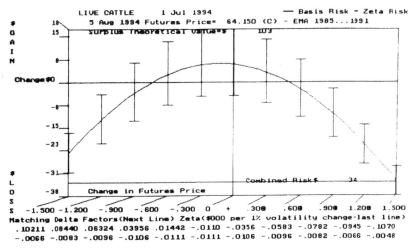

Table 14.12d *Risk Analysis Graph of a Long Condor.*

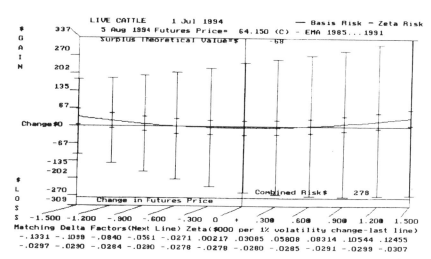

Table 14.12e Risk Analysis Graph of a Short Calendar Spread.

from the passage of time. All are exposed to changes in the implied volatility but the strategy with the highest vega value is the short straddle.

Finally, when we compare the short calendar spread to these previous strategies, the result is completely different. Suppose, the trader returns to his RAP spreadsheet and clears out the long condor. In its place, he "buys" a 64.0 August call by putting a +1 in the QTY cell above its price and "sells" a 68.0 October call by putting a -1 in the appropriate cell. As an aside, the strike prices are different because the levels of the underlying futures are also different. The August Live Cattle futures price is 64.150 and the October Live Cattle futures price is 68.250. The objective of the short calendar spread is to be delta neutral and vega negative. To achieve this, the trader must buy and sell at-the-money options. Thus, the call options bought and sold are for different strike prices but are relative to their underlying asset both at-the-money. When this has been done, the risk graph is evaluated. The result (in Table 14.12e) is somewhat surprising.

The shape is entirely different than the other vega negative strategies. As one would expect, the short calendar spread is gamma positive and thus has a slightly smiling shape. But much worse: the surplus theoretical value of the position is -$68. This means the position is actually losing the theoretical edge. This occurs because to be vega short with a calendar spread, one must buy the nearer term option and sell the longer term option. When the trader buys the August 64.0 call, he is paying a 27.54% volatility for it. Given the trader expects the volatility to drop to 15%, clearly this is a losing proposition. On the other leg of the strategy, he is selling the October 68.0 call at a 19.80% volatility of which he expects to make 4.80 volatility percentage points. These numbers can be found in Table 14.7. Therefore, it is not difficult to see why this position is a "loser" overall. To compound matters, the short calendar spread could also lose $278 overnight principally from a change in the spread relationship between August and October futures. Clearly, the trader would rule out the short calendar spread as a candidate for the best strategy to benefit from a drop in the implied volatility to 15%. That leaves the first four strategies. But which one is best?

When comparing the surplus theoretical values and combined overnight risks of the four possible strategies, it makes sense to combine all the results in one table to ease comparison. This has been done in Table 4.13.

Strategy	Short Straddle	Short Strangle	Long Butterfly	Long Condor
Surplus Theoretical Value	$644	$605	$38	$103
Combined Overnight	$169	$156	$13	$34
Risk Ratio of Surplus/Risk	3.810	3.878	2.923	3.029

Table 14.13   Comparison of Theoretical Values, Risks and Ratios of Theoretical Value/Risk for the Possible Vega Negative Strategies.

If the trader was simply attempting to maximise his theoretical edge, then it is clear that he would sell the August 64.0 straddle. However, while the other strategies have less of an edge (especially the long butterfly and condor), could not the trader just increase the size of his holdings in these other strategies to achieve a similar level of theoretical edge as the straddle? That is instead of doing one long condor with a surplus theoretical edge of $103, he would initiate six long condor spreads and achieve an edge of $618. The answer is yes. Then, he could compare the theoretical edges of the spreads directly. The same comparison can be achieved by simply dividing the surplus theoretical edge by the overnight risk. This has been done for you in Table 14.13. This implies that the number of times the surplus theoretical value will cover the overnight risk will not depend on the number of times the strategy is multiplied. When this is done, it is clear that the short strangle is the best strategy to choose to maximise the return for the risk assumed. However, one caveat must be made. Since, the choice of the trading strategy only depends upon our viewpoint on the implied volatility (vega), it must be considered that all of these positions are also gamma negative. If the trader also holds to the viewpoint that the actual volatility in the market will be low during the period until the expiration of the option, he would again choose the short strangle as the best strategy given his viewpoint. If on the other hand, he is concerned about being short gamma going into expiration, then he would choose between the long butterfly and long condor. If this were done, the analysis in Table 14.13 will once again help him choose. The long condor has a higher ratio of the surplus theoretical value to the combined overnight risk and would therefore be the better of the two strategies.

530

In this chapter, I have shown how the theoretical concepts presented throughout this book are practically applied by market makers. Clearly the introduction of computerisation has had as big an impact on the success of option markets as any other factor. It could very well be that the increased use of powerful and low cost computers is directly related to the extent options markets have grown world-wide.

15: Structure Of Exchange Traded Options Markets

In this chapter, I will examine how exchange traded options markets function. Initially, I will explain the role of the Clearing House and the mechanics of margining at a typical futures and options exchange. Then, I will examine in detail the structure of four option markets that have different structures: the Philadelphia Stock Exchange, the European Options Exchange, the Option Market (Stockholm) and the Chicago Mercantile Exchange. At that point, I will finish the chapter with a discussion of a new kind of margining system that is based upon the risk analysis techniques in Chapter 14.

THE CLEARING HOUSE AND ITS ROLE

A Clearing House can be defined as an organisation that guarantees performance and settlement of all exchange traded contracts. In the case of a typical exchange, this task is undertaken by a Clearing House which is owned by the exchange (as is the case with the Chicago Mercantile Exchange) or is an independent body (like the London Clearing House which clears all the trades on the London futures and options markets and is a division of the International Commodity Clearing House).

The Clearing House plays a crucial role in the operations of every exchange. Once a contract is entered at the futures or options exchange and the confirmation has followed, the Clearing House steps in - so to speak - and assumes the opposite side to each transaction. It, therefore, becomes the ultimate buyer for every seller and the ultimate seller for every buyer. Let us assume you place an order with your broker to buy a 350 call option on Gold futures. Your broker passes the order on to his trader on the floor of the exchange (COMEX in this example) and the order is entered into the trading pit. Suppose the order is executed. That means another trader has agreed to sell this 350 Gold call option to your agent (which is the floor broker acting on your behalf). What risks (apart from the price risk of the option) would you potentially have to face? You could potentially face a credit risk and/or default risk if the trader on the opposite side experiences either financial difficulties (credit risk) or fails to fulfil his side of the deal upon your exercise of the option (default risk). Therefore, if you are depending on your counterparty (the individual on the other side of your deal) to perform, you will have to monitor his financial health to make sure that the contract will be honoured upon exercise. To reduce these risks (and the costs you would have to incur to keep an eye on the counterparty), all transactions after they are consummated are reported immediately to the futures or options exchange and then passed on to the Clearing House. Then, the Clearing House provides a note of confirmation to you and your counterparty. In the confirmation note, the Clearing House indicates that the opposite side of the transactions (for both sides) has been taken over by it. In this example, the Clearing House would inform you that it is the seller of the 350 call option. Any future obligations or rights you have received from the transaction are now held against the Clearing House. The same applies to your counterparty, the seller of the call option, who is now obligated to perform to the Clearing House. The overall market risk of this transaction to the Clearing House is flat because it is buying the 350 call on Gold from the option seller and selling the 350 call option on Gold to you. The risks that the Clearing House assumes are those concerning credit worthiness and potential default.

The net effect of this arrangement is that the Clearing House becomes the seller of all contracts bought and at the same time it becomes the buyer of all contracts sold. Its role is to stand in the middle of all transactions and guarantee the fulfilment of each and every contract. How does the Clearing House protect itself against the risks outlined above? This is done through the mechanism of margining which I will discuss now.

THE MECHANISMS OF MARGINING

To understand the concept of margining, I will once again return to the world of gambling. In the card game of poker, before the participants can play, a deposit has to be placed in the centre of the table by each and every player. This deposit is known as ante and that is the "stake" that each player must put into the "pot" before receiving cards. As the hand proceeds, more money is put into the "pot" reflecting each player's viewpoint of the final result. When the hands are laid down one of the players wins and can take all the money that was in the "pot". To begin the next round, each player must once again put the required ante into the pot to continue playing. If he fails to do so, he is not allowed to play that hand. The winner in the previous hand has the choice to either take all of his money from the table and then replace the ante for the next round or he can leave the ante for the next hand in the "pot" and take out the net proceeds he has won.

The concept of margining at a futures or options exchange works in a similar way. Each participant must "ante" up a deposit with the Clearing House (which is acting like the "pot"). Each day, as the futures or options contracts settle, the hands of all the participants are laid on the table, so to speak. The winners are those who have profited during the trading day from the change in their contract value and the losers are those who have experienced an adverse move in the market. The amount of gains or losses are then taken from the "pot" and the winners receive the profits and the losers have the amount of the equivalent loss debited from their margin account by the Clearing House. To continue trading the next day, both the winners and the losers have to make sure the minimum "ante" remains in the "pot" (the Clearing House) and generally this implies that the losers have to put more money in.

This is repeated every trading day and every day it is possible that the Clearing House may have to shift funds from the accounts of the losers to the winners. Since each participant in the market must deposit this "ante" with the Clearing House, the credit or default risk to it is that on any particular day one of the participants will not be able to pay the loss that occurred during that trading day. To minimise the credit risk, the Clearing House requires all market participants to deposit a margin in cash (or post a suitable security such as a stock portfolio) to cover any losses that could potentially occur. The worst possible loss that could occur during a single trading day is determined by the exchange where the futures or options contracts trade and this amount is called the initial margin (in our poker example this is comparable to the ante). If during the next trading day, a participant is unable to maintain the balance in the "pot" of some minimum amount (known as the maintenance margin), his position will be offset by the Clearing House on the floor of the exchange at the best price available and any remaining funds in the account will be returned to that participant. If the loss exceeds the initial margin, then the participant must pay the difference. If he is unable to do so, then his broker is next in line to pay the loss and if the broker is also unable to do so. then the General Clearing member (that the broker clears through) is liable. If the General Clearing member has defaulted as well, then the rest of the General Clearing members will get together and make up for the loss. Finally, if all the General Clearing members have gone down as well, the Clearing House will reach into its pocket and cover the loss (by drawing from its capital). This system works remarkably well and the futures industry points with pride to the fact that no individual trader has ever failed to receive his profits in a futures or options contract because of a default.[1]

To discuss the mechanics of margining at a typical futures or options exchange, I will take the reader though a simple example of buying a Bund futures contract at the London International Financial Futures Exchange (LIFFE). Let us imagine that the Bund futures market is currently trading at 87.14 and we want to be exposed to the German government Bond market via the Bund futures. At the same time, someone else has an opposite viewpoint and therefore wishes to sell the Bund futures. A contract is agreed upon at 87.14 and consummated. Then both sides of the transaction are assumed by the Clearing House. Thus, we are now long one Bund futures contract with the Clearing House and the seller is short one Bund futures contract with the Clearing House. In order to ensure the performance of both trades and to protect itself against default risk, the Clearing House requires a cash guaran-

---

[1]There was a problem on the London Tin Futures Market once when a consortium of traders cornered the Tin market and then were unable to deliver the tin. However, after closing the exchange for a period, the contracts were eventually settled and the exchange resumed trading.

tee, which is the initial margin (of 6,250 D-marks). This cash can be thought of not as a "down payment" which is the case with stock market margin but rather as a "Guarantee Bond" to assure the integrity of the positions from one day until the next.

The rationale for margin is the consideration that the Bund futures price could change from one day until the next and if it does change the Clearing House will be at risk from the losing party. Suppose that tomorrow Bund futures price increased to 87.25, in this case, we are the winners and the Clearing House will transfer DM 275 to our margin account (87.25 - 87.14 x DM25 per point). The DM275 will come directly from the Clearing House, but will be ultimately debited from the account of someone who was short the Bund futures. Since the total number of buyers and sellers must be equal, it is irrelevant which individual account is debited because the clearing house will draw the losses from all short positions in aggregate. The proceeds will be exactly equal to what is required to pay the aggregate long positions. Somehow and from someone, the money will be drawn to provide the DM275. Then, the Clearing House will look at all the accounts of those holding positions with it and determine if they still have enough funds for the next "hand". If not, they will require more money (in cash) to be deposited to cover the variation. This payment is referred to as variation margin. This process of daily revaluation of all positions is known as marking-to-market. Marking-to-market is similar to our poker game in that after each hand, each gambler knows how much he has. With futures and options markets, the Clearing House essentially divides up all daily profits among the winners and pays the profits from the losers. It is as if the contracts are broken each day (settled up) and re-established at the closing price of that day. Over time, the amount in the margin account will reflect the cumulative gains or losses that have occurred since the initiation of the trade.

Let us examine what would happen to the long Bund futures position if the Bund futures price continued to rise on subsequent days to 87.85. Each day, marking-to-market would occur and we would be credited an additional amount (of course, if the futures price fell in any one day, our account would be debited) until at the time the futures price settled at 87.85, we would have an additional DM 1,775 in our account above the DM 6,250 we must maintain every day to continue "playing". Conversely, those who had sold the Bund futures by that date would have had to pay in an additional DM 1,775 to remain in the game. The individual we initially traded with may have decided long before to stop "playing" and would do so by offsetting his short futures position by buying a Bund futures contract. So the reader may wonder who is now on the other side of our long futures position. The person that has assumed the short position is the individual that sold the futures to our previous counterparty that closed out his position. However, we never need to know that this has occurred because the Clearing House has stood between ourselves and the counterparty we first traded with and will automatically find a short position that will be opposite to our long position. As far as we are concerned, we do not care who is ultimately on the other side of our trade because the guarantee of the Clearing House makes all short (and long) positions fungible.

THE MARGINING OF OPTIONS AT A TYPICAL OPTIONS MARKET

The Philadelfia Stock Exchange establishes margin requirements for customer positions on all types of options and stocks traded on the Exchange. Once the appropriate margin requirement has been determined, the requirement can be satisfied by either deposit of cash or securities or a letter of credit from an approved issuer. For foreign currency options the margin requirements are as follows: For option buyers and covered writers: no margin is required. For Uncovered option writers: 100% of option premium plus 4% of contract spot value less any out-of-the-money amount, down to a minimum of premium plus 3/4% of contract spot value. For spreads: Where the long position expires before the short position, the spread is treated as two separate positions. Where the long position expires at or after the expiration of the short position, the margin required is the lesser of the margin required on the short position or the amount by which the exercise price of the long call (or short put) exceeds the exercise price of the short call (or long put). For short uncovered straddles or strangles: The combined margin on either the short call or short put (whichever is greater) and any intrinsic value. Both premiums received may be applied toward the total margin due. The initial margin required on a short uncovered position is 100% of option premium plus 4% of the contract spot value less any out-of-the-money amount down to a minimum of the premium received plus 3/4% of contract spot value. Uncovered short positions are marked to market daily with the daily contract spot value and the closing price of the short option. The new premium is then used to calculate the margin required, thereby creating a marked to market margin position. The margin must be met in cash or by fully-paid-for securities where the loan value equals or exceeds the margin requirement. When a transaction creates a margin deficiency, additional margin will be required. Alternatively, a letter of credit from an Exchange-approved bank or trust company may be used. When a member firm is a beneficiary under a letter of credit, certain financial information specific to the member firm must be made available to the exchange. Additional margin requirements must be settled promptly to reduce the margin deficit. The broker must collect this margin immediately, or no later than seven business days following the margin call.

STRUCTURE OF DIFFERENT OPTION MARKETS WORLD-WIDE

Broadly speaking, three forms of options markets presently exist: (1) the open outcry market, (2) the open outcry market with a specialist or market-maker and (3) the electronic or computer-based system. Pure open-outcry systems exist at a number of futures and options exchanges world-wide, examples of which include the Chicago Mercantile Exchange (CME) and the European Options Exchange (EOE) in Amsterdam. The Chicago Board Options Exchange (CBOE) and the Philadelphia Stock Exchange (PHLX) trade options with the open outcry/specialist system. This requires a market-maker to supply representative bids and offers to the market at all times. The Options Market in Stockholm (OM) also employs a market-maker system but most transactions are handled electronically and crossed on a computer without the necessity of an open outcry auction process. In this section, I will examine each of these systems to explain how they are structured, the composition of the exchange's membership, any international co-operation that may exist, how the process of trading occurs, the mechanisms of clearing and finally, how risk is addressed from the point of view of the ultimate guarantor.

The Philadelphia Stock Exchange

Background
The Philadelphia Stock Exchange (PHLX) was officially established in 1790 and trades a variety of cash and derivative instruments. Linkage through the International Trading System enables a broker or market maker on the PHLX floor to display his or her own customers' orders in other market centres. The PHLX also conducts a primary market for more than 100 stocks not listed on other exchanges.

Since 1975 the PHLX has traded stock options and the exchange now lists more than 75 such options. Currently, the PHLX is the only US stock exchange to trade in currency options and offer contracts in British pounds, German marks, Japanese yen, Swiss francs, Canadian dollars, French franc, Australian dollars, and the ECU. All these are against the US dollar. The PHLX also trades British Pound/Deutsche Mark and Deutsche Mark/Japanese Yen.

The PHLX also trades seven Sector Index Options: Bank Index, Big Cap, OTC Index, Gold/Silver Index, Phone Index, Utility Index, Value Line Composite Index.

The exchange operates two subsidiaries:
(1) Stock Clearing Corporation of Philadelphia, which handles money and stock transfer after trading.
(2) Philadelphia Depository Trust Company, which physically stores stock and bond certificates for members.

Membership
The PHLX is regulated in the United States by the Securities and Exchange Commission (SEC). There are two categories of stock exchange members: Those who work on the trading floor, and those who execute orders through other members on the floor. Members on the floor perform one of four functions:

(1) The Specialist: a specialist is registered and thus obligated to perform certain functions related to maintaining an orderly market. This may include trading for his own account. The specialist also maintains an order book acting in the capacity of agent.

(2) The Floor Broker: the floor broker acts as an agent for the customer. It is his responsibility to execute orders at the best price. This can be done through his employing firm or with other firms.

(3) The "Two Dollar" Broker: the term is a misnomer with today's negotiated commission rates. This member, for a fee, executes orders for other members, including floor brokers. Typically, he is used when the floor broker is very busy.

(4) The Market maker: like the specialist, is obligated to assist maintenance of an orderly market. He adds liquidity to the market by buying and selling for his own account.

Regular membership on the PHLX provides access to the equity floor. Access to the options floors are provided by a full-privilege seat. Seats are bought and sold in accordance with supply and demand. However, the exchange's admissions committee imposes basic membership requirements; individuals must exceed 21 years of age and must be affiliated either with a partnership or corporation registered as a broker/dealer with the Securities and Exchange Commission. A special feature of US stock markets is the existence of a member known as a specialist. This member is almost without exception a major brokerage institution or bank. This member is required "to make a market on the exchange at competitive prices to the best of his ability commensurate with his position and with prevailing market conditions".[2] These market makers assure that markets exist with real bid and offer prices. In the foreign currency options, large international brokers and banks act as market makers depending on which currencies they specialise in.

Clearing
The Central Clearing House, Stock Clearing Corporation of Philadelphia (SCCP), a wholly-owned exchange subsidiary was established in 1870. The SCCP settles each of its members accounts for the stocks they have traded and cash received or paid. An exchange member need not be a direct member of a clearing corporation but each must make the appropriate arrangements to have their trades settled. Many smaller dealers clear through existing clearing members. Exchange members who join only one clearing corporation specify that all trade settlements be directed to the member's clearing corporation. In reality the control of the massive trading activity is an extremely complex process. For activity which is settling, members are required to pay or collect the net settlement amount and in this respect the clearing corporation has assumed responsibility for orderly settlement of trading activity. The clearing services offered by other registered clearing agencies are generally comparable. However, the SCCP does offer margin accounts to members which permits them to purchase stock without paying the full amount of the cost. This financing enables members to gain a greater leverage by maintaining, in cash only, a percentage of the cost of the securities.

---

[2]Philadelphia Stock Exchange Rule Book, page 2145.

Margin Requirements
(SEE ABOVE)

Option Settlement
The Options Clearing Corporation (OCC) provides two methods by which OCC Clearing members and/or Clearing member clients can deliver currencies arising from foreign currency option exercises and assignments. These are:

(1) "Regular Way": the Clearing member must deliver the US dollar payment to OCC's agent bank two days prior to settlement day which is four days after tendering an exercise notice to OCC, and

(2) Delivery-vs.-Payment: the Clearing member instructs its agent bank (for currency options) to pay US dollars and in return receive foreign currency (for call-holder or put-writer) or pay foreign currency to receive US dollars (for call writer and put holder).

Summary
The PHLX trades a variety of option contracts including stock options/index options and foreign exchange options, the trading is conducted physically on the exchange floor. The specialist system assures orderly markets. The roles of the members are determined by their categories of membership; specialists and market makers are required to maintain orderly markets.

Orders are executed through floor brokers who act as agents for customers and are responsible for executing orders at the best price. Customers must ensure that margin accounts are kept with sufficient cash or collateral with margin requirements being calculated on the type of trade and value of the underlying contract. Settlement can be carried out through the exchange's own clearing corporation or that of another exchange.

The European Options Exchange

Background
The EOE opened in Amsterdam in 1978 trading American-style options (options that can be exercised at any point during the option's existence). The 12,602,453 contracts traded in 1993 make the EOE one of the largest option market inside Europe. The options and futures are cleared through the European Options Clearing Corporation (EOCC).

Membership
At the end of 1993 a total of 384 companies and individuals were registered as members of the EOE. The membership categories are as follows:

Public Order Member (POM): POMs are entitled to both accept orders from non-members and to trade for their own account, but all orders must be executed by a Floor Broker on the floor of the EOE.

Public Order Correspondent Member (POCM): POCMs may accept orders from investors for their own account but only for execution through a POM acting as intermediary.

Floor Broker (FB): FBs execute orders on the floor of the EOE for other members or for members of participating exchanges or for their own account.

Market Maker (MM): MMs trade for their own account and are obliged to make a market in one or more of the option classes to which they are assigned.

Off-Floor Trader (OFT): may have orders for his own account executed on the floor by a Floor Broker.

Clearing Member (CM): a CM is entitled to settle transactions effected on the floor of the EOE through the intermediary of a clearing organisation, recognised by the EOE, with which he is associated.

Members of the EOE must provide to each client (on request) a statement showing the client's open position in each option series in which the client has conducted a transaction.

A client may only exercise an option or effect a closing transaction through the EOE member bank or broker in whose books the open position appears. A client can, however, ask for his position to be transferred to another member of the EOE prepared to accept his account. The EOE is authorised to set limits on the maximum number of options that can be held or written by an investor acting by himself or in concert with others; the EOE can determine that excess positions are liquidated.

Clearing
The EOCC maintains two separate accounts for each Clearing Member: a Public Account, (an aggregate of contracts held for POMs in each clearing currency), and a Traders Account, (reflecting options held for the account of each Floor Broker, Market Maker and off-floor trader). Every Clearing Member may enter into clearing contracts with other members but at any one time a member is only permitted to have one clearing contract. Each business day the EOCC issues to each Clearing Member daily reports including: position reports, margin reports, deposit statements and settlement statements.

On the basis of these statements, the Clearing Member must make provisions on a daily basis to settle the statements.

Margin Requirements

As long as a Clearing Member is obligated to the EOCC as a writer under an options contract, the Clearing Member must maintain the requisite margin. At any time during any business day, the EOCC may recompute the margin and issue a Daily Margin Report to a Clearing Member. Within one hour of the issue of the Margin Report, the Clearing Member must provide the Maintenance Margin shown to be required. At any time, the EOCC may require a Clearing Member to provide a "variation margin" beyond the margin otherwise required if it is determined that such variation margin is necessary. Each POM is free to require additional margin requirements from his clients. Margins can be met by a cash deposit or securities with a POM. An increase in the requirement may make an additional deposit necessary.

Margin calculations are based on the actual price of the option plus a percentage of the actual price of the underlying value, the calculation also considers the exercise price of the option and volatility. The margin percentages are set out every month. The following minimum margin requirements apply:

1) Uncovered written calls: The price of the option plus a percentage of subtracting the exercise price from twice the price of the underlying value.

2) Written put options: The price of the option plus a percentage of the result of subtracting the price of the underlying value from twice the exercise price.

For combinations, an opening purchase of options increases a long position. An opening sale increases a short position and a closing transaction reduces a position. Other lower margin calculations apply to certain combinations, for example, to spreads. The margin requirement for call spreads is the long exercise price less the short exercise price and for put spreads the short exercise price less the long exercise price. The EOE has permitted uncovered options writing, on condition that security is provided, worth in principal not less than the current option premium, plus a percentage (of the difference between twice the price of the underlying value and the exercise price for calls and twice the exercise price and the price of the underlying value for puts). The percentage is set at regular intervals by the EOE. Further margin information is provided in a publication from the exchange "Minimum Margin Requirements".

Exercise Procedure

A client who wishes to exercise an option must notify his EOE member bank or broker. The latest time at which this can be done is specified in the rules of the option agreement. Under the rules of the EOE, the exchange is authorised to set limits on the number of options that may be exercised by a single holder within a specified period. Put and call classes are separate and are not added together. When options are exercised, an EOE member bank or broker who acts as an agent for option sellers is selected by random to deliver the underlying value (where a call is exercised) or buy it (where a put is exercised). The relevant EOE member bank or broker will use its own assignment method to determine which client is to be called on to meet his obligations.

Delivery of and Payment for Underlying Value
The underlying value must be delivered to a financial holding institution nominated by the EOCC. The EOCC reserves the right to determine that exercised options are settled in cash and not by delivery.

Clearing Fund
Every Clearing Member guarantees to the EOCC the performance of every other Clearing Member and in accordance with this, each Clearing Member pays an initial contribution. Both the initial maintenance and specific maintenance contributions are payable in cash or approved government securities. At the end of each month, the EOCC calculates the daily average open position of every Clearing Member. From this figure, the EOCC determines the monthly maintenance contribution. If a member defaults, the EOCC applies this maintenance contribution deposited by the defaulting Clearing Member. If this is insufficient to meet the deficit then the EOCC can apply every other Clearing Member's maintenance contribution to make up for the deficiency.

Summary
The EOE is a floor-based exchange for options and futures modelled after the Chicago Board Options Exchange. The EOE can restrict the maximum number of options that an investor can hold by himself or when acting in concert with other investors. The EOCC clears transactions on behalf of exchange members and produces four daily reports including a margin report. A Clearing Member is obligated to the EOCC to maintain the requisite margin and at any time during the day maintenance margin can be required. The exact margin requirements are based on the open contract, the "weightings" placed on such contracts and the average open position of the member over the previous month. In the event of the default of a Clearing Member, funds of that Clearing Member will be applied to the deficit. If this is insufficient, then any additional shortfall will be covered by funds placed with the EOCC by every other Clearing Member.

Stockholm Options Market (OM)

Background
Swedish trading in standardised options began on 12 June 1985. The options were standardised call options relating to six stocks traded on the Stockholm Stock Exchange. By the end of 1985 average daily turnover was about 5,000 contracts. The turnover continued to rise and by August 1990 amounted to about 34,000 stock options contracts related to thirteen underlying stocks. In March 1986, OM introduced standardised call and put options on the Swedish five-year Treasury

Note (interest rate options). The average volume at the end of 1990 amounted to 3,755 contracts daily. Since, December 1986, OM introduced index options, related to the OMX stock market index, turnover has risen sharply with the product accounting for more than 60% of total volume, an average of 35,000 contracts per day. From 3 August 1987 Swedish non-residents have been able to trade these OMX options. OM's sees itself "as a neutral marketplace and clearing house for trading in derivative instruments" (SOM Overview 1988, p.3). OM has a trading system based on an electronic marketplace. Within this system buyers and sellers meet electronically with deals being closed automatically. Additionally, OM provides a parallel system where buyers and sellers meet in telephone-based block order trading. Swedish banks, brokerage firms and independent market-makers are linked to the OM. Due to Swedish laws and regulations, all customer transactions must take place via Swedish banks or brokers. OM acts as a party to each option contract (i.e. OM acts as seller vis-à-vis the buyer and as buyer vis-à-vis the seller). OM effectively guarantees each option so that a holder of an option is assured of exercising his or her rights. Since the OM is the counterparty to each contract, the buyer and seller have no rights or obligations to anyone other than the OM. OM guarantees through its system of collateral and own capital resources that each option is fulfilled. To ensure this guarantee can be fulfilled, OM allocates pre-tax earnings to a special untaxed reserve to build up a clearing fund (guarantee risk reserve). This reserve now amounts to SEK 317,284,000.

Ownership

According to OM publications, the OM has approximately 1,800 shareholders. The owners comprise the following: all Swedish banks and brokerage firms active in the options market in 1990, AB Investor, Forvatnings AB Providentia, Investment AB D. Carnegie and Co., AB Volvo through the subsidiary Fortos AB, the insurance companies, Skandia and Trygg-Hansa.

Organisation of Trading

OM's options trading is based on an electronic marketplace with integrated clearing. Each transaction with OM as a buyer is matched by an identical transaction with OM as seller; thus the OM is neutral. The marketplace and clearing functions are integrated by computer. When an order is transacted it is cleared immediately. Parallel to the electronic trading is telephone trading with the OMs electronic system still used to quote prices, distribute information and clearing. OM officials act as the telephone [block order] brokers.

The Electronic Market System

Parties linked with the electronic terminal-based system place bid and offers via their own terminals. The orders are ranked in accordance with the criteria of price, time and whether the order is from a market-maker or end customer. Sixty-five terminals are currently in existence.

The Broker Function

Orders over ten contracts (block-orders) are usually executed via OM's block order brokers. Best prices are immediately distributed to market participants via the OM system, which ties into newswire services such as Reuters. Each transaction is recorded on the system after it occurs. Interbank and intrabank trading is also permitted. These transactions, which are not made in the marketplace, are still recorded on the OM's electronic order book. The OM computer system is not equipped to execute special orders e.g. spreads or combinations. The OM broker must display the order onto a wall board display and monitor it continuously. Block order prices are not binding on the OM. Legally, the block order only represents an expression of interest.

Clearing

OM records all transactions in the account of the broker's customer, each of whom has his own account at the OM. Each customer has an account number and therefore remains anonymous. In the morning following a trading day, the broker receives a report containing settlement notes and lists of collateral pertaining to the broker's total account and to the broker's individual customer accounts. Since the OM guarantees the fulfilment of each option it writes, it must ensure all options written to OM will be fulfilled. Collateral arrangements make brokers responsible for their customers. If the customer fails to meet obligations to the OM, the broker must intervene.

Margin Requirements

OM's margin system is designed to protect OM as a clearing house against the risk of non-performance by a customer. The system computes - per product and per customer - the margin requirement for each account at the close of each trading day, expressed as a collateral balance. OM sends a notice of the collateral balance to the broker for the account of the customer. If there is a negative balance, collateral must be provided. The collateral is normally provided to the broker by the customer as an obligation to pay for option transactions. A broker that is not a Swedish bank must in turn provide collateral in the same amount to the OM. Alternatively, at the broker's approval, all or part of the collateral balance may be provided directly by the customer to the OM. The collateral must be provided to the OM or broker by 11:00 am of the first trading day following the day in which the change in collateral balance is attributable. The cash margin is as follows: The total net value of long positions with positive net value, less the adjusted basic amount for all short positions at the close of each trading day.
Adjusted basic amount is the higher of:

a) 25% of the value of the stock at the close of trading (daily closing value), plus or minus the net value of the option, or
b) a minimum, per short position, of five percent of the daily closing value of the stock.

The collateral balance equals the positive net value of long positions less the adjusted basic amount for short positions. If the balance is negative, collateral must be provided.

Delivery Capacity
In accordance with a regulation of the Swedish Bank Inspection Board, delivery capacity is required of the writer of a stock call option and the buyer of a stock put option. Delivery may be fulfilled by deposit of underlying stocks or deposit of a long call. If the long call is out of the money, a supplementary cash deposit is required.

Reporting of Deals Closed
OM prepared settlement notes (which show transactions made by the broker for customers) are delivered to the broker the morning following the transaction together with any collateral/deposit account details. The broker must then in turn prepare settlement notes for his customers. On settlement day, the third day following a transaction, the customer's account is debited or credited in the amount of the premium and fees.

Summary
The OM is an electronic marketplace and links up dealers by a screen-based dealing system. Block orders are conducted by telephone and prices for these orders are treated "subject". The OM has its own guarantee risk reserve in the event of default. Clearing is conducted by the exchange's own electronic system with brokers being responsible for their clients' obligations. The margining system computes the margin requirement per product and per customer, cash or collateral must be provided to the broker or in the case of non-Swedish Banks directly to the OM. In the near future the OM plans to update the margin requirements continuously to cater for "exceptional" markets.

The Chicago Merchantile Exchange (CME)

Background
In 1982, the CME opened its first option contract with options on Deutschemark futures. Rapid growth in the interest of futures and options has led to expansion and development of other option contracts, namely other currencies, interest rate futures, commodity futures and Stock Index futures. In 1984, an international trading link was established with the Singapore International Monetary Exchange (SIMEX). The "offset" arrangement on futures contracts (options are not offered on the SIMEX link but are offered on GLOBEX) provides a full day and night trading cycle. While the two exchanges maintain separate clearing houses, audits, compliance and surveillance departments, the contracts are completely fungible. In

1992 the CME's GLOBEX electronic after hours trading system was launched. The CME is a non-profit corporation consisting of approximately 2700 members. There are three divisions; the Chicago Mercantile Exchange, where agricultural contracts are traded, the International Monetary Market (IMM) division for the trading of currency and interest rate futures, and the index and option market (IOM), trading stock index futures and options on futures.

Function of the Exchange
"The exchange provides a physical location where floor traders can trade specific futures and options contracts, and, through the auction process, discover a price".[3] Buyers and seller do not deal directly. The actual financial transaction is conducted by a third party, the Clearing House of the exchange. The clearing house is charged with the proper conduct of delivery procedures and adequate financing of the whole operation and deals only with clearing members. Each clearing member must be a member of the exchange (although not all exchange members are clearing members). The clearing house settles all transactions at the end of each day's trading by interposing between the two transactors and guaranteeing the contractual obligations of both parties. All CME members are approved by the Exchange's Board of Directors. Like the markets they trade, the memberships themselves are traded freely and actively at current "market prices". All members are given equal access to the market by the process of open outcry. By a combination of shouting and hand signals each trader becomes his own auctioneer openly declaring bids and offers ready to transact. This full open outcry method of trading fosters the liquidity necessary for an efficient market environment.

Organisation of Trading
The membership of the CME is made up of independent traders as well as representatives of major brokerage firms, banks and institutions. Members can trade futures contracts on physical commodities financial instruments, or options on futures, depending on the type of exchange seat they hold. Delivery of the traded instrument is rare with the contract normally closed out with an offsetting transaction (99% of the time contracts are offset rather than delivered upon). The marketplace is made up of the traders in the pits, floor traders and floor brokers. Floor brokers execute orders for the accounts of the Exchange's member firms.

Trade Execution Orders are received by firms on the CME floor. These orders are then relayed to the pit by an order clerk. Different contracts are traded in separate pits. No trading may occur outside the designated pit (except for physical transactions). In compliance with exchange rules floor brokers and traders may only announce bids or offers if they are equal or better than the existing market. When a transaction occurs, participants make a written record and a CME employee enters the price into the computerised reporting system. This price is displayed on electronic boards and stored for later use.

---

[3]According to A World Marketplace, a Chicago Mercantile Exchange publication, page 6.

Clearing

The Exchange's Clearing House is the repository for all transactions that occur on the trading floor. Ultimately, the capital of the Clearing House (from its members) protects all customers. In addition, in 1969, the Exchange created a trust fund for further customer protection. Customer protection is therefore, achieved by regulating the relationship between member firms and customers and protecting clearing members of the exchange against non-performance by any other CME member. However, the first line of customer protection lies with members themselves.

The Commodity Exchange Act requires that each clearing member firm maintain a prescribed level of capital so any insolvency has no direct effect on customer funds. In addition, the Exchange administers financial surveillance which monitors clearing members and where appropriate can impose higher capital requirements than those of the Commodity Futures Trading Commission (the US government regulator for futures and options on futures).

The CME trust fund is a second level of protection existing to insulate customers against the insolvency of a clearing member (this now has approximately $60 million in capital, see Annual Report). The final level of protection then goes to the Clearing House capital and all solvent clearing members. In addition, the Exchange secures payment directly from each of its clearing members, so that the Exchange can insert itself between every transaction it clears. By acting as a buyer to each seller and a seller to each buyer the Clearing House can guarantee that any customer's gain will be realised regardless of any possible default from the party with the opposite position.

Performance Bond (Margin)

Clearing members are required to collect from customers a minimum initial performance bond on futures contracts which thereafter must remain at a minimum maintenance level. Margin levels are generally related to prevailing volatilities.

The CME requires gross margining i.e. long and short positions cannot be offset to give a margining figure. The "gross" system assures that necessary margin exists, and that funds have been segregated for the purpose. The initial margin, net capital and position requirements are intended to limit short term losses so they can be absorbed by a firm and secondly by the Clearing House without disrupting business.

Should a clearing member fail to meet obligations to the Clearing House, the Exchange may apply that member's security deposit and any other available assets to discharge the liabilities of that member, if a shortfall still exists the security deposits contributed by CME members may be used to discharge liabilities. Any remaining requirement is found from solvent members (and ultimately the capital of the Clearing House).

Daily Settlement

All transactions conducted on the exchange are settled daily. As a result, every account holding futures positions is adjusted daily in a process called marking to market. A loss on a position is treated as a debt to the Clearing House which must be made good before trading begins on the next business day. This loss or gain adjustment is known as variation margin. Variation margin protects the Exchange since its debt exposure is limited to one day's price fluctuation. The exchange demands this variation margin from the Clearing members. They in turn are required to make margin calls on their customers. If the ultimate customer fails to meet his obligation, the clearing member can close the position of the customer and apply any proceeds remaining in the margin account to settle with the Clearing House. If funds are insufficient, the Clearing member must either apply other resources or default. As discussed before, other mechanisms then take place to settle all accounts before the markets can open.

Summary
The CME's financial safeguards regulate and protect member firms and their customers. Firms must maintain capital requirements and segregate customer funds. The CME Trust Fund is available in an emergency situation. "Margining" of open positions with daily settlement by both clearing members (and their customers) limits the potential for injurious collapse of a clearing member or customer because any risk is confined to daily variations. The Clearing House deals only with clearing members and settles all transactions at the end of the day's trading by interposing between the two transacting parties and thereby guarantees the contractual obligations.

On 6 of December 1990, at the CME a new era in futures and options margining began with the introduction of the Standard Portfolio Analysis of Risk system (SPAN). This system is now used at 25 exchanges worldwide and SPAN has become the industry standard. Previously to this system, the CME had margined options on futures with a simple system similar to the system outlined above for the PHLX. However, as I discussed in Chapter 14, risk management of options is a complicated business. The delta is only one element in a multifaceted risk management measurement problem. The ideal system for margining and risk management would be to apply the methodology underlying the RAP program to accurately assess the true risk of the portfolio of transactions and then charge a margin based upon the worst case scenario loss. By applying essentially the same methodology as the RAP program, the SPAN system approaches this ideal.

THE SPAN SYSTEM EXPLAINED

On 2 April 1991, the London International Financial Futures Exchange (LIFFE) also decided to adapt the SPAN system to margining option positions. As the ultimate counterparty to every trade and guarantor to the markets, the London Clearing House (of the LIFFE) is at risk to the default of a Clearing Member. To cover its risk exposure, the LCH requires an initial margin to be placed by each participant who holds open positions in the market. At most options exchanges worldwide, when one buys an option, one must immediately pay a premium. The Clearing

House accepts this payment and as far as it is concerned there is no additional risk from the option buyer because he had already surrendered the amount which is the most he can lose (the premium). For the option writers, most exchanges will require that this premium is held at the Clearing House on behalf of the option writer. In addition, the option writer must post additional margin because his loss potential is unlimited. At the LIFFE, the system is different and the settlement procedure for options on futures is closer to the settlement of futures contracts which was outlined above. LIFFE will margin both buying and selling options positions rather than requiring the immediate payment or receipt of a premium.

An immediate problem with this approach is how much to charge as margin since the risk of options will not be the same as the risk of the underlying futures contract. The solution to this problem is found with the portfolio risk evaluation I discussed in Chapter 14. Recognising this fact, the London Clearing House has incorporated the concept of portfolio management of options into determining how risky an option position is and can easily utilise this number to determine the margin required for the portfolio of futures and options as a whole.

The SPAN system simulates how a portfolio of transactions would react to changing market conditions. The margin requirement is equal to the largest possible overnight loss that could occur (exactly as I determined with the RAP system in the last chapter). Together with the LIFFE, The London Clearing House sets a range of possible futures moves overnight as well as ranges for volatility changes. Then the SPAN system calculates a "RISK ARRAY" for each futures and option contract. Each risk array gives the calculated profits or losses for these contracts under sixteen different scenarios. These scenarios can be seen in Table 15.1. By valuing positions using these arrays, the SPAN system determines which is the worst scenario for the portfolio of futures and options and assigns the initial margin accordingly.

1	Futures Unchanged	Volatility Up
2	Futures Unchanged	Volatility Down
3	Futures Up 1/3 Range	Volatility Up
4	Futures Up 1/3 Range	Volatility Down
5	Futures Down 1/3 Range	Volatility Up
6	Futures Down 1/3 Range	Volatility Down
7	Futures Up 2/3 Range	Volatility Up
8	Futures Up 2/3 Range	Volatility Down
9	Futures Down 2/3 Range	Volatility Up
10	Futures Down 2/3 Range	Volatility Down
11	Futures Up 3/3 Range	Volatility Up
12	Futures Up 3/3 Range	Volatility Down
13	Futures Down 3/3 Range	Volatility Up
14	Futures Down 3/3 Range	Volatility Down
15	Futures Up Extreme Move (Cover 35% of Loss)	
16	Futures Down Extreme Move (Cover 35% of Loss)	

Table 15.1 What are the Sixteen Different Scenario.

An outstanding feature of the SPAN system is that it will accurately take into account when positions offset the risk of other positions, yielding a net margin. The SPAN system only affects the margin implications of options on Bund futures, the Bund futures themselves will be margined as was outlined above.

How The Risk Arrays Are Constructed

As I discussed in Chapter 3, option on futures (or forward) prices are sensitive to changes in the price of the underlying futures, volatility and time to expiration. In the construction of the RISK ARRAYS, all these elements are taken into account. The futures scanning range is the largest futures price move that the Clearing House requires initial margin for. For example, with the current futures margin at DM 6,250, this represents a futures price move of 250 basis points. So if the closing futures price of a Bund futures contract was 86.55, then "futures up 3/3" (in Table 15.1) would imply a future price of 89.05 and the SPAN system would evaluate the profit and loss at that point. The category of "futures down 1/3" would imply a futures price of 85.72 (1/3 of 250 basis points) and again the SPAN system would evaluate the profit and loss of the portfolio at that point. In addition to the movement in the underlying Bund futures, the SPAN system also covers the largest volatility move that might reasonably be expected to occur in one day. This is combined with the futures price movements to yield fourteen of the possible sixteen scenarios. The other two scenarios (at the bottom of Table 15.1) are for extreme moves in the price of the Bund futures. This extreme range is defined as twice the normal futures overnight range and would be equal to 500 basis points up or down. However, all these parameters can change and may be revised by the Clearing House after consultation with the LIFFE.

Examples Of Span Initial Margin Calculations

Suppose that you have the following position: long one (1) March Bund call option at a strike price of 80.50. The SPAN risk array for this trade might look like Table 15.2. In this table, the profit and losses have been determined for each of the sixteen scenarios and the margin is determined by looking down the column for the maximum loss, which is the largest positive number (note: gains are negative values). In this case, the maximum loss is on line 14 at DM 4725, therefore the basic initial margin would be DM 4725.

Let us now look at another example of how SPAN works with a more complicated position. Suppose that you instead had a portfolio containing the following positions: short five (5) March Bund futures, long one (1) 80.50 March Bund call option, and long five (5) 74.50 March Bund put options. To determine the initial margin required for this portfolio, once again, the sixteen scenarios would be

1	-125	Futures Unchanged	Volatility Up
2	150	Futures Unchanged	Volatility Down
3	-2000	Futures Up 1/3	Volatility Up
4	-1850	Futures Up 1/3	Volatility Down
5	1550	Futures Down 1/3	Volatility Up
6	1975	Futures Down 1/3	Volatility Down
7	-3975	Futures Up 2/3	Volatility Up
8	-3900	Futures Up 2/3	Volatility Down
9	3025	Futures Down 2/3	Volatility Up
10	3550	Futures Down 2/3	Volatility Down
11	-6000	Futures Up 3/3	Volatility Up
12	-5975	Futures Up 3/3	Volatility Down
13	4175	Futures Down 3/3	Volatility Up
14	4725	Futures Down 3/3	Volatility Down
15	-4725	Futures Up Extreme Move	
16	2100	Futures Down Extreme Move	

Table 15.2 Example of a Simple Risk Margin Calculation 80.50 Bund Call Option.

evaluated and the worst loss would then be the initial margin. The RISK ARRAY for this portfolio can be seen in Table 15.3. The profit or loss for each scenario is determined by first multiplying each array value by the appropriate position size (plus for long and minus for short) and then adding across each row to get a total loss for the overall portfolio in that scenario. The reader can see that the greatest loss occurring is associated with scenario number 12 and is equal to DM 25,275. Therefore, this would be the basic SPAN initial margin required by the Clearing House to hold this portfolio overnight.

Line	Future	Put 74.50 Strike	Call 80.50 Strike	Total Loss DM
1	-5 × 0	5 × -25	1 × -125	-250
2	-5 × 0	5 × 0	1 × 150	150
3	-5 ×-2075	5 × 0	1 ×-2000	8375
4	-5 ×-2075	5 × 0	1 ×-1850	8525
5	-5 × 2075	5 × -25	1 × 1550	-8950
6	-5 × 2075	5 × 0	1 × 1975	-8400
7	-5 ×-4175	5 × 0	1 ×-3975	16900
8	-5 ×-4175	5 × 0	1 ×-3900	16975
9	-5 × 4175	5 × -50	1 × 3025	-18100
10	-5 × 4175	5 × 0	1 × 3550	-17325
11	-5 ×-6250	5 × 0	1 ×-6000	25250
12	-5 ×-6250	5 × 0	1 ×-5975	25275
13	-5 × 6250	5 ×-100	1 × 4175	-27575
14	-5 × 6250	5 × -25	1 × 4725	-26650
15	-5 ×-4375	5 × 0	1 ×-4275	17600
16	-5 × 4375	5 ×-125	1 × 2100	-20400

Table 15.3 Example of a Simple Risk Margin Calculation Portfolio of Bund Futures.

Each of the scenarios automatically takes into account the passage of time over-night and like the Risk Analysis Programme (RAP), SPAN also allows for intra-month charges to be added to the basic risk margin calculation. In this case, the intra-month spread credits will be deducted to produce the final initial margin figure.

The Variation Margin

The variation margin for options however is independent of the SPAN system out-lined above (because the SPAN system simply determines the initial margin). The amount of variation margin that will be credited or debited from participants accounts depends only on how much the price of the option has changed from one day until the next. For example, suppose that a particular call option on Bund futures has a price of 50 basis points. The initial margin will be determined by the SPAN system as defined above. Suppose that the next day, the Bund futures price is unchanged and the implied volatility of the market has increased resulting in the option's price increasing to 70 basis points. The variation margin is determined by the difference between the prices of the call option from one day until the next. So, the variation margin which would be paid to a call option holder on this day would be DM 500 (and the call option seller would be debited this DM 500 amount). To calculate the variation margin for options on Bund futures, one will simply multi-ply today's tick change from the previous trading day by the tick size (DM 25 for Bund futures) and the number of contracts.

The reader must be aware that these margin requirements and methods for margin estimates will change from time to time. To keep up to date, one should contact either one's broker, the exchange where one's futures or options contracts trade or the Clearing House of that exchange periodically to make sure of the current state of affairs.

16: Accounting, Regulation And Taxation Issues For Options

The last chapter of this book addresses the subjects of operational issues, accounting and taxation around the world[1].

REGULATIONS: A GLOBAL SURVEY

Australia

Accounting: The operation of brokers in the futures and options industry is governed by a combination of the Corporations Law, Australian Stock Exchange ("ASX") and Sydney Futures Exchange ("SFE") Rules and Regulations. The ASX Rules and Regulations deal with the operation of exchange traded options, while the SFE Rules and Regulations deal with exchange traded futures. Under the Corporations Law, brokers are required to produce audited financial statements and to maintain proper books and accounting records. The Australian Accounting Standards Board has released an Exposure Draft ED59 - Financial Instruments which covers in general how these products should be treated. Under ED59 the broker must consider whether these transactions have been undertaken for hedging or trading purposes. In the situation where they are undertaken for trading purposes they must be valued at net market value, whereas hedge accounting is used for hedge transactions, i.e. the financial instrument is treated in the same manner as the underlying transaction being hedged. The requirements contained within ED59 are largely similar to those within the International Exposure Draft, ED40.

Currently, AASB1012 specifies the accounting treatment applicable to options and futures contracts entered into as hedges of foreign currency exposures and is broadly consistent with SFAS52. In the absence of any other Australian standards, international and US standards and practices are generally followed.

Regulation: Regulations of futures and options contracts under the Corporations Law is overseen partly by the self regulation of the exchange houses themselves and partly by the Australian Securities Commission (ASC).

---

[1]This chapter was supplied by Arthur Anderesen, London and first appeared in Futures and Option World.

Foreign Companies which do business in Australia must register under the Corporations Law Brokers and other advisors on futures and options must be licensed by the Commission before they may provide such financial services. Client property (such as funds) has to be held in separate designated accounts and dealt with only in accordance with the Corporations Law.

The Commission is entitled to enquire into all futures and options activities and can demand both written material and affidavits from any connected person.

Tax: Where futures and options are used as part of normal trading activities, whether directly or to hedge underlying trading transactions, the gains are taxable and the losses deductible from income.

Gains and losses on futures transactions will, however, only be taxable or deductible when the positions are closed out, i.e. marked to market gains and losses are not presently recognised for Australian tax purposes. Those who buy and sell options for general business purposes (e.g. financial institutions, or to hedge inherently revenue transactions, e.g. interest or trading stock) may deduct option premiums paid, and will be taxed on those received. Consistent with this, gains or losses resulting from the exercise of options will be taxable. Gains and losses on derivatives used to hedge foreign currency exposures (relating to capital transactions) will usually be taxable and deductible respectively. Gains and losses resulting from hedging other capital transactions are covered by the capital gains tax provisions.

The Australian revenue authorities are continuing to review the basis on which financial instruments (including futures and options) are taxed. In the course of this review, the Australian Taxation Office has altered its interpretation of the law as to the manner in which interest rate swaps are taxed in Australia, i.e. payments on bona fide interest rate swaps entered into on or after 21 May 1992 should be taxed on a daily accruals basis.

The Australian Government announced in its Budget on 18 August 1992 that a comprehensive legislative code for the taxation of financial instruments will be introduced.

It is intended that the new regime, which is to be implemented on a prospective basis, will tax financial arrangements (which is to include "contracts used in the provision of credit and in the management of exposure to financial risk") on an accruals basis, thus spreading gains and losses over the term of the financial arrangements.

The revenue authorities will continue consultation with financial markets participants prior to introduction of the new tax regime.

Belgium

Because of the extensive demand for an effective hedging instrument for the large Belgian Government bond market and the growing liquidity of the secondary bond market, a market in futures on Belgian Government bonds (BGBs) has recently been organised: the Belgian Futures and Options Exchange (Belfox). The market, although limited at first to interest rate futures, has recently been extended to options on Petrofina and Delhaize shares and has been extended to options on the index BEL-20 and BGB futures.

Accounting: Belgian accounting principles are determined by law. The Belgian Commission on Accounting Standards renders advice on the application of the accounting law to specific transactions and situations. The Royal Decree of 23/9/92 covering financial statements of banks, covers the treatment of futures and options. Commercial and industrial companies, not covered by the decree, are included in a report by the Commission. This published extensive conclusions on accounting for options on shares. Similar conclusions are expected on futures. The general accounting principles of prudence, fairness, matching, etc. should however be observed.

As a general rule, the substance over form principle is a predominant factor in accounting issues. The Commission (as well as the Royal Decree ruling the financial statements for the banking sector) differentiate between transactions entered into for speculative and hedging purposes.

For speculative transactions, the mark-to-market principle is generally applied, with unrealised gains being, in principle, deferred. Hedging transactions should be valued symmetrically, i.e. any revaluation surplus or shortage should be offset against the revaluation result on the hedged item. The time cost of the hedging instrument could be isolated and the reduction in value separately recognised.

Accounting for interest flows is generally based on the actuarial method, i.e. the internal rate of return at inception of the transaction.

Regulation: Belgium faced a financial Reform Act by the end of 1990. The Financial Reform Act was governing three main items:

- Redrafting of the legal form of the Stock Exchange Markets;
- Reorganisation of the status of the Stock Exchange Brokers (replacement of the individual brokers by agreed brokerage companies);
- Reinforcement of the principle of the centralisation within the Stock Exchange

Also, a Royal Decree relating to the creation and organisation of the Belgian Futures and Options Exchange was enacted. This new market is managed by a private body, the SC Belfox, who will play the role of Market Authority and Clearing House. Belfox drafted the Market rules for futures duly approved by the Ministry of Finances and is controlled by the Belgian Banking and Finance Commission.

Having opened a market for share options in mid June 1992, Belfox has now regulated options on the BEL-20 Index, as well as futures on government bonds and the BIBOR 3 month contract.

Taxation: There are no specific tax rules in Belgium with respect to futures or options. Taxable income should be determined according to the accounting rules unless the tax law provides for specific exemption. Consequently, the way the futures or options transactions are recorded in the accounts will determine the tax regime.

The distinction between "hedging" and "speculative" transactions will also prevail for tax purposes. However, the application of the general principles leaves (to a certain extent) the possibility of anticipating or deferring certain gains or losses and costs generated by or associated with these instruments. Any tax planning opportunities will therefore mainly concentrate on the timing of the profit and loss recognition. These opportunities may however be significant in relation to the utilisation of tax loss carry forwards, non refundable tax credits or anticipated changes in tax rates.

Canada

Accounting: Canada has no authoritative pronouncements addressing the accounting treatment for derivatives but generally the method used depends on the nature of the derivative.

If the derivatives are being used for the designated purpose of hedging activities exposed to price or interest rate risk, and their use reduces that risk, then gains and losses will be deferred. The timing of the recognition of such deferred gains and losses varies according to the specific asset or liability. For non-hedging transactions, mark-to-market accounting is recommended, i.e. realised and unrealised gains and losses should be recognised in the income statement currently. Alternatively, bought options can be stated at the lower of cost and net realisable value, and written options at the higher of sale proceeds and market value.

Regulation: There is a complex regulatory framework covering the Canadian securities industry and derivative transactions. The ultimate authority for regulation of the securities industry rests with the Provincial Securities Commissions under the relevant securities legislation but the audit supervision and enforcement functions have largely been seconded to self-regulatory organisations such as the Investment Dealers Association of Canada and the various exchanges. The securities commissions monitor the effectiveness of these self-regulatory bodies in the audit and compliance areas.

Capital margin requirements for hedge positions have recently come under great scrutiny and the self regulatory authorities have amended their by-laws to clarify the principles relating to margin calculations for inventory and client hedge positions margin offsets.

Tax: Gains and losses arising from transactions involving derivative products can be on income or capital account. Gains and losses arising from trading or hedging trading positions with derivatives as part of normal trading activities are taxed or deducted as part of income. Similarly, if derivatives are used to hedge or mitigate risk associated with regular business operations such as interest rate risk, any gains or losses should also be on income account. Income methods of reporting give rise to a full deduction for accrued losses and fully taxed accrued gains. The timing of the recognition of gains and losses is generally determined by the timing of financial statement recognition. However, it is possible to deviate from such financial statement treatment for tax purposes.

Gains and losses are treated on capital account where derivatives are not used for hedging operating cash flows or where such gains and losses do not arise from normal trading activities. Capital reporting means that only three-quarters of any loss may be deducted, and then only against capital gains, and only three-quartersof any gain is included in income. Gains or losses on capital account arise on a realised basis once the related contracts have been closed out.

The differentiation between income treatment and capital gains treatment is not clear in many cases. This is primarily due to the fact that the Canadian legislation related to derivative products is not well developed. Much reliance is placed on the administrative practice of the taxation authorities and general tax principles.

Denmark

Accounting: For banks and brokers extensive rules have been set up and these are supervised by the Danish Supervisory Authority of Financial Affairs. The rules are under constant review. However, no specific regulation has been laid down for other traders, and general principles are applied.

Professional traders must recognise realised and unrealised gains and losses in their income statement at market value and unrealised gains must be credited to a restricted revaluation reserve in the equity account.

Non-professional traders must account for losses in their income statements on a current basis whilst gains are deferred until realised. Hedge accounting is applied where a transaction fulfils the hedging criteria.

Regulation: Trading on the FUTOP market in futures and options takes place at the Copenhagen Stock Exchange (CSE). Trading at the CSE is supervised, cleared and guaranteed by the Guaranteed Fund for Danish Options and Futures. Only professional traders who are approved members at the CSE are allowed to trade on the CSE. Both the Guarantee Fund and the CSE clearing and exchange members are under the supervision of the Supervisory Authority of Financial Affairs.

Except for margin deposits, no regulatory limitation exists for investors wishing to trade in options and futures through the approved members of the Guarantee Fund for Danish Options and Futures.

Foreign participation and transactions involving foreigners are not restricted in any way. The Margin rules are as follows:

- 4% of size for bond futures
- 12% of size for stock index futures
- premium plus 4% for written bond options

Tax: New tax legislation has been implemented as of 1 July 1991. This new law has two major areas: Futures and options based on shares and futures and options based on all other.

The Main Principle in the law is that gains are taxable and losses can be deducted in the taxable income. Gains and losses should each year be based upon both realised and unrealised gains and losses, i.e. open contracts are marked to market for tax purposes.

However, losses arising from futures and options based on shares cannot be deducted in other income. These losses can only be deducted in income from futures and options contracts to the same share. Certain additional restrictions apply to individual investors. No stamp duty is charged on future and options trading.

France

Accounting: France has brought out new futures and options regulations comparatively recently. These suggest an approach based on the transaction being classified as either hedging or speculation.

Speculative gains and losses should be accounted for at mark-to-market on a current basis, whilst those arising from hedging transactions should be accounted for over the period of the hedge.

Regulation: All those entitled under French regulations to trade futures and options in France must be approved by the regulatory organisation, the Clearing House (Chambre de Compensation). Transactions undertaken by French residents on foreign currency must be carried on through an intermediary (agreed bank). However, French residents may carry out a transaction on interest rate or indices in foreign derivatives without using an intermediary.

Tax: The tax treatment of derivatives trading by resident companies is governed mainly by recent legislation as clarified by Administrative Comments dated 20 April 1988. Contracts on non-hedging transactions on all futures, forwards and options that are quoted or traded "on a market or by reference to a market" must be marked-to-market at year end, and the resulting gain or loss included in current taxable income. On contracts traded outside a market the unrealised gains can be deferred until after the contract settled.

Where contracts are traded specifically as a hedge against risks from transactions in the subsequent year, and disclosure is made to the tax administration, tax on unrealised gains may be deferred until the contracts are settled.

Where contracts are traded specifically as a hedge against exchange risks on future operations, and disclosure is made to the tax administration, tax on unrealised gains may be deferred until the hedge operation is settled. Positions may be offset with the following limitation: where one position has a gain which has not been taxed, the fraction of the loss (realised and/or unrealised) on the offsetting position corresponding to the untaxed gain is not deductible. In such cases, subject to the appropriate disclosure, the deduction is held off until the gain is taxed.

Germany

Accounting: According to German accounting principles each asset and liability has to be evaluated separately. As an exception, micro hedge accounting is applicable if some restrictive requirements are met including that the terms of both the futures or options positions and the underlying asset or liability are identical or very close. Macro hedge accounting in general is not accepted. A mark to market evaluation does not exist. Non-realised losses have to be accrued for, whereas profits can only be shown in the financial statements if realised, e.g. through a closing transaction. Purchased options have to be capitalised at original cost, premiums received by the writer can only be shown as income if realised. If the option is not exercised by the holder at expiration date, its book value has to be written off. The purchase or sale of futures is regarded as a pending transaction and therefore an off-balance sheet item. For anticipated losses a respective accrual has to be set up. Variation margins as such do not yet affect the profit and loss account.

For trading stocks of futures and options the Banker's association proposes a combined valuation of all contracts with the same underlying. If there is a net loss an accrual must be stated. In case of a net profit this should not be recorded. If futures and/or options are included among financial instruments in a separate maintained portfolio under certain conditions a combined valuation is acceptable.

Regulation: Amendments to German Law have made futures trading also binding for private customers. These amendments, which include trading in precious metals (but not trading in commodities), are allied to the opening of the German options and financial futures exchange ("DTB, Deutsche Terminbörse") early in 1990. Under these regulations, private customers are required to sign a risk disclosure statement detailing the risks associated with futures and options contracts, which have to be periodically renewed.

In order to become a member of the German options and futures exchange applicants must have at least a branch office registered and operating in Germany. A securities lending system does exist which allows writers of options more flexibility, as a result the volume is increasing. Within certain restrictions German investment funds and insurance companies are allowed to trade in options and futures.

The current products at DTB are stock options, long and medium term BUND-futures, the future on the DAX (German stock index with 30 major shares) and also an option on the DAX and options on all 3 futures. Encouraged by increasing volumes at DTB further products will follow. For trading on the DTB, a collateral deposit is required. The deposit has to cover obligation of trading. It can be made by means of a deposit of securities with the DTB's portfolio at the German clearing house ("DKV, Deutscher Kassenverein") or a cash deposit with the central bank ("LZB, Landeszentralbank").

Tax: The tax treatment of futures and options for business investors follows the accounting treatment. Profits are taxed as income at standard rates for individual or corporate income tax and municipal trade tax on income. Corporation's and individual's holdings of options are subject to capital taxes. For private investors, premiums received by the writer are taxed as income at standard rates. On 28 November 1990 the Supreme Tax Court neglected to regard the premiums as tax free gambling profits. Further it neglected to deduct premiums paid for closing transactions as well as to offset losses suffered in the underlying assets or liabilities against the premium.

Following recent court decisions, those gains and losses that arise on the disposal of an option are treated as net capital gains. Gains must be short-term (under 6 months), and worth more than DM999 per year, before they will be subject to tax. It should be noted that for private investors this treatment is still subject to current discussions with the tax authorities. The current position on gains from futures is that they are tax free to private investors because they are seen to be gambling profits. This follows a recent Supreme Court ruling on currency forward contracts and should be applicable to all cash settled futures contracts.

It has to be considered that the taxation rules refer to the treatment of products traded before the opening of DTB. However, a new official statement of the Federal Finance Ministry on the taxation of options and futures can be expected, which could result in some important changes in the taxation for private investors. There is no longer a stock exchange turnover tax or stamp duty. Options and futures are not subject to value added tax.

Hong Kong

Accounting: At present derivatives accounting procedures have not been formally set up. A number of different procedures are currently used and disclosure within financial statements is generally poor. There is a need for standard accounting policies designed to recognise the economic reality of the transactions. It is generally accepted that mark-to-market methods are sufficiently reflective of the economic basis of speculative transactions to be used by active traders.

To define a transaction as hedging, the US accounting standard treatment would usually be applied. Hedging transactions would normally be accounted for so as to be in line with the underlying transactions.

Regulation: Trading is regulated by the Commodities Trading Ordinance and the rules of the Futures Exchange. The SFC (Securities and Futures Commission) enforces the rules and regulates brokers. Brokers must comply with regulations concerning levels of capital and liquidity and segregation of client funds. Trading of futures (such as interest rate and commodity futures) takes places on the Hong Kong Futures Exchange. Banks also trade OTC options amongst themselves.

Tax: Capital gains or profits earned "offshore" are not liable to Hong Kong tax. Thus gains are made on futures exchanges abroad though brokers outside Hong Kong will be exempt from Hong Kong profits tax (although they may be liable to tax in that location abroad).

Hong Kong sourced profits resulting from a trade or business carried on in Hong Kong are liable to tax. This is governed by the location where the activity causing the profit took place - known as "operations test". This test is applied to gains and losses on derivatives trading by financial institutions in Hong Kong, and the timing of taxation will generally follow the accounting treatment. Although capital profits on-shore are non-taxable it would be difficult for a financial institution to show that profits from futures and options were capital as the hedging transactions relate to underlying assets that make up part of the trading stock of the business. Non-financial institutions and other companies will also have profits measured by the operations test, and the tax treatment of derivatives used for hedging purposes will match that of the underlying assets. This speculative use of derivatives will be treated as giving rise to taxable gains and deductible losses, whilst where the underlying assets or liabilities are capital, no Hong Kong tax will arise.

Irish Republic

Accounting: There are no accounting standards designed specifically for futures and options, so accepted accounting standards are applied to provide a method that reflects the underlying economic effect of the transaction. Where derivatives are used to hedge a position, the accounting treatment of the future or option contract is matched to that of the underlying asset or liability, and gains and losses may be offset between the two.

Financial institutions using derivatives should mark them to market and include the gain or loss within their profit and loss account. As this method is not in line with the rules of valuation in the Companies (Amendment) Act 1986, disclosure will be necessary. Non-financial companies speculating in derivatives may defer the recognition of unrealised gains until they have been realised.

Regulation: Trading in Ireland takes place on IFOX (Irish Futures and Options Exchange) and is regulated by the Central Bank Act 1989, enforced by the Central Bank. IFOX also has a "guarantee and compliance" officer, who records and controls such things as exposure, position limits and risk management.

Four futures contracts are traded:

- A future on a 20 year Irish gilt
- A future on a 3 month Dibor
- A future on a short gilt
- A future on the Irish Stock Exchange index

Tax: As no prescriptive tax legislation exists for futures and options and no guidelines are available to date, profits and losses from derivatives are taxed according to general principles, and in practice follow the treatment applied in the UK.

Profits and losses from speculative trading or arising from hedges of trading transactions are taxed as normal trading income. Where the taxpayer uses derivatives to hedge a capital asset or liability and does not deal in futures and options, then capital gains tax treatment will be afforded to the transaction. Gains will be taxed at 40%.

However the long gilt futures contract traded on IFOX is exempt from tax, as are dealings in financial futures and traded options carried out by pension funds.

Italy

In 1992 the Italian Futures market (MIF) was created. This market trades contracts on the Italian BTP 10 year government bond.

Accounting: Contracts used to hedge positions should be accounted for in line with the underlying instruments. Futures transactions carried out for trading purposes are marked-to-market and option premiums are suspended and valued to market at year end. Provisions must be set up for unrealised losses on unmatched positions, and gains on options should be accounted for when realised.

Regulation: No restrictions now exist to prevent transactions in foreign currencies. Hence, by operating via a bank authorised to deal in currencies, Italian residents can operate fully on futures and options exchanges.

Tax: All gains and losses arising from futures and options are exempt from tax for individuals and taxed as normal income for professional traders (whether individuals or companies). All Italian investors are liable to pay the transfer taxes which apply in the foreign markets. Where an option is exercised, the premiums paid for the cost of the contract is treated as the cost of the underlying instrument. If the option is left to expire, the premium is deducted when the option is abandoned. Premiums are taxed when cashed and losses arising from written options are deducted on realisation. For tax purposes hedging accounting is not permitted. The exchange of uniform terms contracts (Options and Futures) regarding Italian Government Bonds traded at the related Stock Exchanges are not subject to stamp duty (0.09%).

Japan

Accounting: The general accounting treatment of futures contracts is as follows:

- Upon opening of the futures contract: No accounting entry is required for the futures contract (it is an "off-balance sheet transaction"). Margin payments shall be recorded as an asset, whereas margin receipts shall be recorded as liability.
- Upon fluctuation of the market value of the futures contract: No gain or loss of the futures contract shall be recognised.
- Upon settlement or closing-out of the futures contract: Gain or loss of the futures contract shall be recognised at the time of settlement or closing-out either in the Income Statement or as an adjustment to the acquisition or sale price of the underlying asset.

The general accounting treatment of options contracts is as follows:

- Upon opening of the option contract: No accounting entry is required for the option contract (it is an "off balance sheet transaction"). Option premium paid shall be recorded as an asset, whereas option premium received shall be recorded as liability.
- Upon fluctuation of the market value of the option premium: No gain or loss of the option contract shall be recognised.
- Upon close-out or expiry of the option contract: The gain or loss of the option contract shall be recognised at the time of close-out or expiry in the Income Statement.
- Upon exercise of the option contract: The premium (together with the strike price) shall be capitalised as the cost of the underlying asset.

The above applies to most forms of futures and options other than currency futures and options held by the banks. In the latter case, currency futures margins and option premiums should be carried in the balance sheet and marked-to-market at the bank's reporting date.

Please note these are general principles. Different treatment sometimes applies according to the nature of the business operation.

Regulation: In Japan, there is no one central body regulating the trading of futures and options contracts. The relevant legislation and administrative body depends on the particular instrument or commodity underlying the contract.

For example, the following contracts are governed as set out in the adjacent table. The Financial Times Trading Law covers all financial futures and options except those based on securities. This law covers futures and options traded on the Tokyo International Financial Futures Exchange, which commenced operation in 1989. The principal contracts traded on this exchange are the Euroyen 3 month interest rate futures and options contracts. A new law called the "Commodity Investment Act" was passed in 1991 to regulate emerging domestic commodity funds in Japan.

Tax:

Futures:

Gains and losses from the future transaction are recognised at the time of settlement or closing-out for both corporate and individual tax purposes. No mark-to-market rule is applied upon fluctuation of the market value of the futures contract.

Corporate Tax:

Gains and losses from the future transactions are taxed with other income at the normal tax rates. Effective combined tax rate is 51%.

Individual Tax:

Treatments differ depending on whether or not taxpayer's transactions are considered as business activity.

Business income:

If considered business activity, gains or losses are treated as business income and then taxed with other kinds of income at the standard progressive tax rates from 15% to 65% including inhabitants tax.

Miscellaneous income:

If not considered business activity, gains or losses are treated as miscellaneous income. Gains are taxed with other income the same way as business income, but losses may be neither off-set against other kinds of income other than miscellaneous income nor carried back or forward.

Option premium:

Tax rule on option transactions depends on various factors including the nature of the underlying option property and the life of the option.

Where the underlying property is of a type that is includible in the inventory of the option holder, the entire cost of the option must be capitalised. In the event that the option is exercised, no gain or loss is recognised; instead, the cost of the option is added to the purchase cost of the underlying property. If the option is sold or expires, gain or loss is recognised in the taxable year of sale or expiration. No mark to market valuation is applied during the holding. Where the underlying property is not of a type that is includible in the inventory of the option holder, the timing of gain and loss recognition may depend on the option's remaining life. The cost of a short term option is fully deductible as a loss in the year of purchase. However, the cost of a long-term option would be amortised over the option's remaining life. For this purpose, short-term options are considered options that have remaining lives not exceeding 1 year from the date of acquisition. Incidentally, premiums on deep in-the-money options may not be deductible when paid. There is a potential for exposure, as the entire premium paid or received must be capitalised or deferred until sale, exercise or expiration for Japanese GAAP purposes; this is different from the historical practice described above.

Exchange Market Tax Listed commodity futures are subject to exchange market tax at 0.001%. Options premiums are also subject to exchange market taxes at 0.01%.

Luxembourg

Accounting: The Luxembourg Monetary Institute has issued instructions for banks and other financial institutions which govern accounting treatment of futures and options. For normal commercial companies, no specific regulations cover futures and options and generally accepted accounting principles apply. When items are valued in the accounts the prudence principle must be applied such that only real-ised profits may be taken into account. Gains and losses resulting from hedging ac-tivities may be deferred. The Luxembourg Monetary Institute has issued regula-tions for investment funds which set investment limits for futures and options. Mark-to-market accounting should be applied by investment funds.

Regulation: All companies and individuals doing business in Luxembourg are re-quired to be registered under company law. Legislation has been passed that re-quires all professionals in the financial intermediary sector to be approved by the Luxembourg Monetary Institute prior to commencing their activities. This law also establishes minimum capital requirements for companies carrying on such activities.

Tax: All losses on futures and options transactions are deductible from income (whether realised or otherwise) but only those gains that have been realised will be subject to tax. Unrealised gains are not taxed until such time as the contract is set-tled. Hedging profits and losses are deferred for tax purposes. Futures and options transactions in investment funds are not subject to any income tax at the fund level in Luxembourg.

Netherlands

Accounting: There is very little Government regulation concerning accounting for derivatives. Consequently, common practice applies international, generally ac-cepted accounting principles, largely complying with the existing regulations of the

567

Anglo-Saxon practices. These practices call for professional corporate derivative traders to account for transactions and position to market rates, ("mark-to-market" method).

However, if a position is recognised as investment portfolio, valuation is normally based on amortised cost. For non-professional traders, the distinction between hedging and speculative transactions is made. Hedging positions should be valued according to the same principle as applied for the positions being hedged ("symmetry" method). Speculative positions should be valued at cost-or-lower-market. Some non-professionals choose mark-to-market their positions, netting off unrealised losses and gains, taking the losses of a debit balance and deferring the profits of a credit balance.

One should note that a "hedge" is not strictly defined in any regulation or law; individual corporations are to organise the criteria by themselves.

Regulation: Securities legislation governing derivatives was brought in to protect the public from unprincipled dealers. The most recent regulations came into force in May 1986 and regulation is thus carried out by the exchanges and implementation of the Securities Trading Act and the Securities Trading Decree. Brokers may only act in derivatives transactions with professional issuers, dealers and investors, unless the transaction is made by a licensed person. Licences are given only after the financial situation and the background of the applicant has been accepted by the Dutch Ministry of Finance. Members of certain bodies, such as US and Swiss stock exchanges, are exempt from these rules.

Tax: The Netherlands do not have a general capital gains tax for individuals. A capital gain can be taxed only in very specific situations, for example when a profit is realised as a consequence of insider trading. Except in these specific situations and for those individuals who are trading, there is no income tax or capital gains tax impact on individuals with gains and losses resulting from transactions in futures and options. However, derivatives are brought in to net equity for the calculation of net equity tax. They are taxed on the 1 January value at 0.8%. In the case of professional traders, prudent business principles are applied. Until fiscal year 1990 the tax authorities have accepted a system whereby long positions are valued at the lower of cost and market value, while short positions at the higher of cost and market value. In this way realised gains/losses are treated as normal trading income and expenditure whereas unrealised profits can be deferred and unrealised losses included. In practice, however, this leads to a reduction in the value of the securities to a rather unrealistic level.

Under the new system of valuing stock, options and futures, general prudent business principles will continue to form the basis for their fiscal valuation. However, the new system also proposes to categorise securities which form part of a fund as a separate group. For each group, a choice should be made as to whether all securities are valued at market value or at lower cost price. For both long and short positions, this new system would mean that tax payments can no longer be deferred, as they were under the old regime. Whether or not the new valuation method is acceptable will have to be decided in a court case. Arthur Andersen has entered into an agreement with a major player on the Dutch securities market to challenge this new system in court.

Singapore

Accounting: Recommended Accounting Practices 4 contains guidelines for accounting for financial futures. Foreign currency transactions are regulated by the Statement of Accounting Standard 20. The above accounting standard and practice differentiate between the use of derivatives for speculative purposes and their use for hedging. There is currently no accounting standard for options. In general, reference would be made to the accounting standards and/or practice adopted by the US and the UK where the accounting treatment of a transaction is not covered by a Statement of Accounting Standard or Recommended Accounting Practice.

Hedging transactions should be treated in the same manner as the underlying asset or security. Where hedging or investment in foreign companies is effected by foreign currency transactions, the related profits and losses should be taken to shareholders' interests. Gains and losses on speculative contracts are usually accounted for on mark-to-market basis and should be taken into the profit and loss account in the year they arise.

Regulation: The main regulatory body in Singapore, the Monetary Authority of Singapore (MAS), empowered by the Futures Trading Act 1986, regulates the futures and options market. In addition, Singapore International Monetary Exchange (SIMEX) and the RAS Commodity Exchange regulate member firms and individuals in accordance with their rules and regulations. There are minimum requirements on reporting, auditing, capital levels and separation of client funds ard maximum limits on the daily movements in contract prices.

Brokers, dealers and pool operators in futures must be licensed as futures brokers or futures pool operators. Any person who carries on the business of advising others on futures contracts must be licensed as futures trading advisor. However, holders of the futures brokers licence need not apply for the futures trading advisor licence.

Tax: Traders in futures and options (whether companies or individuals) are taxed on trading profits at the following rates:

- companies and non-resident individuals at 27%
- resident individuals at progressive rates of up to 30%

Non-residents with no presence in Singapore may be exempt from tax. Gains and losses from hedging transactions are taxed/deductible (or not taxed/deductible) in accordance with the underlying asset or liability. A concessionary rate of 10% will be applied to income from "relevant transactions" derived by the following persons:

- Members of SIMEX;
- Offshore banking units of financial institutions (ACUs);
- Approved Oil Traders (AOT) (restricted to oil futures income);
- Members of RAS Commodity Exchange Limited (restricted to income from RSS3 futures transactions);
- Approved Headquarter companies (OHQ);
- Approved Finance and Treasury Centre (FTC);
- Approved International Commodity Trading companies (AIT).

All of the following conditions must be satisfied before a transaction is regarded as a "relevant transaction" for the 10% tax concession:
- the transaction must be in gold bullion, gold, financial (other than Singapore dollar), oil or RSS 3 futures;
- the transaction must be carried out on a specified exchange (i.e. SIMEX, CME, CMEX, Liffe, CBOT, Sydney Futures Exchange, any gold exchange/market, IPE, NYMEX (specified petroleum futures only for both IPE and NYMEX), Kobe Rubber Exchange (RSS3 only), RAS Commodity Exchange (RSS3 only) or Tokyo Commodity Exchange (RSS3 only); and
- the transaction must be with an ACU, a SIMEX member, a member of the RAS Commodity Exchange, an AOT (for petroleum futures contracts only), a non-resident with no permanent establishment in Singapore or an overseas branch of a Singapore resident company.

This 10% tax concession has been extended to include profits from spot transactions in designated currencies with specified persons. The transaction must be with a non-resident, another member of SIMEX or and ACU.

Foreign investors making gains on futures and options contracts from funds managed by an approved fund manager or ACU, OHQ, FTC or Approved Trustee Company are exempt from tax. Also, non-residents are exempt from paying withholding tax on interest received from SIMEX members on margin deposits for transactions in gold, gold futures and financial futures. Non-trading (i.e. speculative) capital gains earned by individuals are not subject to tax.

South Africa

Accounting: In South Africa, any change in the market value of futures, options, swaps and forward rate agreement contracts should be recognised in the Income Statement in the period in which the change occurs, except in cases where the contract qualifies as a hedge for activities exposed to price or interest rate risk. If the contract qualifies as a hedge, the accounting for the changes in market value should be related to the changes in the value of the hedged items.

Regulation: Futures trading in South Africa began in 1987 when a local bank introduced futures contracts on Stock Exchange indices and acted as a clearing house.

South African Futures Exchange (SAFEX) commenced operations in 1990 and operates under rules approved by the Registrar of Financial Markets and is controlled by the Financial Markets Control Act, which came fully into operation on 10 August 1990. SAFEX's membership consists of merchant banks, stock brokers, futures brokers, institutions and commercial banks. All of the 60 or so members must own (or lease) at least 1 SAFEX seat (of which 120 are in issue) in order to be able to trade. The market is three-tiered, with clearing members who guarantee all trades done in the market, non-clearing members (either broking or non-broking) who must clear trades through a clearing member, and clients who may only trade through a broking member.

Futures available include All Share Index, All Gold Index, Industrial Index, Gold Price, Long Bond and Short Term Interest Futures. The Bond Market Association (BMA) is the association formed as the self regulatory body to be empowered, under licence, by the Registrar of Financial Markets for the regulation of fixed interest securities market.

Membership is comprised of deposit taking institutions, issuers, investors, stock brokers and independent intermediaries. The BMA was inaugurated in June 1989 and the application for licence was envisaged during 1993. A formal Traded Options Market (TOM) was launched on 24 January 1992 by the Johannesburg Stock Exchange. Options available include options on SAFEX Futures, SA Bonds and Government Stock, and Equities and Johannesburg Stock Exchange derivatives.

Since no formalised exchanges exists in South Africa, all options on SAFEX Futures and SA Bonds and Government Stock are traded on an OTC basis. However, there is a distinction between standardised and non-standardised options.

Tax: Since there is no specific legislation relating to derivative instruments, each transaction or series of transactions must be examined in accordance with general principles. Gains and losses are usually recognised immediately for taxation purposes. Those arising from trading or the hedging of speculative underlying transactions are taxed as normal trading income. There is no capital gains tax in South Africa and consequently gains and losses arising from hedging of capital transactions do not attract any tax.

Whether or not a specific transaction is of a capital or revenue nature is determined in accordance with the interpretation of the South African courts. However, increased legislation is expected during the forthcoming year that will regulate the tax treatment of the above mentioned derivatives.

Spain

Accounting: Only the Bank of Spain circulars sent to financial institutions which apply specifically to banks, savings banks etc. refer to accounting rules for financial futures and options traded in organised markets. Although it does not include significant changes in this area, Circular 4/1991 stipulates the method of recording futures transactions, which include futures and financial options. Circular 4/1991 standardises and structures the treatment of these transactions with regard to the following aspects:

- Definition of futures transactions.
- Redefinition of organised markets.
- Definition of hedging transactions, relating to interest rate risks and to exchange and market risks.

This Circular also distinguishes between hedging and non hedging transactions: In the case of hedges, the resulting income or loss on the basis of the revenues or costs arising from the hedged asset. Transactions carried out on organised market and outside organised markets are also distinguished. Transactions on organised markets must be valued at market prices. The market value of assets acquired will be determined as follows:

- Based on their market price in organised markets.
- Based on the appraisal thereof by an entity registered with the Bank of Spain (if the assets are property).
- Based on the underlying book value per the audited balance sheet (in the case of holdings in unlisted entities).

Regulation: A Royal Decree regulating the official futures and options markets was approved in 1991. This Decree establishes a stringent guarantee system to safeguard trading on this market. Under this Decree, the CNMV (Spanish Securities and Exchange Commission) has strong control and supervisory powers. Specifically, it is empowered to authorise the general conditions for options and futures contracts traded on the market and to decide, if appropriate, the exclusion of such contracts from trading. However, there is a market governing company whose purpose is to safeguard the rights of the investors, transparency in the setting of prices and market security. The largest shareholder of this governing company (MEFF Sociedad Holding de Productos Financieros Derivados, S.A.) which comprises the former MEFFSA and MOFEX, is the State holding company Argentaria, which encompasses the holdings of Banco Exterior, Banco de Credito Industrial (BCI) and Caja Postal in this market.

Tax: As derivative financial products markets have only recently begun to trade, a specific tax regime for futures and options has not yet been developed. Current legislation suggests that income from trading in derivatives may be treated as a capital gain, and would not be subject to withholding tax at source as though it were income from capital. The treatment of income from trading in derivatives as a capital gain has been approved in a recent non-binding ruling issued by the tax authorities.

Sweden

Accounting: Any profits arising from trading in futures and options must be accounted for on a realised basis. Unrealised losses must be provided for and may be netted off within a futures and options portfolio. Net unrealised gains may not be recognised. Until income from an option is realised the seller must account for the premium received as deferred income. If, at the balance sheet date, options have not been realised a provision for potential losses on exercise must be set up. Options purchased should be held in the balance sheet at the lower cost and net realisable value.

Regulation: Most of the exchange control legislation in Sweden has been abolished. Payments made to or received from foreign countries must, however, be made through a currency bank, and non-residents trading in derivatives must also go via either a currency bank or a stockbroker. Debt instruments such as Swedish bonds must be deposited with a stockbroker or a foreign currency bank.

Tax: Current legislation has been significantly augmented by the rules on options introduced in January 1991. Those for whom dealing in derivatives and other securities is a regular business are taxed according to normal business income rules (30%) with the right to fully offset losses. This would include banks, stockbrokers and insurance companies. Also for other investing companies the tax rate is 30% on profits. Companies that do not deal in derivatives and other securities, however, have a limited right to deductions for losses on shares and securities similar to shares. For these companies, it is only possible to offset losses from the sale of such securities against gains from the sale of the same securities.

As from 1992, the effective tax rate on capital gains for natural persons from the sale of shares and equity-linked instruments is 25% instead of 30%. Income from capital is taxed at 30% for income years 1993 and 1994. From 1995 all income from capital will be taxed at 25%. Losses are also treated in the same source of income. Certain limitations on setting off losses apply.

For taxpayers where the provisions regarding income from capital apply, the following is the position on sales and purchases of options. Those selling options are taxed on the premium received at standard income tax rates. The cost of the premium is treated by the buyer as the cost of the underlying asset. The length of the option may have taxation implications for the issuer.

- If the life of the option is up to one year, the tax liability for the premium received will arise in the year in which the issuer is relieved from his liability under it (e.g. expiry/exercise of the option). For taxation purposes grant and exercise are treated as a single transaction.
- If the life of the option is more than one year, the premium received is taxed separately in the year in which the option was issued.
- However, if the life of the option is more than one year, but the issuer is relieved from his liability under it during the same calendar year that the option was issued, the premium is treated in the same way as for options with a life of up to one year. This means that the treatment is as for a single transaction. If the option is offset or expires, the owner is taxed on the cash settlement (less the premium) at the time of settlement. If the options are exercised, call options are taxed when the shares are sold (the premium added to the initial value of the shares) and put options are taxed at the time of exercise (the premium deducted from the capital gain).

Switzerland

Accounting: Accounting guidelines as issued by Soffex (The Swiss Options and Financial Futures Exchange) state that derivatives can be marked-to-market provided that:

- the derivatives are traded on an exchange by banks on a regular basis and
- the trading is sufficiently executed and regulated.

Where trading is of a non-professional nature, losses must by accounted for as soon as they arise, whereas unrealised gains must not be accounted for. Where futures and options are used for hedging purposes, however, hedge accounting may be used to defer results over the life of the hedge.

Regulation: The basic premise on which Soffex is based is that of self-regulation. The responsibility for setting the rules and regulations lies with the directors and to ensure that non-Soffex members also follow these regulations circular letters have been issued by the Swiss Bankers Association and the Federal Banking Commission which bind all banks and members of the Association. The Swiss Bankers Association has also developed new rules regarding capital adequacy and diversification of credit risks including derivative financial instruments.

The day to day running of the trading and clearing system and the surveillance and compliance is the responsibility of Soffex. As the system is fully automatic it provides a complete audit trail.

Tax: In Switzerland the tax treatment of income is generally determined by the accounting treatment used. Thus the method of taxation used for futures and options follows the accounting treatment. Gains made by individuals on derivatives trading are exempt from federal tax as long as the trading activity does not qualify as professional business. Those gains which can be defined as private capital gains are also exempt from tax in all but one of the 26 Cantons. Net capital gains are however taxed in the 26th Canton.

Trading in futures and options will not incur duty (except in cases of physical delivery of securities) and options held by individuals are subject to regular wealth tax. No withholding tax is charged to Soffex.

United Kingdom

Accounting: No accounting pronouncements relate specifically to futures and options. It is generally accepted that the accounting treatment should be consistent with the underlying economic substance of the transaction. Mark-to-market accounting gives a close approximation of the economic reality in the case of speculative trading, and is becoming generally accepted for active traders. However, futures positions and purchased options may alternatively be stated at the lower of cost and market value and written options at the higher of proceeds and market value. Once a transaction fulfils the necessary criteria to be defined as a hedge, the accounting treatment of the transaction should follow that of the underlying asset or liability.

These principles are consistent with those embodied in the British Bankers Association Exposure Draft on commitments and contingencies.

Regulation: All those involved in futures and options trading, in the United Kingdom and internationally, are governed by the Financial Services Act 1986. The regulatory structure consists of the Treasury, Department of Trade and Industry and self regulation by the markets themselves (as governed by the Securities and Investments Board (SIB). One of the four self regulatory bodies (SROs) under the SIB is the SFA (Securities and Futures Authority). This organisation has primary responsibility for authorising and supervising member institutions. SROs have the power to investigate members' compliance with the rules set by them on matters such as capital adequacy, segregation of client funds and business conduct; if necessary, they can institute disciplinary proceedings.
The SIB has issued rules covering the use of futures and options by the unit trust industry. These empowered existing funds to use futures and options for the purposes of efficient portfolio management. In addition, these allowed specialist futures and options funds to be set up in the UK for the first time.

Tax: The 1990 Finance Act has granted exemption from tax on derivative transactions for authorised unit trusts and exempt approved pension funds. The basic tax treatment afforded gains and losses depends on whether they are the result of trading (when they are taxed as income) or of hedging (when they are taxed in accordance with the underlying asset or liability). The definition of hedging is of particular importance to investment trusts because they are exempt from tax on capital profits and only subject to tax on income. Hence, if they could show the hedged portfolio was capital, no tax would arise.

Following the 1988 Statement of Inland Revenue Practice the grey area that has traditionally caused difficulty in the taxation of futures and options has partly been cleared up, although many difficulties do still remain.

United States of America

Accounting: Futures contracts (with the exception of foreign currency, forward placements and delayed delivery contracts) are dealt with by FASB Statement 80. The currency exception is partly dealt with by FASB Statement 52, although where no specific rules apply the concepts of FASB 80 are generally applied. Accounting treatment differs according to whether the derivatives were used for hedging or speculative positions are marked to market and unrealised profits and losses resulting from a change in market value must be recognised on a current basis. In the case of hedged positions market value changes are recognised as income only when the allied change in the price or interest rate of the underlying asset is recognised.

Regulation: The SEC (Securities and Exchange Commission) regulates equity options. The CFTC (Commodity Futures Trading Commission) governs the commodity, futures and options exchanges. The rules for all futures commission merchants, such as segregation of customer funds, capital adequacy, client relationships and trade reporting, are regulated by the CFTC.

Tax: Whether profits and losses resulting from options other than section 1256 contracts not utilised as a hedge, are treated as capital or ordinary depends on the property underlying the option. If capital asset treatment applies and the option is held for more than one year, long term capital gains and losses will be recognised when the option is disposed of. Any premium paid will be treated as a non-deductible capital expenditure. Any premium received is not included in income at the time of receipt but will be recognised at the time of exercise, expiration or disposal.

Section 1256, Contracts-Regulated Futures Contracts, Foreign Currency Contracts and Dealer Equity Options trading on qualifying exchanges and certain forward fx contracts traded in the interbank market, may be taxed under the year end mark-to-market rules. Unrealised gains and losses are marked to market at year end and treated as 60% long term and 40% short term capital gain or loss. Adjustments to basis are made when the position is closed.

In certain cases Section 1256 Contracts are used for hedging purposes. Generally the mark-to-market and 60/40 rules will not apply where the hedge is entered into in the normal course of the tax payer's trade or business to reduce the risk of the price change, currency fluctuation or interest change and where the transaction is identified as a hedge. Gain or loss on the transaction is ordinary.

For corporations, there is currently no difference in tax rates between capital and ordinary income, but capital losses may only be deducted to the extent that they offset capital gains. Under new legislation individual taxpayers may receive a benefit for net long term capital gains versus net short term capital gains and ordinary income.

Appendix

WORLDWIDE EXCHANGES TRADING OPTION CONTRACTS

Next to the name of each exchange, in brackets, is its abbreviation (when available) followed by the name of the city where the exchange is located (when necessary).

1. Argentina

Bolsa de Comercio de Buenos Aires, Sarmiento
- Equities (22)
- Public Bonds (Pesos)
- Public Bonds (US$)
- Cattle Index (Pesos)
- Cattle Index (US$)

Mercado de Futuros y Opciones SA (MERFOX), Sarmiento
- Live Cattle (US$)
- Live Cattle (Pesos)
- Live Cattle (DMK)

2. Australia

Australian Options Market, Sydney
- Equity Options (47)
- Long Term Equity Options (15)
- Twenty Leaders Index
- Gold Index

Sydney Futures Exchange (SFE) Limited, Sydney
- 50 Leaders Share Price Index
- All Ordinaries Share Price Index
- 90 Day Bank Accepted Bills
- 10 yr T-bonds
- 3 yr T-bonds

3. Austria

Österreichische Termin und Optionenbörse (ÖTOB Clearing Bank AG), Vienna

· Stock Options (American Style
· ATX (European Style)

4. Belgium

Belgian Futures & Options Exchange (BELFOX), Brussels
· Traded Stock (6)
· Bel 20 Index (BXO)
· Belgian Government Bond Futures (BGB)

5. Brazil

Bolsa Brasileira de Futuros, Rio de Janeiro
· Gold
· Cash Commercial US Dollar
· Cash Floating US Dollar

Bolsa de Mercadorias & Futuros, São Paulo
· Gold
· Foreign Currency
· Arabica Coffee

Rio de Janeiro Stock Exhchange, Rio de Janeiro
· Stock Index
· Individual Stocks

6. Canada

Montreal Exchange, Montreal
· 10 year Government of Canada bond Futures (OGB)
· Bond Options (3)
· Equity Options Short-Term (22)
· Equity Options Long-Term (4)

Toronto Futures Exchange (TFE), Toronto
· Silver
· Toronto 35 Index (European Style)
· Toronto 35 Index Participation Options

Vancouver Stock Exchange (VSE), Vancouver
· Gold (European Style)

Winnipeg Commodity Exchange (WCE), Winnipeg
· Canola (American Style)

· Canadian Barley (Domestic Feed) (American Style)
· Barley (Western Domestic Feed) (American Style)
· Feed Wheat (American Style)
· Flaxseed (American Style)

7. Denmark

Copenhagen Stock Exchange and the Guarantee Fund for Danish Options and Futures(FUTOP).
· KFX Stock Index Futures
· Danish Government Bonds Futures: Bullet Loan 8% 2003 Futures
· Danish Stocks

8. Finland

Finnish Options Market (FOM), Helsinki
· FOX Index (European Style)
· Currencies:
· USD American
· DEM American
· SEK American
· GBP Stocks

9. France

Marché des Options Négocialbles de Paris (MONEP), Paris
· On 30 Equities (American Style)
· CAC 40 Index Short-Term Options (American Style)
· CAC 40 Index Long-Term Options (European Style)

MATIF SA, Paris
· ECU Bond
· Notional Bond
· 3 Month Pibor

10. Germany

Deutsche Terminbörse (DTB), Frankfurt
· Equity Options
· Dax Index
· Dax Index Futures
· Bund
· Medium-term Bund (Bobl)

11. Hong Kong

Hong Kong Futures Exchange Limited (HKFE), Hong Kong
  · Hang Seng Index

12. Japan

Kansai Agricultural Commodities Exchange (KANEX), Osaka
  · Raw Sugar

Osaka Securities Exchange, Osaka
  · Nikkei 225

Tokyo Grain Exchange, Tokyo
  · US Soyabeans
  · Raw Sugar

Tokyo International Financial Futures Exchange (TIFFE), Tokyo
  · Three month Euroyen

Tokyo Stock Exchange, Tokyo
  · Topix Options
  · 10 Year Government Bond Futures

13. Netherlands

European Options Exchange (EOE), Amsterdam
  · Equities (40)
  · Government Bonds
  · EOE Index
  · MMI Index
  · OMX Index
  · XMI Leaps
  · Dollar
  · Jumbo Dollar
  · Dutch Top 5 Index
  · Eurotop 100 Index
  · Gold
  · Guilder Bond

14. New Zealand

New Zealand Futures & Options Exchange (NZFOE), Auckland
  Forty Index

· NZ 3 Year Government Stock
· 90 Day Bank Bills (BBO)
· NZ 10 Year Government Stock
· Equities (5)

15. Norway

Oslo Stock Exchange, Oslo
· Bergesen
· Saga Petroleum
· Norsk Hydro
· Hafslund
· Nycomed
· OBX - Index
· XC4L

16. Singapore

Singapore International Monetary Exchange (SIMEX), Singapore
· Eurodollar
· Euroyen
· Nikkei Stock Index
· D-mark
· Japanese Yen

17. South Africa

Johannesburg Stock Exchange (JSE), Johannesburg
· All Share Index
· All Gold Index
· Share Options

South African Futures Exchange (SAFEX), Johannesburg
· All Share Index
· All Gold Index
· Industrial Index
· Gold Price
· Long Bond
· Short-term Interest

18. Spain

Meff Renta Fija, Barcelona
· 90 Day Mibor

· 3 Year Government Bond
· 10 Year Government Bond
· Monthly Options on 10 Year Government Bonds

Meff Renta Variable, Madrid
    · Equities (3) (American Style)
    · IBEX 35

19. Sweden

OM Stockholm AB, Stockholm
    · Stock Options (Approx 22 Free Issues)
    · Stock Options Long Term (Approx 22 Free Issues)
    · OMX Stock Index (Based on 30 Stocks)
    · OMX Stock Index Long Term (Based on 30 Stocks)

20. Switzerland

Swiss Options & Financial Futures Exchange (SOFFEX), Zurich
    · Swiss Market Index
    · Equity Options (5 Shares)
    · Low Exercise Price Option (5 Shares)

21. United Kingdom

International Petroleum Exchange (IPE), London
    · Gas Oil
    · Brent Crude

London Commodity Exchange (LCE), London
    · Robusta Coffee
    · No 7 Cocoa
    · No 5 White Sugar
    · Baltic freight Index (Biffex)
    · EEC Wheat
    · EEC Barley
    · Potatoes

London International Financial Futures & Options Exchange (LIFFE), London
Interest Rate Options
    · Long Gilt
    · 3 Month Eurodollar
    · 3 Month Sterling

· German Government Bond
· 3 Month Euromark
· Italian Government Bond
· 3 Month Euroswiss
Equity Options
· Equities
· FTSE 100 Index (American Style Exercise)
· FTSE 100 Index (European Style Exercise)

The London Securities and Derivatives Exchange (OMLX), London
· Swedish Stock Options
· Long Stock Options
· OMX Index
· Long OMX Index (European Style)
· EOE
· Eurotop 100 Index

22. United States of America

American Stock Exchange (ASE), New York
· Major Market Index
· S & P MidCap 400
· XMI LEAPS™
· Japan Index
· Institutional Index
· Biotechnology Index
· LEAPS on the Biotechnology Index
· EUROTOP 100 Index
· Computer Index
· Oil Index
· Pharmaceutical Index
· LEAPS on the Pharmaceutical Index
· Morgan Stanley Cycle Index
· Morgan Stanley Consumer Index
· North American Telecommunications Index
· Options on more than 375 Equities
· LEAPS™ on Equities
· S & P MidCap LEAPS

Chicago Board Options Exchange (CBOE), Chicago
· Equity Options
· LEAPS® (Long term Equity Anticipation Securities®)
· S & P 100 Index OEX®

- OEX LEAPS®
- OEX CAPS™
- S & P 500 Index SPX™
- SPL
- S & P 500 Index NSX
- SPX LEAPS®
- SPX CAPS®
- S & P 500 end-of-quarter (SPQ)
- FLEX™ (S & P 100 and 500)
- Russell 2000® Index (RUT)
- Russell 2000 Index LEAPS®
- FT-SE 100 Index (FSX)
- CBOE BioTech Index (BGX)
- CBOE Bio Tech Index LEAPS®
- Priority Super Share (ZIS)
- Appreciation Super Share (ZAS)
- Protection Super Share (ZPS)
- Income and Residual Super Share (ZYS)
- Short Term Int Rate (IRX)
- Long Term Interest Rate 5 year yield (FVX) LEAPS® (VXV)
- Long Term Interest Rate 10 year yield (TNX) LEAPS® (VXN)
- Long Term Interest Rate 30 year yield (TYX) LEAPS® (VYY)

Sector Indices
- S & P Bank (BIX)
- S & P Chemicals (CEX)
- S & P Retail
- S & P Health Care (HCX)
- S & P Insurance (IUX)
- S & P Transportation (TRX)
- CBOE Computer Software (CWX)
- CBOE Enviroment (EVX)

Chicago Board of Trade (CBT), Chicago
- Corn
- Soyabeans
- Soyabean Meal
- Soyabean Oil
- Wheat
- Oats
- Silver
- US Treasury Bonds
- 10 Year Treasury Notes
- Municipal Bond Index

- Wilshire Small Cap Index
- Eastern Catastrophe Insurance
- National Catastrophe Insurance
- Midwestern Catastrophe Insurance
- Mortgage backed Securities
- Five Year US Treasury Note

Chicago Mercantile Exchange (CME), Chicago
- Pork Bellies
- Live Cattle
- Feeder Cattle
- Live Hogs
- Broiler Chicken
- FT-SE 100 Index
- Goldman Sachs Commodity Index
- S & P 500 Index
- S & P MidCap 400
- Russell 2000
- Major Market Index
- US Treasury Bills
- Libor
- Eurodollar
- Australian Dollar
- British Pound
- Canadian Dollar
- Deutschemark
- Japanese Yen
- Swiss Franc
- French Franc
- Deutschemark/Japanese Yen
- Three-month Euromark
- Rolling Spot™ British Pound
- Rolling Spot™ Deutschemark
- Lumber
- Nikkei 225 Stock Average

Coffee, Sugar & Cocoa Exchange Inc (CSCE), New York
- Coffee C
- No 11 Sugar
- Cocoa
- Non Fat Dry Milk
- Cheddar Cheese

Commodity Exchange (COMEX), New York
- Copper
- Gold
- Silver
- 5 Day Gold
- 5 Day Silver
- 5 Day Copper
- Eurotop 100 Index

FINEX, New York
- US Dollar Index
- ECU

Kansas City Board of Trade (KCBOT), Kansas
- No 2 Red Wheat
- Mini Value Line

MidAmerica Commodity Exchange (MIDAM), Chicago
- Soyabeans
- Wheat
- Gold
- Corn
- US Treasury Bond
- Rough Rice

Minneapolis Grain Exchange, Minneapolis
- Hard Red Spring Wheat
- White Wheat
- Oats
- Frozen Shrimp

New York Cotton Exchange (NYCE), New York
- Cotton
- Cotlook World Cotton™
- Orange Juice

New York Futures Exchange (NYFE), New York
- NYSE Composite Index
- NYSE Utility Index
- CRB Index

New York Mercantile Exchange (NYMEX), New York
- Crude Oil

· Heating Oil
· Gasoline
· Platinum
· Natural Gas

New York Stock Exchange (NYSE), New York
· NYSE Composite Index ® NYA
· NYSE Utility Index ® NNA,VNA,LNA
· Equity Options (155 Stocks)

Pacific Stock Exchange (PSE), San Fransico
· Wiltshire Small Cap Index
· Equity Options (240 Stocks)
· LEAPS®

Philadelphia Stock Exchange (PHLX), Phildalphia
· National OTC Stock Index
· Value Line Composite Index
· Gold/Silver Stock Index
· Utility Stock Index
· Australian Dollar
· British Pound
· Canadian Dollar
· Deutschemark
· French Franc
· Japanese Yen
· Swiss Franc
· ECU
· Deutschemark/Japanese Yen
· British Pound/Deutschemark
· British Pound/Japanese Yen
· Long Term Currency Options
· Month end Currency Options
· Equity Options (227 Stocks)
· Leaps®
· Value Line LEAPS®

Index